AF361567

BLISSFUL BLINDNESS

BLISSFUL BLINDNESS

SOVIET CRIMES UNDER WESTERN EYES

DARIUSZ TOLCZYK

TRANSLATED FROM POLISH BY JAREK GARLIŃSKI. EXPANDED BY THE AUTHOR

INDIANA UNIVERSITY PRESS

This book is a publication of

Indiana University Press
Office of Scholarly Publishing
Herman B Wells Library 350
1320 East 10th Street
Bloomington, Indiana 47405 USA

iupress.org

This publication was supported by a grant from the National Programme for the Development of Humanities in Poland, financed by Polish Ministry of Education and Science, and prepared in collaboration with the Tischner Institute of Cracow (project no. 3aH15022183).

First printing 2023

Cataloging information is available from the Library of Congress.

ISBN 978-0-253-06708-1 (hardback)
ISBN 978-0-253-06709-8 (paperback)
ISBN 978-0-253-06711-1 (ebook)

CONTENTS

NOTE ON TRANSLITERATION FROM THE CYRILLIC TO THE LATIN ALPHABET

Traditional and familiar English transliterations of Russian names are used in the body of the text (i.e., Gorky not Gor'kii; Dostoevsky not Dostoevskii; Tyutchev not Tiutchev, etc.). When references are made directly to the Cyrillic originals (for instance in endnotes and bibliography), the Simplified US Library of Congress Transliteration System is used (i.e., Gor'kii, Dostoevskii, Tiutchev, etc.).

BLISSFUL BLINDNESS

Escape from Truth

Does it still make sense today to cultivate memories of the twentieth century's terrible past—concentration camps, mass terror, persecution, and genocide? I often ask my American students about it. They say yes, it does. At least a few among them usually refer to the famous maxim by George Santayana: whoever forgets history's catastrophes is doomed to repeat them. An optimistic, rational view of history shines through Santayana's words, reflecting his assumption that humankind, despite dark moments, can learn from its own mistakes.

And yet, so far, the evidence in favor of Santayana's view is no more convincing than the evidence supporting the opposite conclusion—that the only lesson we learn from history is that it does not teach us anything. Those who take that view can easily cite recent examples of mass murder, terror, and persecution. They often argue that dwelling on past evils does more harm than good, generating an endless cycle of retribution and vengeance. To transcend this vicious circle and stop repeating history, some say, we must forget it, not remember it. This sort of thinking has a long-standing tradition. Within days following the murder of Julius Caesar, Cicero, speaking in the Roman senate, postulated that the recent events be forgotten for the common good (*oblivione sempiterna delendam*).[1] European peace treaties reaching back at least as far as the Treaty of Verdun in 843—when Charlemagne's grandsons, Lothar, Ludwig of Germany, and Charles of France, settled their struggles for succession—have repeatedly called upon warring parties to let go the memories of recent hostilities, carnage, and atrocities. Nietzsche, in his musings on the advantages and disadvantages of historical memory, noted that the inability to forget the traumas of the past can constrain our capacity for living in the present. Persistent emphasis on remembering tends to deprive people and nations of the spontaneity that is crucial in confronting the challenges and experiencing the joys of life. This spontaneity—a necessary condition of progress—stems in part from the naivete and youthful ignorance of historical experience.[2] As Wisława Szymborska writes:

> Those who knew
> what this was all about
> must make way for those
> who know little.
> And less than that.
> And at last nothing less than nothing.
> Someone has to lie there
> in the grass that covers up
> the causes and effects
> with a cornstalk in his teeth,
> gawking at clouds.[3]

At first glance, this kind of debate over remembering versus forgetting may seem irresolvable, but only until we recognize a common limitation shared by both sides. Each of them, in fact, focuses on the same pair of questions: How can *we* (and our future heirs) benefit from the terrible fate of the victims? And is remembering more beneficial *for us* than forgetting, or is it the other way around? The entire controversy looks quite different, however, when we transcend this pragmatic perspective and cross over to the ethical dimension by asking not how we can *benefit* from the victims' peril but what we *owe* them as fellow humans.

Forgetting historical evil for the sake of future good means, among other things, forgetting the victims—at least to some degree—for the sake of peace. What the signatories of peace treaties between nations usually had in mind were victims on both sides. Pledges to forget past atrocities were meant as mutual concessions on the survivors' part, intended to break the cycle of retributions and avoid repeating history. But how are we to apply this idea to the totalitarian evil of the twentieth century? Here, we no longer deal with victims on one side or the other of this or that struggle but with victims of genocide, slavery, oppression, and persecution—crimes perpetrated on innocent people by omnipotent powers.

Totalitarianisms annihilated their victims in a dual sense. They eliminated them physically but also strove to annihilate all traces left by them in the memory of others. A survivor of Dachau recalled, "The SS guards took pleasure in telling us that we had no chance of coming out alive, a point they emphasized with particular relish by insisting that after the war the rest of the world would not believe what happened; there would be rumors, speculations, but no clear evidence, and people would conclude that evil on such a scale was just not possible."[4] In Stalin's Russia, Nadezhda Mandelshtam, the widow of the poet Osip Mandelshtam who perished in the Gulag, wrote, "All the murderers, provocateurs, and informers had one feature in common: it never occurred to them that their victims might one day rise up again and speak. . . . They thought that everybody sent to the next world or to the camps had been eliminated once and for all. It never entered their heads that these ghosts might rise up and call their gravediggers to account."[5]

In this light, forgetting the victims of totalitarianism can be, and has often been, judged a sort of complicity with their executioners. It has been described as granting—albeit inadvertently—a modicum of moral satisfaction to the oppressors while simultaneously denying the victims the only compensation a society free from totalitarianism can offer: the symbolic compensation through memory. Bruno Bettelheim, a survivor of the Nazi camps in Dachau and Buchenwald, commented: "If we remain silent then we perform exactly as the Nazis wanted: behave as if it never happened."[6] Antoni Ekart, the author of a Gulag memoir, quoted an inscription on a wall of a punishment cell: "Damned be he who leaves here and remains silent."[7] Primo Levi put it even more bluntly in the poem-admonition opening his memoir of Auschwitz:

> I commend these words to you.
> Carve them in your hearts
> At home, in the street,
> Going to bed, rising;
> Repeat them to your children,
> Or may your house fall apart,
> May illness impede you,
> May your children turn their faces from you.[8]

Today, whenever the topic of Nazi crimes resurfaces in the West, it practically goes without saying that remembering these crimes is our moral duty. Everyone seems to be in agreement, at least on the level of public debate, that forgetting is not a morally valid option: it would mean abandoning the victims to oblivion and inadvertently granting their oppressors a modicum of moral satisfaction.

And yet, motivation so simple and fundamental as the ethical obligation to remember the victims often loses its clarity and urgency as soon as the topic of Soviet communism arises. Instead, the opposite tradition—the one favoring oblivion—often makes its swift and unexpected comeback. My American students who say yes to the question of whether it makes sense today to dwell on the memories of the twentieth century's atrocities are often surprised to learn about communist crimes. Some wear T-shirts with a hammer and sickle, Lenin, Trotsky, or Mao. If these outfits are meant as some sort of youthful antibourgeois provocation then it goes almost unnoticed: hardly anybody seems to be shocked. On the contrary, their college professors chuckle along. Nobody seems disturbed by the immensity of human suffering and death inflicted under these symbols by communist regimes not only in the USSR but also in China, Cambodia, North Korea, Eastern Europe, and so on.

Why does contemporary Western public discourse, sensitive to the historic evil of Nazism and to all that is associated with it, seem so uncommitted, ambiguous, and at times oblivious toward the evil perpetrated by Soviet communism? Of course, next to the greatest crime of Nazism, the Holocaust, anything, including even Stalin's atrocities, is likely to pale in comparison. But this does not explain the oblivious attitudes to Soviet crimes. These attitudes did not result from the overwhelming impression of the Holocaust on Western minds. The key motivations behind Western ambiguities regarding Soviet crimes were formed long before the Holocaust. They developed in the 1920s and matured in the 1930s, when Stalin had no rivals as Europe's greatest mass murderer, and hardly anyone was able to imagine the horrors awaiting European Jews under Nazi power in the imminent future. And even then, during World War II, the emerging truth about the Holocaust was initially dismissed by Western Allied leaders, and it took decades for its awareness to enter the mainstream Western culture.[9] Today, we tend to forget this slow and reluctant Western response to the Holocaust. Instead, we choose to focus on positive memories. Remembering Hitler's crimes evokes distant reminiscences of a historic moral victory. Although the Western democratic powers showed little interest in stopping the Holocaust when it was happening, they confronted and defeated Hitler in a bloody war (waged together with Stalin) and rooted out his ideology. Remembering the long-defeated Nazi evil can therefore serve as an indirect source of moral satisfaction. The present sense of moral legitimacy of the democratic West has been founded largely on the victory over Nazism in 1945. Today it is easy for everyone to feel a part of this legacy. Demonstrating this sort of sentiment costs nothing and, at the same time, constitutes a universally expected gesture that helps everyone feel good about themselves.

Things are quite different with regard to the communist evil. The history of Western reactions to the darkest aspects of Soviet totalitarianism is far from morally clear. For a long time, the Soviet regime paid lip service to the ideals of freedom, equality, and fraternity while committing multiple crimes against humanity: it killed, terrorized, enslaved, and persecuted millions of people for reasons often difficult to understand even to this day. Of course, Soviet crimes were condemned by many in the West, especially during the Cold War, but these condemnations were neither universal nor consistent. Instead, exposing Soviet crimes has often been treated within Western public discourse as something questionable and controversial. At the same time, Western public elites were very good at finding reasons for ignoring, dismissing, and often justifying Soviet atrocities. Survivors who were fortunate enough to find themselves in the free world and who attempted to expose the truth about the human condition in Soviet prisons and camps often encountered a wall of silence, reluctance, and hostility. Julius Margolin, a Polish-Jewish survivor of the Gulag, wrote in 1947:

> Here, among the free people of the West, I understood the depth of the tragedy of those who remain in bondage. On this side of the barbed-wire fence, I ran into a stone wall of pusillanimity and betrayal. . . . Indeed, it is enough to mention victims of the Gulag and, all of a sudden, people who in any other situation seem filled with truly angelic goodness and democratic sensitivity to the smallest imperfection in the world start growing sharp fangs, display absolute moral deafness, and their hearts harden—just as in the story of Doctor Jekyll and Mr. Hyde.[10]

Many other Gulag survivors who made it to the West had similar things to say. In the West today, we tend to forget this. Remembering communist evil, just like remembering Nazi evil, inevitably evokes recollections of Western responses to this evil at the time it was committed. Popular cultural recollections of the war against Hitler perpetuate a sense of pride. But the situation is much more complicated when the crimes of Stalin are concerned. Therefore they are more likely to be left alone. So it is perhaps not surprising after all that my students, who have been educated in schools where little if anything is said about the Red Terror, the Great Famine, the Gulag, and the Great Terror, can speak with sincere eloquence about the moral duty to remember the victims of twentieth century's atrocities while sporting T-shirts with the hammer and sickle.

Gauging the Inconceivable

So how and why did those now often-forgotten Western dismissals, rationalizations, and denials of communist evil come into being? We should start by mentioning some objective factors that contributed greatly to these responses. First of all, unlike the evidence of Nazi crimes, the evidence of Soviet terror—the Gulag, mass murders, and mass persecution—was generally not directly available to the West. Western armies never liberated the Gulag in the way they liberated Nazi camps, stumbling upon and promptly showing the whole world fresh manifestations of horror: piles of corpses and crowds of emaciated and dehumanized prisoners. While Westerners could see the conclusive truth about Nazism with their own eyes, the horrors of Soviet communism could generally be confronted only indirectly, through the testimony of survivors.[11] In order to accept the truth about these horrors, one first had to believe those who spoke about them. And believing is only for those who wish to believe. The facts regarding Bolshevik crimes could be learned in the West only from words—*someone's* words. Such words are always questionable. They can be confronted with different words uttered by someone else. Along with survivors' testimonies, other references to the Gulag, collectivization, show trials, etc. were also heard in the West, but they meant something completely different. They were fabricated or inspired by Soviet propaganda.

Soviet propaganda proved impressively effective in its efforts to deceive, corrupt, pressure, and manipulate many Western opinion makers. In addition to propaganda books, films, and other materials, special showcase camps and prison wards were maintained in the USSR in order to dupe foreign visitors into believing that the survivors' reports about Bolshevik atrocities were nothing more than anti-Soviet propaganda. Returning from visits in these establishments, Western intellectuals, writers, artists, journalists, clergymen, businessmen, and politicians often praised the Gulag as the world's most humane system of resocialization. In 1933, when at least five and a half million people died in the Great Famine and the Gulag grew rapidly, the American journalist Maurice Hindus wrote about the labor camps: "Vindictiveness, punishment, torture, severity, humiliation, have no place in this system. . . . During the period of confinement, criminals experience no other hardships than the enforced separation from home. Unless they violate the light discipline that they must observe they never are made to feel the yoke of the stigma of prison life. . . . Indeed the prison exists not for punishment but for ministration."[12] Other Westerners went even further in their praise of Stalin's humanitarianism. Their enthusiastic comments, books, and articles would fill an entire library. The list of Western apologists of the Gulag, the Great Famine, the Great Terror, and other Soviet crimes against humanity includes a host of famous names such as George Bernard Shaw, Sidney and Beatrice Webb, Harold Laski, Romain Rolland, Theodore Dreiser, Bertolt Brecht, André Malraux, Jean-Paul Sartre,

Edouard Herriot, Vice President Henry Wallace, Frederic Joliot-Curie—to mention just a few.

In light of the lack of direct evidence, Western reactions to Soviet crimes were always based on a choice as to whom one should believe: the survivors or Soviet propaganda? Westerners had to decide for themselves which of the two sources of knowledge about Soviet reality—survivors' accounts and Soviet propaganda—seemed more credible, and which of these two diametrically opposed realities seemed more probable.

Traditional criteria of probability did not prove very useful when applied to the Soviet reality. The truth was that Stalin's crimes transcended the conventional limits of the probable and the thinkable. It was often difficult to find in these crimes any familiar pattern of sense, need, or purpose. Robert Conquest commented, "What happened in Russia under Stalin could not be understood or estimated in any commonsensical fashion, if by common sense we mean notions that sound reasonable and natural to the democratic Westerner." He attributed many Western denials of Soviet abuses of power "not necessarily to prejudice in favor of the Soviet regime and of Stalin, but at least prejudice in regard to certain events or interpretations of them as inherently unlikely."[13] Martin Malia, writing about Soviet crimes, concluded,

> The figure most commonly advanced for the number of deaths during Stalin's twenty-five years in power—from collectivization, the Great Terror, and the routinized postwar terror taken together—is twenty million. Yet whatever the final estimates may turn out to be, it is already clear that we are dealing with atrocity on a scale requiring seven zeros to express. But few in the West guessed anything like the extent of the catastrophe at the time. And how many in the West recognize it even today? Surely, the average person's inability to believe the unbelievable was always a major cause of the West's highly uneven record in grappling with the Soviet enigma.[14]

François Furet made similar observations. Tackling the question of what made so many Western intellectuals blind to Stalin's crimes, he wrote:

> This blindness resulted . . . from an inability to gauge and to judge totally unfamiliar phenomena. . . . Nothing like it had ever existed. Never had any state in the world taken as its purpose to kill, deport, or enslave peasants. Never had a modern political ideology played a similar role in establishing a tyranny so perfect that those who feared it had nonetheless to hail to its foundations. Never had a dictatorship possessed so much power in the name of a falsehood so complete and yet so compelling. No one of these characteristics . . . is intelligible from the examples of the past or from within a familiar conceptual framework.[15]

The unbelievable nature and scale (by the pre-Holocaust standards) of Bol-shevik crimes were not the only reasons why so many Westerners, especially the well educated, refused to believe the survivors' testimony and instead pre-ferred to believe Soviet propaganda. What seemed equally important was the nature of the propaganda. Many Westerners appeared to give credence to So-viet lies because they were so outrageous. In a Gulag memoir, Barbara Skarga quotes a fellow prisoner saying, "You know, a small lie is always exposed, but a big one has a strange persuasive power. It is easy to believe it because it is hard to imagine the authorities would be capable of such colossal mystification."[16] What Skarga means is that it is generally hard to imagine lies so absolute as to be invulnerable to their own absurdity. The situation when a liar, caught in the act, keeps lying with his self-confidence apparently untouched, and indeed instead of feverishly backpedaling even multiplies his lies without any apparent reason, usually confounds us. It often makes people question their own point of view and, finally, search the lie for some kernels of truth. Sylvia Margulies commented on the Potemkin-style shows for foreigners: "Just as Hitler rec-ognized the potency of the 'big lie,' the Soviet regime realized that the more preposterous the facades, the more likelihood that the visitors would be taken in, for they would find it incredible that a country at the stage of development of the Soviet Union would go to such length in attempts to fool foreigners."[17]

Another factor that made Soviet propaganda easier to believe was that many Westerners remained skeptical regarding the credibility of survivors of Soviet camps and atrocities. The fact that these survivors had been incarcerated or subjected to other punitive measures in the USSR was often interpreted in the West as circumstantial evidence that they were active enemies of the Soviet state. Therefore, their accounts could be viewed as biased and unreliable. In the years following World War II, unprecedented numbers of memoirs of the Gulag and other Soviet atrocities appeared in the West. Most were written either by Poles released from Soviet camps and prisons after the Polish-Soviet agreement in 1941 or by Soviet "displaced persons" who refused to return to their homeland after the war. The Polish survivors were often dismissed as prejudiced against Russia, and Soviet refugees were suspected of collaborating with the Nazis during the war (why else would they refuse to return to their Soviet homeland?) By contrast, many Western deniers of Stalin's atrocities belonged to cultural and intellectual elites and were perceived as trustworthy and convincing.

The Art of Denial

As we have seen, there are various objective factors that have influenced West-ern reactions to Soviet crimes: the dearth of direct evidence, the unbelievable nature of these crimes, the inconceivable impudence of Soviet propaganda, and the assumed unreliability of survivors' testimonies. But the most important reasons behind the long-standing Western denials of the dark side of Soviet communism were of a more subjective nature—that is, they originated in the hearts and minds of Western observers and commentators.

Those Westerners who chose Soviet propaganda over survivors' accounts of Bolshevik crimes tended to display three types of attitudes. Some simply found the Soviet propaganda version of truth more credible and genuinely believed it. Others did not believe it but behaved as if they did. And, finally, there was the most peculiar—but quite common nevertheless—category of Western public opinion makers who found it very hard indeed to find this propaganda believable but who did their best to suppress their own doubts in order to convince themselves to accept the Soviet version of truth contrary to their own knowledge and reason. While those who genuinely believed Soviet propaganda were often motivated by the objective factors already mentioned here, the two remaining groups seemed prompted largely by subjective motivations. The most important of these motivations were ideological, economic, and political in nature.

The Bolshevik revolution and the actions of the Soviet regime were, from day one, treated in the West differently from the way facts are commonly treated. In the eyes of many influential Western public figures, these phenomena were part of a reality of a new and special kind, no longer subject to ordinary criteria such as truth and falsehood, good and evil. Many believed that the ultimate victory or defeat of the Bolshevik experiment would supply the answer to a question the West had been grappling with ever since the Enlightenment: Is radical, revolutionary transformation of the world for the better actually possible? Or, to state the opposite, are the attempts to destroy the old world in order to build the new and better one doomed to end in a tragedy because they are rooted in excessive arrogance? Both the left and the right invested much of their ideological capital in the outcome of the Bolshevik revolution. Each side anxiously expected to be proven correct, focusing meanwhile on whatever facts seemed to support its ideological agenda and largely disregarding those that did not. As a result, the truth about Soviet Russia was trumped by ideology to such an extent that any statement on the subject was likely to be treated as an ideological pronouncement rather than a comment on objective reality.

The fundamental moral dilemma of the left boiled down to the question: where does the outer limit of necessary violence lie beyond which the noble goal no longer justifies the means? Grappling with this question, the left was always split on the issue of Soviet communism. While some judged the Bolsheviks by their actions rather than words, others developed a growing aversion to facts. The less one knew about the real communism, the easier one could avoid the uncomfortable question of means and ends. In this context, the alternative version of facts, steadily fed by Soviet propaganda, was all the more welcome. Denying witnesses' testimonies and believing this propaganda helped protect faith in revolutionary ideals from encroaching skepticism.

But even those sympathizers of the Bolshevik experiment who became aware of its oppressive nature often managed to find good reasons for denying survivors' accounts and pretending to believe Soviet propaganda. Recent research into Soviet archives shows that fewer apologists of Stalin than we were inclined to think were, in fact, successfully duped by Soviet propaganda. Instead, more of them made the conscious choice of misrepresenting the truth because they felt compelled to choose between Soviet communism and its enemies, supposed or real. Telling the truth about the Soviet regime was considered taboo by many because they believed that it would automatically provide support to enemies of communism. These enemies—the bourgeoisie, the reactionaries, the fascists, the Nazis, the American imperialists, the CIA, Joseph McCarthy, etc.—had one thing in common: they tended to be treated by many Western public opinion makers as an evil much greater and certainly more directly threatening than Soviet communism. A peculiar ethical and intellectual phenomenon of the twentieth century is the number and prominence of opinion makers who considered truth not as a goal in and of itself but as a mere instrument of ideology and politics.

An important motive behind the willful concealment of truth was a peculiar concern of some members of the intellectual elites for the common man in the West. Some of them claimed that even if Stalin's regime was nothing more than a barbaric tyranny, Western workers who suffered capitalist injustice could still believe in and hope for the Soviet version of a better world to come. Some public opinion makers who espoused this view were fully aware that this hope was false, but even such a hope seemed better than none. At least it offered the common man something to believe in, or so they reasoned. Telling the masses the truth about Soviet communism would deprive them of any hope whatsoever.[18]

Still, these explanations do not fully suffice. However popular these attitudes were among the Western apologists of Soviet communism, some displayed a more complex and ambiguous approach. Their minds often seemed suspended between knowledge and ignorance, truth and falsehood, as if they knew and at the same time did not know. As time progressed, more and more of them realized, or at least strongly suspected, that despite inaccuracies or even exaggerations characteristic of personal witnesses, the survivors of Bolshevik atrocities were generally telling the truth. But this was a kind of truth not everyone wanted to accept. Can one refuse to accept truth once one knows it? Is it possible to deny that two times two equals four? Dostoevsky posed these questions a long time ago.[19] The answer is yes, it can be done.

Trying to understand Western responses to the dark side of communism, we often need to step outside the realm of rational ideas and motivations because what we are talking about here is a historic manifestation of a deep and timeless conflict between the human need for knowledge and a no less human need for faith. This conflict was often resolved in favor of faith and against knowledge. Kingsley Amis, a British intellectual who supported Stalin for more than a decade and finally lost faith in communism, commented, "We are dealing with a conflict of feeling and intelligence, a form of willful self-deception whereby a part of the mind knows full well that its overall belief is false or wicked, but the emotional need to believe is so strong that that knowledge remains, as it were, isolated, powerless to influence word or deed."[20]

The imperative of not criticizing the Soviet regime was not just a matter of individual preference. On the contrary, it became a socially accepted and often required norm in many Western discourses, especially those concerning intellectuals in the period of high Stalinism from early 1930s until the thaw after the dictator's death. Even people of such stature as Albert Camus found out about the power of the milieu. The literary salons of Paris under the sway of Jean-Paul Sartre practically ostracized Camus after he dared to criticize communism in *L'homme révolté*.[21]

For many people on the left who were initially sympathetic toward the revolution, Bolshevik atrocities constituted the main source of moral hesitations between supporting and condemning the Soviet regime. Some of them resolved this dilemma by rejecting Soviet communism altogether. Others tried to preserve the dream by focusing on inner splits in the Bolshevik leadership. From the late 1920s on, some of them managed to mentally separate Stalin's violent and oppressive communism from the supposedly more pure and idealistic communism represented by the exiled Leon Trotsky. Many others either learned how to live with unresolved questions or accepted violence as the only way the word of ideology could become the flesh of the new humanity. Glorification of violence passed in some circles for expressions of antibourgeois rebellion. Hannah Arendt perceived this as an important factor underlying the attractiveness of totalitarianism. She wrote in *The Origins of Totalitarianism*, "Since the bourgeoisie claimed to be the guardian of Western traditions and confounded all moral issues by parading publicly virtues which it not only did not possess in private and business life, but actually held in contempt, it seemed revolutionary to admit cruelty, disregard of human values, and general amorality, because this at least destroyed the duplicity upon which the existing society seemed to rest."[22]

But ostentatious expressions of the Bolshevik taste for violence were, in fact, discouraged by Stalin's propaganda. Although quite common in Soviet literature and media in the early 1920s, they gradually lost their prominence and almost disappeared with the advent of the 1930s.[23] By then, the Soviet leadership recognized that open aggrandizement of Bolshevik brutality did more harm than good in the context of the immediate pursuits of Soviet foreign policy. With the initial strategic agenda of the global proletarian revolution put on hold, the very survival of the Soviet regime and the prospect of creating a modern military-economic order capable of defeating the world bourgeoisie in the future depended on a period of peace and cooperation with the world bourgeoisie in the meantime. The only source of modern technology necessary for Soviet modernization was the capitalist West. In fact, many Western capitalists and political leaders were eager to do business with the Bolsheviks, but the image of the Soviet regime as the hotbed of bloodthirsty revolutionary fanaticism discouraged some of them. These businessmen and politicians did not want to be viewed (or to view themselves) as partners and enablers of a barbaric tyranny.

All the Bolsheviks needed to do was pay attention to this sort of attitudes and respond in the appropriate fashion. By the late 1920s, they coordinated their propaganda efforts in order to project to the West an image of a normal, progressive country led by a rational and deeply humanitarian government concerned with peace and well-being of its citizens. The lengthy period from the late 1920s to 1945 was the time of both the greatest Soviet crimes and the greatest willingness in the West to deny these crimes. It was also the time of the Great Depression, Hitler's rise to power, and World War II. The ideological motivations of some of the Westerners who denied Soviet atrocities were matched by the economic motivations of others. In 1937, during the Great Terror, the United States became the world's largest economic partner of the USSR. The American companies that built Soviet industry at this time were paid to a considerable degree with funds obtained by the Soviet government from the exports of Soviet grain, gold, and timber—all three of which were directly related to the Great Famine and the Gulag. The Kolyma slave-labor gold mines were developed partially in response to President Roosevelt's policy of the gold standard, which created extraordinary demand for Soviet gold and turned the American government into Stalin's strategic customer. Addressing the "rumors" about the deadly labor camps, US Secretary of the Treasury Henry Morgenthau, reassured the Soviet representative in the US, Konstantin

Umansky, that "the methods [the Soviets] used [in order to provide the gold] were of no interest to the American government."[24] Later, in 1944, Vice President Henry Wallace, accompanied by Owen Lattimore, visited the goldmines of the Kolyma and managed to not notice the forced labor there. Both Wallace and Lattimore published enthusiastic reports from their visit.[25]

The growth of Soviet-Western trade in the 1930s enhanced Stalin's position as a political partner of the West. In addition, Hitler's rise to power in Germany motivated many in the West to adopt a polarized view of the world, one in which Stalin appeared as the only viable counterweight to fascism and Nazism. Within this paradigm, criticizing Stalin was often viewed as supporting (albeit inadvertently) Hitler. In Western political culture, the language of politics always drew rhetorical resources from moralistic traditions. Political and economic alliances were therefore customarily explained in moral terms. As a result, even the most blatant crimes committed by partners and allies of Western democracies were almost routinely covered up and whitewashed. Thus, active denial of Soviet crimes became a key element of the Western allies' policy during World War II. In light of this pro-Soviet propaganda, the subsequent rapid switch from the wartime lionization of Stalin to his Cold War vilification had two results. On the one hand, it created an atmosphere in which many survivors of Stalin's atrocities were welcomed to address Western audiences with their stories. But on the other, it unintentionally undermined the credibility of these witnesses. If Stalin, the hero of yesterday, could suddenly become the villain of today, then which of the two mutually exclusive truths was true? In fact, both of them looked very much like products of political agendas. Therefore, some asked, why should one believe that the numerous accounts of Stalin's crimes published in the West soon after World War II were anything more than exaggerations and fabrications supporting the new anticommunist politics of the Western establishment?

In trying to understand Westerners' attitudes toward communism, we should not forget that they were often shaped by unique combinations of personal circumstances and relationships. Martin Amis, son of Kingsley Amis, compiled a list of factors that motivated his father's pro-Stalinist position: "middle-class guilt; 'an unfocused dissatisfaction with the way things are' . . . or unusual hatred of the status quo; a desire to scandalize parental, or paternal, conservatism; and the not quite entirely delusional sense that you were involving yourself directly in world affairs."[26] This list could easily be expanded. Personal factors should never be underestimated as sources of political emotions, views, and actions. Soviet public-relations specialists possessed a sober understanding of this issue. Angelica Balabanoff, who served as the secretary of the Communist International under Lenin (and thus can be considered very well oriented in these matters), wrote later that Western visitors, before being skillfully indoctrinated and duped in the Soviet Union, were divided by the Soviet authorities into four categories: superficial, naive, ambitious, and venal.[27]

Stalin's death and its aftermath provided an important breakthrough in Western responses to Soviet atrocities. Nikita Khrushchev's selective denouncement of Stalin's crimes in 1956 left many Western apologists confused and worried. Jean-Paul Sartre commented that publicly admitting these crimes was a grave mistake.[28] Others welcomed the thaw as proof of the alleged reformability of Soviet communism. Still others abandoned their pro-Soviet sentiments altogether. Although great numbers of survivors' accounts of Soviet atrocities had been published in the West ever since the Bolshevik revolution, it was Aleksandr Solzhenitsyn's *The Gulag Archipelago* in the mid-1970s that changed Western attitudes to this topic more than any other text. It is clear now that Solzhenitsyn's work provided the breaking point beyond which Soviet communism never regained the aura of moral legitimacy in the West, even though its apologists did not quite disappear. Since then, the edifice of the Soviet "big lie" began to fracture beyond repair until it finally collapsed.

Today its ruin still stands, obscuring our view of the twentieth century. It will continue to obstruct the view so long as the inconvenient memories of Western dismissals of Soviet crimes remain largely unaddressed. And I do not mean unaddressed by academic historians but by mainstream Western culture. Given time, unattended ruins tend to evoke nostalgia—a desire to relive a past whose memory has never been fully confronted and that therefore turns into a myth. This is how we end up repeating history.

1

Dreaming of Russia

Long before the Bolshevik revolution, Russia played a peculiar role in Western views of the world. Always enigmatic, though not as culturally remote as China or India, Russia was for centuries treated in the West as a screen on which the Western imagination projected its own dreams, hopes, and fears. The scarce information that was available on Russia was usually passed through a thick filter of various Western ideas, concepts, and intellectual customs, which often had little or nothing to do with Russian reality. Emerging through this filter, the image of Russia often represented not much more than a set of projections intended to confirm the accuracy of one or another Western ideology, belief, or phobia. The empirical, rational or just commonsensical criteria of truth that were normally applied by Westerners commenting on their own environment tended to lose their clarity and binding power when applied to Russia.

In 1917, when the Bolsheviks seized power in Petrograd, two great myths superimposed themselves at once on the Western imagination: the myth of revolution and the myth of Russia. Without taking this fact into account, it is impossible to understand the Western world's later attitudes toward Soviet crimes. The myth of Russia first took shape in the West in the eighteenth century. Until then, Russia remained little known to the Western world. Back in the eleventh century, when Yaroslav the Wise ruled in Kiev, Kievan Rus' was a European power recognized by its European partners. The Swedish king gave away his daughter to Yaroslav in marriage, while marriages of Yaroslav's daughters to princes and kings of France, Norway, and Hungary reflected the position of Kiev in Western politics. Soon, however, the schism between the Roman and Byzantine churches—and the fragmentation of the Kievan state into smaller principalities—followed by the Tatars' lengthy rule over most of Rus', isolated this country from the West for a long time. The Duchy of Moscow, which emerged as the new hegemon of the eastern parts of Rus' and eventually assumed the title of the Russian Empire, did not break this isolation, and Russian contact with the West remained slight. From time to time, papal Rome nurtured hopes of converting the Muscovite rulers to Catholicism, and projects for unity with Muscovite Orthodoxy appeared. But these ideas went nowhere, and Moscow and the West persisted in their relative cultural alienation from one another.

Russia's image in the West changed quickly at the start of the eighteenth century, when Peter the Great launched the transformation of the Muscovite state from backwater into modern European power. Western observers promptly realized that this was not empty rhetoric on Peter's part. In the Great Northern War, the Russian army, modernized along Western lines, soon defeated Sweden, one of the European powers of the day, and extended its hegemony over the Polish-Lithuanian Commonwealth. A Russian fleet appeared in the Baltic. It was quickly understood in the West that a powerful new player had entered the European stage and that henceforth its interests would have to be considered.

The lightning speed with which Peter was transforming his state into a new European power amazed not only Western political and military strategists but also leading lights of the Enlightenment. Before Enlightenment ideologues embraced radical solutions of improving society and establishing the rule of reason—including revolution, overthrowing monarchies, and introducing the republican order—they tended to entrust their hopes in the reason and will of the (enlightened) monarchs. The greater the power such a monarch possessed over the hereditary nobles, local magnates, gentry, bishops, abbots, priests, and finally the rest of his subjects, the more successful he could be in overcoming the resistance of traditionalism on the way to a new and better social order.

The ideologues understood, however, that without being able to call on convincing historical and current examples, their designs were likely to be taken for just another utopian ideal or theoretical fantasy of the kind that had long been found in Western literature. What set them apart from most intellectuals of the past was the fact that many of them were no longer content to be *only* writers. They wanted to mold the real world and influence history. Intellectuals of the Enlightenment tried to present numerous European rulers as examples of rational reformers and benefactors of humanity. This was a time in which rulers themselves made efforts to gain this kind of status among intellectuals. No European king, prince, or emperor was able to serve as an ideal model, however. Firstly, Europeans were too well aware of their monarchs' defeats and weaknesses, their successes notwithstanding. They also knew too many unambiguous details casting a pall over their rulers—and, as the expression has it, familiarity breeds contempt. Secondly, these were, after all, European rulers—that is, they ruled in countries where the monarch's power, even if called absolute, was never fully absolute. The extent and nature of this power were defined by centuries of tradition involving the struggles, negotiations, agreements, and compromises with local magnates, the aristocracy, and the Church. A European ruler was always to a greater or lesser extent subject to some law, or at least tradition, binding him. The legitimacy of his rule, as well as the loyalty of his vassals and subjects, was based on a great many factors not entirely under his control.

Russia was another matter. The land was sufficiently distant and unknown so that the concept of "Russia" suggested nothing concrete apart from some rather vague ideas about its rulers' actions. When saying "Russia," Westerners imagined the enigmatic figure of the tsar but usually knew nothing about Russian society and its people. Hence the West's vision of Russia was remarkably free of the cognitive dissonance that usually comes from knowing too much and that as a rule prevents one from quickly arriving at comfortable generalizations about a country. When speaking of the radical reforms instituted by Peter that resulted in a rapid transformation of Russia into a continental power, no one saw their social and human implications. Thus, the same qualities that were sought after with questionable success in Western rulers were much easier to find in the intriguing and mysterious figure of the Russian emperor, an unambiguous example of an enlightened monarch capable of transforming a country—even one so backward—according to the principles of reason. As for Russian society itself, the object of the transformation, it remained invisible from afar and had no voice at all. Thus it was unable to confirm or to deny what was being written or said about it in the West. It could easily be imagined as pliable material—a sort of clay that might be shaped according to an energetic ruler's sensible design. Leibniz, for example, described Russian society as a sort of tabula rasa—an ideal proving ground for a mind creating a marvelous new world. He saw in contemporary Russia a religious Civitas Dei combined with a philosophical *république des lettres*.[1]

Meanwhile, the "top-down revolution" carried out by Peter was so successful because, among other reasons, Russia was not a Western country but rather a state based on the cult of the ruler and the principle of unquestioning obedience. Peter employed this absolute power with maximum degree of ruthless effectiveness, using wholesale coercion and forced labor as principal methods.

Unsurprisingly, no one abroad paid any attention to the human costs of Peter's reforms. Tales of the forced laborers' fate lived on only in folk legend, repeated fearfully, and were completely unknown beyond the borders of the empire. In some of these tales, Peter's spectacular brutality was addressed, and he was portrayed as the Antichrist. But for a long time the West was unaware of this view of his reforms.

The most influential Western admirer of Peter at the time was Voltaire. He expressed his views initially in his *History of Charles XII*, written after Peter's death. There, Voltaire praised Peter's victory over the Swedish king Charles XII in the Great Northern War. The court of Tsarina Elizabeth, Peter's daughter, saw in the French luminary of the Enlightenment a potential ally and commissioned him to produce an extensive work on the emperor himself. Voltaire carried out the task, giving the West *A History of the Russian Empire under Peter the Great*—a model image of Russia, seen at the time as the most complete embodiment of the enlightened idea of a rational state. He praised Peter's reforms as the "most momentous event in the history of Europe since the discovery of the New World."[2] Turning directly to Western readers, he commented: "The rulers of long-civilized countries can only tell themselves: if a man could be found in the wastes of frozen Scythia who simply by the strength of his own genius could achieve so much, how much could we achieve in countries where the work of centuries makes everything easier?"[3]

Voltaire's services to the Russian court did not end here. Indeed, they reached their peak only during the reign of Catherine II. At the start of her reign, the new empress had to grapple with serious problems regarding her international image. The European courts were well aware that the energetic empress had won the Russian crown through plotting against her husband, Peter III, which culminated in a palace coup. Furthermore, shortly after the coup, Peter III lost his life in highly suspicious circumstances, raising concerns that he had been murdered on his wife's instructions. Catherine was systematically building her own public image by playing the part of the perpetuator of Peter the Great's reforms. Soon she became a prominent patron of the Enlightenment. No one was better suited to play the role of Catherine's Western advocate than Voltaire himself. Voltaire had just lost the generous support of Frederick II's Prussian court and was casting about for a new patron. And so a mutually beneficial collaboration was struck between the "sage of Ferney" and the "Semiramis of the North."

In this he was not alone. Soon Denis Diderot also took on the role. After a lengthy period corresponding with Catherine, the distinguished *encyclopédiste* paid her a personal visit in St. Petersburg. He saw up close the country that he had been vigorously praising (from afar) as the embodiment of the ideal of an enlightened polis and felt unpleasantly disenchanted. However, he discreetly kept this view to himself. The "Semiramis" was generously supporting Diderot from her own purse, including purchasing his personal library and then granting him lifelong access to its books, plus an ample salary for being its custodian.

Western European commentators largely regarded Catherine's Eastern European conquests in terms that were in striking parallel to Western colonial conquests in Africa, Asia, and America. They were seen as noble efforts whose aim was to introduce order into the realm of chaos and to bestow the benefits of real civilization on the natives. As for the countries and peoples conquered by Russia at the time, they were viewed as chaotic and primitive hordes in need of the civilizing power of the empire. This applied to the Crimea as much as it did to Poland.

With a view to reinforcing this image of Russia, in 1787 Catherine invited the Austrian emperor Joseph II along with a group of Western dignitaries for a visit to her recently conquered southern territories stretching to the Black Sea. Before the guests embarked on a specially constructed raft in order to join the "Semiramis" on a trip down the Dnieper, Prince Grigory Potemkin, one of Catherine's lovers and the governor of these conquered lands, reportedly organized a series of "living tableaux" along the banks of the river to represent the happy people spontaneously greeting the supreme authorities and their guests. According to contemporary accounts and subsequent legend, the Potemkin villages—or rather stage sets masquerading as reality—looked quite real. The peasants' houses, farmyards and clothes, as well as the exceptionally healthy and picturesque livestock, all testified to the remarkable success of the empire's civilizing mission.

Western luminaries who praised the Russian Empire were usually unaware—or at least appeared to be unaware—of facts running counter to their official view of Catherine as a model ruler of the Enlightenment. This was even despite a series of Catherine's decrees that deepened the enslavement of Russian peasants. In 1747, before Catherine's reign, the widespread Russian practice of buying and selling peasants as property had been given legal status. And beginning in 1760, landlords could deport them to Siberia for disobedience. After her accession in 1762, Catherine went even further. In 1767, her decree deprived peasants of the right to lodge complaints of brutality and cruelty against their masters. In 1785, a further decree by the "Semiramis of the North" officially defined the status of the peasants as their owners' chattel, and the punishment for complaints was increased: those complaining now faced exile for life as forced laborers in the state mines of Nerchinsk in Siberia.

Catherine's harmonious relations with her Western admirers did not, however, last forever. Two years after the famous trip down the Dnieper, the foundations of the Western order were shaken: revolution had broken out in France. If up until now the leading lights of the Enlightenment could easily imagine Russia as the embodiment of their utopian dreams of a rational state, then Catherine's decisive reaction to the news from France must have come as an unpleasant surprise to many. On the orders of the "Semiramis of the North," distinguished representatives of the Enlightenment in Russia Alexander Radishchev and Nikolai Novikov found themselves imprisoned. The empress had the former sentenced to death for writing a critical novel set in contemporary Russia. As a sign of clemency, his penalty was subsequently reduced to exile in Siberia. After Catherine's death in 1796, her successor Paul I allowed Radishchev to return from exile. Radishchev committed suicide in 1802. Novikov received a fifteen-year prison sentence. He, too, was released only after Catherine's death and never resumed his public activity. In 1791, when the first European Enlightenment-style constitution was ratified in Poland, Catherine immediately ordered armed intervention, crushing all signs of resistance, and eventually erased the country from the map of Europe with the help of the monarchs of Prussia and Austria.

This situation, however, did not last long. Soon, Western elites found new reasons for seeing an advocate of progress and a herald of freedom in a subsequent Russian emperor. Alexander I—Napoleon's conqueror—was fêted in Vienna, London, and Berlin, where one of the main squares was named after him as the liberator of Europe from the Corsican usurper's yoke. Young Alexander's highly publicized deliberations on the benefits of constitutional monarchy immediately earned him the enthusiasm of many advocates of progress throughout the West. The model American republican Thomas Jefferson held high hopes for the tsar.

While Alexander may have initially allowed himself to dream of reforms—his tutor, the Swiss intellectual Frédéric-César de la Harpe, had exercised influence over him in this regard—he ultimately never introduced them and quickly ceased dreaming of them. In any event, La Harpe himself, feeling discouraged, soon left Russia. In contrast to Alexander, his successor, Nicholas, never even dreamed of reform, either as a young man or later. He began his reign in December 1825 by crushing the attempt at a coup by a group of young army officers imbued with republican ideals. He then relentlessly tracked down and crushed every sign of criticism or dissatisfaction among his subjects. Unlike Catherine and Alexander, he made no effort at all to impress the West as a "progressive" ruler. Quite the opposite: he openly proclaimed the ideal of autocracy—that is, the unquestioning obedience of subjects to the ruler, whose will was law. For Nicholas, traditional Russian despotism was not something to be shamefully hidden under a layer of fine words about respect for freedom, the primacy of laws, and other ideals of the Enlightenment. The tsar was proud of the fact that, unlike in many Western countries, perfect order reigned in his empire.

And indeed, order did reign. Nicholas's Russian critics were pursued by the police, put in prison, deported in chains to hard labor, exiled to Siberia or other distant places, conscripted into the army for many years, and sent to the far reaches of the empire so they would have no contact with their own social milieu. As the Poles learned after their unsuccessful uprising in 1831, cruel punishment awaited rebels. The lesson was imparted on multiple occasions to the nations of the Caucasus region. In 1848–1849, it turned out that Nicholas was able not only to maintain order effectively in his own empire but in fact willingly imposed his order in Europe, where rebellious subjects were attempting to change the political status quo. In the eyes of Western intellectuals, the Russia of Nicholas I had lost the progressive aura that it had acquired during the time of his predecessors. It had now earned itself the epithet of "gendarme of Europe." This, however, in no way spelled the end of Western dreams about the mysterious country on the eastern edge of the continent.

It was at this time that a modern ideology of the state developed in Russia based on the conviction that autocracy was the natural expression of the hopes and aspirations of Russians, whose way of thinking was different from that of Westerners. The advocates of this view claimed that all those who tried to judge the Russian state and its society using Western ideas—such as civic and religious liberties, freedom of speech, private property, and so on—were mistaken. The authors and supporters of this new Russian ideology claimed that Russians preferred other values—such as a sense of community or a deep attachment to their ruler—over those so prized in the West. They often argued that even if there were Russians who thought otherwise, they did so because they were alienated from their own people; instead of identifying themselves with their native values, they were parroting Western ideas. In this view, a Westerner was quite unable to understand Russia. In fact, even Russians themselves were often unable to understand it completely. Those who tried were largely educated in Western notions and traditions; their minds had been contaminated with foreignness. Only "simple" folk, especially illiterate peasants, were true representatives of the Russian way of living and thinking. They were, however, unable to formulate and proclaim their ideas on national and international stages. And so, the tsar, "the father of his people," having been joined with them in a mystic union, spoke on their behalf.

The theory of the Russians' deep-rooted difference from Westerners had not come originally from Russian thinkers. In fact, the idea arose in German philosophy at the turn of the eighteenth and nineteenth centuries and the writing of Johann Gottfried Herder, its pioneering proponent. Unlike Leibniz, Voltaire, Diderot, and many other European intellectuals who had earlier willingly and generously expressed opinions about Russia, this Lutheran pastor, born in the East Prussian town of Mohrungen (today Morąg), was not a total stranger to that country. An inhabitant of East Prussia, he had spent four years as a child under Russian occupation and later lectured for five years in Riga, a predominantly German-speaking city in the Russian Empire. Although he never fully mastered the Russian language, while in Riga he wrote an ode in German to Peter the Great in which he praised the Russian emperor, repeating the well-known tropes of Leibniz and Voltaire. His views, however, soon diverged from the norms of the Enlightenment. Reflecting on the laws governing history, Herder came to the conclusion that there was no universal model of civilization shaping different nations to varying degrees. Instead, Western civilization was the result of the influence of different peoples' separate, specific cultures. This civilization develops, Herder argued, by going through phases of domination by one culture or another. In this process of development, "older" cultures, after fully realizing their potential, are successively challenged and replaced by "younger" ones. After the eras of domination by Greek, Roman, Romanesque, and Germanic civilizations, claimed Herder, the Slavs' time was approaching. In the German pastor's opinion, the most creative and unadulterated sources of this civilization could be found in the culture and customs of the simple Slavic folk. The Slavs (Herder was thinking above all of the Russians) were gentle agricultural workers who loved peace and domestic virtues. They shunned conflicts and wars and made reluctant soldiers. It is truly hard not to be astonished how this idyllic image of gentle Slavic pacifists was later used to formulate the ideology of the Russian Empire—a thoroughly militaristic police state.

This is not the first nor the last paradox involving Western perceptions of Russia. Throughout almost the entirety of the nineteenth and twentieth centuries, this country exercised such an influence over the West's imagination partly because it was seen precisely as something eluding the rational, commonsensical views that Western minds had relied upon to explain the world. While social and political reality in Western Europe appeared to be growing more predictable and explicable in the language of the bourgeois ideals of safety, relative wealth, common sense, and moderation, Russia remained an intriguing mystery. It was an enigmatic and never fully understood country

of great potential, heading into the future on its very own path—a civilization
that had not yet realized its goals and of which anything could be expected.
Many Western and Russian intellectuals, whether supporters or opponents of
tsarist rule, agreed on one thing: Russia, unlike the "older" Western cultures,
was simply in its youthful stage—a phase of maturing and staking out its own
identity. Hence the actual, existing Russia was simply a foretaste of some future, fully developed Russia, about which nothing definite could yet be said.
The poet Fyodor Tyutchev wrote:

> You cannot grasp Russia with your mind
> Or judge her by any common measure,
> Russia is one of a special kind
> You can only believe in her.[4]

Tyutchev was an ardent eulogist for the empire. The Polish poet Adam
Mickiewicz, however, was anything but. Nevertheless, he also saw in Russia a
mysterious future potential. This country appeared to him, as it had earlier to
Leibniz, as "a wide-spread page prepared for God to write." But unlike the German philosopher and his successors, the Polish poet did not entrust his hopes
to the Russian rulers. He left open the question of the country's future destiny.
Mickiewicz described Russia thus:

> This level plain lies open, waste, and white,
> A wide-spread page prepared for God to write. –
> Will he trace here his message from above;
> And, using for his letters holy men,
> Will he sketch here his writ of faith again,
> That all the human race is ruled by love
> And offerings remain the world's best prize?
> Or will that fiend who still the Lord defies
> Appear and carve with his oft-sharpened sword
> That prisons should forbid mankind to rise,
> And scourges are humanity's reward?[5]

For Mickiewicz, the equestrian statue of Peter the Great in St. Petersburg
was an allegory of Russia seen as a riddle awaiting its solution in the future.
He wrote:

> His charger's reins Tsar Peter has released;
> He has been flying down the road, perchance,
> And here the precipice checks his advance.
> With hoofs aloft now stands the maddened beast,

Champing its bit unchecked, with slackened rein:
You guess that it will fall and be destroyed.
Thus it has galloped long, with tossing mane,
Like a cascade, leaping into the void,
That, fettered by the frost, hangs dizzily.
But soon will shine the sun of liberty,
And from the west a wind will warm this land. –
Will the cascade of tyranny then stand?[6]

Pushkin adopted this allegory from Mickiewicz for polemical purposes in the laudatory, though essentially ambivalent, vision of the Russian Empire in his narrative poem *The Bronze Horseman*:

Where will you gallop, charger proud,
Where next your plunging hoofbeats settle?
Oh, Destiny's great potentate!
Was it not thus, a towering idol
Hard by the chasm, with iron bridle
You reared up Russia to her fate?[7]

Both authors of these broad, resonant metaphors, like numerous other commentators speaking about Russia, believed that whatever would eventually be written on the blank sheet, and wherever the hooves of Peter's horse landed, it would have great significance for the future of the world. The Romantic vision of the history of civilization as a process of displacing "old" cultures with "younger" ones had a great influence on Western minds. There could be no doubt about Russia's "youthfulness" in civilizational terms. At the same time, the speed and dynamism of its development from the time of Peter continued to astonish. A backward, obscure province had not only become a European power during the Enlightenment but also, by the second half of the nineteenth century, Russian cultural achievements had become a major inspiration for Western culture. Russian literature, which had been developing through imitation of European models since the late seventeenth century, revealed to the outside world literary works that Western readers recognized as an organic and creative part of their own culture—one they also often valued even more than the contemporary works of Western writers. Western readers recognized their own world in the novels of Dostoevsky, Turgenev, and Tolstoy. They could examine their own most pressing concerns and dilemmas in a new light, one that illuminated everything more clearly and let them penetrate more deeply beneath the surface of reality. In the freshness of these contemporary Russian literary masterpieces, one could discern marks of the dynamism and energy of the "younger culture" that was outstripping the "older" Western one. The creative power of Russian literature was seen by some as a harbinger of the arrival of new, broader civilizational currents, flowing this time not from west to east, but from the opposite direction.

This steady stream of cultural and artistic sensations from Russia lasted without interruption until World War I. The great Russian novels were followed by the great Russian theater of Chekhov's plays and Stanislavsky's directing. Tchaikovsky, Anton Rubinstein, Borodin, Rimsky-Korsakov, and Mussorgsky were played in concert halls and opera houses all over the world. At the beginning of the twentieth century, performances of Diaghilev's *Ballets Russes* with music by Stravinsky, choreography by Fokin, set design by Nikolai Roerich and Leon Bakst, as well as the incomparable balletic artistry of Vaslav Nijinsky and Anna Pavlova, were all the rage. The abstract painting of Kandinsky and Malevich led the way in avant-garde art. The Western imagination, electrified by these and other achievements of Russian artists, dreamed prophetic dreams and eagerly projected them onto Russia.

Over the course of the nineteenth century, the Western bourgeois socioeconomic worldview found a relatively stable outlet for its aspirations in a capitalist economy and liberal politics. But at the same time, radical critics of this bourgeois worldview—on the left and right alike—sought alternative social and civilizational models. Following in the footsteps of eighteenth-century utopia seekers, each side was often ready to detect these alternative models and inspirations in the same place in that mysterious but fascinating country where, with an ounce of imagination, one could find answers to all of the West's ills and dilemmas: Russia.

The man who more than anyone else inspired the European right's utopian dreams about Russia in the early nineteenth century was Joseph de Maistre. He knew Russia much better than most of those in the West who pontificated about it, both before and after him. This French monarchist and political critic of Napoleon was in Russia during the Napoleonic Wars as the ambassador of the king of Piedmont-Sardinia. Living there, he was unable to ignore the fact that Russia, even under the rule of the young Alexander I, was still an autocracy unparalleled in Europe. But this was precisely what de Maistre found to be the Russian monarchy's greatest asset. Contrary to the belief in man's positive nature that lay at the heart of both nineteenth-century liberalism and socialism, de Maistre saw man as essentially a morally tainted creature, unable to resist sinful temptation. He maintained that only moral discipline imposed from above by a traditional monarchy based on religious ethical foundations was capable of creating social order and shielding people from descending into chaos, anarchy, and crime. De Maistre believed that while in the West the foundations of traditional social and moral order were disintegrating under the blows of the French Revolution and its successors, both liberal and radical, Russia represented a bastion of ancient values and a real hope for their rebirth.

This line of thinking was welcome in Russia, where official state ideology soon combined de Maistre's views with the Slavophile tradition emanating from Herder's thought. This ideology, established under Nicholas I, assumed its mature, official form in the last two decades of the nineteenth century under the pen (and watchful bureaucratic eye) of Konstantin Pobedonostsev, the principal guardian of political correctness in the Russian Empire during the time of Alexander III. But even before Pobedonostsev became the empire's chief ideologue, thoughts such as these had already been explored by Dostoevsky, especially in his later work. Indeed, Dostoevsky later inspired a great many Western thinkers, artists, and readers who were seeking ways to escape the shoals of bourgeois thinking while simultaneously rejecting faith in the revolutionary, socialist prophecies of the European left.

For the most part, a certain ambivalence toward Russia could be felt in right-wing European circles. On the one hand, the Russian Empire was presented as a bastion of traditional values, unsullied by the bourgeois miasma of liberalism. On the other, however, it was hard to ignore the traditional image of Russia as a seat of "oriental" barbarity—an image hardly fitting the conservative ideals of rebuilding old, preliberal Western culture. One of those who tried to reconcile these contradictions in his own way was Nietzsche. He maintained that civilization in the West, in order to free itself of the bourgeois snare, must first be swept away by new barbarians. Destroying what is already sick and infertile, the barbarians would infuse it with vital strength and youthful energy, thus reviving its culture. Citing the example of ancient Rome, Nietzsche asked: "Where are the barbarians of the twentieth century?"[8]

At the turn of the nineteenth and twentieth centuries, these barbarians were awaited in the West with growing impatience. The Greek poet Constantine P. Cavafy expected them; Oswald Spengler and a great many others had their theories about their imminent onslaught. Nietzsche himself not only asked about "the barbarians of the twentieth century" but provided answers too. Of course, at the time no one better fit the role of barbarian-reformer in Nietzsche's (and not only his) imaginary world than Russia—long seen as a country of limitless potential, where everything appeared larger, less inhibited, more radical, and wilder than in the well-organized but sterile West. Nietzsche prophesied: "The sign of the next century will be the arrival of the Russians in the world of culture. The great goal, contact with the barbarians, the revival of art, splendid youth, marvelous madness and real strength of will."[9] At the end he claimed: "Russia must come to dominate Europe and Asia."[10]

Right-wing opponents of the bourgeois order tried to see in Russia the source of renewal for what they understood as the traditional Western civilization. At the same time, left-wing opponents of the bourgeoisie were thinking along similar lines, although their language was different, and they championed different goals. The tradition of the European left in the nineteenth century was based on the conviction that the revolutionary ideals of 1789—liberty, equality, fraternity—had not been realized and that the work of the French Revolution had to be completed by toppling the rule of the bourgeoisie and liberating the people. However, revolutionary outbursts in Europe usually ended in failure. After the essentially disappointing results of 1848, the second half of the nineteenth century saw capitalism grow at a breakneck pace alongside its liberal political institutions, deepening the disillusionment of those counting on a speedy revolution and radical change. Yet the stronger capitalism became, the more left-wing movements developed hoping to replace it with a more equitable system. If the advocates of utopias in the Enlightenment had looked hopefully toward Russia, trying to perceive in successive Russian rulers the builders of the kingdom of reason, in the second half of the nineteenth century the socialist heirs of the Enlightenment once again began to look more carefully in the direction of that enigmatic land. However, they no longer sided with the empire's rulers but instead with the men and women who had for some time been trying to bring about a revolution in Russia.

In the 1860s, the attention in the West turned seriously to the Russian radicals. The Russian revolutionary movement was growing quickly and evolving in search of the most suitable policies and methods. In the 1870s, the Land and Liberty movement tried to broaden revolutionary consciousness by explaining to the peasants that they should rise up against unjust tyranny, overthrow the tsarist regime, dispossess the landowners, abolish private property, and then live in a better world. For the most part, the effect of these efforts was the opposite of the one desired: the people, instead of bringing about a revolution, often simply handed over the speakers to the police. In the face of this evidence of the people's "immaturity," these efforts were soon abandoned, and the revolutionaries decided to work "on the people's behalf," until the people matured enough to realize where their own interests lay. This operating model prevailed in the Russian revolutionary movement from this point on, the most famous example coming years later with the activities of Lenin and the Bolsheviks. Meanwhile, a wing of the Land and Liberty organization turned into the terrorist group the People's Will, whose activities focused on assassinations of government officials. Their tactics often included bombs, which also killed many innocent people. Following the successful attempt by the People's Will on the life of Emperor Alexander II in 1881, the police broke up the organization, and a wave of repression swept through Russia.

The changing attitude of Karl Marx toward Russian radicals illustrates the growing interest in them on the part of the Western left. At first, Marx was one of the most implacable critics of Russia. He saw it as a backward country, basically incapable of generating a socialist revolution. In his view, Russia was a center of reaction, a feudal land without a proletariat, that is, without the one social class capable of carrying out a revolution and introducing socialism. According to Marx, socialism could be introduced only where a developed capitalist economy already existed, so it was pointless to look in the east. By the logic of the author of *Das Kapital*, Russia could only be an obstacle on the road to realizing the communist utopia. Yet over time, after learning about the Russian socialists' determination, Marx became more intrigued. Russia was the first country to translate *Das Kapital* and to discuss it seriously at a time when few people in Germany itself were interested, and Engels had resorted to writing glowing reviews and publishing them under a variety of pseudonyms in order to arouse interest in his friend's work. Eventually Marx began to attach so much importance to the Russian revolutionary movement that he strove to learn Russian in order to be able to read Russian socialist ideologues Nikolai Chernyshevsky and Petr Lavrov in the original, as well as to be able to follow economic and social changes there.

Marx's ideological kinsmen and heirs attached a growing significance to Russia, at least from the time when his principal rival at the heart of the international revolutionary movement, the Russian Mikhail Bakunin, became the greatest authority among Western anarchists. In 1905, when a revolution broke out in Russia, culminating with what were (for that country) far-reaching reforms, there was a growing tendency to see Russia as the center of events in the world socialist movement. Martin Malia writes: "For the first time in history a tremor in Russia's internal life touched off reverberations that were felt in the farthest corners of the West, indeed outside the West. St. Petersburg was beginning to lay claim to the role that radical Paris had played throughout the nineteenth century. In fact, though no one suspected this at the time, the capital of the tsars had already produced most of the theories, and the leadership, that would soon propel it far beyond any radicalism that had ever emanated from Paris."[11] Never before had Western revolutionaries so literally and directly pinned their hopes on Russia. Earlier, the tradition had been to project dreams onto an ideologically enhanced image of this country, usually silently counting on the ignorance of a Western public that was incapable of comparing the image with its original. Now, however, a growing number of Western ideologues and revolutionary activists not only theorized but actively cooperated with Russian radicals, taking their opinions seriously, and often acknowledging them as their political allies and ideological mentors. Listening to Kropotkin, Plekhanov, or Lenin, many looked to Russia with growing hope. Much was expected of it.

While critics of the bourgeois West—both on the left and the right—tried to see in the inscrutable Russian sphinx an omen of some better (or at least more interesting) future, some relatively rare Western observers challenged these impressions from time to time. In 1839, during the reign of Nicholas I, a French aristocrat, the Marquis Astolphe de Custine, made a journey to Russia. This conservative intellectual went there to find living proof of de Maistre's vision. He most likely wanted to see with his own eyes that bastion of traditional values and describe it as a model of renewal for corrupt Western societies.

What he found, however, was the opposite of what he was ostensibly seeking. He saw in Russia a type of regime unknown in the West. Instead of discovering the spiritual benefits of Russian autocracy, de Custine observed frightening moral desolation. He saw a society based on fear of the official power that permeated all social relations and reduced them to a ubiquitous master/slave structure. The image of a master brutally beating his coachman, with the latter treating his horse no less cruelly, became for de Custine an alarming symbol of Russian autocracy. In his extensive work *Russia in 1839*, published after his journey, de Custine described as follows the nature of authority and the society in that country:

> A monarch who agrees to be seen as more than a mortal assumes the responsibility for all the evil that heaven can send down to earth during his reign.
> A touchiness unknown elsewhere results from this political fanaticism. An accident is treated as a matter of state, as a lack of the respect conferred on the Tsar by God. An unfortunate twist of fate is seen as the start of a revolt, nature's independence is seen as a bad example. A fly that flies at an inopportune moment during a ceremony at court humiliates the tsar.[12]

In St. Petersburg, de Custine was received by Nicholas I, who explained to him that "despotism exists in Russia, it is at the heart of my government and is in tune with the temper of the nation."[13] De Custine left Russia completely disenchanted, knowing already that tsarist despotism was no answer to the inadequacies of bourgeois society. He described what he had seen as something much worse than the West's current ills. He saw the Russian Empire as a tyranny, one in which "the tyrant demands of his people not only submissiveness, but happiness under this burden, with a smile on their faces."[14]

De Custine's book on Russia provoked a great deal of interest in Western intellectual circles. And not only in Western ones. Alexander Herzen wrote:

> This is undoubtedly the most interesting and sensible book that a foreigner has written about Russia. . . . This book makes difficult reading for a Russian, one's head droops, one's arms drop; it is hard to feel the terrible truth and it is sad that a foreigner had to hit the sore spot. . . . This book is torture to me, like a stone crushing my chest; I do not even look at the faults, the essence of de Custine's view is accurate; it is a terrible society, and that country is Russia. His gaze is humiliatingly perceptive.[15]

De Custine's picture of Russia arouses controversy to this day. Some historians accused him of exaggeration by highlighting the dark side of Russian reality. Even if they were right, it is hard to deny this vision its prophetic quality. This sentiment was best expressed by the twentieth-century American expert on Russia George Kennan, who observed that de Custine had delved so deeply into the internal logic of Russian autocracy that his enhanced portrait had in essence described the Russia of a hundred years later—Stalin's Russia.

Russian authorities, who always tried to control their country's image abroad, initially saw de Custine as a valuable political ally and attempted to show him those things in Russia that he ought to appreciate. They assumed that a positive account from the pen of a French intellectual would repair the dismal reputation that the Russian Empire had acquired after the brutal suppression of the Polish uprising in 1831. De Custine realized, however, that he was being manipulated. This too he described. His book undermined the visions, welcomed by the Russian authorities, of tsarist autocracy as a bastion of traditional conservative values.

A propaganda campaign in the West was immediately orchestrated by St. Petersburg in an attempt to damage de Custine's credibility. Pamphlets and articles began to appear. Yakov Tolstoy, an agent in Paris of the Third Department of His Imperial Majesty's Chancellery, published two pamphlets attacking de Custine; Ksawery Łabęcki, a Pole and a senior adviser to the tsarist foreign ministry, brought out a similar pamphlet in French, German and English; Nikolai Grech (Mikołaj Grecz), another Pole and an *homme de confiance* of the head of the Russian secret police, wrote a polemic against de Custine in French and in German. Grech even hired at Russian expense the French writer Hippolyte Auger, who willingly took on the work of writing a vaudeville ridiculing de Custine. However, the heads of the secret police in St. Petersburg, generals Dubelt and Benkendorf, abandoned the idea of staging the vaudeville in Paris, fearing that overly brazen propaganda might create the opposite of the effect intended. The Russian authorities also tried to encourage Honoré de Balzac—who was in love with Countess Ewelina Hańska, a Polish aristocrat and Russian subject—to write a pro-Russian panegyric to draw attention away from de Custine's critical reflections. The writer, however, refused.

If de Custine's book represented the most serious challenge to right-wing dreams of Russia, Joseph Conrad's novel *Under Western Eyes*, published in 1911, made short work of the idealized Western view of the Russian revolutionary movement. Conrad knew Russia incomparably better than any contemporary Western intellectual. As a small boy, he had spent four years in penal exile—initially in Vologda, then in Chernigov—accompanying his parents, who had been sentenced for antigovernment activities in Russian-occupied Poland. His mother died in exile, and at the same time in Poland two of his uncles were killed in the 1863 uprising against Russian rule, while two other uncles ended up in Russian prisons. Russia's dark side, carefully concealed from the West by the authorities in St. Petersburg, was the world of Conrad's childhood.

In his novel about Russia he depicted the struggle between tsarist despotism and revolutionaries as "senseless desperation, provoked by senseless tyranny." In Conrad's far-from-optimistic view, Russia was so thoroughly imbued with tyranny and contempt for the freedom and dignity of the individual that even in the event of the success of a revolution, nothing new should be expected. Anticipating the Russian Revolution, Conrad wrote: "The ferocity and imbecility of an autocratic rule rejecting all legality and in fact basing itself upon complete moral anarchism provokes the no less imbecile and atrocious answer of a purely utopian revolutionism encompassing destruction by the first means to hand, in the strange conviction that a fundamental change of hearts must follow the downfall of any given human institutions. These people are unable to see that all they can effect is merely a change of names."[16]

The novel *Under Western Eyes* was not a success in England. It was only after the Bolshevik revolution that some Western critics rediscovered the book, seeing prophetic elements in Conrad's work. They encountered, however, vigorous resistance from those who preferred to see in Bolshevik Russia the long-awaited embodiment of Western projections and dreams of a more just and sensible world. And these were legion.

2

Ex Oriente Lux

A Brave New World

In November 1917, the Bolsheviks seized power in Russia after an armed coup, accompanied by slogans echoing the rhetoric of the French Revolution. For many people on the European left, an old dream of completing the unfinished Revolution of 1789 took on new life. This was a historic moment when two great myths of the West—the myth of revolution and the myth of Russia—intersected. At the same time, reports started to emerge of the unprecedented scale of atrocities committed in the name of the revolution: mass murder, rapes, torture, executions of hostages, and the illegal incarceration of people in prisons and concentration camps.

Immediately after coming to power, the Bolsheviks made no systematic attempt to conceal from the world the fact that they were employing terror and violence. Like their French Jacobin predecessors, they announced that in order to bring beneficial results for humanity, revolutions cannot avoid having victims, especially in the early stages. When open opposition to the Bolsheviks was crushed in the space of a few years, the new authorities, despite initial promises, were in no hurry to set up a democratic government. On the contrary, the terror deployed during the Civil War became institutionalized, and although in the 1920s its bloody dynamic slackened for a time, it became an intrinsic element of the Soviet system henceforward. This was also the time when the Bolsheviks, after a short period of reveling publicly in their own crimes, began to conceal them from the world. World public opinion became a target for increasingly systematic Soviet propaganda, which industriously constructed Russia's image abroad.

Meanwhile in the West, starting from the moment Lenin seized power in Russia, the subject of Bolshevik violence and terror was shrouded in the haze of ambiguity. Western perceptions of revolutionary violence were based on information that, more often than not, was difficult to confirm. It usually arrived secondhand and frequently bore the mark of propaganda. In such an atmosphere, even demonstrable facts could be questioned relatively easily or simply rejected out of hand. Bolshevik violence quickly became a sensitive subject, not just in Bolshevik propaganda but also in Western debates on Soviet Russia. Some Westerners willingly gave credence to the reports of Bolshevik atrocities; others denied them on principle. From the very beginning, this was a particularly awkward subject for those inclined to believe in the noble intentions and great promise of the Bolshevik revolution and for those who tried to view the Bolsheviks as potential political or economic partners. The controversies surrounding the topic of Soviet crimes would never fully dissipate but would indeed persist as long as the Bolshevik state existed. Their consequences linger in the West's consciousness (and subconscious) to this day.

While the Bolshevik regime appeared to Western public opinion like a new incarnation of the eternal Russian sphinx, events within Russia were acquiring their own momentum. Violence lay at the very heart of the communist doctrine of class warfare, in addition to forming the crux of Bolshevik political tactics. Violence was the reflexive response of the new revolutionary regime to the basic problems of the country it now ruled. How did one retain political power? How did one ensure the people's cooperation with the regime? How did one develop the economy? Soviet Russia became a country where terror, violence, and coercion became not only a tool in the Bolsheviks' struggle to retain power but were employed systematically as an instrument to control the people, the economy, culture, and daily life. Perhaps the most distinctive new institution, one which permanently carved terror and violence into the social fabric of the new state, was the system of concentration camps, or as they were later known, "corrective labor camps." These would go down in the history of the twentieth century under the acronym that was adopted in 1930: the Gulag.[1]

The beginnings of the Gulag are inextricably linked with the introduction of Soviet rule in Russia and are a clear indication of the Bolshevik leaders' attitude to the people of the country in which they had seized power. As is often the case with revolutions, it had proved much easier to seize power than to govern. The armed putsch in Petrograd had brought Lenin and his group quick success, but it soon became apparent that the new rulers were essentially quite unprepared to run the country. Their attention, however, focused not on the people's immediate needs (all they had to offer was a limitless repertoire of slogans about the glorious future) but on the issue of staying in power. Initially viewing Russia as the first beachhead for the imminent world revolution, the Bolsheviks deferred addressing specific problems of the country to the time in the near future when the forces of world communism would take global control. In the meantime, they concentrated on overcoming the resistance of class enemies.

Class enemies existed in the Bolshevik mind in two forms. First, there was the real enemy, who was resisting and actively opposing the new regime. This enemy had to be destroyed. In order to achieve this, a civil war was unleashed in Russia, a conflict that would soon consume several million human lives. But in addition to the real enemies, the Bolshevik leaders' attention was focused also on potential enemies. Membership in the classes defined by Marxist-Leninist doctrine as hostile—the bourgeoisie, the middle class, the landowners, the clergy, the intelligentsia, the wealthier peasantry (virtually everyone except the poorest members of the proletariat, laborers and farmhands)—was adequate grounds to be included in the gallery of class enemies. Yet membership of the proletariat itself (in whose name the Bolshevik leaders spoke, even though very few of them came from this group) was also no protection against accusations of class hostility. On more than one occasion, Lenin and his associates explained that many Russian proletarians were in fact imbued with an incorrect class consciousness and that it was time to educate them. Meanwhile, they had to be treated uncompromisingly and, if necessary, harshly. In these circumstances, the sole bearer of the proletariat's true class consciousness was its vanguard, that is, the leadership of the Bolshevik party: Lenin and his associates. Thus, a dictatorship of the proletariat in absentia was set up in Russia.

Active enemies were physically liquidated, while potential enemies (and there were inevitably huge numbers of these) had to be neutralized. The institution that was well adapted to this task was the concentration camp. In the summer of 1918, barely a few months after the putsch in Petrograd, Lenin's regime was facing a crisis. As Richard Pipes writes, "There exists solid evidence that by the summer of 1918, when the Bolsheviks launched the terror, they were rejected by all strata of the population except for their own apparatus."[2] In a surviving telegram from August 1918 to Bolshevik commissars in Penza, Lenin, in typical fashion, orders the application of "mass terror [in other words mass executions] of kulaks, priests and white guards," while he recommends that "suspicious elements" should be imprisoned "in a concentration camp outside the city."[3] Camps like this already existed in many places. In short order following the socialist Fanya Kaplan's failed attempt to assassinate Lenin, on September 5, 1918, the authorities announced a "decree on red terror," officially sanctioning arbitrary killing and incarcerating people in prisons and camps without trial.

This authority was granted to the Extraordinary Commission for Fighting Counterrevolution and Sabotage, commanded by Felix Dzerzhinsky, which has gone down in history as the Cheka.[4] In addition to pursuing and liquidating active enemies, the Cheka's duties included "safeguarding of the Soviet Republic from class enemies by means of isolating them in concentration camps."[5]

In setting up concentration camps in Russia, the Bolsheviks were following Western colonial models of terrorizing and controlling local populations. In 1897, the Spanish had set up such camps in Cuba in the process of quelling the uprising there. The Spanish governor of the island, General Valeriano Weyler y Nicolau, resolved to cut off the insurgents from sources of aid from the local population. To this end he ordered the "reconcentration" of the population in special camps. Those who failed to follow this order were treated as insurgents and were liable to be the target of armed operations. The Spanish colonial authorities' actions were immediately criticized in the American press for being profoundly inhumane. It should be pointed out that at this time the United States was competing with Spain for control over Cuba. The moral stigma attached to the Spanish methods did not prevent the Americans from employing similar methods in their own overseas territories in the Philippines, captured from the Spanish, where in 1900 the US forces set up concentration camps on the island of Mindanao.

Around the same time, the British introduced concentration camps in South Africa during the Boer War. Quashing Boer resistance, British commander Lord Kitchener applied scorched-earth tactics, depriving the local population of its homes and livelihoods and putting them in concentration camps. Within a few months around twenty thousand people, including numerous children, had died of disease in the camps. These events caused a commotion in British public opinion, mainly thanks to reports by Emily Hobhouse, a British aristocrat known for philanthropic work. She wrote: "Maintaining camps like these is nothing but the murder of innocents."[6] Under pressure from the press and public opinion, the British government stopped using the camps. However, the Germans adopted the idea in 1904 when the native peoples of Herero and Nama staged an uprising in German South-West Africa. The German authorities used the African prisoners in the camps as slave labor and managed to obliterate great numbers of the native people by either killing them or deporting them to the desert and depriving them of food and water.

In adopting these colonial methods, the Soviet authorities were the first to apply them to their own population. During the Civil War, the Bolsheviks routinely treated people held in concentration camps as hostages. These practices, along with other atrocities, did not entirely escape the attention of the West.

In the midst of the Civil War, on February 22 and 24, 1919, British diplomat Sir C. Eliot telegraphed his superior in London, Lord Curzon, from Vladivostok with specific details of recent Bolshevik atrocities in the Yekaterinburg area. Here is an extensive extract from this cable. The facts, reported in dry official tones, tell more than could any commentary, hence I quote at length:

Sir C. Eliot to Earl Curzon (Received February 23, 1919): Following report of 71 Bolshevik victims [that is, victims of Bolsheviks] received from consular office at Ekaterinburg, dated 19th February:

Nos. 1 to 18 Ekaterinburg citizens (first three personally known to me) were imprisoned without any accusation being made against them, and at four in the morning of the 29th June were taken (with another, making 19 altogether) to Ekaterinburg sewage dump, half mile from Ekaterinburg, and ordered to stand in line alongside of newly-dug ditch. Forty armed men in civil clothes, believed to be Communist militia, and giving impression of semi-intelligent people, opened fire, killing 18. The 19th, Mr. Chistoserdow, miraculously escaped in general confusion. I, together with other consuls at Ekaterinburg, protested to Bolsheviks against brutality, to which Bolsheviks replied, advising us to mind our own business, stating that they had shot these people to avenge death of their comrade, Malishev, killed at front, against Czechs.

Nos. 19 and 20 are 2 of twelve labourers arrested for refusing to support Bolshevik Government, and on 12th July thrown alive into hole into which hot slag deposits from works at Verhisetski near Ekaterinburg. Bodies were identified by fellow labourers.

Nos. 21 to 26 were taken as hostages and shot at Kamishlof on 20th July.

Nos. 27 to 33, accused of plotting against Bolshevik Governments, arrested 16th December at village of Troitsk, Perm Government. Taken 17th December to station Silva, Perm railway, and all decapitated by sword. Evidence shows that victims had their necks half cut through from behind, head of No. 29 only hanging on small piece of skin.

Nos. 34 to 36, taken with 8 others beginning of July from camp, where they were undergoing trench-digging service for Bolsheviks to spot near Oufalay, about 80 versts from Ekaterinburg, and murdered by Red Guards with guns and bayonets.

Nos. 37 to 58, held in prison in Irbit as hostages, and 26th July murdered by gunshot, those not killed outright being finished off by bayonet. These people were shot in small groups, and murder was conducted by sailors and carried out by Letts, all of whom were drunk. After murder Bolsheviks continued to take ransom money from relatives of victims, from whom they concealed crime.

No. 59 was shot at village of Klevenkinski Verhotury district, 6th August, being accused of agitation against Bolsheviks.

No. 60, after being forced to dig his own grave, was shot by Bolsheviks at village Mercoushinski, Verhotury district, 13th Julty.

No. 61 murdered middle of July at Kamenski works for allowing church bells to be sounded contrary to Bolshevik orders, body afterwards found with others in hole with half head cut off.

No. 62 arrested without accusation, 8th July, at village Ooetski, Kamishlov district. Body afterwards found covered with straw and dung, beard torn from face with flesh, palms of hands cut out, and skin incised on forehead.

No. 63 was killed after much torture (details not given), 27th July at station Anthracite.

No. 67 murdered, 13th August, near village of Mironoffski.

No. 68 shot by Bolsheviks before his church at village of Korouffski, Kamishlov district, before eyes of villagers, his daughters and son, date not stated.

Nos. 69 to 71, killed at Kaslingski works near Kishtin, 4th June, together with 27 other civilians. No. 70 had head smashed in, exposing brains. No. 71 had head smashed in, arms and legs broken, and two bayonet wounds.

Dates in this telegram are 1918.

. . .

Sir C. Eliot to Earl Curzon—(Received February 25, 1919)
My telegram of 22 February. Following from consul at Ekaterinburg:
Nos. 72 to 103 examined, 32 civilians incarcerated and taken away by Bolsheviks with 19 others at various dates between 9th July, 7th August, 27th July, all 51 having been declared outlaws. Official medical examination of 52 bodies (of which 32 examined, Nos. 72 to 103 not identified), found in several holes; 3 from Kamishlof revealed that all had been killed by bayonet, sword, and bullet wounds. Following cases being typical: No. 76 had 20 light bayonet wounds in back; No. 78 had 15 bayonet wounds in back, 3 in chest; No. 80, bayonet wounds in back, broken jaw and skull; No. 89 had 2 fingers cut off a wrist, upper jaw hacked, mouth slit both sides, bayonet wound shoulder; No. 98, little finger off left hand and 4 fingers off right hand, head smashed; No. 99 had 12 bayonet wounds; No. 101 had 4 sword and 6 bayonet wounds.

These victims are distinct from 66 Kamishlof hostage children shot by machine guns near Ekaterinburg beginning of July, names not obtainable.[7]

If we compare early Bolshevik camps with their colonial predecessors, they seem to call to mind the German camps in South-West Africa. In both places, inmates were treated with utmost brutality and often turned into slave laborers.

On June 28, 1918, Trotsky recommended that the "bourgeoisie" and the "kulaks" be forced in camps to do "the worst kind of work."[8] Trotsky was supported by Dzerzhinsky who, on February 17, 1919, wrote in a report on the work of the Cheka:

> Along with sentencing by courts it is necessary to retain administrative sentencing—namely, the concentration camp. Even today the labor of those under arrest is far from being utilized in public works, and so I recommend that we retain these concentration camps for the exploitation of labor of persons under arrest: gentlemen who live without any occupation [and] those who are incapable of doing work without some compulsion; or, in regard to Soviet institutions, such measure of punishment ought to be applied for unconscientious attitude toward work, for negligence, for lateness, etc. With this measure we should be able to pull up even our very own workers.[9]

Concentration camps served not only to isolate "suspicious elements" as well as "class aliens" but were to be a method of mobilizing the workforce in the Soviet economy—either by means of direct coercion or as a threat and punishment for the unproductive, the poorly disciplined, or even for the chronically late. On April 11, 1919, the party Central Executive Committee issued a decree specifying: "Subjects to internment in the camps of forced labor are individuals or categories of individuals concerning whom decisions had been taken by organs of the administration, Cheka, Revolutionary Tribunals, People's Courts, and other Soviet organs authorized to do so by decrees and instructions."[10] To put it simply, the communist authorities could lock up anyone they wanted.

The closer the Bolsheviks came to final victory in the Civil War, the more helpless they became when faced with the question of how to deliver the economic conditions that their country needed to survive. In this kind of situation, they instinctively resorted to violence and coercion. Lenin and Trotsky believed that this was simply a temporary problem, one that would solve itself in the not-too-distant future when socialism would be introduced into Russia. Meanwhile, the situation appeared paradoxical when examined in the context of Marxist doctrine. Marx assumed that socialism could be built only on a "base" of a highly industrialized capitalist economy. But such a "base" did not exist in Russia at the time. Nor was there a massive urban proletariat—that is, the social class that was to take power and build the communist utopia. By seizing power (in the name of the temporarily absent proletariat), the Bolsheviks had thus created a political and social "superstructure" that, in the absence of a "base" was floating in the air, contrary to the laws of physics and "scientific socialism." Hence, both the practical task of providing their own country basic living conditions and the theoretical demand of reconciling reality with ideology meant that for the Bolsheviks, reviving and modernizing the Russian economy as quickly as possible was absolutely essential.

Trotsky believed that forced labor would be the flywheel of the Soviet economy. To skeptics he would reply that "the unproductive nature of compulsory labor is a liberal myth."[11] In this situation, concentration camps were for Trotsky an obvious pool of slave labor, so they had to be expanded and developed. A decree of the Bolshevik Central Executive Committee of May 12, 1919 called for the creation of forced labor camps for at least three hundred people in each provincial capital. Toward the end of 1919 there were twenty-one such camps in Russia, whereas a year later there were as many as 107. At the same time, discipline modeled on the labor camps was introduced into many areas of the economy. Anne Applebaum writes: "Even at this early stage in Soviet history, the line between 'forced labor' and ordinary labor was blurred."[12]

Using forced labor, the Bolsheviks did not have to resort to copying German colonial methods in Africa. Indeed—to quote the opinion of the historians David Dallin and Boris Nicolaevsky—in no other country did forced labor traditionally play such a key economic role as it did in Russia.[13] Here, they meant Imperial Russia. The history of the Russian Empire's economic eastward expansion, starting at least in the seventeenth century, as well as the history of the economic development of the Urals, Siberia, the Russian Far East, the Arctic, and Sakhalin, were inextricably linked with the history of penal deportations and forced labor.

In the last decade of the nineteenth century, Chekhov wrote on the fate and living conditions of convicts, their families, and descendants on the island of Sakhalin. His extensive reportage, *Sakhalin Island*, was the result of a trip he had undertaken for this purpose to this most remote corner of the Russian Empire. Meticulously researched and documented, Chekhov's account focuses on criminal inmates and exiles while conspicuously avoiding the topic of political prisoners, unpublishable under imperial censorship. Setting off for his voyage to Sakhalin in 1890, Chekhov wrote in a letter to his publisher:

> We have sent *millions* of people to rot in prison, we have let them rot casually, barbarously, without giving it a thought, we have driven people in chains for thousands of miles through the cold, infected them with syphilis, made them depraved, multiplied criminals, and we have thrust the blame for all this on the red-nosed jail-keepers. Today all of educated Europe knows that it is not the fault of the jailers, but rather of all of us—and this is none of our concern, this is not interesting![14]

So the Bolsheviks were in no way pioneers of employing systematic forced labor in Russia. Right from the start, however, they distinguished themselves from their predecessors by the scale of oppression and by the degree of ruthlessness, brutality, and cruelty they employed. In the first years of Bolshevik rule, Lenin's and Trotsky's energetic battle with the "liberal myth of the unprofitability of slave labor" quickly brought results in the form of mass hunger and the increasing destruction of the economy. At the start of the 1920s, at least five million people died of starvation in Soviet Russia.[15] With the world revolution's failure to materialize, the revolutionary regime in Russia found no other choice than to make a temporary compromise with reality: they relaxed for the time being the system of coercion and allowed the revival of a very limited form of free market. When they stopped shooting peasants and putting them in prison for selling agricultural produce (that is, when the NEP was introduced), famine vanished, and basic goods began to appear in shops.[16] For some foreign observers, life in large Russian cities began—at least at first glance—to resemble normal life. For the ideologically driven Bolshevik leaders, however, this compromise between ideology and reality did not represent a new direction. On the contrary, it appeared as something forced, unnatural, even shameful. It was, at best, a tactical pause in the revolutionary struggle for a better tomorrow. Extending this state of affairs for too long smacked of betraying fundamental communist ideals.

In this "transitional" phase following the Civil War, when the immediate threat to the Bolshevik regime had passed, the institution of the Soviet concentration camp was far from dying a natural death. Instead, the camp system was reorganized. A great many local camps and prisons, hastily constructed during the Civil War and the Red Terror, were now closed down, and the authorities began concentrating prisoners—both old and new—in the bourgeoning complex of camps on the Solovki Islands and in the area of the White Sea. Apart from criminal convicts, this was the destination for the main categories of Soviet political prisoners, including still-surviving representatives of the prerevolutionary "enemy classes": former landowners, businesspeople, civil servants, imperial army officers, clergy, members of every political party and organization except the Bolsheviks (for the time being), as well as other "suspicious" people.

The heart of this complex of camps was the medieval monastery on the Solovki Islands. Converting churches and monasteries into prisons and camps become a widespread Bolshevik practice. The previous inhabitants—the clergy— were often left there as prisoners. In the case of the Solovki monastery, however, using it as a prison was nothing new. Because of its extensive fortifications and remote, isolated location, Russian tsars used the monastery as a place of incarceration for particularly troublesome political prisoners. Throughout pre-revolutionary Russian history, around three hundred people were imprisoned on the Solovki Islands. In September 1923, when the Solovki concentration camp was officially opened, there were 3,049 prisoners. In January 1931, 71,000 inmates were held in the Solovki camp system.[17]

The early Solovki years imprinted themselves on the memory of many inmates above all as a period of wild cruelty and barbarity. Punishments included leaving inmates naked in the frost in winter. In summer, they were tied to posts in the forest filled with mosquitoes. Some measures were more refined: many accounts mention forcing prisoners to sit for many hours on horizontal bars without being able to touch the ground with their feet. Those who fell off or jumped down were beaten. Victims were killed in a variety of ways: most frequently they were simply shot, but there were also more elaborate methods: for example the "balan," which involved pushing a bound prisoner down the stairs (all 365 of them) at Sekirnaya Mountain, where the camp's main penal confinement was located. The most common and daily method of destroying the prisoners, however, was through a combination of hunger and physical labor.

In the 1920s, Soviet Russia's principal export—and source of highly coveted hard currency—was timber. Much of it came from the logging done by the Solovki slaves. Thus, the authorities began to see the Solovki camps primarily as an economic asset. If earlier camp inmates had been tormented often chaotically, in the second half of the 1920s this would be done to them systematically and rationally with an eye toward profits. The Solovki camps became a place difficult to describe using traditional concepts. The exploitation of the inmates was described by the authorities in purely economic terms. Cruelty, ruthlessness, and terror became indispensable elements in the camp system, but they did not figure in the language of the authorities. They spoke instead of taking advantage of economic resources, completing plans and production norms, implementing new methods of rational management, and so on. The authorities allocated production norms for inmates and introduced a strict equivalence between achieving these norms and the quantity and quality of food received. The idea was to use hunger to force the inmates to maximize effort. Camp commandants, under constant pressure from their superiors to raise production and revenue, kept increasing these norms. This system was devised by Naftali Frenkel, a criminal prisoner who, as a reward, was promoted to become one of the most important administrators of the camp system. His invention became the curse of inmates in Soviet forced labor camps for decades.

As a result of this system, inmates fell into a vicious circle: in order to escape hunger they had to overwork themselves until they were no longer able to keep it up. Then their rations fell, weakening them even more. Thus they were pushed on a downward slope, often leading gradually to total physical and mental exhaustion and then slow dehumanization and death. Individuals in the final stages of this journey, on the edge of humanity and close to death, were derisively called a *dokhodiaga* ("goner"), a "shit eater," or a *fitil* or "wick" (like the wick of a guttering candle).

In order to force inmates to do this murderous work, the authorities did not necessarily have to guard every one of them. The system devised in the Solovki camps was meant to have the inmates guarding one another and urging each other on. Norms were often calculated on the basis of whole brigades and not individual inmates. As a result, stronger prisoners often did not tolerate weaker individuals in their brigades who were incapable of completing what was usually a target set impossibly high. Instead of solidarity, the prisoners were supposed to be motivated by mutual animosity. A *dokhodiaga* could not usually count on any compassion, for he was, after all, a burden to the rest of the brigade. Janusz Bardach captured this fundamental dimension of the camp life in the title of his Gulag memoir, *Man Is Wolf to Man*.

Humanitarian Jailers

When seeking the right words to describe the Solovki camps, survivors very often called them hell. By 1926, the English-speaking public could read the book *An Island Hell* by a former white guard officer, Sozerko Malsagov, who had escaped from the islands a year earlier.[18] The reality of this hell, however, exceeded conventional imagination. For alongside the murderous work, the shootings, the starvation, and the tortures, the camp's orchestras played marching music, the camp's choirs sang lively Bolshevik songs, a camp theater staged plays (often comedies), a camp paper *The Solovetsky Islands* was published (with its indispensable "funnies"), camp painters displayed portraits of Bolshevik leaders, and so on. This grotesque combination of phenomena belonging to apparently separate and incompatible orders of reality can be understood only in the context of the Soviet rhetoric and ideology of the time.

The communist authorities—not only in Russia but also in every other country ruled according to the communist doctrine—were always busy suppressing public discussion about the differences between reality and its official representation. The constant tension between reality and ideology in Soviet Russia can be seen as a result of a dual role played by the latter. On the one hand, ideology served to deny and distort facts, especially the crimes committed by the regime in power. But at the same time, it also represented a model by which the authorities tried to transform the current reality—or at least so they claimed. In the language of the Bolshevik state, words and facts did not align in any way that was logical or predictable for citizens. What one saw with one's own eyes and what one heard from official (i.e., the only) Soviet media represented two separate worlds. The regime solved this contradiction by requiring citizens to disregard their own perceptions and knowledge of the world, while at the same time carefully listening to official propaganda; they were henceforth to treat what they heard from their masters as the final and irrefutable truth on every subject. Those who could not master this technique in time ran the risk of unpleasant consequences. It was for these laggards, among other categories of people, that new places for work in the camps were being created.

The simultaneous existence of two ostensibly incompatible ways of treating inmates on the islands—brutal terror on one hand and practices more reminiscent of an educational institution than a concentration camp on the other—derived initially from the fact that two kinds of prisoners were kept in the Solovki camps at the same time: criminals and "class enemies." The Bolsheviks treated each of these two categories differently. This difference was rooted in the so-called class theory of criminality, officially proclaimed as part of Marxist-Leninist ideology. According to this theory, common criminals were victims of the unjust social order in the prerevolutionary world. By depriving them of other opportunities in life, bourgeois society left them no other choice but to resort to crime. In the revolution's initial phases, Bolshevik leaders often treated thieves and bandits as allies in overthrowing the old order. They represented a "class element socially close to" the proletariat. The Bolshevik program of the expropriation of the propertied classes on a national scale entailed the nationalization and collectivization of factories, banks, shops, townhouses, private homes, personal savings, furniture, works of art, and so on. On an individual scale, this simply meant theft and robbery. Among the Cheka's responsibilities, for example, was "securing" the possessions of victims of the Red Terror and turning them over to the government for safekeeping. Initially, this was a significant source of revenue for the new regime. The murdered Tsarina's jewels alone, which the Cheka killers sent in suitcases to Moscow, were worth around $100 million. The lowest estimates of the value of the plunder taken by the Soviet authorities from religious sites and monasteries was two and a half *billion* gold rubles.[19] The slogan that gained the Bolsheviks the support of the lumpenproletariat was Lenin's cry: "Plunder what was plundered!" The leader of the revolution himself set the example: he received from the Cheka a suit, shoes, a belt, and suspenders taken from some victim. As a conscientious person, he even made out a receipt for them.[20]

Widespread, uncontrolled plundering carried out by emboldened criminals could not, of course, be left unchecked for long, and the new regime had to move quickly to establish control over the new situation. Ironically, Lenin himself was once robbed at gunpoint during a car trip through Moscow by emboldened gangsters who took his wallet and Rolls-Royce but failed to recognize him. On ideological grounds, however, common thieves, bandits, petty swindlers, and murderers were treated as fallen members of the proletariat, who—instead of thinking of the socialist society's common good—continued to plunder, steal, swindle, and murder for their own benefit. In short, they were falling behind on their path of developing a proper class consciousness. Seemingly unable to overcome pernicious habits inherited from the past, they needed help—that is, they had to be resocialized. The reference to resocialization almost automatically placed official Bolshevik rhetoric in the context of Western theories of criminality that were seen as humanitarian, progressive, and modern. In Russia itself, a great many prerevolutionary liberal theoreticians of the resocialization of criminals, such as Professors Gernet, Isayev, and Lyublinsky, looked hopefully to the Bolshevik regime following its official announcement that a basic goal of the Soviet penal system would be the reeducation and resocialization of criminals.[21]

For many of the supporters of progressive and humanitarian theories of resocializing criminals, Bolshevik rhetoric inspired enthusiasm and hope. In Western societies, both theories and practical attempts to resocialize criminals had been in existence for several decades. Yet it was hard to see the results as impressive. From the perspective of class theory of criminality, one could conclude that the lack of success in resocializing criminals in the West was because they eventually returned to the same society that had pushed them onto the wrong path in the first place. But here the Bolsheviks proposed a completely new, radical, and seemingly definitive solution to this problem. Instead of persevering in the same vicious circle of resocialization followed by recidivism, they swept away the old criminogenic social order and replaced it with a new one. By abolishing unjust social conditions, they were abolishing the deepest roots of criminality at the same time. Or so they maintained.

In terms of this official rhetoric, the Solovki labor camps appeared as a place where criminals were transformed into members of the new society. Such a vision could successfully rouse the enthusiasm not only of idealist Marxists but also many other proponents of a modern, liberal approach to criminality throughout the world. The less someone knew about Soviet prisons and camps, the easier it was to summon up this kind of enthusiasm. And yet some of the creators of the Soviet penal system (particularly those in the People's Directorate of Justice, the Cheka's rival initially supervising criminal law enforcement) took these theories quite seriously, especially in the early days. Hence the appearance in the Solovki camps of theaters, clubs, and choirs singing of a better future.

Unsurprisingly, criminals' attitude toward these theories of resocialization was usually sarcastic, derisive, and purely pragmatic. From the very beginning, these humane theories also conflicted with other, more important, tasks assigned to the camps by the authorities, such as eliminating "class enemies" and the exploitation of slave labor. When these priorities collided, the humane theories lost as a rule. Soon, all that remained of them was window dressing—humane hot air and empty gestures used for show, especially during official visits to the camps. Over time, these gestures became the Bolsheviks' beloved propaganda party piece, put on before specially invited guests from the West.

Romantic Executioners

While the Bolsheviks spoke officially about criminals in a most humane and generous way, they treated their "class enemies" quite differently. This was no accident but rather a consistent expression of the basic tenets of Bolshevik ideology. A radiant future, one in which even yesterday's criminals would become models of human rectitude, was possible only after the annihilation of the forces of reaction, darkness, and backwardness by the vanguard of the proletariat. In this revolutionary struggle, the future of mankind was at stake. Every moment of weakness or indecision in the face of a class enemy could derail the engine of history. If up to this point Russian revolutionaries from various periods had always been dogged by the question of whether the noble goals justified the violent means of achieving them, the Bolsheviks were remarkably free from such qualms. In their view, violence was an essential condition of achieving communism. In order to bring the revolution to a successful conclusion, the proletariat needed to abandon any vestiges of traditional morality. Above all, the communist revolution meant a moral revolution.

Lenin was explicit on this point on numerous occasions. Speaking to young activists in 1921, he explained that "our morality is entirely subordinate to the interests of the class struggle of the proletariat. . . . We say that morality is what serves the destruction of the old exploitive society and the unification of all workers around the proletariat, which is creating the new society of Communists. . . . We do not believe in eternal morality."[22] Nikolai Bukharin wrote at the same time that the ethics of the proletariat is nothing other than behavior leading by the shortest route to the seizure of power and the founding of communism. Any other moral principles are bourgeois fetishes.[23] The Bolshevik author of the 1923 work *On Morality and Class Norms* Evgeny Preobrazhensky proved that all absolute moral norms are fiction, created by the ruling classes to fool the proletariat and to keep it in slavery. The only correct attitude was proletarian class morality, whose yardstick was behavior dictated by the interests and will of the collective.[24]

In line with these principles of class ethics, actual human deeds—murder, rape, theft, plunder, fraud—were morally neutral. They could be good or bad only in terms of the question of whose class interests they would advance. If they served the interests of the proletariat, not only were they not bad, but they deserved a reward and were to be encouraged. But mere mortals were never able to fully understand what served the interests of the proletariat and what harmed them. Even proletarians themselves could not be even-handed judges, since after all, as Lenin was given to point out, many workers continued to carry the treacherous infection of bourgeois morality. So in the meantime, Lenin and his associates reserved the right to decide in matters of class morality on behalf of the vanguard of the proletariat. For all practical reasons, the interests of the proletariat could be identified with the political interests of the Bolshevik authorities. Whoever stood in their way (consciously or not) was not only a political opponent but an enemy of the people (a term borrowed from the French Revolution), a class enemy (its updated Marxist-Leninist variant) but also—on the basis of class morality—simply a criminal. The moral duty of the revolutionary proletariat was to sweep obstacles off the road to communism and to eliminate class enemies. Lenin warned the Bolsheviks not to come under the harmful influence of traditional moral values and treacherous acts of conscience. He asserted that "sentimentality is no less a crime than speculation in time of war."[25] Using his own brand of eloquence, Trotsky added: "We must rid ourselves once and for all of the Quaker-Papist babble about the sanctity of human life."[26]

Revolution understood in this way immediately acquired its own romantic rhetoric. Soviet speakers, propagandists, editors, writers, and poets threw down a challenge to the world, showing contempt for the outdated concepts of good and evil. In 1918, when the Red Terror was announced, the poet Vasily Knyazev wrote in a poem characteristically entitled *The Red Gospel*:

> Hey you! Blind from birth!
> Convinced moralists!
> Isn't it time to take a good look?
> Ah ha!
> The devil take your morality,
> The revolution is bringing death to your morality

. . .
Here is a message from the second Christ . . .
Dearly beloved, who know no pity.
. . .
Our enemy should be shown no mercy.
He's down, but . . . still he lives? Stab him!
Only he who knows how to hate
Can enter the Kingdom of Earth.
It's no matter that we are few!
We shall force the herd, used to the whip,
To follow us.
We know the only straight path to Paradise.
Death to whoever dares
To stand in our way![27]

Knyazev was echoed by a far superior avant-garde poet, Vladimir Mayakovsky, named posthumously by Stalin as a classic of Soviet literature. In his famous 1920 poem *150,000,000* he writes:

Bullets, fill the air!
Rake over the timid!
In the thicket of stragglers,
ring out, Parabellum!
. . .
We'll
     finish you off,
          world-romantic!
Instead of faith,
    in our soul
        we've got steam
           and electricity.
No beggars here!
      We'll pocket the wealth of all worlds!
If it's old, kill it.
      Use their skulls as ashtrays![28]

In a stage production of *Mystery-Bouffe*, written two years earlier on the first anniversary of the Bolshevik attack on the Winter Palace, Mayakovsky introduced the character "Man of the Future" exhorting:

Come unto me
all you who have calmly stabbed your enemy,

and then walked away from his corpse
with a song on your lips!
Come,
unforgiving one!
You have the first right of entry
into my kingdom –
which is earthly, not heavenly![29]

Mayakovsky played this character himself and spoke this parody of the New Testament at the play's premiere, directed by Vsevolod Meyerhold. In another work, similarly inspired by the Red Terror, Mayakovsky wrote: "Enough of singing about the moon and the seagull, I shall sing of the Cheka." He advised young people: "Any youth thinking over his future,/ deciding on whom to model his life, I shall tell, without hesitating: Base it/ On Comrade Dzerzhinsky."[30]

A few months before the premiere of *Mystery-Bouffe* and following the failed attempt by Fanya Kaplan to assassinate Lenin, the mouthpiece of the Red Army, *Krasnaya Gazeta*, thundered: "Without mercy, without sparing, we will kill our enemies in scores of hundreds. Let them be thousands, let them drown themselves in their own blood. For the blood of Lenin . . . let there be floods of blood of the bourgeoisie—more blood, as much as possible . . ."[31] Demyan Bedny, Trotsky's and Stalin's favorite poet, was turning these kinds of challenges into a new type of proletarian poetry. Addressing the soldiers of the white army, he called on them to kill their own officers:

Death to the vermin! Exterminate them all!
And having done away with this damned vermin,
Freed from the yoke of the ruling hordes,
One after another, by regiment and platoon,
Come join our brotherly ranks![32]

As we can see, the Bolshevik "revaluation of values" (to use Nietzsche's phrase) stirred up considerable enthusiasm among Russian writers and artists. True, this phenomenon was amplified by the fact that those artists living in Russia who saw things differently were forced to remain silent. In Soviet literature of the 1920s—even leaving aside propaganda—one discerns at every step a strident and unconcealed fascination with Bolshevik violence, brutality, and cruelty. The main heroes in this literary and rhetorical trend are the men of the Cheka (Chekists)—strong men in leather coats, steeped in romantic myth, who appear both threatening and fascinating. In his famous novel *The Naked Year* (1921), Boris Pilnyak wrote of them: "Men in leather coats gathered on the second floor—Bolsheviks. Every one well-built, wearing a leather coat, good looking, every one strong with locks tumbling in ringlets from under his cap down to his shoulders, each with distinctive cheekbones, tight lips and quick movements. The finest from the puny, misshapen Russian nation."[33] Mayakovsky tirelessly sang the praises of the Cheka's titanic strength and effectiveness:

> The class
> paw
>   lies on the exploiter
> From the Lubyanka
> the paw
>   is the Cheka.[34]

Peering into the hearts of these supermen in leather coats, Soviet writers sometimes discovered internal dilemmas worthy of Shakespearean heroes. For instance, the eponymous hero of Ilya Ehrenburg's 1923 *Life and Death of Nikolai Kurbov*, the Chekist Kurbov, is the kind of person who has never managed to rid himself of the vestiges of bourgeois morality. Unable to resolve himself to arresting a female class enemy in love with him, he acknowledges his own guilt toward the revolution and sentences himself—to suicide. Kurbov has shown weakness and clearly has failed to pass the exam for a new hero. Other literary characters prove more successful, however—real Soviet men of action, for whom shallow sentimentalism is foreign. One such hero is the Chekist Bezais, from Viktor Kin's novel *On the Other Side*. "Life was simple for Bezais," writes Kin. "He believed that world revolution would come if not tomorrow, then the day after tomorrow for certain. He did not agonize, he asked no questions, he kept no diary. And when someone said at the club that the night before the merchant Smirnov had been shot on the other side of the river, he said: "Well, it had to be done" since he could find no other use for merchants." Reading Dostoyevsky's *Crime and Punishment*, Bezais is beside himself with astonishment: "all this chattering about one old woman."[35]

While the Chekist Bezais demonstrates a healthy class consciousness untainted by sentimentality, the hero of Alexander Tarasov-Rodionov's 1922 novel, *Chocolate*—another Chekist named Zudin—proffers a philosophical reflection: "I ordered a hundred hostages shot," he admits, "and never considered whether or not they were guilty. What is guilt? Is a bourgeois guilty for being a bourgeois? Is a crocodile guilty for being a crocodile?"[36]

On the vast battlefield where social classes collided, the individual was no more than a "zero" and an "absurdity," as Mayakovsky put it elsewhere. At best he could be seen as a representative of one social class or another, which in itself was reason enough to decide someone's life or death. In November 1918, Martins Latsis, a deputy chief of Cheka in Ukraine, explained to his subordinates the Soviet position on this question: "Don't look at the paperwork for proof as to whether the suspect acted or spoke against Soviet power. The first question to be asked is to what social class does he belong, who were his parents, and what were his education and profession. Those questions should decide his fate. That is the point of Red Terror."[37]

In terms of the Bolshevik worldview, a person's life or fate had no value or meaning of its own. Sacrificing human lives, freedom, dignity was in this context an essential condition for the victory of the proletariat and was thus seen as something praiseworthy, as an expression of revolutionary virtue. Chekists—the people who killed, enslaved, and tortured in the name of the revolution—were the "midwives" of a better future. They carried out acts for which the romantic heroes of the past lacked the requisite ruthlessness, hobbled as they had been by sentimental feelings.

The fascination with Bolshevik violence that gripped many writers, artists, and intellectuals did not end with literary projection but reached into real life. Isaac Babel, for instance, before becoming famous as the author of *Red Cavalry*, had worked for the Cheka during the Civil War. Vyacheslav Polonsky wrote in his reminiscences on Babel: "His thirst for blood, death, murder, all kinds of atrocities and an almost sadistic liking for suffering limited his range of interests. He was present when death sentences were carried out, he observed shootings, he amassed a huge amount of material on the revolution's cruelties."[38] Demyan Bedny, calling in his poetry for the white "vermin" to be killed, was an example of a creative artist who did not stop at words, but—as befitting a revolutionary romantic—was able to turn them into deeds. When the Cheka had finished interrogating Fanya Kaplan, who had been captured after her attempt on Lenin's life, the commander of the Kremlin guard Pavel Malkov shot her in a garage: Bedny, according to his own account, helped Malkov burn her remains in an oil drum.[39]

The scribbling class's fascination with the men of action was reciprocated. Many a Chekist was flattered by the writers' interest. And then there were those who for a moment put down their revolver and picked up a pen. In Georgia, which had only recently been conquered by the Bolsheviks, the local Cheka published an anthology of amateur verse written by Chekists in 1921 entitled *Smile of the Cheka* [*sic*]. One of the poet-butchers, Aleksandr Eyduk, writes:

> There is no greater joy, nor more beautiful music
> Than the crunch of a broken life and bones.

Thus our eyes dim
And passion surges in our breast,
I want to write on your sentence
The single inexorable sentence: "Up against the wall! Shoot him!"[40]

Beginning with the revolution and up to the Stalinist Great Terror in the late 1930s, one could observe an arresting phenomenon in Soviet Russia: artists and Chekists often sought out each other's company. British historian Donald Rayfield notes that

> *Chekisty* and poets were drawn to each other like stoats and rabbits—often with fatal consequences for the latter. They found common ground: the need for fame, and image of themselves as crusaders, creative frustration, membership of a vanguard, scorn for the bourgeoisie, an inability to discuss their work with common mortals. There was an easily bridged gap between poet who aimed to *épater le bourgeois* and the chekist who stood the bourgeois up against the wall.[41]

The Polish literary scholar Tadeusz Klimowicz has called this phenomenon "the moth syndrome."[42] In Soviet cultural salons, artists and Chekists met regularly. Yakov Agranov, a high-ranking official in the Cheka (later the OGPU and NKVD), who oversaw investigations, arrests, and interrogations of writers (he was the one to interrogate the poet Nikolai Gumilev, who was shot in 1921), was a regular at the salon held in the apartment of Vsevolod Meyerhold and his wife, the actress Zinaida Reich. He also appeared often at the salon run by the literary critic Osip Brik and his wife, Lili Brik, who was Mayakovsky's muse and lover. It was, in fact, Agranov who gave Mayakovsky the pistol that the poet used to shoot himself on April 14, 1930. In the 1930s Agranov also became a regular visitor at Maksim Gorky's salon. But Soviet writers' and artists' social connections reached higher than Agranov's rank. Head of the secret police Genrikh Yagoda, Agranov's superior, attended receptions at Meyerhold's and Gorky's. Indeed, Stalin himself would drop by with his entourage at Gorky's literary soirees.

This intimacy did not end at conversations and joint literary-Chekist parties (a gypsy troupe would sometimes be brought round to Meyerhold's salon at midnight) but spilled over into personal lives. Yagoda was the brother-in-law of the communist writer and literary apparatchik Leopold Averbakh. He also did his best to seduce Gorky's daughter-in-law Timosha—whether successfully or not is unclear.

The romantic cult of revolutionary violence, which had blossomed in the 1920s, was rather quickly becoming a nuisance for the Bolshevik authorities.

At first, just after the revolution, it had been encouraged since it inculcated the appropriate "revolutionary attitudes." Soon, however, with victory in the Civil War achieved, Bolshevik leaders began to have a different view of the aims of Soviet propaganda, especially when it came to foreign countries. With the dream of the world revolution deferred to some unspecified future date, the Bolshevik authorities had to focus on rebuilding the economy and forging a military force capable of defeating the world bourgeoisie when the next opportunity presented itself. This required building economic relations with the capitalist world, which was the only source for needed technologies.

To this end, the Bolsheviks first had to placate Western elites and shift public opinion, convincing their would-be partners that Soviet Russia was a normal country with a pragmatic and stable government—in other words, a country in which one could invest. Parading the Red Terror and revolutionary violence did not help to create such an image. The Soviet authorities were now interested in concealing the atrocities and abuses of power from Western public opinion. As time passed, these efforts became much more organized and produced remarkable results.

Fellow Travelers and Prophets of Doom

The Bolshevik revolution in Russia affected different social circles in the West in different ways. It undoubtedly had the greatest influence on the imagination of intellectuals—that is, people more inclined than others to see the world in terms of ideas, abstractions, and generalizations. As Martin Malia writes,

> Russia's relationship to the West was stood on its head. She ceased being Europe's laggard Eastern train; she now embodied, or claimed to embody, Europe's most advanced ideal, Socialism. And this claim, for the first time since her entry into the concert of Europe, made her the continent's premier power ideologically. For the next seven decades she would be judged less as a nation than as humanity's pilot socialist society—that is, when she was not seen as a second coming of the Tatars.
>
> As if in doubt himself, the symbolist bard of October, Aleksandr Blok, in 1918 summoned the West to reflect in awe and trembling on the riddle of the Russian Sphinx. For the rest of the century the world would indeed stand before it in perplexed interrogation: Was Red October truly a socialist dawn amidst the night of war? Or was it a new descent into darkness and despotism?[43]

Thanks to Lenin and his Communist Party, the myth of revolution that dated back to the assault on the Bastille once again emerged in the minds and hearts of many Western writers, journalists, artists, scholars—that is, people inclined to speak publicly about the future of the world. The intellectuals fascinated or at least intrigued by the Bolshevik revolution were not composed solely of followers of Marxism and other declared sympathizers of socialism. There were also people with previously undefined views who simply saw the Bolshevik revolution as inspiration for the rest of humanity to create a better world of equality and freedom, with no more prejudice, exploitation, and senseless, bloody wars. This way of viewing the communist revolution was significantly emboldened by the fact that this revolution was happening in Russia, a country that had occupied a very special place in the Western imagination. Russia was too remote and too poorly understood for the specific knowledge of its history and contemporary events to interfere with a projection of Western myths, wishes, and dreams. In order to be able to continue imagining Bolshevik Russia as the harbinger of a better future for all, it was necessary to develop an ability not to notice Soviet crimes—or, at least, to justify and rationalize them. But, after all, the West had a rich tradition of glorifying ruthless regimes in prerevolutionary Russia, especially at the time of the Enlightenment; all that was required now was to follow the paths mapped out by Voltaire and Diderot 150 years earlier.

The Bolsheviks immediately appreciated this favorable atmosphere among some Western cultural and intellectual elites. They viewed Western sympathizers as potentially valuable allies and supporters—an important channel of influence on public opinion abroad. In his writings and speeches, Trotsky called them "fellow travelers." Lenin has been credited with coining an earthier phrase, "useful idiots," but no direct evidence has been found supporting this claim.

The day after the Bolshevik revolution in Petrograd, the American journalist John Reed became perhaps the best-known prototype of a fellow traveler. Before he was turned into a communist icon, he was a young, ambitious newspaper reporter, a restless soul seeking adventure outside of his upper-class comfort zone. In 1910 he graduated from Harvard and three years later went to Mexico to write reports on Pancho Villa's peasant revolution. In the early years of World War I, he worked as a war correspondent in Italy, France, the Balkans, and East Central Europe and found himself in Petrograd at the time of the Bolshevik coup. He now considered himself a socialist; he knew less about Russia than Mexico and did not speak a word of Russian. Fascinated with the communist revolution, he quickly made contact with the Bolshevik leaders, who immediately saw in him a potentially useful agent of influence and fed him their own version of current events. This completed Reed's gradual evolution from journalist into revolutionary activist. He gave expression to his newfound knowledge on the Russian Revolution in his book *Ten Days That Shook the World*. It immediately became a great sensation, although its reception in left-wing circles in the West was not clear-cut. American socialists in no way shared Reed's initially uncritical enthusiasm for Lenin and Trotsky, and in 1919 Reed was expelled from the party. But by now he was a man converted to Bolshevik communism. Together with a group of similar enthusiasts for the land of Soviets, he founded the Communist Labor Party of America and became a functionary of the Comintern. Once only a fellow traveler, he was now evolving into a Soviet operative. In Soviet Russia, he met Emma Goldman, an American anarchist recently deported there by the US government. Initially supportive of the Bolsheviks, Goldman quickly grew critical of their oppressive policies. She would later write about it in her 1923 book, *My Disillusionment in Russia*. Reed told Goldman that the victims of the Cheka fully deserved their fate. Not too much time elapsed, however, before Reed himself began to awaken from his fascination with the Soviets—at least according to his friend, Benjamin Gitlow, an American radical who would later abandon and denounce his pro-Soviet involvement. If Reed indeed became disappointed in the Soviet regime, he did not live to make it public; he came down with typhus in Russia and died in October 1920. The Bolsheviks immediately surrounded his figure with the cultish aura of a revolutionary martyr and turned him into a model to follow for Western lovers of proletarian revolution. His remains now lie in the Kremlin wall behind Lenin's mausoleum.

There was no lack of similar supporters of the Bolshevik regime in its early stages. One such supporter, Captain Jacques Sadoul, was a member of the French military mission to Russia in 1917. Fascinated by the Bolsheviks, he joined the Red Army in order to fight against enemies of the young Soviet state. He soon shared his enthusiasm with the public back home. His first book, *Vive la République des Soviets!* was published in French in Moscow in 1918 and used by Bolsheviks as insurrectionist antiwar propaganda for the troops of the French expeditionary corps in Ukraine. It was followed a year later by *Notes on the Bolshevik Revolution*, published in Paris.[44] The foreword for the latter book was written by Henri Barbusse, a writer held in esteem by many as a moral authority for his relentless criticism of the bloody harvest of World War I. Barbusse saw in Soviet communism a source of hope for a better world without senseless wars. He became a steadfast admirer of the USSR and later a leading eulogist for Stalin who specialized in whitewashing his crimes. As for Sadoul, he was sentenced to death in France for his involvement on the Bolshevik side against French forces, but a few years later he was retried and acquitted. He became a functionary of the Comintern and later returned to France, where he had a long career as a relentless spokesman for Soviet causes and, like Barbusse, a distinguished apologist for Stalin's crimes.

Another French officer fascinated by the Bolshevik revolution, André Marty, played an active role in organizing a mutiny among the French forces intervening in Odessa in 1919. Just as in the case of Sadoul, however, France forgave Marty this betrayal, and he was pardoned in 1923 after receiving an initial sentence of twenty years' hard labor. His ex-convict status in France and his Soviet fame as a revolutionary hero did not prevent him from being elected to the French National Assembly in 1924, when he also became a member of the Politburo of the French Communist Party. Later, he fought in the Spanish Civil War, where he conscientiously oversaw the Stalinist purges in the Communist International Brigades. But his faith and obedience to the Kremlin did not last forever. In 1952, the French Communist Party expelled him for criticizing Soviet policy in Eastern Europe.

Revolutionary fervor and verbal support for the Soviets among Western fellow travelers did not always translate into a willingness to take risks and make sacrifices. After visiting Soviet Russia in 1919, the American intellectual Lincoln Steffens claimed: "I have been to the future and it works." According to William Bullitt who traveled with Steffens, he coined this phrase on the train in Sweden before setting foot in Russia.[45] For years, numerous Western admirers of the land of Soviets repeated this famous phrase. As for its author, he subsequently managed to find more reason for circumspection in a private letter from 1926, explaining: "I am a patriot for Russia, the Future is there; Russia will win out and it will save the world. That is my belief. But I don't want to live there."[46] In Steffens's mind, as in the minds of many other enthusiasts of the Bolshevik regime, Russia had a special mythical status—and myth may not be the most comfortable place to live.

Meanwhile, in order to protect one's dreams about the Bolshevik utopia from brutal confrontation with reality, one had to know how to ignore or deny the crimes of the Red Terror. This required some mental effort but was not very difficult, since the information about them was usually fragmentary, chaotic, and often contradictory. Western fellow travelers successfully employed a variety of techniques to drown out disturbing news and to avoid troubling conclusions about the Soviet experiment. The palette of possibilities was rich and varied, ranging from complete denial by way of feigning ignorance to building intellectual constructs justifying the crimes committed during Lenin's rule.

Initially, one of the most creative minds in this area was Pierre Pascal. Like Marty and Sadoul, he was a French officer who found himself in Russia at the time of the revolution and, like them, he immediately became fascinated with Soviet communism. Pascal's views represented an original, if not outright bizarre, blend of communism with religious thinking. Pascal saw the Bolshevik revolution as a momentous step in humanity's religious awakening from the long spiritual torpor of capitalism and materialism. Pascal's thinking echoes Aleksandr Blok's famous poetic vision in *The Twelve*. In the conclusion of Blok's poem, written in the winter after the Bolshevik revolution, the figure of Jesus Christ appears at the head of a band of plundering, raping, and murdering Bolsheviks. In Pascal's view, just like in Blok's, Bolshevik revolution was enveloped in a mystical aura. Pascal noted in his diary entry for December 26, 1917, that the Bolshevik revolution was the realization of the Christian principles according to the "Russian spirit."[47] Thereafter he was convinced that the Bolsheviks had become the incarnation of the will of God in the history of mankind.

This conflation of apocalyptic vision and Bolshevik rhetoric was not unusual at the time. In 1920 Pascal put his thoughts into the book *In Red Russia*. Despite a most unorthodox interpretation of the revolution, his views elicited no opposition from the Bolshevik authorities, especially since they were not aimed at readers in Russia. The book was published in French, in Petrograd, having been passed by the Soviet censorship with a Western readership in mind. Pascal wrote in it of the Red Terror: "The terror has passed and, quite honestly, it never existed. The word "terror," which carries a specific meaning for a Frenchman, always made me laugh there [in Russia], given the moderation, sweetness, and cheerfulness of the terrible Cheka accused of implementing it."[48]

Over time, however, ever greater efforts of will were needed to believe such denials. Reports from witnesses of Bolshevik crimes cropped up too often and too persistently in the West. Faced with early reports of mass atrocities in Russia, US President Woodrow Wilson decided to organize a fact-finding mission on the ground there and, if possible, to negotiate diplomatic relations with the Soviets. In 1919, before the Treaty of Versailles was drafted, he sent a young diplomat, William Bullitt, to Russia accompanied by Lincoln Steffens. Both Bullitt and Steffens were Soviet sympathizers. On their return, Bullitt reported that the rumors of mass violence and terror were greatly exaggerated, assuring the US Congress that "the Red Terror is over" and "executions are extremely rare."[49] In 1924 Bullitt married Louise Bryant, the widow of John Reed. He continually urged the US government to establish diplomatic relations with the USSR. When this came to pass in 1933, President Roosevelt appointed him the first US ambassador to that country. With the opportunity to take a longer and closer look at the land of Soviets, Bullitt changed his views, however—as indeed did many Western supporters of that country, including Pascal himself—and he eventually became an eloquent critic of Soviet communism.

Lincoln Steffens also spoke out about the Red Terror. But instead of denying its existence as Bullitt had done, he tried to exculpate its perpetrators. He stated that "the Bolshevik leaders regret and are ashamed of their red terror."[50] Bryant took a somewhat different approach. Despite John Reed's reported disillusion with Bolshevik Russia (if it was indeed true), she found herself a spot in the limelight of his legend and enjoyed a reputation in Western salons as the first lady of the radical American left. From where she lived on the French Riviera, she would issue commentaries on Bolshevik Russia—writing, for example, that "It was [Dzerzhinsky's] duty to see that the prisoners were quickly and humanely disposed of. He performed this grim task with a dispatch and an efficiency for which even the condemned must have been grateful, in that nothing is more horrible than an executioner whose hands tremble and whose heart wavers."[51] Praising "Iron Felix's" alleged revolutionary humanitarianism, Bryant added that the Cheka was by no means a Soviet invention. "Even we ourselves have a Cheka," she argued, "but we call it a Department of Justice."[52]

The views of Western fellow travelers on Bolshevik terror were not limited to denying it, to justifying it, or to assuring people that even if the terror had existed, it had already ended. Much more audacious voices were heard too. The cult of Bolshevik violence that had reverberated so loudly in Soviet Russia from the Revolution through the 1920s had also crossed Soviet borders and, whether the leaders in the Kremlin liked it or not, resonated in the West. Here, too, it found its most enthusiastic proponents among writers and artists, especially in avant-garde circles, the members of which were always searching for new ways to scandalize audiences and continually build up their own antibourgeois mythologies.

The avant-garde cult of revolutionary violence was not limited to a fascination with Bolshevik deeds but often reflected profound psychological and moral affinities between the new totalitarian ideologies later deemed to be poles apart: communism and fascism. One needs only look at the treatment of the subject of violence by the Italian futurists, especially Marinetti, who were fascinated with fascism and compare it with Mayakovsky's rhetoric. Both poets, like many of their literary confrères, saw in antibourgeois revolution not just a political upheaval but also a moral revolution: the sweeping away of antiquated concepts, such as, for instance, the traditional opposition of good and evil, and replacing them with a new and more modern morality. Louis Aragon, one of the leaders of the French poetic avant-garde and a sympathizer of the Bolshevik revolution, summed it up succinctly: "The blue eyes of the revolution burn with cruel necessity."[53]

The French poet clearly took Mayakovsky's loud praise for the Cheka as a model. In his 1931 work, *Prelude to the Cherry Season*, Aragon wrote:

I sing the GPU we need in France
. . .
I call for the GPU to prepare the end of the world
. . .
Long live the GPU, true image of materialist splendor
Long live the GPU; down with Chiappe and the *Marseillaise*
Long live the GPU; down with the pope and the bugs
Long live the GPU; down with money and banks
Long live the GPU; down with the cheating East
Long live the GPU; down with the family
Long live the GPU; down with infernal laws.[54]

Aragon, in addition to ideological motivations, seemed to also have very personal reasons for feeling particularly close to the Soviet security apparatus. His life companion, Elsa Triolet, was the sister of Lili Brik, the captivating hostess of a Moscow literary and artistic salon frequented by the flower of Soviet political police. Lili combined the roles of wife to the literary critic Osip Brik with being the muse and lover of Mayakovsky, while at the same time (according to Donald Rayfield and others) working as a secret collaborator of the GPU and, most likely, keeping an eye on both gentlemen.[55] When Aragon was writing his hymns to the GPU, Mayakovsky was already dead—a year earlier he had shot himself in the heart. The French bard of the Soviet security agencies, however, had a long life, throughout which he remained faithful to the Kremlin.

Like Aragon, Bertolt Brecht seemed inspired by revolutionary violence and cruelty. He wrote in his 1930 play *The Measures Taken*:

What base act would you not commit, to
Eradicate baseness?
If, at last, you could change the world, what
Would you think yourself too good for?
Who are you?
Sink into filth
Embrace the butcher, but
Change the world: it needs it![56]

While some tried either not to notice Bolshevik violence or to see in it a condition of humanity's future happiness, others—usually positioned at the opposite pole of the ideological spectrum—perceived in it the imminent catastrophe of world civilization. There were many people with an antibourgeois mindset among the Western critics of Bolshevism. They were often characterized by a Nietzschean ambivalence toward Bolshevik barbarity. Ruminating on Russia in 1922, Herman Hesse prophesized the annihilation of Western civilization: "Already half of Europe, already at least the Eastern half of Europe is on its way to chaos, is heading drunken in a holy hallucination headlong into the Abyss, and it sings at the same time, sings out with a drunken hymn, as Dmitrii Karamazov sang."[57] René Fülöp-Miller, like Pierre Pascal, saw in the Russian Revolution a historical phenomenon with metaphysical significance—"the eruption of an elemental spiritual destiny."[58] In contrast to Pascal, however, he did not claim that it opened the way to the Kingdom of God. Oswald Spengler, following Nietzsche, regarded Russia (this time it was the Bolshevik Russia) as the incarnation of a young, barbarous spirit bringing destruction to rotten Western civilization but also as a promise of its future rebirth.

Nearly all such reactions to the Bolshevik revolution were linked by a specific rhetorical style, one that in some ways divorced the phenomenon of Soviet barbarity from reality, ascribing it automatically to some fatalistic, elevated concept of a "higher power," the "spirit of history," and other apocalyptic constructs. Soviet terror perceived thusly could easily be turned into just another figure of speech in the minds of the Western public—prone to be received as a literary hyperbole rather than a description of facts. One reason for this was the sheer scale of crimes in Russia, which exceeded the norms of plausibility through which the West perceived reality up until the Holocaust impacted its consciousness, albeit with a significant delay.

Reactions to such a catastrophic image of Bolshevism were often far-fetched. At one end of the spectrum was the fatalistic vision of Soviet communism as a global cataclysm and a harbinger of the encroaching destruction of Western civilization. This kind of fatalism was often accompanied by attempts to accept communism as an element of supposedly irrevocable historical and metaphysical destiny. This attitude was championed in the West by, among others, Nicholas Berdyaev, a Russian émigré thinker who influenced many non-Marxist views of Russia at the time. He reached the conclusion that the Bolshevik dictatorship was a new incarnation of a young Russian civilization destined to breathe new life into the sclerotic West.

The polar opposite of this approach was an ideological call to arms in the name of defending the West from Bolshevik barbarism. A radical version of this call to arms required the West to renew itself first. According to this approach, the bourgeois-liberal order had to be destroyed and, on its ruins, the knightly spirit of the West, one capable of standing up to and defeating the eastern horde, had to be rebuilt. One of those to develop such ideas was Alfred Rosenberg, a young Baltic German born and raised in the former Russian Empire. Rosenberg soon inspired another young German radical by the name of Adolf Hitler.

Fears and Calculations

Not just ideological projections or romantic dreams, positive and negative alike, influenced the development of the image of the new Bolshevik regime in Western minds, of course. Western political and economic elites had their own often pragmatic motives that affected their views of Soviet Russia. The Bolshevik coup d'état immediately stirred fears about the stability of the social order in the West. For many, the events in Russia served as proof that a small but disciplined and ruthless revolutionary organization was capable of seizing control of a world power. Moreover, this organization appeared to be part of a wider international movement openly espousing the ambition of overthrowing the prevailing political and economic world order. That these were not just idle concerns appeared to be borne out, for instance, by the bloody revolutionary events in Germany and Hungary in 1918 and 1919. Western governments anxiously kept watch for similar events in their own countries, which had seen their own share of labor unrest and workers' riots.

Such fears were apparent in the United States. From the very start of the twentieth century, American authorities struggled to contain a spate of anarchist terrorist activity. On September 6, 1901, President William McKinley was assassinated by a young anarchist, Leon Czolgosz. While World War I was raging in Europe, terrorist attacks were stoking growing anxieties in America. On October 13, 1914, bombs exploded in St. Patrick's Cathedral and St. Alphonsus Church in New York City. On July 22, 1916, a bomb went off during a parade in San Francisco, killing ten and wounding forty. Concurrently, anarchist organizations in the United States were printing and distributing hundreds of publications calling on workers to start armed action, to strike, to destroy factories and equipment. Pamphlets came out with practical instructions on how to build bombs. In April 1919, a mail package bomb addressed to Georgia Senator Thomas W. Hardwick exploded, blowing off the hands of his housekeeper and injuring his wife. Soon, the US postal service managed to intercept twelve other package bombs before they reached their destinations. They were addressed to politicians and public figures, including Attorney General A. Mitchell Palmer, Oliver Wendell Holmes Jr. of the Supreme Court, New York City Mayor John Francis Hylan, J. P. Morgan, John D. Rockefeller, and a number of governors, congressmen, mayors, and other prominent officials.

In June 1919, another coordinated mailing of bombs to nine public officials was organized by the anarchists. Attorney General Palmer was targeted again, but the bomb exploded prematurely, failing to kill Palmer and his family.

In September 1920, the anarchist Mario Buda drove a horse-drawn cart loaded with dynamite and cast-iron bolts onto a busy intersection on Wall Street. The explosion killed thirty-eight and injured hundreds. By this time, Attorney General Palmer had started a massive antianarchist campaign, in which about 10,000 people were arrested and about 3,500 held in detention. The American authorities were inclined to link these attacks with Bolshevik activity, given that Bolshevik cells, financed and directed from Moscow, had in fact been operating in the US for some time. These cells were coordinated by Ludwig Martens, who had been sent to New York for that very purpose. In October 1919, according to data provided by the US government, at least five hundred publications spreading communist and anarchist propaganda in many languages were coming out in America.[59] A month earlier, two communist parties had been formed: the Communist Party and the Communist Labor Party, whose cofounder was John Reed. Both parties were bitter rivals, but on orders from Moscow, they merged in May 1921. The new unified Communist Party of the United States was supervised by the Communist International in Moscow and carried out its political directives. At the time, the American Communist movement had about 34,000 members, of whom 27,000 were immigrants speaking a variety of languages other than English.

The government had a poor understanding of Bolshevik ideology, not to mention Soviet strategy and politics. It also knew little about the communist networks at home. In 1919, the government resolved to do better. The Bureau of Investigation created a new General Intelligence Division (also known as the Radical Division) in order to tackle the issue and appointed as its head a young, ambitious officer named J. Edgar Hoover. Under a new set of laws known as the Sedition Act, Hoover got down to work, and as early as December 21, 1919, he had 249 foreign nationals suspected of revolutionary activities in the US placed on a ship, the USS *Buford*, and deported from the United States to Russia. A year later, the Bolshevik coordinator Martens himself was expelled. After his return to Russia, he was placed in charge of Soviet metallurgy. On August 9, 1920, a few days before the Battle of Warsaw, when it seemed as if nothing could stop the Bolshevik offensive in Central Europe, the US government laid out its attitude toward the Bolshevik regime in stark terms. Secretary of State Bainbridge Colby declared:

> In the view of this Government, there cannot be any common ground upon which it can stand with a Power whose conceptions of international relations

are so entirely different to its own, so utterly repugnant to its moral sense. There can be no mutual confidence or trust, no respect even, if pledges are to be given and agreements made with a cynical repudiation of their obligations already in the mind of one of the parties. We cannot recognize, hold official relations with, or give friendly reception to the agents of a government which is determined and bound to conspire against our institutions; whose diplomats will be agitators of dangerous revolt; whose spokesmen say that they sign agreements with no intention of keeping them.[60]

The Red Army's defeat at the outskirts of Warsaw mollified the American authorities, who came to the conclusion that the specter of world revolution had been halted.

But revolutionary radicals were not the only supporters of the Soviet regime in the West. Much of the incentive for staying silent on the subject of Bolshevik crimes came from circles far removed from revolutionary sympathies—that is, the world of big business. The thinking of many of its representatives on the subject was thoroughly pragmatic. They saw in Bolshevik Russia above all a potential business partner. They recognized that the new regime, if it wanted to survive, would sooner or later have to start cooperating economically with the West. The fact that the Bolsheviks had executed or imprisoned most of the Russian capitalists and seized their property did not seem to give pause to these Western enthusiasts of trade with the new Russia. To a certain extent, such facts served as a warning, but they were also often seen as convenient circumstances. Any natural business competition had been eliminated and the playing field had been cleared for new businessmen eager to make money in Russia. There was no lack of takers. They seemed undiscouraged by the violent rhetoric of the Bolsheviks openly preaching the destruction of the world bourgeoisie. "No group promoted collaboration with Soviet Russia more assiduously and more effectively than the European and American business communities. The Bolsheviks exploited their eagerness to do business by having them pressure Western governments for diplomatic recognition and economic assistance," notes Richard Pipes.[61]

Indeed, when Soviet representatives traveled to France in 1920 to explore the possibility of setting up trade deals, the representative of the bourgeois right—and later a proponent of collaboration with Hitler—Anatole de Monzie advised them to "tell Lenin that the best way to win France over to doing business with Russia is through the businessmen of France. They are our only realists."[62] In Germany, also in 1920, the Soviets encountered similar reactions: Hugo Stinnes, the president of the German Association of Industrialists and (just like de Monzie) later a supporter of Hitler, was known to be "favorably disposed towards Russia and her experiments." According to the later memoirs by the artist Yuri Annenkov who claimed to have had seen Lenin's personal notes, the Bolshevik leader wrote: "Telling the truth is a bourgeois superstition. On the contrary, it is the end that sanctifies the lie. While chasing profits in the Soviet market, the world's capitalists will close their eyes and thus change into deaf and dumb blind men. They will give us credits that will help us to maintain communist parties in their countries and, by supplying us with essential materials, will rebuild the war industry we need for our future victorious attacks on our suppliers. In other words, they will be working towards their own suicide."[63]

One country where the willingness to trade with Soviet Russia was quickly reflected in government policy was Great Britain. Among the advocates of establishing trade links with the Bolsheviks as soon as possible was the prime minister himself, Lloyd George. In his official statements, the simple desire for profit was translated into the language of higher goals. Lloyd George expressed a view, often repeated by businessmen profiting by trading with despotic regimes, that trade ultimately modifies behaviors and turns brutal political radicals into gentle pragmatists. "The moment trade is established with Russia, Communism will go," the head of His Majesty's Government asserted in 1920.[64] Referring to the failed British military intervention in Russia, he claimed: "We have failed to restore Russia to sanity by force. I believe we can do it and save her by trade. Commerce has a sobering effect in its operations. The simple sums in addition and subtraction which it inculcates soon dispose of wild theories."[65] He was echoed in this by the leader of the British Labour Party Ramsey MacDonald: "In supporting the Russian Revolution we are not necessarily taking sides either for or against the Soviets or Bolsheviks. We are recognizing that during a Revolution there must be Jacobinism, but that if Jacobinism be evil, the way to fight it is to help the country to settle down and assimilate the Revolution."[66] In British politics of the day, the influence of Soviet Russia's uncompromising opponents was diminishing. They were led by such intransigent anticommunists as Winston Churchill, a staunch advocate of the military intervention in Russia and the eradication of the Bolshevik regime.

Some original Bolshevik relationships with Western businessmen proved long-lasting. Armand Hammer, for instance, remained closely involved with the Kremlin until his death in 1990. In 1921, when the American press raised the issue of US citizens in Soviet jails, the American industrialist Washington Vanderlip visited Russia on business. The Bolshevik authorities immediately got in touch with him, promising him enormous concessions. The American

businessman was invited to visit the prison where some of his fellow countrymen were being held. On his return home, Vanderlip shared his positive
impressions of the Soviet prison. In the *New York Times*, Vanderlip enthusiastically praised conditions for prisoners in Soviet Russia, admired the "spotless
cleanliness of the prison kitchen," and appreciated the "nutritious prison food."
The Soviets shortly thereafter released some of the Americans. One of them,
Jacob Rubin, commented in a letter to the *New York Times* on Vanderlip's public
professions of praise about the Soviets:

> I desire further to call to the attention of Washington B. Vanderlip that he
> cannot make such wild statements misrepresenting the true state of affairs
> in Soviet Russia because he has obtained concessions and contracts. . . . I am
> willing and ready to meet Washington B. Vanderlip any place and any time at
> a public meeting and prove to the American people that every word uttered
> by said Washington B. Vanderlip in reference to the conditions in Soviet Rus-
> sia . . . is false. I further agree to prove to the American people in public debate
> with said Washington B. Vanderlip that the concessions and contract such as
> he has obtained from Soviet Russia were granted to him for only one purpose,
> and that is to make propaganda for Soviet Russia under the subterfuge of
> commercialism.[67]

Besides the business world, Soviet apologists could also be found in Western
political circles ostensibly quite opposed to communism. Soviet Russia's greatest political ally in the West at the time became Germany, and this had little to
do with German Marxist revolutionaries, who were defeated in 1919 and had
little direct influence on the country's policies. On the contrary, the proponents
of Germany's political alliance with Moscow's proletarian internationalists
were the German nationalists—the very ones who had recently dealt ruthlessly with the German communists' attempted revolution. Humiliated by the
defeat in World War I, the German nationalists searched for opportunities for
Germany to emerge from its postwar isolation. In their view, an alliance with
postwar Europe's other great outsider—Bolshevik Russia—provided just such
an opportunity. Both countries, marginalized by the Versailles treaties, needed
one another in their efforts to regain their prewar status as European powers.
The German Chancellor, Joseph Wirth, claimed in 1919, "The only chance I see
for us to rise again as a great power is for the German and Russian people to
work together as neighbors in friendship and understanding."[68]

In the German nationalists' thinking about Soviet Russia, the issue of the
revolutionary goals of communism was relegated to second place in the light
of practical political goals—above all else, the expected benefits of mutual

rapprochement. Ideology was replaced by geopolitics. The key issue that linked the Bolsheviks and the German nationalists was a desire to counter the effects of the Versailles treaties as soon as possible. Their most immediate geopolitical concern was the elimination of the independent Polish state that was reborn between Germany and Russia. Both governments consistently worked toward a rapprochement and by 1922 had signed an appropriate pact at Rapallo. Thus, the first Western country had officially accepted the Bolshevik regime as the legitimate Russian government and an ally in international relations.

Western advocates of economic and political relations with the new Russia were keen that as little attention as possible be focused on Soviet crimes. The moral outrage sparked by reports of Bolshevik barbarity prevented the creation of an atmosphere conducive to rapprochement with the Soviets. The Soviet authorities were well aware of the willingness of the Western business world and political establishment to overlook communist crimes. By reinforcing views favorable to the Kremlin, the Soviets saw a way of achieving their own goal of escaping isolation on the international stage. They could clearly see the Western desires to view Russia as a country governed by a civilized, rational administration, and they were ready to create such an image for Western use. In order for this image to appear credible, however, more than simple propaganda was needed. Propaganda was much more effective when it was transmitted, knowingly or not, by the Western media themselves. Among these media, the most useful were those enjoying a widespread reputation for being objective and reliable.

What the Papers Said

Among the Bolshevik leaders and activists were quite a few people who had spent a great deal of time in the West before the revolution. They understood how the press there worked and how to use it for their own ends. With the outbreak of the revolution, Russia had become a hot topic for the Western media. Newspapers competed for access to the newest and most reliable news on the momentous events in that country. The Bolsheviks realized very early on how to reap political benefits from this situation. They were in the position to control which Western newspapers and reporters could gain access to coveted news from Russia and which ones were denied. The main criterion was the propaganda value of specific correspondents and newspapers to the Bolshevik regime. Correspondents who were unwilling to have the Bolshevik authorities sign off on their copy had to count on being expelled from the land of Soviets. Thus, their papers would be deprived of direct information on Russia, placing them in an unfavorable position in relation to other competing publications.

The Soviet authorities expected political loyalty from the Western media and made no secret of this. To stay clear of the threat of expulsion, Western correspondents, often pressured by their own editors at home, submitted their copy to the press office of the Soviet Commissariat for Foreign Affairs to be censored. Soviet censors unceremoniously struck from this copy any information on Bolshevik crimes, prisons, and camps, as well as anything that did not suit the Kremlin's current propaganda line. Moreover, the correspondents themselves knew the rules of the game and often on their own initiative steered clear of controversial topics to avoid falling afoul of the Soviet authorities. Malcolm Muggeridge, at the time one of these correspondents, recalled: "One took [dispatches] in to be censored, like taking an essay to one's tutor at Cambridge; watching anxiously as they were read over for any frowns or hesitations, dreading to see a pencil picked to slash something out." When Muggeridge attempted to question the Soviet censor as to why he had crossed out some of his material, he was told: "You can't say that because it's true."[69]

At the same time, media outlets and journalists willing to work with the Soviet authorities could count not only on priority of access to important information but sometimes also on more tangible expressions of gratitude from the Kremlin. From 1920, for example, the British *Daily Herald*, the organ of the Labour Party's radical wing edited by George Lansbury, was secretly funded by Moscow and played the role of mouthpiece for Soviet propaganda. Some Western correspondents in Moscow admitted years later to falsifying reports, whether out of opportunism or out of a feeling of ideological kinship with the Bolsheviks (although undoubtedly one did not conflict with the other). M. Phillips Price, the *Manchester Guardian*'s Moscow correspondent, recalled forty years later: "I did not let the narrative speak for itself, but expounded my own views, as if I had been listening to the speeches of Lenin and Trotsky and were repeating something of what I had heard."[70]

The most notorious star of this style of journalism was the longtime Moscow correspondent for the *New York Times* Walter Duranty. In 1920, he was a young and promising reporter in the paper's Paris bureau when he was temporarily posted to Moscow. Like a shot, he picked up on Moscow's rules of the game and mastered them to perfection. Within a short time, he had so managed to ingratiate himself with the Bolshevik authorities that they communicated to the *New York Times* editors their willingness to accredit Duranty as the paper's permanent Moscow correspondent. It should be added that the *New York Times* was treating Russia rather cautiously at this point and without any specific political angle. The paper had published early reports of Soviet terror and repression. The October/November 1919 edition of *Current History Magazine of the New York Times* published the memoirs of the French journalist L. Nadeau, who had been arrested in the summer of 1918 in Moscow by the Bolsheviks and held in prison for five months. In July 1921, on the pages of the same magazine, L. Paswolski published a lengthy article on Bolshevik prisons that presented the Cheka's method of taking hostages.

Duranty's reporting was well received by most Western sympathizers of the homeland of the proletariat. The American journalist denied the rumor of mass starvation in 1921. In the 1930s, he also denied the famine, terror, executions, mass deportations, and slave labor. In his pieces, he consistently presented the Soviet leadership as a group of sensible liberals and pragmatists ready to work with the West for mutual benefit. Directly and indirectly, he encouraged American capitalists to establish closer economic relations with the USSR and politicians to recognize as soon as possible the Bolshevik regime as the legal government in Russia. On the subject of Soviet atrocities, he claimed that they were to a great extent the product of Western propaganda, and that law-abiding citizens of the USSR had nothing to fear from the security services. In short, Walter Duranty sent nothing but good news from the USSR.

In return, Duranty received gratitude in both countries. In Moscow, among the foreign correspondents, diplomats, and Soviet high society, he acquired the reputation of a bon vivant. Malcolm Muggeridge alleged in his diary that Duranty was on a handsome retainer from the Soviet secret police.[71] Duranty was also valued on the other side of the Atlantic. In the US, he enjoyed the reputation of a leading authority on Soviet issues.

The reports from most of the other English-speaking Moscow correspondents in the 1920s and 1930s were generally of similar nature, although there were some exceptions. For instance, Soviet propagandists failed to tame the *Christian Science Monitor*'s Moscow correspondent, William Henry Chamberlin. Like many of his colleagues, he was initially positively disposed toward the Bolsheviks. Working in the USSR, however, he soon saw through the official propaganda and described his observations in a 1934 book *Russia's Iron Age*. Henceforth he became a consistent critic of the Soviet regime and wrote reviews of memoirs by Soviet camp survivors for the *Chicago Tribune*.

While Walter Duranty's reporting from Moscow in the *New York Times* provided a glaring example of the Western press's collaboration with Soviet propaganda, the London *Times'* attitude can be seen as an opposite example. From the start, its editors did not accept interference by the Soviet propaganda machine in articles on Russia in their paper. Consequently, the Soviet authorities did not grant it accreditation. The *Times*, however, did not bend. Information on Russia reached the paper mainly through its bureaus in Berlin and Riga.

By not having its own reporters in Moscow, the paper became the most reliable source of news on Russia in the English-speaking world.

While Walter Duranty was denying the "rumors" of Soviet violence in the *New York Times*, the London *Times* provided information on Soviet crimes and abuses of power. The English-speaking public learned, for instance, about the Bolshevik crackdown on the Russian Orthodox Church; the trial of Patriarch Tikhon; the transformation of churches and monasteries into prisons and camps; the priests imprisoned on the Solovki Islands on the basis of "administrative measures"; bishops Ambrose, Aleksey, and Gleb working in the Solovki camps as cleaners, handymen, and porters; and the exile for life of metropolitans Cyril, Nikander, Arseny, and so on. "It would be idle to pretend that these unfortunates had committed serious crimes, political or otherwise," reported the *Times* about the clergy persecuted in Soviet Russia. "They are persecuted simply as a part of the Bolshevists' anti-religious campaign. Those suspected of political activities were summarily shot in the early stages of the revolution."[72]

The journalists at the *Times* based their reports and analyses on the sources that were available to them at the time, often the personal testimony of escapees and secondhand information. It is only now that we have access to documents confirming the veracity of many of these accounts. Lenin's secret directive of March 19, 1922, on the subject of expropriating the possessions of the church has survived in the Soviet archives. The leader of the October Revolution ordered that "we can (and therefore must) pursue the acquisition of church valuables with the most ferocious and merciless energy, stopping at nothing in suppressing all resistance. . . . The greater the number of the representatives of the reactionary bourgeoisie and reactionary clergy that we will manage to execute in this affair, the better."[73]

Throughout the 1920s, a stream of reports on Bolshevik violence and abuses of power trickled out of Russia to the West. In the initial phase, a large number of citizens of Western countries were released who had been in Russia during the revolution and who had more or less accidentally ended up in Soviet prisons and camps. In 1920, for example, Andrey Kalpashnikov, a member of an American Red Cross mission who had been arrested by the Bolsheviks and had spent five months imprisoned in the Peter and Paul Fortress in Petrograd, published his prison memoirs in the United States.[74] In May 1921, the *Atlantic Monthly* published letters from a Soviet prison in Riga written in 1919 by Baron von Mengden, who had managed to survive when Latvian forces took the city. Two years later, the American economist Elgin Groseclose published his memoirs of Soviet arrest, *Prisons of Despair: An Experience in the Russian Cheka* in the same journal.[75] Reports on the Soviet system of oppression were continually updated as new escapees and witnesses appeared in the West. During the 1920s, Soviet borders were not yet as tightly sealed as they would become in Stalin's era. Escapees from the camps in the Solovki Islands soon appeared. Two of them, former officers in the White Army, Sozerko Malsagov and Yuri Bessonov, published books detailing their experiences in 1926 and 1928 in both English and French.[76]

In many circles in the West, however, those voices were dismissed and denied, especially when they came from people such as Malsagov and Bessonov who were actively engaged in the struggle against Bolshevism. It was not particularly difficult to ascribe political motives to them and to undermine their credibility—especially since so many day-to-day reports in the respected mainstream press seemed to contradict what these "fugitives from utopia" were saying. It was partly thanks to media such as the London *Times* that the mainstream English-language press still offered a space for debate about the reality of Soviet communism. But not everyone wanted to take advantage of this space. This is how Richard Pipes has described the general atmosphere surrounding the subject of Soviet Russia in the West in the 1920s:

> The outside world heard muffled reverberations of the Bolshevik terror
> from newspaper accounts, reports of visitors, and Russian refugees. Some
> reacted with revulsion, a few with sympathy: but the prevalent response was
> one of indifference. Europe preferred not to know. It had just emerged from
> a war that had claimed millions of lives. It desperately wanted to return to
> normalcy; it felt incapable of absorbing still more stories of mass death. So
> it lent a willing ear to those who assured it, sometimes sincerely, sometimes
> deceptively, that things in Red Russia were not as bad as depicted, that the
> terror was over, and that, in any event, it had no bearing on its own destiny.
> It was, after all, the exotic, cruel Russia of Ivan the Terrible, Dostoevsky's
> "underground men," and Rasputin.[77]

Eyes Left

Clearly, Western reactions to Bolshevik terror and persecution did not always match simple ideological and political divisions in society. We have already mentioned that many Western denials of Soviet crimes came from the least expected places, like the business world and political establishment. But the surprising truth about these reactions does not end there. In the decade following the Russian Revolution, some of the most serious problems encountered by the Bolshevik regime as it tried to conceal its crimes from the world came once again from the least expected direction—namely, the left.

The socialist circles were the only group in the West that knew Lenin and his party not just from reports in the media or casual encounters. This was a cosmopolitan environment that Russian radicals and revolutionaries, especially those in exile, had belonged to since long before the revolution. International socialist circles were in a state of permanent ideological and political dispute that divided their members into mutually critical or outright warring parties, factions, groupings, camps, wings, coteries, etc. Long before coming to power in Russia, Lenin's faction, which had broken away from the Russian social democrats, had counted both supporters and opponents among the Russian and international socialist movement. In Russia, it had competed with the Mensheviks, who came from the same social-democratic roots, and with the Socialist Revolutionaries (the SRs), who enjoyed substantial social support during the revolution. There were also the Russian anarchists. All these Russian groups had their friends and allies in the West and stayed in touch with them.

The moment the Bolsheviks came to power in Russia, Western socialists began to split in terms of their attitude toward the Bolshevik regime. Some felt that the Bolshevik revolution was the first step toward overthrowing world capitalism and realizing the proletariat's dreams. Thus, the new regime in Moscow had to be emphatically supported. Others took the opposite view: they felt that the Bolsheviks had betrayed socialism by crushing democracy and introducing a dictatorship; this was not the dictatorship of the proletariat they claimed but of their own faction. Rosa Luxemburg reacted to the Bolsheviks dissolving the Constituent Assembly in January 1918 and rapidly suppressing freedom of speech, association, and assembly in Russia: "Freedom only for supporters of the Government, only for members of the Party, no matter how numerous they may be, is no freedom. Freedom is always the freedom for him who thinks differently."[78] A great many Western socialists hesitated between support for and criticism of the Bolshevik regime.

After coming to power, Lenin's regime immediately began to deal with its ideological kinsmen in Russia, seeing them as competitors for power. The new inhabitants of the Kremlin had reasons to fear this competition since in the only election held under revolutionary conditions, the SRs decisively defeated the Bolsheviks. The Bolshevik response was, as usual, violence, arrests, and terror. However, Lenin and his group realized from the beginning that repression of their ideological kinsmen and recent allies would not go unnoticed in Western left-wing circles and could significantly weaken their support for the Kremlin.

The Bolsheviks adopted a dual-track approach toward other socialists. On the one hand, they systematically liquidated their left-wing political opposition,

while on the other they worked to minimize the negative echoes of these actions in Western left-wing circles. For this reason, the Kremlin was initially
willing to compromise: it granted the arrested SRs, Mensheviks, and anarchists
the official status of political prisoners. None of the members of any of the non-
revolutionary political parties liquidated by the Bolsheviks were afforded this
status. Nor were former aristocrats, landowners, industrialists, clergy, white
guardsmen, tsarist officials, and all the other de facto political and often entirely arbitrarily detained prisoners. Quite simply, they were "class enemies,"
with all the ominous consequences that term implied. The prisoners officially
classified as political were afforded privileged treatment. In the Solovki camp,
for example, they were housed separately in much better conditions than the
rest of the prisoners. They received better food and were not forced to work.
In a word, these conditions, if not necessarily as humane as those that many
socialist activists had experienced in tsarist jails before the revolution, were
much better than those in which "class enemies" were kept. Left-wing political
prisoners behaved just as they had done in tsarist jails: they staged protests,
loudly claimed their rights, went on hunger strikes, and so on.

Just after the Bolshevik revolution, a group of Russian socialist activists
held in considerable esteem in the West approached the new authorities with a
request for permission to reactivate the Political Red Cross, a prerevolutionary
organization helping left-wing political prisoners. Still uncertain of their newly
seized power, the Bolsheviks agreed. The head of the organization was Maksim
Gorky's former wife, Yekaterina Peshkova, supported by, among others, the
legendary People's Will activist, Vera Figner, who had spent long years in tsarist captivity. Henceforth the activists of the Political Red Cross tried to stay in
touch with the political prisoners, organizing material assistance, delivering
parcels, carrying letters, as well as keeping public opinion in the West informed
of their fate. Thanks to reports from the Political Red Cross, Western public
opinion in the first half of the 1920s was relatively well informed on the situation
of socialists and anarchists imprisoned in Soviet Russia. At the same time, news
about other victims, who were suffering a far worse fate in Soviet prisons and
camps, was largely suppressed and falsified. Socialist prisoners, conscious of
the attention focused on them by their Western comrades, stiffened their opposition even more: they wrote protests and statements, which they sometimes
even managed to have smuggled and publicized in the West.

For the Bolsheviks, some of the most awkward situations usually arose during the frequent international conventions and meetings of left-wing organizations. In 1921, at the Third Communist International, the SR delegation read out
a letter from imprisoned comrades who claimed that their fate in Soviet Russia

was worse than it had been in tsarist Russia. On June 22, 1922, the London *Times* reported in depth on the trials of socialists in Moscow. A group of socialist observers from the West, led by Emile Vandervelde, attended the trials. However, the Bolshevik authorities did not permit them any contact with the accused. On his return Vandervelde declared that this "so-called trial is nothing more than an insulting and deliberately-staged farce." The *Times* commented on this piece of information:

> The Bolshevists . . . have been demonstratively arranging mock trials, as though for the express purpose of displaying their contempt for justice. . . . The foreigners who came to defend the prisoners, have been insulted in the streets of Moscow, violently attacked in the Soviet press, and brow-beaten in the Court. Their speeches were misinterpreted, they were kept under close guard, and prevented from consulting with Russian colleagues and friends. Finally, a heavy bill for the expenses of their maintenance was contemptuously flung in their face. . . . Hundreds of Socialists and non-Socialists have been summarily shot by the Bolshevists on such [false] charges and on no charge at all. Thousands of men and women are now confined in filthy prisons and concentration camps, without knowing what they are accused of and without a prospect of even a mock trial. . . . Those who may be inclined to pin their faith to the word of the Bolshevists should take warning that the risk in so doing was never greater than it is now.[79]

The Soviet authorities organized a propaganda counteroffensive against the Political Red Cross's activities and critical voices from the Western left. The same year, 1922, the Bolsheviks set up the International Red Aid organization, or MOPR in Russian. Its aim was to bring humanitarian aid to political prisoners in capitalist countries. This activity and the propaganda effort surrounding it were meant to distract the attention of Western left-wing circles from Soviet camps and prisons. In 1924, an international conference organized by MOPR was held with appropriate fanfare to announce that the organization already had four million members throughout the world.[80]

However, the effect of these propaganda efforts was at best mediocre. In the first half of the 1920s, the Bolsheviks had not yet decided on the final closing of information channels on the situation of imprisoned members of left-wing parties. They were still wary of being criticized and isolated by the Western allies of the SRs, Mensheviks, and anarchists.

The following story illustrates the actual state of affairs at this juncture. In December 1922, the secretary of the French anarchist United Federation of Metalworkers, Lucien Chevalier, fruitlessly attempted to get a meeting with Trotsky while on a visit to Moscow. He wanted to complain to Trotsky about the treatment of Russian anarcho-syndicalists by the Bolshevik regime. Trotsky avoided Chevalier, who did not give up. Unable to meet with Trotsky in person, Chevalier wrote him a letter, later published in the French trade union publication *Le Métallurgiste*.[81] In the letter, Chevalier mentioned by name a twenty-two-year-old anarchist named Mollie Steimer being held in a Soviet jail.

Despite her young age, Mollie Steimer was known not only in anarchist circles but was also well known to the US federal authorities. She had been born in a Ukrainian shtetl in 1897 and had emigrated as a fifteen-year-old with her parents to New York in search of work. Like thousands of Jewish women immigrants from Eastern Europe, she got a job as a garment worker in New York City. She also made friends with the young members of a Jewish anarchist group with whom she lived in a commune in Harlem. They read Bakunin and Kropotkin in the original and put out a Yiddish paper called *Storm* (*Der Shturm*).

In August 1918, the police arrested Mollie for distributing leaflets calling on American workers to follow the Russian example and start a proletarian revolution at home. The leaflets proclaimed: "Will you allow the Russian Revolution to be crushed? You; yes we mean you, the people of America! The Russian Revolution calls for the workers of the world for help."[82] Mollie Steimer was sentenced under the Sedition Act to fifteen years in prison for revolutionary activity in time of war. This undeniably draconian sentence aroused protests from left-wing activists and intellectuals. Some of those protesting were Roger Baldwin, Lincoln Steffens, and the later Supreme Court Justice and legal adviser to President Roosevelt, Felix Frankfurter. Mollie Steimer did not serve her entire sentence. Instead, she was placed on the SS *Estonia* and deported to Russia on November 1, 1921. In New York, a representative of the Soviet government praised her and her comrades as heroes of the oppressed American working class. On December 16, 1921, Mollie Steimer reached the capital of the young homeland of the proletariat.

Here, however, unpleasant surprises awaited her. After less than a year, on November 1, 1922, Mollie again found herself in prison, this time a Soviet one. News of her arrest rippled through Western anarchist circles, and it was then that Chevalier brought up her case in Moscow. Mollie was fortunate. This was a time when the Bolsheviks were trying not to discourage Western anarcho-syndicalists. Instead, they were trying to bring them into line, using the Red International of Labor Unions based in Moscow. Therefore, from time to time, they would make a magnanimous gesture toward them, releasing some Russian anarchists from jail at the request of their Western comrades. In April of the previous year, they had, for instance, permitted a group of anarchists held in

Moscow jails to emigrate. In this context, Trotsky decided to accede to Chevalier's request to have Mollie Steimer released. After all, her political significance was very modest. He received Chevalier, and after talking to him, the Soviet authorities stopped hounding her, though only for a time; a few months later, she was back in jail. When she threatened to go on hunger strike, her interrogator was astonished: "Does she think she is dealing with the American police?"[83]

Eventually, on September 27, 1923, the Soviet authorities deported her from Soviet Russia to Germany together with her partner, Senya Fleshin, a man with a strikingly similar biography. Mollie Steimer saw their deportation as still more unwarranted persecution. With time, however, she must have realized that she had been extremely fortunate. Had she remained in the homeland of the proletariat, her chances of surviving would have fallen dramatically, probably eventually to zero. On leaving Russia, Mollie settled with Fleshin in Berlin, where they opened a photography business. When Hitler came to power, they left for Paris, and when in 1940 the armies of the Third Reich arrived there too, they left for Mexico, where they again ran a photography business, this time right to the end. Mollie Steimer died in July 1980 at the venerable age of eighty-three. At that time, workers were striking in communist Poland and Solidarity was being born.

But let us return to the 1920s. Most left-wing prisoners in the land of Soviets were decidedly far less fortunate than Mollie Steimer. In 1923, the Bolsheviks consolidated their control both over political prisoners and the communication channels through which information on these political prisoners leaked out. Most of the officially recognized political prisoners previously held in various prisons and camps were moved to the Solovki Islands. The Political Red Cross continued to have access to them in theory, but owing to the difficulty in reaching the islands, contacts of this kind were now possible only if the authorities themselves organized them.

But this did not greatly affect the public attitudes of Western left-wing circles toward the Bolshevik regime. For instance, in August 1924, at a congress of British social democrats at the Manchester Hotel in London, the Mensheviks' émigré representative, Anatoly Baykalov, presented the situation of the socialists in Russia. Summing up his presentation, the London *Times* commented that in the Soviet state, "the principles of Socialism and Democracy are trampled underfoot and the people were deprived of the rights essential in a civilized country. The Socialists were being more bitterly persecuted under the Soviet Government than they had been in the time of the Czar. Thousands of Socialists were in prisons and concentration camps and the Soviet seemed determined to exterminate Russian Socialism."[84] In response to Baykalov's statement, British social democrats adopted a stance critical of the Kremlin, and the proceedings' chairman, MP William Cluse, reminded everyone that "the Social Democratic Federation … was the only party to take up the attitude of hostility to Bolshevism."[85] This took place at a time when news was trickling out of bloody events taking place in the Solovki camp. On December 19, 1923, a group of political prisoners on the islands had organized a protest. The guards ordered the protesters to return to their huts. When they refused, the Chekists opened fire, killing six prisoners.

In January 1925, a British trade union official named John Turner attended the International Trade Union Congress in Moscow with the intention of looking into the issue of left-wing activists imprisoned there. He began by submitting an official inquiry to the Soviet authorities, to which they responded by proposing a personal visit to the Solovki Islands. The following day, however, they stated that the weather prevented such a trip. Nevertheless, Turner caught up in Leningrad with an anarchist recently released from the camp and learned from her of the abuses of prisoners on the islands. In his report on Soviet Russia, Turner stated that there was no freedom of speech, no freedom of the press, no freedom of assembly, and that people were sent to concentration camps merely on "suspicion of counterrevolutionary convictions." The London *Times* summarized Turner's conclusions: "A person who attracts the attention of the authorities … is immediately arrested and subjected to cross-examination. If the authorities are not satisfied with his replies he is certain to be kept in prison."[86]

A few months later, the Soviet efforts to conceal the truth about political prisoners suffered a serious blow. The International Committee for Political Prisoners published an extensive set of documents in English testifying to the fate of left-wing political prisoners in the USSR. This substantial volume contained letters, statements, appeals, and other testimony by left-wing political prisoners that had been smuggled out of Soviet camps, prisons, and places of forced exile. Numerous Soviet resolutions and regulations that had been used to deprive people of their freedom were also presented in the book. In all, 140 documents were made public.[87]

It was difficult for the Soviets to discredit the collection as politically motivated propaganda cooked up by the bourgeois enemies of the revolution. Activists of the International Committee for Political Prisoners made it perfectly clear that they sympathized with socialist ideas. But they did not accept that one socialist faction would suppress the activities of the others, let alone do so violently. Not only did such behavior weaken support for the Bolshevik cause in the eyes of the left in the West, it also jeopardized the whole socialist experiment. As the thinking went, the sooner the Bolsheviks, urged on by world public opinion, abandoned these shameful practices, the faster the new Russia would gain the consolidated support of the left in the West. Thus, appeals were made simultaneously to the Bolsheviks' conscience and to their political sense in order to make it known just how badly persecution of the socialists was hurting their image in the eyes of potential allies in the West.

The volume's editor, Isaac Don Levine, ensured that it received maximum publicity. He asked numerous eminent cultural figures for comments. Twenty-two of them responded to this appeal, and their letters were printed as a special foreword to the book. The attitudes of some of these respondents to the issue of Soviet repression of the left hardly differed from those of the editors. The English writer Arnold Bennett announced: "I am not prepared to regard the Soviet Government as worse than those of other countries," then stated, "And so long as the present severe repression continues Western nations will conclude that the existing Soviet authorities feel their position insecure. Cooperation with the advanced elements of the West is rendered difficult by a prolongation of a reign of terror . . . especially in view of the fact that many, if not most, of the present victims are as sincere advocates of the November Revolution as the communists themselves."[88] The editor of the London *New Leader*, H. N. Brailsford, also appealed to the Soviets' political sense, writing: "The suppression of the freedom of speech, printing and association in Russia under a workers' government endangers its future and delays, by its ugly example, the acceptance of Sovietism by other peoples."[89] Albert Einstein, in turn, expressed cautious optimism, believing that under the pressure of Western public opinion the Bolsheviks would soon have to change their behavior. He wrote:

> All serious people should be under obligation to the editor of these documents. Their publication should contribute to affecting a change in this terrible state of affairs. For the powers that be in Russia will be compelled to alter their methods after the appearance of these letters in print, if they desire to continue their attempt to acquire moral standing among the civilized peoples. They will lose the last shred of sympathy they now enjoy if they are not able to demonstrate through a great and courageous act of liberation that they do not require this bloody terror in order to put their political ideas in force.[90]

Harold Laski echoed these appeals to the Bolsheviks' political sense in his commentaries on Soviet concentration camps. He wrote:

> Western Socialists can hardly fail to feel that the refusal on the part of the Soviet Government to give their Socialist comrades the chance of a creative life is a blot upon their record which makes exceedingly difficult the frank resumption of cordial relations. It has made many in England who welcomed

the Revolution feel strongly that the splendor of its purpose is marred by the tyrannical suppression of men whose loyal service to the ideals is beyond question. No communist in Russia who came to the West but what would discover that the task of his Socialist comrades abroad would be far easier if he was prepared to treat Russian political prisoners with generosity and justice.[91]

The writer Rebecca West took the same line but did not spare the Soviets sharp words, criticizing them boldly for their political short-sightedness:

[The Soviet government] must give its citizens the right to free speech, free association, and a free press; and it must treat its political prisoners as if it were sane and a stable government and not a frightened old woman who has seen a mouse. If it fails to do so, we in England cannot compromise our position by supporting it; for that would be to render ridiculous and inconsistent our demand, which is a vital part of our movement, that those liberties should be the birthright of our fellow-subjects in India, in Egypt, and in the British Empire generally.[92]

Knut Hamsun took his criticism of the Soviets much further than West. Instead of trying to convince the Bolsheviks that better treatment of socialist prisoners would bring them long-term political benefits, he raised the question of the relationship between the Bolsheviks' slogans and their actions:

If there is a spark of the early fire left in the breasts of the rulers of Russia today—and we still cling to the belief that there is—they cannot permit the conditions disclosed in these letters to develop and drive root until the last humanitarian currents of the Revolution are polluted beyond redemption. If the friendliness of the intelligentsia of Western Europe is at all valued in Moscow, these thousands of imprisoned idealists should be set free at once and their energies and knowledge employed for the common good. . . . May the publication of these letters awaken the conscience of the Soviet leaders and give them the spiritual courage necessary to demonstrate that justice is not dead in Russia.[93]

Some of the commentators tried to dismiss the significance of the Soviet abuses of power rather than revise their own good opinion of the Kremlin. In this effort, the old Russian tales of the good tsar and the bad officials found new meaning. Sinclair Lewis came to the conclusion that the Soviet authorities simply did not know what was happening in Soviet camps and prisons: "I believe that [the Soviet authorities] themselves may well be ignorant of what is going on in their prisons, just as even our highest officials in America are often completely ignorant of what really goes on in our prisons and slums, and that they will hear the appeal of these outsiders, who have no selfish demand but only the longing to be able to trust Russia."[94] In this, he was echoed by Bernard Kellerman: "It is unbelievable that the Russian government, which identifies its aims with humanity and human dignity, can know of these conditions in the prisons and this martyrdom of the political prisoners. Probably it has been shamelessly lied to and deceived by its commissars and investigators."[95]

Some went even further. Upton Sinclair was evidently so wrapped up in criticism of American abuses of power that he turned out to be tone-deaf to the Soviet ones. He wrote:

> I am greatly shocked to discover that conditions of [political] prisoners in Russia are about the same as the conditions of political prisoners in the state of California, of which I am a citizen. . . . I feel more moved to activity on behalf of these prisoners than on behalf of prisoners in Russia, concerning whose fate I know only indirectly. I recognize the right of a state to protect itself against those who actually commit crimes of violence against it; I understand that such acts of political crime have been committed in Russia, as for example the attempt to assassinate Lenin. Nothing of the kind has happened in recent years in the United States, and none of the political prisoners in California have charged against them any acts of violence. In this respect, therefore, it appears that the state of California is far behind the government of Russia in its standard of civilization.[96]

Romain Rolland adopted a similar attitude: "But there are almost identical things going on in the prisons of Poland; you have them in the prisons of California, where they are martyrizing the workingmen of the IWW; you have them in Jugoslavia; you have them in the English dungeons of the Andaman Islands, into which have been cast the Indian patriots. Each week similar cries of sorrow and accusation come to me from some country of the world."[97]

Bertrand Russell demonstrated a markedly different approach to the Bolshevik regime and the issue of disregard for human rights. Right after the end of the war, Russell visited Russia with a delegation from the British Labour Party to take a closer look at the new system. He did not, however, succumb to the charms of his Bolshevik hosts, including Lenin himself. He found the Leninist regime to be simply despotic and henceforth stuck to that view. In a letter to the International Committee for Political Prisoners he wrote with his usual irony:

> Misled by Western Socialists, the statesmen of Great Britain, France, and America regard the present holders of power in Russia as idealists and therefore dangerous. If they will read this book they will become convinced

of their error. The holders of power in Russia, as elsewhere, are practical men, prepared to inflict torture upon idealists in order to retain their power. There can be no reason why Western imperialists should quarrel with these imperialists of the Northeast, or why Western friends of freedom should support them until there is a radical change in their treatment of political opponents.[98]

Thomas Mann also wrote bitingly about the Bolsheviks: "I read that in one of these martyr bodes, where these letters were written, and which was formerly a church, they have removed all the religious images and symbols, and have put in their place the pictures of Lenin, Trotzky and Marx. I don't know how Lenin and Trotzky feel about this proceeding, but I am sure that Karl Marx would turn in his grave if news from the world of these letters should force its way through to him."[99]

Many writers and intellectuals responding to Levine's call held no illusions as to the actual moral nature of communism—both in theory and in practice. Karel Čapek unambiguously denounced the communist regime:

Do you, who organize or carry on terrorism against human souls, have any belief in the soul, in conscience, in something which is good and wonderful in mankind? If you do not believe in these things then you have no right to be a people's rulers; if you believe in any moral order, and if, despite that, you continue to act in such a manner as appears from the weighty and desperate testimony given by these martyred people, then woe be unto you; for you have betrayed man in his historic struggle against brutal atavism. You say that the world's bourgeoisie is against you; but a greater force than that is opposed to you, the conscience of the world is against you. And conscience is, and will be, more and more, a political and international factor; you have defeated your own cause by depriving yourselves of this ally.[100]

Arthur Schnitzler did not even count on any attempts to appeal to communist consciences. He came straight out and said,

At the present time, when Terror as an element of public policy is recognized as legitimate, not only by the underlings of government but also by its leaders, at such a time there is no injustice, no knavery, no barbarity which is not excused by the convenient and cowardly pretext of political necessity. You wish, my dear Mr. Levine, to make an appeal to the Bolshevist rulers to give up or at any rate to relax their regime with regard to their political opponents.... The very fact that such an appeal at all has become necessary leaves small hope that it will be of much avail. Yet if, nevertheless, that should turn out to be the case even in a modest degree, we must not imagine it would be because our appeal touched the heart of the jailers: for to persons who think mainly along political lines even humanity will only be a pawn in the game and never a moral necessity.[101]

The great Danish literary critic Georg Brandes also harbored no illusions about the communist promises. His words recall Conrad's images in *Under Western Eyes*: "The Russian Revolution had bettered nothing. Cruelty and contempt for the right to liberty have remained the same. It has taken a century to break the arbitrary power of the Czars. That has been accomplished, and in place of this power there is another, just as stupid and cowardly, a thousand times more hypocritical."[102] Maurice Maeterlinck noted that the world was becoming so accustomed to Soviet barbarity that it treated it as a normal state of affairs about which simply nothing could be done. He wrote: "This drama is being played out at this very moment at the other end of the earth; and the civilized world is so weary of protesting in vain against the Soviet abominations that it no longer takes the trouble to raise its voice."[103]

This swelling chorus of criticism reverberating in Western left-wing circles in reaction to the growing number of new reports on the fate of political prisoners in Russia alarmed the Soviet authorities. In response, the Kremlin started playing hide-and-seek. In July 1925, the Bolsheviks announced proudly to the world that they were no longer holding political prisoners on the Solovki Islands. And indeed, this was partly true. However, they neglected to mention that, first of all, they were speaking only of people officially classified as political prisoners—that is, Mensheviks, SRs, and anarchists. As for the remaining political prisoners, the "class enemies," nothing changed for them. Indeed, during the winter of 1925–26, a quarter of the six thousand prisoners on the islands died from an epidemic.[104] Secondly, the Soviet authorities had forgotten to add that there were no political prisoners on the Solovki Islands for the simple reason that they had been transferred to more inaccessible camps near Tomsk and Verkhneuralsk, where conditions were worse than on the islands.

Meanwhile, Soviet propaganda pretended as if there were no more political prisoners in Russia and that the Solovki camps had been completely closed. The leader of the Soviet trade unions, Mikhail Tomsky, publicly stated in the presence of French and Belgian trade union representatives that the Soviet authorities had dismantled the remains of the machinery of terror and coercion, as it was no longer needed after the end of the Civil War. In a more intimate group at a party conference in Leningrad, the same Tomsky, no doubt feeling more at ease, permitted himself greater honesty and humor: "Under the dictatorship of the proletariat, three or four political parties can exist, but only when one is in power and the others are in prison."[105]

However, this maneuver turned out not to be entirely effective. Even in Tomsk and Verkhneuralsk, political prisoners found ways to smuggle letters out to the West, exposing the Bolshevik game of hide-and-seek. Eventually the authorities decided to make a simple semantic change: the status of political prisoner was abolished. Those who had previously enjoyed this status were now put on an equal footing with the other prisoners. In this way, political prisoners finally disappeared from the Soviet Union. They joined the uniform mass of camp inmates—the slaves of Soviet communism, tormented by hunger and murderous work. Now they could only dream of the good times when they had written protests and gone on hunger strikes, and when their Western comrades had taken an interest in their fate and exerted influence on the authorities in Moscow. The 1930s were approaching, the time of the great leap to socialism— the era of the Gulag, collectivization, Great Famine, and Great Terror.

3

In the Soviet Theater of Life

The 1930s were the most oppressive and deadly years in Soviet history, marked by brutal collectivization, the Great Famine, a vast expansion of the Gulag, and finally the Great Terror. It was also the time of a momentous growth of pro-Soviet sentiments in the West. More often than before, Western commentators, ostensibly trying to find out and comprehend what was happening in the Soviet Union, were in fact describing not what *was* there but what they *wanted to be* there. And what more and more of them wanted to find was something positive. Comparing the sympathetic attitudes of many American intellectuals toward the Bolsheviks in the 1920s and 1930s, a former American correspondent in Moscow, Eugene Lyons, noticed that

> in the early years of the Russian experiment American eulogists were relatively few. Their books showed a romantic, almost lyrical acceptance of the revolution. The facts, no matter how harsh, were usually admitted and assimilated as part of the agony of birth. . . . But in the years now under discussion [the 1930s] the attitude is quite different. There is for most part a literature of apologetics, ranging from panicky rationalizations and self-deception to deliberate concealment.[1]

Even if many Western opinion makers still found it difficult to eradicate doubts about the Bolshevik regime, it nevertheless became easier now to formulate justifications for refraining from talking, writing, and finally even thinking about them. It is fair to say that the desire to learn the truth about the Soviet Union was supplanted, to a larger extent than before, by concern about who might benefit from this truth. Many among those who suspected, or even knew, that the truth about the Bolshevik regime had its increasingly dark side were nevertheless inclined to avoid discussing it publicly, because they believed that this would benefit the wrong causes—capitalist exploitation, social injustice, imperialism, reaction, and finally fascism and Nazism. This anxiety, which had been present among foreign sympathizers of the Bolshevik revolution since 1917, now informed Western attitudes on a much broader scale.

This significant change in Western responses to Soviet crimes between the 1920s and 1930s was, in fact, rooted in a confluence of two processes, the first originating in the Soviet Union, the other stemming from the West. Toward the end of the 1920s, the Soviet leadership decided to use direct violence and forced labor on a large scale in the course of the rapid modernization of the country. As a result of forcible collectivization in the early 1930s, millions of Soviet peasants were robbed, deported, imprisoned, enslaved, starved to death, or killed outright. The large numbers of peasants in custody were treated by the authorities as a pool of cheap forced labor, and so the Gulag quickly expanded, reaching unprecedented dimensions and becoming an important component of Stalin's economic policy.

At the same time, the modernization of the USSR also required a significant improvement in economic—and to a considerable degree political—relations with the Western world that presented the only source of the modern technologies necessary for Soviet industrialization. The prospect of this new level of cooperation with the bourgeois West depended to a significant degree, however, on the ability of the Bolsheviks to distract the attention of Western public opinion away from the methods being used to modernize the USSR, namely mass oppression, terror, and coercion. In order to reach this goal, West-directed Soviet propaganda was boosted and fine-tuned to a degree unknown in the previous decade.

But this newly enhanced propaganda, as spectacular as it was, would not have influenced Western minds to the extent it did if so many of its targets did not have their own reasons either to believe it or at least to treat it as an excuse for dismissing revelations of Soviet atrocities. The primary reason for this increased readiness to accept Soviet propaganda at the beginning of the decade was the Great Depression. The anxious search for viable alternatives to the crisis-ridden capitalist system led many toward acceptance of the Soviet system, or at least its propaganda image. This growth in pro-Soviet sentiment was not limited to capitalism's critics and foes. Among those who hoped to save the capitalist West by reinvigorating its economy were many who believed that expanding trade relations with the USSR could help reach this goal. Some of the strongest advocates of this new economic prospect were businessmen hoping for profits. These attitudes provided strong motivation for evading the issue of Soviet atrocities. Later on, pro-Stalin sentiments received a major boost after Hitler came to power in Germany in 1933. Communism figured in the minds of many as the key counterforce to Nazism and fascism. Thus Stalin was viewed with growing conviction as the world's best hope against Hitler. Naturally, Soviet propaganda did everything possible to reinforce this perception. In light of these developments, a peculiar symbiosis emerged between the designers of this propaganda and its Western consumers and contributors. Both sides found vital reasons to remain committed to this relationship.

The Leap Forward

Lenin's death in 1924 was followed by a period of internal power struggle among Bolshevik leaders. This postponed for a few years an issue that the Soviet regime had to face sooner or later: if the Bolsheviks seriously intended to realize their basic ideological goals, in the name of which they had seized power, they would have to complete the unfinished transformation of the economic structure of the country. After the enforced nationalization of industry and trade, which had been alleviated temporarily by the New Economic Policy, the time was coming for the collectivization of agriculture. Communist doctrine did not tolerate private farming. This meant that the new rulers of the Soviet Union had to undertake the gigantic task of expropriating the peasants' land, livestock, buildings, farming equipment, and crops. Tens of millions of Soviet people had to be forcibly deprived of their most valuable possessions and turned into laborers in the state-controlled economy.

In addition to this unfulfilled ideological requirement of collective ownership of the entire economy, the Soviet Union still presented a paradox in light of Marxist doctrine. It was a country where the communist political superstructure, suspended in midair against the Marxist laws of historical gravity, waited for its own economic base to be built underneath it.

But economic modernization seemed necessary not only in order to satisfy the requirements of Marxist doctrine. Even more pressing were practical concerns. With the Bolsheviks' hopes for worldwide revolution shelved until an undefined opportune moment in the future, Stalin, who defeated his rivals in the internal Soviet power struggle at the end of the 1920s, seems to have understood that the prospect of leading the world revolution to its future victory would depend on his ability to transform Russia into a major military and economic power. Only this could ensure the regime's security and safeguard its interests in the international arena—at least until the time was ripe to deliver the coup de grâce to the world bourgeoisie.

Apart from Marxist-Leninist dogma, Stalin looked to Russian history for a suitable model for his vision of modernizing the Soviet Union, and he seemed to find it in Peter the Great. In 1928, as ideas about how to achieve this modernization were ripening, Stalin stated during a session of the Central Committee: "When Peter the Great, conducting business with the more advanced countries in the West, feverishly built mills and factories, to supply the army and strengthen the defenses of the country, it was a special sort of effort to leap clear of the confines of his backwardness."[2] Stalin knew very well that Peter's relentless brutality was effectively erased from official Russian history and did not evoke critical reactions abroad. On the contrary, the tempo of Peter's modernization-by-coercion aroused deference and admiration in the world. The new Soviet dictator believed, as Peter had, that the mass effort of forced laborers commanded by the state authorities was an effective method of quickly modernizing Russia. The Bolsheviks—a doctrinaire regime in charge of a fledgling economy—were incapable of mobilizing a sufficient workforce with positive material incentives. And yet workers had to be dispatched to the remotest corners of the Soviet Union to build roads, railways, canals, and mines in order to enable the exploitation of formerly inaccessible natural resources. Already in 1928, it was clear to the Soviet leaders that a significant portion of this job should be done by forced labor.

That year the Politburo called a special commission, headed by the Justice Commissar of the Russian Soviet Federal Republic Nikolai Yanson, to explore how to use forced labor most effectively. Yanson belonged to the initially quite numerous group of senior Bolshevik activists with considerable foreign experience. He left Russia after the revolution of 1905 and spent a lengthy period 1907–1917 in the United States, where he became an activist in the Socialist Party of America. It was not Yanson, however, but Genrikh Yagoda—backed by Stalin—who had the most influence on the commission's decisions. Yagoda, then the deputy (and future successor) of the chief of the Soviet political police Vyacheslav Menzhinsky, claimed that Russia's prisons and camps were already too full and that funds were lacking to build new ones. For these reasons, he suggested creating more new "camps which will make rational use of labor." "We are contending with a multitude of problems, attempting to attract workers to the north of the country," he argued. "If we send many thousands of prisoners there, we will be able to exploit the natural riches of the North . . . what can be achieved in those regions is well exemplified by Solovki." Yagoda's vision did not end with the short-term exploitation of northern riches. It opened the prospect of developing and colonizing vast territories in the Arctic, Siberia, and the Soviet Far East—inhospitable to humans, yet economically valuable to the state. He elaborated: "With various administrative and economic measures we can force the freed prisoners to remain in the North, and thus we will populate these remote regions."[3]

Of course, Yagoda's proposal was nothing new in Russia. It corresponded with traditional methods of developing and colonizing the most distant lands of the Russian Empire with convicts and exiles. The contemporary Soviet model of forced labor—the Solovki camps—had already been turned into a principal producer of timber, a key Soviet export item and a vital source of hard currency at the time. And the Soviet government was in desperate need of hard currency in order to buy Western machinery and technologies necessary for modernizing the economy. Consequently, Yagoda and other Bolshevik leaders, including Stalin, believed that the Solovki experiment in forced labor should be developed on a wider scale and applied in various branches of the economy. And so it was done. Instructions from the Soviet authorities in June 1929 transformed the entire Soviet penitentiary system into a de facto system of penal labor. The new guidelines stated that all prisoners sentenced to over three years of confinement were to be sent to labor camps, which should be established wherever they were required—first of all, in remote, inaccessible areas with abundant natural resources.[4] These camps were now placed under the unified jurisdiction of the political police—the Cheka (which was transformed and renamed the OGPU [*Ob"edinennoe gosudarstvennoe politicheskoe upravlenie*—The All-Union State Political Administration]). In 1930, this system of forced labor was integrated within a new branch of the OGPU, named *Glavnoe upravlenie ispravitel'no-trudovykh lagerei i kolonii* [The Main Administration of Corrective-Labor Camps and Colonies]—GULag for short.

New camps grew quickly all over the far-flung territories of the USSR. Methods already tried and tested in Solovki were now employed throughout the Gulag in order to push the prisoners to the limits of their strength. Those who did not fulfill the production targets received less food. The Stalinist plan for industrializing the country was no less ambitious than the reforms of Peter the Great. The first Five-Year Plan (1928–1933) aimed to accomplish an industrial revolution in Russia in five years. Consequently, production quotas in these camps increased even more than before. Work under such brutal conditions destroyed the workers, but this did not discourage the authorities. Mass arrests became a method of replenishing and expanding the overexploited slave labor force. One of the responsibilities of the OGPU was to keep resupplying the camps with new prisoners.

At the beginning of the 1930s, a seemingly infinite source of forced labor became available in the Soviet Union as a result of Stalin's decision to push for a speedy completion of the collectivization of agriculture. The methods of implementing this campaign remained true to Bolshevik standards. Poor peasants were pitted against wealthier ones, who were referred to as the *kulaks* (*kulak* meaning "fist" in Russian). In the depths of the provinces, where no foreign correspondent could penetrate and from which no news could reach the outside world, the Bolsheviks employed unchecked brutality. The authorities, eager to export grain to Western countries in return for industrial technologies and equipment, placed unrealistic demands on peasants in some regions and decided to forcibly confiscate all grain—including seed grain—from those areas that did not meet the quotas. This policy was implemented so ruthlessly that it turned into a genocidal campaign, causing a massive famine in parts of the country, especially in Kazakhstan, parts of the North Caucasus, and, to the greatest extent, in Ukraine. As a result, some 5.5 to 6 million people starved to death in the Soviet Union.[5] Peasants arrested in the process of collectivization were treated as a large pool of slave labor. They were forced to build not only the new roads, railroads, canals, and mines, but also new camps for themselves and their successors. The Bolshevik regime was turning millions of its subjects into the compost from which the future flowers of the communist utopia were to grow.

Setting the Stage

Among the issues preoccupying the architects of the Soviet road to communism via collectivization and the Gulag was the question of how the West would react to this expansion of terror and state slavery in the USSR. The issue was raised during the meetings of the Yanson Commission in 1928. A member of this commission, Vladimir Tolmachev, the commissar of internal affairs of the Russian SSR, remarked that news of the development of the Gulag could elicit negative reactions abroad.[6] It had not been easy to hide the system of state terror and violence from the world thus far. Therefore, one could expect that the radical expansion of this system would be all the more difficult to conceal. The problem of Western reactions to such violence always occupied the attention of the Bolsheviks, but at the beginning of the 1930s it took on additional significance. Stalin's modernization could only succeed under conditions of economic exchange with industrialized capitalist countries. In this context, the image of the USSR in the eyes of its potential Western trade partners was politically vital.

From the moment the Bolsheviks came to power, their regime paid special attention to shaping and controlling its own image abroad. As we have already seen, during the 1920s Soviet propaganda produced undeniable accomplishments in this field, but there were still large gaps: Soviet propagandists were not always consistent in their efforts. On the one hand, the regime tried to present itself to the West as a normal state that had just overcome a difficult period of internal conflicts and was now ready to implement its humanitarian ideals of universal justice, equality, and welfare. Numerous fellow travelers—from left-leaning idealists to pragmatic businessmen and politicians eager to make deals with the Soviets—supported and popularized this image in the West. The Bolshevik leaders had plenty of opportunity to recognize that this humanitarian rhetoric was quite effective not only in reinforcing the pro-Soviet attitudes of many Western communists but also in turning some noncommunist Westerners into Soviet sympathizers.

At the same time, some radical Western admirers of Bolshevism cultivated a romantic image of the Soviet regime as the firebrand of the world revolution whose flame would soon destroy the old world and liberate its suffering masses. The image of the bloody Cheka executioners in leather jackets was as exciting for some revolutionary-minded Western radicals as it was repugnant to many other people in the West. For some time, this romantic myth did more harm than good for Soviet intentions to establish relations with the West and win supporters among noncommunist Westerners. At the twelfth session of the Enlarged Executive of the Comintern (the Communist International) in 1926, Mikhail Tomsky, the general secretary of the Red International of Trade Unions, tried to explain to foreign communists that violent slogans, which might be appropriate for initiated comrades, should be avoided in mobilizing noncommunist supporters in the West. Instead, he urged, more vague and all-inclusive catchphrases, such as "world peace," should be used.[7]

By the late 1920s, the Soviet authorities seemed to understand that if they wanted to find new Western economic and political partners, they had to stop provoking anxiety and outrage abroad. The time had come to effectively play down the bloody revolutionary rhetoric. Stalin wanted to be presented abroad first and foremost as a judicious and pragmatic leader, committed to peace and striving to liberate his country from centuries-long backwardness. His potential Western partners were supposed to feel good in helping him attain this goal.

An international framework of organizations of "friends of the new Russia" had already existed in many countries since the early 1920s. Some of these organizations and associations originated spontaneously, while others, such as the "International Workers' Aid," were created by the Kremlin and run by its agents of influence. The Soviet authorities strove to control these structures, but most of the people involved in them seemed unaware of the level of manipulation to which they were exposed. The Bolshevik regime treated this loose network of organizations with considerable flexibility, seeing in them a key instrument that would play for noncommunist audiences in the West a tune glorifying the Soviet Union as the harbinger of universal peace and human rights. The "friends" of the new Russia were systematically fed the message that supporting the Soviet regime was tantamount to protecting world peace and humanitarian progress—a proposition that, on its face, seemed unquestionably noble but also vague enough to appear attractive to many well-wishers abroad. In any case, the slogan "hands off Russia" sounded much more acceptable to them than the original Bolshevik rallying cries, such as "death to the bourgeoisie," "show no mercy to the enemy," "rob what has been robbed," "set the world on fire," and so on.

While trying to avoid heavy-handedness, the Soviet authorities strove to exert as much control as possible over their Western allies in public relations without discouraging and alienating them. In 1927, the International Congress of Friends of the Soviet Union was organized in Moscow. A thousand delegates came from forty-three countries. The Presidium of the Congress, composed of Scott Nearing, Diego de Rivera, Paul Vaillant-Couturier, Karl Gei, Alfred Kurella, and Robert Sievert, issued a bulletin setting out the Congress's agenda. In a typically Soviet way, the bulletin was then "edited" by Konstantin Umansky, a key Soviet apparatchik in charge of external propaganda.[8] At the end of its deliberations, in November 1927, the International Congress of the Friends of the Soviet Union issued the final resolution. The draft was then secretly submitted for review to Aleksei Rykov, the chairman of the Council of People's Commissars at the time. In his comments, Rykov reinforced the priority of the Congress as "turning [these noncommunist "friends" of the Soviets] into our defenders in the capitalist world."[9]

Within the new, dominant Soviet narrative of peace and humanitarianism, the Gulag constituted a sore point. All rhetoric aside, the basic problem boiled down to the question of how to intensify state slavery while simultaneously convincing the West that no such thing existed in the USSR.

Already at the beginning of the radical expansion of the Gulag, this problem assumed quite a concrete and pressing form. In 1930, Soviet timber exports—the primary source of hard currency for the Kremlin—came under threat of boycott and embargo by the United States, Great Britain, and France. The low production costs of Soviet timber from the forced labor camps allowed its sale in Western markets at low prices, which were protested by both the Western timber industry and the trade unions. In August 1930, the leader of the American Federation of Labor, William Green, criticized Soviet timber dumping as "industrial piracy," and called for a boycott, explaining that its low price was the result of slave labor.[10] The US Congress passed the Tariff Act the same year, which contained Section 1307, stating: "All goods . . . mined, produced, or manufactured . . . by convict labor or/and forced labor . . . shall not be entitled to entry at any of the ports of the United States. . . . 'Forced labor,' as herein used, shall mean all work or service which is exacted from any person under the menace of any penalty for its nonperformance and for which the worker does not offer himself voluntarily."[11]

A debate erupted in the American press and within the US government on whether this ban should be used against the import of Soviet timber. Naturally, the Soviet authorities and their Western mouthpieces protested that there was no truth in the allegations linking the Soviet timber industry with slave labor. In the *New York Times*, Walter Duranty cited Soviet statements that lumberjacks were among the best paid workers in the USSR; their salaries could reach the equivalent of $150 a month ("if energetic"), while the average salary of a qualified worker was about $60. Duranty admitted: "While it is true the lumber camp workers include 'kulaks' who have been transferred from their homes on account of opposition to the collective farming movement or for other reasons, they are not regarded as criminals, much less convicts." According to Duranty, these people cut timber in the Solovki camps without coercion in hopes of joining the Soviet professional lumberjack trade union. Duranty explained that they were tempted by the high pay and the prospect of quickly regaining full civil rights, curtailed as a result of their unfriendliness to the government that collectivized their land and property.[12]

The reactions of Soviet authorities to Western discussions regarding Soviet timber exports were quick, showing how closely Moscow monitored this issue. The Soviets continued the policy of deception begun in 1925 in response to the publication of *Letters from Russian Prisons*. On April 7, 1930, before the passing of the Tariff Act, they used a characteristic semantic trick, changing the official name of the camps from "concentration camps" (*kontsentratsionnye lageria*) to "corrective labor camps" (*ispravitel'no-trudovye lageria*). According to later testimonies by former prisoners, one of the methods employed by Soviet authorities in response to the timber debates was the game of hide-and-seek. The Soviets removed officially convicted prisoners from some cutting sites and replaced them with penal exiles who had never received formal court sentences; foreign visitors were then invited to these sites. In other places the timber was originally cut and loaded by prisoners, but in the ports, in the presence of foreigners, it was reloaded onto foreign ships by regular workers.[13]

Regardless of all the above, the US Treasury Department introduced an embargo on Soviet wood pulp and matches, but it lasted only a week before being quickly and effectively quashed by the US State Department. Those American business circles that had long sought to expand economic cooperation with the USSR fought against conditioning it on Soviet respect for human rights. In their view, discussions on this subject were not good for business, yet the debate continued. In December 1930, newspapers reported that workers at the paper mill in Piercefield, New York, discovered a message written in pencil, in Russian, on one of the blocks of wood pulp delivered from Arkhangelsk, informing about the appalling work conditions there.[14] In February 1931, the US Congress still deliberated the question of whether imports of products of slave labor from the USSR should be limited, but with no effect. The embargo project did not even make it to the floor for a vote.

A similar debate erupted in Great Britain. The Conservatives, led by William Joynson-Hicks (the Viscount Brentford) and Winston Churchill, openly criticized Soviet state slavery, advocating for a trade embargo. "Are we, a Christian, civilized nation, to stand by while these things are being done?" Joynson-Hicks referred to the brutal treatment of women in Soviet camps as he spoke on March 6, 1931, at a rally organized by the Trade Defense Union Against the Soviet Economic War in London's Albert Hall.[15] The Labour Party's prime minister, Ramsay MacDonald, however, opposed economic sanctions. In doing so, he used quite peculiar argumentation. On January 19, 1931, he stated in Parliament: "Information which has now reached me suggests that the timber industry in Northern Russia, including felling, removing, sawing, and shipping, is at present carried on not only by means of convict and compulsory labor but also by free labor. It would therefore be impossible to prove legally that any particular consignment of timber was made or produced in 'a foreign prison, jail, house of correction or penitentiary.'"[16]

Meanwhile, reports from Russia awakened the concern of the British Anti-Slavery Society. It conducted an investigation and published the *Report on Russian Timber Camps*, authored by Edward Bateson and Sir Alan Pim.[17] The authors confirmed the existence of a system of state slavery in the USSR. Similarly, the London *Times* did not leave any doubts on this matter, condemning the camps and calling for a boycott of Soviet exports. An embargo on Soviet timber was also considered for some time by the French government. André Tardieu, the minister of agriculture, confirmed this on February 12, 1931, in response to a question from Senator Edouard Néron concerned about a possible crisis in the French lumber industry.

By the end of 1931, however, the Soviet authorities could breathe a sigh of relief and even congratulate themselves. The debate on Soviet timber quieted down, and Western governments decided not to pursue an embargo against the

USSR. The Soviet leadership could now see more clearly the extent of the desire of many Western politicians and businessmen to close their eyes to Bolshevik abuses of power in order to do business with Russia. Soviet propagandists were, of course, ready and eager to play on these desires. Though the borders of the USSR were by now much tighter than in the 1920s, and the information coming out of the country was filtered more effectively, the Gulag was becoming a far larger phenomenon and, therefore, was increasingly difficult to conceal. Not waiting for another controversy to erupt over Soviet slave labor, Moscow seized the initiative and developed a more systematic propaganda campaign to undermine the credibility of current and future revelations about the Gulag and other Soviet atrocities.

The conventional wisdom that the best defense is a good offense found its new implementation. If state slavery could not be completely concealed, then it had to be flaunted. Of course, this had to be done with a twist: namely, a particular way of viewing and understanding the Gulag had to be firmly implanted in Western discourses. The Bolsheviks always appreciated the creative role of language as the key that opens and closes people's minds. And so, instead of shamefacedly hiding the Gulag, the Soviet authorities boasted about it to the world. Quite a few Western opinion makers not only believed them but eagerly joined in.

Reforging Brains

The Stalinist transformation of the Soviet Union in the early 1930s has often been dubbed the "second Soviet revolution." If the immediate goal of the first revolution was the irreversible destruction of the old order, the second focused on constructing the new order. To this end, the dominant emotional and ideological theme of Soviet propaganda had to change. Unchecked class hatred, elemental resentment, and spontaneous revenge—emotions so useful in the process of destroying enemies and gaining power—often become troublesome in the process of reorganizing and governing society after power is won. These sorts of collective emotions could no longer exist in their original, spontaneous, and anarchic form but had to be closely controlled by the new revolutionary regime in power. This is especially true when a new regime strives to achieve the monopoly of deciding when, how, and against whom these powerful feelings are to be channeled. In the meantime, other, more constructive collective emotions have to be aroused and placed at the center of government-controlled public discourse. The "second Soviet revolution" demanded propaganda different from the first one.

The theme of bloody, epic struggle between the old and the new, which dominated earlier Bolshevik rhetoric, had to give way to new themes of moral and political unity and to the vision of the entire Soviet society standing shoulder to shoulder, with a song on its lips, ready to fulfill the tasks set by the Communist Party. The consolidation of power meant more to Stalin than merely controlling all political, social, cultural, and economic life in the country. The Soviet leadership was not only supposed to be universally praised, but it also had to control how, when, and in what manner it was praised. Spontaneity in this area, as in every other area of Soviet life under Stalin, was not looked upon kindly. In a country where everything had a political significance that was fully understood only by the highest authorities, there was no room for improvisation—even when it came to praising Stalin himself.

Efforts were undertaken in the early 1930s to more closely control the language of Soviet propaganda, domestic as well as international. The provocative cult of revolutionary violence, present throughout Soviet art, literature, theater, and popular propaganda in the 1920s, all but disappeared in the early 1930s. While quieting the romantic cult of Bolshevik violence, Soviet propagandists simultaneously reinforced the other, parallel theme associated in Soviet public discourse with Bolshevik prisons and camps already in the 1920s—namely, the theme of humanitarian resocialization and reeducation. If previously the humanitarian rhetoric of reeducation was typically applied to the topic of common criminality—while the topic of class warfare was associated rather with the bloody exploits of unflinching heroes in leather jackets—now the demarcation between class enemies and common criminals was somewhat blurred. Peasants incarcerated during collectivization were often treated as class enemies and criminals at the same time. The logic behind this was quite simple: Since the state took away their land, buildings, farm equipment, animals, and, finally, their food, it would be incorrect to maintain that they were punished for defending *their* property. Instead, they should be viewed as thieves and robbers trying to steal *collective* property. Thus, Soviet propaganda portrayed them not only as enemies of the state but, at the same time, as common criminals. These enemies/criminals—"counterrevolutionary terrorists," "saboteurs," "thieves," "wreckers," and "foreign spies"—were presented as responsible for most hardships suffered by the Soviet people.

Selectively obscuring the distinction between class enemies and common criminals had yet another implication. Both categories of people became subject to the rhetoric of resocialization, formerly applied by Soviet propaganda to criminals. The most hardened enemies were supposed to be physically eliminated (their numbers were to rise dramatically in the late 1930s), but the remaining ones could be depicted, like criminals, as people lost in the corrupt ways of the prerevolutionary world and, therefore, in need of resocialization, just like the homeless orphaned children portrayed in many Soviet publications with humanitarian overtones. One of the central theses of Stalinist propaganda held that the more secure the Bolshevik regime felt itself to be, the more liberal would be its policy toward this sort of people. This implied that if there had indeed been some instances of harsh treatment of politically suspect elements in the past, it was because the Bolsheviks were forced to act in such manner under direct threat posed by the enemies of the revolution, both foreign and domestic. But with the domestic enemies defeated and the foreign ones proven largely ineffective, the Bolshevik authorities, motivated (as always) by humanitarian ideals, were willing to help those Soviet citizens who felt lost and had difficulties developing the appropriate class consciousness. These men and women (and indeed children) would not be abandoned but given the opportunity to find a place for themselves in the new society. An underlying implication of this discourse was that this generosity of the Bolshevik authorities toward the people could be reversed whenever the regime felt insecure again. This meant that any criticism of the Soviet authorities (foreign, of course, since domestic criticism was silenced) could worsen the fate of Soviet subjects as it could make their masters feel threatened. Upon a closer look, this was nothing more than a new and subtler form of the old Bolshevik practice of using their subjects as hostages.

The place where the confused elements of Soviet society could rid themselves of harmful habits and ideas in order to be reborn as new Soviet people was, of course, the Gulag. Within this new rhetoric, the Chekists (as the OGPU men were still called) who ran the camps were no longer presented as the bloody supermen of yesteryear. On the contrary, now they appeared as kind-hearted tutors and thoughtful therapists. Thanks to their care, former criminals and enemies were transformed in the Gulag into new, grateful members of the great Soviet family. But this transformation could not be effected until the Gulag inmates learned to view themselves and the whole world around through the prism of Soviet propaganda—that is, until the language of this propaganda became the only language in which they would speak and think.

This idea of inner transformation, known as *perekovka,* or "reforging," became one of the central themes of Soviet propaganda in the late 1920s and early 1930s—until 1937. The metaphor of reforging was rooted in traditional metal symbolism (melting, tempering, forging, casting, etc.), used in many cultures since antiquity to describe various initiation rites. In these rites, the individual is subjected to trials—sometimes painful and risky—in order to discard the immature self and be born again on a higher plateau of consciousness. The key measure of success in this Soviet parody of initiation was the admission by a prisoner of his own guilt as well as his unconditional, enthusiastic, and active submission to his new "mentors." Just as outside the Gulag, a basic practical indicator of the prisoner's progress on the path of this supposed internal rebirth was the fulfillment of planned production targets. Needless to say, in practical terms the physically weak stood little or no chance of achieving this sort of initiation. During the first half of the 1930s, *perekovka* provided the mandatory framework within which the topic of the Gulag was publicly addressed in the Soviet Union.

One of the most peculiar elements of *perekovka* was the fact that Gulag victims—especially, but not exclusively, during the early 1930s—were required to actively contribute to the creation and maintenance of this fiction. The people forcefully placed in the labor camps were not only supposed to expend the last of their strength for the sake of the Soviet economy but were also expected to create the impression that they accepted their bondage, humiliation, deprivation, and exploitation with gratitude and enthusiasm. Camps were plastered with slogans such as: *Chestnym trudom iskupaem nashu vinu* (With honest work we redeem our guilt) or *Trud est' delo chesti, delo slavy, delo doblesti i geroistva* (Work is matter of honor, matter of glory, matter of valor and heroism). Enthusiasm expressed by some prisoners was often feigned in hopes of a shortening of a sentence, a transfer to a lighter work regiment, a promotion from a laborer to a supervisor, or simply as a scheme to get an extra bowl of soup and not starve to death.

Some of the cleverest prisoners pursued privileges offered by jobs in the internal propaganda system in the camps. The Gulag authorities published 261 different periodicals written and edited by prisoners for prisoners.[18] The biggest camp newspaper was *Perekovka*, with a circulation of thirty thousand copies in the camp complex serving the construction of the Stalin White Sea–Baltic Sea (Belomor) Canal in the years 1931–1933. The construction of the Belomor Canal was the apogee of the theatricalization of the Gulag by Soviet propaganda in the early 1930s. It was the first giant construction project of the period completed exclusively by forced labor. Stalin set an exacting deadline and entrusted the Gulag authorities with responsibility for the entire project. Instead of using expensive equipment, masses of cheap slaves built the canal with shovels, axes, wheelbarrows, and crowbars. The project was, of course, completed on time. The exact number of victims of this Soviet economic success story remains disputed. Nick Baron, Anne Applebaum, and some other historians estimate about 25,000 dead, noting that this figure does not include prisoners released due to severe illness and exhaustion who died shortly thereafter.[19] Unofficial Russian folklore whispered that the canal, like Petersburg two centuries earlier, was built on the bones of slaves.

But this, of course, was not reflected in *Perekovka* and other propaganda publications. Instead, they were full of euphoric reports about brigades of inmates brimming over with desire to best one another at work. These reports were complemented with countless stories of former *kulaks*, wreckers, and other class enemies who, thanks to the Gulag, were born again as exemplary Soviet citizens and heroes of socialist labor.

Naturally, a different picture altogether emerges from accounts by escaped survivors. Ivan Solonevich, a Russian sports journalist, was incarcerated in the Belomor construction camp in 1933 after being caught trying to secretly leave the country. He finally managed to escape from the camp to Finland in the summer of 1934. His Gulag memoir was published abroad, initially in Russian, and soon it was translated into many languages.[20] Solonevich describes his meeting with the editor of one of the local branches of the *Perekovka*, a man named Markovich. Upon finding himself alone with Solonevich, Markovich greeted his fellow journalist: "If you have never seen a perfect idiot before in your life, please look at me." It turned out that Markovich, a Russian Jew, emigrated before the First World War to the United States, where he accumulated a significant fortune—some thirty thousand dollars. A sympathizer of the Bolshevik revolution, he returned to the Soviet Union in the mid-1920s. However, his fortune quickly enriched the coffers of the fatherland of the proletariat, and Markovich himself landed in the Gulag. There, his views underwent an understandable change. In a confidential conversation with Solonevich, Markovich explained where his ideological verve as an editor of the *Perekovka* came from.

> "You know, Ivan Lukyanovich," said Markovich, thoughtfully gazing at his "creation," "in a decent country a paper like this would not be thought fit for a public lavatory, if you'll excuse the expression."
>
> "Then why don't you let it go to the devil?"
>
> "What would I do without it? After all, I must serve my appointed time. Seeing that I've somehow entered the Socialist Paradise, I'll have to play the part of a Socialist saint. This isn't America. That I know quite definitely: haven't I paid nearly $30,000 and five years' Camp confinement for that information? ... Tell me now, what person in Moscow has a better layout than I have here? ... I've got a room to myself, I get a good dinner, naturally, not without grafting a bit—but I get it. And supposing I need a new pair of trousers tomorrow, shan't I get them? I'll get them—the Soviet Press can't be allowed to run around trouserless!"[21]

Markovich undoubtedly belonged to the category of prisoners who quickly learned to play their roles in the Soviet theater of lies. He learned how to use sober cynicism in order to protect himself in the midst of the dehumanizing world of the Gulag. Confident in his own ability to survive through cunning, he secured for himself a privileged position in the camp. But these survival tactics had their own dangers. A Polish survivor of the Gulag, Barbara Skarga, wrote about victims who tried to play the game of ideological accommodation with the system:

> The ideology works because its power reaches further than violence. . . . It creates a camp-appearance, a camp-idea. . . . There are no winners and losers who feel mutual hatred . . . there are only the strict, but good, shepherds and the lost sheep, full of gratitude for all the efforts [of the shepherds]. There are no masters and exploited slaves; there are only the authorities . . . dear to our hearts, representing the higher authority in Moscow, the kind-hearted father Stalin, and there are we who desire to give the last of our strength for the sake of the wondrous fatherland. . . . There are no executioners and victims—murdered, torturers, terrified, or fighting to the end for a scrap of human dignity. No, the camp administration plays the role of unhappy fathers, who, with deepest regret, much punish their own children . . .
>
> In such a way the prisoner, as all Soviet citizens, enters the realm of lies. If he dreams of survival he must brace himself. He must speak the same language as his oppressors, repeat the same phrases. . . . He can do this cynically, knowing that it is a game. But he can easily go too far in this game, stand too stiffly at attention at the sight of the commander, bow too obsequiously to the supervisor, overzealously denounce a new slacker. He may finally start believing in the game, at which point sad is his fate. Before his body fails, his soul will fall.[22]

Many survivors agreed that fear, starvation, violence, cold, and physical exhaustion, coupled with a relentless requirement to lie and pretend, could force people to stop believing their own minds in order to better accommodate their tormentors. Julius Margolin commented:

> The main difference between the Soviet camps and detention camps in the rest of the world is not their huge, unimaginable size or the murderous conditions found there, but something else altogether. It's the need to tell an endless series of lies to save your own life, to lie every day, to wear a mask for years and never say what you really think. In Soviet Russia, free citizens have to do the same thing. Dissembling and lies become the only means of defense. Public meetings, business meetings, encounters on the street, conversations,

even posters on the wall all get wrapped up in an official language that doesn't contain a single word of truth. People in the West can't possibly understand what it is really like to lose the right to say what you think for years on end, and the way you have to repress the tiniest "illegal" thought you might have and stay silent as a tomb. That sort of pressure breaks something inside people.[23]

The legitimization of the Gulag in Soviet propaganda of the 1930s heavily depended on the voices of prisoners praising their oppressors. These praises were elicited, manipulated, and exploited by Soviet public-relations specialists who presented them to foreign audiences. Many foreigners, in turn, took those praises at face value (or at least pretended to do so) and reconfirmed them in their own comments and reports. Thanks to this kind of propaganda, the Soviet labor camp did not appear abroad as a dark secret but as something quite transparent and accessible to scrutiny. Referring to their "encounters" with "real prisoners," scores of "objective observers," both domestic and foreign, assured the world about the harmony between the humanitarian theory of *perekovka* and its practical application in the Gulag. By doing this, they dissipated the misgivings of many doubters as well as undermined the credibility of many Gulag survivors seeking to tell their stories to the world.

Writers at Work

Best suited for the role of "objective observers" were people who enjoyed international fame and credibility and were not recognizable in popular opinion as communist partisans. Around 1928, when Yanson's Commission was still planning a strategy for the radical expansion of forced labor, no Russian suited this role better than Maksim Gorky. At the time, Gorky lived in Sorrento, enjoying a worldwide reputation as a fiercely independent writer. A Bolshevik sympathizer and personal friend of Lenin's long before the revolution, Gorky won additional recognition abroad for his bold criticism of Bolshevik lawlessness and violence in the early period following the 1917 coup.[24] Using his old contacts with Lenin and other Bolshevik leaders, Gorky helped many Russian writers, artists, and intellectuals in the initial few years after the revolution—he stood behind them and provided them with material support, jobs, and other aid. When he realized that his ability to continue these efforts was diminishing (he was unable to save the poet Nikolai Gumilov, Anna Akhmatova's former husband, from execution in August 1921), he left the Soviet Union in disgust in October 1921. The following year, he protested—along with Anatole France—against the show trial of Socialist Revolutionaries in Soviet Russia. He did not, however, identify himself with the "white" Russian political émigré community and never burned his bridges. The Bolshevik regime never denounced Gorky either.

In a few years, Gorky became increasingly frustrated with life abroad. His worldwide fame was slowly fading, and his wealth was diminishing. Meanwhile, the Soviet political police were busy surrounding Gorky with agents and making him increasingly dependent on the Bolshevik regime. Yagoda enlisted Petr Kryuchkov, Gorky's personal secretary, as an agent of the OGPU. From him and other spies, the Soviet political police learned details of Gorky's life, ideas, plans, hesitations, and doubts. Well aware of the writer's frustrated ambitions, his hungry ego, and his financial concerns, the OGPU generously supported him with their own funds. The writer refused neither money nor expensive gifts, such as, for instance, a car paid for by the OGPU.

In late 1920s, not only Yagoda but Stalin himself started wooing Gorky back to the USSR. The famous writer was assured that the status of the patriarch of Soviet literature awaited him on his return. Naturally, both sides understood that Gorky's new role would be contingent upon his availability and loyalty to his patron in the Kremlin. In 1928, Gorky began a series of highly publicized trips to and around the USSR. But he still tried to avoid burning bridges: until 1933 he spent winters in Italy and the remainder of the year in Russia. Stalin and Yagoda kept their side of the deal, at least for a few years. Gorky was immediately surrounded in the Soviet Union with exceptional splendor and lavished with honors. The writer received several villas and practically unlimited financial resources at his disposal. He was treated like royalty, traveled in a special railroad salon car, and even smoked cigarettes specially imported for him from Egypt. At his request, any book published anywhere in the world was brought in for his reading pleasure. Tverskaya Street, the main street in Moscow, was renamed in his honor. The name of the city in which he was born, Nizhny Novgorod, was changed to Gorky. Throughout the Soviet Union, streets, theaters, schools, academic institutes, factories, and collective farms were named after him. No writer in the history of world literature was surrounded by such an official cult in his lifetime as Gorky was in the USSR. After 1933, when the writer was denied permission to travel abroad, he realized that he was, in fact, trapped in a gold cage. But it was too late to complain. He died in 1936, and his status as a Soviet icon outlived that of Stalin himself.

Meanwhile, Gorky's triumphant trips to and around the Soviet Union in 1928 and 1929 immediately resulted in a cycle of reports, *In and About the Soviet Union*. In these accounts, he praised the new Soviet reality, clearly showing his Kremlin sponsors that they could indeed depend on him. Gorky's itinerary, planned primarily by the chief of the secret police, Yagoda, included a short visit to the Solovki camp in June 1929. Gorky, playing the role of a citizen of the world and an independent observer, was to confirm the veracity of Soviet propaganda about the Gulag. He was also supposed to provide a highly credible counternarrative in response to the revelations contained in the 1925 *Letters from Russian Prisons* and the 1926 Solovki memoir by Sozerko Malsagov.

A theatrical show was staged throughout the Solovki camp especially for Gorky's benefit, perhaps in an effort to minimize the writer's potential moral hesitations, should they arise. Witnesses remembered the Solovki's main torture chamber at Sekirnaya Mountain being repainted and suddenly transformed into a reading room. Clean linens appeared in the barracks prepared for show, and tablecloths and flowers adorned the tables of the cafeteria. Gorky's visit stirred up hopes among political prisoners who remembered his principled criticism of the Bolsheviks following the revolution of 1917. Some expected the famous writer to stand up for them. According to some survivors, prisoners were forbidden from approaching the honorable guest under penalty of death. It seems that Gorky was not unaware of the charade. Witnesses reminisced later that he could not restrain himself from expressing his disgust at the spectacle. Visiting the "reading room" at Sekirnaya Mountain, he noticed that some of the prisoners, whose job was to sit there and pretend to read newspapers, were holding the newspapers upside down, trying to make him aware of the manipulation. He reportedly walked up to one, turned his paper right side up, and left without a word. Seeing the clean linens in the camp hospital he walked out, immediately muttering "I don't like parades."[25]

But in a photograph taken at Solovki during the visit, the writer stands with a serene expression on his face in the company of Chekists. Next to him stands his son Maks and daughter-in-law Timosha, dressed in a fashionable Chekist-style leather outfit. Today we know for sure that Gorky's eyes and thoughts reached deeper than the Solovki stage decorations. In his personal travel notes from the trip to Solovki, he wrote: "Like a dog: I understand everything yet remain silent."[26]

In reality, he was not silent at all. On the contrary, he dutifully fulfilled his sponsors' expectations. The journal *Nashi dostizheniia* (*Our Achievements*) had the honor of printing his long report entitled "Solovki." It was, predictably, a paean to the miracle of reeducation through labor, and the Solovki camps were presented in it as the crowning achievement of Bolshevik humanitarianism. Describing the prisoners, the writer reached conclusions identical with the propaganda matrix: "The psyche of people thrown into anarchy by their past is thoroughly transformed. Socially dangerous people are transformed into socially useful ones, professional criminals turn into highly qualified workers and conscious revolutionaries."[27] It comes as no surprise that the writer could at the end conclude with a straight face: "In my opinion, the conclusions are clear. Camps such as Solovki are needed."[28]

Gorky—a citizen of the world—did not hesitate to place the Solovki concentration camp in an international context. He wrote: "If any 'cultured' European society dared to conduct in its own country an experiment such as this colony, and if this experiment yielded fruits such as ours, this country would blow all its trumpets and boast about its accomplishment. . . . Is it because of our modesty or for some other, perhaps less noble, reason that we do not know how to write about our achievements even when we see them and try to describe them?"[29]

Gorky's sponsors at the Kremlin and the Lubyanka appeared to be fully satisfied with his attitude. Four years later, as if in response to Gorky's conclusions about excessive Soviet modesty, they decided to make the Gulag an object of spectacular celebration. This is precisely what happened with the construction of the White Sea Canal. The fanfare surrounding this largest Soviet slave labor project to date was supposed to effectively drown out all testimonies of fugitives as well as criticisms from abroad.

The propaganda campaign praising the White Sea Canal was crowned in 1934 with a special book, *Belomor*. It was not penned by a single author but represented a collective effort of Soviet writers. In this manner, the Gulag propaganda was taken to a higher level. This was a new step in the overall strategy of creating the impression of maximum objectivity. Clearly, the objectivity of the testimony of any individual observer, even the most authoritative, could not equal the collected opinions of many witnesses who mutually confirmed their observations and conclusions. In August 1933, the OGPU organized a visit of a group of no fewer than 120 Soviet writers to the newly built canal. The writers had a series of meetings with (selected) prisoners, supervisors, and local authorities. Of course, the literati were constantly accompanied by OGPU men. They understood what was expected from them. They also knew that refusing an invitation to participate in this project carried grave risks. Yet Mikhail Bulgakov, for example, managed to talk himself out of it, blaming his fragile health. In a twist of historical irony, he was never arrested and died from natural causes in 1940.

Most of the others did not even try to refuse. On the contrary, many writers actively sought this assignment. The group that went to the canal included some of the most popular and acclaimed Soviet literary stars of the time, such as Mikhail Zoshchenko, Boris Pilnyak, and the comedy-writing duo Ilya Ilf and Evgeny Petrov. The fact that many participants of this project had some politically problematic episodes in their earlier lives seems to have played a role in motivating them to cooperate with the OGPU. Viktor Shklovsky, for example, had sympathized with the Mensheviks in the past, and was recognized in the 1920s as a leading formalist critic (an increasingly dangerous label in the 1930s). The background of Prince Dmitry Svyatopolk-Mirsky was even more troublesome. This son of the Minister of Interior in the Russian Empire had fought in the Civil War on the side of the Whites. He managed to emigrate to England where he lectured in the School of Slavonic Studies at the University of London. His *History of Russian Literature* is widely read to this day by students at English-speaking universities. In England, Prince Mirsky's views evolved quickly, and he became increasingly sympathetic to the Soviet regime (in this, he resembled some of his British colleagues). In 1931, he joined the Communist Party of Great Britain and published a book, *Lenin*—a sincere confession of his new faith. Finally, in 1932, he decided to act consistently with his convictions and took the next logical step: he returned to his communist homeland, ready to prove his loyalty to the Soviet authorities.

Mirsky was not the only former émigré among the authors of *Belomor*. Aleksei Tolstoy had also fought in the White Army and managed to leave Russia. Having spent just a couple of years in Paris and Berlin, he returned in 1922, and ingratiated himself with the Bolsheviks to the point of becoming one of the most reliable literary spokesmen of the regime. In the 1930s he enjoyed a celebrity status, prestige, and luxurious lifestyle second only to Gorky himself. Another participant in the *Belomor* literary project, Vsevolod Ivanov, in contrast to Mirsky and Tolstoy, had fought in the Civil War on the Red side but in the late 1920s was attacked by Soviet critics for writing about his wartime experience with insufficient Bolshevik zeal. His contribution to *Belomor* was an important step on his road toward regaining the regime's trust and becoming a leading Socialist Realist writer. Valentin Kataev, the author of the celebrated 1932 classic production novel *Time Forward*, was also a veteran of the Red Army and rising star of Soviet literature. Bruno Jasienski, on the other hand, was a foreigner trying to find his place in the Soviet literary establishment. He earned some recognition and notoriety as a young Polish futurist poet and self-styled dandy shortly after World War I. A committed communist, he left Poland for Paris, where he lived from 1924 to 1929. Expelled from France for disseminating subversive propaganda (his novel *I Burn Paris* had just been published in *L'Humanité*), he settled in the Soviet Union where he befriended Yagoda and started a promising career as a Soviet writer and literary official.

Each of the writers involved in writing *Belomor* had his or her own particular reasons to take part in this unprecedented enterprise. Viktor Shklovsky hoped to get his brother Vladimir released from the White Sea Canal camp.[30] Some other authors, like the young proletarian writer from Magnitogorsk Aleksandr Avdeenko, candidly offered somewhat simpler motives. Describing the writers' voyage in a reserved train car through the hungry Soviet countryside to the White Sea camps, he mentioned the conditions created for the literati by the OGPU: "We ate and drank whatever we wanted, and however much we desired. Smoked sausage. Cheese. Caviar. Fruit. Chocolate. Wine. Cognac. We didn't have to pay for anything."[31] Added to this was the prestige that, in Avdeenko's opinion, came from participating in a project sponsored by the highest authorities, along with literary heavyweights, including Gorky himself. The latter did not take part in the trip due to declining health but headed the editorial committee of the *Belomor* volume and personally wrote the first and last chapters. Gorky's fellow coeditors of the book were Leopold Averbakh (Yagoda's brother-in-law, famous for being a fanatical watchdog of communist orthodoxy in Soviet literature of the time) and Semen Firin, the OGPU chief of the White Sea Canal project. It is most likely the only such case in the history of world literature where a great writer and concentration camp commander worked together on a literary work.

From the group of 120, thirty-six authors were selected to participate in writing the book.[32] The selection of authors underlines their diversity. The communist zealot Averbakh neighbors the "humanist" Gorky, the repenting formalist Shklovsky, the former Polish futurist Jasienski, the London intellectual Mirsky, the outstanding humorist Zoshchenko, and so on. These writers had held deeply divergent views in the past, but now all of them appeared reconciled and unified in the Soviet spirit. If such diverse authors were capable of speaking in one voice in a common proclamation of the firsthand truth about the Gulag, then who could contradict this truth by presenting his own individual—and therefore inevitably subjective and controvertible—testimony? *Belomor* was supposed to seem truer than truth itself.

The book appeared in 1934, decorated with a portrait of Stalin on the first page (Yagoda found himself on the second). Photographs of enthusiastic prisoners adorned this unusual volume. They were taken by the famous artist Aleksandr Rodchenko, who took this opportunity to demonstrate his successful transformation from an avant-garde futurist into a Socialist Realist. Quite predictably, the book set forth the well-known *perekovka* theme of Soviet propaganda, presented by the authors in the form of direct impressions, personal observations, conversations with guards and prisoners, overheard stories, and so on. The guiding motif, repeated endlessly in various configurations, was the miraculous transformation of enemies and criminals into new happy and productive Soviet people. This motif was woven into the larger historical narrative of the great transformation of backward Russia into a modern giant, accomplished thanks to the brilliant leadership of the Communist Party and the humanitarian idealism of the political police. The Gulag and the construction of the canal symbolized this transformation and made the reader anticipate more and even greater miracles to come in the land of Soviets.[33]

Applause from Afar

While the mandatory rapture about *Belomor* lasted in the USSR, a team of Soviet translators and editors began translating the book into English. In the process, they considerably changed the original in order to make it more effective for Western consumption. In their attempt to make the book appear more believable, the editors deleted many fragments of the Soviet original describing in quite fantastic terms the miserable fate and cruel oppression of the working masses at the hands of Western bourgeois regimes. The book appeared in the United States in the fall of 1935. Its English-language editorship was officially credited to Amabel Williams-Ellis, who back in August 1934 had been invited to the First Congress of the Soviet Writers. In her introduction, Williams-Ellis informed readers that in the book they would find the answers to such questions as, "What happens to political prisoners in the USSR: does a Soviet labour camp differ from a concentration camp in, say, Nazi Germany?" She announced: "For the first time we are here told the story of what goes on in a Russian labour camp"—as though no one before had ever written about Soviet camps.[34]

Belomor was received in the United States with extensive reviews. John Chamberlain wrote in the *New York Times* that hearing in the past about politically motivated "sabotage" in the USSR had made him suspect the OGPU of manufacturing such accusations in order to gain more forced laborers to complete various construction projects of the Five-Year Plan. But these doubts were dispelled when he read *Belomor*. He admitted that while he still could not entirely rid himself of the impressions made upon him by the memoirs of recent escapees from the Gulag, such as Tatiana Tchernavina, Vladimir Tchernavin, and Georgy Kitchin, he was equally unable to deny the verity of *Belomor*. Ultimately, he found a way to overcome this dilemma by concluding that though there were perhaps incidents of abuse like those described by the escapees from the Gulag, this did not diminish the fact that *perekovka* was effective and successful. After all, without extreme enthusiasm on the part of the prisoners, the realization of such ambitious projects in such a short timeframe would be impossible, the *New York Times* reviewer reasoned. And he had irrefutable proof of this in the form of the *Belomor* volume.[35]

At the same time, Western correspondents and visitors to Moscow reported about an unusual play being shown there. Soviet theater, which had long enjoyed the attention of Western cultural elites, was tackling the subject of the Gulag. The play, *The Aristocrats* by Nikolai Pogodin, takes place on the building site of the Belomor Canal, and the prisoners and Chekists are its protagonists. At the beginning, the former are presented in a negative light: professional criminals drink alcohol, play cards, steal, and use vulgar language. As if this were not enough, they mock the educational efforts of the Chekists, notoriously avoid work, and look for opportunities to escape. The worst among them are a professional thief, Kostya the Captain, and his lover Sonya—a prostitute, thief, drug addict, and alcoholic.

But not surprisingly to anyone familiar with the main tenets of the *perekovka*, Pogodin's hardened criminals turn out to possess ample positive qualities after all. Under the hard shell of brutality hide sensitive hearts and minds. The Chekist Gromov—a patient mentor and a true father figure to the prisoners—notices this. His methods of reeducating prisoners show remarkable success: a heart-to-heart conversation over tea between a Chekist and Sonya leads to Sonya's miraculous illumination. Shortly afterward, an unrecognizably transformed Sonya swears she will never raise a glass to her lips again, not to mention stealing, whoring, and other former vices. She becomes a shock worker at the canal building site.

With Kostya, however, it does not go so easily. He continues to joke about *perekovka* like an unruly schoolboy. But what then are the OGPU methods for? Gromov, a sophisticated educator and expert in psychology, decides to win Kostya's trust in a way both bold and ingenious. He entrusts Kostya, a professional thief and violent criminal, with the responsibility for guarding the food and clothing warehouse, and finally, as incredible as it sounds, he makes him guard weapons as well. Kostya feels so touched by this show of trust that he undergoes an internal transformation and, surely enough, becomes a shock worker. Finally, on the festive day of the canal's completion, Kostya and Sonya are released early as a reward for their exemplary work effort.

In the play's finale, the Chekists and the reforged prisoners celebrate the canal's completion together. One of the transformed criminals sings:

> A bandit's life I used to lead,
> A life as black as night.
> To work I thought there was no need,
> I robbed and shot at sight.
> A life like this was sure to bring

> A sentence on the new canal.
> For me it's been a second spring,
> I want to live and work and sing.
> The past is but a dreadful dream,
> A thing I must forget.
> Now tears of joy begin to stream—
> Mine aren't the only tears, I bet.[36]

Gromov gives a speech which sums up the message of the play: "Yes, comrades, it's true, our destinies have become intermingled and in this intermingling of thousands of lives there is much that is touching, much of the highest and best in humanity. Why will the White Sea Canal be famous?" For those in the audience who might not yet know the right answer, Gromov spells it out: "People once rejected by society, outcasts, lost, and even enemies, are today recognized and highly valued by their country."[37]

Although Pogodin's play was widely shown and praised in the Soviet Union at the time, the Western public had little opportunity to admire it on stage.[38] But soon enough, the screen version of *The Aristocrats* (entitled *The Prisoners*) produced by Mosfilm and directed by Evgeny Chervyakov, made it to Western movie theaters. On February 19, 1937, enthusiasts of Soviet cinema filled the Cameo Theater in New York City to catch the American premiere of the touching story of the transformation of Kostya the Captain and others in the Gulag. The movie began with an introduction by Maksim Gorky, in which the great writer solemnly attested that the story was true to life.

Many viewers must have immediately associated the film with a popular Soviet classic of 1931, *The Road to Life*. Ordered by the OGPU under Yagoda, *The Road to Life* was the first Soviet sound movie. It told a story of the successful resocialization of homeless juvenile criminals in the corrective labor commune run by the OGPU in Bolshevo outside Moscow. Dedicated to "a great friend of children, Feliks Dzerzhinsky," *The Road to Life* popularized the new humanitarian image of the Soviet political police in the early 1930s. In all fairness, this early presentation of the youth version of the *perekovka* paradigm on film was quite an outstanding work of cinematic art. By the end of the 1920s, Western audiences had already learned to admire masterpieces of Soviet propaganda film directed by Eisenstein, Pudovkin, and Dovzhenko, so *The Road to Life* was immediately noticed and enjoyed tremendous international success. The audience at the first Venice Film Festival in 1932, organized by Mussolini's government, voted to recognize the film's director Nikolai Ekk with the prize for the best director. According to *Komsomolskaia pravda*, by November 1932 *The Road to Life* was playing in twenty-seven countries.

So when *The Prisoners* appeared on screen in New York, the *New York Times* reviewer Frank Nugent called it "an adult sequel to *The Road to Life*." Although Nugent did not question the credibility of the *perekovka* theme as such, he remained quite sober regarding its portrayal in the film. "Some of Pogodin's conversions are understandable and logical, but there are others which we must swallow whole and at some peril to our mental digestive process," he noted.[39]

Why then did so many Western commentators so eagerly allow themselves to be convinced or duped by this sort of propaganda throughout the 1930s? After all, many accounts by former Soviet prisoners and other witnesses of the Gulag were being published in the West at the time. These reports and memoirs tended to confirm and complement one another, thus creating a fairly consistent testimony that seemed at least bound to question, if not outright undermine, these Soviet propaganda efforts. Let us keep in mind that as early as 1926 Sozerko Malsagov's memoir from the Solovki, *An Island Hell*, appeared in London.[40] Just two years later, a French writer, Raymond Duguet, published *Un Bagne en Russie rouge* (A prison in red Russia), a book based on accounts by numerous survivors and escapees. Anne Applebaum calls Duguet's book "for sixty years . . . the most complete source on [Solovki] in the French language."[41] In 1928 and 1929, French and English translations of Yuri Bessonov's prison and camp memoirs appeared along with the camp memoirs of Finnish businessman Boris Cederholm, who was imprisoned by the OGPU under the charges of espionage.[42] The early 1930s brought quite a few studies of Soviet camps—for example, William A. Fairburn's *Forced Labor in the Soviet Union* and *The Conscription of a People* edited by the Dutchess of Atholl, as well as the aforementioned report by Alan Pim and Edward Bateson.[43] In 1933, a collection of letters from camp inmates appeared in London with an introduction by Hugh Walpole. At the same time, Viking published a sensational, though undoubtedly embellished, memoir by Leo Nussimbaum (writing under the pseudonym Essad-Bey) entitled *OGPU—The Plot against the World*.[44]

The number of firsthand testimonies about the Gulag available in the West kept growing throughout the 1930s. In 1934, Tatiana Tchernavina published in London and New York her memoir *Escape from the Soviets*.[45] This former curator at the Hermitage in Leningrad, together with her husband, biologist Vladimir Tchernavin, and their thirteen-year-old son Andrei, escaped from the Soviet camps to Finland—the most common route for escapees from the Gulag at the time. Her recollections of the Gulag, written while still in a Finnish hospital just after escaping Russia, did not pass unnoticed in the West. On May 20, 1934, the *New York Times* ran a double review by J. Donald Adams of Tatiana Tchernavina's book coupled with *Winter in Moscow*—an intimate account of the loss of pro-Soviet illusions by a former British press correspondent in Moscow, Malcolm Muggeridge. Adams called Tchernavina's memoir "one of the most moving and convincing testimonies of the human experience" that he would ever come across. It was, in his words, "a book for future generations" that would be read "when the present Kremlin regime is only an episode of ancient history." Tatiana Tchernavina's husband, Vladimir, published his Gulag memoir in English in 1935, not long before the appearance of the English version of *Belomor*.[46]

Shortly before and after the American publication of *Belomor*, the Western public also had the opportunity to read the newly released memoirs of an anonymous Russian female survivor under the pen name Olga Dmitrevna, as well as a book by a Finnish businessman named Georgy Kitchin. Kitchin was arrested in the Soviet Union in 1928, accused of espionage and held for four years in a Leningrad prison and northern camps. As a result of an inquiry by the Finnish authorities, the Soviets allowed him to return to his country.[47] Another prisoner the Soviets permitted to leave was Julia de Beausobre, who was released in 1934 in exchange for a ransom as a result of persistent pleas and inquiries by her former English governess. Four years later, her camp memoirs appeared in English.[48]

But that was not all. The same year, 1938, a book by Croatian communist Ante Ciliga, was published in French. Ciliga had moved ten years earlier to the USSR only to find himself arrested and placed in a camp for his Trotskyist sympathies. After protests from Western left circles he was released and deported from the USSR in 1935. His book (published in English in 1940) became one of the early examples of what would later be called the "literature of disillusionment." It complemented earlier books by communist believers disenchanted with Soviet reality, such as Panait Istrati's reminiscences published in the volume *Vers l'autre flamme* (1929). Ciliga noted that only those imprisoned in Soviet Russia were able to understand the true essence of communism.[49] Ivan Solonevich, an ardent anticommunist and the author of the most popular testimony of the Gulag in the 1930s, *Russia in Chains*, reached similar conclusions.

As we can see, revelations about the Gulag were not lacking in the West during the decade preceding World War II. However, their influence on Western minds—particularly those shaping public opinion—was negligible in comparison with the influence of Soviet propaganda.[50] Why?

To Tell or Not to Tell

Never before were so many Westerners so determined to believe in the positive image of the Soviet state as in the 1930s. While many factors contributed to this development, the most important breakthrough in Western attitudes to Soviet communism was certainly linked with the aftershocks of the crash of the stock market in October 1929. Within days, the relatively stable image of Western society and economy suddenly crumbled—not only in the eyes of its leftist critics but also among many moderates, liberals as well as people quite uninvolved in politics.

Antibourgeois sentiments, always strong among Western intellectuals and cultural elites, gained a new momentum. "One could not help being exhilarated at the sudden and unexpected downfall of this stupid, gigantic fraud," the American literary critic Edmund Wilson said of the economic crash, which he viewed as the collapse of capitalism.[51] The feeling of deep disillusionment with Western life often had moral underpinnings. Many saw in the crisis the first sign of the unavoidable downfall not only of the Western economic system but also the entire flawed civilization. Decades later, Scott Nearing reminisced about the time of the Great Depression: "I said adieu to Western civilization first because I was disgusted with its professions of belief in Christian doctrine of 'love God and serve your neighbor' coupled with its hypocritical practice of 'every man for himself and the devil take the dropout.'"[52]

Facing the crisis, people of various political persuasions anxiously sought alternatives to what they saw as a compromised world of greed, selfishness, duplicity, wastefulness, and chaos. New cravings for utopias emerged in the West. Once again, many eyes turned east to a very little-known country in which the Western world had traditionally envisioned alternatives to its own inadequacies and cures for its own ills. They looked to Russia.

Stalin's Russia appeared to Westerners largely through the prism of Soviet propaganda. What they kept hearing about was an impressive country, full of energy and enthusiasm, where enormous economic challenges were boldly undertaken and where the word "unemployment" was unknown.[53] Soviet documentaries, newsreels, photographs, posters, books, and magazines projected images of smiling young workers, tractors rushing across fields, golden ears of wheat, factory chimneys belching smoke to the accompaniment of joyful songs, rousing marches, and imposing parades. All of this presented a shocking contrast when compared with Western documentaries, newsreels, photographs, posters, books, feature films, and magazines showing despondent unemployed workers waiting in long soup kitchen lines, tons of wheat and sugar being dumped into the sea, closed factories, and police dispersing desperate crowds. "The apparent success of the Five-Year Plan has affected the morale of all the rest of the world—and of the Americans surely not least," Edmund Wilson wrote from the vantage point of his New York apartment. "After all," he opined, "the Communist project has almost all the qualities that Americans glorify—the extreme of efficiency and economy combined with the ideal of a herculean feat to be accomplished by common action in the atmosphere of enthusiastic boosting—like a Liberty Loan drive—the idea of putting over something big in five years."[54]

The hunger for an optimistic alternative and the ensuing desire to believe in the Soviet model grew strong enough in the minds of an increasing number of Western public opinion leaders to make them take Soviet propaganda at face value. One did not need to be a communist, or even a socialist, to look toward the Soviet Union in hopes of finding there a positive inspiration or a viable alternative to the decaying West. Often people of moderate and liberal views became ardent sympathizers of Stalin's regime. Hugh Dalton, the British Labour Party parliamentarian who would later become one of the key ministers in Churchill's cabinet during World War II, expressed his views from the 1930s:

> There was no unemployment in the Soviet Union. Here was no "industrial depression," no inescapable "trade cycle," no limp surrender to "the law of supply and demand." Here was an increasing industrial upsurge based on a planned Socialist economy. They had an agricultural problem, we knew, in the Soviet Union, but so had we in the capitalist West, where primary producers had been ruined by the industrial slump. We knew that in Soviet Russia there was no political freedom. But there never had been under the Russian Czars and, perhaps some of us thought, we had over-valued this in the West, relatively to the other freedoms.[55]

Such thoughts, emotions, and desires prompted quite a few Western opinion makers to allow themselves to be manipulated by the Soviets. Some of them managed to see what they chose to see and ignore what they decided to ignore. Others could not help noticing the evidence of massive oppression behind the Soviet facade and yet felt compelled to conceal what they knew or suspected. Awareness of many imperfections in Stalin's state did not have to interfere with its ostensible acceptance. These attitudes, resulting in various forms of denial, often had a peculiar additional motivation. "We decided to look upon Soviet Russia sympathetically if only for the reason that defenders of the western capitalist status quo were so afraid of it and told so many lies about it," Granville Hicks admitted.[56] John Dos Passos presented similar reasons for consciously concealing the truth about the Soviet Union. He admitted that he was motivated by the "fear of writing something that would be seized on by anti-Soviet propaganda in the West. That was a period in which American capitalism seemed a much greater danger to the Russian experiment than the other way around."[57]

These statements by Hicks and Dos Passos illustrate a key factor motivating many Westerners either to refuse to notice disturbing aspects of Soviet reality or at least to conceal them from the public view. This factor can be described as the politicization of truth. In this light, the question of what was really happening in the Soviet Union lost its importance as it was trumped by a different question—namely, whose political interest would be served if the truth is publicly admitted? Eric Hobsbawm explained this attitude:

> Modern political choice is not a constant process of selecting men or measures, but a single or infrequent choice between packages in which we buy the disagreeable part of the contents because there is no other way of getting the rest, and in any case because there is no other way to be politically effective . . . the communist intellectual, in opting for the USSR . . . did so because on balance the good on his side seemed to outweigh the bad.[58]

Once the "package" was chosen, everything in it had to be accepted and justified—or at least overlooked—in the name of some assumed political effectiveness. Such a politicization of truth about the Soviet Union was made quite easy by the fact that troubling knowledge about this country's evils relied almost always on controvertible personal accounts of survivors and escapees and more or less accidental observations by a few visitors. These sources could easily be challenged by different accounts and observations—especially those provided or inspired by Soviet propaganda.

Sometimes the truth about the real communism was politicized, concealed, or deformed out of a peculiar sense of moral obligation. Antoni Słonimski, an acclaimed Polish poet and critic, gave an insightful account in his 1932 book *Moja podróż do Rosji* (My journey to Russia) of the moral vacillations that almost led him to lie about his impressions of the Soviet reality. Słonimski described his return from the USSR:

> In the evening, I am back in Warsaw. . . . A porter is carrying my suitcase and we talk while waiting for a taxi. I feel an inexplicable desire to tell him that I am returning from Russia.
>
> "Well, how are things going there?"
>
> In this quiet question, I hear the trust which people from the proletariat feel towards the party comrades. I must admit that I enjoy this atmosphere of communion. I would like to tell him something that would make us even closer to each other. I read in his tired eyes the answer he would like to hear from me. I am sure that if I told him "Things are going well over there,

comrade," he would carry my suitcase fast and easy to the cab, and he would smile. Finally, I answer:

"It is hard to tell in a few words. It is bad and good at the same time."

Now I know what the porter thinks about me. For him, I am an enemy. There are no positions in between. Whoever is not with us is against us. I am riding through the city with a feeling of stifling solitude.[59]

Słonimski was not the only cultural celebrity who balked at ruining the dreams of the common people about the "workers' paradise" in the USSR. Whether these dreams were real or only projected by these celebrities is another question. One must admit that, in contrast to many other intellectuals placed in similar situations, Słonimski felt compelled to remain honest. Instead of choosing moral comfort stemming from a confirmation of the hopes of the "common man" at the expense of truth, he admitted to his uneasy feelings about Soviet reality.

Eugene Lyons, after his return in 1934 from the USSR, where he had spent six years serving as a press correspondent, candidly described his own hesitations in an essay, "To Tell or Not to Tell," published in the June 1935 issue of *Harper's*. In it, Lyons recalled his thoughts in 1928, the year he started his job in Moscow: "'Whatever happens,' I pledged in my own mind on my way to Soviet Russia, 'I shall never attack the Soviet regime. No matter how disappointed I may be in the Bolshevik reality, I shall keep the disappointment to myself.'"[60] This promise, however, proved harder to keep than Lyons expected. "My initial reactions to the physical scene were distressingly unsatisfactory," he wrote about his stay in Russia.

> The sympathy stirred by the spectacle of suffering—even the suffering of social outlaws and class enemies—seemed an alarming symptom of ideological weakness, and I held on grimly to slogans of ruthlessness. Real Bolsheviks, I observed, were not merely indifferent to this suffering but took a perverse pride in it, as a sort of testimonial to their strength and purpose . . .
>
> Terror became a tangible presence. Prison camps multiplied, executions without trial became so commonplace that they lost their "news value." . . .
>
> There was something soothingly anesthetic about the metaphors of class war—economic fronts, agrarian fronts, socialist fortresses, victories and defeats.
>
> When I paused to consider my own state of mind, I was dismayed. The certainties I had brought with me had somehow lost their firm texture. My stomach was not strong enough to digest the Soviet reality. The spectacle of disaster, oppression, arbitrary power, pain, and death all around me could not be reduced to simple Bolshevik arithmetic of price-paid-for-the-future.[61]

As a result of this increasing cognitive dissonance, the very notion of truth about Soviet communism plunged Lyons into a moral dilemma. He confessed:

> I could not fix the precise point in time when the Hamletian alternative, to tell or not to tell, had first presented itself. In the beginning I had felt guilty *toward the revolution* whenever I reported anything uncomplimentary about the Soviet scene. Later I had begun to feel guilty *toward the Russian people* when I concealed or toned down such things. It was this recognition of the Russians as human entities, with certain minimal human rights and a capacity for human pain, quite aside from their historical function as experimental material, that signalized the change in me.[62]

But even Lyons's moral awakening from ideological slumber did not spare him from the temptation described by Słonimski of misleading the Western masses by confirming the version of truth they supposedly desired to hear. Writing about a visit to America in 1931, in the midst of the Great Depression, Lyons admitted the following: "In America the old inhibitions, the anxiety to save face for the revolution, were victorious in my mind. . . . For millions the epic of a Russia where unemployment had been abolished spelled hope. . . . I took the easiest and pleasantest course of sustaining these hopes."[63]

These moral hesitations, however important the role they played, were not the only motivation reinforcing Lyons's resistance to the idea of telling the truth about Russia. Other motivations were somewhat less principled. Lyons belonged to a small number of public intellectuals who would ever admit them. "By 1934 exaggerated faith in the Soviet experiment had become the intellectual fashion among the people for whose good opinion I cared most," he noted. "It was clear to me what sort of account of Russia the intellectual elite preferred to hear. . . . They asked questions about Russia and appeared horrified if I failed to give the prescribed answers. . . . The desire to 'belong,' not to be a political dog in the manger, was a powerful inducement to silence, or at least to cautious understatement."[64]

Stalin to the Rescue

The politicization of truth about Stalin's regime was not limited to ideological friends of the Soviet Union. It was also practiced by those who strove to rescue the capitalist economy and preserve the Western way of life. By the 1930s, the circle of those eager to do business with the Soviets grew exponentially. At the time of the economic crisis in the West, coupled with forcible modernization in the USSR, many politicians and industrialists saw an opportunity for overcoming domestic slumps by intensifying trade relations with Stalin. The results of the debates surrounding the import of Soviet timber in 1930–1931 demonstrated the strength and reach of these attitudes in the West.

As these debates were coming to a close, a number of Western politicians were invited to the USSR, including William I. Sirovich—a US congressman and president of the Industrial National Bank in New York. Duly impressed by what his Soviet hosts told and showed him during his six-day visit, Sirovich announced on his return that he strongly believed in the Stalinist path of economic development. He did add, however, that Stalinism was an "ideal Slavonic civilization, but one that would not work in an Anglo-Saxon country." The congressman opined that establishing economic relations with the Soviet Union would end the economic crisis in America as the former could constitute a perfect market for American surplus exports for the next fifty years. In his speech, Sirovich did not hesitate to reassure those Americans who might have recently come across reports of slave labor in the USSR. He mentioned that, according to what he was told, there were not more than some forty thousand forced laborers "sent to prison camps for crimes political and otherwise" but that this constituted a small percentage of the population so therefore there was really nothing to be concerned about.[65]

During this time, the Soviets—who were seeking official US recognition and the intensification of Soviet-American trade—carefully monitored moods in the American political and business establishment. The head of the Soviet Information Bureau in Washington, Boris Skvirsky, reported, "Events indicate that in times of crisis Americans add considerable importance to Soviet markets and the threat of their loss works to our advantage. . . . We should be aware of the strength of our current position and should be prepared to take advantage of it."[66]

They did take advantage of it quite effectively. In the first half of the 1930s, the diplomatic and economic relations between the USSR and the Western world expanded rapidly. Western advocates of this process were vitally interested in propagating an acceptable image of Stalin and his regime. They welcomed the dismissals of the Gulag topic and its replacement by the "humanitarian" myth of *perekovka* that, even if it did not entirely agree with the reality, at least mollified public opinion toward political and economic partnership with Stalin. The new president of the United States, Franklin Delano Roosevelt, sworn in on March 4, 1933, was a major advocate of the development of political and economic relations with the USSR. Like many in the American business world, he saw in it an opportunity for stimulating exports and speeding American recovery from the crisis. The Japanese offensive in Manchuria in 1931 additionally motivated his quest for a prospective alliance with Soviet Russia in order to stave off the growing power of Japan in the Pacific and Far East. On November 17, 1933, Roosevelt's energetic efforts proved successful, and the United States officially recognized the Soviet regime. Roosevelt strove to convince American opponents of this move that the Soviets would, in exchange, free prisoners of conscience, refrain from supporting revolutionary activities within the United States and repay a portion of the enormous debts incurred by Russia in the United States prior to the Bolshevik revolution. The Soviets did not fulfill any of these promises. Nonetheless, the appetites of American businessmen and politicians for more trade with Soviet Russia were large enough to sign a trade agreement on July 13, 1935, anyway.

In fact, Soviet-American trade had already been flourishing. Before the trade agreement was signed, multiple American companies invested in the USSR and cooperated with the Soviet government. Their role was instrumental in the completion of most of the large industrial projects of the Five-Year Plan. The giant industrial architecture firm Albert Kahn designed 521 factories in the USSR. General Electric played a pivotal role in the construction of the famous Dneprostroy dam and other power stations. Henry Ford signed a record-breaking forty-million-dollar deal with the Soviets and built a Soviet Ford factory in Nizhny Novgorod (soon renamed "Gorky"). At the same time, outdated Ford models, withdrawn from production in the United States, were assembled in Moscow. Thanks to this deal, Ford was able to better weather the Great Depression: while closing some of his American plants and laying off American workers, he expanded his business in the Soviet Union. For the USSR, this spelled the beginning of a domestic car industry.

Western companies operating in the Soviet Union needed a skilled labor force capable of handling modern technology. They could not carry out their projects without Western engineers, technicians, and specialized workers—at least until new Soviet crews could be trained. Western newspapers, besides multiple reports about the depths of crisis and unemployment at home, ran advertisements for new jobs opening up for Westerners in the Soviet Union. These ads seemed to provide additional evidence confirming that articles and reports of numerous travelers, correspondents, celebrities, intellectuals, and public figures describing the wonders of the Soviet world were not mistaken. In this atmosphere, some Westerners sought a better life overseas, in the land of Soviets. In the early 1930s, ships full of people passed by the Statue of Liberty at the gateway of New York Harbor, but they were sailing away from the traditional destination. People crowding the decks parted with their American homeland and looked eastward with hope.

A miner from Denver wrote in a letter to the *Moscow News*, a Soviet newspaper published in English especially for the English-speaking immigrants in the USSR: "Give us a chance to come to the Soviet Union. We are willing to work hard; to endure hardships, if need be. Here we have hardships, hunger too and no hope. Over there, you are building for tomorrow. Let us come and help. We will be satisfied with bread and carrots."[67] It was not unusual for workers laid off from Ford's plant in Detroit to move to the USSR in order to find employment in Ford's plant in Nizhny Novgorod. Some of their compatriots found jobs in the Stalingrad tractor factory and many other factories, steel works, mines, refineries, electric plants, and other industrial projects built and operated in the USSR by American companies.

Either/Or

The tendency to politicize the truth in regard to the Soviet Union gained additional strength in Western democratic media and public discourses after Hitler was appointed chancellor of Germany in 1933. In the years to follow, more people than ever seemed ready to accept the belief that capitalism and liberal democracy were living out their final days and the future belonged to one of the two mutually hostile new ideologies: communism and fascism. Fascism and Nazism, especially in their early stages, awoke the interest and sympathy of a certain number of prominent intellectuals and artists, among them such figures as Gabriele d'Annunzio, Filippo Marinetti, Oswald Spengler, Ernst Jünger, Martin Heidegger, Charles Maurras, Louis-Ferdinand Céline, and Ezra Pound. But the majority of Western intellectual and cultural elites perceived fascism, and especially Nazism, as a direct menace to civilization. Even most of those who did not try to avoid and dismiss information about the Bolsheviks' barbarity viewed fascism and Nazism as threats much more direct, concrete, and urgent than a cruel but somewhat distant and exotic tyrant in Moscow. Many expected an all-out confrontation between Hitler and Stalin.

In this atmosphere, more and more people who had not previously believed in Stalin's humanitarianism nevertheless felt a new kind of pressure to make a political choice between him and Hitler. Soviet propagandists and diplomats worked hard to imprint this conviction on Western consciousness. Stalin played the role of the anti-Hitler before Western audiences, thus eliciting special treatment. According to this dualist paradigm, quite successfully implanted by the Soviets and their allies in many Western minds, exposing Stalin's crimes or criticizing his regime was tantamount to lending support (albeit inadvertently) to Hitler. The question of what communism was became increasingly less important than the question of how communism could defeat fascism and Nazism.

As early as June 1935, Eugene Lyons commented:

The brutalities of Hitlerism in Germany momentarily provided a post-factum justification for their counterpart in Russia. I visited Hitler's Reich several times and found a scaled-down version of the practices which had horrified me in Russia. . . . Concentration camps, purgings, arbitrary arrests, and executions—all the machinery of unbridled dictatorship—were being installed. The Nazis made no secret of the fact that they modeled their political household upon Bolshevik patterns. Nazi firmness, like Bolshevik firmness, covered a multitude of excesses. I asked myself: must one choose between two sets of frenzied cruelties?[68]

More and more leaders of Western public opinion felt they did have to choose. For many of them choosing against Hitler meant taking the side of Stalin. Comparing the two totalitarian regimes became a taboo in many intellectual circles. The antifascist sentiment often brought together people of various views. Political divisions among communists, socialists, and even mainstream liberals often became less vital than ever when viewed in the light of the Nazi challenge. Stalin's legitimacy in the eyes of the Western world was growing as quickly as Hitler's was diminishing. On October 14, 1933, Hitler's Germany left the League of Nations and on September 18, 1934, Stalin's Soviet Union became its new member. "I am a Communist because I am a liberal," Stephen Spender admitted in 1937.[69] Ernest Hemingway stated that whoever opposed the communists was "either a fool or a knave."[70] Malcolm Muggeridge wrote about many of his British fellow intellectuals of that time: "Stalin became their antidote to Hitler; Marxist hate should abolish Nazi hate, and Marxist falsifications correct Nazi ones."[71]

In the light of anticommunist oppression championed by the fascists and Nazis, the communists became widely identifiable in the West, first and foremost, as victims of violent dictatorships. It was as if the parts of victim and oppressor were cast, and Westerners had considerable difficulties moving beyond this opposition and imagining victims who might also be oppressors. Some intellectuals who were aware of Bolshevik crimes nevertheless managed to find them morally superior to the same sort of crimes committed by the fascists and Nazis. Lenin's idea of "class morality" came in handy. According to it, people's actions have no intrinsic moral value, and what makes them good or evil is whether they serve *us* (the communists struggling for progress) or *them* (our reactionary enemies). At an antifascist meeting of Revolutionary Writers and

Artists in 1933, André Gide spoke about political regimes employing violence. Comparing the Nazis and the Soviet communists, he asked: "Why and how does it happen that, in this case, I support something that I would condemn elsewhere?" Then he answered his own question: "In the German terror, I see a return to the most hateful past. But in the construction of the Soviet society I see a limitless promise of the future."[72]

In the late 1930s, the position of Stalin as the global leader of the epic struggle against Nazism and fascism became even stronger. The passive attitude of the key Western democracies toward the Spanish Civil War, contrasted with the direct involvement, on opposite sides, of the USSR and Nazi Germany (along with fascist Italy), reinforced the notion of the decline of Western democracy and strengthened Stalin's image as the anti-Hitler. The actual role played in Spain by Soviet agents was largely ignored and covered up by a myth focused almost exclusively on the idealism of the communist participants of the war.

The popular slogan "No enemies on the left" in reality often meant a ban on criticizing the Soviet regime and its actions. When George Orwell tried to publish his reportage from the Spanish Civil War, *Homage to Catalonia*, in which he described the campaign of terror perpetrated by the Stalinist forces against other republicans, he was turned down by Victor Gollancz, the publisher of the Left Book Club in London. A series of Orwell's articles on the same topic was rejected by the editor of the *New Statesman*, Kingsley Martin. Orwell finally found a publisher for *Homage to Catalonia*, and it appeared in the United Kingdom in 1938, but it was not published in the United States until 1952.[73] The only translation that appeared in Orwell's lifetime was into Italian in 1948. In 1968, Martin still defended his actions from thirty years before: "I would no more have thought of publishing them than of publishing an article by Goebbels during the war against Germany."[74]

4

Wonderland

Pilgrims in the Theater

Soviet propaganda of the 1930s could not have been as effective as it was had it solely relied on its own materials, books, films, articles, and reports. A key factor in its success stemmed from the fact that those who (directly or indirectly) discredited testimonies of witnesses and survivors of Soviet atrocities were not just people clearly identifiable as communists and other supporters of the Soviet regime. At the turn of the 1930s, when a widespread Soviet propaganda campaign was launched in order to project the image of the USSR as an idealistic regime devoted to providing a better life for its people, Soviet leaders did not know that history would work to their advantage in the way it did and that soon Western audiences would be eagerly searching for reasons to exculpate Stalin.

A key element of Soviet propaganda regarding state terror and slave labor was the illusion of credibility—a fabricated impression of direct, objective, unbiased, and therefore authoritative observation of reality. In fulfillment of this strategy, the Soviets welcomed foreign celebrities, intellectuals, social activists, and other leaders of public opinion in order to provide them with opportunities to "see for themselves" that Bolshevik rule was, indeed, deeply humanitarian and that rumors about communist oppression were nothing but falsehoods and exaggerations fabricated by enemies of the Soviet Union.

These visits were carefully handled, and their effects were often meticulously orchestrated. Guests—especially those whose words commanded attention in the West—were often inconspicuously (although sometimes quite clumsily) manipulated by various guides, interpreters, assistants, drivers, hosts, "accidental passersby," and other Soviet agents trained to handle foreigners. As already

noted, Soviet authorities were particularly interested in Western cultural celebrities and other public opinion leaders who were not immediately identifiable in public as communists but were widely considered as fair and impartial
observers. The most desirable among them were, of course, people who showed
potential for being persuaded, impressed, flattered, duped, bought, corrupted,
pressured, or blackmailed into seeing what their Soviet handlers wanted them
to see or, at least, writing what they wanted them to write.

The Bolshevik art of manipulating foreigners was as old as the Bolshevik regime itself. As already mentioned, according to Angelika Balabanoff, Western
visitors in Lenin's time were evaluated and classified by their Soviet handlers
upon arrival according to four categories: superficial, naive, ambitious, and venal.[1] In all likelihood, each category was presented with a slightly different set
of incentives. While it was certainly difficult to find the ideal types representing
each category, it seems that those categorized as "venal" were the most convenient to handle because, as Richard Pipes points out, "having no ideals to begin
with, they were immune to disillusionment."[2] However, in Pipes's view, it was
not they but rather the "naive" ones who seemed to account for the majority of
Western visitors managed by Soviet public-relations specialists. "They believed
that man and society could be made perfect," as Pipes describes them, "and
since the world which they knew was far from perfect, they readily accepted
Communist ideals for Communist reality."[3] For their sake, Potemkin villages
were built, and various situations were orchestrated in which their dreams and
beliefs in the Soviet brave new world could be confirmed and reinforced.

The selection of the right kind of visitors was an important issue. The international network of societies of the "friends of the Soviet Union" proved useful
not only in spreading Soviet propaganda abroad but also in wooing people who
could be expected to reflect and reinforce this propaganda in their own public
statements. Upon entering the USSR, these Western visitors were handled by a
series of Soviet institutions. The tasks of these agencies sometimes overlapped,
although they seemed to specialize in catering to different categories of foreigners. Western labor activists were usually managed by the Comintern (Communist International) and Profintern (Labor International), while the USSR
Chamber of Commerce and its more specialized branches devoted to various
countries dealt with Western businessmen. At the same time, the Soviets designated several agencies to take special care of Western intellectuals, writers,
artists, and celebrities. Which representative of this category was handled by
which institution depended to a considerable degree on his or her political
views and the extent of his or her fame. Western communists were usually
managed by specialized branches of the Comintern. Openly communist and

procommunist writers were often cared for by the Bureau of Revolutionary Literature, established in 1925 and transformed into the International Union of Revolutionary Writers (MORP) in 1930.[4] A member of the Union, the Irish writer Liam O'Flaherty, described its activities as mobilizing "the principal writers of the world under its control, for the purpose of demoralizing capitalism and encouraging the working class of the world to make war on their oppressors."[5]

At the same time, prominent noncommunist, or not openly communist, intellectuals and cultural celebrities were usually handled by VOKS (*Vsesoiuznoe obshchestvo kul'turnoi sviazi s zagranitsei* [All-union society for cultural relations with foreign countries]). VOKS was established by a decree of the Council of People's Commissars in August 1925 specifically for the purpose of influencing, converting, and manipulating Western cultural elites. Its founder and head (until 1929) was Olga Kameneva, the wife of Lev Kamenev and sister of Trotsky. She was a seasoned propagandist with rich prerevolutionary experience of life in the West. During the famine of 1921–1923, she worked at the forefront of the Bolshevik propaganda campaign against the American Relief Administration—an organization that saved the lives of millions of Russians but was perceived by the Bolshevik leaders as an impediment to Soviet power. In 1923–1925 Kameneva headed the Committee for Foreign Aid, established by the Bolsheviks and determined to liquidate foreign humanitarian aid and push the remaining foreign charities out of Russia. The organization took over foreign donations for starving Russian peasants, and Kameneva managed to embezzle some of these funds to finance Soviet propaganda and public-relations efforts aimed at Western cultural elites, including the creation of VOKS. As she reported later, not without pride, in a secret document only recently discovered and quoted by Michael David-Fox, "In essence the material side of the cause was funded with bourgeois money: from the leftovers from bourgeois organizations giving aid to the starving."[6] In 1929, after Trotsky's fall from power, Kameneva was dismissed from VOKS and replaced by Fedor Petrov. In 1934, the job went to Aleksandr Arosev.

VOKS operated under supervision by the Communist Party and in close collaboration with the secret police. It coordinated a variety of activities, such as collecting information on a large number of important Western cultural figures, publishing and disseminating ample propaganda materials in the West, also orchestrating visits of important foreign intellectuals, writers, politicians, journalists, artists, and other celebrities. VOKS provided them with guides and interpreters whose regular duties included spying on their customers and writing detailed reports about their behavior, opinions, attitudes, interests, habits, and weaknesses. These guides (many of them attractive women) were also expected to engage the visitors in political discussions and try to influence their views to reflect Soviet propaganda. Both the guests and the guides were often placed under the additional surveillance of OGPU and, later, NKVD agents. "*They* were everywhere foreigners were," a VOKS guide, Raisa Orlova, wrote later about the secret police role. "We knew that every recorded conversation we had with foreigners was forwarded to the NKVD."[7] VOKS organized events, filled auditoriums with the right kind of audiences, planned and orchestrated "spontaneous" encounters with "the Soviet people" as well as with Soviet officials and celebrities, and made sure the visitors saw only what they were supposed to see. The main agency that helped VOKS in handling foreign celebrities in the 1930s, and that also catered to ordinary tourists and lesser intellectuals, was the Intourist, established in 1929.

Foreign intellectuals and celebrities placed under the care of VOKS were fed with ideas and impressions markedly different than most of their communist counterparts handled by other institutions, usually under the jurisdiction of the Comintern. When Liam O'Flaherty visited the VOKS offices—after being welcomed, as a trustworthy communist, by the International Union of Revolutionary Writers—he was astounded by the difference in tone. He wrote, "Not a word did he [the VOKS representative] speak about the revolution, or about the liberation of the world proletariat. He was concerned solely with the aggrandizement of his country, Russia."[8]

On some occasions the guides failed to keep everything under control and guests would notice things not intended to be noticed. The guides were trained to divert their guests' attention and explain away those unexpected encounters. Sometimes the secret police would step in and take things into their own hands. Tamara Solonevich, the wife of Ivan Solonevich, was a translator assigned in 1926 to a delegation of English workers. In her memoir, *Notes of a Soviet Translator*, published after the Solonevichs' escape, she wrote about a homeless child trying to catch the attention of the guests. One of the armed agents following the delegation simply shot the child in front of her and out of the sight of the foreigners.[9] It was a considerable risk for Soviet citizens to attempt to enlighten the foreigners that they were being duped and manipulated. Even outsmarting the secret police and all the guides and handlers did not guarantee success. Sometimes the guests were equally dangerous. For example, Michael David-Fox writes about a Soviet man who tried to warn a delegation of Scandinavian workers about the charade created for them. They turned him in to the OGPU.[10]

In the early 1930s the Soviet Union became a fashionable destination among Western intellectual elites. "The entire British intelligentsia has been in Russia this summer," Kingsley Martin wrote in 1932.[11] Of course, not only British intelligentsia showed up in droves. Some Western travelers set out on their voyages in a way reminiscent of pilgrims peregrinating to holy and miraculous sites. They went there with complete sets of firm beliefs in their minds. Their most important goal was, quite obviously, to strengthen their faith, not to expose it to some sort of verification. Malcolm Muggeridge described them:

> On their way to the Soviet Union they were in a festive mood: like a cup-tie party on their way to a match, equipped with rattles, colored scarves and favours. Each of them harboring in his mind some special hope; of meeting Stalin, or alternately, of falling in love with a Komsomolka, sparkling eyed, red scarf and jet black hair dancing the *carmagnole*; above all, with very enlightened views on sex, and free and easy ways. In any case equipping themselves with special, authoritative knowledge which would enable them to embellish their articles and lectures. . . .
>
> In their dealings with the crew and the stewards they were punctilious in cultivating an egalitarian attitude; the word "comrade" was often on their lips. . . . These fellow-passengers provided my first experience of the progressive elite from all over the world who attached themselves to the Soviet regime, resolved to believe anything they were told by its spokesmen. For the most part they were academics and writers—the clerks of Julien Benda's *La Trahison des clercs*; all upholders of progressive causes and members of progressive organizations, constituting a sort of Brechtian ribald chorus in the drama of the twentieth century. Ready at any moment to rush on to stage, cheering and gesticulating . . . a western version of the devotees of Krishna who throw themselves under the wheels of the great Juggernaut.[12]

Julian Huxley—himself an experienced admirer of the land of Soviets—advised those who were going there for the first time, "It is no good viewing everything Russian through your own imported atmosphere, for that merely acts as a distorted lens to the facts . . . the visitor to Russia must attempt to discard some of his bourgeois ideas about democracy, religion and traditional morality, his romantic individualism, his class feelings, his judgments of what constitutes success, and pick up what he can of the atmosphere in which the Russians live immersed."[13]

Many followed Huxley's advice, knowingly or not. John Strachey wrote, "Even today . . . before a classless society has fully emerged, there is perceptible an exhilaration of living which finds no parallel in the world. To travel from the capitalist world into Soviet territory is to pass from death to birth."[14] Strachey wrote about this supposed exhilaration in the Soviet Union in 1932, when scores of Soviet people were starving to death as a result of ongoing collectivization. In 1937, a year marked by the Great Terror, Lion Feuchtwanger made observations quite similar to Strachey's:

> I came to the Soviet Union from countries where complaints are the general rule and whose inhabitants, disconnected with both their physical and spiritual conditions, crave change. . . . The air which one breathes in the West is stale and foul. In the Western civilization there is no longer clarity and resolution. . . . One breathes again when one comes from this oppressive atmosphere of a counterfeit democracy and hypocritical humanism into the invigorating atmosphere of the Soviet Union. Here there is no hiding behind mystical, meaningless slogans, but a sober ethics prevails.[15]

With this kind of attitude on the part of many visitors, and with the expert help of Soviet public-relations specialists, these pilgrimages often fulfilled the expectations of both the pilgrims and their hosts. The guests were eager to experience epiphanies and did not stray—literally or figuratively—from the paths prepared for them by their handlers. Malcolm Muggeridge recalled:

> Their delight in all they saw and were told, and the expression they gave to this delight, constitute unquestionably one of the wonders of our age. There were earnest advocates of the humane killing of cattle who looked up at the massive headquarters of the OGPU with tears of gratitude in their eyes, earnest advocates of proportional representation who eagerly assented when the necessity for a Dictatorship of the Proletariat was explained to them, earnest clergymen who walked reverently through anti-God museums and reverently turned the pages of atheistic literature, earnest pacifists who watched delightedly tanks rattle across the Red Square and bombing planes darken the sky, earnest town-planning specialists who stood outside overcrowded ramshackle tenements and muttered: "If only we had something like this in England!" The almost unbelievable credulity of these mostly university-educated tourists astonished even Soviet officials used to handling foreign visitors.[16]

Pondering this historic spectacle of gullibility and confusion, one should not underestimate the role played by Soviet appeals to the personal vanity and material interest of some Western visitors. The hosts went to great lengths to make them feel important. Writers, artists, philosophers, journalists, scientists— whether they enjoyed international fame or were hardly recognized at home for their work—were often treated in the Soviet Union like royalty. This sort of treatment became much more frequent in the 1930s, after the Soviet handlers heard many complaints from their earlier guests about poor hygiene, bad food, and shoddy accommodations in the 1920s. In the decade marked by the Great Famine and the Great Terror, Western visitors—especially those considered particularly useful by the Soviet authorities—were put up in luxurious hotels at no charge, showered with expensive gifts, and flattered by nearly everyone they met, including high-ranking Soviet leaders. They almost uniformly referred with amazement to the extent of Soviet hospitality. John Burrell, an American engineer, reminisced in 1932—at the time of mass famine—about banquets with "silver plates, cut glass dishes, flowers, fine linen, many courses of excellent food, and a table covered with wines and liquors."[17] During their stay in the USSR in 1934, the French literary couple Marguerite and Jean-Richard Bloch were provided with a private railway car, which had a library, a study, a kitchen, a cook, and two attendants. The car could be coupled to various trains according to the guests' orders—all provided at the hosts' expense.[18] Duly impressed, Jean-Richard Bloch wrote in his journal about the Soviet regime, "They want to raise the level of human life, intellectual and material, above everything that capitalism has reserved for its financial oligarchy . . . I don't think a greater task has ever been attempted since the origins of humankind."[19] Liam O'Flaherty, describing a lavish banquet organized in his honor by the International Union of Revolutionary Writers, soberly noted that it was "worthy of a worthier person than myself."[20]

What astonished many Western writers, artists, and intellectuals was the extent of their alleged fame and significance in the Soviet Union.[21] Some were even received by top Soviet leaders, including Stalin himself, who made a very positive impression on most of them. "I have never met a man more candid, fair, and honest. . . . Everyone trusts him," H. G. Wells wrote after meeting Stalin in 1934.[22] The impression of wide recognition in the Soviet Union—not only by peer intellectuals, writers, and artists but by ordinary people as well—was not limited to the most famous Westerners. On the contrary, many intellectuals and artists who never enjoyed fame in any shape or form in their own countries were praised and treated as world-class celebrities during their visits to the USSR. Ignored and underestimated at home, they felt important, appreciated, and loved as soon as they entered the land of Soviets. Eugene Lyons referred to Moscow as "a paradise for misfits from abroad."[23]

The hosts did not stop at verbal flattery. Indeed, they often put their money where their mouths were. Soviet literary and cultural officials approached many Western guests with generous offers to publish or exhibit their work in the Soviet Union. Eugene Lyons learned, shortly after his arrival in Russia, that his biography of Sacco and Vanzetti was published in Russian translation, and it was selling like hotcakes. Royalties promptly followed.[24] Contracts offered by

Soviet officials to selected Western authors often exceeded anything they could dream of in their own countries. Arthur Koestler wrote that he was invited to the Soviet Union in order to write a book called *The Soviet Land through Bourgeois Eyes*. This happened when he was a communist believer, before his definitive disillusionment with communism in 1938. At that time, he had not yet published a single book, but he was nevertheless treated by his Soviet hosts almost like a literary giant. He reminisced later:

> When I arrived in a provincial capital, say in Tiflis, I went to the local Writers' Federation, where I produced my Comintern letter. The Secretary of the Federation thereupon arranged the usual banquets and meetings with political leaders and members of the intelligentsia of the town, appointed somebody to look after me, and put me in touch with the editor of the local literary magazine and the director of the State Publishing Trust—in this case the Trust of the Georgian Soviet Republic. The editor of the magazine declared that it had been for many years his dearest wish to publish a story by me. I handed him a copy of a story published some time ago in Germany; and the same day a check for three or four thousand roubles was sent to my hotel. The director of the State Publishing Trust asked for the privilege of publishing a Georgian translation of the book I was going to write; I signed a printed agreement form and was sent another check for three or four thousand roubles. (The salary of the average wage-earner was at the time 130 roubles per month.) I thus sold the same story to eight or ten different literary magazines from Leningrad to Tashkent, and sold the Russian, German, Ukrainian, Georgian and Armenian rights of my unwritten book against advance payments which amounted to a small fortune. And as I did this with official encouragement, and as other writers did the same, I could wholeheartedly confirm that Soviet Russia was the writer's paradise and that nowhere else in the world was the creative artist better paid or held in higher esteem. Human nature being what it is, it never occurred to me that my contracts and cash advances had been granted not on the strength of my literary reputation, but for reasons of a different nature.[25]

The typical program of a foreign tour of the USSR included visits to showcase industrial plants, electric stations, collective farms, schools, hospitals, and so on. Although quite a few foreign visitors were skeptical or outright critical about what they saw in the USSR, their voices were often unheard as many of them chose to keep their critical impressions to themselves. Those who did speak out exerted incomparably less influence on the public discourse outside of the anticommunist circles than their predecessors did in the 1920s. Attitudes toward the Soviet Union, which shaped Western public discourse in the 1930s in significant ways, can be exemplified by an event described by William C. White, an American living in Russia at the time. He witnessed the visit of a group of Western tourists in a Soviet printing shop. One of the visitors, a female teacher from Brooklyn, examined a modern printing press and commented: "Really, that is remarkable. . . . Such an amazing invention could be produced only in a country like yours, where labor is free, unexploited, and working for one end. I shall write a book about what I have seen." When the visitors saw the back of the machine, they had to try very hard to conceal a certain awkwardness. There was a sign: MADE IN BROOKLYN, N.Y.[26]

The Land of the Happy Prisoners

The usual list of sites proudly presented to foreign guests as evidence of the progressive and humane nature of the Soviet state included prisons and labor camps. They were supposed to appear to the visitors as educational facilities where Stalin's pedagogues realized the humanitarian program of social therapy for criminals through labor. Of course, what the hosts showed the guests was a staged version of Soviet prisons and camps. By the 1930s, Soviet propaganda specialists were well versed in these sorts of stage effects. One of the methods used to this effect was exposing these visitors to "ordinary Soviet people" played by OGPU agents and Party or Komsomol activists. In 1926, for instance, a delegation of German workers and a group of American intellectuals were brought to Kharkov (Kharkiv) prisons. There, they had a frank conversation with political prisoners who assured them that life in prison was very good indeed. Little did the Western visitors know that their interlocutors were OGPU agents posing as inmates.[27]

With time, entire showcase camps and prisons were tailored to propaganda purposes. The most famous of them in the 1920s were selected sections of the Lefortovo and Sokolniki prisons, while in 1930s it was the juvenile correctional labor commune in Bolshevo. Lefortovo and Sokolniki were conveniently located in Moscow, so that groups of foreign tourists could reach them quickly and comfortably. Bolshevo was some twenty kilometers outside Moscow, and visitors were often transported to it in buses supplied by Intourist. The Bolshevo commune was created in the early 1920s as a successful experiment in resocializing young offenders, especially homeless orphans. Widely recognized for its accomplishments, it was converted into a showcase location exemplifying for foreign visitors the idea of the *perekovka* in the Gulag. In fact, Bolshevo was anything but representative of Soviet orphanages, not to mention the Gulag.

The juvenile inmates in Bolshevo enjoyed exotically luxurious conditions and a great deal of freedom and positive attention. For many of them, this was the true ticket to the good life. But there was one silent condition—absolute cooperation with the authorities. The alternative was a return to regular Soviet prisons for juvenile delinquents where the conditions were as exotically horrible as they were luxurious in Bolshevo.

During the Westerners' visits to these and other show prisons and camps, the eloquent guides and hospitable camp officials lectured the guests about the cutting-edge approach to resocialization of criminals in the Soviet Union, and the prisoners willingly confirmed these lectures with their own stories. The guests were expected and encouraged to publicly share their observations back in their home countries. Many were happy to use this demonstration to form generalizing opinions about Soviet prisons and camps. Ella Winter, in her 1933 book *Red Virtue*, written after a journey to the USSR, reported:

> Crime, according to Soviet law, is the outcome of antagonisms existing in a society divided into classes; it is always the result of faulty social organization and bad environment. The word "punishment" is not approved of: it has been replaced by the phrase "measures of social defense." . . . Sentences are short and once the sentence has been served the miscreant is readmitted into everyday life with no . . . scar of shame, no brand of having been a "convict." . . . Soviet criminology seems to assume that the "criminal" is not a criminal. He is not to be treated as an outcast. . . . He is an "unfortunate," sick, weak or maladjusted and must be trained to become . . . a functioning member of society. This theory is carried out in practice in the communes run by the OGPU.[28]

Maurice Hindus was an experienced American reporter in the USSR, and it would be quite difficult to believe that he was duped by Soviet propaganda. Nevertheless, he commented on Soviet prisons in 1933:

> The Soviets are acting on the assumption that it is not the criminal who is under obligation to society but that society is under obligation to the criminal. Implacable environmentalists, they believe that under normal conditions of living the human animal . . . would not commit antisocial acts. . . .
>
> On good behavior which is easy in Soviet jails, as easy as in Soviet schools, the sentence is pared down. Constant amnesties on the occasion of revolutionary holidays bring further reductions. During the period of confinement criminals experience no other hardships than the enforced separation from home.[29]

Two years earlier, Walter Duranty explained in the *New York Times* that the main purpose of the forced labor camps was "to remove subversive individuals from their familiar milieu to a remote spot where their potentially harmful activities will be nullified—the Bolsheviki add kindly, 'where such misguided persons will be given a chance to regain by honest toll their lost citizenship in the Socialist Fatherland.'" Duranty compared the Gulag to early colonial communities in Virginia. He wrote: "Each concentration camp forms a sort of 'commune,' where everyone lives comparatively free, not imprisoned, but compelled to work for the good of the community. They are fed and housed gratis and receive pay for their work, though on a lower scale—perhaps one-third is the average—than the outside rates."[30] At the same time, Sherwood Eddy argued that the Soviet "penal system is one of the most advanced, the most modern and redemptive in the world. . . . The man whom the capitalistic society brands as criminal they count a little brother who has gone wrong, perhaps through no fault of his own, because of poverty, ignorance, neglect or social injustice."[31]

Five years later, Anna Louise Strong informed her American readers that "the labor camp is the prevalent method for handling serious offenders of all kinds, whether criminal or political. . . . The labor camps have won high reputation throughout the Soviet Union as places where tens of thousands of men have been reclaimed."[32] Strong spent much time in the Soviet Union and obviously knew more about it than most of the Western tourists. She was instrumental in founding *Moscow News*, the English-language paper in Moscow, which adamantly wooed many American engineers and skilled workers to emigrate to the USSR in the early 1930s. Strong was also a friend of Eleanor Roosevelt. The Roosevelts used to invite her and inquire about life in the Soviet Union. Listening to her stories about the rapid development of the Soviet economy at the time of the crisis in the West, President Roosevelt reportedly wondered how Stalin could afford to *buy out* all these Russian factories.[33]

The American Pulitzer Prize–winning playwright Elmer Rice belonged to the select few who had the opportunity of relating contemporary Soviet Socialist Realist theater to contemporary Soviet reality. While in Moscow, he was invited to a performance of Pogodin's *The Aristocrats* at the Realistic Theater and then driven to the showcase camp in Bolshevo. Watching the performance, Rice experienced some initial reservations as to its realism. All doubts disappeared, however, as soon as the American traveler saw the accomplishments of the *perekovka* in Bolshevo. He shared his thoughts and impressions with the readers of the *New York Times*: "Undoubtedly, Pogodin has drawn a somewhat idealistic picture. But I myself visited Bolshevo, near Moscow, and saw firsthand what can be done in the way of human rehabilitation. This community, founded twelve or fourteen years ago entirely by habitual criminals, is now a thriving and orderly industrial town of 12,000."[34]

Western visitors to Soviet prisons and camps naturally tried to compare them to penitentiary institutions in their own countries. A British communist activist, Pat Sloan, wrote in his book *Soviet Democracy*:

> Compared with the significance of that term in Britain, Soviet imprisonment stands out as an almost enjoyable experience. For the essence of Soviet imprisonment is isolation from the rest of the community, together with other persons similarly isolated, with the possibility to do useful work at the place of isolation, to earn a wage for this work, and to participate in running the isolation settlement or "prison" in the same way as the children participate in running their school, or the workers their factory.[35]

In his other book, with the equally telling title *Russia without Illusions*, Sloan added: "The Soviet labour camp provides a freedom for its inmates not usual in our own prisons in this country [the United Kingdom]."[36]

Pat Sloan was a communist, and so his outlook could have been seen by some as perhaps biased by his political allegiance. But opinions similar to his came very often from seemingly unprejudiced and objective observers—and even from scholars. Harold Laski, a famed British political scientist who, back in 1925, had publicly pleaded with the Bolsheviks for more restraint in their repressive policies, warning them that they might lose support among the Western left, now undertook a journey to the country of the Gulag. Having talked with functionaries of the Soviet justice system as well as with some inmates, he concluded in his book *Law and Justice in Soviet Russia*: "No one who has seen over a Russian prison, and compared that experience with a visit to one in England, can doubt that the advantage is all on the Russian side."[37] For example, Soviet "prisoners have absolute quiet in the reading rooms where they have a good supply of newspapers, periodicals and books. . . . Wireless, classes in cultural and vocational subjects, gymnastics, books, dramatic performances, concerts both for, and by, the prisoners, a prison newspaper, in which the right to make complaints is an essential feature, all these are universal." The British scholar was "struck by the excellent relations between the prisoners and the warders, and the sense of men who were living a useful life untainted by that torture of separation from the power to fulfill personality which is the dominant feature of our own system."[38] Laski's book was treated in the English-speaking world as a serious analysis of the Soviet justice system.

What Harold Laski examined in the somewhat dry language of a scholar, George Bernard Shaw discussed in the lighter style of an essayist. After his visit to a showcase prison for women, he concluded: "None of these women would have been better off as innocent persons earning their living in an English factory."[39] Reading some of Shaw's comments about the Gulag, one must admit that not without reason was he called the master of paradox. "In England," he wrote, "a delinquent enters [the jail] as an ordinary man and comes out as a 'criminal type,' whereas in Russia he enters . . . as a criminal type and would come out an ordinary man but for the difficulty of inducing him to come out at all. As far as I could make out, they could stay as long as they liked."[40]

These remarks by Shaw about Soviet prisoners reluctant to leave their cozy prisons or labor camps when their sentences were over were echoed by the eminent British jurist and Labour Party politician D. N. Pritt in his article "The Russian Legal System." Pritt visited the Gulag in 1932 with an inquiry delegation sent there by the Fabian Society. He described his firsthand observations: "There is none of the restriction and futility created by the over-regimented life of so many English prisoners. . . . Small wonder that in such a 'prison' a substantial part of the population . . . nevertheless prefer to continue living in the 'prison' bringing up their children in the surroundings which helped themselves back to normal life."[41] Anna Louise Strong made quite similar observations: "So well-known and effective is the Soviet method of remaking human beings that criminals occasionally now apply to be admitted [to the Gulag]."[42]

At first glance, these reports seem nothing but grotesque examples of the gullibility of foreign visitors duped by their Soviet handlers, but there are paradoxical reflections of truth in them. This truth, however, was far too shocking and unfathomable for these pilgrims to contemplate, let alone understand.

A Garden in Full Yield

During collectivization in the early 1930s, some regions of the Soviet Union were subjected to famine so terrible that, in the eyes of their many inhabitants, the Gulag—as devastating as it was—seemed to offer a better chance of survival than staying at home. True, prisoners at the Belomor Canal were notoriously undernourished and many starved. Their average daily rations amounted, at least officially, to about thirteen hundred calories. But this was two or even three times as much as collective farmers in Ukraine received in 1932 and 1933—that is, if they got anything at all.[43] Many got nothing. Denying food was one of many forms of punishing peasants for their insufficient level of cooperation during collectivization or simply for not meeting the impossible grain requisition norms imposed on them by the government at the beginning of the decade.

While VOKS entertained Western guests in Moscow and other showcase locations, Stalin closely monitored the progress of his collectivization policy in remote provinces. Initially, local party officials sent him alarming reports requesting intervention and aid. He ignored them, however, giving priority to grain export to the West in exchange for the hard currency so vital to his plans of turning the USSR into a military and industrial power. Soon, entire villages were dying of hunger. On June 18, 1932, the day following Stalin's refusal to send aid to Ukraine, a Komsomol member wrote to the Ukrainian headquarters of the party in Kiev: "Collective farm members go into the fields and disappear. After a few days their corpses are found and, entirely without emotion, as though this were normal, buried in graves. The next day one can already find the body of someone who had just been digging graves for others."[44]

Internal documents of the party and political police as well as witnesses' descriptions regarding the life of Ukrainian peasantry at the time of collectivization often sound downright grotesque. Authorities at all levels received countless secret reports like this one:

> Citizen Gerasimenko ate the corpse of her dead sister. Under interrogation
> Gerasimenko declared that for a month she had lived on various rubbish,
> not even having vegetables.... Citizen Doroshenko, after the death of his
> father and mother was left with infant sisters and brothers, ate the flesh of his
> brothers and sisters when they died of hunger.... In the cemetery up to 30
> corpses have been found, thrown out at night, some gnawed at by dogs...
> several coffins have been found from which the corpses have disappeared....
> In Sergienko's apartment was found a corpse of a little girl with the legs cut off,
> and boiled meat.[45]

The OGPU—which had the best firsthand knowledge of the situation—noted: "Families kill their weakest members, usually children, and use the meat for eating."[46]

The more news about this massive calamity reached Stalin, the more ruthless and sadistic his response became. He purged the Ukrainian branch of the Communist Party and OGPU of those officials who sent requests for aid and those who demonstrated insufficient resolve (meaning brutality) in dealing with starving population. On August 7, 1932, he introduced a new and tougher law that defined all agricultural produce as state property and obliged the local authorities to punish peasants with immediate execution for possession of food beyond prescribed rations. "Thus a starving peasant could be shot if he picked up a potato peel from a furrow in land that until recently had been his own," Timothy Snyder explains.[47]

Some desperate starving mothers smuggled their infants to towns and cities begging for food or trying to give them away to strangers in hopes of saving them from imminent death at home. Arthur Koestler, who lived in the USSR and traveled through Ukraine at this time, saw children held by their mothers up to the windows of his train. He remembered them, many years later, as "horrible infants with enormous wobbling heads, sticklike limbs, and swollen, pointed bellies."[48] But he did not write about it until he parted with his communist beliefs later on.

The Soviet authorities did their utmost to keep the famine secret. Though occasional independent reports and testimonies of escapees did appear in the West, they were systematically dismissed by the Soviet propaganda machine and its Western allies. In 1930, Gareth Jones, a twenty-five-year-old assistant to former British prime minister Lloyd George, made a trip to Stalino (today Donetsk) in eastern Ukraine. Jones had one definitive advantage over most Western travelers to the USSR—he could communicate in Russian. It was not long before he began to realize what was happening around him. In the summer of 1931, Jones traveled again to the Soviet Union in order to closely investigate the famine. This time he carefully explored the situation and, upon his return, anonymously published a book, *Experiences in Russia 1931: A Diary*.[49] This was the first significant public exposure of the Soviet famine abroad and the first clear public indictment of Stalin's collectivization policy. But Jones was not quite done yet. He went once again to the USSR in early 1933. He got his visa only because the Soviets did not know who authored the damaging book on collectivization. This time he traveled from Berlin, where he worked as a press correspondent.

Upon his return from the USSR to Berlin, Jones gave a press conference and wrote a press release about the Soviet famine, published immediately in the *Manchester Guardian*, the *New York Evening Post*, and other newspapers. "I walked along through villages and twelve collective farms," he reported, and

> everywhere was the cry, "There is no bread. We are dying." This cry came from every part of Russia, from the Volga, Siberia, White Russia, the North Caucasus, and Central Asia. I tramped through the black earth region because that was once the richest farmland in Russia and because the correspondents have been forbidden to go there to see for themselves what is happening. . . . In the train a Communist denied to me that there was a famine. I flung a crust of bread which I had been eating from my own supply into a spittoon. A peasant fellow-passenger fished it out and ravenously ate it. I threw an orange peel into the spittoon and the peasant again grabbed it and devoured it. . . . "We are waiting for death," was my welcome, "but see, we still have our cattle fodder. Go farther south. There they have nothing. Many houses are empty of people already dead," they cried.[50]

Jones gave his press conference in Berlin on March 29, 1933. But just six days earlier, the German parliament passed the Enabling Act, giving Hitler dictatorial powers, and the news from Germany overshadowed Jones's report. Moreover, this news galvanized Hitler's opponents in the Western world, many of whom now felt even more compelled to place their hopes with Stalin. And since revelations about the Soviet famine were repeatedly mentioned by Hitler's propaganda, this made it easier for Hitler's opponents to dismiss the whole topic as Nazi spin, as many of them did.

But the Soviet authorities would not leave this issue unaddressed. On March 31, their trusted collaborator, Walter Duranty, dismissed Jones's revelations. He wrote an article in the *New York Times* titled "Russians Hungry But Not Starving." Jones responded on May 13, also in the *New York Times*. He took on not only Duranty but also other Western journalists whose comments on the famine did not differ much from Duranty's. "Journalists," Jones wrote, "are allowed to write, but the censorship has turned them into masters of euphemism and understatement. Hence they give 'famine' the polite name of 'food shortage' and 'starving to death' is softened down to read as 'widespread mortality from diseases due to malnutrition.'"

Jones was banned by the Soviet authorities from entering the country again, and Duranty continued denying the famine. His denials were increasingly more vehement as the numbers of famine victims mounted. On September 14, 1933 (by which time millions had already died of starvation in various parts of the USSR, including the North Caucasus), he wrote in an article entitled "Abundance Found in North Caucasus": "The use of the word 'Famine' in connection with the North Caucasus is a sheer absurdity. There a bumper crop is being harvested as fast as tractors, horses, oxen, men, women, and children can work.... There are plump babies in the nurseries or gardens of the collectives.... Village markets are flowing with eggs, fruit, poultry, vegetable, milk and butter at prices lower than in Moscow."[51] On November 8, 1933, the day following the sixteenth anniversary of the Bolshevik revolution, Duranty opined that the rumors about the Soviet famine were nothing other than political propaganda aimed at derailing the process of granting the Soviet Union official recognition by the United States—"an eleventh-hour attempt to avert American recognition by picturing the Soviet Union as a land of ruin and despair."[52]

Nine days later the United States granted official recognition to the USSR. The Roosevelt administration had worked very hard to make this happen, and Walter Duranty was recognized for his contributions. Duranty enjoyed great prestige in the American cultural, political, and economic establishment as a leading expert on Soviet affairs. He personally briefed FDR about the Soviet

Union, advocating for the recognition.[53] Back in May 1932, he received a Pulitzer Prize for the "erudition, depth, objectivity" as well as "exceptional clarity" of his reporting from the Soviet Union.[54] Of course, he knew much more of what was really going on in the Soviet Union than he shared in his reporting. On occasions he even remarked about it in private. At a party with British diplomats, he reportedly said that "Ukraine has been bled white. . . . It was quite possible that as many as ten million people may have died directly or indirectly from lack of food in the Soviet Union during the past year."[55]

As Jones pointed out, Duranty was not the only Western journalist looking the other way when millions starved to death in the Soviet Union in 1931–1933. To be sure, foreign journalists were forbidden to go to the areas where famine was especially lethal. Interestingly enough, however, the Soviet authorities did not seem exceedingly worried about the possibility of Western correspondents going after the real news and reporting it to the outside world. Konstantin Umansky—the Soviet official who censored foreign press reports from the USSR and had a lot of influence over the accreditation of foreign correspondents—met these correspondents in a Moscow hotel and simply instructed them on how they were supposed to write about the famine. Eugene Lyons, then the United Press correspondent and present at the meeting, wrote later: "We admitted enough to soothe our consciences, but in roundabout phrases. . . . The filthy business having been disposed of, someone ordered vodka and zakuski, Umansky joined the celebration, and the party did not break up until the morning hours."[56]

What worried the Soviet authorities more than the presence of Western journalists was Ukrainian survivors escaping from famine-stricken areas to neighboring Poland. These escapees tried to tell the world about the horrors in Soviet Ukraine. The Polish authorities were initially willing to listen and believed what they heard but ultimately decided not to take any official steps to investigate or publicize these revelations. The Polish government had just finalized a long process of negotiating a nonaggression treaty with the Soviet Union. The treaty was signed in July 1932, and Poland did not want to complicate relations with its eastern neighbor by initiating what the Soviets would surely rebuke as a hostile propaganda campaign. Some Polish media, however, did raise the issue and the Ukrainian minority in Poland (about 4.5 million strong at the time) also strove to turn the world's attention to the famine. In the fall of 1933, Cardinal Theodor Innitzer of Vienna tried to appeal for aid for the Ukrainian victims, only to be ridiculed by the Soviet authorities for spreading false rumors and meddling in the internal affairs of the USSR.

In order to undermine the credibility of Jones's reports and Polish and Polish-Ukrainian discussions of the famine in the summer of 1933, the Soviets invited former French prime minister Édouard Herriot to visit Ukraine. The visit was carefully orchestrated; it represented a true accomplishment of Soviet propaganda theater. Herriot, accompanied by French journalist Geneviève Tabouis, was taken to many locations between August 26 and September 9 in order to "see for himself" that the Ukrainian famine was nothing but a bunch of lies spread by enemies of the Soviet Union. Before Herriot's arrival in Kiev, electricity was installed in many houses. Along the streets where Herriot was driven, shop windows, normally empty, were filled with goods (not for sale but for visual effect, suggesting prosperity). Cars were brought from other cities and driven by communist activists on the streets during Herriot's visit, to make an impression of a bustling and thriving city. Pedestrians were instructed how to dress and how to behave on the day of the visit. Special food supplies were transported wherever Herriot went. These efforts proved successful, and Herriot did not disappoint his handlers. On his return, he shared his observations with the Western public: "I crossed the Ukraine. So! I assure you that it looked like a garden in full yield. You tell me that this land is reputed to be going through a depression right now? I cannot speak of what I have not seen. And heaven knows, I made them take me to afflicted areas. All I witnessed, however, was prosperity."[57] Whether the French politician was indeed duped by his Soviet handlers remains a question. The truth is he was chosen for this high-profile visit because Soviet authorities knew he was deeply committed to his long-standing political vision of a Franco-Soviet rapprochement and would do everything possible not to jeopardize it. Stalin and his lieutenants knew well in advance that Herriot had urgent reasons not to notice the Ukrainian famine.

George Bernard Shaw, the master of paradox who wittingly remarked on Soviet prisoners reluctant to leave camps, never comprehended the real irony behind his own comments. On his way to the Soviet Union in 1931, he gave a public display of his disbelief in the rumors about hunger in the land of the proletariat. When the train stopped on the Polish-Soviet border, he ostentatiously threw his food out the window. Later on, he assured everyone that during his Soviet visit he was fed (and even overfed) with exquisite food. One evening, during a banquet in Moscow's Metropol Hotel, he was approached by Sonia Chamberlin, wife of *Christian Science Monitor* correspondent William Henry Chamberlin. As a Russian, she was more aware of the famine than most of the foreign guests at the banquet. She told Shaw that ordinary people in the Soviet Union felt sorry that he had not thrown his food away when he was already within the Soviet borders. The food thrown out by Shaw could have saved some lives. Shaw responded in his usual style—by showing off his famed wit. He reportedly looked around the banquet hall and asked Mrs. Chamberlin,

"Where do you see any food shortage?"[58] On hearing Shaw's remarks on the Soviet famine, Malcolm Muggeridge wrote in his diary, "He is a preposterous old fool."[59]

Shaw stuck to his denials when Jones's revelations about Soviet famine reached the Western public along with other witnesses of the collectivization disaster. On March 2, 1933, Shaw and twenty other "recent visitors to the USSR," not mentioned by name, signed a letter to the editor of the *Manchester Guardian*, denouncing reports on the famine and slave works in the USSR. The signatories viewed those reports as evidence of a "blind and reckless campaign to discredit" the Soviet Union and as "inflammatory slander" aimed at derailing Stalin's Five-Year Plan. Shaw and the other tourists contrasted their Soviet impressions with the dire situation of the working masses in the West:

> We desire to record that we saw nowhere evidence of such economic slavery, privation, unemployment and cynical despair of betterment as are accepted as inevitable and ignored by the press as having "no news value" in our own countries. Everywhere we saw a hopeful and enthusiastic working-class, self-respecting, free up to the limits imposed on them by nature and a terrible inheritance from tyranny and incompetence of their former rulers, developing public works, increasing health services, extending education, achieving the economic independence of women and the security of the child and in spite of many grievous difficulties and mistakes which all social experiments involve at first (and which they have never concealed nor denied) setting an example of industry and conduct which would greatly enrich us if our systems supplied our workers with any incentive to follow it. We would regard it as a calamity if the present lie campaign were to be allowed to make headway without contradiction and to damage the relationship between our country and the USSR.[60]

A New Civilization

Gareth Jones was not the only outspoken Western visitor to notice the famine. Malcolm Muggeridge, who at the time served as a Moscow correspondent for the *Manchester Guardian*, took a train ride to Dnepropetrovsk, where the Soviets had built a giant power plant. On his way through Ukraine, he did not avoid noticing hungry children begging for food at provincial railway stations. Shaken by what he saw, Muggeridge described his impressions in anonymous reports for the *Manchester Guardian*. Soon his British editors started pressuring him to pay less attention to the famine; too much emphasis on this topic was not welcome. In reply, Muggeridge quit his job at the *Guardian*. He gave speeches back in England, in which he not only criticized the nature of the Bolshevik regime but also exposed the many ways this regime corrupted and duped Western fellow travelers. In 1934, he published the novel *Winter in Moscow* based on his experience and observations in Russia.

Muggeridge's public speeches and his book were received with reluctance and hostility by many British intellectuals. Among the people most disappointed by Muggeridge's views were Sidney and Beatrice Webb. The Webbs belonged to the most prominent British intellectual elite. Sidney Webb was one of the founders of the London School of Economics. His ideas vitally contributed to the economic and political philosophy of the Labour Party at the time. In the 1920s, the Webbs were moderately critical of the Soviet regime, but the Great Depression turned them into adamant advocates of planned economy, so they joined the ranks of Western sympathizers of the country of Five-Year Plans. In 1932 and 1933, they toured the USSR and accepted at face value most of the propaganda served to them by their Soviet handlers. Of course, like most Western commentators on the Soviet Union, they knew no Russian. When Muggeridge published his exposure of the Soviet charades, the Webbs did not believe him. As a matter of fact, they found his comments so fantastic that they started considering him all but mentally disturbed. Their embarrassment was confounded by the fact that Muggeridge was married to Beatrice Webb's niece, Kitty. Beatrice wondered in her personal diary whether "psychoanalysis and early treatment in the nursery and the school" could have saved her nephew-in-law from his apparent mental instability.[61] In order to make sure that Muggeridge's revelations about the famine were nothing more than expressions of his anti-Soviet obsession, the Webbs invited the Soviet ambassador, Ivan Maisky, to their country home in Passfield and asked him to comment on the topic. Mr. Maisky "comforted us about the food shortage," Beatrice wrote in her diary.[62] At that point, Mr. and Mrs. Webb knew for sure that they were right and Malcolm Muggeridge was wrong.

The Webbs were working at the time on their book *Soviet Communism: A New Civilisation?* In it, they addressed the topic of collectivization and the rumors about the famine. They admitted that some degree of force was used in collectivization but considered it necessary for the greater good. Indeed, they acknowledged that "something like a million families" might have suffered. But despite all, the Webbs concluded that "candid students of the circumstances may not unwarrantably come to the conclusion that . . . the Soviet Government could hardly have acted otherwise than it did."[63] In fact, the attitude the Soviet government demonstrated during collectivization—as harsh as it might have been—not only deserved justification on the part of the British scholars but won their outright praise. "Strong must have been the faith and resolute the will of the men who, in the interest of what seemed to them the public good could take so momentous a decision," the Webbs wrote.[64] Robert Conquest characterized this comment by the Webbs as "words which might equally be applied, by any wishing to do so, to Hitler and the Final Solution."[65]

In their book the Webbs recited what they had been taught in the USSR about the nature and role of the Soviet political police. They praised "the considerable social services rendered by its uniformed staff" and extolled "its achievements of a reformatory character."[66] As an example of these achievements, the Webbs mentioned the White Sea Canal. "It is pleasant to think," they wrote, "that the warmest appreciation was officially expressed of the success of the OGPU, not merely in performing a great engineering feat, but in achieving a triumph in human regeneration."[67] Before the publication of their book the Webbs consulted with important Soviet experts. During his trip to Russia in 1934, Sidney Webb submitted sections of the manuscript to the chief of VOKS, Aleksandr Arosev, with a kind request for critical comments. How important this book was for the Soviets can be illustrated by the fact that Arosev felt obliged to ask Lazar Kaganovich, one of Stalin's most trusted lieutenants, for instructions on this matter.[68] In March 1935, the Webbs invited Ambassador Maisky again for a weekend in Passfield to run the manuscript by him. Once again, the Soviet diplomat obliged. The book was published later that year and hailed in Great Britain as a scholarly analysis of Soviet economy and society.

In subsequent editions, the authors deleted the question mark from the original title. They no longer had any doubts, at least officially, that Soviet communism was indeed a new civilization. In 1943 Beatrice wrote in her diary: "We have lived the life we liked and done the work we intended to do; and we have been proven to be right about Soviet Communism: a new civilisation."[69]

A Tourist's Story

The belief that somewhere, in a distant land, humanity's most pressing problems are resolved by a "new civilization" seemed to have great therapeutic value—especially for those who could reinforce this belief with what they thought was a firsthand experience. This sort of therapy was not so different from that offered by vacations on various paradisical islands. The Soviet Union offered a vacation from reality but with all the appearances of the real world. In fact, vacation tours, in the literal sense, of Soviet prisons and camps became quite popular in the West in the 1930s. These tours were advertised and reviewed in the travel sections of magazines and newspapers, next to advertisements of group pilgrimages to Lourdes, rafting expeditions down German rivers, tours of English castles, Egyptian antiquities, and so on.

On April 14, 1935, for instance, the travel section of the *New York Times* featured one such piece, entitled "Trips to Soviet Prisons," which publicized the tours organized by the Union Tours travel agency under the direction of one Joseph Fulling Fishman. Here is the offer. The tourists cross the Atlantic on the *Normandy* cruise ship and, having reached the USSR from the Baltic Sea, enjoy the historic marvels of Leningrad and Tsarskoe Selo. But the main focus of the tour is on modern Soviet attractions. The organizers invite the tourists for a boat excursion along the Belomor Canal, a visit to a labor camp in Medvezhegorsk, and a visit to the Novinskaya women's prison in Leningrad. Later on, the tour participants are taken to Moscow, where they meet representatives of the National Commissariat of Justice and listen to their presentation on the cutting-edge methods of resocializing criminals. But the vacation offer of the Union Tours in the USSR was wider and more diverse than that. The *New York Times* reminded its readers: "This is only one of many groups that will head for Russia during the summer; many will observe operations and others will remain in one or another of the Russian universities to study more intensely the philosophy of the new Russia."[70]

Returning from the exciting land of the Soviets to the mundane reality of their own countries and lives, these Western tourists could find hope in remembering what they had experienced and what their Soviet hosts had told them. Personal experience demonstrated to them that there was indeed a country thanks to which faith in a better future for humanity was still possible. In order to keep this faith alive, they only had to ignore negative rumors casting a shadow on this sunny picture of Stalin's domain.

Among numerous foreigners visiting the Gulag in the 1930s, few had an opportunity to deepen their knowledge of the Soviet labor camps by revisiting them as inmates. Jerzy Gliksman was one of them. Later, he compared both experiences in a memoir illuminating the relationship between the onstage performance in the Gulag propaganda theater and the reality behind the scenes.

Gliksman, a young Warsaw lawyer with a doctorate from the Sorbonne, was a socialist. He earned recognition as a defense counsel and legal adviser for socialist trade unions. Soon he became a representative of the Jewish Labor Party (the Bund) in the Warsaw City Council. His 1935 visit to Moscow started in quite a typical fashion: a luxurious hotel, lavish banquets, champagne, caviar, gourmet Russian dishes, and the charming company of a young and attractive female VOKS guide. Every day Gliksman was driven to factories, cultural centers, hospitals, and museums. Among the latter, the Museum of Atheism (in a former church, naturally) and the Museum of the Revolution made a distinct impression on him.

In the evenings he enjoyed Moscow's theater productions. He loved good theater and was very intrigued when he heard that Pogodin's *The Aristocrats*, a play about the Gulag, was being shown in Moscow. Gliksman did not miss the opportunity to see *The Aristocrats* and Pogodin's humanitarian vision of the transformation of man in the Gulag made a great impression on him. But, like Elmer Rice, he did not feel entirely convinced of the verisimilitude of what he saw on stage. A hint of doubt remained. Wasn't the play a bit too sugary to be true? On the following day, Gliksman asked his attractive female guide whether he might be able to see a real camp. He had heard about such visits before but did not really expect his request to be answered positively. Much to his surprise the guide told him that, luckily enough, the VOKS was organizing a tour of the corrective labor colony in Bolshevo on the next day.

The next morning, Gliksman took a seat on an Intourist bus filled with foreign visitors. There were journalists, writers, artists, academics, and trade union activists from Great Britain, France, Belgium, Mexico, and the United States. Many of them were guests invited for the Moscow celebrations of the anniversary of the Bolshevik revolution on November 7. On their way to Bolshevo they praised the goodwill and openness of the Soviet government, which had nothing to hide from the world and even made its prisons open to outside scrutiny. "What other government in the world would as easily agree to such a visit?" travelers kept asking.[71] A French-speaking older gentleman in a pince-nez commented:

> Unfortunately I have not seen Pogodin's play . . . but I did study several professional books on Soviet law, and I am really charmed. We, the Western European jurists, talk a great deal about reforming the old, rusty penal codes; but they, in Russia, actually did something about it. We punish our criminals, we lock them up in prisons. But do these people improve as a result? What advantage does our society at large derive from their treatment? The Russian system of labor camps is an ideal solution. It gets important construction work done for the country, and it changes the character of the criminals through labor. The Russians may indeed be proud of accomplishments such as the Byel . . . Byel . . . —well, I always forget the name of the canal.

"You have in mind the *Byelomor* Canal," the VOKS representative who was in charge of our excursion cut in. Then he added with a smile, "So that you might recall this name with greater ease, I have something for you here." He then distributed to every person two packages of excellent Russian cigarettes which it was very difficult to obtain in the stores. On each box was an inscription reading *Byelomor Canal Cigarettes.*[72]

When the tourists reached the juvenile labor colony in Bolshevo, their impression matched their expectations. "I am sorry you see it in autumn," the guide remarked. "In summer it is even more beautiful here. Greenery and flowers are then all over the camp."[73] Still, even in late autumn the place looked more like a vacation spot than a labor camp. In cozy residential buildings the visitors noticed immaculate white linens and spotless bathrooms. The inmates worked energetically and with a swagger in halls decorated with portraits of the camp's leading shock workers. The tourists were informed that the prisoners chose their own work according to their individual talents and interests; some preferred woodworking, others elected tailoring and still others took pride in building sleds for children. The presence of foreigners did not make much of an impression on the prisoners because—as the guards explained—they were quite used to it. After work, not longer than six hours per day, the inmates studied in evening schools (once again, clean and airy classrooms and sympathetic teachers). When studying was over, there was still time left for amateur theater, movie shows, discussion clubs, playing musical instruments, and so on.

The dinner in the camp cafeteria turned out to be both tasty and nutritious. As coffee was served, the guests learned that the prisoners themselves elected their own self-government, administration, and supervisors. Only the camp commander was a regular NKVD officer; actually, it turned out, he was a professional educator as well. Apparently, the cooperation between the prisoners' self-government and the camp commander was excellent. If a prisoner did something against the rules, he was judged by a jury elected by his peers from his peers. But such cases were extremely rare, the visitors were told. And, of course, nobody even thought of escaping from this camp. "After our guide had finished his really touching speech, I saw tears in the eyes of an elderly English lady," Gliksman writes. "They were tears of appreciation and joy. 'Wonderful! Wonderful!' she kept repeating. 'How beautiful the world could be!' a French movie director who happened to be sitting at my side whispered to my ear."[74] In order not to leave any doubt in the minds of the foreigners, the guide suggested that they talk freely with prisoners without witnesses. Gliksman knew Russian and took advantage of this opportunity. "The inmates repeated almost everything we had been told by our guide. They were happy in the camp, they said. Everything was just ideal; nothing could be better."[75]

There was, it seemed to the guests, no end to these pleasant encounters. In the evening, the hosts took them to a correctional colony for former prostitutes currently working as seamstresses. By a fortunate coincidence (of course), the colony's director spoke fluent English, French, and German. A few guests expressed some reservations: "Perhaps the fallen women thought it humiliating to be visited and stared at?" But one of the attendants reassured them: "They are used to these visits. Foreign tourists are brought on a visit here almost every evening."[76]

After his return to the hotel, Gliksman compared Pogodin's play he had seen on a Moscow stage to the "real life" encountered in Bolshevo. He knew reports about the horrors of the Gulag and collectivization but, after his Soviet visit, he seriously doubted their accuracy. "Was it really possible that all I had seen was only artful propaganda, make-believe, mere fiction?" he kept asking himself. He found it hard to believe in such colossal deception. "Perhaps the Great Russian Revolution had achieved something new and progressive in the treatment of prisoners, if only criminal prisoners," he reasoned. "Perhaps we had not fully realized Russia's accomplishments in this field." Touched by what he saw in Bolshevo, he seemed unaware that earlier that same year, on April 7, a decree was issued in the Soviet Union lowering the minimum age of full criminal responsibility, including the death penalty, from sixteen to twelve. Later on, he reminisced about his first visit to the land of Soviets: "Then, in 1935 in Moscow, I never dreamt that I should be in a position to study at close quarters and in great detail Soviet justice and especially Soviet prisons and camps, and see how prisoners, guilty and not guilty, criminals and 'counter-revolutionaries,' adults and adolescents, honest and 'fallen' women alike, were really treated."[77]

The opportunity to deepen his knowledge of the Gulag came five years later, after the joint invasion of Poland by Hitler and Stalin in September 1939. Having found himself in eastern Poland under Soviet occupation, he shared the fate of hundreds of thousands of Polish citizens. Arrested by the NKVD, he ended up in prison in Oszmiana (now Ashmyany in Belarus), where he spent long nights hearing the cries of tortured people. His ultimate destination was the Gulag. But this time he was not driven there in an Intourist bus.

After nearly two years in Soviet prisons and camps, Gliksman's views changed rather dramatically from those he held in 1935:

> The Soviet *lagers* are in fact institutions practicing slave labor. . . . Openly and cynically, without any trace of concern for appearances, the camp inmate is therefore treated simply as a forced supplier of needed work. . . .
>
> The treatment he receives from the camp authorities hurts and kills all vestiges of a man's inner moral values. In practice, the living, feeling, and thinking human being does not exist. The camp authorities are interested

solely in extracting the maximum of labor from the prisoner whose value is measured by the number of cubic feet of earth dug or the amount of timber felled. And since the supply of camp inmates is almost inexhaustibly large, and the expended and weakened can easily be replaced by fresh human material, hardly anybody concerns himself with the prisoners' lives and health. The human being, the individual, is only an insignificant unit, a dead cipher in the involved account of this kind of planned economy.[78]

Jerzy Gliksman could count himself among the lucky. In August of 1941 he was released from the Gulag with other Polish citizens (to whom we will return later). Before he left the camp, a female prisoner named Sarah, not fortunate enough to be counted among the citizens of Poland, told him: "You can do one thing for us, and one thing only. . . . Should you really succeed in getting abroad—and I most sincerely hope you will—tell all you know about us. . . . Tell the West." On his way out of the camp, Gliksman approached another prisoner left behind, Professor Strovsky. "'Professor,' I said softly as we parted. 'I shall never forget you!' And then I repeated Sarah's words, "I shall tell the Western World about you.' But Strovsky shook his head. 'They won't want to believe you anyway,' he said."[79]

Dissonances

Not all voices critical of Soviet oppression were doomed to remain unheard in the 1930s. Those that achieved some resonance in the West often made the Soviet authorities quite concerned and, sometimes, inclined to accommodate the critics. The Victor Serge affair was an example of this relative capacity of Western opinion makers to influence Soviet decisions. Serge, the son of Russian émigrés, born and raised in Belgium, was imprisoned during World War I for subversive activity. Once released, he moved to his parents' homeland, Russia, and joined the Bolsheviks. In internal party debates he supported Trotsky's positions. At the time of Trotsky's expulsion from the Bolshevik Party and his exile abroad, Serge was also expelled from the party and briefly arrested. But Stalin was not ready yet for the definitive purge of the Trotskyites. Serge settled in Leningrad and in 1929 published (in Paris) a book critical of Stalin.[80] He was arrested again in 1933 and deported to Orenburg with his wife and son.

This happened when millions of peasants dying of hunger in the Soviet Union did not attract much of the world's attention. But unlike those peasants, Victor Serge was known to some vocal Westerners who cared about him. Although most of the French left was silent on Serge, a group of Trotskyists and other disillusioned ex-admirers of the Soviets, such as Boris Souvarine and

Pierre Pascal, tried to inform Western public opinion about him. In June 1935, they decided to use the International Writers' Congress in Paris as the stage on which they would present their cause to the world.

The idea of the Congress was conceived by the Soviet authorities as a part of the propaganda campaign targeting the Western literary establishment. The Soviets paid for the Congress and expected their most famous Western literary advocates to come up with a show of support for Stalin. Ostensibly the Congress was to be focused on defending the world's culture from fascism and praising Stalin as humanity's greatest hope in this struggle. But Stalin's principal literary ambassador, Gorky, did not attend. The writer blamed his health, which was probably a legitimate reason, although some historians speculate that Gorky's absence might have been a sign of his growing disillusionment with his patron. In any event, Stalin might have been somewhat disappointed, even more so as some of the most awaited participants pulled out at the last moment. Romain Rolland, instead of coming to the Congress, chose this particular moment to travel to the Soviet Union and, during his stay there, to pay a personal visit to Gorky. George Bernard Shaw and H. G. Wells did not come to Paris despite invitations and neither did Thomas Mann, Ernest Hemingway, or Theodore Dreiser. In this situation, the stars of the Congress were André Gide and André Malraux, as well as the always dependable Henri Barbusse and Louis Aragon, plus Aldous Huxley, Virginia Woolf, and E. M. Forster. There was also a group of German anti-Nazi émigré celebrities, including Bertolt Brecht, Lion Feuchtwanger, Johannes Becher, and Thomas Mann's brother Heinrich.

The key organizer of the Congress was Willi Münzenberg, the most influential animator of the Soviet international propaganda machine at the time. Münzenberg had begun his brilliant career in Bolshevik public relations as the founder of the International Workers' Aid organization created out of Lenin's initiative back in 1921. Ever since then, he had been playing a central role in motivating and organizing numerous organizations, networks, and initiatives, formal and informal alike, engaged in propagating Soviet viewpoints and interests abroad. Fellow travelers and other noncommunist "friends of the new Russia" were his purview. In François Furet's words, "His usual quarry was the intellectual, who had more influence and more vanity than the ordinary mortal. He compelled writers, philosophers, and artists to sign in as bona fide combatants, so that he could mobilize them instantly."[81] In organizing the Paris Congress, Münzenberg was helped by two Soviet literary men entrusted by Stalin with handling foreign writers and intellectuals—Ilya Ehrenburg and Mikhail Koltsov (who were, in turn, overseen by the Party boss of the Soviet Writers' Union, Aleksandr Shcherbakov). The Soviet delegation to the Paris

Congress also included Nikolai Tikhonov, Aleksei Tolstoy, Vladimir Kirshon, Isaac Babel, and Boris Pasternak. The last two were added to the list rather reluctantly, in response to personal requests from Malraux and Gide.

But the absence of some principal superstars was not the greatest disappointment Stalin had to endure during the Congress. While the tone of the speeches and discussions generally reflected the expectations of the Soviet organizers, some conversations took a wrong turn, and the name of Victor Serge was heard repeatedly. For Stalin, this probably constituted a signal that Trotsky's sympathizers were trying to hijack his Congress. Among those who raised the issue of Serge's deportation were Magdelaine Paz, André Breton, and Henry Poulaille. Finally, Gaetano Salvemini, an Italian writer with indisputable antifascist credentials who lived in exile in the United States, spoke on the Congress floor: "I would not feel as though I had the right to protest against the Gestapo and the Fascist OVRA if I endeavored to forget about the existence of a Soviet political police. In Germany, there are concentration camps, in Italy there are penitentiary islands, and in Soviet Russia there is Siberia."[82] Salvemini publicly asked a question that few Western cultural celebrities seemed to stumble on at the time: "Is the bitter cold of Siberian villages, to which ideological opponents of the regime are exiled any better than German concentration camps?"[83] It is important to remember that at the time of the Paris Congress Stalin's victims could be counted in millions while Hitler was only taking his first steps on the road to becoming the mass murderer we know.

The Soviet delegates to the Congress tried to dismiss the issue, but their efforts were not entirely successful: the topic of Victor Serge was only partially swept under the rug. It turned out this was not the first time Stalin was unwilling to risk exposing himself to too much criticism and too many doubts on the part of the very people he wanted to be his cheerleaders in the West—at least for the moment. Victor Serge was released and allowed to emigrate from the USSR shortly afterward. Perhaps if Western intellectuals cared just a little more about other Soviet victims, they might have been able to save more lives and mitigate, at least by a small margin, the brutality of the Soviet system of repression.

If the critical voices at the Congress did indeed have real impact on Stalin's decision to let Serge go, the Soviets never publicly admitted to budging under this sort of pressure. What made this decision undoubtedly easier for Stalin was the fact that Romain Rolland, Stalin's principal Western apologist, pleaded for Serge in a conversation with the dictator during his visit in Moscow. As already mentioned, when the Congress deliberated in Paris, Rolland journeyed to the USSR at Gorky's invitation, which may have made Stalin anxious. If Gorky and Rolland's ardor for Stalin was indeed cooling, then losing their outspoken support at the sensitive time of the Paris Congress would have been a debacle for Soviet propaganda. In any case, the fact remains that the Soviets played it very carefully.

It should be noted that Rolland was initially very critical of the Bolshevik revolution, a stance that was influenced by none other than Gorky. Like Gorky, Rolland initially abhorred Bolshevik violence, deceptiveness, disdain for individual liberties, and tyrannical methods of governing. In 1921–1922, he expressed this sentiment in a highly publicized debate with the unapologetically pro-Bolshevik Henri Barbusse. Trotsky, in *Izvestiya*, called Rolland a "pretentious individualist."[84] In 1927, Rolland stated: "On Bolshevism, I have in no way changed. The bearer of high ideas (or, rather, since thought has never been its forte, the representative of a great cause), Bolshevism has destroyed it (and them) by its narrow sectarianism, its inept intransigence, and its cult of violence. It has given rise to Fascism, which is a sort of reverse Bolshevism."[85] But, starting around 1928, Rolland's views evolved and, by the mid-1930s, he became a leading fellow traveler and admirer of Stalinism—though he never formally joined the Communist Party. His affection for Stalinism resulted rather from the typical vague projection of humanist and pacifist beliefs upon the idealized image of the Soviet Union as the greatest hope for world peace and justice. Once again, it was Gorky who seemed to play a key role in this evolution of Rolland's views about Soviet communism. At the time, Gorky had already abandoned his critical attitude toward the Bolshevik regime and was in the process of being anointed by Stalin as the grand master of Soviet literature.

Rolland's views seem to have also been affected by an increasingly intimate relationship with his Soviet translator, editor, representative, and admirer, Maria Kudasheva, whom he married in 1934. Kudasheva, whose views appear to have been enthusiastically pro-Soviet, moved to France in 1929 in order to live with Rolland, but she always remained in close contact with Soviet institutions vitally interested in the French writer. Kudasheva's political beliefs aside, her tireless loyalty to the Soviet authorities might very likely have been influenced by the fact that her son from a previous marriage, Sergei, was not allowed to leave the country with her but remained in Moscow. Whether she was a regular Soviet secret police agent remains uncertain for now, but it would be a daring assumption that there was no such connection. In any case, in the mid-1930s, her correspondence with Mikhail Apletin, the secretary of the International Union of Revolutionary Writers, and with the Foreign Commission of the Union of Soviet Writers, amounted to two or three letters per week.[86] Via Gorky, Kudasheva, and various cultural apparatchiks like Apletin and VOKS chief Aleksandr Arosev, the Soviet authorities monitored Rolland's life, his ideas, and concerns. Using the same channels, they also kept making more or less subtle attempts (it seems mostly successful) to gently steer his attention, thoughts, and emotions in politically expedient directions. Rolland was always cautiously treated by his Soviet handlers as a fellow traveler, a "friend of the Soviet Union," and not as "one of *our* men" (communists). He was a highly valuable asset of Soviet propaganda, and the Soviet authorities greatly appreciated his services, turning him into perhaps the most celebrated Western intellectual in the Soviet Union.

When Rolland showed up in the USSR in June 1935, he was given a royal reception. Upon his arrival, the writer was informed that a Russian translation of his collected works had just been published in the Soviet Union in a very large print run. He was transported in a special luxury train car and stayed in a six-room apartment in the Savoy Hotel. A special nurse and a secretary were constantly at his disposal, not counting other personnel, such as translators, guides, drivers, and servants. "I am surrounded with parental care by the Council of People's Commissars," he noted with gratitude in his diary.[87] Stalin personally welcomed him at the Kremlin: "I am happy to talk with the greatest writer in the world."[88] Rolland responded with an oration worthy of imperial courts: "Dear Comrade Stalin, please allow me to thank you for inviting me. You probably know what your name and your personality mean for us, and how reassured we are by the awareness that you of all people are the leader of this great country of the new world, of which we are proud and in which we place our hopes. I am happy I can shake your hand and I want to say that I am moved by the expressions of interest which accompany me in your country, and especially by your invitation to rest in your villa."[89] A few days later, Rolland met Stalin again in Gorky's mansion. The ruler came with his entourage, including Molotov, Kaganovich, and Voroshilov. On another occasion, Rolland met Genrikh Yagoda, who immediately aroused his sympathy and whose eyes the French writer described as "honest and kind."[90]

But Rolland did not stop at panegyrics alone. In his conversation with Stalin he touched upon some controversial issues, including Victor Serge. Research in declassified sections of Stalin's personal archive has revealed telling details about this conversation. Rolland did not challenge the validity of Serge's punishment. On the contrary, by admitting that "I am completely sure that he deserved his punishment," he distanced himself from Serge's Western advocates. But he immediately pointed out that "it was necessary to explain this fact to the mass of friends of the USSR."[91] What Rolland appeared to be concerned with was not Serge himself but the troubling need for some explanation of the reasons behind Serge's punishment in order to assuage growing doubts among some Western "friends of the Soviet Union." Thus Rolland reassured Stalin about his loyalty. He simply appeared to be asking for further instructions on how he should serve the Soviet cause more effectively. Was he sincere, naive, cynical, or savvy?

Perhaps he was sincere after all. In a letter to Jean-Richard Bloch, written back on November 15, 1934, Rolland expressed his feelings about Serge: "Like you and Barbusse, I haven't the slightest regard for S[erge]." But in the same letter, he admitted what really concerned him about the publicity around Serge: "For a year, the S. case has done disproportionate damage to Western public opinion, growing worse with each passing month."[92] This sort of attitude was reminiscent of many Western supporters of the Bolshevik regime who worried much more about Stalin's Western image than about the fate of his victims at home. Back in 1925, some writers publicly expressed similar feelings in the introductory remarks to *Letters from Soviet Prisons*. Most of them still believed that by making their criticism public, they would pressure the Soviet regime to reexamine its repressive measures. By the 1930s, however, concerns of this sort were voiced confidentially and not in public anymore. Before talking with Rolland, Stalin was approached by Bloch, Barbusse, and Georges Duhamel, all of whom expressed similar anxieties about "the S. case."

The Soviet dictator might have already decided that the Western campaign for Serge's release was becoming too damaging at the moment. If so, then Rolland might have provided him with an opportunity to demonstrate to Western leftist circles that he can be placated by those loyal to him rather than pressured by his critics. One thing seems certain: without the Western protests regarding Serge, Rolland would have had no reason to express to the Soviet leader his worries about the image of the Soviet Union abroad. As a result, it is more likely that the fate of Victor Serge would have been sealed just like the fates of the Trotskyists under Stalin in the years to come.

All things considered, Rolland was not as naive as he might appear. In fact, he became aware that he was being manipulated during his Russian visit. In Moscow, he privately talked with Maria Kudasheva's son, Sergei, who expressed his anxiety about the growing atmosphere of oppression, especially since Sergei Kirov's assassination in Leningrad in December 1934.[93] In his private diary Rolland noted: "The dictatorship still exists but it tries to mask itself (they did everything so that I would not notice it)."[94] But he kept these observations to himself. In public, he was quick to send Stalin a signal that he understood and appreciated the rules of the game. Before his trip back home, he wrote to Stalin that it was his and, indeed, all of humanity's obligation to defend the Soviet Union. "From this duty—you know this, dear comrade—I have never retreated, and will never abandon it as long as I live."[95]

Before Rolland's book about his 1935 trip to the USSR was published, the author expressed his admiration for Stalin and Stalinism in an essay "Retour de Moscou," which appeared in the October issue of *Commune*. The status of Rolland as the supreme cultural friend and defender of the Soviets in the West was thus cemented. By November 1937, the number of copies of Rolland's works published in the Soviet Union reached 1.3 million.[96]

A Sudden Awakening

Although Rolland did not take part in the Paris Congress, the Soviet authorities had good reasons to be satisfied with his visit in June and July 1935. So when a year later André Gide arrived at the Soviet capital, they hoped for similar results. Gide was at the pinnacle of his fame and presented a great asset for Soviet propaganda. His support for communism was grounded in a typical antibourgeois rebellion and fed additionally by his personal revolt against his own bourgeois family background. While exposing the hypocrisy of French capitalism and colonialism, Gide almost automatically admired their alleged antithesis—Soviet communism. By the mid-1930s, Gide became one of the most prominent spokesmen for the Stalinist version of antifascism. He was involved in international campaigns on behalf of communists arrested by Hitler's regime—including Ernst Thälmann and Georgi Dimitrov. He sat on numerous antifascist and pro-Stalinist committees and boards. In 1935, he published *The Vatican Cellars* in the communist *L'Humanité*. Gide's role in organizing the Paris Congress additionally emphasized his position as Stalin's leading apologist, so that Mikhail Koltsov recommended him to Stalin as the next high-profile guest.

The Soviet handlers treated Gide in Russia to a similar set of impressions and incentives as they did Rolland a year earlier. Before his departure for Russia, Gide learned from the Soviet press that four hundred thousand copies of his works sold in a few months in the USSR.[97] Upon his arrival, he was informed that three hundred thousand postcards with his portrait appeared in the "Homeland of the Proletariat." He was lavished with luxury and flattery and surrounded by attentive translators, guides, and servants. Gide met Soviet literati and cultural dignitaries as well as "ordinary Soviet people" enamored of his writing. The only notable difference between him and Rolland was that he was not received by Stalin. Just after Gide's arrival, on June 18, 1936, Gorky died. His funeral was a great celebration. Stalin and Molotov carried the coffin. Gide was asked by Mikhail Koltsov to deliver a eulogy. He obliged.

But the Soviet techniques of seduction that had worked so well for scores of Western celebrities failed to make the right impression on Gide. Instead, they backfired. Unlike so many foreign luminaries duped by Soviet propaganda, or at least pretending not to notice the charades played around them, Gide balked. "The immense privileges that I was offered amazed and terrified me and I was afraid of being seduced and corrupted," he reminisced later on.[98] He left Russia not just unimpressed by the Soviet "new civilization" but disgusted by it. Moreover, unlike many other cultural celebrities, he did not leave this feeling to himself but expressed it loud and clear in his short book *Retour de l'U.R.S.S.* (Return from the USSR), published by Gallimard very soon after his return.[99] Describing his Soviet impressions, he came to conclusions quite unmentionable in the cultural circles to which he belonged at the time: the essence of life in communism was the absence of freedom. Like another French traveler to Russia a hundred years earlier, the Marquis de Custine, Gide described life in the USSR as symptomatic of a society terrorized, enslaved, and deceived. He wrote: "What is demanded now is resignation and conformism. What is expected and required is approval for everything that is happening in the USSR; what they want to effect is for this approval to be not reluctant but sincere, even enthusiastic. The most surprising thing is that this is actually achieved. At the same time, the tiniest protest, the smallest criticism, is punishable with the most severe penalty and immediately silenced. And I doubt whether in any other country, including Hitler's Germany, the spirit is less free, more humiliated, scared (terrorized) and enslaved."[100]

Retour de l'U.R.S.S. was a sensation. It sold between one hundred and two hundred thousand copies in two months. Within a year, it was reprinted ten times and translated into fourteen languages. For the Soviet authorities and their Western supporters, it was an act of treason. Louis Aragon insinuated in *Commune* that Gide's book was linked with a propaganda campaign conducted by the Nazis.[101] Romain Rolland launched an attack in *L'Humanité*: "This bad book is in fact a mediocre book, an incredibly trivial, superficial and immature book full of contradictions. If the book has created a considerable stir, it is definitely not because of its worth—it is worthless—but because of the rumors that surround Gide's name and the exploitation of his fame by the enemies of the USSR, always on the lookout and ready to use any weapon against it that falls into their malicious hands."[102] In comparison to a number of books published at that time by fugitives from the USSR and serious critics of communism—for instance Boris Souvarine's *Staline*—Gide's account seems quite superficial and at times naive. But it was the latter that caused a worldwide response while the former were hardly even noticed outside their niche audiences. The reason was simple: *Retour de l'U.R.S.S.* was written by a literary star.

Gide had the courage to step outside a convenient set of clichés obscuring the view of the Soviet regime and to speak out about it at a time when such talk was virtually inadmissible in his milieu. He did not back down while being attacked for destroying the antifascists' unity in the face of the Spanish Civil War. Instead, he read testimonies of Soviet fugitives and personally talked with some of them. In response to his critics, he published in 1937 *Les retouches à mon Retour de l'U.R.S.S.* (Afterthoughts on the USSR, 1938), in which he wrote about Stalin's victims: "I see these victims, I hear them, I feel them all around me. Last night their stifled cries awoke me; today their silence dictates these lines. No one is intervening in *their* favor. All the right-wing journalists use them, moreover, to stir up the regime they execrate; those who hold dear the idea of justice and liberty, those defending Thälmann, the Barbusses, the Romain Rollands, have said nothing, are saying nothing; and around them the immense proletarian crowd is blinded."[103] Addressing his fellow writers, Gide asked: "Comrades, confess that you are beginning to get uneasy; and you ask ourselves with increasing anxiety in the face of the Moscow trials, for instance, 'To what lengths shall we have to carry our approval?' Sooner or later, your eyes will be obliged to open. Then you will ask yourselves—you, the honest ones—'How could we have kept them shut so long?"[104]

In a very roundabout way, *Retour de l'U.R.S.S.* became an important book for the Russian intelligentsia under Stalin. It was denounced and banned in the Soviet Union, of course, and perhaps no one there, with the exception of a few literary apparatchiks entrusted with foreign relations, read it at the time. Nevertheless, its very existence was sometimes seen there as a sign of hope that not everyone in the world turned a blind eye to the human fate under communism. In the years 1939–1941, when new prisoners were coming to the Gulag from the recently conquered territories of Poland, some incarcerated Russian intellectuals began asking them whether they knew the famous book by André Gide—and if they did, then could they tell them about it? Gustaw Herling recalled: "A young medical student from Leningrad, with a girlish face . . . once, in the latrine, asked me in a whisper if I had read Gide's *Retour de l'U.R.S.S.*, for judging by the articles in the Soviet Press it must be a very interesting book."[105]

5

Stalin Presents

Calculated Pandemonium

Despite some glitches, the Soviet authorities had good reasons to be satisfied with the results of the propaganda campaign covering up their crimes and abuses of power in the early and mid-1930s. All in all, Western opinion-making elites turned out to constitute quite receptive audiences for the Stalinist spectacle of the *perekovka* and the "new civilization." In the second half of the decade, however, this spectacle was transformed into something even bolder and more challenging. The Soviet masters of deception took their art into a new dimension. The traditional principles of stage realism, based on the effect of verisimilitude, became less and less constricting. The poetics of Stalin's great performance became increasingly surreal.

In the period 1936–1938, Soviet society was overcome by a devastating wave of arrests, incarcerations, executions, and deportations, which passed into history as the Great Terror. In its peak period of 1937–1938, the NKVD arrested 1,575,000 people and executed 681,692 of them—according to its official record.[1] Estimates of the real numbers tend to be higher, around 750,000.[2] If we take the 470 days of the most intensive terror and divide the official number of victims by the number of days, we will get the number of 1,450 people shot every single day. This means, one human being was killed every minute, day and night, for fifteen months and twelve days.[3] At the same time, the Gulag overflowed with new prisoners. Back in January of 1934, just after the White Sea Canal had been built, the system had 510,307 inmates. By January 1, 1938, the numbers had grown to 1,881,570.[4] These figures did not account for people deported to labor colonies instead of regular camps. Neither did they include persons who died of hunger, exposure, violence, and exhaustion in the forced labor system or during the months-long transport to and between prisons and camps. For comparison, the number of prisoners in Nazi concentration camps in the same year reached about twenty thousand. Before the Holocaust set new records for mass murder, the NKVD executioners were certainly the world's most prolific killers. For example, between August 8, 1937 and October 19, 1938, in Butovo outside Moscow, one of many killing fields, a team of just twelve NKVD men managed to shoot 20,761 people. In the same period, the total number of death sentences in Nazi Germany amounted to 267.[5]

Until recently, the Great Terror was customarily viewed as Stalin's paranoid purge of real and imagined communist rivals, which spilled over into the rest of society. Survivors who tried to describe it later were mostly members of the educated classes, many of whom once belonged to the communist establishment. For many of them, the Great Terror was shocking because of its seemingly random and unexpected nature. In reality, the Great Terror, as random as it might have seemed to many victims and witnesses, was the result of Stalin's careful calculations and deliberate policies. Its lethal edge targeted specific categories of Soviet people, among whom neither communists nor members of the intelligentsia were the most prominent.

For decades, Stalin's specific motives behind the Great Terror were a matter of speculation among Western commentators and historians. After the collapse of Soviet communism, when new sources became available, some historians advanced a convincing explanation of the genesis of the Terror, rooted in Stalin's geopolitical concerns and anxieties. In the mid-1930s, after nonaggression agreements had been signed by Poland and Germany and by Germany and Japan, Stalin suspected these three countries of preparing a joint invasion against the USSR. There were no such plans in reality, but the Soviet leader was aware that each of these countries had single-handedly defeated Russian forces within the recent thirty years (Japan in 1905, Germany in World War I, and Poland in 1920). He was especially anxious that a joint invasion might be supported by internal uprisings and conspiracies against his regime—just as the Bolshevik conspiracy in 1917, supported by Germany, internally toppled the Russian government. He became determined to identify his potential internal enemies and to destroy them by a series of preemptive strikes.[6]

The list of suspects included Stalin's former opponents in the party, the military, the political police, and the rest of the Soviet power structure—starting with those people who could be linked to Trotsky or at least suspected of such sympathies. Ultimately, Stalin targeted all the members of the Soviet elites whom he did not trust. The further he went, the more distrustful he became.

The largest categories of suspects, however, were the *kulaks* and select ethnic minorities. The *kulaks* had already been "liquidated as a class" during collectivization, but many of them were still alive, often in penal labor colonies to which they had been deported. Stalin must have had no doubts that these peasants hated him for what he had done to them and their families. So he seemed to suspect that, in case of war, they (as well as their friends and relatives) might rebel against his power and support his foreign enemies and domestic rivals. In order to prevent this, he decided to have them purged.

Lists were compiled on the basis of old NKVD files of *kulak* deportees. To speed up things, quotas were sent from Moscow to local NKVD offices specifying how many arrests were expected to be made, how many people should be killed, and how many sent to the Gulag. The local officials and NKVD chiefs, in fear of being perceived as unworthy of Stalin's trust, tended to behave like model Soviet shock workers: they not only fulfilled the plans but also asked for permission to arrest and kill more people. Torture was widely employed in order to extract false admissions of guilt and testimonies incriminating others. On July 21, 1937, torture was formally authorized and encouraged by Stalin as a method of interrogation. Some NKVD officers boasted that they could get anyone to confess to anything.

A key element of the Great Terror that has not been fully accounted for until recently was the fact that Stalin and the NKVD extensively used national categories to choose their victims. 247,157 people were killed on national grounds—for being Polish, Finnish, German, or Latvian. As members of these minorities, they were automatically suspected as foreign spies and conspirators. Among a series of nationalities targeted by the NKVD, the Poles occupied the dominant position. In the "Polish operation," against an imaginary Polish espionage network, the NKVD arrested 143,830 people, 111,091 of whom were shot.[7] Altogether, as Timothy Snyder points out, "as of the end of 1938, the USSR had killed about a thousand times more people on ethnic grounds than had Nazi Germany."[8] The nature of the Great Terror cannot be grasped without noting that of the 681,692 people executed by the NKVD in 1937–1938 on political grounds, the victims of actions against the *kulaks* and select national minorities accounted for 625,483—more than 90 percent.[9] This fact has been overlooked in the West until recently.

An important novelty of the Great Terror, one the West *did* pay a lot of attention to, was that it targeted unprecedented numbers of communists, including many high dignitaries. Suddenly, a high position in the Soviet hierarchy became a source not only of power and prestige but also of daily fear. By late 1937, none of the people in power, including members of the Politburo, could feel entirely safe. The official image of the Soviet regime assumed surreal characteristics. Almost every day, Soviet media surprised the public at home and abroad with sensational revelations about more and more Soviet leaders, revolutionary heroes, and communist activists of all levels who turned out to be Polish, German, and Japanese spies, terrorists, as well as agents of the international bourgeoisie. This stood in stark contradiction to the inner logic of the dominant propaganda of the early 1930s. The *perekovka* claimed that "class enemies" were mostly confused people unaware of what was good for them. *The Aristocrats, Belomor,* and countless reports, articles, and films—foreign and domestic—demonstrated that, thanks to successful reeducation in the Gulag, the "class enemies" were disappearing and turning into conscious and well-adjusted Soviet people. According to the *perekovka* vision, the time was near when there would be no more "class enemies" left.

Instead, a quite contrary vision of Soviet society emerged in the Soviet media of the late 1930s. The enemies not only failed to disappear but suddenly multiplied everywhere. Even worse, they were exposed as hiding in the very heart of the Communist Party. Most of the Bolshevik leaders of the revolution and Civil War, such as Trotsky, Zinoviev, Kamenev, Bukharin, Radek, Pyatakov, Tomsky, Rykov, and others turned out to be enemies of communism. Among the 139 members of the party's Central Committee, 98 were exposed as enemies. Out of the 1,996 delegates to the party's Seventeenth Congress in 1934, 1,108 were convicted as foreign spies and anticommunist agents. Even the leadership of the Red Army turned out to be a nest of enemies: Stalin's people had to shoot three out of five marshals, thirteen out of fifteen army commanders, fifty out of fifty-seven corps commanders, and eight out of nine Red Navy admirals. In this unstable world, only one thing remained certain: the cause of the proletariat had only one defender beyond any suspicion—Stalin himself. Other than that, anything seemed possible.

Nothing Is What It Seems

Many ordinary people in the Soviet Union remembered previous violent campaigns of the Bolshevik regime and therefore were not necessarily astonished by this one. But for most of the communist victims it was a shock. Fate seemed to mock them. They were arrested on false charges and often forced by torture (especially beginning in the summer of 1937) to admit to crimes they had never committed. If they were fortunate enough to avoid execution, in the camps and prisons they encountered hundreds and thousands of other people convicted on similarly absurd charges. In the minds of many communist victims, the sense of order in the universe was seriously challenged.

Eugenia Ginzburg, a lecturer in Marxism-Leninism married to the party leader in Kazan, was arrested in 1937 for allegedly participating in a terrorist Trotskyite conspiracy. She spent eighteen years in prisons, camps, and confined settlement. Later on, she reminisced about her initial efforts to explain her predicament. "A Communist held by the Gestapo—I would have known exactly how to behave. But here? Here I had first to determine who these people were, who kept me imprisoned. Were they fascists in disguise? Or victims of some super-subtle provocation, some fantastic hoax? And how should a Communist behave 'in prison in his own country'?"[10]

In prison in their own country, not all communists lost faith in communism. Many were quite used to thinking about themselves as a separate, enlightened caste of society, and this attitude seemed to help some to save their ideological beliefs and ignore the facts. They typically viewed themselves as victims of an unfortunate mistake while often considering other, noncommunist prisoners to be rightfully punished. Based on this assumption, some of them behaved in prisons and camps like representatives of the regime and viewed their fellow prisoners as enemies.

With time, however, it was difficult for some of these people to avoid noticing that prisons and camps were full of other communists who also claimed to be victims of the same sort of mistake. A troubling question loomed: how many individual mistakes could really have been made? Some communist prisoners tried to solve this puzzle and keep their faith intact by thinking—just like Eugenia Ginzburg in the initial stages of her arrest—that their fate was the result of some "fascist" conspiracy in the political police or Soviet government. Some hoped that as soon as Stalin discovered this conspiracy, he would immediately restore order: the innocent communists would be separated from the real enemies and restored to their former positions of power.

There was also a less optimistic explanation: what if Stalin did know everything and stood behind this assault against the "old Bolsheviks"? To some true believers this could mean only one thing: Stalin was not the legitimate Bolshevik leader but a usurper. Therefore, the old Bolsheviks in Stalin's prisons and camps were, in fact, martyrs of the communist faith. In addition to these principal mental strategies of defending the ideological faith, there was one more. Perhaps, at the current stage, the interest of the party required a sacrifice whose true significance was unknown to the victims. Even though they did not understand the ultimate reasons for their victimization, they had to prove their unconditional loyalty to the party, even if the party demanded a false admission of guilt or false testimony incriminating innocent people. After all, according to Bolshevik class morality, everything that furthered the holy cause of the proletariat was good. And who else, if not the party and its organs (NKVD), knew better what this cause required at a given moment? Such mental strategies not only helped many imprisoned communists to protect their faith but also allowed some to view themselves as being morally in opposition not to their real victimizers, but to noncommunist victims.[11]

Many Bolshevik henchmen and propagandists mentioned in this book became Stalin's victims. Yagoda was arrested in March 1937. He was convicted in a show trial on March 15, 1938, and shot for, among other things, allegedly ordering the assassination of Gorky. Gorky's death in 1936 was probably natural, although Stalin's role in it is still a matter of discussion. Yagoda was replaced by Yezhov who was arrested, in turn, on April 10, 1939, and executed on February 4, 1940. Nikolai Yanson, the head of the special committee that planned the expansion of the Gulag at the end of the 1920s, was shot on June 20, 1938. Vladimir Tolmachev, the member of the committee who was anxious about Western reactions to the radical expansion of forced labor, was killed as well. Olga Kameneva—Lev Kamenev's wife, Trotsky's sister, and the first chief of VOKS back in the 1920s—had, of course, no chance of surviving. Dismissed from her post in 1929, after Trotsky's emigration, she followed her husband's fate as did their two sons (the younger being still a minor). Kameneva's husband was shot in 1936, her sons in 1938 and 1939; her brother was assassinated in Mexico in 1940, and she was killed in 1941.

The current chief of VOKS at the time of the purges, Aleksandr Arosev, did not fare any better. Like many Soviet functionaries who had wide contacts with the outside world, he was arrested as a foreign agent. Being married to a foreigner (his wife, Gertrude Freund, was Czech) only made things worse for him. He was sentenced to death on February 8, 1938, and executed two days later. Some foreigners who lived in the USSR and publicized favorable views of the Soviet regime, followed the same path. One of them was Rev. Julius Hecker, an American (though Russian-born) Methodist Episcopal pastor. Having moved to Soviet Russia with his American wife and daughters, he reportedly gave up his US citizenship and wrote books about religion in the Bolshevik state, including *Religion under the Soviets* (1927), *Moscow Dialogues: Discussions on Red Philosophy* (1933), and *The Communist Answers to the World's Needs* (1935). On a winter night in 1938, the NKVD came for Rev. Hecker. He was shot on April 28, 1938.

The purges did not spare people and institutions glamorized in Soviet propaganda, including the correctional labor commune in Bolshevo. Following Yagoda's arrest, its longtime chief, the NKVD officer Matvei Pogrebinsky, committed suicide. The NKVD arrested more than four hundred people in the Bolshevo commune; many of them were executed, and the showcase commune was closed on January 1, 1939.[12] The same fate was shared by most of the Chekists praised in *Belomor*. As a result, the book had to be banned, withdrawn from libraries, and most of its copies destroyed. Men whose photographs adorned the volume—such as the chief of the Gulag system Matvei Berman and the OGPU bosses of the canal construction, Kogan and Rappoport—were exposed as enemies and did not survive the purges. Neither did many other founders and leaders of the Gulag. Fedor Eikhmans (the former commander of the Solovki) and Eduard Berzin (the head of the Vishera and Kolyma camps) died with bullets in their heads. The men who replaced them did not last long either. Berman's replacement, Izrail Pliner, was executed in the same year as his predecessor. Interestingly enough, Naftali Frenkel, the architect of the system of work quotas and food rations in the camps, belonged to the narrow category of those high officials of the political police who survived the purges. Stalin made sure he was spared.

Many literary eulogists of the Cheka and OGPU followed in the footsteps of their heroes. The NKVD shot the author of *The Red Gospel*, Vasily Knyazev, on November 10, 1937, and Viktor Kin, the author of *On the Other Side*, in December. Aleksandr Tarasov-Rodyonov and Boris Pilnyak were killed in 1938. Some authors of the *Belomor* book shared the fate of their protagonists. Both of Gorky's fellow editors of the book were exposed as enemies of the people. Leopold Averbakh was arrested in April 1937, sentenced to death on June 14, 1937, and executed on August 14, 1939. Semen Firin lost his life when Stalin purged his boss, Berman, and the rest of the OGPU management of the White Sea Canal construction. Bruno Jasienski, who had emigrated from Poland to France and then, from France to the Soviet Union, was arrested and charged with espionage for Poland and France. He received his death sentence on September 17, 1938.

Prince Dmitry Svyatopolk-Mirsky ultimately failed to win the trust of the Soviet authorities. Living abroad for so many years before his return to the Soviet Union made him simply too untrustworthy to be left alone at the time of the frantic search for foreign spies. On January 26, 1937, the main organ of the Soviet Writers' Union, *Literaturnaya Gazeta*—to which Mirsky had frequently contributed his articles—called him a "dirty Wrangelian," referring to Mirsky's White Army service under General Wrangel in the Civil War. This sort of public denunciation often was the prelude to imminent arrest. This happened to Mirsky in the summer of 1937. And so Mirsky inhabited the world of the Gulag, the place he had praised so wholeheartedly four years earlier in *Belomor*. Even though he was found guilty of no specific crime, he was sentenced to eight years in the camps for *suspected* espionage for Great Britain. Had he been convicted for *actual* espionage, his sentence would have most likely been death.[13] According to NKVD documents, Prince Mirsky arrived at the Kolyma camps in September 1937. Unlike the candidates for the reforging described in *Belomor*, however, he was too weak to meet the labor quotas. By February 1939, he was classified as medically unfit for work—in the Gulag slang, he was a *dokhodiaga*, meaning "goner" or "living corpse." His ordeal lasted until June 6, 1939, when he was pronounced dead.[14]

Mikhail Koltsov and Vladimir Kirshon, whom Stalin had entrusted with controlling the public relations damage caused by the Serge affair at the Writers' Congress in Paris, in 1935, experienced a fate worse than Serge's. When Kirshon was shot on July 28, 1938, Koltsov was still viewed by the unsuspecting public as one of Stalin's most trusted men in literature and propaganda. A correspondent for *Pravda* in the Spanish Civil War, Koltsov was an important conductor of the choirs of Western communist propaganda regarding Spain. *L'Humanité* often reprinted his *Pravda* articles. Ernest Hemingway used him as the prototype for the character of Karkov in *For Whom the Bell Tolls*. "Karkov, coming from *Pravda* and in direct communication with Stalin, was at this moment one of the three most important men in Spain," he wrote.[15] The novel's protagonist, Robert Jordan, "had liked Karkov. . . . Karkov was the most intelligent man he had ever met . . . they had become friends."[16] In a conversation with Robert Jordan, Karkov did not fail to make clear references to Stalin's purges. "We detest with horror the duplicity and villainy of the murderous hyenas of Bukharinite wreckers and such dregs of humanity as Zinoviev, Kamenev, Rykov and their henchmen," he said. "We hate and loathe these veritable fiends. . . . Certainly we execute and destroy such veritable fiends and dregs of humanity and the treacherous dogs of generals and the revolting spectacle of admirals unfaithful to their trust."[17]

Stalin's real-life actions were more surprising than Hemingway's fiction. Instead of rewarding Koltsov for his service in Spain, the Soviet dictator had him arrested and tortured. The roles suddenly changed, and now Koltsov was treated in the Soviet press with the same sort of epithets he had used against "enemies of the people" not long before. When *For Whom the Bell Tolls* appeared in the United States in 1940, Koltsov had already been convicted and executed (on February 2) as an agent of German, French, and American intelligence. One of the reasons behind his demise seemed to be Stalin's disappointment with the results of Gide's visit back in 1936. Six days before executing Koltsov, NKVD men shot Isaac Babel, who had also been convicted as a spy. Babel had had the misfortune to be one of the lovers of Evgenia Khayutina, editor of the prominent literary magazine *The USSR Under Construction*. She later married Yezhov. When Yezhov's time came to be arrested and tortured in April 1939, among those he denounced were Khayutina's former lovers, including Babel. Khayutina was already dead at the time; she had committed suicide on November 19, 1938. Vsevolod Meyerhold and his wife Zinaida Reich, the hosts of the memorable parties enjoyed by artists and Chekists alike, did not fare better than Babel and Koltsov. Meyerhold was arrested on June 20, 1939. On July 15, Zinaida Reich was found dying in their apartment with her eyes gouged and seventeen knife wounds. The NKVD tortured Mayerhold for months and finally shot him on February 2, 1940, the same day they shot Koltsov. Two days later, they shot Yezhov himself.

The Art of Swallowing

In the eyes of the Western public, the Great Terror appeared mainly as Stalin's struggle against his opponents inside the Soviet power elite. Three show trials against former Bolshevik dignitaries performed in Moscow in front of foreign journalists and diplomats between the summer of 1936 and spring of 1938 dominated the attention of the West and distracted it from the mass terror all over the country. Western commentators were often puzzled and wondered whether the charges against the defendants in the Moscow trials were indeed legitimate. While many Soviet communists in Stalin's prisons viewed their own fate as the result of some unfortunate mistake, some Western commentators were unwilling to go even that far and believe in such mistakes. Instead, they did their best to trust official Soviet announcements about enemies and spies exposed and brought to justice. Jerome Davis, for instance, reassured his readers that "in the main these trials are genuine and the men guilty."[18]

Many pragmatic Westerners reasoned that no leader of a country, even a brutal dictator, would engage in an unwarranted destruction of his nation's elites. Stalin did much to reinforce this reasoning in the West. The Moscow trials were orchestrated so that the most prominent Bolshevik defendants admitted their guilt before the eyes of the world. In doing so, the defendants were to deny the credibility of their actual and potential defenders abroad. This was quite an audacious scenario. Preparing the first great performance of this sort—the Zinoviev-Kamenev trial in August 1936—Stalin had to take a considerable risk into account. What would happen if some defendants refused to play their parts or played them so unconvincingly that the entire show flopped? Warned by his lieutenants against the risk of unfavorable Western responses, Stalin allegedly said, "Never mind, they'll swallow it."[19] Stalin's reaction was reported in the

West by Walter Krivitsky, a Soviet intelligence officer who defected in 1938. In the following year, Krivitsky's book, *In Stalin's Secret Service*, was serialized in the *Saturday Evening Post* and received much public attention.[20] On February 10, 1941, Krivitsky was found dead in the Bellevue Hotel in Washington, DC, with a fatal gunshot wound in his head and three suicide notes by his bed.[21]

If Stalin's attitude regarding the risks of the show trials was, indeed, as nonchalant as Krivitsky reported, the Soviet leader knew what he was doing. For many years, choirs of foreign admirers had given him ample reasons to feel confident of his capacity to dupe the Western public. Many years later, Robert Conquest commented: "The fact that so many did 'swallow' it was thus certainly a factor in making the whole Purge possible. . . . The trials, in particular, would have carried little weight unless validated by some foreign, and so 'independent,' commentators."[22] The series of high-profile theatrical performances masquerading as court trials took place in the grand column hall of the House of Trade Unions—the same place where George Bernard Shaw had participated in the official celebrations of his seventy-fifth birthday back on July 26, 1931. The show trials started on August 24, 1936, with Zinoviev, Kamenev, and fourteen lesser ex-Bolshevik leaders as the defendants. Everyone, with the single exception of Ivan Smirnov, publicly admitted to conspiring to kill Stalin, bring Trotsky to power, and overthrow the Soviet order. Sixteen death sentences concluded the spectacle. The performance ended, followed by real-life executions.

The second performance took place in January 1937, starring Karl Radek, Georgy Pyatakov, Grigory Sokolnikov, and fourteen others. Four of them, including Radek and Sokolnikov, were spared death sentences and sent to prison instead; the others were shot. (Later, however, in 1939, Stalin changed his mind and ordered the secret killings of Radek and Sokolnikov in prison.)[23] In March 1938 the curtain went up again. This time, Yagoda moved from the director's chair to the defendants' bench, where he was accompanied by Nikolai Bukharin, Aleksei Rykov, and eighteen others. The main prosecutor, Andrei Vyshinsky, declared: "Time will pass. Thistle and grass will grow on the graves of the despicable traitors, covered with eternal contempt of the honest Soviet people, the entire Soviet nation. And above us, above our happy country, our bright sun will shine merrily with its cheerful rays."[24] Vyshinsky's predictions came true, though not entirely: People shot by the NKVD did not have graves.

Many Western apologists for Stalin, well trained in the art of swallowing Soviet propaganda, behaved in a predictable manner—they kept swallowing. In all fairness, for many people who did not experience life under Soviet rule, there was something fundamentally puzzling in the fact that so many former revolutionaries—some of whom had risked their lives for their beliefs in the past—did not even attempt to deny the charges and to make their innocence known to the world. It was hard to believe that they wasted the last opportunity to expose this humiliating charade and instead willingly doomed themselves. Even those observers who did not quite believe in the defendants' guilt often found their behavior difficult to explain. Many Western spectators seemed so puzzled that they did not even try to consider whether the defendants might have been subjected to torture or blackmailed with promises to spare their own and their families' lives. Jerome Davis opined:

> The accused were tried in open court with representatives of the whole world listening in. There was not then and is not now a scintilla of evidence that any of them had been tortured. They knew they were facing death, and yet did not protest innocence although the world would have been prone to believe them. The defendants were ex-revolutionists who had never confessed under the Tsar's regime to save their lives or their families.... It so happens that I was chairman of the Legislative Commission on Jails in the State of Connecticut for many years. I have seen hundreds of criminals who confessed when confronted with overwhelming proof of their guilt.[25]

In Davis's view, things seemed not much different in Moscow than they were in the state of Connecticut. Many other commentators reached similar conclusions. Like Davis, Upton Sinclair found it difficult to imagine that Bolsheviks might simply have tortured their victims into admitting guilt: "Over and over I ask myself: Is there any torture, any kind of terror, physical, mental or moral, which would induce them to do such a thing [i.e., to confess uncommitted crimes]?"[26]

Lion Feuchtwanger, who was present at the 1937 trial, commented in his book *Moscow 1937*, published shortly afterward: "I was forced to accept the evidence of my senses, and my doubts melted away as naturally as the salt dissolves in water. It cannot be denied that the most impressive feature of the confessions is their precision and coherence.... If a producer had had to arrange this court scene, years of rehearsal and careful coaching would have been necessary to get the prisoners to correct one another eagerly on small points and to express their emotions with such restraint."[27] Feuchtwanger was an antifascist icon whose credentials went back well before the Nazi takeover in Germany. A German-Jewish literary star, he escaped Nazi persecution and settled in the French Mediterranean resort of Sanary-sur-Mer. His journey to Moscow to witness the January 1937 show trial was an initiative of Mikhail Koltsov, then the chief of the Foreign Commission of the Union of the Soviet Writers. Associated with the fiasco of Gide's 1936 visit, Koltsov seemingly tried to redeem himself in Stalin's eyes by arranging for a high-profile propaganda book on the Moscow trials to be written and published in the West. He chose Feuchtwanger for the author of this prospective book because of his international stature and anti-fascist credentials. As we know, this did not save Koltsov.

According to recently published research in Soviet archives, Feuchtwanger was not duped by what he was shown in Moscow by his handlers. On the contrary, he seemed quite perplexed. His VOKS translator and guide (doubling as a spy), Dora Karavkina, anxiously reported Feuchtwanger's negative comments to her boss, Arosev. "In his opinion, there is no freedom of speech in the USSR," Karavkina wrote about Feuchtwanger on December 14, 1936, shortly after his arrival.[28] The Comintern chairman, Georgi Dimitrov, met Feuchtwanger in Moscow before and after the show trial and noted Feuchtwanger's critical comments in his personal diary: "1. It is incomprehensible why the accused committed such crimes. 2. It is incomprehensible why all the accused are admitting everything, knowing that it will cost them their lives. 3. It is incomprehensible why, apart from the confessions . . . no sort of evidence has been produced. . . . The trial is conducted monstrously."[29] After the first visit with Dimitrov, Feuchtwanger told Karavkina (in full confidentiality, of course) some details of their conversation. Karavkina, in turn, provided her supervisors with a meticulous account of Feuchtwanger's comments. "He told me," she wrote, "about his visit to Dimitrov, who received him at home for dinner. He went there especially in order to discuss the Trotskyite trial. He said that Dimitrov was very nervous in talking about it and took one and a half hours to explain it to him, but 'did not persuade him.' Feuchtwanger then declared to me that this trial is being considered abroad in a very hostile light and that it is seen in the same category as the Reichstag Fire Trial."[30] Reading Karavkina's reports, Aleksandr Arosev probably grew anxious that Feuchtwanger's visit might end with a fiasco just like Gide's. He regularly wrote about his concerns to the three most important men in the USSR at the time—Stalin, Yezhov, and Molotov—asking for instructions. In all likelihood, expecting a disaster, he was trying to dissociate himself from the very idea of inviting Feuchtwanger in the first place and to proactively shift the entire blame on Koltsov.

Both Arosev and Koltsov must have been relieved when Feuchtwanger's book, *Moscow 1937*, appeared shortly after his return from the USSR. As we know, neither of the two men enjoyed this feeling for long, but this was no fault of Feuchtwanger. The German writer delivered exactly what he was expected to deliver. He not only never publicly shared his objections about freedom of speech in the USSR, the veracity of the Moscow Trials, and other controversial topics, but wrote exactly the opposite of what he had been saying privately in Moscow. He passionately defended the trials and informed the world that, at the time of his visit, "the entire city of Moscow felt satisfied, harmonious and even happy."[31]

Ludmila Stern, who examined Russian archival evidence of Feuchtwanger's visit in the USSR, interprets his stunning change of mind as a genuine result of his conversation with Stalin. "Stalin was clearly prepared for his conversation with Feuchtwanger," she writes. "He had been clearly informed about his visitor, his queries and frame of mind: Karavkina's reports, which reached Stalin via Arosev, provided ample material on Feuchtwanger. Feuchtwanger was swayed by Stalin's charisma and was persuaded by his slow but weighty and consistent arguments, which alleviated his previous doubts and which he reproduced in his book. As a theater lover, Feuchtwanger fell under the spell of Stalin's spectacle, and later the spectacle of the trial."[32] This might have been so, but there is another possibility as well: perhaps, just like so many other Western visitors to the USSR, he willfully sacrificed the truth for what he believed to be the politically right thing to say. In the great dichotomy between Hitler and Stalin, he took Stalin's side.

Feuchtwanger's book was published very quickly in the West and had a large print run. Two hundred thousand copies also appeared in the Soviet Union. The author explained, among other things, why the Soviet Union was a democracy in 1937: "Democracy is government by the people, dictatorship is government by an individual. But if this individual represents the people as ideally as is the case with us here, do not democracy and dictatorship become one and the same thing?"[33] Feuchtwanger was repeatedly characterized by his critics as "perhaps the most nauseating of the Western apologists for the Moscow trials." To use John V. Fleming's words, this was "a considerable insult, given the strength of the competition."[34]

One of Feuchtwanger's strongest competitors was undoubtedly the German playwright Bertolt Brecht. He proclaimed: "Even in the opinion of the bitterest enemies of the Soviet Union and her government, the trials have clearly demonstrated the existence of active conspiracies against the regime.... All the scum, domestic and foreign, all the vermin, the professional criminals and informers, found lodging there. The goals of this rabble were identical with the goals of the accused. I am convinced that this is the truth, and I am convinced that it will carry the ring of truth even in Western Europe, even for hostile readers."[35] In 1935, Brecht reportedly said to Sidney Hook about the Soviet communists arrested in preparation for the first Moscow show trial: "As for them, the more innocent they are, the more they deserve to be shot."[36] In 1936, the NKVD arrested Brecht's former mistress and one of his principal actresses, Carola Neher. He responded to this news by saying: "If she has been condemned, there must have been substantial evidence against her."[37] Carola Neher died in the Gulag six years later. In a private conversation with Henry Pachter of the City University of New York, Brecht allegedly explained his lack of moral scruples about cheering for the Soviet jailers and executioners: "Fifty years hence the communists will have forgotten Stalin but I want to be sure that they will still read Brecht. Therefore I cannot separate myself from the Party."[38]

In France, Romain Rolland took the stage to deliver a passionate defense of Stalin's Great Terror. On January 6, 1937, he wrote in *L'Humanité*:

> It is now, when hatred pours from fascism of all stripes, and every kind of rabid reaction is aimed at the USSR—in this hour when the USSR is suffering from treacherous and wild attacks, even from countries of the socialist camp that should be proud to fight alongside the USSR, which seek instead to discredit it out of the fear and envy provoked by its enormous successes and its peaceful conquest of minds throughout the world—it is now that I want to pledge to the Soviet Union my loyalty and my unshakeable attachment to its great people and its leaders.
>
> Dead or alive, I shall always be with the youth and people of the USSR in their ordeals and battles, their joys and pains, in their Herculean labors, cleaning up the quagmire of the ancient world to build a new world on a purified land. I shall also be with them when the final victory unites them with the peoples of the world.[39]

But when the terror hit close to home, and Rolland's personal friends in the USSR became targets, he lost his rhetorical zeal and, indeed, tried to plead for the lives of Aleksandr Arosev and Nikolai Bukharin in agonizing letters to Stalin. He received no response. At the time of the 1938 Moscow trial, Rolland wrote privately to Bloch: "The Moscow trial is excruciating. I don't want to write here about the matter, we'll talk about it." In the same letter, he went on to explain the nature of his discomfort. Just like three years earlier, at the time of the Serge affair, Rolland worried most of all about the reputation of the Soviet Union in the West. "The effects [of the trials] on the whole world, especially France and America, will be disastrous," he wrote. "Wouldn't the best friends of the USSR deem it urgent to send by the quickest possible means a message (a closed message, not to be published) to the Soviet authorities, imploring them to consider the disastrous political consequences—for the Popular Front, for the reconciliation of the socialist and communist parties, for the common defense of Spain—of a sentence condemning the accused to capital punishment?"[40] From this time on, Rolland no longer praised the Bolshevik regime; however, he never criticized Stalin either. One should not forget that his wife's son, Sergei, lived in Moscow. In May 1939, Rolland tried to use his influence in the USSR to secure a permission for Sergei to visit them in France, but Sergei was never allowed to leave the USSR.

Meanwhile, the communist organ *L'Humanité* did its best to legitimize the Moscow trials. On February 8, 1938, Marcel Cachin commented in it on the beginning of the third trial: "And if the crime is proved, and admitted, let no one be surprised by the severity of the judges. . . . The idea instead should be to imitate the vigilance of Soviet judges against saboteurs and traitors to the fatherland. No doubt our Spanish friends understand the implications here."[41] The reference to the "Spanish friends" was an expression of support for the violent action of the Stalinists against the Trotskyists and anarchists (POUM) in Barcelona, in May 1937. When *L'Humanité* ran the article, the leader of the POUM, Andrés Nin, had already been tortured and murdered under the supervision of the NKVD in Madrid, and the show trial of other POUM leaders had yet to take place in Barcelona.

Among many communists locked up by the Stalinists in Spain was Karl Bräuning, a German who fought in the International Brigades. He managed to escape. In December 1939, he wrote about his captivity in a letter to a friend:

> What we lived through in July was horrible and cruel. Dostoevsky's *House of the Dead* is nothing in comparison. . . . And we were so hungry that we were often delirious. I'm half the man I used to be, just skin and bones. We were ill all the time and had no strength left at all. There's no difference between men and animals when you get down to that stage, it's just pure barbarism. Fascism still has a lot to learn from those bandits; it's culture and luxury in comparison. It must have been written in our files that we were literally to be worked to death by legal means, because that's exactly what they tried to do.[42]

When the Spanish Republic fell in the spring of 1939, 3,961 Spanish communists, as well as many other refugees, found political asylum in the Soviet Union. Some of them were taken directly to the Gulag; many others joined them there soon. In Soviet prisons and camps, they met communists from other countries. Stalin's agents proved astonishingly effective in carrying out the purges abroad. True, some foreign communist activists resided in the Soviet Union and did not even have to be lured in. For instance, many German communists had fled Hitler to the safety of the homeland of the world proletariat. One of them, Susanne Leonhard, wrote many years later in her memoir: "From Hitler's Germany, a country in which walls had ears, I escaped to the Soviet

Union, but, in the summer of 1936, the surveillance and the fear of informers were with no doubt worse [there] than they had been in Berlin in 1933–1934. People were afraid of saying a single heretical word. One was paralyzed by fear whenever one caught oneself thinking a heretical thought."[43] Leonhard was deported to the Gulag but survived to tell the tale. Others were not so fortunate. Among those killed were members of the Politburo of the German Communist Party, Heinz Neumann, Hermann Rammele, Fritz Schulte, Herman Schubert; a former secretary of the Central Committee, Leo Flieg; and editors of the party's paper, *Die Rote Fahne*, Heinrich Süsskind and Hugo Eberlein. Similarly, the bloody dictator of the failed Hungarian revolution of 1919, Béla Kun, was shot along with his former commissars. Many foreign communists showed up promptly when summoned to Moscow, seemingly in good faith, thus making themselves available for arrest.

Among all the communist parties abroad, the Polish one was the least trusted by Stalin. Its activists were routinely jailed and executed during the Great Terror either as members of Trotskyite conspiracies or as Polish agents, or both at the same time. Having killed or imprisoned nearly all Polish communist activists available to him, Stalin did not even bother replacing them by people he could trust. Instead, he disbanded the Polish party altogether in 1938. Some of its functionaries, who served prison terms in Poland at the time as Soviet agents and could not come to Moscow when summoned, ended up inadvertently saving their lives.

Some communists, not just inside but also outside the Soviet Union, tried to outdo each other in proving their loyalty to Stalin. Wide streams of accusatory reports, written by Western communists against other Western communists, flowed to Moscow. In one such report, on June 23, 1937, André Marty of the French Communist Party reported to the secretary general of the Comintern in Moscow that the representative of the Comintern in France, Eugenius Fried, was a suspicious character because he had not been arrested thus far by the French police.[44] Killing distrusted foreign communists did not necessarily require their presence in the Soviet Union. For instance, on August 26, 1937, the body of Rudolf Klement, a candidate for chairman of the new Trotskyist International, was found in the River Seine. Three years later, the NKVD finally reached Trotsky, killing him at his home in Mexico.

Among the Western communist activists who cautiously evaded the Soviet trap was Willi Münzenberg, the maestro of the propaganda choirs of Western fellow travelers. In the fall of 1937, Stalin reportedly told the chief of the Comintern, Georgi Dimitrov: "Münzenberg is a Trotskyist. When he arrives, we will arrest him without fail. Try to entice him to come here."[45] But Münzenberg stalled, initially blaming health problems. Instead of reporting to Moscow, he stayed in France. Expelled from the German Communist Party, he publicly announced his break with the communist apparatus but not with communist ideology.[46] Later, in June 1940, after the German invasion of France, he tried to escape to the South of France and then perhaps to North Africa. He failed, and his body was found months later hanging from a tree. The police investigation ruled out a suicide but failed to identify the perpetrators.[47]

In 1937, the number of Western pilgrims to the USSR decreased by 65 percent as the official Soviet paranoia about spies intensified. The authorities became much more selective about their invitations. No Soviet official wanted to be accused of allowing a spy or an enemy into the Soviet Union. All people who came in contact with foreign visitors had reasons to fear arrest. Among the Westerners considered sufficiently trustworthy and important to become official guests in 1937 was Victor Gollancz, one of Münzenberg's key collaborators in the United Kingdom. Gollancz created and ran a network of pro-Soviet propaganda organizations, including the Left Book Club—a publishing series with 44,800 regular subscribers in 1937, a system of 1,500 left-wing discussion groups, and the monthly magazine *Left News*. He arrived in Moscow on April 30, just in time to admire the May Day parade on Red Square. Among many Soviet showcase locations, Gollancz visited the Bolshevo labor colony (then still in operation) and the Moscow-Volga Canal. Little did he know that, just two days before his arrival in the USSR, the chief NKVD commander of the Moscow-Volga Canal construction, Semen Firin, a veteran of the Belomor Canal and Gorky's fellow editor of *Belomor*, had been arrested. Two hundred other NKVD officers working at the canal were arrested in the following days and executed later. Some, like A. Sorokin, acted quickly and managed to kill themselves before arrest. On April 30, an official celebration was organized as the first ship sailed on the new canal. An eyewitness recalled: "The festivities were going on at the canal, the cheerfulness was accompanied by anxiety and fear. The sound of music was mixed with sirens and horns of the vans carrying the victims away."[48] On May 11, while still in the USSR, Gollancz publicly admitted: "For the first time, I have been completely happy . . . while here one can forget the evil in the rest of the world."[49]

Some Western intellectuals were busy inventing rhetorical ways to reconcile their doubts regarding the legitimacy of the Moscow trials on the one hand and their desires to continue supporting Soviet communism on the other. At a party thrown by *The Nation* for André Malraux, the French writer said: "Just as the Inquisition did not affect the fundamental dignity of Christianity, so the Moscow trials have not diminished the fundamental dignity of communism."[50]

Other cultural celebrities were somewhat less hesitant and more blunt. George Bernard Shaw commented: "We cannot afford to give ourselves moral airs when our most enterprising neighbour [meaning the USSR] humanely and judiciously liquidates a handful of exploiters and speculators to make the world safe for honest men."[51]

An American Story

With the Great Depression and Hitler in power in Germany, the Soviet Union's position as an economic and political partner of Western democracies was increasing. Good relations with Stalin were viewed by some Western leaders as a wise political investment. One of these leaders was Franklin Delano Roosevelt. His attitude to the Soviet regime seems to have been reflected in his choices regarding the appointments of the US ambassadors to Moscow. After the official recognition of the Bolshevik regime in 1933, the job went to William Bullitt, a well-known Soviet sympathizer. But during his Moscow tenure, Bullitt was disabused of his earlier dreams and ideas and became deeply critical of the Kremlin. Before his return in 1936, he wrote in an official report to the State Department: "The problem of relations with the Government of the Soviet Union is . . . a subordinate part of the problem presented by communism as a militant faith determined to produce world revolution and the 'liquidation' (that is to say murder) of all non-believers. . . . The final argument of the believing communist is invariably that the battle, murder, and sudden death, all the spies, exiles and firing squads are justified."[52]

Roosevelt did not seem to pay much attention to Bullitt's warnings. In January 1937 his new ambassador, Joseph E. Davies, arrived in Moscow. Davies, a Washington lawyer, was married to Marjorie Merriweather Post, the heiress to a fortune made by her father who created the Postum Cereal Company (later transformed into General Foods). Davies not only made financial contribution to Roosevelt's 1936 reelection campaign but also became its chairman. Although Davies knew next to nothing about Russia, he was keenly aware that his boss in the White House expected him to develop closer relations with the Soviets. Hence he went to considerable lengths to avoid any complications in this area. Soviet-American trade flourished during his ambassadorship; in 1937, the United States sold the Soviet Union goods and services worth $42,892,000, becoming the world's largest exporter to this country.[53]

Just two days after his arrival in Moscow, Davies attended the second show trial. On April 6, 1937, he told American journalists: "A wonderful and stimulating experiment is taking place in the Soviet Union. It is an enormous laboratory in which one of the greatest experiments in the realm of state administration is being accomplished. The Soviet Union is doing wonderful things. The leaders of the Government are an extremely capable, serious, hardworking and powerful group of men and women."[54] Among these "men and women," Davies was particularly impressed by the general prosecutor, Andrei Vyshinsky, whom he watched at the show trial. "The attorney general," he wrote about Vyshinsky later on, "is a man of about sixty and is much like Homer Cummings: calm, dispassionate, intellectual, able and wise. He conducted the treason trial in a manner that won my respect and admiration as a lawyer."[55] As for the trials, Davies reported to Roosevelt that Stalin had exposed "a clear conspiracy against the government" and the defendants' "confessions bore the hallmarks of credibility."[56]

Davies's subordinates in the American embassy, however, had different views. George Kennan, a young second secretary of the embassy at the time, wrote in his memoirs about Davies's service in Moscow: "What mortified us most of all was the impression that the President himself knew nothing about, or cared nothing for, what we had accomplished in building up the embassy in Moscow. . . . Had the President wished to slap us down and mock us for our efforts in the development of Soviet-American relations, he could not have done better than with this appointment."[57] Davies's deputy in Moscow, the experienced career diplomat Loy Henderson, wrote in his memoir that Davies "was much less concerned about the trials, the executions, and the terror than he was at the thought that the purge . . . might mar the picture of Stalin as a benign, idealistic person that he had been trying to paint for the benefit of the president, the Department of State, and the other readers of his reports."[58] The new ambassador's attitude astonished American embassy personnel so much that they even briefly considered submitting a group resignation but did not follow through.

Was it possible that Davies did not comprehend what was really going on in the Soviet Union at the time? This was hardly the case. As early as February 12, 1937, shortly after his presence at the January 1937 show trial, Davies wrote in a letter to his fellow diplomat, William Phillips, the US ambassador in Rome, that the trial was "shockingly horrible."[59] In June 1937, after a trip to London, Davies was reportedly upset by a discovery made by his staff of a listening device above his bedroom in Spaso House—the extravagant Moscow residence of American ambassadors. On July 10, he tried to describe the situation in Moscow in his letter to Sumner Welles, a new undersecretary of state appointed by Roosevelt the same year: "On the face of things everything is quiet. There is nothing unusual on the streets or among the crowds you see, but there are constant rumors, both unverified and authenticated, of prominent people in all sections of life being in prison or liquidated. They seem intent on making men free here even if they have to put every man in prison to do it. It is an extraordinary combination of the strongest, highest altruistic devotion to the purpose of elevating mankind and the proletariat, and the most ruthless, tyrannical cruelty."[60] On October 6, Davies found a way of writing confidentially to Roosevelt himself, bypassing the usual diplomatic channels. "Everything over here is topsy turvy," he confessed. "One could write a brief on the good things they are doing and trying to do, but a dictatorship and a police state brings far more evil than it attempts to cure. Their professed fine purposes are being besmirched by this horrible bloodletting."[61] Many years later, Marjorie Merriweather Post (no longer married to Davies), said in an interview that back in Moscow she was sometimes awakened in the middle of the night by sounds of gunfire. At one such occasion she said to her husband, "I know perfectly well they are executing a lot of those people." Davies reportedly responded, "Oh no, I think it's blasting in the new part of the subway."[62]

Ambassador Davies not only managed to ignore the fates of Soviet people but also remained quite indifferent to the predicament of many Americans trapped in the Soviet Union at the time. Most of the Americans who immigrated to the Soviet Union in the early 1930s in pursuit of a better life did not take long to realize their mistake. In the second half of the decade, they largely shared the destiny of many other foreigners in the "homeland of the world proletariat." Their photographs and cheerful comments about Soviet reality—often featured by Soviet propaganda in early 1930s—were replaced by increasingly frequent reports about new arrests of foreign spies posing as Soviet sympathizers. By this time, most of those Americans anxiously searched for ways to get out of the Soviet Union and return back home, but few succeeded. The gates of the Gulag and the doors of death cells opened for many others.

Many sought help in the American embassy but, more often than not, this help was denied. Some of them had their US passports taken away by Soviet authorities under various pretexts. Usually this was enough for the embassy to turn down their pleas for assistance. On their way out of the embassy and onto the street, they were routinely arrested by NKVD agents. The NKVD did this often in front of the embassy, in full view of American personnel who studiously pretended not to notice anything. As a rule, the embassy personnel did not warn people of the Soviet secret police awaiting them on the street. Such warnings could have put the embassy in an inconvenient position if people refused to leave the premises. The only options left were either to grant them the right of refuge in the embassy or to forcefully remove them. Either option was almost bound to create potential problems. Soon, many Americans living in the Soviet Union were no longer willing to take the risk of visiting their embassy in Moscow. Instead, many of them disappeared quietly into the netherworld of Soviet prisons and camps, while their families and friends in the United States appealed in vain to the American government. Usually no action was taken in Washington, and even when some of these inquiries made it to Davies's embassy, nobody did anything about it there.

In fact, Davies seemed too busy with things other than spending time investigating the fates of American citizens in the Soviet Union. For much of the time, the ambassador could not even be found in the embassy, as he and his wife toured the Soviet Union purchasing Russian art. The Soviets sold large amounts of old Russian artwork in return for hard currency. Of course, most of the artifacts—icons, porcelains, silver, textiles, etc.—had been confiscated by the Bolsheviks from their owners. Some were purchased at very low prices by the state monopoly and resold with high profit. In this way, Mr. and Mrs. Davies created their famous Russian art collection exhibited today at the Hillwood Estate in Washington, DC. When the Davieses did not buy art, they sailed the Baltic on their boat the "Sea Cloud"—reportedly the largest private yacht in the world.

Joseph E. Davies was proud of his service as US ambassador to the Soviet Union. Before his 1938 departure from Moscow, Stalin surprised him by inviting him for an unexpected personal meeting, shaking his hand and thanking him for his cooperation. The Soviet dictator also gave Davies his autographed photograph, which Davies later kept on his fireplace mantle and told his guests about having once talked with this great man. In his later reminiscences, he described Stalin in touching detail. "His brown eye is exceedingly wise and gentle," he wrote about the world's most accomplished mass murderer before Hitler. "A child would like to sit on his lap and a dog would sidle up to him."[63]

The predicament of many Americans trapped in the USSR did not change dramatically after Davies's departure from his post in Moscow. In 1948, for instance, the Soviets arrested Alexander Dolgun, an employee of the US embassy. Dolgun had lived in the USSR since 1933, when his parents arrived in this country in search of work. Like many other Americans, Dolgun's father found a job assembling Fords in Moscow. When Soviet secret police agents forced Dolgun into their car, he protested: "What is it all about? Don't you know you are dealing with a citizen of the United States of America?" When they arrived at the Lubyanka prison, the investigating officer laughed: "Fuck your embassy. That's all you are going to hear from them. That's the end of it. That's all they are good for. You are going to be here for the rest of your life, do you understand that?"[64] This prediction turned out almost correct. Luckily for Dolgun, Stalin's death resulted in the early release of the American from the Gulag in 1956—but he could not return to America until 1971.

The Banality of the Unthinkable

By and large Stalin was right if he expected the West to "swallow" his official version of the show trials. Robert Conquest commented: "In fact, those who 'swallowed' the trials can hardly be acquitted of a certain degree of complicity in the continuation and exacerbation of the torture and execution of innocent men."[65] But for some Westerners the Great Terror and the show trials in Moscow caused an awakening. It was, in fact, not very difficult for an attentive public to expose some tricks used by the prosecutors, who sometimes referred to defendants' secret meetings with foreign agents in nonexistent hotels and to similar "evidence." While many Western visitors in Moscow tried to justify the trials, others tried to expose the charade. A journalist of the Austrian *Neue Freie Presse*, who attended the 1937 trial—the same at which Ambassador Davies and Lion Feuchtwanger were present—reported: "No analogy from modern European history is aroused in western brains when hearing of this deathly tragedy of marionettes. It is necessary to go far back, to the Middle Ages, if one wants to find a similar fervent longing for execution, a similar tired 'only quickly, only quickly the end.'"[66]

The people most knowledgeable about these charades were communists themselves. Among them, Trotskyists played a key role in exposing Stalin's fraud in the West. The enmity between Stalinists and Trotskyists divided Western communists more than ever before. James T. Farrell noted: "There is now a line of blood drawn between the supporters of Stalin and those of Trotsky, and that line of blood appears like an impassable river."[67] Trotskyism became an attractive choice for those who could not deny Stalin's crimes on the one hand but did not want to lose their faith in communism on the other.

Following the first Moscow show trial in 1936, the American Committee for the Defense of Leon Trotsky was established. It brought together a number of intellectual celebrities, including John Dos Passos, Franz Boas, Reinhold Niebuhr, Edmund Wilson, Sidney Hook, and others. The committee organized its own investigation into the charges against Trotsky in order to exonerate him. They decided to question Trotsky and thus give him an opportunity to publicly respond to the accusations presented by the Kremlin. To carry out this task, a special Commission of Inquiry into the Charges Made against Leon Trotsky was created, headed by John Dewey. John Finerty—a renowned lawyer who earned his fame on the left defending Sacco and Vanzetti in 1927—was the commission's chief legal counsel. As for Dewey, he had been one of the most celebrated Western intellectuals in the Soviet Union, on par with such Soviet favorites as Romain Rolland. But his Soviet fame ended definitively as Dewey's commission conducted a series of interviews with Trotsky in Mexico in order to publish the conclusions in a book whose title explained all: *Not Guilty*.[68] While the commission managed to expose some blatant lies presented at the trials, Trotsky used this opportunity to reinforce his image as a pure communist idealist opposed to Stalin's abuse of the cause. On February 9, 1937, he stated in his public address to the commission: "The Moscow trials are perpetrated under the banner of socialism. We will not concede this banner to the masters of falsehood! If our generation happens to be too weak to establish socialism over the earth, we will hand the spotless banner down to our children.... Neither threats nor persecutions nor violations can stop us!"[69]

The Stalinists counterattacked. In March, *Soviet Russia Today* published "An Open Letter to American Liberals," signed by eighty-eight American writers, artists, journalists, social activists, professors, and other intellectuals. The authors stated: "The demand for an investigation of trials carried on under the legally constituted judicial system of the Soviet Government can only be interpreted as political intervention in the internal affairs of the Soviet Union with hostile intent."[70] The list of signatories included Theodore Dreiser, Granville Hicks, Corliss Lamont, Malcolm Cowley, Jerome Davis, Louis Fischer, Lillian Hellman, Max Lerner, Robert Morss Lovett, Col. Raymond Robins, Henry Roth, Maxwell Stewart, Anna Louise Strong, Nathaniel West, and others. It is safe to say that none of them would have ever described the Nazi persecution of German communists as an internal affair of Germany.

In their stand against Stalin's show trials, the Trotskyists, in fact, found themselves on the same side of the fence as anticommunists. In France, the Stalinist propaganda paper, *L'Humanité*, was confronted by the Trotskyists as well as by the conservative *Figaro littéraire*. On July 1, 1937, Boris Souvarine commented in this paper:

In France and everywhere else there are millions of people who are in Stalin's pocket. The editors of *L'Humanité* are identical with the men at *Pravda* when it comes to flattery and sycophancy, and they don't have the excuse that a totalitarian dictator is breathing down their necks. When an academician like Komarov demeans himself in Red Square yet again by asking for more blood, one must bear in mind that if he had not done so, he would have been effectively committing suicide. And with that in mind, what are we to make of men like Romain Rolland, Langevin, and Malraux, who admire and actively support the so-called Soviet regime with its "culture" and "justice," and who aren't forced to do so by hunger or torture?[71]

Interestingly enough, some noncommunist and anticommunist commentators in the West managed to find ways of viewing the Great Terror as a constructive phenomenon. *Le Temps* opined in an editorial on July 27, 1936, before the first Moscow trial started: "The Russian revolution has now entered its Thermidor period. Stalin has understood the impracticality of pure Marxist ideology and the myth of the universal revolution. As a good socialist, but above all as a true patriot, he is aware of the dangers posed to the country by both ideology and myth. His dream is probably a sort of enlightened dictatorship, a paternalism very far from capitalism, but equally distant from the chimera of Communism."[72] This and other Western comments at the time reflected a tendency to understand the Great Terror as a victory of Stalin's moderate pragmatism over the radicalism of the "old Bolsheviks" like Trotsky. Familiar-sounding terms referring to the French Revolution, such as "Thermidor," gave some commentators and their readers an illusory impression of understanding the Soviet phenomena better than they actually did. Other historic references were in use too. When the verdict of the second Moscow trial was announced on January 30, 1937, *L'Écho de Paris* commented: "That Georgian lowbrow has unwittingly joined the ranks of Ivan the Terrible, Peter the Great, and Catherine II. The people he is eliminating are the revolutionaries who have remained faithful to their diabolical cause, madmen filled with a permanent will to destroy."[73]

This sort of thinking stemmed from the fact that, in the eyes of the West, the Great Terror was largely reduced to the show trials and the purges of the Soviet elites. For a long time hardly anyone in the West noticed that the years 1936–1938 brought about a tragedy of the entire Soviet people, especially the Russian peasants and ethnic minorities. Nicolas Werth commented on it in *The Black Book of Communism*:

> As huge, stage-managed events, the trials in Moscow were also a highly effective tactic to deflect the attention of fascinated foreign observers from events that were going on elsewhere, especially the massive repressions against all social categories. For these observers, who had already kept silent about dekulakization, the famine, and the development of the camp system, the events of 1936–1938 were no more than the last act in the political fight that for more than ten years had seen Stalin pitted against his principal rivals. This was the end of the power struggle between the Stalinist "Thermidor" bureaucracy and the Leninist old guard, which had always remained faithful to its revolutionary promises.[74]

This selective view of the Great Terror was reinforced later on, during Khrushchev's thaw following Stalin's death, and dominated Western public discourse until a new picture began emerging slowly, and not without difficulties, after the collapse of Soviet communism.[75]

Under Nazi Eyes

An important key to understanding the Western reluctance to admit Soviet crimes in the 1930s can be found by examining the Nazi views on this topic. The truth is that hardly anyone in the West was more committed at the time to exposing and publicizing Stalin's crimes than the Nazis. Anticommunism was a core element of Nazi ideology, and Hitler's followers were prone to viewing all public exposure of Bolshevik evildoing as evidence supporting Nazi ideas about communism. But while Nazi anticommunist propaganda seemed considerably successful inside Hitler's Germany, its efforts to exploit Soviet crimes in order to mobilize support of the rest of the Western world turned out to be not only largely ineffective but outright counterproductive. By morally condemning the Bolshevik evil, Nazi propaganda almost inevitably revealed its own hypocrisy: a regime famous for using criminal methods in pursuit of political goals was criticizing another regime for doing just that. In effect, instead of persuading the world, Nazi exposures of Stalin's crimes severely undermined many genuine witnesses to these crimes in Western eyes. The Nazis, in fact, made it much easier for many Westerners to dismiss the credibility of these witnesses by associating them with Hitler's anticommunist propaganda campaigns. Even some of those who believed the testimonies of Soviet survivors and defectors nevertheless felt compelled to see them as potentially useful for the Nazis and therefore hard to support publicly.

When viewed in their dynamic historical context, the Nazi attitudes toward communism were, in fact, more complex than popular contemporary narrative would suggest. In the initial stages of the National Socialist movement, in the early 1920s, German sympathies and antipathies toward the Bolsheviks were motivated by factors considerably different than in the rest of Europe. In the Weimar Republic, pro-Soviet attitudes could be found on the nationalist right as well as on the communist left. As noted earlier in this book, important circles of right-wing German nationalists were eager to cooperate with the Bolsheviks in order to challenge and overturn the new European geopolitical order built on the Treaty of Versailles. The Nazis were initially split on how to view the Bolshevik regime in Russia. On the one hand, such National Socialist leaders as Joseph Goebbels and the Strasser brothers advocated some degree of collaboration with the Soviets. Their positive attitude to the Bolsheviks went even further than the geopolitical calculations of many conservative nationalists. They were, in fact, quite impressed with the Bolsheviks' successful coup d'état and their ruthless effectiveness in creating a socialist dictatorship. Goebbels wrote in 1925: "We look towards Russia because it is the country most likely to take with us the road to socialism. Because Russia is an ally which nature has given us against the devilish temptation and corruption of the West."[76] The antibourgeois character of the Soviet regime inspired quite a few right-wing radicals and some Nazi rank and file in 1920s. At the time when Hitler served his prison term after the failed putsch of 1923, some Nazis expressed interest in working together with the communists. They even found communists in Bavaria who responded with eagerness: "You hang the Jews, we'll hang the other capitalists."[77]

On the other hand, the Nazi movement had a strong anti-Bolshevik component championed by, among others, two Baltic German émigrés from Russia, Max Erwin von Scheubner-Richter and Alfred Rosenberg. Scheubner-Richter was killed as he stood next to Hitler during the 1923 putsch, but Rosenberg went on to write books and pamphlets and to become one of the chief ideologues of the Nazi Party. He was born and raised in Reval (Tallinn as of 1918), a predominantly German-speaking city in the Russian Empire. He witnessed the two Russian revolutions of 1917 in Moscow. In 1918, when the Germans occupied the western territories of the former Russian Empire, he volunteered for the German army but was turned down not only for being a Russian citizen but also for being unable to name any references in Germany. Nevertheless, in November 1918 Rosenberg emigrated to Germany and soon joined the Nazi Party. His views on Soviet communism were not far removed from those of some ultranationalist right-wing circles among recent Russian émigrés, particularly those of the Black Hundred.[78] Inspired by such writings as *The Protocols of the Elders of Zion*, Rosenberg viewed Bolshevism as nothing other than a mask for the international Jewish conspiracy. This conspiracy, according to him, not only imposed its rule in Russia but intended to take over the world.[79]

Rosenberg and Scheubner-Richter influenced Hitler's thinking about communism much more profoundly than Goebbels and the Strasser brothers ever did.[80] Just like Rosenberg, Hitler ostensibly believed that communism was a tool of the global Jewish conspiracy. He also considered the Russians and other Slavs to be essentially inferior people (*Untermenschen*)—incapable of either governing themselves or contributing to world civilization. Hitler's ideological vision was focused on the task of creating a new living space (*Lebensraum*) for the German master race in Eastern Europe. In order to accomplish this goal, he planned to defeat the communist (meaning Jewish) masters of the Soviet Union, "solve" once and for all "the Jewish question," dramatically reduce the Slavic population of Russia and Eastern Europe and exploit its remainder as a slave labor force. This racist variation of anticommunism espoused by the Führer prevailed in the Nazi Party and, by the late 1920s, became an intrinsic part of its ideology and politics.

Hitler's rhetoric, especially after his ascent to power in 1933, presented the Bolsheviks as an imminent threat to Germany as well as to the whole of Western civilization.[81] Besides rallying the Germans, he also strove to make the political establishments of England and France believe that Germany was the last line of defense of the West against barbaric Bolshevik hordes poised to invade Europe at an opportune moment. Whether or not Hitler genuinely believed in what he was preaching, a key pragmatic goal of these rhetorical flights in the early 1930s was to convince England and France to revise the Versailles Treaty and allow Germany to rearm.[82]

Although the Nazis were motivated by an anti-Bolshevik ideology, they quietly studied and emulated Bolshevik methods of achieving political goals. Martin Malia commented that like the Italian fascists, the Nazis "adapted the Leninist model . . . to produce their own versions of that great novelty of twentieth-century politics, the one-party state—which is in fact a non-party, mass-mobilization state."[83] Hitler's party faced a task analogous to that of the Bolsheviks, namely the suppression or elimination of the categories of people who stood in the way of their respective utopias. Although the ideological criteria determining who was to be eliminated were, of course, different, many practical problems were quite similar and required similar solutions. The Bolsheviks, who preached class struggle, were committed to liquidating the bourgeoisie, landowners, and *kulaks*, while the Nazis, who professed race warfare, felt compelled to ensure that Jews, Gypsies, Slavs, homosexuals, and mentally or physically handicapped persons no longer threatened the integrity and racial purity of their utopia.

Long before conceiving the Final Solution, the Nazis started by swiftly adopting a series of Bolshevik solutions at home. One of them was the concentration camp. As early as March 13, 1921, Hitler announced in the Nazi organ *Völkischer Beobachter*: "We must stop the Jewish attempts to undermine our nation by locking up their perpetrators safely in concentration camps." Naturally, at that time, Hitler could only refer to one model of a comprehensive, large-scale use of the concentration camps as a method of governing a country: the Soviet model. On December 8, 1921, speaking at Berlin's National Club, Hitler declared his readiness to create concentration camps as soon as he took power in Germany.[84] And indeed, soon after the Nazi ascent to power, the first such camp was opened in Dachau, to be followed by others. Moreover, a new regulation was issued authorizing the Gestapo to send people to concentration camps without formal court sentences. These solutions clearly reflected Soviet models.

By the early 1930s, Goebbels had changed his views about Soviet Russia. Following the party line, he abandoned his early musings about a possible alliance with the Bolsheviks and became the leader of a new Nazi anticommunist propaganda campaign. In 1933, with the Nazi Party in power, Goebbels's Ministry of Propaganda and Popular Enlightenment inspired the foundation of a new institution for coordinating these propaganda efforts, the Gesamtverband Deutscher antikommunistischer Vereinigungen (Coalition of German Anti-Communist Associations), better known as the Anti-Comintern. In 1934, the publishing house Nibelungen Verlag was established to serve this propaganda and soon an exhibit "Bolshevism without a Mask" opened, first in Munich and then moved permanently to Berlin. In 1936, the journal *Contra-Comintern* was founded. Goebbels not only organized this impressive propaganda machine but took the center stage in condemning Soviet communism. At the 1935 party rally in Nuremberg, he spoke of Bolshevism as the "challenge of Jewish-led subhumanity against culture as such."[85]

In harmony with Hitler's rhetoric and Rosenberg's theories, Nazi scholars and writers—such as Hermann Fehst, Theodor Adamheit, Niels Närk, Adolf Ehrt, Rudolf Kommos, and, most importantly, Hermann Greife—laid the ideological framework within which Germans and other addressees of Nazi propaganda were supposed to view the Soviet regime.[86] But the Nazi propaganda specialists knew full well that these monographs and essays could be effective only if they were accompanied by factual revelations of Bolshevik evil and firsthand testimonies to the failure of the Soviet experiment. Once again, the Nazis were determined to undermine the Soviets by using Soviet methods. Goebbels personally studied Soviet propaganda techniques and was quite impressed by their persuasive power.[87] This power was largely attributable to their illusion of credibility, which was achieved by Stalin's propagandists with considerable success thanks to the effect of ostensible objectivity demonstrated by its firsthand "eyewitness accounts." Therefore, firsthand accounts of Soviet "achievements" published by Western fellow travelers were systematically contested by Anti-Comintern publications of firsthand accounts by other Westerners (mainly Germans) as well as Soviet escapees and refugees.

Similar to Soviet propaganda, which used multiple authors in order to enhance the effect of objectivity (for example, in *Belomor*), in 1935 Nibelungen Verlag published a collection of firsthand accounts by twenty-five German specialists who worked in the Soviet Union. The book, entitled *Und Du siehst die Sowjets richtig* (And you see the Soviets correctly), which appeared in the same year as the English translation of *Belomor*, took on not only Soviet propaganda but also Western fellow travelers. The Nazi publication emphasized and exposed fake theatrical effects created by the Soviet authorities for foreign visitors.[88] Not surprisingly, the famine of 1933 and the Gulag were given a lot of attention in this book. But just as *Belomor* (especially its original Russian version) could not refrain from ideological preaching, neither did most of the Nazi counterpropaganda. The authors of the collection—some more than others—were eager to contrast the fear and oppression in the USSR with the supposedly happy and relaxed atmosphere of Hitler's Germany.

Other firsthand accounts of Soviet reality published as Nazi propaganda went even further in their ideological commitments. Maria de Smeth, a Dutch woman, was kidnapped by Soviet border guards off the Crimean coast. In the memoir of her Soviet captivity, *Unfreiwillige Reise nach Moskau* (Involuntary journey to Moscow), she did not stop at describing her experience but went on to explain the Bolshevik oppression of Russia as a result of a Jewish conspiracy and to analyze Soviet misery as a result of mixing of the races.[89] Similarly, Ernst Ertl, an Austrian mechanic, attempted to tell the story of his emigration from his unemployment-stricken country to the USSR, but it ended up as a novellike account of the struggles between Jews and non-Jews in Russia.[90]

In many publications of this sort, genuine facts were mixed in various proportions with ideological projections and embellishments. The Anti-Comintern was particularly eager to exploit stories of Russians who were oppressed by the Bolsheviks and managed to get out of the USSR. Petr Nikolaev, a peasant who escaped to Finland, published his memoir, *Bauern unter Hammer und Sichel* (Peasants under hammer and sickle), through Nibelungen Verlag, and so did Maria Kraft, a Russian German who was allowed to leave the USSR after she married a foreigner.[91] The Nazi propaganda machine also published memoirs by two former Soviet military pilots dismissed from the military service and reassigned to civil aviation, Vladimir Unishevsky and Georg Kravetz. They flew over the Soviet border, to Estonia and Latvia respectively.[92]

Interestingly enough, the most popular firsthand account of Soviet life published by the Anti-Comintern was one least ostensibly committed to the Nazi ideology. Karl Albrecht's *Der verratene Sozialismus* (Socialism betrayed), published in 1938, was reprinted ten times and sold close to one hundred thousand copies before the summer of 1939.[93] Albrecht was a German communist who emigrated to the USSR in 1924 to become a high-ranking Soviet official. He occupied the post of deputy commissar for forestry in the Soviet government when he was arrested in 1932. Forestry was a part of the Soviet economy particularly dependent on slave labor and Albrecht's memoir presented a damaging exposure of the role played by the Gulag in Stalin's modernization effort. He also provided disturbing accounts of Western visitors willfully succumbing to Soviet propaganda. The main theme of Albrecht's critique of Bolshevism was, however, not the well-known Nazi idea of the Jewish conspiracy or the racial inferiority of the Russian people, but the allegation that the Soviet regime betrayed the ideals of socialism. While condemning both Stalin and Trotsky, Albrecht still praised Lenin in his book. Moreover, he praised such German communists and enemies of Nazism as Max Hoelz and Clara Zetkin, both of whom had left Germany for Soviet Russia. Albrecht described the death of Hoelz in 1933 as a murder by OGPU agents and discussed Zetkin's isolation in Moscow before her death the same year. Albrecht himself was sentenced to death by the Soviets. He survived a mock execution before being allowed to leave for Nazi Germany. The Gestapo arrested him on arrival, but he was soon released. One may assume that the Nazis decided that his book about the USSR would be more useful than his imprisonment or death. "As long as I have the strength, I will commit my future work to this one struggle: against Moscow—for socialism," he wrote in the closing paragraph of his book.[94]

The publication of Albrecht's book by Nibelungen Verlag, despite the virtual absence of a clear Nazi ideological agenda, shows that Goebbels's propaganda machine was capable of being more flexible, and perhaps more cunning, than it is usually credited with. In fact, this was not the only account of this type coming out of the Anti-Comintern. Nazi propaganda was vitally interested in publicizing accounts of former communists disenchanted with the Soviet regime. Maria Reese was another such case. This former communist deputy to the Reichstag in the Weimar Republic, and a friend of Clara Zetkin, emigrated from Nazi Germany in 1933 but returned disappointed with communism in 1935. Her memoir, *Abrechnung mit Moskau* (The Reckoning with Moscow), came out from Nibelungen Verlag in 1938.

As the books by Reese and Albrecht suggest, Nazi propaganda experts must have valued this kind of story for helping their cause despite (or perhaps because of) the virtual lack in them of direct Nazi proclamations. The wide success of positive accounts about Soviet life by seemingly nonpartisan fellow travelers might have provided a model for this approach. Alexander Baumeister's *Das endlose Gefängnis* (The endless prison), published in 1936, was similar to Albrecht's and Reese's accounts in this respect. Its focus was not, however, on a communist's disappointment with Soviet communism. Baumeister told the story of Georgy Kitchin, the Finnish businessman who spent four years in the

Gulag before being allowed to return to Finland.[95] In 1935, Kitchin published his own memoir regarding his Gulag experience in English. Both renditions of his story presented quite similar accounts of Soviet forced labor.

Even if Goebbels's propaganda regarding the Soviet Union might have stood a chance of gaining any credibility thanks to its occasional clever avoidance of outright ideological agitation, Nazi public relations specialists made sure this effect was immediately lost—at least in the eyes of people other than Nazi sympathizers. With minor exceptions, the main thrust of the Anti-Comintern campaign was heavy handed and full of blatant lies. "The Great Anti-Bolshevik Exhibition" of 1937 was an example of this approach. Here, some genuine evidence of Stalin's crimes was mixed with Nazi propaganda posters, excerpts from inspirational speeches by Hitler and Goebbels, and all sorts of made-up statistics. The authors explained the roots of the Bolshevik evil in no ambiguous terms. "Bolshevism and Jewry are two words for the same thing," the catalog reads. The intended audiences of this propaganda were not limited to Germans but rather included all of Europe. "Europe should see and recognize the danger of Bolshevism. We will never tire of pointing it out. Without fear, we want to point the finger at the Jew, the instigator, the cause, and the beneficiary of this terrible catastrophe," the explanation went, and a quotation from Goebbels followed: "See, there is the enemy of the world, the destroyer of cultures, the parasite among the peoples, the son of chaos, the incarnation of evil, the ferment of decomposition, the plastic demon of the collapse of humanity."[96]

Having defined the root of Bolshevik evil in such terms, the Nazi propagandists went on to announce: "Peace, however, is Bolshevism's worst enemy, which it must destroy to realize its plans for world domination." Indeed, the Nazi regime presented itself as Europe's greatest champion of peace. "Two worlds meet," the exhibition catalog reads. "Germany is serving all peoples and cultures. Moscow is lighting a torch to set the whole world afire, seeking to build its rule in chaos, a rule that aims to destroy all life through Jewry." To put it briefly, Nazi propaganda offered an almost mirror reversal of the favorite Soviet propaganda paradigm of the time: the black-and-white dichotomy between Stalin and Hitler (one of them being cast as a devilish warmonger and the other as a pure knight of peace). A quote from the Führer accompanied the Nazi exhibition of Bolshevik crimes: "We call on the peoples of the earth to join together against the danger of Bolshevism, if they do not want to fall into the pit of a terrible and unforeseeable fate."[97]

Walter Laqueur summarized the effectiveness of this Nazi propaganda: "In retrospect there is no doubt that the Anti-Comintern helped Stalin more than it harmed him."[98] There were quite a few people in Europe who realized that

Stalin's rule was a deadly tyranny. Publicly demonstrating this conviction and trying to expose Soviet crimes might, however, have seemed much like a positive response to the Nazi ravings and to Hitler's call to "join together against the danger of Bolshevism." To be sure, Hitler did have sympathizers and followers all over Europe and even in America, but by and large not many people outside Germany, especially among Western public-opinion elites, wished to be mistakenly associated with his ideas. Not many wanted their own observations about Soviet communism to be exploited by the Nazis. And, besides, Nazi propaganda almost guaranteed its own demise in the eyes of many of its addressees outside Germany. As Laqueur aptly points out: "Nazism, not to mention its many other abhorred features, believed in the superiority of the German race, and with this basic belief in racial exclusiveness and the inferiority of all other peoples, no genuine international co-operation was possible."[99]

But the indirect effects of Nazi anticommunist propaganda were more peculiar than that. Because of this propaganda, an atmosphere of ambiguity and disbelief surrounded many witnesses and survivors of Soviet oppression who were in no way associated with Nazi ideas and politics. The context often defeated the message. Soviet propaganda used this opportunity to apply the name "fascist" to all statements critical of Stalin. The very topic of Soviet abuses of power appeared to many as controversial and more or less suspect. The Western public discourse of the 1930s was by and large unsuccessful in finding ways of clearing up this ambiguity.

The further into the 1930s, the more absolute the dichotomy between Hitler and Stalin became in the minds of many. By the mid-1930s, the German nationalist ideas of joining forces with the Bolsheviks in order to change the post–World War I order of Europe were suppressed and could be found only in old newspapers, magazines, and books. Some novels from the Weimar Republic, still read in Germany in the 1930s, dreamed about a victorious war fought in the future by a German-Soviet alliance against Poland, the country whose very existence between Germany and Russia was viewed by the imperialists on both sides as a perpetual insult. In a futuristic novel, *Bismarck II: A Novel about the German Future*, written back in 1921, Otto Autenrieth unfolded the bold vision of a great German leader who "attacked [Poland] from Germany and Russia at the head of an enormous army. He subjugated Poland quickly, razed its large cities with bombs, and used hundred-kilometer-long trains to deport all the male population of Poland to concentration camps in eastern Siberia. . . . The Polish nation disappeared from the face of the Earth. One of the most dangerous destroyers of peace in Europe has been pacified for good."[100] Almost ten years later, in 1930, in the novel *Achtung, Hier Deutschland!* published by the

Nazi publishing house Kampf Verlag, a Nazi sympathizer Bert Branden [Herbert Blank] wrote about Germany's future as well, but he subtitled his work *A Contemporary Novel*: "The Reichswehr . . . and a Russian corps first took Poland in pincers. After a brief campaign, in the course of which Warsaw burned down to its foundations, the entire Polish population was deported to Siberia, so that this parasite and destroyer of European peace was finally liquidated, and the territory was divided between Russia and Germany."[101]

For most of the 1930s, when the world was viewed by so many as a future battleground between the two giants, communism and Nazism, this sort of vision no longer evoked anxiety. It seemed nothing more than a distant echo of outdated daydreams. And then came the summer and fall of 1939.

6

A Black-and-White Western

An Autumn Surprise

On September 23, 1939, the inhabitants of Brest-Litovsk were able to witness with their own eyes scenes that only a few months earlier would have been thought a bad dream or absurd joke. Red flags fluttered above the town, some bearing the hammer and sickle, others the swastika. Hitler's and Stalin's troops paraded along the main street, while German and Soviet commanders congratulated one another on their joint victory. Both armies had just achieved the armed conquest of Poland. They thus had completed the first phase of the series of agreements outlined five days later in the secret clauses to the document that has gone down in history as the Ribbentrop-Molotov Pact. The world was still unaware that the countries of Europe, assigned to the "spheres of interest" of either Germany or the USSR on the strength of these secret German-Soviet agreements, were soon to fall in turn to one or other of these allies. In the near future, when Hitler was dealing with Denmark, Norway, Belgium, Holland, France, Greece, and Yugoslavia, Stalin invaded Lithuania, Latvia, Estonia, Romanian Bessarabia, and unsuccessfully tried to conquer Finland.

Meanwhile, *Pravda* in Moscow, which as recently as the summer of 1939 had been fulminating in typical fashion against Hitler's criminal designs, on September 30 joyfully announced that "German-Soviet friendship has been cemented forever." Soviet citizens had learned how to conceal being surprised by anything. During the years of the purges, they had become accustomed to history starting all over again every day and that yesterday's truth in no way had to align with today's. That yesterday's heroes were today's traitors had become quite routine, so why couldn't yesterday's mortal enemy suddenly turn out to be a dear friend? Collective memory in its Soviet version was like a blackboard at school on which a teacher wrote something and then erased it and wrote something else. The trick was to forget yesterday's truth instantly and to learn today's as quickly as possible. There was a high price to pay for getting it wrong.

The Western public had had little training in this kind of thing, however. The alliance between Stalin and Hitler and their attack on Poland had upended the prevailing view of the world in which the two leaders had appeared to the West in mutual black-and-white opposition. For many Western minds informed by this opposition, this was as unimaginable an alliance as one between good and evil, heaven and hell. In the West, Stalin had previously been supported and had been forgiven much, above all because he represented humanity's last hope against Nazism and fascism. For this reason, from the mid-1930s a great many noncommunist parties of the left had worked with Stalin within the framework of the Popular Front. How could this bipolar view of the world be retained in light of the shocking events unleashed in September 1939? How could one continue to support Stalin and not notice the dark side of his rule?

For those harboring such doubts, Soviet propagandists had prepared a new theory, one whose aim was to assuage their agitated minds and consciences. According to it, the USSR's loyal Western supporters needed to realize that Nazi Germany, although ostensibly hostile to communism, was in an "objective" sense its tactical ally, however, because Hitler was the enemy of the world bourgeoisie. Destroying the power of the Western bourgeoisie, which was defended by Great Britain, France, and their ally Poland, in fact cleared the way for communism's future victorious advance.[1] Communist leaders outside the USSR patiently explained to their comrades why they now had to support Hitler. For instance, as Klement Gottwald explained to the communists in Czechoslovakia (which Hitler had already invaded and turned into a Nazi dominion): "We are standing together with German proletariat against Western imperialism and aggression. . . . Our pre-war rallying cries must be changed. Now the slogan of rebuilding Czechoslovakia is a cover for imperialist and anti-Soviet plans."[2] As for Stalin's conquests, it was of course explained to the uninitiated that the newly conquered countries and territories had in fact been liberated, their peoples freed from the bourgeois yoke; they were now welcoming Soviet rule with joy.

As for the most likely reasons for the sudden change in Soviet policy from demonstrative anti-Nazism to an alliance with Hitler, Comintern Head Georgi Dimitrov summarized them in his notes on a meeting with Stalin. Dimitrov took down his boss's statements in the terse language of political fact, without any of the ideological rhetoric that usually adorned Soviet leaders' public statements: "It will be no bad thing if the Germans manage to upset the position of the wealthier capitalist countries (especially England). Hitler, not understanding and not wanting this himself, is upsetting and undermining the capitalist system. . . . We can maneuver and support one side against the other so that they might destroy one another better."[3]

Western communist parties, led for the most part by people devoted to Stalin, supported the new line of their leader in Moscow, although they often had to pay for it with a significant drop in popularity in their own communities. The membership of the Communist Party of the USA, for instance, fell at this time and never recovered its 1937 prominence.

The reaction of the political and opinion-forming élites in the West toward Hitler's and Stalin's joint aggression was not clear-cut. On September 18, the day after Soviet forces entered Poland, the London *Times* criticized the attack. The paper's Helsinki correspondent reported in a dispatch dated September 17: "Today the Soviet Union sent forces across the Polish border to plunge a knife into Poland's back." The writers of an editorial in the same issue of the *Times* treated this act of aggression as the USSR throwing off its mask and showing Stalin's true intentions. The French ambassador in London André-Charles Corbin, in a dispatch to France's prime minister Daladier, summed up the *Times*' position as follows "the ideological backdrop to this conflict has clearly come into focus and . . . the democracies have now found themselves faced with their true enemies: a Hitlerite dictatorship and a communist dictatorship, each one equally dangerous."[4]

For some of those who had earlier been great admirers of Stalin, the pact with Hitler was a dash of cold water, rousing them from a lengthy intellectual stupor. They now joined the company of those whose faith in communism had recently been shaken during the Moscow trials. Victor Gollancz, one of the promulgators of Soviet propaganda in the English-speaking world and someone who had praised Stalin in the dark year of 1937 on the pages of the *Moscow Daily News*, now lost faith in his recent idol. In 1941, he published a collection of articles critical of the Soviet Union, written by people who until recently had been admirers of Stalin, such as Laski or Strachey, as well as known opponents such as Orwell, under the title *The Betrayal of the Left: An Examination and Refutation of Communist Policy*. In this book, Gollancz admitted to his recent manipulations and distortions. He wrote, inter alia: "I accepted manuscripts about Russia, good or bad, because they were "orthodox"; I rejected others, by *bona fide* socialists and honest men, because they were not. . . . I published only books which justified the Trials, and sent the socialist criticism of them elsewhere. . . . I am sure as a man can be—I was sure at the time in my heart—that all this was wrong."[5] Raymond Robins, a long-standing admirer of the land of Soviets and the author of panegyrical conversations with Lenin confessed to being shaken by the Stalin-Hitler pact: "humanity does not deserve to survive."[6]

The reaction of Western governments and public opinion to Stalin's politics was becoming more critical as the Soviet dictator followed one attack with another. On January 1 1940, *Time* magazine announced Stalin as its "Person of the Year," portraying him as a sinister figure. The cover carried a picture of the Soviet despot's mustachioed face, while inside one could read that Stalin "matches himself with Adolf Hitler as the world's most hated man." The USSR was expelled from the League of Nations. The British government, in response to the Soviet attack on Finland, decided to provide the Finns with military aid. The Finnish war began to mobilize Western public opinion against Stalin. Eleanor Roosevelt now expressed publicly her support for the Finns defending their country.

Eleanor's husband, however, reacted somewhat differently. FDR now found himself under pressure both from the US Congress and American public opinion to revise his policy of making concessions to Stalin. Nevertheless, he found a way to continue doing so. Roosevelt hoped that sooner or later war would break out between Stalin and Hitler. Although he tried not to show it, Roosevelt was troubled by the alliance between Stalin and Hitler. Conducting secret discussions with the Soviets through the intermediaries of Acting Secretary of State Sumner Welles and the Soviet ambassador in Washington, Konstantin Umansky (the same man who had until recently been censoring American correspondents' reports from the USSR), he tried to convince Stalin to abandon the alliance with the Germans. When Congress imposed an embargo on Germany after the attack on Poland, Roosevelt managed to save the USSR from a similar embargo. He argued—as Soviet propaganda was later to do when needed—that Stalin's invasion and occupation of eastern Poland was in reality a defensive move, creating a security buffer for the USSR against the Germans.[7]

Roosevelt succeeded not only in maintaining diplomatic relations with the USSR between 1939 and 1941, but trade between the two countries reached a record high during those years. In 1940, when German aircraft using Soviet fuel were attacking Great Britain, the Americans were selling the Soviets goods to the value of $86,943,000. In other words, when compared to 1937, the year the United States became the world's greatest exporter to the USSR, US exports to that country had doubled. At the same time, Soviet Russia was becoming an invaluable source of strategic raw materials for Hitler. Thanks to those supplies, the Germans were able to carry out a number of further conquests in Europe in

1940–41, despite the British economic blockade. During the Soviet-German alliance, on average about two to three hundred trains left the USSR for Germany each month carrying iron ore, chrome and zinc, crude oil, timber, phosphates, platinum, cotton and also, despite the chronic food shortages in the Soviet Union, livestock, and wheat.[8]

As Soviet trains crossed the territory of conquered Poland with their raw materials bound for Germany, they passed trains filled with prisoners going in the opposite direction. These rail "transports" filled with people were headed for Stalin's archipelago of camps and places of exile. There, prisoners from Poland met their companions in misery from the USSR itself, as well as from other countries and territories that had recently been annexed into the great Soviet commonwealth of nations. All of them were meant to build the power of the homeland of the proletariat together.

The Gulag was becoming more international. A Polish prisoner, Marian Czuchnowski, recalled consignments of new slaves arriving at one of the transit camps: "At all times of the day Poles and Russians, Tatars and Chinese, Uzbeks and Ukrainians, Czechs and Spaniards, Hungarians and Sarts, Mordvins and Kazakhs, Belarusians and Jews were shoved into . . . the dirty barber's shop and bath house."[9] Those who had been unable to cope with journeys lasting sometimes for weeks often went straight to the camp hospitals.

> Most of the "transports" were usually dumped on us early in the morning. The corpses were immediately separated from the living and the dying on the square, and they were dragged off by the legs over to the other side to a great flat tarpaulin-covered shed, or if that was full, they were shoved through an open window down a plank into dark underground cellars.
>
> Down there gravediggers were already sorting out the deceased, they stripped the corpses of what was left of their rags, tore their miserable little bundles from their tight fists and made a tall pile of naked bodies, ready to be taken to the cemetery. Trucks drove up to the cellar windows from which, again on a plank, bodies were dragged up and tossed onto the trucks, one on top of the other, tightly and densely, right up to the top. Then spare, slatted side supports were opened up, and the corpses were piled up as high as possible, secured in place with wire, and the whole lot covered with green canvas.
>
> The driver would then speed out of the yard.[10]

The living were herded into slave markets in the great transit camps, where officials from specific camps conducted selections to pick the healthiest and strongest prisoners for themselves. Jerzy Gliksman, the visitor touring the Bolshevo show camp back in 1935, ended up at one of these markets—this time as a slave laborer. This is how he described his second, somewhat different, contact with a camp:

> All day long we were kept in the woods and given neither food nor drink. . . .
> The frost appeared to be increasing and it was impossible to stand still for a single instant. People jumped up and down, beat their hands against their chest and knees, twisting and bending in every direction. In the greyness of approaching evening the scene looked like a gigantic ballet, a grotesque *danse macabre* on a colossal stage. Here and there some dropped to the snow. The guards and officers shouted abuse and ordered the soldiers to remove the sick. They were dragged like logs back to the camp. . . .
>
> All day long I noticed unknown officials, both uniformed and in civilian clothes, wandering among the prisoners, ordering some to remove their *fufaykas*, feeling their arms, their legs, looking over their palms, commanding others to bend over. Sometimes they would order a prisoner to open his mouth and peered at his teeth, like horse traders at a county fair. . . .
>
> This slave market continued the entire day.[11]

In the lands of East Central Europe seized by Stalin, Soviet authorities carried out a program of social change already perfected in the USSR. Beata Obertyńska recalled the start of Soviet rule in Lwów (now Lviv): "They ransacked the house. Immediately upon arrival they carried off the furniture, and poured paraffin all over the books and burnt them on the lawn. An alley of hornbeams was cut down. Now they began chopping down the park."[12] The writer herself, crowded into a freight car with others, was soon on her way under guard to Soviet Asia. The NKVD was getting rid of undesirable social classes posthaste: landowners, moderately wealthy peasants, the bourgeoisie, the middle class, the intelligentsia, the clergy, government and military officials, as well as all "suspicious elements." Whole families were sent into exile, including children and the elderly. By June 22, 1941, in Soviet-annexed Polish territory alone, the NKVD had managed to forcibly repress about a million people—every tenth person living there. At least thirty thousand people had been shot, almost half a million exiled, others conscripted into the Red Army (mainly into work battalions, the *stroybatalyony*) or locked up in the Gulag. It is now calculated that at least a hundred thousand of these people died in the camps and in exile.[13] François Furet summed up that period: "While the Gestapo was establishing its police regime to the west of Poland, [Stalin] began a political purge in his eastern section. Hitler rounded up and ordered the assassination not only of the large Jewish minorities but also of tens of thousands of Poles in the name of anti-Semitic and anti-Slavic racism. Stalin deported and murdered in the name of socialism."[14]

In the winter of 1939–40 Brest-Litovsk was once again the scene of events few people could have previously imagined. On the strength of the secret agreements between Stalin and Hitler, NKVD officials began to round up German and Austrian communists who had sought refuge in the USSR from the Nazis and turn them over to the Gestapo. Stalin had already managed to eliminate a great many of them, but a sizable contingent was still alive in camps and prisons. Among them were Aleksander Weissberg, a Viennese physicist with communist leanings originally from Kraków, and Margarete Buber-Neumann, the wife of a former member of the German Communist Politburo (by then a widow, thanks to Stalin). Both survived to talk about it years later. The train with German communists collected from the Gulag arrived under guard at Brest-Litovsk, and the prisoners were led onto the bridge over the Bug. Here the (recently expanded) Soviet Union ended; on the other side was Nazi Germany with its new colonial possessions. The Gestapo was waiting for the prisoners on the bridge. Margarete Buber-Neumann writes that when the prisoners realized what was happening, two of them refused to cross the frontier. One was a German communist convicted in absentia by a Nazi court, and the other was a Hungarian Jew. The NKVD dragged both of them forcibly over to the other side of the Bug.

Soon, deportations from the conquered territories to the Gulag increased. After four massive operations to deport people from eastern Poland, a fifth was planned. It was to take place during the night of June 27–28, 1941. The NKVD had drawn up lists of people to be arrested, the prison trains' routes had been planned, and space in transit camps prepared. However, the unexpected events of June 22, just five days before the operation was set to commence, thwarted Soviet intentions.

Us and Them

Many people greeted the German invasion of the USSR on June 22, 1941 with relief. The inhabitants of eastern Poland expecting deportation to Siberia must have relaxed, if only for a brief moment. No doubt those in the West who wanted to worship Stalin and preserve their faith in Soviet Russia also felt relief. They no longer had to wrestle with the doubts that the Soviet-Nazi pact had stubbornly raised. After a period of confusion, once again they were easily able to distinguish Soviet light from Nazi darkness. The German attack on Russia was pushing Stalin into the allied embrace of Great Britain and eventually the United States. Churchill was now ready to do anything to make the Third Reich's military machine grind to a halt in Russia. The fulfillment of Churchill's and Roosevelt's hopes now rested on one thing: whether Stalin would succeed in holding off Hitler. Entering into an alliance with Stalin, Churchill was under no illusions as to the nature of the Soviet state or the Bolshevik leader's habits. From the time of the October 1917 coup in Russia, Churchill had been a leader of the anticommunists in the British parliament. He had at first called for armed intervention in Soviet Russia and then had urged isolation for that country. In both cases he had been defeated: both at the hands of bourgeois advocates of increased trade with the USSR and the left-wing supporters of the Soviet regime. He had called the USSR "the sullen, sinister Bolshevik state," as well as "the mortal foe of civilized freedom."[15] During the winter of 1939–1940, he had advocated for military support for Finland in its war with the USSR. His 1941 alliance with Stalin was a temporary political expediency arising from the conviction that Britain's safety at that moment depended on Russia's success against Hitler. Churchill clarified his position in a confidential conversation with his own secretary John Colville: "If Hitler invaded Hell I would make at least a favorable reference to the devil in the House of Commons."[16]

Roosevelt calculated along similar lines: if the USSR was unable to cope with the Germans, the main burden of the war—measured in millions of victims— would eventually fall on the shoulders of the United States. Unlike Churchill, Roosevelt was from the beginning somewhat indifferent to the ideological and moral issues associated with Bolshevism, just as long as the Bolsheviks' revolutionary activities did not directly affect the United States. He believed himself to be a consummate political player, and he consciously saw the source of his greatness in his own pragmatism. In May 1942, he confessed to his friend, the treasury secretary Henry Morgenthau: "You know I am a juggler, and I never let my right hand know what my left hand does. . . . I may be entirely inconsistent, and furthermore I am perfectly willing to mislead and tell untruths if it will help win the war."[17]

Thus the alliance of the Western powers with Stalin was strictly political, dictated by the balance of power in the world. This must have been generally clear to anyone who took the slightest interest in current affairs. The Western public followed Stalin's conquests of 1939–1941 as closely as Hitler's. It was hard not to recall in this context the persistent reports on Stalinist crimes in recent years. The public in Great Britain and the US appeared ready to take on board and accept the strategic reasons for an alliance with Stalin without denying the totalitarian nature of the Stalinist state.

Western leaders took a different approach, however. Instead of clearly presenting the pragmatic nature of their anti-Nazi alliance with Stalin to their electorates, they decided to place their own policies within the context of a black-and-white moral paradigm in which the enemy of evil can only be good. Describing the conflict between Stalin and Hitler in this sort of language required a radical departure from public knowledge. Thus the myth was created of World War II as a battle between absolute good and absolute evil. Within the bipolar domain of this myth, the Western governments could avoid saying aloud that in the battle against one great criminal, the Western world had allied itself with another. The image of the war, championed by the Allies, was meant to be shorn of signs of any kind of moral ambiguity, of all causes of anxiety. It was meant to bring to mind the world of the Western movie genre, where good fights against evil in order to eventually beat it, and where it is impossible to mistake who is on which side: you can tell by the color of the hats. From June 22, 1941, Stalin—Hitler's enemy and ally of the Western powers—wore a white hat: he was on the side of good. In a world divided into *them* and *us*, he was one of *us*. If facts appeared to muddy this picture, then facts be damned. If recalcitrant memory prevented accepting this image of Stalin, then memory be damned.

Stalin's own subjects, trained in the art of being astonished at nothing, gave no public signs of surprise, of course, on learning from their press and their leaders' speeches that Hitler—the USSR's friend only the day before—had always been an enemy of communism and their homeland, while yesterday's enemy Great Britain turned out to be a friend. Public memory in the USSR had long since lost any kind of continuity or logic. Western governments now tried to conduct a similar operation with their own societies, which were far less accustomed to it. Almost overnight, efforts were made to scrub British and American public consciousness of Stalin and Hitler's recent alliance, Soviet aggression in Eastern Europe, and all the crimes committed by the Stalinist regime.

After a time, the results began somewhat ominously to recall the Soviet template. For instance, on January 4, 1943, an American passing by a newspaper kiosk would likely have experienced a certain déjà vu. Just as three years before, Joseph Stalin's mustachioed face stared at them from the cover of *Time* magazine as the new person of the year. This seemed to be the same Stalin but was not the same at all. Instead of a dictator "matching himself with Adolf Hitler as the world's most hated man," *Time* depicted him now as a great statesman, an indomitable leader, a strategic genius and courageous friend of the free world. It was as if the first Stalin had never existed. In January 1943, the new image of Stalin as trustworthy "Uncle Joe" had been so well implanted in the Western media that doubtless this same reader of *Time*, recalling Stalin's earlier image in the same magazine, might have suspected his memory was playing tricks on him.

Any doubts as to who Stalin was, and what his regime represented, seemed at the time—or at least were meant to seem—long since laid to rest. Proof of this was supposed to be the daily press articles, films, books, the language of official communiqués, reports, and commentary. In this regard, the authorities could count on the cooperation of a great many opinion makers—intellectuals, journalists, artists, writers, filmmakers, academics—who by the 1930s had already set up shop in the world of pro-Soviet, antifascist rhetoric. After a period of ideological crisis and confusion caused by the Stalin-Hitler pact, their reassuring dichotomy of communism/fascism had returned redoubled, and they again could devote their labor and talents to taking the right side of it.

Barely a week after the German attack on the USSR, the *New Statesman* published an article by Harold Laski, "Towards Friendship with the Soviet Union." Laski, a distinguished British lawyer and a veteran admirer of Stalin, recalled: "We can learn a great deal from the Soviet Union in all areas relating to criminal law, including the treatment of prisoners."[18] In October 1941, G. H. D. Cole, an eminent historian and president of the Fabian Society, managed to bring out a book, *Europe, Russia and the Future,* in which he deployed a daring vision of Europe after the inevitable British-Soviet victory over Hitler. "Is it not most likely that the problems of Poland, and of the Balkans, and of Hungary, will be solved by their inclusion as Soviet Republics within a vastly enlarged State based of the U.S.S.R.?" wrote the British historian. Cole's thinking, inspired by this optimistic vision, went even further: he declared that he would prefer to see a future Europe under Stalin's rule than experience a return to the hopeless, prewar order on the old continent. "I would much sooner see the Soviet Union, even with its policy unchanged, dominant over *all* Europe, including Great Britain, than see an attempt to restore the pre-war States to their futile and uncreative independence and their petty economic nationalism under capitalist domination. Much better be ruled by Stalin than by the restrictive and monopolistic cliques which dominate Western capitalism."[19]

Encountering the burning enthusiasm of Stalin's traditional advocates, the Allied authorities nevertheless maintained a certain caution by not leaving as delicate a matter as propaganda completely in the hands of these enthusiasts. The Soviet regime's public image was meant to be constructed and managed in a controlled manner under the government's direct supervision. In the United States, the newly formed Office of War Information took care of this. A group of well-known people from the worlds of scholarship and culture found work in it, including the historians Arthur Schlesinger Jr. and Barbara Tuchman, the filmmakers Frank Capra and William Wyler, the poet Archibald MacLeish, the playwright Robert Sherwood and the journalists Richard Hottelet and Elmer

Davis. In Great Britain, the new propaganda line had been clearly laid down by the end of 1941, at a time when the US was just entering the war. In an official memorandum of December 6, 1941, for internal use only, Hugh Dalton, a member of Great Britain's inner governing circle, outlined the main thrust of British propaganda regarding the USSR: "We should take the line that we shall be their comrades [i.e., the Russians'] in the peace as we have been in the war… and that by sharing in the common victory and in the peace-making, and in the planning of a more prosperous world after the war, the future of Anglo-Russian relations will be different from what it has been in the last two decades."[20]

If in the 1930s the Soviet Union had been admired mainly because it supposedly represented a contrast with the tired West, in Allied war propaganda it was the other way around: Stalin's state was praised for its alleged similarity to the West. At the time of war, citizens of the Western powers were supposed to be proud of their own countries, instead of criticizing them and looking for better alternatives abroad. During World War II, linking official patriotism with a pro-Soviet stance became possible and even encouraged in Great Britain and the US. It was easy precisely because, thanks to the media, Westerners were being told that the Soviet Union was reminiscent of the Anglo-Saxon countries. The liberal Catholic journal *Commonweal* even came to the conclusion that the Soviet system was "something like a combination of Washington's, Jefferson's, and Lincoln's [government], and functioning under a similar constitution."[21] *Life* magazine informed its readers that the citizens of the Soviet Union are "a hell of a people" who "look like Americans, dress like Americans and think like Americans." For those readers who had heard something about the NKVD, it was quickly explained that it was nothing more than "a national police similar to the FBI," whose task was to "track down traitors." And if there was still someone who stubbornly recalled rumors of millions of victims of Stalin's collectivization, then *Life* explained: "Whatever the cost of farm collectivization in terms of human life and individual liberty, the historic fact is that it worked."[22]

This kind of propaganda convinced some Americans. For example, in the late summer of 1941, two months after the German invasion of the USSR (but before the United States had come into the war), Edward Speier, a thirty-six-year-old mechanic from Detroit, decided to bring aid to the beleaguered Land of the Soviets. He managed to stow away on a Soviet ship taking American railroad locomotives from California to the Soviet Union. When the vessel docked in Vladivostok, Speier was immediately arrested by the NKVD as a spy. His family contacted the American authorities, and a representative of the US Embassy in Moscow demanded a meeting with Speier. During this meeting, the American diplomat was astonished that Speier, who looked like "a very uncouth person," continually recited glowing praises of the USSR, as well as scathing attacks on the US. Discouraged and disconcerted by this performance, the diplomat shrugged, and the embassy dropped the case. Speier died about eighteen months later in a "transport" to a camp in Karaganda.[23]

President Roosevelt was personally involved in creating Stalin's positive image. He knew too that in this regard he could count on his former ambassador to Moscow, Joseph Davies—an experienced singer of Stalin's praises from the time of the Great Terror. He encouraged him to write a book about the USSR based on his own experiences. Roosevelt knew very well what kind of book he could expect from Davies, who also seemed to have a clear idea of what his boss in the White House expected from him. In December 1941, the book *Mission to Moscow* appeared in record time under Davies's name (it was written, in fact, by two ghostwriters, Spencer Williams and Stanley Richardson, both former journalists in Moscow). The book came out immediately, with 700,000 copies printed, and efforts were made to turn it into a bestseller. It was promptly translated into thirteen languages. Davies did not disappoint Roosevelt and painted a quite angelic picture of Stalin, one worthy of the pens of the greatest panegyrists of the 1930s. From the perspective of his experiences during his Moscow posting, Davies assured his readers that the true aim of Soviet policy was "to promote the brotherhood of man and to improve the lot of the common people." According to the American diplomat, Stalin desired to "create a society in which men may live as equals, governed by ethical ideals."[24] As proof of this, Davies included in the book his own reports from 1937 and 1938 in which he had asserted that the Moscow trials were completely justified.

He was not alone in trying once again to justify the Stalinist purges. An illustrative example of how the Moscow trials could be fit into the framework of pro-Soviet wartime attitudes was demonstrated by Sir John Maynard in his 1942 work *The Russian Peasant*. "The natural result of wholesale prosecutions and punishments is a crop of false charges," he writes about the purges. "But the rank and file has been little touched, and their sympathy with the sufferers has on the whole been small. The Soviet Government did not lose support of the masses by the drastic proceedings of 1936–1938, for the masses believe that the punishments have been deserved: as—in general—they probably were."[25] The British scholar based his knowledge of what Soviet masses believed on meticulous studies of Soviet media and official government documents.

After the appearance of Davies's book, Roosevelt, satisfied with its success, decided to press the advantage. He seemed aware that while the power of the word was impossible to ignore, the real key to the imagination of the masses, especially in America, lay in Hollywood. A few years later, the Warner brothers, owners of Warner Brothers studio, admitted that the president had asked them at a White House dinner to adapt Davies's book for the screen.[26] The studio got to work, and by April 1943 the film version of *Mission to Moscow*—an outrageously distorted tribute to Stalin, directed by Michael Curtiz of *Casablanca* fame—was ready. The film begins with Joseph Davies himself saying on screen that "the Soviet Union was surrounded by so many prejudices and misunderstandings that I recognized it as my duty to tell the truth. . . . Once in Russia I developed a great respect for the Soviet leaders' honesty." The film, needless to say, was widely distributed, and the Office of War Information organized a campaign of praise and admiration. Stalin personally ordered *Mission to Moscow* to be shown in Soviet theaters. The film followed the official line so closely that the Soviet dictator saw no need to censor it. As a reward, Davies received the Order of Lenin from "Uncle Joe." This work was accompanied by a whole series of other pro-Soviet productions of practically all Hollywood studios. American moviegoers had an opportunity to envy Soviet collective farm workers after seeing their happy lives in *Song of Russia* (MGM). They could also admire *North Star*, based on a screenplay by Lillian Hellman and made by Sam Goldwyn's studio, as well as Gregory Peck's film debut as a Soviet partisan fighter in *Days of Glory* (RKO). *Three Russian Girls* (United Artists) and *Boy from Stalingrad* (Columbia) completed the picture.

And yet, despite the orchestrated chorus of praises of Davies's work and its film version, there were critics who could not stomach all the sugarcoating on this celluloid "Uncle Joe." Manny Farber criticized *Mission to Moscow* in the *New Republic*: "This mishmash is directly and firmly in the tradition of Hollywood politics. A while ago it was Red-baiting, now it is Red-praising in the same sense ignorantly. To a democratic intelligence it is repulsive and insulting."[27] The intellectuals associated with the *Partisan Review*, who were in the process of evolving from Stalinism to anticommunism by way of Trotskyism, drew up a joint letter against the lies and "glorification of dictatorship" in the propaganda film. The letter was signed by Alfred Kazin, Edmund Wilson, Sidney Hook, and Dwight Macdonald.[28] Concurrently, the philosopher John Dewey, chairman of the 1937 commission that had highlighted the falsehood of the Moscow trials, warned the American public on the pages of the *New York Times* that *Mission to Moscow* was "the first instance in our country of totalitarian propaganda for mass consumption—a propaganda which falsifies history through distortion, omission or pure invention of facts."[29]

William Henry Chamberlin, a former longtime American correspondent in Russia, wrote in March 1944 that the American authorities' attitude toward the Soviets was based on "a curious mystical belief that if only we trust Stalin enough, no matter what he does, we will be happy ever after. The more Stalin does to undermine our confidence, the more our publicists and statesmen insist on a blind, deaf and dumb cultivation of [that] confidence."[30] Chamberlin's words acquire additional significance when contrasted with the behavior and statements of the man on whom the West depended the most at the time: President Roosevelt. In a confidential statement to William Bullitt, the former US ambassador in Moscow, Roosevelt appears to have given expression to his deepest and most personal convictions about Stalin. The leader of the free world admitted: "I just have a hunch that Stalin doesn't want anything but security for his country, and I think if I give him everything I possibly can and ask nothing from him in return, *noblesse oblige*, he won't try to annex anything and will work for a world of democracy and peace."[31]

What might explain the origin of this paralyzing naivete in the mind of one of the most consummate political strategists of the day? Did Roosevelt believe in the propaganda image of Stalin that he had ordered constructed for his own political use? William Bullitt, a former Soviet sympathizer who had seen a thing or two, was shocked by the president's attitude. George F. Kennan, the American diplomat, liberal, and eminent student of Soviet Russia and a man well versed in Soviet-American relations at the time, remarked on Roosevelt's "almost childish inability to understand Stalin's personality and the nature of his regime."[32] After Roosevelt's death, Kennan remarked laconically: "The truth is—there is no avoiding it—that Franklin Roosevelt, for all his charm and for all his skill as a political leader, was, when it came to foreign policy, a very superficial man, ignorant, dilettantish, with a severely limited intellectual horizon."[33] Yet this astonishing naivete on the part of the Allies toward Stalin—the truly childlike enchantment that seasoned politicians and diplomats experienced around this thug—went beyond Roosevelt's personal illusions. The head of the British Foreign Office, Anthony Eden, confessed to a friend on December 20, 1944, that he had "a real liking for Stalin" who had "never broken his word." Even in 1946, in his instructions to the Foreign Office, Eden insisted that "there was a disagreement in the Politburo and we should concentrate on arriving at an understanding with Stalin who alone had moderate ideas."[34]

Nevertheless, the strenuous efforts by the Allied governments to create a positive image for Stalin, despite employing all available means of persuasion and pressure, encountered problems. The sanitizing of reality by the Western media was somewhat reminiscent of attempts to paint a wall covered in mold—after each coat of paint the wall looks like new, though not for long: one way or another, the mold comes through again. Soon after the signing of the Anglo-Soviet pact of 1941, when the authorities in London and Washington were retuning their own propaganda to a Soviet wavelength, inconvenient witnesses made their appearances on the world stage.

Inconvenient Witnesses

In concluding their pact with Stalin in the summer of 1941, the British government encountered something of a diplomatic problem: Great Britain was still allied with Poland. Although this alliance had done little for Poland in September 1939, when the British (like Poland's other strategic ally, France) had been in no hurry to provide the Poles with any concrete assistance, the Poles continued to behave as loyal allies toward the British. The armed forces organized in the West by the Polish émigré government in London had been fighting alongside the British from Norway to Africa, earning publicity on the British Isles. During the Battle of Britain, Britons followed daily reports on the radio and in the press on the continual series of successes by Polish airmen, about whom the commander of RAF Fighter Command, Sir Hugh Dowding, was to have said: "Had it not been for the magnificent [work of] the Polish squadrons and their unsurpassed gallantry, I hesitate to say that the outcome of [the] Battle [of Britain] would have been the same."[35] The Polish airmen became heroes in the British media: they were written about and photographed, films were made about them (e.g., the popular drama *Dangerous Moon*), and their likenesses were even put up on billboards.[36] British public opinion was aware of Poland's fate under Nazi and Stalinist rule and was on Poland's side.

By allying himself with Stalin, Churchill was de facto making common cause with his ally's enemy. For these and other reasons, the issue of Polish-Soviet relations somehow had to be settled. Consequently, the British put pressure on Poland's prime minister, General Sikorski, to reach an agreement immediately with the USSR. Sikorski set two conditions: the release of all Polish citizens imprisoned or exiled by the Soviet regime and a guarantee of the prewar Polish-Soviet border. The British government succeeded in convincing Sikorski to abandon the second condition for the time being. Sikorski refused to abandon the first.

Stalin agreed to Sikorski's demand and ordered the release of Polish citizens from the Gulag and confined exile. We might add that the Soviet dictator was never under greater pressure than he was then. When Sikorski and the Soviet ambassador in London, Ivan Maisky, were signing an agreement on July 30, 1941, German divisions had been driving practically unchecked toward Moscow for four weeks, beating speed records for advances and taking hundreds of thousands of Soviet soldiers prisoner. Thus developed a situation that was unprecedented in the history of the Soviet machinery of totalitarian violence and propaganda. On the strength of the Sikorski-Maisky agreement, Polish citizens—people who were supposed to have vanished without trace—began to emerge from the numerous camps and places of exile scattered across the whole vast territory of Stalin's empire. The Stalinist regime, which had always attached exceptional importance to ensuring that the truth about the Gulag never get out, was suddenly forced to allow hundreds of thousands of prisoners and deportees to leave the Soviet "other world" that had been previously hidden from outside eyes. Furthermore, the prisoners were released to the care of their own government, which was allied to the Western powers and aware of the injustices suffered by Polish citizens at the hands of the Soviet state.

According to a report by the USSR's principal political police chief Lavrenty Beria, by January 15, 1943, the number of Polish citizens released from camp and exile totaled 389,041. These included 200,828 people of Polish extraction; 90,662 Jews; 31,392 Ukrainians; 27,418 Belarusians; 3,421 Polish citizens of Russian extraction; as well as 2,291 people of other ethnicities.[37] Most of them were in a pitiful state. Tens of thousands died just after being released. Everyone was trying to reach one of the assembly points run in the USSR by representatives of the Polish government in London. One of those survivors, Romuald Wernik, remembered that journey as follows: "After a few days, as we were throwing out the bodies of the dead, and hunger and exhaustion clouded my mind, I had feverish hallucinations that only empty wagons would get there, that all of us would fall by the wayside, marking the route with our corpses. That at our destination someone would open the doors and see that there was nobody there. If he was a believer, he would make the sign of the cross in terror. A phantom train, the 'Flying Dutchman on wheels.'"[38]

The fittest, the strongest, and the luckiest made it. But their nightmare was not yet over, for the Soviet authorities were refusing to supply the assembly points with food and medicines. Those who requested food were told: "You're Polish, let Poland feed you."[39] According to data from the Polish Embassy in the USSR, between December 1941 and June 1942, among the 200,000 Polish deportees assembled in Central Asia around 20,000 died of typhus.[40] This catastrophe, unlike most catastrophes on Soviet soil, was played out under the gaze of Western observers. The fate of seventy-seven thousand Polish children, which included a great number of orphans, troubled them the most. The British and Canadian governments, as well as the American Red Cross, expressed a willingness to evacuate fifty thousand of them. However, the Soviet authorities did not agree, arguing that they had transportation problems.

(Though transportation problems could apparently be overcome when it came to shipping prisoners *to* the camps.) Andrei Vyshinsky, famed for his speeches for the prosecution at the Moscow trials, told the Polish ambassador with his characteristic cynicism that "the Soviet authorities guarantee the welfare of the Polish children."[41] In reality, the Soviet authorities were afraid of the West's reaction to the appearance of such a huge number of children from the Soviet Union—a scene that would have been reminiscent of the living skeletons that the world would later see after the liberation of Nazi camps.

In keeping with international agreements, the Poles were meant to create an army out of these exiles. In March 1942, General Władysław Anders, a recent prisoner in the Lubyanka, now at this army's head, made the dramatic decision to lead his men and other Polish refugees out of the USSR. He knew that great numbers of Poles still remained there who were trying to reach the assembly points. However, he had come to the conclusion that his army was threatened with decimation by hunger and disease. Between March and September, about 115,000 citizens of prewar Poland left Soviet territory. Anders's army would later carry out a crucial assault on Monte Cassino in Italy.[42] Among these 115,000 people brought out of the USSR were about 37,000 civilians, including 18,300 children. An American liaison officer Lieutenant Colonel Henry Szymanski, assigned to Anders's army, sent a detailed report to Washington on the situation of the Polish exiles from the USSR, by then in Iran. In it, he wrote about the Polish children: "It is estimated that 50% have already died from malnutrition. The other 50% will die unless evacuated to a land where American help can reach them." Szymanski added a number of photographs to his report. They were the first of the whole series of pictures of children reduced to living skeletons during World War II. They were taken before the pictures of small prisoners from liberated German concentration camps appeared to the world. But these pictures of the children from Soviet exile were not shown to the world. American authorities hid them in the archives and classified them as secret, as they did with the entirety of Szymanski's report. A secret memo explained: "This document contains information affecting the national defense of the United States within the meaning of the Espionage Laws, Title 18, U.S.C., Sections 793 and 794. The transmission or the revelation of its contents in any manner to an unauthorized person is prohibited by law."[43] As for the children, they were sent all over the world to be settled in refugee camps and orphanages in Iran, Pakistan, India, Lebanon, and Palestine. Some of them ended up in British colonies in Africa, finding shelter in

Uganda, Kenya, Tanganyika, Rhodesia, and South Africa. Some reached New Zealand and Mexico.

While the Western allied governments worked on deflecting the public's attention from topics deemed too "controversial," the scant information on the subject that got through to the West was often so dramatic that it exceeded ordinary limits of credibility. For instance, in 1946 an American of Polish descent in Chicago succeeded in adopting a Polish orphan who had survived Siberian exile and ended up in a refugee camp at Santa Rosa in Mexico. In Chicago, the boy was placed in front of an audience and asked to describe his life in the Soviet Union.

> Hank told them how he and his family were taken from home, about the Red Army soldiers pounding at the door, about having to pack within a half-hour's time, and about their transport in freight cars after waiting on a railroad siding for three days without food and water. He spoke about a young woman passing her infant through the bars, the shouts and the shot, and how every day during their transport the Soviet soldiers removed the dead bodies from the cars and just dumped them by the side of the tracks; about their stay in Siberia, how they existed in the run-down horse barn, and their daily struggle to survive. Near tears he mentioned the death of his mother, and that he was never able to see her grave, that his grandmother had to go and bury her, and her words afterwards: "I had to split her nightgown in order to bury her in it. She was all in pieces, the arms, the legs, the head."[44]

After he had finished his tale, the boy left to the accompaniment of loud comments from the audience: "There is no way it could have been like that; the kid doesn't know what he's saying." And yet most of his audience were Polish Americans, probably with relatives in Poland, and so had had more opportunities than other Americans to hear similar accounts.[45] We should also remember that this was in 1946 and that Americans now knew about the Nazi concentration camps. Many of them had seen newsreel footage and photographs of piles of dead bodies and half-burned human remains in crematorium ovens—the images that canceled the ordinary limits of imagination regarding evil. But in recent public memory Stalin's empire had been at the other end of the spectrum—in the land of good and light.

Meanwhile, despite the best efforts of American and British authorities, it was impossible to silence the voices of 115,000 witnesses and isolate them from the world. Especially since these witnesses often considered it their moral duty to tell the world the truth about the Soviet Union. This desire to bear witness to the truth is common among people who have survived historical catastrophes and mass crimes. Those who manage to get out alive from Nazi camps and ghettos, the Cambodian killing fields, African massacres, and other hells on earth often feel that they have survived on credit, so to speak, and that they bear a moral obligation to testify in the name of those who did not make it. Since the survivors were unable to prevent the victims' physical destruction, the only thing that they can still do for them is to save them from another death—death by neglect and oblivion. If the nightmare of the crime has passed, we should be reminded of it, since—as Santayana put it in a well-known phrase—those who cannot remember the past are condemned to repeat it. And if the crime continues with new victims, then there's even more of a reason to warn the world about it. The many Poles, Jews, Ukrainians, Belarusians, Russians, and others of the prewar Polish Republic who had survived Soviet camps and exile believed and felt no differently.

These witnesses to the horrors of the camps immediately found an audience. The Polish government in London wanted to learn in as much detail as possible about the fate of its citizens in the USSR, knowing that many of them still remained there. Representatives of the Polish authorities carried out surveys among survivors in refugee camps, especially in Iraq and Palestine. In response to these questions, thousands and thousands of people were able to recount their own experiences in Stalin's state. They described how they had been arrested and interrogated, how and where they had been transported, what conditions were like in the prisons and camps, whom they had met there, what slave labor they performed, how the camps were structured and run, and who had died in the Gulag or in exile and how. In this manner, a rich trove of factual material on the Soviet state system of repression and slavery was quickly assembled. Based on it, one could for the first time learn about the system's physical outlines: its structure, geographical extent, and methods used, as well as the conditions in which the victims had lived and died. Previously the West had been able to learn all of this only from individual accounts from the relatively few escapees. Now it had at its disposal a huge, internally consistent body of factual information on the subject. Before Gorbachev's *glasnost* there was no more exhaustive source of information on the Gulag. This material was available to the Allied authorities right from the start. Indeed, it had been collected on British military bases under their owners' eyes. However, the Allied authorities were routinely wary of reacting in any way to this testimony. A British government report that was drawn up only in December 1943 was classified confidential.

The need to bear witness to people's experiences in that "inhuman land" did not end with official surveys. Articles, short pieces, memoirs, and works of literature based on reminiscences quickly began to appear. Polish newspapers and magazines came out in Anders's army. These periodicals began to receive manuscripts written by former prisoners and deportees, for the most part now wearing Polish uniforms. However, the British authorities found a way to deal with this problem too. These publications, although written in Polish, were produced by Polish military units under British command, and thus falling under British military censorship, which took care that accounts of the Gulag and exile did not appear in print. In their place were blank spaces on the pages of the Polish military publications. Gustaw Herling-Grudziński, who at the time was working on the editorial staff of *Orzeł Biały*, recalled that "the blank spaces became a permanent fixture in *Orzeł* and stamped 'withdrawn.' Obviously, all critical remarks about our powerful ally were withdrawn, including articles about the children evacuated from the USSR."[46] Wiktor Weintraub, editor of the magazine *W drodze*, observed the same phenomenon.

In the book *Diabeł w raju* (The devil in paradise), Tadeusz Wittlin recounted the following story. While being held in a Soviet jail in Minsk in the spring of 1941, he encountered a British soldier there, a Sergeant Edward Baldwin. It turned out that Baldwin, a driver from Manchester, had been mobilized in 1939 and had gone with the British Expeditionary Force to defend France from the Germans. During the French campaign in 1940, he had been taken prisoner and sent to a POW camp in the part of Poland occupied by the Germans. He had managed to escape and head east. He assumed that if he managed to cross the Soviet frontier, he would be granted political asylum in the USSR (formally neutral in terms of the German-British war) and would be able to go home. And, with the help of some Polish peasants, he attained this goal. On the Soviet side of the frontier, a surprise awaited him, however: instead of asylum and a return to England, he was met with charges of espionage and packed off to prison. Wittlin recalled that he saw Baldwin for the last time in March 1941, when the guards told him to collect his belongings and escorted him away. The British sergeant did not return to the cell and no more was heard of him. Then came the Sikorski-Maisky agreement, and Wittlin left the USSR together with Anders's army and after a time became editor of a Polish military publication, *Parada*, that was published in Egypt. He wrote an account of Sergeant Baldwin with the intention of publishing it in his paper. He wanted to draw the British authorities' attention to the British soldier's fate, and if he was even alive, perhaps trigger his release. However, the article returned with the annotation "stopped by censor." Wittlin decided to seek an explanation from the British censor in person. Years later he described the conversation:

> "I'm terribly sorry, but we just couldn't pass your excellent piece," a captain of the Intelligence Service told me with exaggerated courtesy at the censorship office, where I had gone for an explanation.
>
> "There's nothing to be done, war claims its victims," he added mysteriously, as if he had discovered a hitherto unknown truth.
>
> "Let us assume that Sergeant Baldwin died in combat. At this stage we cannot offend our great ally. I'm sure you understand."
>
> I didn't.[47]

But it was not only the witnesses of the camps and exile whose lips the British authorities attempted to seal. In 1943, George Orwell tried to get his latest book, *Animal Farm*, published. One after another, publishers rejected the manuscript, seeing in the satirical work an exposé of Soviet totalitarianism. The manuscript was finally accepted, but immediately afterward the publisher pulled out of the agreement. He did this under pressure from the Ministry of Information and wrote a letter to Orwell: "If the fable were addressed generally to dictators and dictatorships at large, then publication would be all right. But the fable does follow, as I see now, so completely the progress of the Russian Soviets and their two dictators [Lenin and Stalin], that it can apply only to Russia."[48] Two years later Orwell wrote: "Any serious criticism of the Soviet regime, any disclosure of facts which the Soviet government would prefer to keep hidden, is next door to unprintable.... These people [in the press and the government] don't see that if you encourage totalitarian methods, the time may come when they will be used against you instead of for you.... If liberty means anything at all, it means the right to tell people what they do not want to hear."[49]

In December 1941, just as the United States was joining the anti-Hitler coalition, London representatives of the Jewish socialist party, the Bund, which had been active in prewar Poland, together with socialist politicians of the Polish émigré government informed the British and American authorities that two Bund leaders had been arrested in the USSR: Wiktor Alter and Henryk Erlich. The two arrested men were both members of the Executive of the Second Socialist International. Alter was known in British socialist circles. During World War I, following an escape from tsarist exile in Siberia, he had spent several years in Great Britain, where he had been active in the British Labour Party. Upon learning of the February 1917 revolution in Russia, he first left for Russia and then settled for good in Poland. Erlich and Alter found themselves in the USSR in 1939 in a similar fashion to so many others: after they had been evacuated from Warsaw to Poland's eastern areas, they had been caught up in the Soviet invasion. They were soon arrested, and as early as July 1941, the NKVD sentenced them by executive order to death, though this was subsequently commuted to ten years in the Gulag. In September 1941, they were released on the strength of the Sikorski-Maisky pact and immediately made contact with representatives of Sikorski's government in the USSR. They were supposed to be sent to London, where they would join the Polish authorities-in-exile as representatives of the Bund. At this time the Soviet authorities suggested that they join the Jewish Anti-Fascist Committee that had just been formed on Stalin's initiative. Alter and Erlich agreed. On December 4, 1941, however, there came an unexpected twist in their fortunes, and they were again arrested by the NKVD.

At the news of Alter and Erlich's latest arrest in the USSR, the president of the International Labor Federation Walter Citrine, alerted by Polish and Jewish socialists, lodged protests with Foreign Secretary Anthony Eden and the leader of the Labour Party, Clement Attlee, for immediate interventions to be made at the highest level. Both politicians avoided taking any significant action, however. The deputy leader of the Labour Party, Arthur Greenwood, did turn to the Soviet ambassador, Maisky, for clarification, but did not even receive a response. A year passed, and in January 1943, in response to repeated pressure from Polish and Jewish socialists, the secretary of the Labour Party, James Middleton, again wrote to Maisky. Shortly thereafter the Soviet authorities received a very determined call for Alter and Erlich to be released, signed by the secretary of the American Federation of Labor, William Green, and a group of well-known American personalities (including Albert Einstein). This time a reply was not long in coming. On February 23, the Soviet ambassador Litvinov informed Green that Alter and Erlich had been shot for anti-Soviet activity. In reality both had been condemned to death in December 1941, but the executions had been postponed. On May 15, 1942, Erlich was found hanged from the bars of his cell window; he had probably committed suicide. Alter was shot in February 1943.

At the news of the deaths of Alter and Erlich, American socialists and trade unionists reacted immediately. On March 30, thirty-five hundred union delegates attended a rally in response to the news from Moscow. The crowd was addressed by the mayor of New York City, Fiorello La Guardia. He said that Alter and Erlich were the "Soviet Union's Sacco and Vanzetti." He was wrong. The execution in 1927 of Sacco and Vanzetti after a murder trial based on circumstantial evidence had caused a storm of protest throughout the world. There was less fuss about Alter and Erlich. When Polish socialists and Bund representatives in London organized a rally in memory of the two men, the British Labour Party, afraid of possibly inflaming relations with Stalin, did not even send an official delegation. Only individual members of the party attended. George Dallas, a member of its executive council, agreed to chair the event in defiance of the party leadership's stance.

The communist *Daily Worker* wrote in a piece on the issue with the headline USSR VILIFIED FOR EXECUTING TRAITORS: "Anti-Soviet propaganda and abuse of the most venomous kind was a feature of the meeting . . . which unfortunately seemed to enjoy the patronage of the British Labour Party, since an Executive member was in the chair." The president of the International of Unionists and Socialists, Camille Huysmans, who spoke at the rally, was also lambasted. The communist paper criticized him for "indulging in fierce attacks against the leaders of the Soviet Union, the Red Army, and the Soviet system."[50] The British press limited itself to short mentions on the whole Alter and Erlich issue. Neither the *Times*, the *Daily Herald*, the *New Statesman*, the *Tribune*, *New Left*, nor *Fabian News* printed a word of criticism of the USSR.

A socialist activist of the Czech authorities-in-exile in London, Josef Belina, attempted to galvanize the leadership of the Czech Socialist Party to protest on behalf of Erlich and Alter. However, the party demanded his silence and concurrently issued a statement supporting the execution of the Bund leaders. "Out of an internal matter of the Polish Socialist movement there should not be created an action of international character," claimed the Czech socialists, adding that "the Soviet Union is engaged in the most terrible war and we believe that she is choosing the means of her defense with conscience."[51]

Paradoxically, it was the Nazis who greatly helped the Allied authorities in deflecting the West's attention from Stalinist crimes. After the outbreak of the German-Soviet war, Nazi propagandists, just as they had before the Ribbentrop-Molotov pact, willingly took advantage of any proof of Soviet crimes in order to discredit the USSR in the eyes of the world. Of course, during the war these efforts caused a reaction quite contrary to the one intended and did so much more widely than in the 1930s, especially in the Allied countries. As a matter of course, the public usually rejected information that came from Nazi propaganda or in some way reminded people of it. And indeed, on the strength of the prewar Stalin-Hitler dichotomy, all kinds of proof of Stalinist crimes often produced a similar reaction.

Before and during the war, the Nazis' textbook anticommunism resonated to a certain extent in Russian émigré circles. For many an émigré, the prospect of a German victory over Stalin seemed the only imaginable opportunity to liberate Russia from Bolshevik rule. One person to espouse these views, at least to some degree and for the time being, was Ivan Solonevich. An escapee from the camps and author of a popular prewar memoir, *Russia in a Concentration Camp*, Solonevich devoted himself to anti-Bolshevik activity in exile. He settled in Bulgaria, where he set up an émigré publication *Golos Rossii*, or *The Voice of Russia*. Not surprisingly, the Soviet authorities showed him no mercy. At the beginning of 1938, Solonevich learned that his father had died in the Gulag. In February, a bomb hidden in a delivery of books exploded in Solonevich's office, killing his wife and the secretary to the editorial board. Solonevich and his son moved to Nazi Germany, where he was granted political asylum and remained under surveillance. Needless to say, his name was added to the lists of people sought in Germany by the NKVD after the arrival of the victorious Soviet army in 1945. He managed to flee to Argentina, however, where he set up a Russian monarchist newspaper *Nasha Strana* (Our land). He was eventually deported to Uruguay, where he died in 1953 following an operation and in circumstances considered suspicious by his circle of followers.

During the war, the Nazis had little trouble finding proof of the criminal nature of Stalinism. The evidence could be plainly seen as the Wehrmacht conquered Soviet territory. Already in the first few days of the German offensive, thousands of bodies of prisoners, hastily murdered by the retreating Soviets, were discovered in Lwów and other locations in prewar Poland that had been occupied by the Soviets. Accounts of the Stalinist purges and the Great Famine of 1931–33, as well as articles on the Gulag and accounts by former prisoners, appeared in newspapers published by the German occupiers in the conquered territories. For instance, a book by Kajetan Klug came out in 1943 in occupied Warsaw titled *Największe niewolnictwo w dziejach. Sprawozdanie z rzeczywistych przeżyć w obozach karnych GPU* (The greatest slavery in history: An account of true experiences in GPU penal camps).

These German initiatives often had a paradoxical effect. The sources and context of these denunciations appeared to invalidate their content, or at least cast doubt on it, since they came from a regime whose crimes had stunned the world. Announcing proof of Soviet crimes in Nazi publications, even if these accounts happened to be accurate, not only stripped this specific information of credibility in the eyes of the free world but often cast doubt subsequently over all other sorts of similar information. At the very least, it strengthened the position of those who were trying to marginalize such proof. But there came a time, however, when this particular effect, like the entire pro-Stalinist mythology of World War II, was put to the test.

Words and Bodies

On April 13, 1943, at 9:15 a.m., German radio announced that mass graves had been discovered in a wooded area near the village of Katyn in the Smolensk region. They contained the bodies of men wearing 1939 Polish Army officers' uniforms. All of them had been killed with a shot to the back of the head. New corpses were being found daily, and by June 1943, 4,143 bodies had been discovered. All signs and circumstantial evidence pointed to these men having been killed by the Soviets in the spring of 1940. Radio stations in every country occupied by Hitler and his allies repeated this sensational news.

Initially, people in the West had no idea how to react to this information. Above all, it had been announced by the Germans, and so its credibility was dubious. Treating the news seriously would have inevitably led to questioning the underlying black-and-white portrayal of the war—one in which Stalin, as an ally of the Western Allies, automatically acquired a positive moral status. Such an image could not be reconciled with the fact that this same Stalin was also committing mass murder. Meanwhile, the Polish government in London had enough information to immediately draw the correct conclusion from the German reports. It had from the start shared this information with its Western allies. After the 1941 Sikorski-Maisky agreement, when Poles released from Soviet camps and places of exile started appearing at assembly points for Anders's army, the men on whom Anders had been especially counting—that is, the officers captured by the Soviets in September 1939—were nowhere to be found. When questioned about this by Generals Anders and Sikorski, Stalin played a sort of comedy routine in front of them. In their presence, he asked Beria whether he by any chance knew where these officers were. After hearing out Beria, he then reassured the Poles that the missing men were en route from camps to the assembly points and should turn up in short order.

On April 13, 1943, when the Germans announced their gruesome discovery, the whole truth was known only to the Soviet leadership. It was an alarmingly banal truth. Its roots went back to the period 1939–1941, which had been so stubbornly expunged from the consciousness of citizens of the Allied countries in the West and the East. During the German-Soviet invasion of Poland, the Red Army took about 240,000 Polish soldiers prisoner. But it turned out that the aggressors were not prepared to house and feed such a large number of prisoners. So Soviet military authorities turned the Polish soldiers over to the police system, which specialized in the routine management of masses of slaves. But it, too, was unable to handle such a large number of prisoners, and so some of them were handed over to the Germans, some were released, and about 37,000 sent off to forced labor. The group of prisoners that attracted particular attention from the Soviets were the officers. Only some of them were professional military men. The majority were members of the Polish intelligentsia who were drafted for the war. They were teachers, academics, doctors, lawyers, civil servants, engineers, journalists, artists, etc. Precisely because they represented the elite of Polish society, the Soviet authorities intended to prevent them from returning to their own country and society. Depriving the country of its leadership was a permanent objective both of Soviet and Nazi invasions of Poland. Both dictators used similar methods, including concentration camps and executions. Petr Soprunenko, an NKVD official assigned by Beria to supervise the Polish prisoners, divided up the officers, concentrating most of them in two separate camps. Some of them he housed in Kozelsk, in the former Optina monastery adapted by the Soviets as a camp. Once this had been a famous center of Russian Orthodox spiritual life; in the preceding century, the famous monk Ambrozii had lived there—a religious mentor for many, including Dostoevsky, who portrayed the monastery and Ambrozii himself as Zosima in *The Brothers Karamazov*. The second group of Polish officers was housed in a former convent in Starobelsk.

The question as to what to do with these prisoners became ever more pressing during the winter of 1939–1940. Especially since after the attack on Finland, the arrival of new consignments of Finnish prisoners was expected. The attempts of the NKVD to recruit Polish officers produced very disappointing results as the men proved overwhelmingly resistant to suggestions of collaborating with Soviet authorities. It appears that the Soviets briefly weighed the possibility of sending the Polish officers to camps in Kolyma or Kamchatka along with other Polish prisoners. In February 1940, Soprunenko reported to Beria that the Polish camps needed to be emptied out to make room for the Finns.

On March 5, a decision was made on finally solving this problem. At a meeting of the Politburo, Beria proposed a formal motion to murder all the Polish officers in the camps at Kozelsk and Starobelsk. Executed along with them would be Polish policemen, border patrol, and forestry service officers, as well as other civil servants held at a camp at Ostashkov. Beria added to this list another 11,000 Polish prisoners, for a total of 25,700 people. The motion stated that they were all "sworn enemies of Soviet power, filled with hatred for the Soviet system of government" and recommended the following: "Examine [their] cases without calling the arrested men and without presenting [them with] the charges. . . . Using the special procedure, apply to them the supreme punishment, [execution by] shooting."[52] The motion passed unanimously. The first to sign it was Stalin, followed by Voroshilov, Molotov, and Mikoyan. Kaganovich and Kalinin, absent from the meeting, probably voted in favor over the telephone, as someone signed for them. It was agreed that the victims were to be kept in ignorance of their fate until the very end. The whole business was, of course, shrouded in secrecy.

The Politburo's decision was implemented immediately. For the sake of proper procedure, the *troika* of senior NKVD officers was assigned—Vsevolod Merkulov, Bogdan Kobulov, and Ivan Bashtakov. The teams of executioners led by the chief executioner from the Lubyanka, Vasily Blokhin, got down to work. The murders were carried out between April 3 and May 13. The prisoners from Ostashkov were shot in the NKVD dungeons in Tver, known at the time as Kalinin. The victims were brought in one by one, shot in the back of the head, dragged out, and thrown onto trucks. Vasily Blokhin not only supervised the executioners' efforts but also took a gun and joined in the work, dressed in his usual leather apron and long motorcycle gauntlets. The executions were conducted night after night, and the trucks were parked near the building with their engines turned on to drown out the shots. The bodies were buried in the village of Mednoye.

Prisoners of Starobelsk were murdered in a similar way in Kharkov and buried at an NKVD center outside town. Meanwhile, the Kozelsk prisoners were killed in the Katyn wood and the NKVD prison in Smolensk. Most of them were executed with a shot to the back of the head as they stood over the trenches that were filling up with corpses. Some of them probably resisted right at the end—their bodies were later found with their hands tied behind their backs and also with coats thrown over their heads and tied with rope around their necks. A number of other Polish victims from Beria's list were killed and buried in Bykivnya outside Kiev. Some were murdered in Kuropaty, Stalin's killing field near Minsk.

The NKVD also tried to arrest those victims' families that were living under Soviet occupation. These were exiled mainly to Kazakhstan. The crime was to remain a secret. The mass graves in Katyn were covered with freshly planted pines. On June 9, 1940, the head of the Gulag, Vasily Chernyshev, reported that the camps in Kozelsk, Starobelsk, and Ostashkov had been emptied and were awaiting new consignments of prisoners. On October 26, Beria ordered 124 executioners and those organizing the executions to be given cash awards. The officers received a monthly salary raise, while the rank-and-file NKVD men were given eight hundred rubles each.

When the Germans announced the discovery of the Katyn graves, the Western media froze, awaiting the Soviet reaction. Both the Soviet press agency TASS and *Pravda* stayed silent until April 15, as did the *New York Times*, the

London *Times* and other leading newspapers in the free world. Finally, on April 15, at 7:15 a.m. Moscow Time, the Soviet Information Bureau broke the silence:

In launching this monstrous invention, the German-Fascist scoundrels do not hesitate at the most unscrupulous and base lies in their attempt to cover up crimes which, as has now become evident, were perpetrated by themselves.

The German-Fascist reports on this subject leave no doubt as to the tragic fate of the former Polish POWs who in 1941 were engaged in construction work in areas west of Smolensk and who, along with many Soviet people, residents of the Smolensk region, fell into the hands of the German-Fascist hangmen in the summer of 1941, after the withdrawal of Soviet troops from the Smolensk area.

Beyond doubt Goebbels' slanderers are now trying by lies and calumnies to cover up the bloody crimes of the Hitlerite gangsters.

The Hitlerite murderers will not escape a just and inevitable retribution for their bloody crimes.[53]

At this moment, the British and American authorities probably felt a sense of relief. But the Polish government in London did not consider the matter closed, and on April 17 contacted the International Red Cross in Geneva about opening an inquiry into the matter of the Katyn massacre. The same day the Germans came out with a similar request, naturally sensing an opportunity to complicate relations in the Allied camp. Each side involved in the matter—the Poles, the Soviets, the Germans, the Americans and the British—was aware that the black-and-white mythology of World War II, maintained in the West with such determination, would be unable to survive a confrontation with the reality uncovered at Katyn. On April 19, *Pravda* published an article under the remarkable headline of "The Polish Helpers of Hitler." The Kremlin thundered:

The slander escalates quickly. Before the ink dried on the pens of the German-Fascist slanderers, the disgusting fabrication of Goebbels and company about the alleged mass murder of Polish officers by the Soviet authorities in 1940 were followed not only by Hitler's lackeys but, strangely enough, by the circles of the [Polish] government of General Sikorski. . . . Those Poles who willingly accepted the Nazi lie and are ready to collaborate with the Nazi executioners of the Polish people will be remembered by history as helpers of the cannibal Hitler.[54]

Two days later Stalin wrote to Churchill and Roosevelt in a secret dispatch:

The fact that this hostile campaign against the Soviet Union has begun simultaneously in the German and Polish press and is conducted in the same

spirit leaves no doubt that there is a contact and a collusion between Hitler—
the Allies' enemy—and the Sikorski government. At a time when the peoples
of the Soviet Union are shedding their blood in a grim struggle against
Hitler's Germany and bending their energies to defeat the common foe of the
freedom-loving democratic countries, the Sikorski government is striking a
treacherous blow at the Soviet Union to help Hitler's tyranny.[55]

Without any apparent objections, the Western leaders adapted to the rules
of the game laid down by Stalin. Henceforth their reactions would be based
on a consistent legitimization of Soviet lies. On April 26, Churchill replied to
Stalin's dispatch to assure the Soviet leader that he had complete confidence
in him, while describing Polish attempts to start an international investigation
into the Katyn affair as a "fraud." He promised to exert pressure on the Polish government to accept the Soviet "truth" about Katyn. Roosevelt wrote to
Stalin in similar vein. "I fully understand your problem," stated the American
president, simultaneously reassuring the Soviet dictator that "Churchill will
find ways and means of getting the Polish Government in London to act with
more common sense in the future."[56]

It appeared that Churchill had no substantial doubts as to who had murdered the Polish officers at Katyn. In a conversation with Sikorski he said: "Alas,
the German accusations are probably true. The Bolsheviks can be very cruel."[57]
That is what he thought unofficially. Officially, however, Churchill's foreign
secretary, Anthony Eden, demanded that Sikorski issue a special statement
supporting the Soviet position that Katyn was a Nazi provocation. Sikorski replied: "Our policy towards the Allies is honest. Force is on Russia's side, justice
on ours. I do not advise the British people to cast their lot with brute force and
to stampede justice before the eyes of all. Therefore, I categorically refuse to
withdraw the Polish request to the International Red Cross."[58]

Needless to say, both Churchill and Roosevelt were much better informed
about Katyn than their official reactions might suggest. In 1943, the British
and American authorities conducted several secret inquiries into the matter.
In June, the British ambassador to the Polish government, Sir Owen O'Malley,
summed up one of these inquiries, which had been conducted under his direction. In his report, O'Malley unambiguously confirmed that the Soviets were
guilty of the crime. He even described the methods used to murder the Poles
at Katyn quite accurately:

> If a man struggled, it seems that the executioners threw his coat over his head,
> tying it around his neck and leading him hooded to the pit's edge, for in many
> cases a body was found to be thus hooded and the coat to have been pierced
> by a bullet where it covered the base of the skull. But those who went quietly

to their death must have seen a monstrous sight. In the broad deep pit their comrades lay, packed closely round the edge, head to feet, like sardines in a tin. . . . Up and down on the bodies the executioners tramped, hauling the dead bodies around and trading in the blood like butchers in a stockyard.[59]

On becoming acquainted with O'Malley's report Churchill told Eden: "We should none of us ever speak a word about it."[60]

The British shared their findings with the Americans. Churchill sent Roosevelt O'Malley's report on August 13. The secret conclusion stated: "The Soviet government has severed diplomatic relations with the Poles in order to conceal its own responsibility for the crime."[61] In any case, the US president had the results of his own secret inquiry, which confirmed Soviet guilt. Roosevelt's special Balkans envoy George Earle presented him with an unambiguous report on the matter, which the president ignored. And when Earle, shocked by this turn of events, announced that he would make his findings public, Roosevelt officially forbade him from making any statements on the subject of the USSR. Soon, Earle was sent on assignment to the Samoa Islands and remained there for the rest of the war. Between April and June 1943, an international commission appointed by the Germans also examined the Katyn graves. German propagandists did not even have to interfere too much in its work. Specialists from Belgium, Bulgaria, Croatia, Czechoslovakia, Denmark, Finland, France, Holland, Hungary, Italy, Romania, Slovakia, and Switzerland reached the only possible conclusion—the Soviets had carried out the crimes in the spring of 1940. After an examination of the graves, a group of specialists from the Polish Red Cross confirmed these findings. The chasm between the facts and the Allied myth of the war attained dimensions that even Roosevelt was unable to tolerate with his characteristic sangfroid. The American president was unable to contain an outburst of anger— against the Poles, for their refusal to confirm Stalin's lies. He shouted, "Wow, what fools [the London Poles] are! I've no patience with them."[62] He then did not fail to assure Stalin that the Poles "are misguided" in their assessment of the facts.[63]

O'Malley, an experienced diplomat, weighed the political and moral dilemmas facing the Allies over the Katyn murders and their discovery. In conclusion to his report on the secret inquiry he wrote:

In handling the publicity side of the Katyn affair we have been constrained by the urgent need for cordial relations with the Soviet Government to appear to appraise the evidence with more hesitation and lenience than we should do in forming a commonsense judgment on events occurring in normal times or in the ordinary course of our private lives; we have been obliged to appear to distort the normal and healthy operation of our intellectual and moral judgments; we have been obliged to give undue prominence to the tactlessness or impulsiveness of Poles, to restrain the Poles from putting their case clearly before the public, to discourage any attempt by the public and the press to probe the ugly story to the bottom. In general we have been obliged to deflect attention from possibilities which in the ordinary affairs of life would cry to high heaven for elucidation. . . . We have in fact perforce used the good name of England like the murderers used the little conifers to cover up a massacre. . . .

This dislocation between our public attitude and our private feelings we may know to be deliberate and inevitable; but at the same time we may perhaps wonder whether, by representing to others something less that the whole truth so far as we know it, and something less than the probabilities so far as they seem to us probable, we are not incurring a risk of what–not to put a fine point on it–might darken our vision and take the edge off our moral sensitivity.[64]

The permanent under-secretary at the British Foreign Office, Sir Alexander Cadogan, commented as follows on O'Malley's report:

This is very disturbing. I confess that in cowardly fashion, I had rather turned my head away from the scene at Katyn—for fear of what I should find there. There may be evidence, that we do not know of, that may point in another direction. But on the evidence that we have, it is difficult to escape from a presumption of Russian guilt.

This of course raises terrible problems, but I think no one has pointed out that, on the purely moral plane, these are not new. How many thousands of its own citizens has the Soviet regime butchered? . . .

And one other disturbing thought is that we may eventually, by agreement and in collaboration with the Russians, proceed to the trial and perhaps execution of Axis "war criminals" while condoning this atrocity. I confess that I shall find that extremely difficult to swallow.

However, quite clearly for the moment, there is nothing to be done. As to what circulation we give to this explosive material, I find it difficult to make up my mind. Of course it would be only honest to circulate it. But as we know (all admit) that the knowledge of this evidence cannot affect the course of action, or policy, is there any advantage in exposing more individuals than necessary to the spiritual conflict that a reading of this dispatch excites?[65]

British and American authorities agreed to act out the charade that the Soviets had created around Katyn, and they did this "off the cuff," so to speak, without much serious consideration of the dilemmas that O'Malley and Cadogan had raised in their secret reports. Quite simply, the Western Allies did everything to uphold the Soviet version of the crimes, while not revealing to the Soviets the extent of their own information on the matter. However, they encountered a number of problems from Polish radio stations in the US, which began openly talking of the Katyn crime and the international commission's findings. Alarmed by such a state of affairs, head of the OWI's foreign-language section Alan Cranston had the OWI authorities threaten to close down the Polish stations if they did not stop discussing the Katyn issue.

How did the Western media react? It is quite astonishing how little interest they showed in establishing the facts and seeking the truth. The Western press on the whole reflexively adopted Stalin's version. Taking as their model the angry Soviet rhetoric aimed at any attempts to obtain the truth, Western newspapers joined the Stalinist smear campaign against the Poles. They condemned the Polish government for even daring to ask the question. On May 10, *Life* and *Newsweek* attacked the Polish government for publicizing the Katyn issue. *Life* called the Poles "the most chip-shouldered chauvinists in Europe," while reminding its readers (in case there was any doubt): "The important thing for us to remember is that no vital U.S. interest is involved in the Russo-Polish dispute.... Since our major self-interest lies with Russia, our diplomats ought not to get too huffy in backing up the Poles."[66] *Newsweek* sneered at Polish attempts at a public exposé of the truth about Katyn, writing that they were the result of "that curious trait of unrealism that led the Polish lancers to charge German tanks and that still permeates Polish politics."[67]

The *New Statesman*, meanwhile, found a way to justify the Soviet crime while not actually fingering the perpetrator. "The Soviet government often with reason, would regard the landed aristocracy and the officer class in Poland in the light of Fascists and class enemies.[68] It was just as if applying the Bolshevik category of "class enemy" justified mass murder (the Nazis also employed a similar semantic ploy when murdering their "racial enemies," such as Jews, Gypsies, and so on). *The Spectator*, however, speculated "philosophically" as to why there was no sense in trying to establish the identity of the perpetrators of the Katyn crime: "There is more to be said for leaving the dead to their sleep. No amount of investigation will bring them to life."[69]

And yet by January 1944 it turned out that clarifying the issue of Katyn was highly desirable. This time it was the Soviet authorities who demanded an inquiry. After recapturing the Katyn area from the Germans, the Soviets established a special commission to prove that the Germans were in fact guilty in Katyn. The outcome was obvious before the investigation started, since the commission's actual title left no doubt on the matter: "The Special Commission to Establish and Examine the Circumstances of the Shooting by the German Fascist Invaders in the Katyn Wood of Prisoners of War—Polish Officers."

The professor of medicine Nikolai Burdenko, whom Stalin had nominated to chair the commission, later supposedly confided in his friend Boris Olshansky on the matter in 1946. According to Olshansky, Burdenko told him that "There is no doubt such Katyns were and will be happening. . . . If you start digging our Mother Russia you will find quite a few such excavations. . . . We had to make a complete denial of the widely spread German accusations. On personal orders of Stalin I went to the place where the graves were found. It was a spot check and all bodies [in the graves] were four years old. Death took place in 1940. . . . Actually, for me as a doctor, the question is clear and there is no argument about it. Our comrades from the NKVD made a great blunder."[70] Olshansky fled to the West two years later and revealed Burdenko's supposed confession.

Meanwhile, the Soviet commission's "findings" of German culpability for the crime appeared to inspire the Western Allies' trust—at least officially. In January 1944, the Soviet authorities organized a special show for the benefit of the West beside the open graves at Katyn. Among the invited public was Kathleen Harriman, the twenty-five-year-old daughter of the American ambassador in Moscow, Averell Harriman, as well as the embassy's third secretary, John Melby. They were accompanied by a group of Western news correspondents. Some of them later described the journey. Judging by these accounts, the visit to Katyn was virtually indistinguishable from the carefully choreographed visits of Western fellow travelers of the 1930s. The English journalist Alexander Werth, who took part in the trip, later recalled in his book, *Russia At War, 1941–1945*: "The whole procedure had a distinctly prefabricated appearance. Altogether, the Russian starting point in the whole inquiry was that the very suggestion that the Russians might have murdered the Poles had to be ruled out right away; the whole idea was insulting and outrageous."[71]

One of Werth's fellow journalists, the *Sunday Times* correspondent Edmund Stevens, recalled in 1989 the trip's details: "We were assigned a special sleeping car and a restaurant car, filled with caviar and other tidbits, which we really missed in the forest."[72] Stevens must have had an uncommonly strong stomach, given that he did not lose his appetite for Soviet caviar "and other tidbits" at the open graves in the wood. Here, Werth's own words best convey the strange atmosphere of the visit:

> On January 15 a large group of Western correspondents, accompanied
> by Kathie Harriman, the daughter of Averell Harriman, the United States
> Ambassador, went on their gruesome journey to look at the hundreds
> of bodies in Polish uniforms which had been dug up at Katyn Forest by
> Russian authorities. It was said that some 10,000 had been buried there, but

actually only a few hundred "samples" had been unearthed and were filling even the cold winter air with unforgettable stench. The Russian Committee of Inquiry, which had been set up, and was presiding over the proceedings, consisted of forensic medicine men, such as Academician Burdenko, and a number of "personalities" whose very presence was to give the whole inquiry an air of great respectability and authority; among them were the Metropolitan Nicholas of Moscow, the famous writer Alexei Tolstoy, Mr. Potemkin [a *nomen omen*—D.T.], the Minister of Education, and others. What qualifications these "personalities" had for judging the "freshness" or "antiquity" of unearthed corpses was not quite clear. Yet the whole argument turned precisely on this very point: had the Poles been buried by the Russians in the spring of 1940, or by the Germans in the late summer or autumn of 1941? Professor Burdenko, wearing a green frontier guard cap, was busy dissecting corpses, and, waving a bit of greenish stinking liver at the tip of his scalpel would say "Look how lovely and fresh it looks."[73]

Then the foreign guests returned to their private carriage in which champagne and other Russian delicacies awaited them.

Despite the undoubted skill that the Soviet authorities had acquired in bamboozling Western guests, the Katyn performance was somewhat unconvincing. On his return from Katyn, Melby stated in his report: "It is apparent that the evidence in the Russian case is incomplete in several respects, that it is badly put together, and the show was put on for the benefit of the correspondents without opportunity for independent investigation or verification."[74] Kathleen Harriman noticed that the witnesses produced by the Soviets "were very well rehearsed and appeared subdued rather than nervous, their pieces having been learned by heart. . . . We were expected to accept the statements of the high-ranking Soviet officials as true, because they said it was true."[75] Melby reported that "all the statements [by the witnesses] were glibly given, as though by rote. Under questioning the witnesses became hesitant and stumbled, until they were dismissed by the Commission." During the train journey back from Katyn, Melby noticed that the representatives of the Soviet Foreign Ministry "were almost unduly anxious on the return trip to be assured that we were convinced." And yet all these observations did not prevent Kathleen Harriman and John Melby from reaching in their reports the only politically correct conclusion. Melby wrote: "On balance, however, and despite the loopholes, the Russian version is convincing."[76] In November 1952, when testifying before a special committee of the US House of Representatives on the subject of Katyn, both Melby as well as Kathleen Harriman changed their minds, and claimed that everything had pointed to Soviet guilt. Of course, a great deal had changed in American politics between 1944 and 1952. In the meantime, both the Americans and their British allies accepted the Soviet version of Katyn without apparent reservation.

On May 5, 1945, when Soviet forces were celebrating the capture of Berlin, and the Western world had long stopped thinking about Katyn, a US Army officer who had recently been released from German captivity showed up at the headquarters of the US 104th Division. He introduced himself as Lt. Colonel John Van Vliet and was carrying pictures of the Katyn graves uncovered by the Germans in 1943. He demanded to be put in immediate touch with the Pentagon. This was soon arranged. It turned out that Van Vliet had been taken prisoner by the Germans in North Africa in 1943 and, together with another US officer, Captain Donald Stewart, had been taken to Katyn, where the Germans had showed him the opened graves of murdered Polish officers. On the basis of the information that the Germans had provided him, Van Vliet was in no doubt whatsoever that the Soviets had committed the massacre. At the Pentagon, he was received by General Clayton Bissell from military intelligence. When he made an extensive report about Katyn, Bissell ordered Van Vliet to keep everything he had told him in utter secrecy, after which he classified the report "Top Secret" and locked it in the files. When five years later efforts were made to find the document, it emerged that it had mysteriously disappeared. It was established that the sole copy had been sent from the Pentagon to the State Department, and specifically to the department run by Alger Hiss, who had been a confidant of Roosevelt and an adviser at the Yalta conference. According to the FBI's Venona files, he was also a Soviet agent, leading one to speculate whether he might have played a role in the document's disappearance.[77]

As the culminating point of the Allied victory over the Nazis, the Nuremberg Trials were also the high point of the black-and-white World War II myth. Sir Alexander Cadogan, who in 1943 had considered the prospect of cooperating with the Katyn murderers to try Nazi criminals in court to be "exceedingly difficult to swallow," now had to swallow more than he had bargained for. The chief Soviet prosecutor at Nuremberg, Roman Rudenko, included the Katyn crime on the indictment sheet against the Nazi authorities. The sole piece of supporting evidence that the Soviets presented in this case was the report of the Burdenko commission. If there was a moment during the trial when Hermann Göring could speak of holding the moral high ground over his accusers, then this was it. "I didn't expect that the Russians would be so impudent to mention Poland," he said. Another of the accused, Baldur von Schirach, commented: "When they talked about Poland, I thought I would die."[78]

This Soviet display of hypocrisy came within a hairsbreadth of causing a scandal. The defense lawyers at Nuremberg easily undermined the credibility of the "material proof" produced by the Soviets. Telford Taylor, who replaced Robert Jackson as the chief counsel for the prosecution, feared that the trial might be compromised in the eyes of the world. He tried to convince his Soviet colleagues to leave the Katyn affair alone. Rudenko stuck to his guns, however. Eventually the British judge Geoffrey Lawrence headed off the whole business by leaving out the Katyn issue in the final verdicts. Nevertheless, the Soviets carried out their own "trial" and hanged a group of German soldiers in Minsk for having committed the crime. These included officers who had been in the area of Katyn during the discovery of the graves and the work of the first international commission in the spring of 1943.

American and British authorities also tried to cover up the Katyn crime after the war, despite the fact that in the late 1940s the black-and-white World War II myth was mothballed and government propaganda took on a completely new tone—this time anticommunist. In 1949, the Polish community in America succeeded in establishing the public Commission on Examining the Katyn Crime, with Arthur Bliss Lane chairing. Lane was the former US ambassador to Poland who had resigned the ambassadorship in February 1947 out of anger at US policy toward Poland, and who a year later had published a book with the telling title *I Saw Poland Betrayed*. The US government–subsidized Voice of America radio station refused to broadcast Lane's speech at the Katyn Commission's opening session. Only in 1951 at the height of the Cold War did the commission succeed in influencing Congress to demand an official inquiry into Katyn. Witnesses were heard, evidence was scrutinized, and the same conclusions emerged. This did not mean a complete and irreversible break with the prevailing policy of silence, however. As late as 1978, during the period of American-Soviet détente, the Voice of America managed to censor a broadcast of a statement by the Polish writer Andrzej Braun, who criticized Poland's communist leadership at a congress of the Association of Polish Writers for censoring the truth about Katyn.[79]

As for the Soviet authorities, they steadfastly lied about Katyn almost right up to the very end of the USSR. In 1988, forty-five years after German radio informed the world about the discovery of the Katyn graves, the leader of the now-waning land of Soviets, Mikhail Gorbachev, allowed some inquiry into the Katyn issue. After the Soviet Union collapsed, a great many Soviet documents from secret files on the subject were released and published.[80] It was only then that the locations of the remaining mass murders of Poles in 1940 were identified: Tver, Kharkiv, and Bykivnya. Forensic experts from Poland were allowed to rebury the bodies and conduct thorough forensic examinations. Thus Katyn became most likely the best documented and evidenced of Stalin's crimes. The Office of the Chief Military Prosecutor of the Russian Federation started an official investigation in order to examine all existing evidence (a few members of the NKVD executioners' teams were still alive and gave depositions in return for immunity). The twentieth century was drawing to a close. The time was coming when World War II could be finally consigned to history. At least, that is what one might have assumed.

Practically all the essential evidence was collected before 1994, but the Russian Office of the Chief Military Prosecutor showed itself in no hurry to end the case with an obvious conclusion. Instead, in 2004, under the new Russian leadership of Vladimir Putin, the investigation was secretly terminated without any concluding statement. This decision was discovered by the public only later after the fact. This was quite a shock for those who had assumed that the only commonsensical way for the Russian authorities to deal with this Soviet crime of the past was to reveal all the evidence, pronounce the obvious verdict, and respectfully allow the Katyn massacres to pass into history. Who could possibly benefit from denying a mass murder committed more than six decades earlier by Stalin's regime? This was the regime responsible not only for Katyn but also for the deaths of millions of Russians. What could possibly be the purpose of avoiding any admission of Soviet responsibility for this crime when the most crucial archival and forensic evidence had already been revealed, studied, and publicized all over the world? And yet, official and legally binding confirmation of Stalin's responsibility proved too much for the Russian authorities. This means that for all legal purposes in Russia, Katyn was neither a crime against humanity nor a political crime and that the perpetrators are still theoretically unknown. Ironically, this astonishing state of affairs is clearly at odds with Soviet tradition, which had always recognized the Katyn massacre as a crime against humanity. Except that, in line with this tradition, the guilty ones had, of course, been the Germans.

Blind Man's Bluff in Kolyma

Four months after Kathleen Harriman and John Melby's trip by private lounge car to Katyn, US Vice President Henry Wallace flew to Kolyma. This was to be the first stage of a journey across the Soviet Far East and Siberia, after which Wallace planned to visit Mongolia and China. On May 23, 1944, an American C-54 transport aircraft carrying Wallace with a small staff flew from Alaska and landed on a Soviet airstrip built two years earlier specifically for American aircraft carrying weapons, ammunition, food, and military and industrial equipment, all part of the US Lend-Lease program. Wallace's aircraft was refueled and took off again. The following day the American guests reached Magadan, the capital of the vast area whose name, Kolyma, had acquired an ominous reputation among prisoners in the Gulag throughout Stalin's empire. For the inhabitants of the Gulag, Kolyma meant hell on earth, the place from which one could not hope to return.

But Kolyma also played a large role in the American economy. A not-insignificant part of the gold held at that time in the vaults of the US Federal Reserve came precisely from here: the mines of Kolyma. When Franklin Roosevelt became president in 1933, he had already drawn up a plan to revive the moribund US economy and to lead the country out of economic depression. One of the plan's key points was the financial policies that he and his friend, the treasury secretary Henry Morgenthau, had worked out to increase the nation's gold reserves. Shortly before this, rich seams of gold had been discovered in Kolyma, and the Soviet authorities had moved with lightning speed to exploit them using slave labor. The life of a slave in Kolyma was short. The inhuman conditions, the Arctic temperatures, the physical exhaustion, the brutality of the supervisors and the cruelty of the camp criminals offered scant chance of survival. But the corpses were continually replaced with new consignments of prisoners and production grew. In this way, the Soviet Union became the United States' principal supplier of gold. Both countries gained from this exchange. The US government bought more or less any amount of Soviet gold, and the surpluses not bought by the Americans commanded high prices in New York, London, and Paris. Advertisements appeared in the *New York Times* urging wealthy Americans to invest in Soviet gold bonds. The Soviets used the hard currency earned from the sale of the gold to buy Western technology and machinery essential for modernizing the USSR and turning it into a military superpower.

As new mass graves filled up in Kolyma, the stocks of gold bars stamped with a hammer and sickle grew in the vaults of the US Federal Reserve. It would not be quite accurate to say that American authorities were unaware how the Soviets extracted the gold. After all, during the gold mines' development they initially needed the knowledge and experience of American engineers and technicians. Not everything could be hidden from them. In 1932, an American engineer in Russia named Raymond Vandervoort told the US State Department that

> a good deal of the labor employed in the gold mines is forced labor and that the casualties among these people are exceedingly heavy and he [i.e., Vandervoort] estimates that 50 to 60 thousand a year die from exposure, hardship,

and cold throughout Siberia. . . . They are the most persecuted people on
the earth. . . . The attitude openly expressed by officials with regard to the
casualties among workers is one of unparalleled hard-heartedness. They take
no notice of the deaths and insist that through these casualties they have less
persons to feed. . . . The Russians butcher and butcher and butcher. There has
been no let-up in the number of executions.[81]

Reports of this kind regularly found their way into the government archives
but elicited no response. Just in case, however, Henry Morgenthau reassured
the Soviets that "the methods they used were of no interest to the American
government."[82]

During 1942 and 1943—the period right before Wallace's visit to Kolyma—
the overall mortality in the Gulag across the USSR was an average of one prisoner in four. The victims succumbed mainly to starvation, illness, exhaustion,
and the cold. In their fight against Hitler, the Soviet state took care of its own
army first of all, while not neglecting the political police. There were not enough
resources for the slaves, however. Stalin decided to organize some of the Gulag's
inmates, especially those sentenced for common crimes, into Red Army penal
battalions where the chances of survival were minimal. However, the prisoners
willingly went to the front, since this at least gave them some hope of avoiding
death by starvation in the camps. Political prisoners—that is, "right-wingers,"
"Trotskyists," or others sentenced for "betraying their homeland," "espionage,"
"terrorism," "sabotage," and so on—had to stay in the camps at least until the
end of the war, irrespective of the length of their sentence. The Gulag chiefs
faced a real problem meeting production targets since the camp workforce
simply grew weaker and died off at an alarming rate. Admittedly, even during
the war, the NKVD still continually carried out sweeps—first among their
own citizens and later among the populations of conquered countries—and
supplied the Gulag with new batches of prisoners, but these also soon flagged
in the inhuman conditions. Unbeknownst to them, the Americans provided
significant help to the Gulag in solving this problem. American canned goods
and flour reached not only the front lines but also the camps. The same was
true of machinery and equipment destined for the Soviet wartime economy.

When American Lend-Lease aid—estimated to be worth eleven billion in
1940s dollars—arrived in the USSR, American ships had to be unloaded in Soviet
ports. This job was often performed by Gulag prisoners. This did not escape the
sailors' attention. J. S. Schulz, captain of the vessel *City of Omaha*, which arrived at
the port of Molotovsk near Archangel, wrote in a report that when kitchen scraps
were being taken off to give to the pigs, a Soviet guard used his bayonet to prod

a prisoner rooting around in the scraps and then shot him. "If a prisoner takes a step in the wrong direction, or commits some minor infraction, they kill him," wrote Captain Schulz. During the same stay in Molotovsk, Soviet guards shot another prisoner on the deck of the *City of Omaha* in full view of the American crew. The captain even had to get the port authorities to take the body off his ship.[83]

Before Vice President Wallace even arrived in Kolyma, rumors of his impending visit began to spread among the prisoners. Elinor Lipper described Wallace's visit in her prison memoirs, which were published in the West at the start of the 1950s. Lipper, a Dutch Jew with Swiss citizenship, had been a communist in the 1930s. When she arrived in the homeland of the proletariat, it took the authorities no more than two months to arrest her. She ended up in Kolyma—in other words, her chances of ever returning to the land of the living fell to zero. After the war, a miracle happened, however: Swiss authorities took up her case in 1947, and Elinor Lipper was granted permission to leave the USSR. It took eighteen months of passing through one transit camp and prison after another for her to leave the country that had once aroused her enthusiasm. Shortly thereafter she produced her Kolyma testimony for the world.

"None of the numerous high commissions ever aroused so much excitement as Wallace's visit to Kolyma during the war," she recalled. Rumors circulating among the prisoners began to assume ever more extravagant forms. Some people maintained that in exchange for American help during the war, the USSR was about to cede Kolyma to the United States. There were heated discussions as to whether under the terms of this transaction Soviet territory would be handed over to the Americans together with the prisoners on it. "It was a typical prisoners' fairy tale, as absurd as it was tenacious. And it received a tremendous stimulus when news came of the impending visit of the American Vice-President," wrote Lipper.[84]

Of course, the Soviet authorities had no intention of showing Wallace the real Kolyma, with its camps, hunger, violence, and death. Just as in the case of countless visits by Western dignitaries before the war, the issue was for Wallace "to see with his own eyes" that all the rumors of Soviet slavery and the horrors of Kolyma were baseless fabrications of anti-Soviet propaganda. There was no show camp in Kolyma along the lines of Bolshevo near Moscow. Therefore, this time it was decided to forgo the fairytales about *perekovka,* to not mention the camps at all, and to show the guest Kolyma as if normal workers were laboring there in everyday conditions. It was decided to remove anything reminiscent of the Gulag from the American guests' field of vision. Even the guard towers along the route that Wallace took were dismantled. Of course, if ever a prisoner found himself in the vicinity of the Americans, then any attempt at contact with them meant voluntary martyrdom. Punishments in the camp were cruel; for example, north of Magadan was a special penal camp called Serpantinka. Little is known about it, since barely a handful of souls survived it. One of them, Olga Adamowa-Sliozberg, wrote that it was so crowded in the huts that "we took turns sitting on the floor—the others had to stand and await their turn. From time to time in the morning the doors were opened and ten or a dozen prisoners were called out. No one responded, and so they then dragged people out and shot whoever came to hand."[85]

Wallace's three-day visit passed without any untoward incidents. Or at least Wallace did not mention anything suspicious in his account of the visit in the book *Soviet Asia Mission*, published in 1946. The American guests were personally greeted in Magadan by the infamous master of life and death over Kolyma prisoners, Ivan Nikishov, head of the NKVD-run slave labor enterprise Dalstroy, dressed for the occasion in a civilian suit. In his book, Wallace wrote: "At Magadan I met Ivan Feodorovich Nikishov, a Russian, director of Dalstroy (the Far Northern Construction Trust), which is a combination TVA and Hudson's Bay Company."[86] He looked at Soviet reality in light of the American propaganda of the day, seeking at every step similarities between Stalin's Russia and Roosevelt's America. "But the Hudson's Bay Company is not run by the police nor does it make use of forced labor," as Elinor Lipper corrected in her memoir. "Furthermore, neither the Hudson's Bay Company nor the TVA shoots its workers if they refuse to go to work."[87]

Meanwhile Wallace ate up everything his Soviet hosts fed him, and two years later solemnly trotted it out in his book. He wrote, for instance, that Nikishov had told him, not without a certain pride, that "twelve years ago the first settlers arrived and put up eight prefabricated houses. Today Magadan has 40,000 inhabitants and all are well housed."[88] Nikishov doubtlessly did not explain to Wallace who these "settlers" were who had so willingly come out to Kolyma. He apparently also did not mention that they had not come of their own free will but usually were crammed onto trains that had traveled east for about a month, with the corpses removed from time to time from the freight cars. One of the prisoners recalled that when his "transport" finally reached the transit camp at Nakhodka near Vladivostok, about 70 percent of those who had survived the journey were suffering from night blindness and diarrhea.[89]

Those among the Kolyma "settlers" who, after reaching the end of the railroad line thought that their torment had ended, were in for a cruel surprise. In the port of Nakhodka they were herded onto ships. These were old American, British, and Dutch freighters, bought up by the USSR and adapted for carrying prisoners: they were fitted with machine guns and metal grates. These vessels sailed north through the seas of Japan and Okhotsk to Magadan. We should add that during the war, these vessels were overhauled for free in American shipyards. British historian Tim Tzouliadis has remarked on this little-known fact as follows: "It was as if the Reich-ministry had arranged to have its railway engines repaired in Philadelphia and then shipped back across the Atlantic to recommence their journeys to Auschwitz."[90] The Americans did not just overhaul the Kolyma ships of death but provided the Soviets with new ones, such as the *Odessa*. These were Liberty ships. After minor modifications (the installation of metal grates and placing guards on the decks) they performed splendidly as floating prisons. The prisoners were crammed into the holds below decks and locked up for several days when the ship sailed close to Japanese territorial waters. This was done out of fear of the interested gaze of Japanese fisherman and the border patrol. The NKVD tossed food down into the holds where a savage battle for survival took place.

In this battle, criminals fared by far the best. "During the entire voyage, which lasted a week, no member of the guard or the ship's crew ever entered the prisoners' hold. They were afraid to, especially when a large number of murderers and bandits were being transported," wrote Elinor Lipper. "None of them took any account of what went on below decks. As a result, during all such voyages the criminals put across a reign of terror. If they want the clothing of any of the counterrevolutionaries, they take it from him. If the counterrevolutionary offers any resistance, he is beaten up. The old and weak are robbed of their bread. On every transport ship a number of prisoners die as a result of such treatment." Lipper recalled her own journey: "We lay squeezed together on the tarred floor of the hold because the criminals had taken possession of the plank platform. If one of us dared to raise her head, she was greeted by a rain of fishheads and entrails from above. When any of the seasick criminals threw up, the vomit came down upon us. At night, the men criminals bribed the guard, who was posted on the stairs to the hold, to send over a few women for them. They paid the guard in bread that they had stolen from their fellow prisoners."[91]

The criminals' brutal domination over the rest of the prisoners did not end with the battle for survival. Sometimes all it took was a bribe, and the guards allowed the jailbirds to "have some fun" on the ships. Their favorite amusement was the "tram," that is, gang rape. Elena Glinka describes this as follows: "They raped according to the command of the tram 'conductor' . . . then, on the command '*konchai bazar*' heaved off, reluctantly, giving up their place to the next man, who was standing in full readiness . . . dead women were pulled by their legs to the door, and stacked over the threshold. Those who remained were brought back to consciousness—water was thrown at them—and the line began again."[92] Janusz Bardach, a Polish prisoner who arrived in Kolyma two years before Wallace, recalled: "Several men attacked each woman at once. I could see the victims' white bodies twisting, their legs kicking forcefully, their hands clawing the men's faces. The women bit, cried and wailed. The rapists smacked them back . . . when the rapists ran out of women, some of the bulkier men turned to the bed boards and hunted for young men. These adolescents were added to the carnage, lying still on their stomachs, bleeding and crying on the floor."[93]

When the ship reached harbor, the dead and the dying were thrown onto the shore, while the living were herded to a transit camp where they eventually ended up in a selection process, commonly called the "slave market." Here their fate hung in the balance. Being sent to "general work," that is to the gold mines, forest work, building roads, and other such tasks, usually meant hunger, cold, fear, and a gradual debilitation—often leading to a complete loss of one's humanity and death. Being sent to the hospital or some ancillary job in the camp could mean survival—at least for a time.

Meanwhile, the more Wallace learned about his hosts, the more he was struck by the similarities between life in the United States and in Kolyma. The first evening in Magadan, the US vice president, together with Nikishov and his entourage, watched *The North Star*—a new Hollywood hit, written by Lillian Hellman, recounting the happy lives of Soviet collective farm workers in Ukraine and their heroic resistance against the German invaders. Wallace had brought a copy of the film with him to Kolyma in order to present it proudly to the head of the camps. "The Hollywood version of life on a Soviet collective farm seemed to amuse the Russians a great deal," remarked Wallace, "although they were warmly appreciative of its friendly spirit." As confirmation of his observations Wallace quoted Mrs. Nikishov's words: "It is marvelous that Americans would produce a picture about us." He then commented: "In making this film, Hollywood built an entire village only to demolish it. Magadan is not such [a] synthetic town. It has solid underpinnings."[94]

The American vice president was probably unaware of the reasons for his NKVD hosts' amusement as they sat in Magadan and watched the fruits of Lillian Hellman's imagination regarding Soviet life. It would probably have been even harder for him to imagine how much he himself must have amused the local NKVD—an American dignitary strolling around Kolyma, unaware that he was playing the part of the fool in a comedy they directed, acted in, and were the only members of the audience who understood the theatrical conventions. Regular bursts of laughter, this time probably in the Kremlin itself, undoubtedly must have greeted the appearance two years later of Wallace's book *Soviet Asia Mission*. Wallace's comments on Hollywood's show villages and the real

Magadan—comments inspired by the fool's progress, staged especially for the naive visitor by the NKVD—must surely rank among the world classics of unintended comic (or more precisely, tragicomic) dramatic effects.

On the second day of the visit, the NKVD took their American guests to two gold mines, which immediately impressed Wallace by the scale of their workings that, in his view, were more extensive than the gold mines in Fairbanks, Alaska. The American politician admired the 350-kilometer road going north from Magadan and the truck repair shops. He did not fail to notice, "The plant has a complete set of machine tools and is able to make on the spot many spare parts such as we might order from Detroit."[95] "He does not say—or does not know—that this highway was built entirely by prisoners and that tens of thousands gave their lives in building it," Elinor Lipper remarks.[96] At the gold mines Wallace had an opportunity to talk with some workers. Or at least that is what he thought he was doing. "The Kolyma gold miners," he writes in his book, "are big, husky young men, who came out to the Far East from European Russia."[97] The people with whom Wallace spoke did indeed look like that. There are photographs of this meeting, although these people were not real "Kolyma gold miners" but Komsomol activists, appropriately rehearsed and dressed in work clothes.

As for the "Kolyma gold miners," their completely different appearance has been described by those who managed to survive and tell the tale. In keeping with general working practices in the Gulag, the energy level of prisoners in Kolyma engaged in extracting gold gradually began to fall, and the smaller the norms were that they achieved, the lower their rations became. In a nutshell, they were "goners." With additional reductions in rations during the war, this would happen very quickly. "Goners" were the lowest caste in the Gulag prisoner hierarchy, like the "muselmänner" in the Nazi camps. One of the prisoners in Kolyma at the time of Wallace's visit described these "goners":

They neglected themselves, did not wash—even when they had the opportunity to do so. Nor did the wicks bother to search for and kill the lice that sucked their blood. The *dokhodyagi* did not wipe the dribble off the ends of their noses with the sleeves of their *bushlats* . . . the wick was oblivious to blows. When set upon by fellow *zeks*, he would cover his head to ward off the punches. He would fall to the floor and when left alone, his condition permitting, he would get up and go off whimpering as if nothing had happened. After work the *dokhodyaga* could be seen hanging around the kitchen begging for scraps. For amusement, the cook would throw a dipperful of soup in his face. On such occasions, the poor soul would hurriedly pass his fingers over his wet whiskers and lick them. . . . The wicks stood around the tables, waiting for someone to leave some soup or gruel. When that happened, the nearest lunged for the leavings. In the ensuing scramble they often spilled the soup. And then, on hands and knees, they fought and scraped until the last bit of precious food was stuffed into their mouths.[98]

The author of this description, a prisoner named Thomas Sgovio, would probably have given a great deal to get near Vice President Wallace. He was, after all, an American, born in Buffalo. His father, a communist activist, had emigrated to the homeland of the world proletariat in 1933. Young Thomas Sgovio, together with his mother and sister, had followed two years later. Thomas's father was employed at the Ford plant in Gorky. Thomas started out as an illustrator in the Soviet publication *Sovietland*, produced by TASS and aimed at Americans just like him and other supporters of the USSR. By 1937, Thomas Sgovio, like his family, no longer had any doubt that they had made a terrible mistake. Their American friends in the USSR were daily disappearing into the maw of the NKVD. Wanting to get out of the USSR at any price, Sgovio went to the American embassy in Moscow on March 21, 1938. The embassy, led at the time by Joseph Davies, was in no hurry to help people like Sgovio, however. Although there were many of them now in desperate straits, they were usually sent away with a receipt. Thomas Sgovio was told to wait for a reply and to go home. The embassy staff knew that applicants leaving the building were routinely arrested by the NKVD but did not bother to warn them. Thomas Sgovio, like very many other people in the same situation, was calmly allowed to leave the embassy, after which he was, of course, arrested. That was how he ended up in Kolyma, where his American origins—the direct cause of his misfortune—probably contributed to his survival. The bored criminals in his hut happily sat and listened to Thomas Sgovio's stories about famous American gangsters like Al Capone and John Dillinger. So he came under the protection of the omnipotent camp bandits and as a reward often received an extra helping of food. His artistic talents also came to his aid: he learned tattooing, a highly prized skill in the criminal world. He soon was employed making signs in the camp. For an extra bowl of soup and a release from general work, the young American from Buffalo wrote in well-formed Cyrillic letters on placards for Kolyma: ЧЕСТНЫМ ТРУДОМ ИСКУПАЕМ НАШУ ВИНУ (With honest work we redeem our guilt).

Vice President Henry Wallace never met his compatriot Thomas Sgovio. Enchanted by his conversations with the "husky young men" in the gold mine, the American dignitary had no idea of the man's existence. During the chats with the "gold miners," Wallace, as befit a meticulous and principled man, did notice a number of suspicious details in their appearance, however. It did not escape his notice that the vigorous Kolyma workers were wearing American rubber boots. The conscientious and perceptive politician recalled that the terms of Lend-Lease did not permit the use of special delivery equipment in the gold mines. Fortunately, the ever-hovering Nikishov calmed his guest's fears, assuring him that the specific boots he had spotted had been bought "for cash in the early days of the war." This apparently satisfied Wallace. He did not inquire whether that was when the USSR had been cooperating with Hitler. Perhaps he didn't have time, since, as he wrote in his book, "the miners asked me to take back a message of solidarity to the people of the United States. Their trade union leader, N. I. Adagin, sent his best regards to Sidney Hillman and Philip Murray."[99] This is not a joke: Wallace in all seriousness writes about the Kolyma gold miners' trade union.

It should be noted that Wallace's concerns about the boots were unjustified. The real Kolyma gold miners did not as a rule wear either American boots or clothes. As for the prisoners, they had a specific attitude toward clothes. The Kolyma veteran Janusz Bardach, recalling a "goner" who collapsed after evening roll call, describes this:

> A group formed around him. 'I get the hat,' one man said. Others grabbed the victim's boots, foot rags, coat and pants. A fight broke out over his undergarments.
>
> No sooner had the fallen prisoner been stripped naked than he moved his head, raised his hand, and stated weakly but clearly, 'It's so cold.' But his head flopped back into the snow and a glazed look came over his eyes. The ring of scavengers turned away with whatever scraps they had, unaffected. In those few minutes after being stripped, he probably died of exposure.[100]

Apart from the boots, no other Lend-Lease items struck Wallace. Clearly the American tractors, trucks, machinery, canned goods, and sacks of flour and cornmeal were well hidden. The prisoners used empty cans to make mugs, oil lamps, pots, pans, stove chimneys, and even buttons. Anne Applebaum comments that it would be hard for the prisoners to imagine "the surprise such ingenuity would have occasioned in the country where the cans had originated."[101]

Kolyma veteran Varlam Shalamov wrote how one Lend-Lease item was used in a way that would have caused even greater astonishment. Shalamov recalled the supply of grease for machinery:

> Ah yes, the machine grease! The barrel was immediately attacked by a crowd of starving men who knocked out the bottom right on the spot with a stone. In their hunger they claimed the machine grease was butter sent by Lend-Lease and there remained less than half a barrel by the time a sentry was

sent to guard it and the camp administration drove off the crowd of starving, exhausted men with rifle-shots. The fortunate ones gulped down this Lend-Lease butter, not believing it was simply machine grease.[102]

Shalamov wrote how the camp authorities decided to use a new bulldozer they had received through Lend-Lease:

> The permafrost keeps and reveals secrets. All of our loved ones who died in Kolyma, all those who were shot, beaten to death, sucked dry by starvation, can still be recognized even after tens of years. There were no gas furnaces in Kolyma. The corpses wait in stone, in the permafrost. . . .
>
> The bulldozer scraped up frozen bodies, thousands of skeleton-like corpses. Nothing had decayed: the twisted fingers, the pus-filled toes which were reduced to mere stumps after frostbite, the dry skin scratched bloody and eyes burning with a hungry gleam. . . .
>
> The camp administration decided that the first job for the bulldozer received from Lend-Lease should not be work in the forest, but something far more important.[103]

In the best tradition of Soviet hospitality toward Western dignitaries, the hosts in Kolyma did not fail to show Wallace the delights of the surrounding country, as well as the local cultural attractions. During a walk in the taiga, Wallace developed a strong affection for Nikishov, who "gamboled about, enjoying the wonderful air immensely," as the American writes.[104] "It is too bad that Wallace never saw him 'gamboling about' on one of his drunken rages around the prison camps, raining filthy, savage language upon the heads of exhausted, starving prisoners, having them locked up in solitary confinement for no offense whatsoever, and sending them into the gold mines to work fourteen and sixteen hours a day, at no matter what human cost," Elinor Lipper commented.[105] In the evening there was the theater. Wallace had an opportunity to admire a performance of music and ballet in the Magadan theater named, appropriately enough, after Gorky. The guest was in raptures. "I don't think," he wrote "I have ever seen anything better put on by the talent of a single city."[106]

On closer examination, this seems hardly surprising. Wallace, of course, did not know that the artists performing for him were hardly "taken from just one town." The group billed as a "Red Army amateur choir" was anything but; the "local Magadan orchestra" was not quite local. Prisoners who performed on the Kolyma stage had, in their previous lives, played, sang, and danced professionally in the best Russian theaters, opera houses, and concert halls. The custom of maintaining an orchestra or a theater company in a camp dated from the triumphal period of *perekovka*. For camp commandants, this was an element of genteel decorum as well as a source of prestige; for the prisoner-artists, work on the stage represented an opportunity to survive away from murderous labor and in tolerable conditions. Just as in numerous Nazi concentration camps, prisoners in many a Soviet camp were herded off to work to the sounds of a camp orchestra.

Wallace, much taken with the Kolyma performers, did not have time to congratulate them in person for the successful show, however; as Elinor Lipper writes, "He never met any of these actors because immediately after the curtain fell they were loaded aboard a truck and returned to the camp."[107] In any event, prisoners knew what awaited them if they failed to keep the big secret. Thomas Sgovio reminisced, "One word or sign that we were prisoners would be considered an act of treason."[108] They needed no reminding that this quite simply would mean being shot.

Applauding the Kolyma performance, Wallace probably did not imagine that the theater was itself simply an element in another, larger theater, all around him at every step. He probably also did not realize that there was a moment when the whole three-day performance staged especially for him in Kolyma almost came undone. During a visit to a state farm near Magadan, Wallace fell into a conversation with the female pig farmers who'd been introduced to him. Wallace, being an agricultural expert himself, asked some technical questions. He was answered with a troubling silence. Wallace did not know that none of the women understood what they were saying because all of them worked in the prison administration in Magadan and had been dressed up as pig farmers. The real state farm workers, prisoners, were of course locked up far away from the guests. However, the interpreter was up to the task and immediately distracted Wallace.

Later, when visiting the town of Magadan, the American dignitary was pleasantly surprised by the abundance of Russian products in the stores. He did not fail even to go into one of them to buy some small local product. However, the inhabitants of Magadan were even more astonished than Wallace, for they had never yet seen such abundance in the stores. For two years they had been only able—if they were very lucky—to use their ration cards to buy a few basic products, usually supplied by the Americans. "Then Mr. Wallace went home," wrote Lipper, "and published his enthusiastic report on Soviet Asia. The watch towers were put up again, the prisoners sent out to work again, and in the empty shop windows were to be seen nothing but a few dusty and mournful boxes of matches."[109]

When Wallace and his entourage continued their journey after the three-day visit to Kolyma, the producers and leading players in the Kolyma production could toast their own success. The performance had been a triumph. Additional confirmation of their artistry later came in the form of *Soviet Asia Mission*, the book in which Wallace described not only everything precisely the way that his hosts had wanted but also proposed far-reaching conclusions on the nature of the Soviet state and on the prospects for future Soviet-American cooperation on the basis of these impressions from the journey. "The Russian and American people instinctively like each other," he wrote. "Roosevelt instantly felt at home with Stalin. Neither the Russians nor the Americans want to use modern technology as an instrument of war. We want to raise our own standards of living and we do not want to exploit other people."[110] Vice President Wallace, like President Roosevelt, was a strong proponent of expanding trade with the USSR, seeing an opportunity for great postwar profits for both countries. He saw Stalinist Russia as a future global partner for the US in a new and better postwar world order. Had Roosevelt not dropped Wallace as his running mate in favor of Truman in his successful 1944 reelection bid, then in April 1945, after the death of Roosevelt, Wallace would have become president of the United States.

Until recently it was believed that Wallace had no idea whatsoever of the existence in Kolyma of slave labor camps. This seemed extremely unlikely, given the number of accounts on the subject available to the American public, not to mention the government. But the US vice president said not a word about them. Is it possible that he really didn't know? Such an assertion might be tenable if not for a report that lay for many years in the secret Soviet archives. This document, written by Nikishov after Wallace's visit and sent to Beria, reveals that Wallace had in fact approached the Dalstroy authorities for permission to visit a camp, but this permission had been denied. As we can see, this did not negatively impact his visit, nor did it affect his enthusiastic attitude toward Soviet reality that he communicated to the American public.[111]

If Wallace did have any doubts or hesitations during his Kolyma visit, we might assume that his most important traveling companion, Professor Owen Lattimore, helped set him straight. Lattimore had visited the USSR before the war and was a person no one could have accused of being ignorant of Soviet reality, much less naivete. We can assume that as a guest of the land of Soviets, he was seen by his Soviet minders as "ambitious." In the US, he had developed a reputation as an authority on Central and East Asia. Raised in China, where his parents taught English, he was the author of books on China and Mongolia, as well as the US government's leading expert on policy toward those countries during the war. Those who knew Lattimore or had read his books could have no doubt as to what kind of image of the USSR this academic was ready to promulgate.

Lattimore had been able to travel in Mongolia in the early 1920s and was widely considered to be a top US expert on that country. From 1926, the Soviet occupation authorities in Mongolia had barred entry to all foreigners. Despite this, Lattimore seems to have hoped that being on good terms with the Soviet regime would help him to obtain a unique opportunity to travel around Mongolia. Thus he described this de facto Soviet colony as a democratic and independent country, when the Soviet authorities were deporting and executing the Mongolian elites, destroying the native religious culture, and forcibly collectivizing the countryside.

In 1932 and once again in 1934, the Soviets suppressed uprisings in Mongolia, and two years later Stalin acknowledged that the time had come to introduce Mongolia into the League of Nations, a step that required the help of Western friends of the USSR. An official in the Soviet Foreign Ministry named Igor Bogolepov received instructions from its head, Litvinov, to contact Lattimore about this issue. The professor wasted no time in getting down to business. As the leading expert on Mongolia, he assured US ambassador in Moscow William Bullitt that the country was independent, and he denied that it was in any way under Soviet influence. As it so happened, Bullitt knew the situation in Mongolia, however, since he had earlier heard the confidential confessions of the Soviet Deputy Commissar of Foreign Affairs Lev Karakhan, who had personally overseen the suppression of the most recent Mongolian uprising. Karakhan had told Bullitt that he had resolved the problem quickly and effectively. "All I had to do was oversee the purge. In a country of nomads, there are only 300 or 400 people who count. All I did on a given night was to have about 400 seized by our OGPU men, and I had them shot before dawn and installed the people that the Soviet government wanted, and Mongolia is now completely ruled by the OGPU."[112]

But this rather compromising slip-up in no way deterred Lattimore from further pro-Soviet statements. In September 1938, he defended the Stalinist trials on the pages of *Pacific Affairs*: "Verbatim records of the trials are entirely credible. . . . A great many abuses have been discovered and rectified. . . . Habitual rectification can hardly do anything but give the ordinary citizen more courage to protest, loudly, whenever he finds himself victimized by 'someone in the party,' or 'someone in the government.' That sounds to me like democracy."[113] At the same time he went on about Yezhov: "As to the suggestion that the new head of the secret service is likely to abuse his power just as Yagoda did, it is obvious that the publicity given in the Soviet Union itself to Yagoda's turpitude is a safeguard against any such thing."[114] In 1941, Roosevelt decided that Lattimore was the most competent person to whom he could entrust the delicate task of serving as US adviser to General Chiang Kai-shek in China. The US president had based his decision on the recommendation of his personal envoy to China, Lauchlin Currie, who was a confidant of his, a friend of Lattimore's, and apparently an agent of Stalin's intelligence service.[115] In 1944 Lattimore was appointed head of the Pacific section of the Office of War Information (OWI).

After Wallace and Lattimore's visit to Kolyma, *National Geographic* published an article in December 1944 by Lattimore entitled "New Road to Asia." The account of Kolyma it contained in no way differs from Wallace's impressions of the trip. According to Lattimore, Kolyma was strikingly similar to industrial areas in the Western United States, and if it differed in any way, it was definitely in Kolyma's favor, where "Instead of sin, gin and brawling of the old-time gold rush, extensive greenhouses growing tomatoes, cucumbers, and even melons, to make sure that the hardy miners get enough vitamins."[116] We should add that Lattimore had not made this up; there *were* greenhouses in Magadan. Of course, they were not there for the "hardy miners," but for the head of Dalstroy, Nikishov and his wife Gridasova. Lattimore also mentions Nikishov and Gridasova, noting that they were sensitive, well-educated people, music lovers, and art connoisseurs. Reading Lattimore's raptures in *National Geographic*, Elinor Lipper remarked: "What would Dr. Lattimore think of a man who, having visited the Nazi camps of Dachau and Auschwitz, afterwards reported only that the SS commandant of the camp had 'a sensitive interest in art and music'?"[117]

It would be better to pass over in silence Wallace and Lattimore's visit to Kolyma, along with their later accounts. It is hard to treat them as anything but a black farce in which hollow laughter is the only possible psychological response. In this farce, representatives of the free world were seen as laughingstocks by amused criminals, a group of thugs who yet again had decided to prove to the world that the truth did not exist and that what we understand by this concept is nothing but a version of events dictated by the most powerful—or simply the most brazen. "Who will take responsibility for such statements as this," wrote Elinor Lipper about Wallace's and Lattimore's accounts, "if someday the camps of Kolyma are thrown open to the inspection of the whole world, as the camps of Dachau and Auschwitz were open? Would these words bear repetition when the mounds of frozen corpses under the snow are one day disinterred to testify to what the Soviet Union really is?"[118] The trouble is that the camps of the Gulag, unlike the Nazi camps, were never liberated and so were never opened up for all the world to see.

7

The Curtain Falls, the Show Goes On

Victory

The victory over Hitler turned out to be Stalin's crowning achievement. The Soviet dictator had begun the war invading Poland as a partner of Nazi Germany, and he ended it as a hero of the free world. Together with the leaders of the United States and Great Britain, he dictated the new postwar world order. While admiring the heroism and sacrifice of the Soviet troops, the Western Allies were silent about Stalin's victims. Whether a given citizen of the USSR perished at the front, was murdered by German military or police forces, died of hunger and disease in a German camp, or suffered a similar fate in a Soviet camp or exile was often a question of chance. Sometimes it depended on that person's ethnic origin.

After the German invasion of the USSR in 1941, Stalin continued uprooting and deporting national minorities who for one reason or another did not enjoy his trust, even though many had lived in Russia for centuries. As early as the end of August 1941, despite the retreating Red Army's enormous losses, Beria managed to detach a special NKVD corps of almost fourteen thousand men commanded by Ivan Serov to carry out the armed pacification of the Volga Germans. By the end of September, the NKVD had managed to send 230 fifty-car rail "transports" carrying German exiles from the Volga to Kazakhstan and Siberia—altogether about 450,000 people. Throughout the Soviet Union, 1,209,430 people of German descent, or 82 percent of all the Germans in the USSR, were arrested and exiled or sent to the Gulag.[1]

In 1943, as Soviet forces regained areas of the USSR that had been occupied by the Germans, this persecution affected various ethnic groups. In the fall of

1943, the NKVD, under the direct supervision of Ivan Serov and Bogdan Kobulov, set about deporting peoples from the south of the USSR and the Caucasus, who had always caused problems for the Russian authorities. Thus open season was declared on the Chechens, the Ingush, the Karachays, the Crimean Tatars, the Balkars, and the Kalmyks. In this way, about nine hundred thousand people were deported to the East. In 1944, the populations of Greeks, Crimean Armenians, Bulgars, Meskhetian Turks, Kurds, and Caucasian Khemshins were removed from Crimea and the Caucasus. For this operation, nine hundred American Studebaker trucks, supplied to the Soviet Union as part of the Lend-Lease program, came in very handy. One of the Crimean Tatar deportees recalled later: "In the tightly shut wagons, people died like flies because of hunger and lack of oxygen, and no one gave us anything to eat or drink. In the villages through which we passed, the people had all been turned against us, and they had been told that we were all traitors, so there was a constant rain of stones against the sides and doors of the wagons. When they did open the doors in the middle of the steppes in Kazakhstan, we were given military rations to eat but nothing to drink, and we were told to throw all the dead out beside the railway line without burying them."[2] Another recalled: "They had deported thirty families from our village. There were one or two survivors from five families. Everyone else died of hunger or disease."[3] At the end of these deportations, the Supreme Soviet of the USSR awarded its organizers—Beria, Serov, Kobulov, and Sergey Kruglov—the Order of Suvorov First Class.

It is difficult to establish precisely how many deportees managed to survive after arriving at their destinations. Those who entered the Gulag between 1941 and 1945 had a worse chance of surviving than inmates at other times. According to reports from the Gulag administration, during this period 932,260 people died in the camps from hunger, exhaustion, illness, and "other causes." This number does not include deportees in confined settlements and those who did not survive the journey.[4]

Of course, one did not have to be a member of one of the USSR's untrustworthy peoples to end up in the Gulag, or in exile during the war. People were still sent there for the same reasons as they had been before the war. The reign of terror did not even leave frontline Red Army units unscathed. Soviet soldiers were often more afraid of the NKVD and the Soviet military counterintelligence (SMERSH) than the enemy. Merit and decorations were no protection from the camps. One soldier who learned this lesson was a young artillery captain named Aleksandr Solzhenitsyn. During lulls in the fighting in East Prussia, he corresponded with a former schoolmate, Nikolai Vitkevich, who was also serving as a frontline officer in another unit. In personal letters, both soldiers criticized Stalin, whom they also took the liberty of calling *pakhan* ("the boss" in criminal slang). In February 1945, they were arrested for this by SMERSH. Solzhenitsyn got eight years in the Gulag, and Vitkevich ten; both were also sentenced to lifelong internal exile.

NKVD and SMERSH detachments followed right behind the Soviet forces moving west. They carried out arrests among the local populations, usually on the grounds (or the pretext) of collaboration with the Nazis. This was as true for Soviet territory as it was for the conquered countries of East and Central Europe, where the ground was being laid for Soviet occupation or for future puppet governments designated by Stalin. In addition to real or alleged collaborators, the first to end up in Soviet prisons and camps were members of various national liberation movements fighting during the war against the Germans (and other enemies and rivals) without Stalin's authorization. At the same time, politically active people were being hunted down, as were representatives of local elites who had demonstrated independence and who could in the future play a role in social resistance to Sovietization.

During 1944 and 1945, Ukrainians began to stream into the Gulag in large numbers, followed a little later by Lithuanians, Latvians, Estonians, and eventually Hungarians, Romanians, and of course Germans (not counting POWs). Entering the territory of prewar Poland, Soviet forces immediately set to liquidating the Polish resistance movement, above all Home Army (AK) detachments and the structures of the Polish underground state. The Polish London government's Western allies did not protest when "transports" of captured AK soldiers headed east for the camps, using the same route that Polish citizens of the eastern borderlands had taken in 1940–41 during the Nazi-Soviet alliance.

On March 28, 1945, six weeks after Roosevelt, Churchill, and Stalin's historic meeting at Yalta, a different meeting was to take place in Pruszków near Warsaw between representatives of the USSR and local representatives of the Polish London government to discuss the situation in Poland and Polish-Soviet relations. Sixteen leaders of Underground Poland arrived at the invitation of the Soviet authorities' representative, General Ivanov. This turned out to be a trap, however, and the supposed Ivanov was NKVD general Ivan Serov. Instead of talking to the Poles, Serov and his armed subordinates seized them and flew them out from Warsaw's Okęcie airfield to Moscow. The Soviets told the surprised British and Americans that there had been no kidnapping and that all rumors on that subject were Polish inventions. At the beginning of May, when Soviet forces were attacking Berlin, a further surprise awaited the Western Allies. The Soviets now claimed that yes, they were holding the Polish government's representatives in the Lubyanka but only because they had turned out to be enemies of the USSR—and Nazi collaborators.

On June 18, five weeks after Germany's capitulation, a show trial began in Moscow that was organized along already well-rehearsed lines. This time the accused were leaders of Underground Poland. As before, Stalin was counting on the fact that if the accused were forced publicly to admit to false charges, the West would be satisfied with the Soviet version, and that despite the obvious lies it would simply shrug off its Polish allies' protests. Stalin's public "proof" that the Polish underground state was in fact an anti-Soviet—thus ipso facto pro-Nazi—conspiracy appears to have been intended to make it easier for the American and British authorities to withdraw assistance to the Polish government in exile in London and to recognize the Stalinist crew in Poland as the legitimate Polish government. Indeed, in July, this is exactly what happened.

The Polish defendants were put in the dock and surrounded by soldiers carrying rifles with fixed bayonets. This farce was played out before the whole world. Representatives of the US and British embassies, as well as the Western press, took their seats in the hall. Vasily Ulrikh, presiding judge in the Moscow show trials of the 1930s who'd obligingly handed down a string of death sentences at the authorities' behest, took his seat at the judge's table. Nikolai Afanasyev and Roman Rudenko appeared as prosecutors. Rudenko would play to a larger audience the following year as the Soviet chief prosecutor at the Nuremberg trials. The Soviet-appointed "defense" spoke on behalf of the accused. To the dismay of some of the accused, the "defense" confessed on behalf of their "clients" to false charges, expressed remorse and asked the court for leniency. The show trial lasted three days. The defendants were given prison sentences, with the exception of Kazimierz Kobylański, Stanisław Michałowski, and Józef Stemler-Dąbski, who were acquitted. Some of the men never saw release, including General Leopold Okulicki, the commander of the Home Army, one of the three largest anti-Nazi resistance movements in Europe. He was dead by the end of 1946. According to official Soviet documents, he died on the operating table in the Butyrki Prison hospital. Stanisław Jasiukowicz, the highest-ranking secret representative of the Polish London government in Nazi-occupied Poland, and Jan Stanisław Jankowski also did not live to see the end of their sentences.

Once again Stalin had not miscalculated: the Western Allies again seemed undismayed at this Moscow performance. The British ambassador in Moscow even stated that "no one got the death penalty; the accused were able to defend themselves." The London *Times*, known in the 1920s for its principled attitude toward Soviet terror, now stated: "This judgment should come as no surprise to anyone who has followed the Polish government's anti-Soviet activities." These were by no means isolated views in the West.

At the end of the war many Soviet people expected that the system of state terror would be relaxed in the USSR. Many assumed that victory would have a pacifying influence on the Soviet dictator and would finally provide him with a feeling of security. Yet not for the first time, Stalin surprised those who believed that they knew how to read his mind. Instead of liberalization, the USSR saw further tightening of the screws. The prisons again filled up, and the Gulag blossomed. With the aid of the secret police, Stalin was building up and strengthening totalitarian control over society after a time of relative chaos and improvisation forced on him by the war. After swallowing new countries in East and Central Europe, his empire now had to digest them. At the same time, the Soviet economy required immediate rebuilding, and there was a shortage of manpower. Over twenty million Soviet citizens had lost their lives in the war, most of them men in their productive years. To maintain the recently acquired status of world power in these conditions represented an enormous challenge. The Soviet regime had a tried and trusted method for this: terror and coercion. Starting at the end of the war, the system of state enslavement again began to expand. According to NKVD documents, in 1945 there were 1,460,677 inmates in the Gulag; five years later there were as many as 2,561,351. These figures did not include exiles living under police supervision, often in conditions little better than those in the camps. The number of such exiles was usually at least equal to that of inmates. Historians calculate that tens of millions of people cycled through the Gulag system during Stalin's rule. Anne Applebaum accepts an approximate and somewhat conservative figure of 28,700,000 forced laborers, including regular Gulag prisoners as well as people deported to special settlements.[5]

Going Home

In the period immediately preceding and following the war's end, the Western Allies did not limit themselves to closing their eyes to Stalin's crimes. Nor did they recoil from an active involvement in Soviet operations in Europe to hunt down people in the name of "repatriation." At the end of the war, around five million Soviet citizens found themselves in Germany and in countries recently occupied by it. For the most part these were prisoners of war, people shipped out by the Germans to labor, inmates of Nazi concentration camps, exiles of all kinds, as well as soldiers in formations that had voluntarily fought alongside the Germans. These soldiers had largely been recruited from Soviet POWs and deserters, or from people in Soviet territory occupied by the Germans. Among them were also former White émigrés. Different motives had led them to serve in formations under German command. Soviet POWs had often done so to try to avoid dying of hunger in German camps, where they were methodically starved. About three million of them were starved to death. In the case of numerous Soviet national minorities, it was often hope for liberation from the Soviet empire. A frequent motive shared by many regardless of their ethnicity was the desire to defeat the Bolshevik regime. Soviet citizens volunteering for these formations, especially Soviet soldiers taken as POWs by the Germans in the early period of the war, usually knew about Hitler only what they had been told by Soviet propaganda, which they often disbelieved on principle. Since this propaganda portrayed every one of Stalin's victims as a criminal, then it was not difficult to dismiss its entire message and treat Hitler's crimes the same way—as an invention of Soviet propagandists. Of course, the Nazi invaders quickly demonstrated to local populations the real nature of their regime. Soon many collaborationists ended up involved in Nazi crimes. When victory came, Soviet authorities had no intention of letting any members of these collaborationist formations get away. Furthermore, they also had no intention of allowing other Soviet citizens who happened to be abroad—including millions of POWs, prisoners of German camps, and slave laborers—to decide their own fate.

From the moment that Allied forces began to liberate Stalin's former subjects from German camps, the Soviet dictator demanded that the Allies immediately transfer all Soviet citizens to Soviet control. The Western Allies began immediately to implement Moscow's demands, carrying out the task zealously and nearly always without the consent of those affected. As early as October 1944, the first British shiploads of Soviet POWs sailed secretly from Liverpool to Murmansk. German U-boats were still prowling the Atlantic. Shortly thereafter, on November 11, Soviet authorities set up a Repatriation Board commanded by General Filip Golikov who announced: "The Soviet regime is most concerned about the fate of its children who were dragged into Nazi slavery. They will be respectfully received back home like honest children of the fatherland. The Soviet government believes that even Soviet citizens who under the threat Nazi terror committed acts that went against the interests of the USSR will not be held responsible for those actions, provided that these people are prepared to carry out their normal duties as Soviet citizens upon their return."[6] The Allies, as can be seen, took Stalin's concern for his lost "children" scattered throughout Europe seriously; by January of 1945, they had managed to deport about 322,000 Soviet citizens to the USSR.

At the Yalta Conference in February 1945, Roosevelt and Churchill signed a secret clause at Stalin's request granting him the right to "repatriate" all those people who on September 1, 1939, had been Soviet citizens and who currently were "outside the borders of their homeland." According to this agreement, Soviet citizens who had served in Nazi military formations or who had collaborated with the Germans would be "forcibly repatriated." However, the British and the Americans willingly used force also against other subjects of Stalin they managed to seize in Europe. Soviet authorities would soon have so many "repatriates" on their hands that on May 11, 1945, barely three days after Germany's capitulation, they already had a hundred screening camps with space for a million people up and running. In January 1946, in order to simplify organizational structure, these camps were put under the Gulag administration.

The "repatriation" operation was conducted with such gusto that the screening camps soon began to run out of space. Between May 1945 and February 1946, 4,200,000 people passed through them. The Soviet authorities were so "concerned" about these people that only around 58 percent of them were released.[7] The remainder were drafted into the armed forces, sent to forced construction units (*stroybaty*), deported to Siberia, Kazakhstan, and other distant places in the USSR, or sent straight to the Gulag (often with ten- or twenty-year sentences). A Soviet Army soldier who had been captured by the Germans during the war was seen by the Soviet authorities as a traitor of sorts. The duty of a real Soviet was to have died for Stalin. Remaining under German occupation, not to mention living in Germany itself (for example as a forced laborer or POW), was grounds for suspicions of collaboration. In the Soviet tradition, of course, there was never a clear demarcation between suspicion and proof of a crime. What was important was that the economy of the USSR, ravaged by the war, needed new hands. This meant that the Gulag awaited new slaves.

Hunting down former Soviet subjects continued all over Europe at least up to the fall of 1946, and in some areas even longer. Sometimes Allied commanders were unclear who exactly was to be forcibly repatriated to the USSR and who was not. On August 25, 1945, the commander of the American Seventh Army, General Alexander Patch, inquired of the US European Theater of Operations headquarters if indeed he was to hand over former Soviet POWs to the USSR against their will. This inquiry was sent to Washington and received a reply that "all Soviet citizens who were in the territory of the Soviet Union on September 1, 1939, must be repatriated, without regard to their personal wishes and, if need be, by force."[8]

Long before the Yalta Conference, British Foreign Secretary Anthony Eden had no illusions as to what fate awaited many repatriated Soviet citizens. On

September 3, 1944, he had stated in confidence that "if we do what the Soviet Government want and return all these prisoners to the Soviet Union, whether they are willing to return or no, we shall be sending some of them to their death."[9] Yet this had no effect on the Allies' attitude at Yalta. After signing the "repatriation" agreement, they did what they could to abide by it to Stalin's complete satisfaction.

The Allies' operation took on its most dramatic form from the end of May to the beginning of June in Austria. On May 9, 1945, the first day after the German capitulation, the headquarters of the Cossack Corps fighting under German command, located near the Austrian border, contacted the headquarters of the British Eleventh Armoured Division to discuss capitulation terms. The Cossacks were interested in only one thing: they were prepared to surrender to the British without a fight in exchange for a guarantee that they would not be handed over to the Soviets. They received such a guarantee. They laid down their weapons and, assuming that they were prisoners of the British, set up several camps in the Drava Valley. The Cossacks were accompanied by their families who had managed to escape from their homes before the arrival of the Red Army. Among the Cossack elders were also White émigrés with their families. Neither they nor the families of the men in the Cossack Corps were covered by the secret clauses of the Yalta treaty on forcible repatriation. In addition to this, the British were of course bound by the guarantees that they had given to the Cossacks in exchange for them surrendering without a fight. Altogether there were over thirty-five thousand people in the Cossack camps on the Drava. Trusting the British assurances, they gave no thought to escaping and awaited further developments on their fate.

The British authorities, however, had not the slightest intention of keeping their promise. General Charles Keightley, the commander of British V Corps, received an order to contact the Soviets and to hand over all the inhabitants of the Cossack camps to them. In order to expedite the operation, this intention was not revealed to the Cossacks. When the officer responsible for contact with the prisoners, Major Rusty Davies, heard of the plan, he wanted to have nothing to do with this treacherous undertaking. "They had implicit faith in me," he recalled. "They believed every word I told them."[10] So he asked for a transfer, but this was refused. It was explained to him that it was precisely because of the trust that the Cossacks had in him that he had been assigned an important role in the intended operation. He was to deceive the POWs and then, at the last minute, to convince them of the pointlessness of resistance. Many years later General Keightley recalled: "The repatriation of the Cossacks was of course an order from Army Group and certainly stemmed from Westminster, probably from Winston [Churchill] himself. Whether we were happy about the operation or not, therefore, really did not come into it."[11] In a direct order to his men General Geoffrey Musson, Keightley's subordinate, was more specific: "If a person or body of people attempts to escape, you will order them to halt by shouting at them. If they deliberately disregard your order and run away, you will open fire, aiming at the legs if you think that this will be enough to stop the attempted escape. If not, shoot to kill."[12]

On May 28, the British summoned all the Cossack officers to a meeting with the commander-in-chief of all British forces in that area of Europe, Field Marshal Harold Alexander. About fifteen hundred officers climbed onto trucks. After being driven out of the camps, instead of having a meeting with the field marshal they were handed over to the Soviets. Thus, the soldiers and civilians remaining in the camps were deprived of their leaders. June 1 was the date designated for handing them over to the Soviets. After a time, Major Davies informed them of what was about to happen, also stating that if they followed orders quietly, families would not be split up. "They were quite horrified when I told them, and I was petrified myself, to be quite frank with you," he recalled in an interview many years later. "Looking back I realize that they could have torn me limb from limb if they'd wanted to. . . . They didn't shout at me or attack me, they just pleaded. They couldn't believe that I was doing this to them. You see, they had implicit faith in me. That's the horrifying thing about it. That's why I feel so sick about the whole thing."[13] The Cossacks' reaction was different from what Davies had been expecting: they refused to submit voluntarily to repatriation but did not fight back either. Instead, they drew up a letter for the British in which they stated: "We prefer death than to be returned to the Soviet Russia, where we are condemned to a long and systematic annihilation,"[14] and they began a hunger strike. Witnesses stated that during the night of May 31 to June 1 the Orthodox service was conducted in the camp for their souls.

On the morning of June 1, the service continued. "We would pray in the fields, we would pray continuously, without pause," recalled Olga Rotovaya. "We were convinced that the British would not lay hands on people who were praying."[15] They hoped in vain; British soldiers started implementing their orders. "It was terrible," recalled Major David Shaw commanding the Second Battalion Royal Fusiliers. "We had to manhandle them and force them into trains at the point of a bayonet."[16] Rifle butts, bayonets, and clubs were used. The Cossacks used passive resistance. Commanding the operation in the main Cossack camp near the town of Lienz, Major Davies recalled: "The people formed themselves into a solid mass, kneeling and crouching with their arms locked around each other's bodies. . . . Terrified and hysterical people threw themselves on their knees before the soldiers begging to be bayoneted or shot to death as an alternative of loading."[17] Then a group broke out of the encirclement, some of them managing to escape across a bridge over the Drava into the nearby woods. Others, seeing no chance to get away, threw themselves off the bridge into the river, and some of them lost their lives. The suicides began. Witnesses—both escapees and British soldiers—recall mothers jumping into the river holding children in their arms. Chasing the fugitives through the woods, the soldiers found hanging from trees the bodies of Cossacks who preferred to die rather than to return to their homeland. Major Davies recalled a Cossack who shot his three children, his wife, and then himself. Finally, on June 7, General Keightley reported that the operation in the Drava Valley was over. About thirty-five thousand Cossack "repatriates" ended up in Soviet hands.

The Soviets, however, alleged negligence. They insisted that the fugitives hiding in the woods be captured immediately, and British authorities zealously complied with the demands. As a show of goodwill, they even allowed Soviet "observers" to join British search teams. But the British soldiers were beginning to question their orders. From the beginning, many of them had felt that they were engaged in something shameful. The longer the operation lasted, the more a feeling of disgust grew, and it began to show. A chaplain in one of the British battalions named Kenneth Tyson wrote that the men "had to make themselves blind and deaf to heartbreaking protests, to act unyieldingly and to use force."[18] John Pinching, another officer taking part in the British "repatriation" operation, said of the unwilling "repatriates": "They should never have been sent back. We all felt very badly about it."[19] One of the soldiers driving the Cossack families, Corporal Donald Smith, recalled loading people onto trucks: "We helped the aged, who were praying all the time. Some of the children had been separated from their parents. Some were, I think, too shocked even to cry or pray, but climbed into the vans quietly to squat in a corner. I was at this point sickened."[20]

The mood among the British troops was slowly growing mutinous. Supervising the railway convoys of "repatriates" the commanding officer of the Second Battalion London Irish Rifles, Colonel Bredin, recalled:

> I spoke to people who had seen prisoners being shot and I think there was
> clear evidence that shootings took place. Anyway, my men were quite sure
> of it and we heard enough about it to be sure that it was not the sort of
> thing that we ought to be having a hand in. We also got reports that there
> were suicides on the trains, people jumping off or cutting their throats with
> bits of broken windowpane. A fairly serious situation arose with the soldiers

very nearly getting to the point of saying, "Sorry, sir, we won't obey your orders." . . . They'd seen plenty of carnage during the war, but this was one thing they would not put up with.[21]

A similar fate awaited other POWs from units formed of Soviet ethnic minorities who had served alongside the Germans. As early as February 1945, about eight thousand men of the 162nd Turkmen Infantry Division were handed over to the Soviets near Taranto. The British officer responsible for their deportation by ship to Odessa, Major Dennis Hills of the Eighth Army, realized that either death or the Gulag awaited them in the USSR. His duty to obey orders did not lessen his sense of taking part in a shameful operation that stained the honor of a British officer. He knew that the British high command was cynically reneging on its own promises that had saved Allied lives. If the British had not assured the men of the Turkmen Division that they would not be handed to the Soviets, they would certainly have fought a bloody battle to the end, knowing as they did the price of surrender. Taking part later in other "repatriation" operations, Major Hills tried to save as many "repatriates" as possible from being forcibly returned to their communist homeland. The British authorities swiftly reacted, and Major Hills was demoted. Interestingly enough, no formal charges were lodged concerning his attitude to Soviet "repatriation." In this way the issue was hushed up. Officially, Major Hills was reprimanded for unbecoming conduct by exercising at dawn in the square in Trieste.[22]

Unwillingness to carry out "repatriations" also spread among US soldiers. They began to ignore orders to use force to hand citizens of the USSR over to the Soviets. The authorities, moreover, did not punish these men; in the event of a court martial it was likely that defense counsel would call the Yalta agreements inhumane and thus in violation of international law. A number of senior commanders protested. Field Marshal Alexander openly came out against the British Foreign Office, which was continually pressing the military authorities to satisfy every Soviet demand on "repatriation." On August 23, Alexander wrote to the War Office on the subject of Soviet "repatriates": "Such treatment, coupled with the knowledge that these individuals are being sent to an almost certain death, is quite out of keeping with the principles of democracy and justice as we know them. Furthermore, it is most unlikely that the British soldier, knowing the fate to which these people are being committed, will be a willing participant in the measures required to compel their departure."[23] The issue was raised in the papers. On October 4, 1945, General Dwight Eisenhower, Supreme Allied Commander Europe, issued an order to halt temporarily forcible "repatriation."

Soon, however, it started up again. The Western Allies were pursuing and catching Soviet citizens at least up to September 1946. One of the commanders of Russian formations that had collaborated with Hitler, General Meandrov, remarked in a British camp just before being handed over to the Soviets: "It is not just we who refuse to return to the Soviet Union; there are tens of thousands of 'traitors to the people.' Nothing like this has ever happened before in the history of any nation. Aren't the reasons for this mass defection clear to the world? Or does the world not want to understand?"[24] Clearly, Meandrov and his subordinates should have been investigated and charged whenever needed for their wartime behavior. Yet he was certainly right about one thing: the world really did not want to understand the reasons for the desperate attempts at flight from "repatriation" by many former Soviet subjects.

The French authorities immediately joined the crowd of those zealously tracking down Stalin's subjects. By October 1, 1945, they had managed to hand over to the Soviets around ten thousand people from their zone of occupation in Germany. But that was not all that they had to offer Stalin. The French authorities allowed the NKVD to set up seventy transit camps inside France but outside French jurisdiction. It was to these camps, out of view of the French police or any other authorities, a place where the NKVD had unlimited power, that people were brought and subsequently vanished. This went on until 1947, at a time when tens of thousands of French citizens from Alsace and Lorraine were in Soviet camps. During the war they had been drafted by the Germans into the Wehrmacht and sent to the Eastern Front. The Soviets then called on them to desert, promising them the possibility of fighting in General de Gaulle's forces. They did not keep their promise, however, and surrendering Alsatians and Lorrainers went not to join de Gaulle but to Soviet camps. There were twenty-three thousand of them in the largest camp in Tambov, where ten thousand of them died.[25]

The forcible "repatriations" led to hardly any public protest. There were of course some critical voices in the press but on a limited scale. On June 11, 1947, the Conservative MP Harold Nicolson tried to raise the matter in the House of Commons. The following day in the Paris *Le Monde*, a lawyer named Galiniak made the case for treating forcible repatriation as incompatible with international law. At the end of the summer of 1947, the socialist publication *Masses* published an article exposing the NKVD camps in France:

> One can easily imagine Genghis Khan, at the height of his powers, closing his frontiers to prevent his slaves from running away. But it is hard to imagine that he would be granted the right to extradite them from abroad. . . . This is a true

sign of our postwar moral decay. . . . What moral or political code can possibly be used to oblige people to go on and live in a country where they will live and work as slaves? What gratitude does the world expect from Stalin for turning a deaf ear to the cries of all the Russian citizens who have taken their own lives rather than return home?[26]

On this note, World War II and the history of the anti-Hitler coalition came to an end. The American historian George Fischer called the forcible postwar repatriation of Stalin's subjects an "indelible stain on the honor of the West."[27]

Old Allies, New Enemies

In March 1946, in the town of Fulton in President Harry Truman's home state of Missouri, Winston Churchill told the faculty and students of Westminster College that

> from Stettin in the Baltic to Trieste in the Adriatic, an iron curtain has descended across the Continent. Behind that line lie all the capitals of the ancient states of Central and Eastern Europe. Warsaw, Berlin, Prague, Vienna, Budapest, Belgrade, Bucharest and Sofia, all these famous cities and the populations around them lie in what I must call the Soviet sphere, and all are subject in one form or another, not only to Soviet influence but to a very high and, in many cases, increasing measure of control from Moscow.[28]

When the former prime minister of Great Britain spoke in Fulton, Allied hunts for unwilling "repatriates" to the USSR were still going on. But the speech was a sign of the collapse of the wartime anti-Hitler coalition. For the first time since the start of the alliance with Stalin in 1941, a Western statesman had publicly recognized the Soviet empire's despotic and aggressive nature. Radical changes were coming in Western policies and propaganda toward the USSR.

A sudden shift now could be observed in the Western powers' rhetoric, one reminiscent of the somersaults of Stalinist propaganda in the 1930s, when yesterday's heroes of progressive humanity turned overnight to be its most dangerous enemies. Stalin—until recently officially venerated by the Allied leadership as a great friend of the free world and a conqueror of Nazi tyranny—once again became a barbarous tyrant in their eyes. Within a year of Churchill's speech in Fulton, President Truman introduced a new US doctrine toward the USSR and the communist world. This was the doctrine of containment, according to which the Soviet empire was identified as an antagonist of the US. The Cold War had begun—or, to use Martin Malia's description of it, "the Third World War that never took place."[29]

American and British authorities, who had until recently been trying to cover up Soviet crimes and silence witnesses, now willingly discussed Stalinist atrocities and let witnesses speak. Between 1946 and 1947, two Russian émigré Menshevik historians working in the United States, David Dallin and Boris Nicolaevsky, produced the most extensive study of the Gulag at that time: *Forced Labor in Soviet Russia*.[30] They based their work on accounts by Polish prisoners and exiles collected by the Polish London government after Anders's army had left the USSR in 1942. During the war, the Allies had classified such accounts as secret to block their publication. Dallin and Nicolaevsky supplemented this material with numerous accounts by former subjects of the Soviet empire who were abroad during the war and had then managed to avoid the forcible "repatriation." They were greatly helped in this by Soviet secret police documents that fell into German hands during their offensive in the USSR and were then seized by the Allies. Up until now, the Western public had dealt only with individual accounts by victims of the Soviet camps, but now it received a systematic, general work on the subject. Dallin and Nicolaevsky's work was greeted with interest by the American press. William Henry Chamberlin discussed it at some length in the *Chicago Tribune*.[31] The paper also published a small map of Soviet camps drawn by the American magazine *Plain Talk* on the basis of details established by Dallin and Nicolaevsky. "This map exposes better than a million words could the nature and character of Soviet power, as well as the convictions that guide it," commented the paper on November 14, 1947.

Numerous escapees from the Soviet empire who had previously encountered enormous difficulties in publishing their camp and prison testimony were now actively encouraged to do so. Newspapers and journals—until recently silent on the subject—now willingly carried reviews and discussions of Gulag memoirs. On February 23, 1947, the *Chicago Tribune* printed William Henry Chamberlin's review of a book by a Polish witness of the Gulag, recently printed in the United States, called *The Dark Side of the Moon*. It was published anonymously for fear that the author's friends and family living in Poland might be affected by Soviet persecution. T. S. Eliot wrote an introduction. Chamberlin described the book as "one of the most disturbing accounts of man's inhuman behavior to man. This book," he wrote, "should be mandatory reading for every member of the UN Committee on Human Rights. Americans have a moral duty to read it, even if this is shocking and unpleasant."[32] Today we know that the author of this book was Zoe Zajdlerowa, an Irish woman who married a Polish army officer and lived in Poland before the war. In 1939, she found herself under Soviet occupation and soon followed the typical Polish pattern of arrests and deportations. Saved by Anders's army, she was given access to the Polish government's collection of testimonies by survivors of Soviet camps and confined settlements. The head of the Polish government, General Sikorski, asked her to write in English a book presenting to the world the fate of Stalin's Polish prisoners. Soon afterward, Sikorski died in a mysterious plane crash on July 4, 1943. Zoe Zajdlerowa kept her word. About a year after her book was reviewed in the *Chicago Tribune*, on February 1, 1948, John Thompson wrote in the same paper about the English-language publication of Andrzej Korwin-Romański's Gulag memoir *Prisoners of the Night*.

Wartime survivors of the Gulag—Poles, Russians, Ukrainians, Jews, and people of other nationalities who managed to end up in the West—left a huge trove of memoirs. Most of this testimony was for a long time accessible only in the original languages. Clearly, its chance of reaching a Western audience depended on being translated into Western languages. Some succeeded in conquering this barrier, and their work generally attracted notice in the West. As early as 1945, Józef Czapski's *Souvenirs de Starobielsk* came out in French, as did Ada Halpern's camp testimony, *Liberation—Soviet Style* in English.[33] The same year, Kazimierz Zamorski and Stanisław Starzewski published in Rome in French under the noms de plume of Sylwester Mora and Piotr Zwierniak a collective work of accounts by Polish survivors entitled *La Justice soviétique*, while a Russian sailor and Gulag escapee named N. N. Nikitin published in English in Boston his personal reminiscences under the evocative title *Why I Could Not Live in Soviet Russia*.[34] In 1948, Jerzy Gliksman's *Tell the West* was published in English, and a year later the camp memoirs of Antoni Ekart and Julius Margolin appeared in French.[35] That same year, 1949, the public in the US and Great Britain was able to read a full edition of Vladimir Petrov's memoirs. Petrov was a former law student in Leningrad, who after spending six years in Kolyma, ended up in Ukraine, where the German occupation found him. He fled ahead of the advancing Red Army and after the war managed to reach the United States.[36] Also in 1949, Margarete Buber-Neumann published her memoir of Stalin's and Hitler's camps in German, English, and French.[37] Two years later, Alex Weissberg's and Elinor Lipper's accounts came out in English, and Gustaw Herling-Grudziński published *A World Apart*.[38] Shortly afterward Anatol Krakowiecki told the French public about Kolyma.[39] The list could go on, especially since many books published in one of the Western languages were often translated into others and sometimes reissued under another title.

A compendium of accounts by thousands of Polish inmates of the Gulag from Anders's army formed the basis of an official report by the American Federation of Labor (AFL) *Slave Labor in Russia*. This report was presented to the UN together with a motion to start an investigation into slave labor in the

USSR. The authors of this document stated that "in spite of the Allied victory, the world is perturbed to a very high degree by communications which seem to indicate that the evils we have fought to eradicate, and for whose defeat so many have died, are still rampant in various parts of the world."[40] When the US motion to begin an investigation into the Gulag reached the UN, the representatives of the USSR and its satellite countries did everything to block it. During the debate on February 16, 1949, the Soviet representative Semyon Tsarapkin held the podium for ninety minutes, thus preventing a vote being taken on the issue. The next day it was the representative of the Polish People's Republic, Juliusz Katz-Suchy, who took over the baton and used the same tactics. Such stalling techniques kept the topic of the Gulag off the UN agenda for some time but did not manage to preempt it for good. In June 1950, the UN and the International Organization of Labor organized the Ad Hoc Committee on the Forced Labor, which examined allegations of forced labor in twenty-four countries. In this context, the topic of the Gulag drew some international attention. The committee published its final report in March 1953, shortly after Stalin's death. New hopes for positive changes in the USSR arguably resulted in softening the critical language of the report.[41]

Meanwhile, the sudden shift by the authorities in the US and Great Britain from their wartime pro-Soviet policy to Cold War anticommunism was showing its side effects. While Churchill was talking of an iron curtain and Truman was announcing his doctrine to contain communism, the momentum of the propaganda campaign praising "Uncle Joe" persisted through sheer inertia. Bookstores still carried Wallace's *Soviet Asia Mission* praising Stalin and Kolyma. As for Wallace, he ran for president in 1947 on a platform of strengthening ties with the USSR. At the same time, a quite new official anticommunist and anti-Soviet language was already being heard. This sudden volte-face by the American authorities must have elicited consternation among those whose memory was sound and who had not forgotten Roosevelt's recent delight with Stalin and the propaganda around it. It was hard not to ask about the origin of this abrupt change and question who the real Stalin was: good old "Uncle Joe" or a demonic criminal?

In short, the authorities of the Western powers—who had already twice changed their opinion of Stalin since the beginning of the war—had undermined their own credibility. They were demonstrating to the world that for them, the truth was simply a matter of prevailing political expediency. People who attempted to set up a moral equivalency between Soviet communism and the democratic West had been handed a useful argument. Those who sought to reject the incriminating evidence about communism now could claim that the postwar criticism of Stalin's rule was in fact just another political ploy on the part of the authorities and the "establishment" in the West. Once again the truth had become politicized.

It was easy enough then to extend this feeling of mistrust or suspicion to the accounts of numerous Gulag survivors that were now appearing in the West. These accounts could easily be seen as part of a broader anticommunist propaganda campaign dreamed up by the Western authorities for political gain. Public opinion shapers who were inclined to dismiss Gulag testimony often tried to frame it as motivated by political prejudice and an anticommunist agenda. The authors of Soviet camp memoirs were usually well aware of the reluctance regarding their testimony in the West. Unlike witnesses of Nazi atrocities—after all, few needed convincing about the evil nature of Nazism—these authors were motivated by an obligation to reveal the dark truth about Soviet communism that was hidden behind the deceptive facade. For example, a former prisoner in Kolyma, Vladimir Petrov, claimed in his memoirs that "years in the camps have developed within me an implacable, relentless and all-consuming hatred for everything Soviet and communist."[42] But statements like this were often treated as a reason or a pretext to undermine the credibility of Gulag testimony. The witnesses were declared political opponents of the USSR, the argument went, and as such they could not be viewed as objective and credible. Of course, on the basis of similar premises, one could equally undermine the accounts of former inmates of Nazi camps—after all, those who wrote about Auschwitz or Mauthausen did not conceal their anti-Nazi feelings, and so according to the same twisted logic they too could be accused of a similar lack of objectivity.

The sudden change in the Western authorities' attitude toward the USSR caused some of Stalin's admirers to accuse them of rank ingratitude. As soon as Hitler had been defeated at a cost of many millions of Soviet lives, Stalin was no longer useful to the West and was thus excluded from the winners' enclosure to be treated as a criminal and a pariah. That was the picture of East-West relations promoted by Soviet propaganda and its Western sympathizers. This propaganda fell on fertile ground in circles traditionally friendly toward the USSR. In a foreword to the camp memoirs of Julia de Beausobre, the left-leaning writer Rebecca West gave this warning in 1948: "To write of Russia today is dangerous. I do not allude to the obvious material danger that, as has occurred more than once in the United States and on the Continent of Europe, one may afterwards be found dead in a hotel bedroom, having, apparently, committed suicide. That is a danger which the courageous must face as part of this very disagreeable day's work. I allude to the danger that what one says, if it is not condonation of all Russian practices, may be taken as propaganda for the idea of declaring war on Russia."[43]

The effects of Western anticommunist crusades during the Cold War were often the opposite of those expected. An especially vivid example of this was the activities of the senator from Wisconsin Joe McCarthy and his special committee appointed by Congress to protect against communist infiltration of the United States. McCarthy and his associates not only showed themselves largely ignorant on the subject of communism but also used undemocratic and illegal methods that were eventually exposed. In fact, to a significant extent McCarthy inadvertently discredited American anticommunism and often involuntarily helped those who were intent on undermining the credibility of testimony on Stalinist crimes.

Among those to appear before McCarthy's committee were the 1944 visitors to Kolyma: Henry Wallace and Owen Lattimore. Testifying on October 17, 1951, Wallace explained that he had had the wool pulled over his eyes during his visit to Kolyma. "I was not going out of my way to find slave labor," he admitted. "The Russians were going all out to impress me."[44] In the meantime, Wallace had managed to change his view of the Soviet Union. Two years earlier he had read Vladimir Petrov's Kolyma memoirs and had reportedly experienced a real shock. Shortly after he met Petrov and believed his testimony. The two men reportedly became friends. Wallace publicly apologized to the American people for his misguided support of Stalin. J. Edgar Hoover, the head of the FBI, leading anticommunist and a political opponent of Wallace, was not moved by these apologies by the former vice president: "Old bubble head has seen the light at last, but all too late."[45]

Lattimore behaved quite differently from Wallace. In the spring of 1950, he was summoned to appear before the committee to respond to McCarthy's suspicions of being a Soviet agent. Lattimore displayed his indignation before the committee. The committee finally found him guilty of perjury, but the appeals court reversed the verdict. Owen Lattimore had not only been officially exonerated of the charges, but he defended himself in his book *Ordeal by Slander*, which came out in the summer of 1950.[46] Lattimore's book was met with positive reviews in many newspapers and periodicals. A reviewer in the *San Francisco Chronicle* wrote: "Americans owe it to Lattimore and to themselves to read this story."[47] As late as 1968, Lattimore defended his reports from Kolyma in a letter to the *New Statesman*. He also attacked Elinor Lipper, the Kolyma survivor, attempting to discredit her testimony. With a peculiar sort of irony, he suggested that her negative portrayal of the Kolyma boss Ivan Nikishov must have been grossly exaggerated since, after all, she had survived the camps.[48]

The fact that McCarthy bent the judicial process in his investigations and finally broke the law came back to haunt not only him but also the case he was trying to make. It became easier to argue that since communism's accusers had to have recourse to dishonest arguments, this clearly meant that honest means were not sufficient to indict the system. Why, the reasoning went, should credence be given to witnesses who lately had been speaking and writing so often about supposed slave labor camps and other atrocities in the depths of Russia? After all, McCarthy had turned to many a false witness.

In the minds of some people accustomed to thinking in the black-and-white categories of a communism/fascism or Stalin/Hitler duality, Joe McCarthy had now replaced Adolf Hitler as the embodiment of reactionary evil. Imperialist America had assumed the role of Stalin's principal enemy, and anti-communism had become the contemporary embodiment of fascism. Martin Malia observed that "after the defeat of Hitler, his real international role was rhetorically transferred to the United States, and all American policies from the Marshall Plan to Ronald Reagan's Star Wars were stigmatized as a new fascist imperialism. A corollary to this use of antifascism was 'the struggle for peace,' which became a dominant theme in the early 1930s and then again after 1945, as another way to combat the 'war-mongering' powers of the West."[49]

A new anti-Soviet ferment was also starting up among left-wing intellectuals. Doubts that had been sown during the Moscow trials in the 1930s and reignited by the Ribbentrop-Molotov pact once again resurfaced. New, disturbing books began to appear. After his problems with wartime censorship, George Orwell finally managed to publish *Animal Farm*. Arthur Koestler's novel about the Stalinist purges, *Darkness at Noon*, which this one-time communist had published as early as 1940, appeared in French translation in 1945 as *Le Zero et l'infini* and became a bestseller. It sold half a million copies. Orwell's new novel, *1984*, published in 1949, pierced another hole in the rhetorical armor surrounding communist atrocities in the minds of many Western intellectuals. At the same time, British Labour Party member Richard Crossman published *The God That Failed*, a collection of essays by well-known figures from the worlds of culture and politics whose convictions on the subject of communism were evolving from admiration to criticism—Arthur Koestler, Richard Wright, Louis Fischer, Ignazio Silone, André Gide, and Stephen Spender. So once again in the West, two versions of the truth about Soviet communism were in play: the oppressors' version and the victims' version.

The Paris Trials

In the year of 1949, a spectacular confrontation between the two opposing views of Stalinist Russia took place in France. This confrontation has gone down in history as the "Kravchenko and Rousset cases."

In no other Western country did Soviet propaganda receive such a favorable reception as in France. In the postwar years, the French Communist Party was a considerable political force, receiving 30 percent of the votes cast in parliamentary elections. The communists' influence on public opinion was extensive and was partly the function of a wartime ethos still fresh in people's minds. Forgotten was the fact that during the Soviet-German alliance, when France was at war with Germany, the French Communist Party had both in word and deed tried to undermine its own country's war effort and that when Hitler invaded France in 1940, the leader of the French communists, Maurice Thorez, had taken refuge with Hitler's ally, Stalin. After the war, all attention was focused on its later stages, after the German alliance with the USSR had collapsed, emphasizing that the communists had belonged to the most active elements in the French Resistance movement. This attitude of the French communists after 1941 was presented in stark contrast to that of the French right, whose symbol was the collaborationist Vichy government. Many people wanted to forget about Vichy as quickly as possible and to distance themselves from any political views associated with it—often including antipathy toward Stalin. Another factor increasing pro-Soviet attitudes in France was the dramatic rise of anti-American sentiments. Soviet propaganda played on these emotions.

The Kravchenko affair began rather mundanely but quickly became the subject of daily press reports, discussion, and commentary, thus keeping the issue of Stalinist crimes before the eyes of Western public opinion for a long time. The main figure of the affair, Victor Kravchenko, could pass for a positive example of social advancement in the USSR. As the son of a worker, he had earned a degree in metallurgy and had begun a swift rise in his career in Soviet heavy industry. He quite soon was appointed to management positions. He must have enjoyed the authorities' good opinion and trust, since in 1943 he had been sent to Washington as part of a Soviet delegation handling the purchase of technical equipment within the terms of Lend-Lease. On April 3, 1944, Kravchenko eluded his Soviet minders—he "chose freedom." The Soviet embassy immediately demanded that the American authorities seize Kravchenko and turn him over to the Soviets as a "deserter." Anyone who knew anything about Stalin knew exactly what fate awaited Kravchenko should he be handed over. Once again, it turned out that the Soviet Union could count on one of its most trustworthy American admirers, Joseph Davies. The former US ambassador to Moscow shook the tree with his contacts at the State Department and personally tried to convince his friend, President Roosevelt, to deport Kravchenko to the USSR. At the same time, Harry Hopkins, one of Roosevelt's most trusted advisers, assured Roosevelt that Kravchenko could be deported in secret, thus avoiding any unnecessary publicity and scandal. But Roosevelt did not want to risk this, especially since the FBI under the leadership of the anticommunist Hoover had already managed to make the affair public and had warned Kravchenko to go to ground for the time being.[50]

I Chose Freedom was the title of the book that Kravchenko published in the United States in 1946, two years after his escape and a year after Roosevelt's death. The book was an open court case against the Stalinist system. Drawing on his own long years of experience and observation, Kravchenko described a system of widespread coercion, fear, and enslavement. As a Ukrainian, he knew some of the details of the criminal collectivization and famine of the early 1930s. As an engineer in heavy industry, he had personal encounters with the forced labor system. Finally, as a government official, he knew a thing or two about the Stalinist purges, which had engulfed many of his friends and colleagues. Kravchenko's book appeared at the moment when American policy and official government rhetoric toward the USSR had clearly begun to shift from recent wartime admiration toward Cold War criticism. So Kravchenko was not silenced by administrative pressure; on the contrary, his book quickly became a hit. It was translated into nineteen languages. "It is, I believe, the most remarkable and most revelatory report to have come out of the Soviet Union from any source whatsoever," wrote the American commentator Dorothy Thompson.[51] Certainly, Kravchenko could not have written his book in English without help. Today we know that he was helped by none other than Eugene Lyons, who ghostwrote the book: Lyons was the former American correspondent in Moscow in 1928–1934 and the author of the essay "To Tell or Not To Tell." Before Lyons put the final draft on paper, Isaac Don Levine, the editor of the 1925 collective volume *Letters from Soviet Prisons*, wrote down Kravchenko's story and David Dallin, Max Eastman, and William Bullitt became involved in supporting Kravchenko.[52]

Naturally, the Soviet authorities did not take this blow lying down. Kravchenko began to receive anonymous threats, and the communist press openly attacked him, accusing him of anti-Soviet lies and libel. Riding this propaganda wave, the publication *Soviet Patriot*, put out by the Soviet Ministry of Foreign Affairs, announced in October 1947 that Kravchenko had worked with American intelligence and that as a member of a Soviet delegation in Washington, he had been selling the Americans secret documents from safes in the Soviet embassy. The publication also claimed that Kravchenko was not the author of *I Chose Freedom* and that the book had been a series of false statements prepared at the request of the Truman administration. A month later the same theme appeared in the French communist weekly *Les Lettres françaises*.

An article under the headline "How Kravchenko Was Fabricated" and signed by a certain Sim Thomas exposed the alleged secret machinations on the part of American intelligence that had accompanied the appearance of Kravchenko's book. The author of the article claimed to have personal connections to an anonymous American OSS agent who had provided him access to classified material. According to Thomas's account, Kravchenko was a regular drinker, a rake, and a gambler who fell afoul of his bosses during his stay in Washington. Waiting to be sent home in disgrace, Kravchenko supposedly undertook work for the OSS in return for the Americans paying off his gambling debts and offering him political asylum in the US. Without a doubt, Thomas asserted, *I Chose Freedom* had been confabulated and put together for the use of American anti-Soviet propaganda. The facts in it were outrageous lies, while Kravchenko was an "abject creature," "a vulgar traitor," "an enemy of France and an enemy of the warring Allies," in a word "a puppet whose plainly visible strings were 'made in the USA.'"[53]

Kravchenko sued *Les Lettres françaises* for libel. A Paris court set January 24, 1949, for the start of the case. The Western press covered the approaching trial in depth. Kravchenko was aware of the strength of French communism and the extent of pro-Soviet sympathies in France. In his own admission, he had deliberately chosen France as the stage for his own confrontation with Soviet propaganda. He could just as easily have sued the American communists who were printing similar attacks on him. He wrote:

> I had deliberately chosen to take action in France, however, because there I could most effectively carry out the purpose of my book—the fight against Communism. A libel suit against a Communist newspaper in the United States would have been of little importance, for there the Communist press won no credence outside of the circle of devoted readers. . . . But France stood in the very forefront of the European battle against Communism. The French Communist party was large and powerful, having polled in recent elections some 30% of the votes. Here was a political and strategic position which Moscow had to defend. That was one of my principal reasons why I chose to attack in France.[54]

Kravchenko and his Western supporters, including Eugene Lyons, Isaac Don Levine, and Max Eastman, were well aware that his clash with *Les Lettres françaises* would be a public confrontation with the whole Soviet system. That was what they wanted. They realized that ultimately it was not a question of the editors of the publication Kravchenko was suing being able to prove the truth of their accusations against him. The question was whether Kravchenko himself would be able to prove to the court and the public that his critique of the Stalinist regime was based on facts. In order to achieve this, he needed witnesses. To this end he turned to the numerous exiles from the USSR, former POWs and forced laborers for the Nazis who had managed to avoid the hue and cry of the postwar "repatriations." Many of them were still in DP (displaced persons) camps. His appeal brought immediate results. Kravchenko recalled:

> The response was astounding. The letters began arriving in tens, then in hundreds and finally in thousands. They came from every country where camps of refugees from the paradise of Stalin or the inferno of Hitler existed. [...] It seemed that every DP in Europe wanted a chance to pour out before the western world the bitter story of his life under the Soviet regime. The letters came from Russians, Ukrainians, Belo-Russians and others, persons of all ages, of both sexes, of every imaginable profession, of all classes of society.[55]

Kravchenko chose his witnesses carefully. On the one hand, he did not want people with families still under Soviet rule, since they would undoubtedly become targets of Stalinist reprisals or would be convenient for blackmailing the witnesses. On the other hand, Kravchenko tried to weed out declared political opponents of the Soviet regime, as well as anyone who could in any way be suspected of collaborating with the Germans during the war. He knew that during the trial the communist side would attempt to discredit his witnesses. Yet despite this care on the part of Kravchenko, the Soviet authorities lost no time in resorting to their permanent repertoire of propaganda and pressure, publicly accusing Kravchenko's witnesses of collaborating with the Nazis and demanding that the French government deport them to the USSR. And when the French government refused, the TASS agency announced to the world that "the French government dares to invite into a French court persons whose very presence in France is offensive. . . . This is clear evidence of the fact that the Kravchenko trial is a machination in preparation for an anti-Soviet war, organized by the American Intelligence Service."[56]

The propaganda storm against Kravchenko employed simple yet tried-and-trusty methods. French communist publications, with *L'Humanité* in the lead, published various calumnies that Soviet state propaganda then quoted as representing the overwhelming attitude of French public opinion. "Attempts at undermining Soviet demands by French ruling circles have aroused the indignation of progressive society in the French capital," announced TASS on the basis of commentary in *L'Humanité* on the subject of supposed war criminals among Kravchenko's witnesses. After the start of the trial, the French Association of Friends of the USSR called a rally for February 3 in Paris attacking

Kravchenko as an anti-Soviet defamer and an agent of American imperialism. Yellow banners appeared in the street with the sign: KRAVCHENKO IS AGAINST FRANCE. Underneath they read:

> In the midst of war, Kravchenko betrayed his country! At the time when Russian blood was flowing for the liberation of France, he tried to sow discord among the Allies, to the applause of Hitler and of Goebbels. Today, WHEN THE GERMAN THREAT IS RE-APPEARING, the same Kravchenko is again playing the game of the enemies of France by trying to harm the Franco-Soviet alliance, the basis of the security of our country. . . . WHO WILL REFUTE THE SLANDERS OF KRAVCHENKO?[57]

Reading these words, one may get an impression that Kravchenko joined the Germans during the war, France was liberated by the Soviet Union, and the United States is France's enemy. In the anti-Kravchenko campaign, the anti-American card was played continually. "Kravchenko is only a pawn in an outdated game," wrote columnists in *Les Lettres françaises*. "Formerly these urinators of copy came to us from Germany. Today they are imported from America. But whether Hitler or Truman inspire them, as long as there are Kravchenkos, there will be free men to answer them."[58] Familiar anti-American refrains were invoked loudly at the start of the proceedings. The paper's editors, Claude Morgan and André Wurmser, spoke for *Les Lettres françaises*. In an opening statement Wurmser thundered: "This is a case against opinion, which French morality, the Constitution of the French Republic and the Declaration of the Rights of Man most expressly reprove. . . . It is a political trial which a foreign propaganda means to use to undermine the friendship of our country with a third nation. . . . It is a prosecution undertaken by foreign interests to interfere in the internal and external policy of France."[59] The foreign power meddling in France's internal affairs was of course the US, while the country France was friendly with was naturally the USSR: the Paris editor did not even have to spell that out.

However, the case began embarrassingly for *Lettres françaises*. The author of the article defaming Kravchenko, Sim Thomas, failed to appear in court. Wurmser and Morgan explained that Thomas had not come from the United States for fear of reprisals, but neither Judge Durckheim nor most of the press believed this evasion. The mysterious American with OSS contacts simply did not exist. The person claiming that Kravchenko was a fabrication was himself a fabrication.

The rest of the trial was a series of embarrassments for the Paris paper's editors. They called as witnesses well-known figures in public life who earlier had shown admiration for the wonders of Soviet civilization, had visited the Gulag in the 1930s, and had written enthusiastic books about this. Stalin's well-known admirer and the dean of Canterbury, the Reverend Hewlett Johnson, appeared before the court as an eminent expert on Soviet matters. He was to demolish the credibility of the descriptions of starvation in Ukraine and conditions in the camps. The well-known cleric could be counted on for such things. In the dark year of 1937, Hewlett Johnson had made a trip to the USSR from which he had returned enchanted. Two years later he had published a book entitled *The Socialist Sixth of the World*. In it he wrote, among other things, that "the communist puts the Christian to shame in the thoroughness of his quest for a harmonious society. Here he proves himself to be the heir of the Christian intention."[60] Now, in 1949, the dean of Canterbury decisively assured the court and the French public that he had a profound knowledge of the USSR, having visited that country twice and having spoken with the most representative personalities in Soviet public life. This knowledge entitled him to state that complete freedom of the individual existed in the USSR. In a rhetorical gesture he threw his authority onto the scales, calling out: "If Kravchenko is telling the truth, then I am lying." He clearly expected that his words would produce a wave of polite denials, but they produced laughter in the public gallery.[61]

Among the witnesses called by *Les Lettres françaises* were senators, generals, members of parliament, former ministers, academics, philosophers, writers, and even a marquis, Emmanuel d'Astier de la Vigerie. Kravchenko's witnesses testifying against the homeland of the proletariat were workers, peasants, engineers, and doctors. Kravchenko wrote: "There was a bitter irony in this contrast. The prosperous and successful persons opposite had come to the courtroom to defend a regime which proclaimed itself the protector of the workingman. Into the same courtroom, to refute that claim, had come the workingmen themselves–my witnesses."[62]

Kravchenko's witnesses were telling their own stories. They described in detail the hunger, the deaths of those close to them, cannibalism, arrest, tortures, executions, and the brutality in the prisons and camps. A Ukrainian peasant from a DP camp, Ivan Pushkar, described his time in a camp in Kolyma. After a two-month journey by train and in the cargo hold of a prison ship to Magadan, Pushkar found himself on a bunk in a transit camp. He described his neighbors in the hut as follows:

An old man named Kiliberda had been condemned to fifteen years for "having been in Spain" (he was illiterate, and couldn't even pronounce the name of the country correctly), "and there having sunk a Soviet ship." Actually he had never been more than five miles away from his village. Not knowing how to write, he had signed his "confessions" with a cross. . . . A stoker named Dotzenko had been condemned to ten years because his father had been, allegedly, a prince possessed of five thousand acres of land before the Revolution. A simple workman, Dotzenko had never seen a prince in his life. But he was condemned in spite of his denials. A priest who was with us had been given fifteen years for having called the people to prayer. . . . After six months of camp life, I became so weak that I was put to work cutting firewood. . . . Some of my companions in misfortune grew so weak that they were sent . . . to the section of those who were dying, from which no one ever returned.[63]

Another witness named Antonov described to the Paris Palace of Justice the interrogation he endured before he was sent to a camp on the construction site of the White Sea Canal. Here are some extracts from his testimony:

At the fourth questioning, the man who was interrogating me (his name was Sologub) called . . . two guards who, after having punched me in the face . . . tied my hands behind my back and my feet too and knocked me down. Sologub ordered them to "rub" my stomach. Rubbing the stomach meant this: One of the guards pressed my head while Sologub himself stood on my feet to hold me still; then another hit me on the stomach with a sandbag, until my stomach swelled considerably. I spat blood and saliva from my mouth. . . . Because I cried out a great deal, Sologub ordered them to gag me and they pushed into my mouth a rag covered with fresh blood and saliva, so I realized that it had already been used for other victims. After some time, I was on the point of losing consciousness. . . . Then they sat me on a chair and asked if I were going to confess and sign the record? I was already speechless, I couldn't talk. . . . So Sologub said: "He doesn't understand very well. Something in his head bothers him. Put a compress on it." This time one of them held me by the feet, another by the shoulders and the third began beating me on the head with a small sandbag. After these tortures I was in such a state that I didn't want to eat; I only wanted to die. . . . [Sologub] ordered the guards to put me into a special cell. . . . I thought I was going to die there. . . . There was no sound; there was no light either. . . . I stayed there for a very long time. No one came to look at me and I was beginning to freeze. I tried to move so as to warm myself. But that was no good, for there wasn't much room to move in and I couldn't turn around. . . . I had to defecate in my clothes, for no one took me out of there and nothing was provided for such needs and I could no longer move even my hands. . . . The fifth day I was only half alive . . . and on the sixth day some men came and opened the door . . . ordering me to crawl out. I couldn't move anymore.

They had an instrument, a kind of crook like the ones used to catch young lambs; with this crook they caught hold of me and pulled me out of there. . . . I fainted. . . . I was awakened by a feeling of great pain. . . . The guards carried me out into the court where it was zero or perhaps even fifteen below zero. As I was wet from my excretions and from vomiting, I quickly began to freeze. . . . I screamed very loudly because I felt my ears and my fingers freezing.[64]

None of this was new; the Western public had already had many opportunities to get to know similar accounts from other Soviet prisoners. New reports were continually appearing in the West on a larger scale than before. However, it took these public testimonies in the Palace of Justice to draw wider attention to the drama that had been going on for so many years in the USSR.

The only well-known person (especially in left-wing circles) on Kravchenko's witness list was Margarete Buber-Neumann, the widow of a former Politburo member of the German Communist Party, Heinz Neumann. Margarete Buber-Neumann had been active in the communist movement from a young age. Between 1921 and 1926, she had been a member of the German equivalent of the Komsomol, the youth communist league, and between 1926 and 1937 she had belonged to the "adult" German Communist Party. After Hitler came to power, the Neumanns left Germany and took refuge first in Spain and then in Switzerland. In 1935, they reached Moscow and moved into the famous Lux Hotel, where the Stalinist regime kept its eye on many highly placed foreign communists. Neumann was arrested in 1937; Margarete was arrested a year later. Her husband's trail went cold, while she ended up in a camp in Karaganda. The Paris public heard yet another tale of the camps. It already knew the subject, but in this witness's tale a new and little-known thread appeared. Margarete Buber-Neumann recounted how in January 1940, on the strength of the Soviet-Nazi agreement, she was handed over by the NKVD—together with a group of thirty other German communists—to the Gestapo on the new Soviet-Nazi border at Brest Litovsk. The Nazis sent Margarete to the Ravensbrück concentration camp. In the Nazi camp the German communist inmates did not want to believe her account of the Gulag and treated her as an enemy spreading anti-Soviet lies. She survived Ravensbrück. When she was testifying before the court in Paris, the attorney for *Les Lettres françaises*, Nordmann, accused her of ingratitude toward the Soviet Union whose troops, after all, liberated the Ravensbrück camp.[65] In his summing-up Nordmann claimed that Margarete Buber-Neumann was lying and that she had left the USSR for Nazi Germany at her own request. "Years later Nordmann offered a semi-apology for the brow-beating of this witness, and, by implication, several other witnesses,"

John V. Fleming writes. "He thought he could discount their testimony because they were either kulaks or Trotskyites. The implication, of course, was that slave labor camps were perfectly appropriate for kulaks and Trotskyites."[66]

Closely observing the involvement of Western communist intellectuals at the trial, Stephen Spender commented: "The intellectual Communists seemed extremely interested in theory, very little in evidence which might conflict with theory. For example, I never met any who had the slightest interest in any side of Russia which was not the Stalinist propagandist presentation. It does not surprise me that during the Kravchenko case in Paris, Communists and fellow travelers should have volunteered to give evidence against the book *I Chose Freedom* though they had no pretensions to any knowledge of Russia. From their point of view all they had to know was that Kravchenko was opposed to the Soviet System. This proved he must be wrong."[67] The trial ended in a spectacular defeat for the French communists. It was a no less embarrassing failure for Soviet propaganda on the international stage. Henceforth, the Soviet authorities never again confronted fugitives from the USSR and witnesses of Soviet crimes in direct, open debate. Yet such a clear fiasco for the Soviets did not convince every observer. A significant segment of influential French circles remained impervious to facts.

Kravchenko described the Paris trial in his next book, *I Chose Justice*. In January 1966, he was found dead in his New York apartment. His death was ruled a suicide. The London *Times* published an obituary of him on January 26, in which it presented Kravchenko's *I Chose Freedom* and his lawsuit against the French communist paper as a "reprehensible Cold War action," as if the Paris trial had established nothing.[68] Thirteen years after Kravchenko's death, the editor and publisher of *Les Lettres françaises*, Claude Morgan, Kravchenko's adversary in the courtroom, published his autobiography, *Les Don Quichotte et les autres*, in which he admitted that "Kravchenko was right." He admitted too that just after Kravchenko's death he had wanted "to pay him homage, but it was as yet too early."[69]

Indeed, the people from the *Lettres françaises* circle appeared to have learned nothing from their defeat. Or perhaps instead they came to the conclusion that they had nothing to lose. Simply put, they dug in their heels. The echoes of the Kravchenko case had barely died away in the press when the editors of *Les Lettres françaises* again found themselves in court accused of libel. As before, the case concerned truth and lies about the Gulag.

The case was brought on November 5, 1950, by David Rousset, a former Trotskyite who had been active in the French Resistance and then a prisoner in Nazi concentration camps. Rousset was known to the French public as the author of a book about the German concentration camps, *L'Univers concentra-tionnaire*, which had received the Prix Renaudot in 1946. Rousset was extremely interested in news from the still-functioning Soviet camp system. Eight months after the end of the Kravchenko trial, on November 12, 1949, he called in *Le Figaro litteraire* on former inmates of Nazi camps to show solidarity with Stalin's prisoners and called for a public inquiry into the Gulag. In February 1950, his appeals proved successful, and he organized the International Committee Against Concentration Camp Regimes.

The communist press reacted to Rousset's appeal just as if the Kravchenko trial had never taken place, as if Soviet crimes had not been confirmed before the eyes of the world. *Les Lettres françaises* again, just as if nothing had happened, led the press attacks claiming that the so-called atrocities of the Soviet camps were simply a creation of anticommunist propaganda. The editor of *Les Lettres*, Pierre Daix, like Rousset a former inmate of Nazi camps, wrote that "the camps of re-education of the Soviet Union are the achievement of the complete suppression of the exploitation of men by men; the decisive sign of the effort by victorious socialism to achieve the liberation of men from this exploitation in liberating also the oppressors, slaves of their own oppression."[70] Margarete Buber-Neumann commented on this new campaign in an article in the *Figaro Littéraire* under the evocative title "An Investigation into Soviet Camps. Who is worse, Satan or Beelzebub?" And when a statement appeared in *Les Lettres* that David Rousset, in his writing about Soviet camps, had falsified a quotation from the USSR penal code, Rousset took its editors to court.

Unlike Kravchenko's witnesses, who had for the most part been ordinary people from DP camps, Rousset called as witnesses former Gulag inmates with names that were not unknown, especially in left-wing circles. Now appearing before the Paris court were Western communist activists and supporters of the USSR who had sought shelter in Stalin's state but had ended up in camps and prisons there instead. Among them there were two people who, ironically, perhaps owed their survival to the fact that the NKVD had in 1940 handed them over to the Gestapo: Margarete Buber-Neumann, whom we have already met, and Aleksander Weissberg. There were also those who, thanks to Polish citizenship, had left the homeland of the proletariat with Anders's army. Others had managed to escape across the border or had been freed at the request of Western governments.

Rousset chose his witnesses in such a way as to preclude from the start his adversaries' favorite argument that anyone saying anything against Stalin's country was motivated by anticommunist ideology and politics. Rousset's witnesses' left-wing credentials were at least as good as, and often even better, than those of the editors of *Les Lettres françaises*. Rousset's witnesses had the undeniable advantage over their opponents in that they had had an opportunity to compare their own ideas about communism with real communism as practiced in its homeland. The fact that many of Rousset's witnesses were Jewish deprived communist propaganda of yet another weapon, which it had employed lavishly in the Kravchenko case: insinuating that witnesses must have a pro-Nazi past.

The first witness for the prosecution to appear before the Paris court was a slight, slim woman obviously suffering from stage fright. This was Elinor Lipper. She had been released barely two years earlier at the request of the Swiss authorities. She had spent ten years in Kolyma. Her memoir of the camp had just come out in Switzerland in German, and an English translation was in the works. It was precisely in that book that Lipper had described with inimitable irony the visit of US Vice President Wallace and Owen Lattimore to Kolyma in 1944. She was immediately attacked in the courtroom by the lawyers representing *Les Lettres françaises*, claiming that her personal misfortune and experience in the USSR proved nothing. Elinor Lipper was the first of an unusual gallery of figures who would pass through the courtroom, testifying against communism and its accomplishments.

These included Jerzy Gliksman, whom we have also already met. In his memoir, *Tell the West*, published in 1948, he had described in detail Soviet methods of coercing and exploiting people in the Gulag. Gliksman left the Soviet Union with the Polish army of General Anders and so did yet another witness of David Rousset, Józef Czapski. Czapski was a Polish painter born in an aristocratic family. Drafted to the Polish army for the war in 1939, he was captured by the Soviets and kept in the officers' camp in Starobelsk. Transferred to another camp, he avoided execution with other Polish POWs in 1940. Released after the Sikorski-Maisky agreement in 1941, he joined the Anders Army and was appointed by his superiors to conduct a search for the missing officers whose bodies were later found in Katyn. Czapski left the USSR with the Anders Army, and after the end of the war lived in Paris. By the time of the Rousset trial, Czapski's memoirs from his Soviet captivity had been published in French: *Souvenirs de Starobielsk* came out in 1945 and *Terre inhumaine* in 1947.

Another author of Soviet camp memoirs recently published in the West who now appeared as a witness in the Paris court was Julius Margolin. His *Journey to the Land of the Zek* had appeared in French in 1949, and so the French public had had some time to absorb it between the Kravchenko and Rousset cases. Margolin, a philosopher from Pinsk with a doctorate from the University of Berlin, was a Zionist. In 1936, he had emigrated from Poland to Palestine. In 1939, he had been visiting Łódź when the German invasion caught him. Like many

Polish Jews, he fled east, stopping in his hometown of Pinsk. Here, however, he was arrested by the NKVD. He arrived in the Gulag with a five-year sentence. He was released as a Polish citizen and eventually made it back to Palestine.

The next witness, Margarete Buber-Neumann, needed no introduction to the editors of *Les Lettres*. The English version of her memoirs from Soviet and Nazi camps had just appeared, the first part of the German original having come out in 1945. In her introduction to this unusual comparative study of the two murderous tyrannies, the author professes that she had written it "to let the world know on the basis of first-hand experience what can happen, what must happen when human dignity is treated with cynical contempt."[71] We should recall here that among Western left-leaning intellectuals, any attempts to compare Nazism and communism were usually greeted with angry criticism. While Margarete Buber-Neumann, fully qualified to make such comparisons, was testifying before the Paris court, another woman, Hannah Arendt, was preparing a book for publication in the US that analyzed Nazism and Stalinism as two expressions of a broader phenomenon that had been earlier called "totalitarianism" by some writers. The book was entitled *The Origins of Totalitarianism* and would become the subject of far-reaching debate among the Western intellectual elites in the future.

In addition to Margarete Buber-Neumann, one other prisoner appeared in the Paris courtroom who had been among those handed over to the Gestapo that same day in Brest Litovsk. This was Aleksander Weissberg. "It turns my stomach to see a German testifying before a French court," was how one of the defense team of *Les Lettres françaises* greeted him.[72] Of course, Weissberg was not German but a Jew from Kraków educated in Vienna. Enchanted by the lure of the USSR, he had moved there in 1931, where he began to work as a physicist in a scientific institute in Kiev. The purges in the 1930s swept him up too. He went through prisons and camps until in the winter of 1940 he was handed over to the Gestapo. The Nazis sent him as a Jew to the Kraków ghetto. He survived the Holocaust by managing to escape from the ghetto and later joining the Polish insurgents in 1944. In 1948, he succeeded in getting out of communist Poland and managed to settle in Sweden and, in the early 1950s, in Paris.

In order to silence the absurd and insulting attacks by the lawyers for *Les Lettres*, Weissberg presented his left-wing credentials. This took the form of a letter that had been written by a group of eminent Western physicists when Weissberg had been in a Soviet prison. The letter's signatories testified that he was an unblemished communist, a man wholly and completely committed to the Soviet Union. Among those who had signed the letter were Albert Einstein and Frédéric Joliot-Curie. The latter was a faithful active member of the French

Communist Party. He had also recently appeared as a witness for *Les Lettres françaises* at the Kravchenko trial. Now Weissberg presented moral testimonials to the Paris court from this distinguished propagandist. Ironically, a victim of communism had to prove his credibility by producing a communist résumé or relying on the good opinion of communists.

Long-silenced echoes of the Hitler-Stalin pact of 1939–1941, of the Stalinist purges, prisons, and camps emerged in Rousset's witnesses' testimony to the Paris court. There was also no lack of reverberations from the Spanish Civil War. One of its communist heroes appeared in the courtroom: Valentin Gonzalez, known by his nickname El Campesino—a man about whom Ernest Hemingway wrote in 1940 in *For Whom the Bell Tolls*: "He was a brave; tough man; no braver in the world. But God, how he talked too much. And when he was excited he would say anything no matter what the consequences of his indiscretion. . . . He was a wonderful Brigade Commander though in a situation where it looked as though everything was lost. He never knew when everything was lost and if it was, he would fight out of it."[73] In addition to his military accomplishments, El Campesino was also famous for his ruthless oppression of peasants in areas under his control. After the defeat, El Campesino, like many Spanish communists, took refuge in the USSR. During World War II he found himself in Uzbekistan where he suffered from hunger, and in order to survive he led the life of a bandit. Eventually, during an escape over the mountains to Persia, he was captured and ended up in NKVD custody. Despite being tortured, he did not sign a false confession. With a three-year sentence (unusually mild for the time) he went to the camps in Vorkuta. Working in a mine, he had an accident. He was taken to the hospital from which he escaped, being resolved at all costs to get out of the USSR. This time he succeeded and made it to Persia. In 1952, shortly after the Rousset trial, Valentin Gonzalez's memoir *El Campesino. Life and Death in Soviet Russia* came out.[74]

Most of Rousset's witnesses were joining a swelling current of testimony by former communists and supporters of Soviet Russia whose fate it had been to discover communism's dark side, and who spared no effort to share their experiences and observations with the world. This current had already appeared a long time before, when admirers of early Bolshevism, like Pierre Pascal, Panait Istrati, or Victor Serge, had seen it with their own eyes and had not hesitated to produce books with their views. Soon others, such as Ante Ciliga and Arthur Koestler, emerged. At the turn of the 1940s and 1950s, during the period of greatest tension in the propaganda war between the US and the USSR, testimony by disillusioned communists introduced a new element into the Western public debate: it broke down the comfortable moral opposition between left and right, between Stalin and Hitler, inherited from the 1930s and strengthened over the course of World War II. In some circles where being left-wing was mandatory in order to have any kind of credibility, powerful dissent was being created. This dissent appealed especially to the imagination of people who had difficulty making an equivalence between left-wing views and pro-Soviet attitudes.

There was yet another reason why witnesses called by Rousset to testify before the Paris court operated in new circumstances compared to earlier witnesses to the Gulag in the West. During the short interval between the Kravchenko and Rousset trials, the parameters of the debate on communism had visibly changed. Toward the end of June 1950, the Congress for Cultural Freedom had been held in West Berlin, and an international organization of the same name had been established. This was the West's, more specifically the US government's, political response to the Soviet-sponsored International Peace Conference organized in August 1948 in Wrocław, Poland. The Congress for Cultural Freedom was the first large-scale attempt to energize Western intellectuals in order to stem Soviet propaganda's influence on cultural, intellectual, artistic, and media life in the West. The Congress was officially funded by the American Federation of Labor, but in reality, the money came from the CIA, though very few of the participants in the Congress were aware of this fact. Information about it came to light only in 1967, leading to a predictable furor and a crisis of legitimacy for the Congress.

Meanwhile, however, the organizers of the Congress managed to assemble a great many top-tier figures from various circles of the Western intellectual elite. The most active were disillusioned communists, often with Trotskyite roots. Among the organizers were the writer Arthur Koestler, the former secretary of the German Communist Party and current mayor of West Berlin Ernst Reuter, the former member of the leadership of the Italian Communist Party Ignazio Silone, as well as the American Sidney Hook, formerly known for his procommunist views. About 150 writers, artists, scholars, politicians, and journalists signed a declaration supporting the Congress in 1950. Among French intellectuals David Rousset himself, as well as such ideologically varied figures as André Gide, Raymond Aron, Denis de Rougemont, and the Congress chairman Jules Romains, became involved in the Congress's activities. Benedetto Croce, John Dewey, Karl Jaspers, Bertrand Russell, Jacques Maritain, and Salvador de Madariaga were honorary vice chairmen. Among the German delegates to the Congress was a group of prewar émigrés from Nazi Germany, including Carl Friedrich, Golo Mann, and Wilhelm Röpke. Also playing active roles were Aldous Huxley and Richard Crossmann from Great Britain, the Swiss François

Bondy, the theologian Richard Niebuhr from the United States, the American trade union activist Irving Brown, and the journalist Melvyn Lasky. Among those to send greetings and expressions of support were Eleanor Roosevelt, John Dos Passos, Upton Sinclair, André Malraux, Claude Duhamel, Victor Gollancz, Louis de Broglie, Julian Huxley, and Carlo Levi. The presence of people who until recently had been unable to find a common language is striking. Yesterday's lyricists of the USSR, like Upton Sinclair, John Dos Passos, or André Malraux were now signing their names next to implacable opponents of the regime—men of the moderate left like Bertrand Russell as well as lifelong opponents of Marxism such as Raymond Aron.

The Congress for Cultural Freedom proposed a new language for the Western debate on communism—one that was particularly important for the left. Its essence was treating the traditional divide between the left and right as a category that should no longer cloud the truth about communism and its homeland. In his speech in Berlin, Arthur Koestler questioned this division as secondary in terms of the new twentieth-century reality that was dominated by the confrontation of democracy and totalitarianism of both brown and red varieties. Hannah Arendt's book *The Origins of Totalitarianism* provided the theoretical framework for the ideological stance of many people involved with the Congress. Comparing the fascists' and communists' motives and methods, Arendt called attention to the meaning of concentration camps as the quintessence of totalitarianism in both its variants. The truth about the Gulag acquired a new status for many intellectuals in the West. It became the subject of investigations and thought, without being immediately trumped and dematerialized by the traditional Stalin/Hitler, imperialism/socialism, left/right dichotomies that had previously insisted that people close their eyes to communist evil.

The atmosphere surrounding Soviet communism and its dark side had now changed compared to the time before and during the war. Before the war, it had been possible to ignore reports on the Gulag, the purges and the terror by pointing to the scarcity of evidence. Now there was so much proof available, and the number of witnesses so great, that these traditional excuses made little sense. Socialists, communists, soldiers from the Red Army and the Anders Army, women, men, children, Catholics, Orthodox, Protestants, Muslims, Jews, Poles, Germans, Russians, Ukrainians, Tatars, and so on were telling the West virtually the same story about the USSR. In the face of such clear and unambiguous reports, one could either accept the facts—or stop dealing with them altogether.

Indeed, those who went on denying the existing evidence of Soviet crimes seemed almost ostentatiously uninterested in facts. In order to understand the motivation of numerous Western intellectuals who continued steadfastly to deny witnesses' testimony about the USSR, we should perhaps stop questioning their knowledge and instead concentrate on the issues of faith, psychology, and politics. In order to explain their attitude, many of these intellectuals could probably repeat Tertullian's motto, "Credo quia absurdum" (I believe because it is absurd). An attitude that Nietzsche had once characterized as "a refusal to see something one sees—a refusal to see something because one can see," became an acceptable part of their discourse.

The truth about the USSR was politicized even more radically than it had been in the 1930s. The clearer and more overwhelming the proof of Stalinist crimes, the more stubbornly it was met with denial in some quarters. A justification of this approach by Sartre has gone down in history: he did not deny the existence of camps in the USSR but claimed that the truth should not be told about them so as not to cause the French proletariat despair.[75] If the French working masses learned the truth about the USSR—as the Parisian intellectual implied—they could suffer painful disillusionment and lose faith in the redemptive power of communism. Robert Conquest commented on Sartre's words as follows:

> Why the labor-camp population should be sacrificed to the (rather smaller) membership of the CGT [French Communist trade union—D.T.] was not clear; nor, indeed, was it ever made plain why the views of the French proletariat, one of the few that has ever come largely under Communist influence, should prevail in world affairs any more than those of the anti-Communist British and American and German proletariats. Nor is it obvious at first sight why falsehood should demand the allegiance even of the intelligentsia. This sort of intellectual and ethical attitude might be treated as a passing aberration, a curiosity of history, and one might have thought that anyone holding it would have forfeited any public standing as a moral arbiter, at least in this sort of sphere. But this does not seem to have been the case, and if only for that reason is worth referring to.[76]

Sartre was not the first to formulate this type of moral dilemma—should the masses be told the cruel truth about the world they live in, or should they be rather fed an optimistic lie? Dostoevsky posed this dilemma with unparalleled perceptiveness in *The Legend of the Grand Inquisitor*. Antoni Słonimski had shared his hesitations with his readers in 1932 describing his return from the USSR. Let us recall that when asked by a porter at the railway station in Warsaw "what it's really like" in the Soviet Union, he had felt in the man's tone hope that the communist dreams would be confirmed by an eyewitness.

But Słonimski decided not to indulge these dreams at the expense of the truth, although at that moment it would have been more convenient morally for him to refrain from disappointing the simple man's hopes.

Sartre had no such scruples. Unlike Słonimski, he had no qualms in advocating for deliberate suppression of truth about the Gulag. In the early 1950s, when many Western intellectuals were changing their views under the pressure of the growing volume of reports of Soviet crimes, Jean-Paul Sartre was evolving in the opposite direction. When David Rousset brought up the topic of Stalin's camps in 1950, Sartre and Maurice Merleau-Ponty attacked him in *Les Temps modernes* not for lying (they neither denied the existence of the Gulag nor argued that it was a benign form of resocialization) but for providing weapons for the enemies of Soviet socialism.[77] In response to Albert Camus's denouncement of the Gulag in 1951, Sartre wrote: "Yes, Camus, like you, I find these camps inadmissible, but equally inadmissible is the use that the so-called bourgeois press makes of them every day."[78] More important than truth was preventing anticommunists from being proven right—because, as the French philosopher concluded, "any anti-communist is a dog!"[79]

After a traditional pilgrimage to the USSR in 1954, Sartre claimed in an interview with *Libération* without batting an eyelid that "complete freedom of criticism exists in the USSR" and that "Soviet citizens criticize their government far more and far more effectively than we do." "If you do not see Soviet citizens traveling freely around the world," the Parisian existentialist explained, "it is not because they are forbidden to do so, but because they do not want to leave their wonderful country."[80] Over twenty years later he stated: "After my first visit to the USSR in 1954, I lied." But in the next sentence he made a typical self-correction: "Actually, lie might be too strong a word: I wrote an article where I said a number of friendly things about the USSR which I did not believe. I did it partly because I considered that it is not polite to denigrate your hosts as soon as you return home, and partly because I didn't really know where I stood in relation to both the USSR and my own ideas."[81]

The Story of a Single Book

The ambiguous and evolving attitudes of Western elites toward Soviet crimes during the Cold War can be explored by focusing on one of the most profound testimonies of the Gulag—*A World Apart* by Gustaw Herling-Grudziński. Herling was arrested by the NKVD in 1940 trying to get out of the Soviet-occupied part of Poland to as-yet-unoccupied Lithuania. His interrogating officer associated Herling's name with Göring's (in Cyrillic script "h" is written "g";

hence the confusion.) This sufficed to send Herling to the Gulag. In a camp in Yertsevo near Archangel, Herling had some initial luck getting into a brigade of porters unloading boxcars carrying food. Later he ended up in a sawmill, then logging and harvesting. Here he encountered camp hunger and exhaustion. Soon, however, came the German-Soviet war and the "amnesty" for Polish prisoners. Fruitlessly waiting to be released, Herling together with several other Poles began a desperate hunger strike. In the Gulag, where everyone was already hungry, this was probably unprecedented. The striking Poles were seen as mad and suicidal, yet the camp authorities relented, and in January 1942 the long-awaited release arrived. After a dramatic journey across Russia, Herling reached the Anders army. On March 30, 1942, he left the USSR together with his unit. By way of Persia, Iraq, Palestine, and Egypt, he reached Italy, where in May 1944 he took part in the fighting at Monte Cassino and on the Gothic Line. After the end of the war, he made it to England. In 1951 his camp testament *A World Apart* appeared in an English edition.

Herling's book on the Gulag went beyond a simple factual description. It was a literary and philosophical reflection on the human condition based on the personal experiences of the writer subjected to the pressure of Soviet dehumanization in a camp. *A World Apart* joined a new, slowly developing, postwar discourse about the human condition, provoked mainly by the moral shock of the Holocaust and Nazi atrocities. Herling described human experience similar in many ways to the Auschwitz experiences described by Tadeusz Borowski, or later by Primo Levi and Elie Wiesel. The questions he posed in *A World Apart* belong to the series of endlessly disturbing questions facing humanity after World War II. Is a human being, subjected in a camp to the dehumanizing pressures of hunger, fear, pain and humiliation, able despite everything to retain his or her own humanity, if we measure humanity by the person's ability to follow his or her free will and moral choices? After the experiences of the totalitarian hells of the twentieth century, are we still able to describe man using the traditional language of moral values, assuming that people are creatures by nature capable to be guided by these values?

Herling, like Borowski, questioned the traditional conceptions of humanity. He described Gulag victims who, before their physical destruction, were subjected to moral destruction. In Herling's eyes humanity's worst tragedy and totalitarianism's greatest evil was that man, guided by his innate instinct to live and to survive, more often than was previously imagined turned out to be able and willing to commit any vile act, all while continuing to be a victim of evil.

"If the recollection of all that happened in Europe during the late war is to have any meaning at all," wrote Herling, "we must forget the principles of every-day morality on which the life of our grandfathers and fathers was founded. . . . There it has been proved that when the body has reached the limit of its endurance, one cannot, as was once believed, rely on strength of character and conscious recognition of spiritual values; that there is nothing, in fact, which man cannot be forced to do by hunger and pain."[82]

This assertion brought to mind the Auschwitz stories of Tadeusz Borowski, which were then known to Polish readers. In fact, Herling wrote his Gulag memoir as a polemical response to Borowski's pessimistic vision of human nature. And yet, unlike Borowski, Herling had discovered in the camps something that allowed him to provide a positive answer to the question posed later by Primo Levi in relation to someone at the depths of degradation in a camp: "Is this a man?" Herling replied "yes," since he had observed in the Gulag that people in inhuman circumstances could be motivated to act not just by animal survival instincts but sometimes also by some separate and uniquely human instinct, even when it was at odds with survival. In *A World Apart*, Herling described how some of his fellow prisoners gathered what remained of their own strength to bring themselves to behave in ways defying the logic of self-preservation. These Gulag slaves suddenly threw down a desperate challenge to their camp masters. These were people who (in the words of Kierkegaard) "fight even when their own reason shows that fighting is impossible, and that it must end in humiliating defeat."[83] But what drove them to this—often hopeless—behavior was deeper than reason.

What Herling discovered in human beings, in the depths of debasement in the camp, was a special, autonomous, and exclusively human instinct for freedom. He wrote, for instance, of a female prisoner who, in the name of love for a fellow prisoner, sacrificed her best chance for survival by rejecting a position as a nurse in the camp hospital. This happened in a world where "love" was considered as nothing more than a currency with which women bought their survival. Another example described by Herling was that of three nuns who had been working in a camp for several years and who one day announced that they would no longer continue working "for Satan." They knew that a death sentence threatened anyone refusing to work in a camp. Such behavior included also the hunger strike begun by the author himself in the camp. In these and other examples of strange and unpredictable human behavior in the Gulag, Herling found spontaneous manifestations of the human instinct for freedom no less powerful than the survival instinct. People urged on by this instinct risked and sacrificed their own chance of survival only to prove to themselves and to the world that despite the hunger, the exhaustion, and the lack of hope, they were able to be guided by their own free will right to the end—in other words they were still human in the fullest sense of the word.

This vision of humanity contained in *A World Apart* alluded to the image of man outlined almost a hundred years before by another inmate of a Russian forced labor camp—Fyodor Dostoevsky. In *The House of the Dead* Dostoevsky had observed and described the deep need of the prisoners to see themselves as free entities. He had written that this need "sometimes ends in anger, in frenzied rage, in insanity, fits, convulsions. So, perhaps, a man who has been buried alive in his coffin and who has woken up in it hammers on its lid and struggles to throw it open, although of course his reason tells him that all his effort will be in vain. But this is not a matter of reason; rather it is one of convulsions."[84] In Dostoevsky's view, it is precisely this irrational instinct for freedom that motivates people to behave in unpredictable ways, often contrary to survival instinct, in order to prove to themselves that free will has not died within them.

Having survived the hell of the Gulag, Herling confirmed and expanded Dostoevsky's conclusions. If a person's humanity can be measured by the ability to behave of one's own free will, often in contradiction to one's survival instinct, then man in the "concentration camp world" of the twentieth century remains, despite everything, a man. His humanity, crushed with methodical brutality by totalitarian butchers, erupts unexpectedly in ways that are often hopeless, strange, and desperate. But it still is humanity.

The fate of Herling's book in the West illustrates the state of Western debate on Soviet crimes during the Cold War. Frankly speaking, Herling was lucky in a sense that most of the Gulag witnesses at that time were not. He sent an extract from his memoirs, translated into English, to the London publisher Heinemann even before he had finished the whole book. It so happened that the publisher sent the manuscript for review to Malcolm Muggeridge, who rated it very highly. *A World Apart* appeared in English in 1951, when the Congress for Cultural Freedom was held in Berlin. Bertrand Russell wrote a short foreword to the book, which automatically caught the reviewers' attention. Russell commented:

Of the many books that I have read relating the experiences of victims in Soviet prisons and labour camps, Mr. Gustaw Herling's *A World Apart* is the most impressive and the best written. . . . Fellow-travelers who refuse to believe the evidence of books such as Mr. Herling's are necessarily people devoid of humanity, for if they had any humanity they would not merely dismiss the evidence, but would take some trouble to look into it. Communists and Nazis alike have demonstrated that in a large proportion of mankind the impulse to inflict torture exists, and requires only opportunity to display itself in all its naked horror. . . . Although the effort is not easy, one should attempt, in reading such a book as this one, to understand the circumstances that turn men into fiends, and to realise that it is not by blind rage that such evils will be prevented.[85]

The book quickly gained acclaim in the English-speaking world. Over the course of the following year, two American editions were published and translations began to appear, first into Swedish in 1952, and a year later into German, Spanish, Chinese, and Arabic, and soon also into Japanese and other languages. In 1958, the book came out in Italy, where Herling lived. Here, however, things took a strange turn, illustrating the political twists regarding the topic of Soviet crimes in that country. Walking around Italian bookstores, Herling discovered that no one knew anything about his book anywhere. He finally concluded that his publisher, Vito Laterza, had printed a very small run. In Herling's view, Laterza had probably not wanted to refuse to publish *A World Apart*, since he was also the publisher of Herling's famous father-in-law, the Italian philosopher Benedetto Croce. But he also very clearly did not want to alienate the left-wing intellectual elite by printing a crushing denunciation of Soviet communism. "Using the language of Orwell, the book was published and not published at the same time," Herling recalled many years later in a conversation with a Polish literary scholar Włodzimierz Bolecki.[86]

This was not as unusual as it may seem. Next to France, Italy was the Western country where communist ideas and politics enjoyed the greatest popular support. In 1948 the Italian Communist Party had 2.2 million members. In the 1953 elections it won 22.6 percent of the votes. At one point the Italian communist newspaper *Paese Sera*, in a piece written by Gianni Toti, even demanded that Herling be deported from Italy. *A World Apart* had to wait until 1965 for a proper Italian edition. This time, one of the leading Italian representatives of the still-growing legion of disillusioned communists, Ignazio Silone, wrote the foreword. Speaking later with Czesław Miłosz, Herling described his position in Italy, especially in the 1950s, as that of a leper. Miłosz, who at that time spent almost ten years in France after his prominent break with the communist authorities in Poland, replied: "I was a leper in France too. We were people to whom people did not want to listen, whom people did not want to see. And this affected not just me, but all writers from Eastern Europe living in the West."[87]

Most interesting of all was the fate of *A World Apart* in France. As early as 1951, when the first English edition of the book came out in London, its French translation, recommended for publication by Gabriel Marcel, awaited publication by the Paris Catholic publisher Plon. The *Figaro Littéraire* published several extracts of Herling's book as advance notice of its imminent publication in

French. However, Plon shortly thereafter withdrew from the agreement with vague allusions to the views of the "new editorial team." "There is no doubt in my mind," Herling said many years later, "that political considerations came into play." The publication of *A World Apart* in France was stopped.[88]

After the rejection of *A World Apart* by Plon, Herling sent the manuscript to Gallimard. Albert Camus replied: "I really enjoyed your book and I have enthusiastically talked about it. However, the final decision was negative, above all for commercial reasons, I believe. I am personally disappointed by this and want to tell you that, in my view, your book ought to be published and read in every country, as much for what it is, as for what it says. With your permission, I shall try to sound out some other publishers."[89]

Camus's efforts were unsuccessful. He died in 1960, and *A World Apart* had still not appeared in France, despite numerous further efforts by a great many people. This astonishing resistance slackened only in the 1980s, when the Spanish writer Jorge Semprun succeeded in convincing the Denoël publishing house that it was high time that this book by a survivor of the Gulag in 1940–42 be brought out. At long last, *A World Apart* came out in France in 1985, thirty-four years after its original publication in England. The book received the Guttenberg Prize and an award from the French Pen Club, while Bernard Pivot devoted a whole episode of his prestigious TV show *Apostrophes* to Herling. When Herling described on the show the fate of *A World Apart* in Sartre's homeland, Pivot exclaimed: "Shame! Shame on us!"[90] This was the time when a new Soviet leader, Mikhail Gorbachev, had just come to power in the Kremlin. Within a few years, the Soviet Union would cease to exist and *A World Apart* would appear on the shelves of Moscow bookstores.

8

The Passing of an Illusion?

Orphaned

On March 5, 1953, precisely on the thirteenth anniversary of condemning 25,700 Polish citizens to death in Katyn, Kharkov, Tver, Bykivnya and other killing fields, death came for Stalin himself. In front of UN headquarters in New York, sixty nations' flags were lowered as a sign of respect. In India, the Parliament interrupted its proceedings with two minutes of silence, and in France the government of Prime Minister Mayer declared three days of national mourning.[1] Bertolt Brecht declared: "The oppressed of all five continents . . . must have felt their heartbeats stop when they heard that Stalin was dead. He was the embodiment of their hopes."[2]

It is unclear what Brecht knew about the thoughts and feelings of the oppressed on all the five continents; what is known, however, is that at the news of Stalin's death, in thousands of camps, hearts beat faster. "It's now or never," reacted Olga Adamova-Sliozberg, "everything will change. It's now or never."[3] In some camps—for instance in Steplag and Vyatlag—the prisoners reacted with shouts of joy, although for the most part they were probably afraid to show their real feelings and went through the motions of the mandatory show of grief and mourning. Fear and the sense of enslavement within the Soviet empire had taken such deep root that to this day it is hard to say which Gulag inmates (as well as ordinary Soviet citizens) publicly lamenting Stalin were feigning grief and which ones had so identified with their role of obedient subject that tears came to their eyes unbidden. Barbara Skarga, a Gulag prisoner from the Polish eastern border lands, recalled the day when her camp learned the news of the death of the standard bearer of peace: "Stalin died. Suddenly Tchaikovsky's

Sixth Symphony came over the camp loudspeakers, followed by Handel, Mozart and Beethoven.... It was already relatively warm, the snow was melting on the taiga, so after work we sat as close as we could to the loudspeaker hanging high on a pole and listened. The supervisors nodded: the *zeks* are mourning Stalin, good girls. In fact, many Russian women prisoners were mourning Stalin for real, hard though it is to believe."[4] Crying out loud or laughing inside (one did not exclude the other), the condemned now hopefully awaited change. "Tension and fear were general, and the expectation that something *must* happen now," Walter Ciszek recalled the reaction to Stalin's death in a camp near Norilsk. "The guards outside and inside the camp had been doubled. . . . Comments on the death of Stalin rippled like an undertow through the camp. The camp officials began to shift prisoners from one camp to another, hoping to separate leaders from their followers."[5]

Signs of uncertainty appeared among Gulag supervisors and guards; many of them suddenly showed more leniency. The inmates, however, began more often to protest and make demands of authorities. Kangaroo courts were springing up to try camp informers and overzealous prison trusties. Strikes and revolts started to break out in the camps, including in Norilsk, Vorkuta, and Kengir. Bloody battles were fought between the security forces and rebellious prisoners. Walter Ciszek recalled:

> The machine-gunners continued firing waist high to pin everyone to the ground. Anyone who tried to get up got hit. . . . I looked back over my shoulder to see rows of corpses and the wounded scattered in the roadway. I could hear the chatter of the machine guns, the curses and moans of the prisoners, shouted commands, and still, rising above it all, the high-pitched screams of the women from the direction of their camp. . . . Some of the leaders of the revolt were found dead in the latrine, with their wrists slashed or their throats cut. They preferred to kill themselves rather than be taken alive.[6]

Lyubov Bershadskaya described an attack using tanks on the striking Kengir camp in June 1954: "I was standing right in the middle and around me tanks were crushing living people."[7]

The prisoners had not been wrong: Stalin's death was the beginning of the end of the Gulag. Changes began at the very top the very next day. Behind them stood none other than the principal political police chief of Stalin's empire, Lavrenty Beria. There was little doubt that after Stalin, Beria was the most powerful person in the empire, exercising as he did control over much of the security apparatus. His behind-the-scenes quest for power in the Soviet police state was not openly questioned by anyone who valued his life. But his was not the absolute power that Stalin had wielded. Beria had to take much more account of the other members of Stalin's orphaned Politburo. Initially they did not come out openly against Beria for fear of their own safety, but they quickly began to plot against him in secret.

Meanwhile, Beria began a speedy review of the Soviet system of state slavery. He knew the system better than anyone. He was fully aware that, contrary to Stalin's belief, the Gulag not only brought no economic benefit, but on the contrary, the cost of maintaining a huge army of guards, administrators, and prisoners, as well as the unprofitability of many substantial Gulag investments, were ruining the Soviet economy. Even before Stalin's funeral, Beria divested himself of formal jurisdiction over the Gulag, handing it over to the Ministry of Justice (with the exception of special camps for political prisoners). On March 22, Beria suspended over twenty large Gulag projects, including the Turkmen canal, the Volga-Ural and the Volga-Baltic canals, as well as the famous "road to nowhere"—the name given to the North Siberian railroad line being built by camp inmates from Salekhard to Igarka. On March 27, he announced an extensive amnesty for Gulag inmates, mostly criminals, which was to affect around 1,200,000 prisoners. On Beria's instructions, 220,000 current investigations were also dismissed. On April 4, less than a month after Stalin's death, Beria officially banned torture. Finally, on June 16, Beria declared his intention to "liquidate the system of forced labor on the grounds of economic ineffectiveness and lack of perspective."[8]

Economic calculation was certainly not the sole motive for Beria's sudden switch from ruthless executioner to liberal reformer. Beria undoubtedly had deep political instincts, and these were now telling him that whoever wanted to become Stalin's successor would have to secure for himself the loyalty and support of the party establishment, security apparatus and the military. The representatives of these key structures of the Soviet state had lived in constant fear under Stalin's control. The pleasure of their master, who held over them the power of life and death, could at any moment change to displeasure. They had ruled and at the same time they had trembled in fear for their own fate and that of those closest to them. This had applied to people at every level of government, from collective farm manager to Politburo member. Thus, the leader of the proletariat's death was greeted by the Soviet governing elite with a collective sigh of relief—skillfully hidden, of course, under a mask of inconsolable grief.

For people in Stalin's inner circle, it was clear that party establishment, the political police, and the army would only support a new leader who would be able to bring them a sense of security while reassuring them of the stability of their power. Beria was perfectly well aware of this. He began right at the top. He had Molotov's wife, Polina Zhemchuzhina (who, on hearing of Stalin's death, had burst into tears) released from the Gulag. He ordered the posthumous rehabilitation of Kaganovich's brother Mikhail, who had been suspected of treason in 1941 but had managed to shoot himself in a Kremlin toilet rather than wait for his arrest. Beria also ordered that Mikhail Kaganovich's widow receive a pension. However, neither Molotov nor Kaganovich showed any gratitude.

These lightning moves by Beria made other members of Stalin's Politburo uneasy. It appeared as if the powerful head of the Soviet security apparatus was trying to build his own power base that would allow him to rise above the other comrades in the highest circle. Knowing Beria's earlier habits, they had ample reason to fear that their future fortunes and chances of survival under Beria's regime could become uncertain. A plot was hatched under the leadership of Nikita Khrushchev and supported by Marshal Georgy Zhukov. The conspirators made a preemptive strike in the summer of 1953. During a meeting of the leadership on June 26, Beria was arrested and secretly transported from the Kremlin—which was guarded by NKVD officers loyal to him—to an undisclosed location under military control. On December 23, Beria was secretly tried, pronounced an "enemy of the people," and condemned to death. His prosecutor was Roman Rudenko, the same man who had accused the leadership of the Polish Underground in Moscow of collaboration with Hitler and the Germans at Nuremberg of the Katyn massacre. This time the list of charges had been carefully chosen so that nothing could inadvertently come back to haunt Beria's accusers and judges. That evening, a great many of Beria's former comrades and subordinates gathered in the execution cell to watch the death of a man whom for years they had treated with reverent respect, secret fear, and even more secret hatred. A special wooden shield had to be installed to protect those present from ricochets. Beria wanted to say something before his death, but Rudenko reportedly ordered a cloth to be stuffed into his mouth. Officers supposedly quarreled as to who would take the first shot. Finally, the honor fell to General Pavel Batitsky. Beria's corpse was burned, and his family was deported to Sverdlovsk.

The killing of Beria did not, however, mean a retreat from the reform policies he had begun. The new (old) leadership seemed to understand why Beria had so hastily transformed himself from executioner into reformer. And even if not every member of the Politburo was in favor of these reforms, it was too late to reverse them. The amnesty for Gulag inmates was continued and began to embrace even more people. In hundreds of cities throughout the USSR, people released from the camps began returning. The world of the Gulag, previously veiled in ominous secrecy, was now revealed to millions of people in personal conversations with and accounts from returning prisoners. These testimonies were for the most part confidential. After all, despite the new reforms, much of the Soviet power structure was staffed by the very same people who had until recently written and read denunciations, investigated, arrested, interrogated, tortured, passed sentences, sent people to camps, guarded them, and killed them.

Meanwhile, the authorities were hastily rehabilitating party and state officials, both living and dead, condemned by Stalin. After coming to power, Khrushchev began to apply Beria's reformist approach in his battle with his recent Politburo allies, now rivals. He portrayed his opponents therefore as potential advocates of a return to Stalinist methods of controlling the power elite. This approach finally reached its logical conclusion. At the Twentieth Party Congress in February 1956, Khrushchev gave a secret (but soon to be famous) speech, in which he accused Stalin of personal responsibility for the purges of the party apparatus. He said out loud what most of the participants at the Congress knew firsthand. Many had been personally involved in the annihilation and victimization of innocent people, although now they appeared deeply shocked by such seemingly unbelievable news.

In this critique of Stalin, Khrushchev not only broke a taboo but also laid out clear boundaries for what Stalin could now be criticized within the party and what should not be discussed. In reality, the new Soviet general secretary attacked his predecessor only for crimes against the Communist party. In his eyes, Stalin's sin had been his unwillingness to share power with the party and his persecution of many devoted communists for reasons that were to them incomprehensible. There was to be no discussion of issues such as the murdering, persecuting, enslaving, and exploiting in camps of millions of innocent people who had never been communists and were not part of the power elite. This sort of discussion would inevitably have led to the question of the communists' moral and political legitimacy to hold power in Russia. Such deliberations, one may quite reasonably assume, held little appeal for the delegates to the Twentieth Congress. In any event, Khrushchev dispelled this kind of anxiety, making it clear to his audience that criticism of Stalin was an internal matter of the party. What was at issue were the "errors and distortions" committed by the Leader, as well as his "cult of personality," and not the crimes against humanity or the legitimacy of the communist regime. There was no need to reveal this criticism to the Soviet people, let alone the outside world.

Khrushchev miscalculated, however, if he did indeed expect the party to keep this a complete secret. Stalin's critic was still thinking along Stalinist lines. It had been much easier to keep things quiet during the Standard Bearer of Peace's time, since idle chatter led to a bullet in the back of the head. Freeing his party comrades from fear, Khrushchev rashly undercut the concept of party discipline. The first to break ranks were the Polish comrades invited to the Congress, who published Khrushchev's speech in the context of internal quarrels within the Polish communist elite. Thus the secret speech by the head of the Soviet party turned instantly into an event with worldwide repercussions.

Revealing Khrushchev's remarks outside the Soviet Union immediately undermined the credibility and authority of those Westerners who for years had been denying reports of communist crimes. It was impossible to refute the fact that the unmasking of Stalin's crimes, even if very selectively, had happened in the Kremlin and had come from the current helmsman of the communist vessel. *Roma locuta causa finita.* "It turned out" that the purges and the camps had not been the invention of anticommunist propaganda, as many influential people in the West had been convincing themselves and others. It is hard to tell how many people in the West were truly shocked by the revelation of the truth about Stalinism, partly because feigning shock became a popular technique to save face on the part of Stalin's recent admirers. Many cheerleaders for the USSR now felt serious anxiety, not necessarily because they had suddenly discovered the ugly truth but rather because they understood that revealing this truth to the world could greatly undermine the system with which they linked their hopes. Bertolt Brecht, nearing the end of his life, remarked: "I have a horse. He is lame, mangy and he squints. Someone comes along and says: but the horse squints, he is lame and, look here, he is mangy. He is right, but what use is that to me? I have no other horse. There is no other. The best thing, I think, is to think about his faults as little as possible."[9]

Jean-Paul Sartre was no less deeply inconsolable. He judged Khrushchev's speech to be "an enormous mistake." "In my opinion," remarked the author of *La Nausée*, "the public and solemn denunciation, the detailed exposition of all the crimes of a sacred personality who had for so long represented the regime, was madness when such frankness was not made possible by the prior and considerable raising of the population's standard of living. . . . But the result was to discover the truth for the masses who were not ready to receive it."[10] At the same time, Frédéric Joliot-Curie insisted in a conversation with Ilya Ehrenburg that the greatest restraint be used when discussing what Khrushchev had revealed. He asked Ehrenburg not to say anything about it in front of his children for the time being. Joliot-Curie had for a long time known about Stalin's prisons and camps. He had even interceded in the 1930s on behalf of Aleksander Weissberg, who had been imprisoned in the USSR. It was one thing to know, though, and quite another to talk about it aloud, especially in front of the children.

But many people committed to retaining their faith in communism viewed Khrushchev's speech above all as proof of the Soviet system's ability to reform itself from within. The Soviet leader, so the thinking went, had criticized the "errors and distortions" that had appeared in the best of systems as the fault of one man: Stalin. Although it was impossible to ignore these "errors and distortions," they belonged after all to the past. What really mattered was that the land of Soviets had just overcome them and was restored to its healthy Leninist core values. With these values thriving again, the revived Soviet Communist Party was back in the business of building a shining future for all. Such was the new party line of the thaw. But despite these efforts at stitching back together the fabric of Soviet ideology that was inadvertently ripped by Khrushchev, this fabric henceforth began to seriously unravel. Although a long time was still to elapse before the final shreds disintegrated, no way was to be found to stop the process.

Meanwhile, a visible erosion of faith developed in the Western world among the "fellow travelers." Richard Pipes described this phenomenon:

> Fellow-travelers were mesmerized by Stalin's tyranny: instead of seeing it as the crassest violation of Communist claims to democracy, they interpreted it as a guarantee of Communism's purity, since by eliminating politics and all the sordid infighting that went with it, it enabled the Communists to concentrate on what they assumed to be the movement's ultimate objective. Paradoxically, as soon as the Communist leaders themselves began to admit to failures and crimes, which happened after Stalin's death, fellow-travelers deserted them in droves. Soon the breed vanished. For the idealistic fellow-travelers, self-delusion was a necessity: they would ignore oppression and mass murder in the name of an ideal rather than subscribe to a more humane policy whose pragmatism robbed them of utopian dreams. The soul of the idealistic fellow-traveler was an eternal battleground. For many, there was a limit to the negative evidence they were capable of rejecting: for them, sooner or later, came the moment of truth–for some, the expulsion of Trotsky, for others, the trials of the 1930s, the Nazi-Soviet Pact, or the suppression of Hungarian liberty.[11]

Martin Malia described as follows the significance of Khrushchev's speech in the West:

> Khrushchev did . . . a supremely important thing, for Soviet Russia and all the world: he destroyed the mystique of Stalin, and with this act there began

the erosion of the mystique of Communism itself. . . . The importance of the speech was not that it told the West anything basic that it did not already know, and still less that it told the full story about Stalin, for it did neither of these things. Its importance lay rather in the fact that the Kremlin itself now certified part of the truth about Stalin; and only such an imprimatur made it possible for that truth to pierce the ideological armor that had hitherto protected the Father of the Peoples. The hypnotic spell that Stalinism had exercised over both adherents and opponents in the West was suddenly broken.[12]

In the past, Western admirers of Stalin, at least the sincere ones, had usually been convinced of his infallibility. At the same time, Stalin's critics had repeatedly been confronted by the incomprehensible invulnerability of Stalinism in face of massive evidence of crimes against humanity, which should have totally discredited Stalin and communism in the eyes of the world. Khrushchev's speech stripped Soviet communism of its mystical aura, an aura that had fascinated some and depressed, or even terrified, others. As Martin Malia summed it up: "With Khrushchev's bold stroke, the greatest mass hallucination in modern history was ended."[13]

Pandora's Box

Nikita Khrushchev had not realized that he had, in fact, opened Pandora's box. Communism, absent the pressure of Stalinist rule by terror—communism with a screw half-loose—immediately began to slip from the control of the Kremlin drivers of the "locomotive of history." Right after Stalin's death, workers in East Berlin came out against the communist authorities. The vanguard of the proletariat sent tanks against them. In June of 1956, a workers' revolt broke out in Poland. Hardly had that been put down (again, by tanks and machine guns), when factional infighting in the Polish leadership intensified, and autumn saw more demonstrations, which almost led to armed intervention by the USSR in its Polish dominion. Toward the end of the year, Hungary revolted, and the world had an opportunity to contrast the Kremlin's rhetoric of thaw with its real intentions when Soviet Army tanks rolled into Budapest, where blood was spilled, and thousands of Hungarians fled across the Austrian border. The USSR's admirers in the West, as well as those who believed in Khrushchev's "communism with a human face," had many an opportunity to reconsider their views. Soon the Soviet viceroy in East Germany, Walter Ulbricht, discovered a simple way to prevent his subjects from escaping en masse from the socialist paradise: he ordered the Berlin wall to be built. In 1962, the attempt to place Soviet nuclear missiles in Cuba almost resulted in a nuclear war between the superpowers.

This unstable image of Soviet communism in the eyes of the West was complemented by memoirs from the recent Stalinist past. After Stalin's death, citizens of Western countries released from the camps in the wave of amnesties began to appear in the West. There were many of them, especially taking into account the masses of released German and Italian prisoners-of-war (those still alive). In addition to the POWs, former Western communists and Soviet sympathizers, who had paid for their dreams of life in the paradise of the proletariat with many years in the hell of the Gulag, now returned home. For the most part, they were aware that in the final analysis they were the lucky ones: their many friends from the West who had been led by the same desire to live in the land of Soviets never lived to see their homes. Not only Western communists were returning but people of many beliefs, trades, and backgrounds previously held in the prisons of the Soviet empire for a variety of reasons.

Many of these former prisoners saw it as their duty to bear witness to the truth about their own fate and that of their comrades in misery. Starting in 1954, right after the Beria amnesty and before Khrushchev's speech, their memoirs of the camps began to appear in the West. They told frequently of their own fascination with idealized communism and of the real communism that they had discovered in the depths of suffering and degradation.

The first in this series of testimony to appear was Joseph Scholmer's *Vorkuta*, which came out in 1954 simultaneously in three languages: German, English, and French.[14] Scholmer was a prewar German communist who had been imprisoned by the Nazis. After the war, he might have been one of those to lay the foundations of the East German communist state, had he not been arrested as early as 1947—that is, before the official founding of the DDR. As a former prisoner of the Gestapo, he already had some experience in this area. Accused of espionage and forced to admit to crimes he had not committed, he made the conscious decision to name a great many East German communist bigwigs during his interrogation, having reached the conclusion that they could use a similar lesson. He ended up in the camps in Vorkuta with a twenty-five-year sentence. As a doctor, he helped prisoners to feign illnesses, saving more than a few lives. He was allowed out after the Beria amnesty.

The fortunes of another German, Wilhelm Fischer, took a different turn. He had never been a communist, but he had had the misfortune to make a name for himself as a designer of navigational instruments. The Soviets, as part of their policy of stripping Germany of assets, arrested Fischer and shipped him off to the USSR. There he ended up in a *sharashka*—that is, one of the secret centers where imprisoned scientists worked. He spent thirteen years in a *sharashka* in a Moscow suburb of Tushino, contributing to the development of Soviet technology. Some of his projects even received a Stalin Prize. Of course, he was not the one to receive the award. In 1958, having been released from the USSR, he recounted his tale to a journalist from *US News and World Report*.[15]

The same year, a book on the Gulag by Jean Nicolas called *Eleven Years in Paradise* came out in France.[16] Its title was self-explanatory. Meanwhile, John Noble, an American, published his memoirs in the US. Noble, the son of German immigrants, had spent the war with his parents in Germany. Arrested there by the Soviets, he had been forced to testify in court against his own father. Released after Stalin's death, he left for the United States. The title of his book, *I Was a Slave in Russia*, also requires no commentary.[17]

Not all Western inmates of the Gulag managed to return from the USSR on the wave of the thaw, however. Many had to wait years for this opportunity. The amnesty was not extended to Walter Ciszek, an American Jesuit of Polish ancestry. He would probably have ended his days in the USSR, and the Western world would have never learned of his fate had the authorities in Moscow not decided in 1963 to exchange him for two Soviet spies picked up by the FBI. Ciszek would not have landed in the Gulag had he not been engaged in church ministry work in eastern Poland in 1939. After the Soviet invasion, he changed his cassock for a workman's overalls while secretly continuing to provide spiritual care. He was arrested in the spring of 1940, interrogated in the Lubyanka and sentenced on the pretext of spying. He was sent to an Arctic camp—a mine in Dudinka—and then to one of the camps around Norilsk. He survived the camp. After completing his sentence, he remained in exile in Norilsk, Krasnoyarsk, and Abakan, continuing to work secretly as a Catholic priest, spreading the Gospel, conducting baptisms, weddings, hearing confessions, and setting up secret parishes. Shortly after returning to the US, he published his memoirs, *With God in Russia*.[18]

Two other Americans, Victor Herman and Alexander Dolgun, waited even longer to be repatriated. Herman had been one of the numerous American supporters of the USSR in the 1930s who had decided to seek a better future in the land of Soviets. Like most of them, he was arrested in 1937. In his memoirs, published only in 1978, he described the lengthy and unusually cruel torture he endured at the hands of the NKVD during his interrogation.[19] As the result of this torture and psychological pressure (for instance, preparations for his execution were played out in front of him), Herman was on the edge of insanity. Starved in a camp near Vyatka, he survived by catching and eating rats. His fellow countryman, Alexander Dolgun, who worked at the American embassy in Moscow and was quickly forgotten by his superiors and colleagues when the Soviet secret police arrested him, survived an inhuman barrage of torture in the Lefortovo and Sukhanovo prisons. He was permitted to go home only in 1971. The world learned about Alexander Dolgun's fortunes four years later in his book *An American in the Gulag*.[20]

The stream of testimony by Western inmates of the Gulag who were released after Stalin's death picked up speed in the 1970s. It was then, for instance, that the memoirs appeared of Aino Kuusinen—a longtime Comintern official and member of Stalinist intelligence. Aino Kuusinen was the wife of the Soviet dignitary Otto Kuusinen, who was meant to be the Bolshevik viceroy in Finland in 1940. He was one of the few high-ranking foreign communists residing in the USSR who survived the Stalinist purges of the 1930s without a scratch. He enjoyed the trust of all the first three helmsmen of the Soviet vessel: Lenin, Stalin, and Khrushchev. The result of this was that not only did he survive intact all the internal settling of scores in the leadership in the Kremlin, but he continued to rise in the hierarchy. Between 1921 and 1939 he was secretary to the Executive Committee of the Comintern, between 1940 and 1957 he held the position of vice-chairman of the Supreme Soviet of the USSR, and between 1957 and 1964 he was even a member of the Politburo. His wife had been less fortunate and had been arrested in 1937. While her husband was climbing ever higher up the ladder of the Soviet hierarchy, Aino Kuusinen spent eight years in the camps in Vorkuta and then until 1955 in internal exile. In 1964, after the death of her husband—who had been buried with full honors due to a Soviet dignitary of the highest rank—Aino Kuusinen visited Finland where her stepdaughter Herrta, a prominent activist in the Finnish Communist Party, lived. At that time, the Finnish authorities were treating the Kremlin with cautious courtesy, so Aino Kuusinen was unable to come out in public there about her own past. But the road to the West was open, and Aino Kuusinen chose freedom. Her flight aroused worldwide interest. In the early 1970s her memoirs appeared in German, Finnish, Swedish, Japanese, Italian, French, and English.[21] The year 1977 saw the republication in English of the memoirs of Israeli prime minister Menachem Begin, a citizen of prewar Poland who had been brought out of Soviet captivity as a soldier in General Anders's army.[22]

These new camp memoirs written by people from the West contributed to a gradual change in the attitude of Western public opinion toward the Gulag. While it is impossible to ignore the significance of this testimony, it played a secondary role in this process, however. Western attention was now focusing more on camp testimony appearing elsewhere—in the very heart of the USSR.

There, from the moment Khrushchev gave his famous speech, a great test had been underway to see whether communism was capable of coping with the truth about itself. After the Soviet leader's speech, numerous citizens of the land of Soviets, especially writers, artists, academics, and journalists, had begun to test the limits of free speech. The subject of the Gulag was central to this test.

It could not have been otherwise. Gulag prisoners, the living dead, were exiting the earthly Soviet equivalent of the other world en masse and unexpectedly appearing back among the living. Often, however, they were unable to find their footing in this land of the living, just as in the earlier accounts of people who had survived Nazi camps and often felt out of place in the world of normal human behavior, cares, and emotions. Apart from these psychological problems, Gulag inmates returning to life often encountered other difficulties. Their wives, husbands, and children had often disowned them during their many years in the camps; sometimes they had been given up for dead. On returning, they sometimes discovered that their spouses had started new families. It also often turned out that the people responsible for the disjointed life of a Gulag victim—the torturers and informers—were still in power, or simply lived nearby, in the same towns or even in the house next door, and had never faced any consequences. The close presence of their former victims was not to their liking. Many returning camp inmates, knowing only too well the price of crossing the authorities, moved into the shadows. They lived in fear that their freedom would not last. There were those too who did not even try to return to their homes but furtively settled in towns near the camps in Siberia, the Arctic, the Far East, or Kazakhstan.

But there were also former prisoners who set themselves a life goal of bearing witness to the hell of the camps on behalf of themselves and their fellows who had not survived to the end. One of these was an ex-convict and, at the time, a physics teacher in Ryazan' named Aleksandr Solzhenitsyn. Arrested in February 1945 by SMERSH, he had experienced some fortune amidst his misfortune, having been sent for a time to a "sharashka" near Moscow. In 1950, he was transferred to a newly opened special camp for political prisoners in Kazakhstan. Three years later, after completing his sentence in the Gulag, he was exiled to the settlement of Kok-Terek, in southern Kazakhstan, where he was meant to spend the rest of his life under police supervision. In any event, this was not a long-term prospect for him since a tumor had been discovered in his stomach. But he was given permission to go to a hospital in Tashkent that, despite his prognosis, managed to cure him. Solzhenitsyn had been gifted a life.

Shortly thereafter, his fortunes again changed unexpectedly: amnesty came, and he walked free, in a manner of speaking. In 1956, he was able to leave Kok-Terek and return to European Russia. He was not allowed to live in Moscow or other major cities, so he settled in Ryazan' and began to teach at a school. He already felt a sense of mission, a debt to be repaid. As he recalled later, he felt that since he had regained his life and his freedom, either fate or God had returned them to him for a reason. He quite quickly concluded (as many survivors do) that this meant bearing witness to what he and his comrades in misery had undergone in the Gulag. So he began to note his own experiences and those of others. His secret plan to write "about everything" began to expand. If he truly hoped that one day Russians would be able to read his work, then only stubborn optimism (or perhaps naivete) could justify the thought that this might happen during his lifetime.

Meanwhile, it was now 1961, and with it came the Twenty-Second Congress of the Soviet Communist Party under Khrushchev's leadership. In the context of infighting in the upper establishment of the party, the Soviet leader was still playing the thaw card. What he needed in order to play his hand was "constructive" criticism of Stalinism coming from the lower reaches of the party. At the congress, Khrushchev once again attacked the Stalinist purges of communists and called for a "broader and more vigorous" discussion of the "errors and distortions." A nonvoting member of the Central Committee, the editor of the leading literary monthly *Novyi Mir*, Aleksandr Tvardovsky, took up his leader's policy and from the congress platform called on Soviet writers to tackle this theme in literature.

Following the sessions at the Congress from Ryazan', Solzhenitsyn recognized that the time had come to speak out and test just how much of the truth about the Gulag the authorities were prepared to reveal. He wrote a tale on the camps, one based partly on his own experiences, and decided to try to get it published in the journal edited by Tvardovsky. This was a bold step but also one not devoid of caution. Solzhenitsyn's story restricted itself to a description of a single day spent in a camp by a typical Soviet noncriminal prisoner, the peasant and soldier Ivan Denisovich Shukhov, who had been encircled by the Germans during the war but had broken through to his own lines only to be immediately arrested by SMERSH. The work contained no direct criticism of the Soviet system, no politics at all. The camp was presented from the point of view of the main protagonist, a man too uncomplicated to spend much time thinking about politics, ideology, or to make any kinds of moral and philosophical generalizations. Without any direct guidance from the author, readers of the story themselves were forced to come to terms with the moral, ideological, and political issues that the topic of the Gulag inevitably evoked.

Legend has it that Aleksandr Tvardovsky, after receiving the typed manuscript, spent the whole night reading it through to the end. What is true is that the influential editor of the monthly *Novyi Mir* immediately decided to use any means at his disposal to publish this work by the unknown provincial teacher. Tvardovsky had not only political reasons but personal ones too. He came from a peasant family that had suffered during collectivization. While he had been building a career as a Soviet writer, editor, and apparatchik, his father and brother Ivan had been wasting away in the Gulag. Tvardovsky was haunted by guilt, and this undoubtedly influenced his attitudes during Khrushchev's thaw. This master of political compromise with the powers that be felt that Solzhenitsyn's story of the Gulag—to which he himself gave the title *One Day in the Life of Ivan Denisovich*—had at that moment a real chance of being published in the USSR, albeit only with Khrushchev's personal support. Without his support, the censors would certainly reject it.

After 1937, when Viktor Shklovsky, in an attempt to improve the fate of his own brother in the Gulag, published the final enthusiastic paean for camp *perekovka*, entitled *Perekovka on the Volga-Moscow Canal*, no work about the camps had appeared in Soviet literature—even traditional praise.[23] The subject was taboo, and *Ivan Denisovich* was meant to break that taboo. Tvardovsky succeeded in convincing Khrushchev's personal secretary, Vladimir Lebedev, to interest his boss in Solzhenitsyn's work. Lebedev promised to help, and shortly thereafter read a few extracts from *Ivan Denisovich* to Khrushchev. The general secretary of the Soviet Communist Party immediately liked what he heard. He supposedly even called his old buddy from Stalin's Politburo, Mikoyan, and told him to listen. Finally, the leader of the Soviet state pronounced: "In this matter I would even go so far as to say that *Ivan Denisovich* expresses the spirit of the Party."[24] *Roma locuta causa finita.* Two days later the Cuban Missile Crisis broke out, and Khrushchev had more important matters to deal with than reanalyzing the meaning of Solzhenitsyn's work.

What had Nikita Khrushchev liked so much about *Ivan Denisovich*? Supposedly what most caught his fancy was the long scene in which the prisoner Ivan Denisovich labors at a building site. At this key moment in the work, Ivan Denisovich is so engrossed in his bricklaying that he even disregards the order to end work and assemble for the return to the barracks. So as not to waste the rest of his mortar, Ivan carries on working, despite fatigue and the cold. He thereby runs the serious risk of going into the solitary punishment cell, where prisoners are tormented with even greater hunger and cold. He fortunately manages to avoid this. Khrushchev, who had previously encountered descriptions of work mainly in Socialist Realist literature or Stakhanovite propaganda, saw in this (ambiguous, in reality) enthusiasm on the part of a slave for his slave labor a sign of Soviet man's boundless devotion to the building of communism.

After all, the heroes of labor, in keeping with the poetics of Socialist Realism, were always model communists. For Khrushchev, however, Solzhenitsyn's Ivan was an illustration of the idea that even camp and the glaring injustices of the "cult of personality" had not managed to crush faith in communism. Indeed, it was precisely this undying faith in communism that allowed prisoners to retain their human dignity in Stalin's camps—this was supposedly the message that the general secretary of the Communist Party of the USSR had found in Solzhenitsyn's story.

Ivan Denisovich appeared in 1962 in the November issue of *Novyi Mir*, and then shortly afterward in book form, with an enormous joint print run of eight hundred thousand copies. Readers rubbed their eyes with astonishment. Here, in the USSR, someone was writing openly about the Gulag from the perspective of an inmate—nay, an innocent inmate suffering for a crime he had not committed. In order to shield readers from potentially radical and dangerous ideas, reviewers hastened to provide explanations that this was a critique of the period of "errors and distortions," not an attempt to find the sources of the evil of the Gulag in the nature of Soviet communism. On December 26, shortly after the appearance of *Ivan Denisovich*, the secretary of the Central Committee, Leonid Ilyichov, explained to the writers summoned to the Central Committee for a meeting: "We should realize that no cult of personality could dim the heroic efforts of the Soviet people. . . . It should be emphasized that the battle with the consequences of the cult of personality in the name of strengthening the Leninist way of life, in the name of maintaining our power and increasing our nation's achievements are one thing, however it is quite another thing to pretend that one is fighting the consequences of the cult of personality, when one is really raising a hand against our ideology and our life, in other words against socialism and communism."[25] *Ivan Denisovich* came out in the USSR because Nikita Khrushchev had included it in the first of these two categories.

Literary critics who saw in the publication of Solzhenitsyn's work the first breach in the wall of lies and silence surrounding the Gulag (as well as those who simply wanted to get into the general secretary's good graces) began to assure Soviet readers and Soviet leadership that Khrushchev had read *Ivan Denisovich* correctly. In an editorial, *Literaturnaya Gazeta* explained that the writer had shown in *Ivan Denisovich* that "Soviet people never abandoned faith in the Communist Party, in Soviet rule . . . even during the most brutal conditions of Beria terror."[26] Writing in *Izvestiya*, the critic Vyacheslav Pallon quoted the opinion of a former Gulag inmate and the prototype for the character of the Captain in *Ivan Denisovich*, who had supposedly said that "it is clear to every reader of this story that, with a few exceptions, people remained people in the camp for the precise reason that in their hearts they remained Soviet people, and that they did not identify the harm that had been done to them with the party and with our system."[27]

Yet the more that was said and written about *Ivan Denisovich*, the harder it became to conceal one thing: even the most creative arguments could not reduce the work to the safe ideological framework proposed both by the authorities and by critics favorably disposed to Solzhenitsyn. The fact remained that there was no suggestion in the text to believe that the enigmatic camp denizen Ivan Denisovich was motivated by any ideological impulses that were characteristic of a "real Soviet person." That type of idea or concept never enters his mind. There is no direct criticism of communism in the story, but there is also no praise or justification of the system. There is just the camp. Solzhenitsyn's debut differed from the overwhelming majority of works of Soviet literature in that it tackled a provocative subject while withholding clear guidelines for the reader on how to solve the resulting moral and ideological questions. For the first time in the history of Soviet literature, the reader was faced with the phenomenon of the Gulag and was treated as an adult; he was left alone with his conscience to draw conclusions on the moral nature of this phenomenon.

It was hardly surprising, then, that soon voices began to be raised in the Soviet press that saw in *Ivan Denisovich* a dangerous attack on sacred communist truths. In the context of growing internal party opposition to Khrushchev, the general secretary was reminded with growing (although not direct) outspokenness that he had misread Solzhenitsyn's story. Only the author himself could refute these voices. At that moment he could accept the Khrushchev interpretation of his own work, claiming that the author's intentions had been precisely a depiction of the triumph of communist values that not even a Stalinist camp could undermine. But he did not do that.

The Soviet authorities quickly realized that they were unable to control what readers chose to think about *Ivan Denisovich*. The regime was faced with a choice: either allow people to question the very nature of Soviet communism and its consequences, or exclude not only Solzhenitsyn's story about the Gulag but also the very theme of the camps and state terror from the sphere of permissible public debate. This was of course a purely theoretical dilemma; surely no one in the higher reaches of the Soviet power structure took the first option seriously. But Pandora's box had been opened. Thanks to the publication of *Ivan Denisovich*, Solzhenitsyn suddenly became the most talked-about person in the USSR. He also immediately gained a following abroad, where his book appeared in many translations. And although shortly thereafter—following Khrushchev's replacement by Brezhnev—Solzhenitsyn was deprived of a voice in the USSR, and around 1966 *Ivan Denisovich* was withdrawn from libraries and condemned to public oblivion, the world awaited his next statements with interest. Unable to publish his novels *The First Circle* and *Cancer Ward* in the USSR, works that dealt with the subject of Stalinist terror, prisons, and the Gulag, Solzhenitsyn would publish them in the West. The Soviet regime would find itself faced with an unprecedented challenge: for the first time, it was being openly criticized in the world by a writer with an international reputation who resided in Russia.

The appearance of Solzhenitsyn's debut story about the Gulag in the USSR had a series of consequences. For the many former prisoners who wanted, like Solzhenitsyn, to bear witness to the fate of man in the Gulag, it was an incentive to follow in the footsteps of the schoolteacher from Ryazan'. As they wrote or prepared their own testimony for publication, they closely followed the public discussion about *Ivan Denisovich*, deducing from it just how extensive the limits of free speech were in Khrushchev's USSR. It was clear that only testimony of a kind that did not undermine communism's moral legitimacy in a way visible to the censors and political watchdogs could be allowed when decisions were made as to publication in the USSR.

One of the people who decided to take advantage of this propitious moment in order to bring out her memoir of the camps was Eugenia Ginzburg. She had spent eighteen years in Soviet prisons, in camps at Kolyma, and in exile in Magadan. In one important respect her memoirs, entitled *Journey into the Whirlwind*, fulfilled the authorities' need for "constructive" criticism of the "cult of personality" much better than had Solzhenitsyn's *Ivan Denisovich*. Unlike Solzhenitsyn, before her arrest Ginzburg had been a party activist and an ardent communist. She had arrived in the Gulag on the wave of the party purges in 1937. In one of the first lines of her memoirs, she describes her state of mind not long before her arrest: "I don't want to sound pretentious, but I must say in all honesty that, had I been ordered to die for the Party—not once but three times–that very night, in that snowy winter dawn, I would have obeyed without the slightest hesitation. I had not the shadow of a doubt of the rightness of the Party line. Only Stalin—I suppose instinctively–I could not bring myself to idolize, as it was already becoming the fashion to do."[28]

Both this profession of faith and the distancing from Stalin seemed to fit Khrushchev's rhetoric of overcoming the "cult of personality" like a glove. In order to leave no doubt in the censors' minds, Ginzburg gave her memoirs the subtitle *A Chronicle from the Time of the "Cult of Personality"* (dropped from the English edition of 1967). As if that was not enough, she also wrote a foreword in which she repeated practically word for word all the mandatory "thaw" incantations. In the first sentences she asserted: "All that this book describes is over and done with. I, and thousands like me, have lived to see the Twentieth and the Twenty-Second Party Congress." At the end of her foreword she also added that "the great Leninist truths have again come into their own in our country and Party! Today the people can already be told of the things that have been and shall be no more."[29] It was supposed to emerge irrefutably from these thoughts that the author had entered a Soviet camp as a devoted (though not to Stalin) communist, and that even eighteen years in the Gulag had not undermined her communist faith. At least that is how the Soviet censor was meant to understand Ginzburg's memoirs. Her son, the writer Vasily Aksyonov, later described his mother's rhetorical efforts as *malen'kaia khitrost'*—a "small ruse."[30]

The body of Ginzburg's memoirs reveals something quite different from what is suggested by the political incantations in the foreword. It is a testament to the writer's deep internal spiritual evolution. Only in prison and camp does she recognize the moral and philosophical emptiness of communist ideological jargon that has hitherto served as her key to understanding the world. Shortly after her arrest, encouraged by her NKVD interrogating officer to implicate innocent people, she refuses, citing her conscience—a concept that the interrogating officer derides as an anachronistic fetish, quite unsuited to Leninist class morality. The officer is right: Ginzburg's communist faith turns out to be weak. Had she really been the true communist believer she wanted to be, she would have subordinated her subjective moral feelings to the overriding interests of the party. Let us recall that Vladimir Ilyich Lenin himself had criticized "vapid sentimentalism" of the conscience and had demanded that the sole moral criterion for a real communist be the interests of the proletariat (in other words, the Communist Party's current directives). When put to the test of ideological fidelity at her interrogation, Eugenia Ginzburg fails. Or, to put it another way, she begins to emerge from her ideological blindness. In the prisons and camps, she would soon open her eyes wider and begin to search for a new language of values, one that she would be able to reconcile with her own conscience. Her book tells of this profound quest. In reality, *Journey into the Whirlwind* delivers a crushing blow to communism's moral pretensions. It does not do that, however, in a direct or open way. Only years later, when writing the second volume of her memoirs and no longer harboring any hope of being published in the USSR, Ginzburg explained the first volume's internal ambiguity:

> I had assigned myself a specific aim: to offer the manuscript to the major journals. Perhaps to *Iunost*. . . . Or–you never know your luck–even to *Novyi*

Mir, which by that time had already published *Ivan Denisovich*. Alas, together with my hopes of publication the missing inner editor came into being. He carped at every paragraph: "You won't get that past the censor." I started looking for more streamlined formulations, and not infrequently spoiled passages that had come out well, comforting myself with the thought that, after all, a sentence or so was not much sacrifice for the sake of publication, of reaching people at last.[31]

Soviet editors were not taken in. Despite her caution and rhetorical efforts, Ginzburg's testament did not appear in the USSR. The manuscript lay in the editorial offices of the journal *Iunost'* until 1966, when its editor in chief Boris Polevoy finally returned it to Ginzburg, laughing at her naïve desire to see *Journey into the Whirlwind* published in the USSR. The same happened to other Gulag memoirs being written at the time in the hope of seeing the light of day in the land of Soviets. The authorities realized that the publication of *Ivan Denisovich* had been a nonstarter and decided to put an end to public discussion of the Gulag. In 1966, the publication house *Sovetskii Pisatel'* rejected a manuscript of an early version of Varlam Shalamov's *Kolyma Tales*. In Shalamov's work there was no direct criticism of communism, yet in the whole of camp literature there was surely no more revealing account of Soviet communism's evil.

Thus, the theme of Soviet crimes once again became taboo in the USSR. Works on the Gulag and the terror written during the thaw and submitted for publication, such as Georgy Vladimov's *Faithful Ruslan*, Lydia Chukovskaya's *Sofia Petrovna*, Vasily Grossman's *Forever Flowing*, and Yuri Dombrovsky's *The Keeper of Antiquities*, could not appear there. Instead, they began to circulate in manuscript form, however, and eventually made it to the West. There they would come out in Russian émigré publications and soon thereafter in translations into Western languages. When this occurred, their authors, threatened with repression in the USSR, often announced that these works had been published without their knowledge or consent. Sometimes, under the pressure of the authorities, they would repudiate their own testimony. For instance, in 1972, the sick and harassed Varlam Shalamov was forced to make a statement in *Literaturnaya Gazeta* that his stories, which had been published in the West in Russian, French, and German, were no longer relevant after the Communist Party's Twentieth Congress. In his statement, Shalamov also mentioned that he had had nothing to do with the publication of his works, that he condemned their appearance in print, and that he remained a law-abiding Soviet citizen. Shalamov died destitute in 1982.

Hope and Confusion

The attitude of many influential Western public opinion makers toward Gulag memoirs had clearly changed from what it had been in Stalin's day. Even communist intellectuals who had previously outdone each other in their expression of devotion to the Kremlin now became less predictable. The French version of *Ivan Denisovich* was published by the same Association of Friends of the USSR that not long before had produced and distributed placards blackening Victor Kravchenko. Pierre Daix, the editor of *Les Lettres françaises*—the very person who had been singing the praises of reeducation in the Gulag and had been accusing David Rousset of lying—wrote an introduction full of praises. An inevitable question arises: Why had it taken so long for these people to start opening their eyes to Soviet crimes? After all, there had been no shortage of material on the subject.

Of course, as we have already pointed out, Khrushchev's speech at the Twentieth Party Congress and the Soviet leadership's further critique of Stalin's methods had been a great influence on this change. But it was also the peculiar nature of much of the newest survivor literature of the Gulag that had a special significance—works such as Solzhenitsyn's *Ivan Denisovich*, or Ginzburg's *Journey into the Whirlwind*, on which Western public opinion was now focused. At first glance, these books did not seem to require the reader to abandon his or her faith in Soviet communism, or at least in a variant of reformed communism "with a human face." For those Western readers who hoped for a kinder and gentler USSR, it was easier to accept the truth about Stalin's crimes if they could view them as "errors and distortions" and not as integral part of the Soviet system itself. The newest wave of Gulag testimony that the West was focusing on more than ever now differed from earlier versions in that it came from survivors living in the USSR. It was difficult to accuse these witnesses of being in the employ of anticommunist forces in the West. Their testimonies were for the most part works of a literary rather than factual nature, and they were written for publication in the USSR. The latter explains to a great extent why they did not contain sharp and direct criticism of the Soviet system. Their authors, in hopes of publishing in Soviet journals and periodicals, deliberately avoided such criticism and left a great deal unsaid. For Soviet readers experienced in reading between the lines, this was enough to appreciate the courage of these witnesses and to look for indirect meaning of such works. At the same time, Western readers—who were not trained in this sort of reading skill—could read them without feeling compelled to view the hell of the Gulag as an integral part of the communist system.

It is worth recalling that even Solzhenitsyn, who was later seen by the world as a determined and uncompromising critic of communism, for a long time did not betray his own views. *Ivan Denisovich* was a deliberately enigmatic work, constructed in such a way that there was no place in it for directly expressed views on the Soviet system. Its reader perceives the reality of the Gulag through the eyes and mind of the main protagonist, a semiliterate Russian peasant soldier, Ivan Denisovich Shukhov, who does not think in terms of abstract ideas and political generalizations. It was precisely because many things were left unsaid that Solzhenitsyn's story had been allowed to appear in the USSR.

The first volume of Eugenia Ginzburg's *Journey into the Whirlwind* seemed even more ambiguous. In 1967, it was translated into English and received with great interest in the West. Readers and critics often read literally Ginzburg's tactical foreword on overcoming the "cult of personality," and on a return "to the truth of Leninism." In other words, her remarks were often read in the West in the way that she had hoped Soviet censors would read them.

Only in the second volume of Ginzburg's memoirs, written later without any hope of publication in the USSR, were readers able to read the writer's commentary on the genesis of the first volume.[32] In the second volume Ginzburg described her own experience in camps as a "the heroine's spiritual evolution, the gradual transformation of a naïve young communist idealist into someone who has tasted unforgettably the fruits of the tree of the knowledge of good and evil."[33] Dispelling any doubt as to the influence of Stalinist prisons and camps on her attitude towards communism and her own communist past, she wrote: "When you can't sleep, the knowledge that you did not directly take part in the murders and betrayals is no consolation. After all, the assassin is not only he who struck the blow, but whoever supported evil, no matter how: by thoughtless repetition of dangerous political theories; by silently raising his hand; by faint-heartedly writing half-truths. *Mea culpa* ... and it occurs to me more and more frequently that eighteen years of hell on earth is insufficient expiation for the guilt."[34]

However, Western readers received these words only after the writer's death (the English translation appeared in 1981). Living in the USSR, she had been afraid to publish them in the West. It should be noted that the frankly written second volume of *Whirlwind* did not generate the same interest in the world outside the USSR as had the first, which was written with an eye to Soviet censorship.

In many Western reactions to the post-thaw wave of literary memoirs on the Gulag emerging from the USSR in the 1960s, a strange paradox may be noted. These testimonies, often written carefully with Soviet censorship in mind, became more palatable to many public opinion leaders in the West than testimonies of survivors who had written directly for Western audiences without trying to outsmart Soviet censors. Many former Soviet sympathizers in the West were prepared to accept the truth about Stalin's crimes but were not necessarily willing to draw from it broader conclusions on the nature of the Soviet system, ideology, and government.

Another factor motivating the growing openness toward Gulag testimony in the West was that these works could now be read as stories about the past. It was not only communist sympathizers and other critics of capitalism among Western opinion makers who hoped the Soviet system would evolve in a positive direction. Since the early 1950s, Western Europe and the United States had been going through a long period of economic stability and prosperity. The need for utopia fell significantly and with it declined the attractiveness of communist Russia as an antidote to the ills of the West. What emerged instead was a new context in which the Soviet regime was to be viewed. These new optics were dominated by the newly acquired status of the Soviet Union as one of the world's two nuclear superpowers locked in a dangerous test of wills with apocalyptic consequences. Mankind was facing an existential threat like no other in its history.

In the atmosphere of the global nuclear tension between the United States and the Soviet Union, the theory of convergence was advanced in the West. Its proponents believed that the only thinkable future of mankind consisted of an imminent gradual disappearance of the mutual antagonism between capitalism and communism. This process should lead to a lasting peaceful coexistence and culminate in the two socioeconomic systems converging. Supporters of this theory held that capitalist and communist systems both had something to offer one another. Therefore, they should have learned from each other and corrected their own shortcomings until they ended up resembling each other. This kind of thinking was presented in canonical form by the Harvard economist John Kenneth Galbraith in his 1967 book *The New Industrial State*. The opposite view, namely the vision of the inevitable clash between the two systems, seemed for many so pessimistic that it felt simply unthinkable.

The economic theory of convergence found its political incarnation in the policy of détente between communism and capitalism. Its principal exponent, Henry Kissinger, stated: "The necessity for *détente* does not reflect approbation of the Soviet domestic structure. . . . The necessity of *détente* is produced by the inadmissibility of general nuclear war under present conditions."[35] This idea defined the basis of US foreign policy toward the USSR. The boundary between a distanced disapproval of communism's "domestic structure" and a silent acquiescence to its human rights violations remained fluid.

After replacing Khrushchev in 1964, Leonid Brezhnev made his mark on the outside world as early as his fourth year at the helm as the invader of Czechoslovakia—a country whose communist government in 1968 was trying to take seriously the idea of reformed communism with "a human face." At the same time, trade relations between the USSR and the West were developing again after a period of mutual isolation, and it became increasingly evident that the Soviets, like the West, wanted to avoid a nuclear confrontation. Many Western observers, in trying to make sense of these different signals from the USSR, tended to see political reality there as a result of a struggle between liberal (détente-minded) and reactionary (aggressive and dogmatic) elements within the Soviet leadership. In their view, gentle pressure needed to be applied to the USSR in order to strengthen the liberal tendencies in the hope that, thanks to them, the Soviet regime would over time lose its forbidding character and, convinced of its own security, would transform itself into a more civilized country, one that resembled a Western nation.

To Freedom and Back

The amnesties of the thaw dramatically diminished the Gulag system but did not entirely bring it to its end. Soon, new political prisoners were sent to the camps. This was no longer the Stalinist Gulag, of course; its scale and methods had changed. The Soviet authorities had moved away from the concept of slave labor as a key element in the development of a socialist economy. Inmates were still used as a workforce, but the vast projects carried out with slave labor were a thing of the past. Political prisoners, incomparably less numerous than before, were usually separated from criminals in special camps. One could still end up in such a camp for criticizing the authorities, now on the basis of the new Article 70 of the criminal code on "anti-Soviet agitation and propaganda," or Article 190–1 on "deliberately spreading by word-of-mouth fabricated falsehoods discrediting the Soviet political and social system." One could also end up there for practicing religion, especially religious education, for which the new Article 142 on "breaking the law on the separation of church and state" was used.[36] However, such crimes no longer carried the penalty of death or twenty-five years in Kolyma—"just" a few years in a camp, where death by hunger no longer decimated the ranks of slaves. By Soviet standards, especially in comparison with Stalin's day, this was undoubtedly great progress.

As soon as the paralyzing Stalinist reign of terror was relaxed, many citizens became more adamant in demanding their civil rights and liberties. This never assumed a mass scale but became noticeable in the West, especially in the

1960s. The camps opened their gates to a steady trickle of Baptists and Old Believers, activists of nationalist movements in Ukraine, the Baltics and Georgia, Jews protesting the authorities' refusal to permit emigration to Israel, as well as various Soviet citizens critical of the authorities. A new generation of Soviet intelligentsia came of age in this period. One of its leading representatives was Eugenia Ginzburg's son, the writer Vasily Aksyonov. After his parents were arrested in 1937, the five-year-old Vasily Aksyonov was forcefully placed in a Soviet orphanage, from which he was later rescued by his relatives. He wrote: "We were born in the thirties, at the height of world and Russian enslavement. We were supposed to become model slaves, but things did not work out that way."[37] Joseph Brodsky (born in 1940) added: "We emerged from under the post-war rubble when the state was too busy patching its own skin and couldn't look after us very well. We entered schools, and whatever elevated rubbish we were taught there, the suffering and the poverty were visible all around. You cannot cover a ruin with a page of *Pravda*."[38]

In the early 1960s, Brodsky—a young poet openly rejecting conformity with the authorities—began to acquire recognition in unofficial Leningrad literary salons. The authorities would not leave it without a response. Brodsky was arrested and sentenced in 1964 to five years in a penal labor colony near Archangel. The official reason was shirking work (a crime in a "country without unemployment"). The court did not accept that Brodsky was a poet since in the USSR only a member of the Union of Soviet Writers could be considered a poet. Brodsky did not belong to the union. The prosecution concluded that "Brodsky is not a poet, but someone trying to write verse. He has forgotten that in our country a person must work, he must create something: machine tools, wheat, as well as poetry. Brodsky must be physically forced to work. He needs to be expelled from a hero city [Leningrad]. He is a parasite, a bum, a freeloader, an ideologically grubby person."[39] But these attacks did not intimidate Brodsky. He famously said before the court that poetry is a gift from God and not an issue of administrative classification.

Western journalists present in court described the trial and Brodsky's attitude. His defiance inspired some other rebellious citizens in the USSR who publicly came to his defense. In order to intimidate them, the prosecutor did not fail to add: "We must examine the moral character of those who have defended him."[40] Some leaders of Western public opinion as well as Soviet dissidents signed protests in which both groups used the same language of human rights. The West's sympathy was now clearly with the accused. From now on, whenever the Soviet authorities wanted to sentence someone on political grounds, they had to take into account the pressure of Western media and public opinion. This pressure sometimes translated into concrete political and economic factors. And the Soviet state, with its economic development and international position dependent once again on stable relations with the West, did not want to see a return to the Stalinist self-isolation of the postwar years.

In Brodsky's case, the active involvement of Western public opinion proved effective. Not quite two years after his sentencing, Brodsky was released from his labor colony. He spent the following four years in Leningrad having many of his works published in the West. In 1972, the patience of the authorities was finally exhausted, and Brodsky was forced to emigrate. One needs to keep in mind, however, that, in Stalin's day, someone like Brodsky would simply have disappeared—to be shot or sent to the Gulag. The Ukrainian dissident Valentin Moroz summed up the changes that had taken place in the Soviet system of oppression since Stalin's death: "People are as ever thrown behind bars and as ever transported to the East. But this time, they have not sunk into the unknown."[41] Anne Applebaum comments: "And that, in the end, was to be the greatest difference between Stalin's prisoners and the prisoners of Brezhnev and Andropov: the outside world knew about them, and above all could affect their fate."[42]

In 1966, the Western media's attention focused on the trial of two writers, Andrei Sinyavsky and Yuly Daniel, arrested back in September of the previous year. Their crime consisted of having published their work in the West without asking the Soviet authorities for permission. For their own safety, they had done this under the pseudonyms of Abram Tertz and Nikolai Arzhak. Sinyavsky (Tertz's) work—especially his novella *The Trial Begins* and essay "On Socialist Realism"—had aroused a fair amount of interest in the West. Among the journals publishing the essay on Socialist Realism had been the French *Esprit*, the Italian *Il Tempo Presente*, the American *Dissent*, and the Polish émigré *Kultura*. Arzhak wrote in the book *Iskuplenie (Redemption)*, published in New York: "The prisons and camps are not closed. That's a lie! The papers lie! There is no difference whether we are inside prison, or prison is inside us! We are all prisoners! The government cannot free us! We need an operation! Cut out, release the camps inside you! You think the Cheka, the NKVD, the KGB put you inside? No, you did. The state is . . . us."[43]

The Soviet state, as always, sensitive as to what could be said about it in the West, decided to teach Sinyavsky and Daniel a lesson. An additional factor arousing the unconcealed ire of the Soviet legal system was the fact that both writers had tried to outfox their state "minders" by publishing their own works under pseudonyms. It was hard to judge just how far the authorities were prepared to go this time in relation to the accused. The memorable political trials of Stalin's day must have been at the back of the minds of Sinyavsky and Daniel. Fear was still very real. In their final statements, they tried to appeal for leniency. Sinyavsky said: "Well, I am guilty. But I am not one of our enemies. I am a Soviet man and my work is not hostile."[44] Daniel said: "Our mistake lies not in having written our works, but in sending them abroad. . . . We deeply regret that our work has been exploited by the forces of reaction so that we have harmed our country. That is not what we wanted. We would ask the court to take note of the fact that we did not have evil intent."[45] For publishing "material vilifying the USSR" abroad, both men were sent to camps: Sinyavsky was given seven years and Daniel five.

Mikhail Sholokhov, at one time a favorite of Stalin and winner of the Nobel Prize in 1965 (he was awarded the prize shortly after Sinyavsky and Daniel were arrested but before their trial), said the following about the Sinyavsky-Daniel trial at the Twenty-Third Congress of the CP USSR: "Now if we had had these types with their black consciences back in the memorable 20s, when we tried people not following strictly limited articles of the legal code, but 'following revolutionary legal consciousness' [Applause], turncoats like these would have received a very different sentence! [Applause]. But now, just look, they are still going on about the 'severity' of the sentence."[46] Long before the sentence had been passed, *Izvestiya* published an article by Dmitry Eremin called *Hypocrites*, using words deceptively reminiscent of prosecutor Vyshinsky's tirades at the trials of the 1930s: "Time will pass and no one will remember them. Pages, yellow with mold, will be rotting in the garbage cans. After all history frequently confirms: libel, be it ever so foul and malicious, will inevitably evaporate in the hot breath of truth. So will it be this time."[47]

This time, however, Eremin's prophecies did not come true. Two weeks after his article, the London *Times* published a protest by Western writers against the arrest of Sinyavsky and Daniel. Among those signing it were Hannah Arendt, W. H. Auden, Saul Bellow, Heinrich Böll, André Breton, Günther Grass, Graham Greene, François Mauriac, Arthur Miller, Alberto Moravia, Philip Roth, William Styron, and Arnold Toynbee.[48] Although the arrest and trial of Sinyavsky and Daniel was meant to be a deterrent to those who took the idea of freedom of speech, as guaranteed in the Constitution of the USSR, too literally, not everyone felt deterred. On the contrary, the Moscow dissidents Aleksandr Ginzburg, Yuri Galanskov, Aleksei Dobrovolsky, and Vera Lashkova collected and published in *samizdat* documents from the Sinyavsky and Daniel trial to protest the unlawful sentence. For this, all four authors were arrested and convicted in 1968 with sentences similar to Sinyavsky's and Daniel's.

While the West was buzzing about these repressive actions, two friends of the accused, Pavel Litvinov and Larisa Bogoraz, wrote a statement denouncing the trial. They passed it out to Western journalists in front of the courtroom, into which only carefully selected individuals were admitted. The statement contained an appeal to the people of the USSR: "Demand the release of the accused from the arrest! Demand a new trial in conformity with all the legal norms and in the presence of international observers! Citizens of our country! This trial is a stain on the honor of our state and on the conscience of every one of us. . . . We are handing this appeal to the Western progressive press and ask that it be published and broadcast by radio as soon as possible. We are not sending this request to Soviet newspapers because that is hopeless."[49] It may seem surprising that they were handing Western journalists an appeal addressed to Soviet citizens. But in fact, the act was perfectly logical. The most effective way to reach the inhabitants of the USSR around the censors was not by way of *samizdat*, since it had very small print runs and reached narrow circles of metropolitan intellectual elites, but through Western radio stations broadcasting in Russian: Radio Liberty, the Voice of America, the BBC. It was mainly thanks to these stations that people in the USSR could learn about many true events taking place in their own country but suppressed in Soviet media. There was still a certain risk attached to listening to Western radio. The penalty for listening to illicit (and thus heavily jammed) radio stations was no longer death or Kolyma, however, but losing one's job, an official transfer from big cities to provinces, denying one's children entry to college, and similar kinds of harassment. There were also attacks by "unknown assailants." Thanks to Western radio stations, the news about new Soviet political prisoners was heard not only in the West but also inside the Soviet empire. Memoirs of witnesses to the Gulag of Stalin's day were also broadcast by Western radio stations to Soviet audiences.

The presence of Western newspaper, radio, and television correspondents in the USSR was instrumental in having information trickle out. The Soviet authorities were unable to control this channel as tightly as they had before, although they did their best. In the 1930s, *New York Times* Moscow correspondent Walter Duranty and others had largely succeeded in whitewashing Soviet crimes before the world. Denying the famine in Ukraine and justifying the Moscow trials, they became the darlings of both their intellectual milieu back home as well as the Soviet authorities. After the thaw, however, Western journalists in the USSR no longer viewed themselves as spokesmen for the Soviet point of view in the bourgeois West. Often it was the other way around. It was precisely an interview with a dissident or smuggling out and publishing notes from a communist prison or camp, that became for many of them the fulfillment of their calling as a journalist and a source of moral satisfaction, or at least an opportunity to earn the plaudits of their readers or editorial bosses.

Information and commentary on Soviet camps and prisons became almost a permanent fixture in the Western media. In his Moscow apartment, the physicist Andrei Sakharov held press conferences for Western journalists on the persecution of Soviet citizens on political grounds. The time came when the American CBS television network broadcast conversations between its Moscow correspondent William Cole and recent Soviet prisoners of conscience Andrei Amalrik, Vladimir Bukovsky, and Petr Yakir. Right afterward—this was in 1970—Cole was expelled from the USSR, but this did not intimidate Western journalists. The media, cultural institutions, and public opinion became increasingly sympathetic to Soviet dissidents. In 1975, Sakharov was awarded the Nobel Peace Prize.

The fact that political prisoners in the USSR were no longer isolated and forgotten was the result of many factors. But in practice, it came down to the attitudes of specific people: on the one hand, Western journalists, editors, politicians, and cultural figures; on the other hand, individual Soviet citizens who risked a great deal in order to obtain and distribute information about the victims of repression to the world. Starting in 1968, the Moscow poet Natalya Gorbanevskaya regularly published *Chronicle of Current Events* in *samizdat* form, a document which quickly became an important source of information on human rights violations in the USSR. Information on the fate of current political prisoners was included in the sections entitled "In the Camps and Prisons" and "In Solitary." This was tangible, detailed information. It provided not only the names of the prisoners, but often those of officials; information was given on actual events, on prisoners' state of health, on the punishments and harassment they suffered, on their location and living conditions. This information had been obtained by *Chronicle* associates at the price of significant sacrifices and risks. They traveled to distant regions where the camps were located, often bribing guards and administrative workers who would smuggle out messages from inmates. Despite strenuous efforts, the authorities were unable to eliminate these practices. Until recently, any actions that might reveal the secrets of the camps would have been unthinkable. The mystique of the Gulag had forever dissipated. Political prisoners were no longer the "living dead." They could see that their oppressors were not in a position to deceive world opinion about their fate. The *Chronicle* was read and discussed on Western Russian-language stations, and soon it was also being published in the West in English. Publishing a report *Prisoners of Conscience in the USSR* in 1975, Amnesty International was able to rely on detailed information from the "Chronicle."

Toward the end of the 1960s, translations of camp memoirs by inmates of the Brezhnev-era "new Gulag" began to appear. In one of the most prominent, *My*

Testimony—published in *samizdat* in 1967 and translated two years later into English and German—the author, Anatoly Marchenko, echoes the memoirs of Gulag survivors from the Stalin era. "When I was locked up in Vladimir Prison, I was often seized by despair. Hunger, illness, and above all helplessness, the sheer impossibility of struggling against evil, provoked me to the point where I was ready to hurl myself upon my jailers with the sole aim of being killed. Or to put an end to myself in some other way. . . . One thing alone prevented me, one thing alone gave me the strength to live through that nightmare: the hope that I would eventually come out and tell the whole world what I had seen and experienced. . . . Today's Soviet camps for political prisoners are just as horrible as in Stalin's time. A few things are better, a few things worse. But everybody must know about it."[50] Marchenko, a worker from Siberia, had served a groundless criminal sentence before he became a political prisoner. He described in his book the terrifying world of criminal camps, a world full of ritual cruelty and ruthless brutality, of homosexual rapes and of the endless bestial domination of the strong over the weak. After completing his first sentence, Marchenko attempted to flee the Soviet Union. Like El Campesino before him, he tried to cross the Iranian border and was caught. This time he was sentenced for a political offense. In a camp for political prisoners, he got to know Yuly Daniel. Thanks to him, he later came into contact with the Moscow dissident world and published his camp memoirs.

Describing his time in a camp for political prisoners, Marchenko emphasized how important it was for the inmates to know that the world remembered them. Unlike in many well-known accounts of Stalinist camps, where people were tormented by a feeling of utter helplessness and loneliness, in the Brezhnev-era camps a dogged battle was going on. Among the inmates of the special camp in Vladimir described by Marchenko (and confirmed by Vladimir Bukovsky), an atmosphere of constant direct action reigned: protests, hunger strikes, and demands were the frequent response to ongoing efforts by the authorities to break prison solidarity. The results of these efforts varied. Some of the inmates were pressured to publicly recant in the Soviet media. Others never did.

Marchenko was never broken. Having served two sentences, he threw down a further challenge to the authorities, publishing *My Testimony* in the West. For this act of insubordination, as well as a letter to *Rude Pravo* supporting the 1968 Prague Spring, Marchenko was rearrested. He spent three years in a far stricter camp, gaining release in 1971. In 1975, he was again arrested and exiled to Chuna. He managed to write his memoirs of a hunger strike in *From Tarusa to Chuna* and began a new book *Live Like Everyone*, which he did not complete.

He was arrested for the fifth time and died in December 1986 in prison in Chistopol. The probable cause of death was the forced treatment he was given after yet another hunger strike. "Anatoly Marchenko died in struggle. His struggle had lasted twenty-five years, and he had never hoisted the white flag of surrender," stated his widow, and the world media picked up her statement.[51]

Marchenko was not the only internationally known figure to die in a Soviet prison at this time. Earlier, in 1972, Yuri Galanskov had died in a camp in Perm, as had the Ukrainian poet Vasyl Stus in 1985. When Marchenko was dying in Chistopol, in Moscow the new general secretary of the Communist Party, Mikhail Gorbachev, was beginning to express the idea of a renewal of the Soviet state and a normalization of relations with the West.

Returning to the 1960s and 1970s, however, there were numerous accounts by inmates of Brezhnev-era camps that appeared in the West at this time. In 1970, Andrei Amalrik, who had been exiled to Siberia in 1965 for "parasitism," published his memoirs in English and in German under the title *Involuntary Journey to Siberia*.[52] A year earlier, his essay "Will the Soviet Union Survive until 1984?" had come out in the Netherlands. The writer did not have to wait long to be rearrested. This time he served part of his five-year sentence in Kolyma. He emigrated in 1976. Pyotr Yakir's shocking memoir *A Childhood in Prison* was published in English in 1972.[53] After his father, a general in the Red Army, had been shot in 1937, Pyotr Yakir lived in Soviet orphanages and then the camps. Even the fact that the authorities from time to time succeeded in forcing people like Yakir to publicly recant their views did not necessarily mean that the West naïvely accepted such statements. They were now more often seen as proof of the repulsive brutality of a regime that would not hesitate publicly to break and humiliate people with whom it disagreed.

Method in Madness

In response to this negative attention from the West in the 1960s and 1970s, the Soviet authorities sought innovative ways to continue to silence and discipline their subjects without the risk of repercussions from the West. One such innovation was based on the political abuse of psychiatry. Instead of locking up disobedient citizens in camps and prisons, the authorities often put them away in psychiatric hospitals and told the world that they were mentally ill and required treatment.

In fact, treating critics of the authorities as insane had a long tradition in Russia. In 1836, under Nicholas I, it was announced that Petr Chaadayev, one of Russia's most outstanding minds, was mad and he was placed under house arrest. This was punishment for writing an essay "A Philosophical Letter" and having it published in the Moscow journal *Teleskop*. Chaadayev had written the essay under the influence of a stay in the West, where he had surveyed Russia from a distance and reached the conclusion that the principal driving force of the Romanov empire was enslaving its own people. "The authorities decided that no person of sound mind could proclaim the views found in the *Letter*," Bogdan Galster commented. "So Chaadayev was formally recognized as mentally ill, forcibly put under medical (and police) supervision, and prevented from publishing for the rest of his life."[54]

In Stalin's early days during the 1920s, ending up in a psychiatric hospital and being diagnosed as mentally ill could mean survival. The other consequence of overly bold or careless words was being shot or sent to the camps—though sometimes the diagnosis of madness did not exclude the Gulag or an execution. For instance, Aleksei Ganin, a poet and friend of Sergei Yesenin who was suffering from mental problems caused by alcoholism, was sent to a psychiatric hospital, which did not prevent the authorities condemning him to death and shooting him in 1925. In turn, Yesenin's son, Aleksandr Yesenin-Volpin, a poet and mathematician born in the same year 1925, was locked up in a psychiatric hospital in 1949 for, among other things, writing a poem that included the phrase "the Great Terror." After about a year, he was sent to a camp in the Karaganda Region for five years. After his release under the Beria amnesty, his time on the outside turned out to be short. As early as 1959, three years after Khrushchev's famous speech and three years before the publication of *One Day in the Life of Ivan Denisovich*, Yesenin-Volpin was again arrested and put in a psychiatric clinic for a year. This was not his last enforced stay in this institution. Yet another stay in 1968 was the result of his dissident activities, which consisted mainly of signing protests against the persecution of other dissidents, including Sinyavsky, Daniel, Galanskov, Ginzburg, Dobrovolsky, and Lashkova. In 1972, Yesenin-Volpin emigrated to the US.

Ten years earlier, in the memorable year 1962, when official criticism of "errors and distortions" reached a peak in the USSR and *One Day in the Life of Ivan Denisovich* was about to be published, a novel called *The Bluebottle* by Valery Tarsis appeared in print abroad. Unlike Sinyavsky and Daniel, Tarsis published it under his own name. Even at the peak period of the thaw, in the eyes of the Soviet authorities this was such a brazen act that it was clearly hard to explain it in any other way than by the author's insanity. Tarsis spent eight months in a mental hospital (the institution known informally as "психушка," or *psikhushka*). When he emerged, he hastened to describe his experience in *Ward 7* (the title was an allusion to Chekhov's story, *Ward 6*, describing an insane asylum in tsarist Russia). He published it abroad in 1964, again under his own name, first in Russian and a year later in an English translation. Vladimir Bukovsky recalls that Tarsis's book "was an enormous success and quickly became a bestseller. From that moment, however, Tarsis behaved as if there were no Soviet authorities: He gave interviews, took part in press conferences, more or less openly sent new manuscripts abroad; he even bought himself a car—to the envy of the whole Writers' House where he was living."[55] Tarsis resigned from the Soviet Writers' Union and spent his time working on a *samizdat* publication called *The Sphinx*. Like Brodsky, Sinyavsky, Daniel, Yesenin-Volpin, and a great many other troublemakers, he soon found himself living abroad.

When the Soviet authorities in the 1960s decided to reinvigorate the Russian tradition of locking up rebellious subjects in mental hospitals, they insisted on using the language of modern psychiatry. To this end, Soviet experts made the exclusive breakthrough discovery of the previously unknown condition of "sluggish schizophrenia." In the opinion of its discoverers, this was a particularly treacherous form of schizophrenia since patients suffering from it did not display typical symptoms of psychiatric illness. Quite the opposite: they behaved apparently normally, were able to work, both scientifically and creatively, and sounded perfectly rational when taking part in public discussions. In fact, however, these unfortunates were suffering from a severe mental disease. Soviet specialists described the symptoms of this mental condition as "the patient's conviction of his own rectitude, an obsession with asserting his trampled 'rights,' and the significance of these feelings for the patient's personality. They tend to exploit judicial proceedings as a platform for making speeches and appeals."[56]

In light of such assertions by Soviet experts, citizens showing signs of "sluggish schizophrenia" were to be grateful that they were living in a country where science had in a timely manner discovered the sources of this condition and where the authorities would not abandon them without appropriate care. Of course, this care had to have an element of compulsion, given the patients' insanity. People stubbornly demanding "rights" for themselves and others were taken away, often in straitjackets, to psychiatric hospitals, where they would spend months, and sometimes years, locked up in the company of people suffering from other mental conditions. The supervision in these establishments was more reminiscent of a prison rather than a hospital. Particularly severe cases, like that of Natalya Gorbanevskaya, Vladimir Bukovsky, or General Petr Grigorenko, were treated with electric shocks, cold showers, drugs leading to torpor and painful side effects, and various sophisticated methods like spinal taps that elsewhere would probably be seen as torture.

The propaganda image of psychiatric treatment that disguised persecution in Brezhnev's and Andropov's day vividly brought to mind the long-forgotten myth of *perekovka*. Both then and now, the oppressors played the caring guardians, while their victims were presented as misfits, acting against their own and society's interests—in short, people needing care and treatment. In both cases the success of the "treatment" was measured in the prisoner-patient's readiness to recant to the authorities and willingly submit to them. In Stalin's day, Gulag inmates were meant to sing cheerful songs, shout joyfully, and write articles praising their persecutors. Victims were expected to be driven by fervor to work beyond the limits of their strength, proving to their masters that they had finally earned their "trust." In Brezhnev's day, the proof of the effectiveness of a wayward citizen's treatment in a *psikhushka* was to be the patient's public statement that he had come to realize the nature of his illness. One was cured when one finally understood that one's previous obsessive dreams of freedom and human rights had simply been the product of a sick mind. If in the 1930s Gulag inmates' "cure" was presented in the West in ideological terms, as treating the underdevelopment of class consciousness with the redemptive method of forced labor, now the language of medicine was used for the same purpose. No doubt it was expected that Western public opinion, which after the 1930s had managed largely to rid itself of excessive enthusiasm for radical efforts to create a new man in the Gulag, would be more inclined to accept the scientific-sounding theories of Soviet psychiatrists than class theories of resocialization.

These hopes, however, turned out to be in vain. News of the incarceration of dissidents in psychiatric hospitals and of their brutal "treatment" methods not only did not soothe the concerns of the Western public but in fact shocked it instead. In 1970, the journal *Survey* exposed Soviet psychiatric abuses, focusing on the case of General Grigorenko, who was held in psychiatric hospitals for criticizing the authorities and protesting against the Soviet intervention in Czechoslovakia in 1968. In 1973, Grigorenko's memoirs and commentaries, *Mysli sumasshedshego* (The thoughts of a madman) were published in Russian in Amsterdam, and in 1976 a collection of *The Grigorenko Papers* appeared in English.[57] In 1971, memoirs of psychiatric abuse written by the brothers Zhores and Roy Medvedev and by Russian Orthodox religious activist Gennadi Shimanov, were published.[58] That same year, extensive documentation on Vladimir Bukovsky's case, smuggled out from the USSR, appeared in the West.

Bukovsky—one of the most tireless critics of the Soviet order—had already become well acquainted with prisons, camps, and psychiatric clinics. Together with professional psychiatrist Semyon Gluzman, he wrote and published in samizdat *A Manual on Psychiatry for Dissidents*, in which he described in detail the system of tormenting people in mental hospitals, as well as ways of resisting. In 1976, after the USSR had signed the Final Act of the Conference on Security and Cooperation in Europe in Helsinki, which included a clause on respect for human rights, the Soviet authorities agreed to release Bukovsky from prison and exchange him for the head of the Chilean Communist Party, Luis Corvalán, recently imprisoned by the Pinochet regime. A ditty began to circulate in Moscow: "They swapped a thug for Corvalán / Where could they find a shit to swap for Lyon'ka?" Lyon'ka was, of course, Leonid Brezhnev.[59] At a press conference in Switzerland on the day after his arrival in the West, Bukovsky was asked how many political prisoners there were in the USSR. One hundred and fifty million was his answer. As for his own political views, he explained to Western journalists: "I am neither from the right-wing camp, nor from the left-wing camp—I am from the concentration camp."[60] A few months earlier another patient of Soviet psychiatry, Natalya Gorbanevskaya, had found herself in the West and now came to welcome Bukovsky at the airport.

As a reaction to the growing evidence of Soviet abuse of psychiatry, the United States Congress began a congressional inquiry into this matter in 1972. Studying the cases of Bukovsky, Grigorenko, Gorbanevskaya, and of many other political prisoners, the American congressmen relied on, inter alia, the testimony of Aleksandr Yesenin-Volpin, who had recently arrived in the West. Western psychiatric organizations were also taking an interest in Soviet mental hospitals. Initially, however, the Western psychiatric establishment seemed confused by reports of Soviet practices. The American Psychiatric Association, as well as the British Royal College of Psychiatrists, reacted with unease to the information on the use of psychiatric clinics to suppress political opposition in the USSR but also warned against relying in such matters solely on reports and not on scientific data.

In the fall of 1971, following a sharp critique of Soviet psychiatric abuse, published by forty-four eminent Western psychiatrists in the London *Times*, the Soviet authorities started actively taming the Western psychiatric establishment. A prominent administrator of Soviet psychiatry, Professor Andrei Snezhevsky, gave an interview for the *Izvestiya*, in which he shared his "feeling of deep disgust at the outrageous fabrication" of these Western specialists. "Cases of the confinement of healthy persons in a psychiatric hospital are absolutely out of the question in our country," he stated. Another star of Soviet psychiatry, Professor Marat Vartanyan, spoke a year later to *The Times*: "I can guarantee there are no sane people detained in psychiatric hospitals in the Soviet Union."[61] The controversy surrounding the Soviet psychiatric abuse evoked a range of responses. When questioned about this issue by the *Observer* in

September 1973, secretary general of the World Psychiatric Association (WPA), Dr. Dennis Leigh, said on behalf of the WPA: "We are not concerned with political matters. We are an association . . . like the United Nations and what our national member-societies do is up to them."[62]

The Soviet specialists in public relations must have felt encouraged by Dr. Leigh's statements because they decided to use him in a delicate propaganda performance that had been prepared with Western public opinion in mind. Just as Western luminaries had once been personally invited to the show camps, so now a similar visit was arranged to Psychiatric Clinic #5 in Stolbovaya Stantsya, where General Grigorenko was being held. Dr. Leigh and his Swedish colleague Dr. Carlo Perris were invited to visit Grigorenko in hospital. So as not to arouse any doubts in the minds of the luminaries of Western psychiatry as to the general's mental state, Soviet specialists informed them ahead of time that the patient was almost cured. He had regained his sanity, they stated, and was soon to be discharged from hospital. But after the guests' arrival at the clinic on October 15, 1973, a number of unexpected complications arose. Suspecting some kind of deception, Grigorenko agreed to talk only in the presence of his wife and a trusted interpreter. The Soviet organizers decided not to run the risk and called the whole thing off. Grigorenko's son, Andrei, wrote later: "Unfortunately, people in the West do not always have a sufficiently clear idea of the Soviet situation and the position of a man behind bars. The fact that the Western psychiatrists who visited Father in the psychiatric hospital did not bother about an impartial translator but were prepared to conduct a conversation through the official Soviet interpreter, can be explained only as an amazing lack of comprehension. Obviously, it did not enter their heads that the translation might not correspond at all to what was said. There is another point. After a conversation in prison conditions, a man remains completely in the power of the administration."[63]

This propaganda glitch did not, however, seem to arouse suspicion on the part of the Western visitors. The only exchange with Grigorenko they managed was a casual question as to how the patient was feeling, to which he replied: "By comparison with Chernyakhovsk, here things are better."[64] Grigorenko was referring to the mental hospital in Chernyakhovsk, where he had been kept before being brought to Stolbovaya Stantsya. On the basis of this remark Dr. Leigh was quoted (or perhaps misquoted?) stating publicly that General Grigorenko had said he was being treated "well."[65]

Dr. Perris described the visit to Grigorenko in the weekly *Stern*. "Unfortunately he did not want to talk to us," stated the Swedish psychiatrist "and without examining and talking to him, we cannot judge whether he is being held in a secure facility justifiably or unjustifiably."[66] Three weeks later, however, the Soviet TASS agency reported, quoting (or perhaps misquoting?) the Swedish newspaper *Expressen*: "Professor Carlo Perris of Sweden testifies that the former General Grigorenko 'is really ill.' 'I consider that my Russian colleagues have carried out a correct diagnosis of Grigorenko.'"[67] Representatives of the Swedish branch of Amnesty International tried to find out Dr. Perris's real views on this matter, but he was reportedly not available for comment.[68]

Meanwhile, Soviet propaganda followed up on this. Barely two days after the aborted performance involving Perris and Leigh, a journalist from *Stern*, Klaus Lempke, was brought to the clinic at Stolbovaya Stantsya along with a photographer. But before that even took place, Academician Georgy Morozov—the president of the Soviet Psychiatric Association and director of the famous Serbsky Institute in Moscow, where many rebellious Soviet citizens were "treated"—had a series of chats with the German journalist, providing him with background information. When Lempke arrived at Stolbovaya Stantsya, he reportedly never even spoke to Grigorenko. The resident psychiatrists talked with him and allowed him to take some photographs. Nor did he meet with Grigorenko's family or friends. However, he studied the general's "case history." Two weeks later, Lempke's article appeared in *Stern* and the Soviet public-relations specialists could congratulate themselves. The German journalist wrote the following about those protesting in the West against Grigorenko being held in a *psikhushka*: "Do they know whether he is well or sick? When did they last see him, talk to him, spend time with him?"[69] It seems that Klaus Lempke was presented with the Soviet theory questioning the sanity of people who openly contested Soviet authority. "Warnings do not deter him," wrote the *Stern* reporter about Grigorenko, "on the contrary, they strengthen him in the conviction that he is the only person who can save the whole country." This sounds very much like a characteristic of a mentally disturbed person. "What is the result of this?" writes Lempke, "his behavior is seen as irrational and self-destructive. Is it any wonder that psychiatrists in this country regard his behavior as unhealthy?"[70] The article aroused a great deal of interest, and soon the London *Daily Express* and *Paris Match* reprinted it.[71]

Despite this and other temporary successes, Soviet propaganda never managed to pull the wool over the eyes of Western leaders of public opinion to the same extent that it had succeeded in doing with *perekovka* back in the 1930s. President of the American Psychiatric Association Alfred Freeman demanded of Soviet psychiatrists that an international commission of experts be formed to make an independent study of the serious criticism of psychiatric abuses in the USSR. The president of the British Royal College of Psychiatrists, Sir Martin

Roth, spoke out in similar terms. The response from the highest reaches of Soviet psychiatry consisted of calumnies. In a letter to the *Guardian*, signed by stars of the Soviet psychiatric establishment—Professors Snezhevsky, Nadzharov, Morozov, and Serebryakova—we find the following phrases: "malicious concoctions," "continuous unseemly attempts to misinform public opinion," "slandering Soviet psychiatry," "propaganda clamor and smear campaigns."[72]

In November 1973, barely a month after the visit to Grigorenko by Drs. Leigh and Perris, and two weeks after the publication of Lempke's article in *Stern*, the Royal College adopted the following resolution at its meeting in London: "The Royal College of Psychiatrists deplores the current use of psychiatry in the Soviet Union for the purpose of political repression, and condemns the activities of doctors who lend themselves to this work." The Royal College also called on the psychiatric associations of fourteen countries to set up an international commission to study the abuses of Soviet psychiatry. "We consider it a matter of urgent necessity that practical steps should be taken in the immediate future," stated the British psychiatrists.[73] In addition, protests by Western psychiatric associations and articles in the press dealing with Soviet abuses of psychiatry were appearing all the time. The WPA secretary general, Dr. Leigh, agreed to have these issues discussed at the World Psychiatric Congress in Honolulu in 1977. The Congress condemned the Soviet practices. Soviet propaganda was clearly losing.

The upper echelons of the Soviet government were following these reactions attentively. Despite the growing criticism in the West, they did not decide to cease the practice that so obviously was embarrassing the Kremlin in the eyes of world public opinion. Quite the opposite. In her history of the Gulag, Anne Applebaum quotes a secret 1976 report by the head of the KGB and eventually Brezhnev's successor, Yuri Andropov, commenting on critical Western opinions on the abuses of psychiatry in the USSR. The document was secretly scanned and smuggled out of Russia by Vladimir Bukovsky who visited Russia in 1992 and was given access to secret Soviet archives by Boris Yeltsin. Back in 1976, Andropov stated:

> Recent data testify to the fact that the campaign has the character of a carefully planned anti-Soviet action . . . at the present time, the initiators of the campaign are trying to draw in international and national psychiatric organizations as well as specialists of good reputation, to create a 'committee' designed to monitor the activity of psychiatrists in various countries, above all in the USSR. . . . An active role in building up the anti-Soviet mood is being played by the Royal College of Psychiatrists in Great Britain, which is under the influence of Zionist elements.[74]

Neither Andropov nor the other leaders of the USSR were willing to draw any other conclusions from this state of affairs except to persist in their error. This example undoubtedly illustrates the growing helplessness of the Kremlin leadership in trying to find new, convincing justifications for their own system of repression. From various internal documents and official statements by the authorities it is difficult to determine whether their authors still wanted to convince the West that their cause was just and the methods were right, or whether they were only desperately trying to convince themselves of this assertion.

The Face of Russia

The fact that the theme of Soviet crimes finally entered the Western cultural bloodstream can be attributed to a significant degree to the effect on public opinion of one man: Aleksandr Solzhenitsyn. His exceptional standing in the eyes of the West was the result of a number of factors. His debut novella, *One Day in the Life of Ivan Denisovich*, was the first account of the Gulag to gain instant worldwide acclaim. Moreover, this acclaim was not impeded by significant ideological opposition on the part of Western defenders of the Soviet régime. Many of them had already become disappointed by Soviet communism. Many others denounced Stalin and now believed in the thaw assertions that the "cult of personality" had been overcome and that the USSR was building socialism "with a human face." *Ivan Denisovich* initially seemed to please both groups. It depicted the Gulag but did not directly criticize the Soviet ideology and system as the sources of totalitarian evil. This reticence left open, at least to a certain extent, the possibility of interpreting Solzhenitsyn's story in the spirit of post-thaw optimism. Criticizing the "errors and distortions" of the Stalinist past did not have to mean undermining the faith in the bright future of the supposedly self-correcting Soviet system. At least for the time being.

Solzhenitsyn skillfully took advantage of the international fame triggered by *Ivan Denisovich*. In the escalating series of confrontations between the writer and Soviet authorities, the Western public found itself increasingly rooting for the former. Living in the USSR, Solzhenitsyn could more or less at any moment count on the attention and support of the Western media and public opinion. It turned out that Soviet authorities had made a colossal mistake by allowing this unknown teacher from the provincial city of Ryazan' to publish his story about the Gulag. Instead of becoming a useful pawn of Khrushchev's faction in the current politics of the thaw, Solzhenitsyn emerged as a serious challenger of the Soviet government, its ideology, and its politics. The central theme in this challenge was the Gulag.

For a long time, the authorities were unaware that following his release from camp, Solzhenitsyn had begun to work secretly on a project that was to fulfill his life's mission. He had defined this mission as bearing witness to the Gulag in the name of those who had never lived to see freedom. He entitled this new book *The Gulag Archipelago*. However Solzhenitsyn imagined presenting this work to the world, one thing seems certain: without the support of Western public opinion and the media, *The Gulag Archipelago*, even if it had been published in the West as it was in 1973, would not have immediately become a work of enormous significance—the book that would bring the word "Gulag" into many languages of the world as one of the symbols of the dark side of the twentieth century.

Before it even came to that, however, Solzhenitsyn had to overcome many obstacles. As his confrontations with the Soviet authorities grew, so too did his international fame, which helped rally the Western public to his cause. In the 1960s, he became in the eyes of the world the most influential public figure telling the truth about the dark side of Soviet reality. In 1969, after publishing *The First Circle* and *Cancer Ward* under his own name in the West, Solzhenitsyn was expelled from the Soviet Writers' Union—just as Pasternak had been thrown out of the same Union after publishing *Dr. Zhivago* in 1957, a novel that was awarded the Nobel Prize a year later. Western writers reacted immediately to Solzhenitsyn's expulsion. The president of the Soviet Writers' Union, Konstantin Fedin, received a protest signed by, among others, Arthur Miller, John Updike, Truman Capote, Kurt Vonnegut, Carlos Fuentes, Yukio Mishima, Günter Grass, Friedrich Dürenmatt, Igor Stravinsky, and—this is not a mistake—Jean-Paul Sartre. Many signatories to this protest also appended their names to a letter published in the London *Times* and signed by W. H. Auden, A. J. Ayer, Graham Greene, Rosamond Lehmann, Muriel Spark, Philip Toynbee, and other Western writers. The letter's authors wrote: "The silencing of a writer of Solzhenitsyn's stature is in itself a crime against civilization. . . . Should this appeal fail we shall see no other way but to call upon the writers and artists of the world to conduct an international cultural boycott of a country which chooses to put itself beyond the pale of civilization until such time as it abandons the barbaric treatment of its writers and artists."[75]

At the same time, the president of the Soviet Writers' Union received a letter from Jean-Paul Sartre, Elsa Triolet, Louis Aragon, and Michel Butor. These veteran glorifiers of Stalin used a new tone that would have previously been quite out of character for them. They wrote, "Yet despite all this, we still wish to believe that . . . there will be found in the high councils of the nation, to whom we owe the Dawn of October and the defeat of Hitlerian fascism, men capable of realizing the wrong that has been done and of putting it right. This–for the common cause for which we live, fight, and die."[76] Incidentally, it is hard today to understand precisely on what grounds these dignitaries of French letters could describe themselves as people dying for a cause.

Having deprived Solzhenitsyn of a voice in a national forum, the authorities were doubtless expecting that the West would soon grow bored with its darling of the day. But this time the authorities' hopes remained unrealized. In July 1970, François Mauriac, together with a sizeable number of French writers, nominated Solzhenitsyn for the Nobel Prize. The members of the Swedish Royal Academy were initially unsure whether, in the event of receiving the prize, he would be forced to repeat Pasternak's gesture of declining the award in 1958 under the pressure of Soviet attacks. The Academy preferred to avoid another international incident with political implications. It also did not want to harm the writer himself by drawing the Soviet authorities' attention to him. However, Solzhenitsyn did not much resemble the subtle and fragile poet from Peredelkino. He had admittedly dreamed of the Nobel Prize—it would put him in the spotlight, where he could even more effectively transmit his message to the world. At the time, the first volume of *The Gulag Archipelago* was already finished and had been smuggled out to the West. The writer's collaborators in the West were just waiting for the signal to publish his magnum opus. The manuscript had already been secretly translated into German and Swedish, and translations into English and French were in the works.

At this moment, an emissary of the Royal Academy arrived in Moscow. He met secretly with a friend of Solzhenitsyn, Lev Kopelev, to sound him out as to how Solzhenitsyn would react to the Nobel Prize. Kopelev dispelled the Swedes' doubts. In the event of awarding the prize to Solzhenitsyn, the Academy could expect him to accept it. Right to the end there was no unanimity on the committee, but finally Solzhenitsyn's candidacy prevailed.

On October 8, a Norwegian correspondent in Moscow, Per Egil Hegge, called Solzhenitsyn and informed him that he had been awarded the prize. Immediately after the official communiqué by the Royal Academy, the Soviet Writers' Union criticized the decision: "One can only deplore the fact that the Nobel Prize Committee has allowed itself to be dragged into a dirty game, played not in the interests of the development of spiritual and literary values, but dictated by political calculations," announced *Pravda* and *Izvestiya* on October 10. In this, they were seconded by *Literaturnaya Gazeta*, *Sovetskaya Rossiya*, *Komsomolskaya Pravda*, and other Kremlin mouthpieces. The English-language *Soviet Weekly* assured its readers that "Solzhenitsyn is a run-of-the-mill writer with an exaggerated idea of his own importance. His tragedy is that he has given in too easily to flattery of people who have no scruples about the means they use to struggle against the Soviet system. But he must surely realize himself that his literary gifts are not only below those of the giants of the past but also inferior to many of his Soviet contemporaries–writers the West chooses to ignore because it finds the impact of truth in their writing most unpalatable."[77] The authors, however, did not specify which contemporary Soviet writers they had in mind.

Soviet papers quoted batches of "worldwide responses" to Solzhenitsyn's prize in the East German, Bulgarian, Czech, and other papers that followed the mandatory line. One of the members of the Royal Academy, Arthur Lundquist, openly opposed Solzhenitsyn's award, claiming that it was a gesture in favor of the enemies of the USSR. "I consider the award of this prize to be a mistake," he stated, and *Pravda* quoted him on December 12, 1970.

The overwhelming majority of Western reactions to Solzhenitsyn's award was, however, decidedly positive. The *Times* of London recalled that one of the aims of the prize for literature established by Alfred Nobel was to honor works filled with idealism and faith in human values, and that few previous winners had fulfilled this criterion as much as had the author of *Ivan Denisovich* and *The First Circle*. Taking advantage of this moment when the eyes of the whole world were focused on him, Solzhenitsyn wrote a letter to the Communist Party's principal ideologue, Mikhail Suslov, suggesting that he was willing to treat all of the authorities' previous hostility toward him as a misunderstanding, if only they would publish his works in the USSR. He suggested that he would be able to accept the Nobel Prize in "more favorable circumstances" (his own words), in other words, he would refrain from withering criticism of the Soviet system before international audiences. The price of this, however, would be to open up Soviet public discourse to the glimmers of truth about communism's dark side contained in Solzhenitsyn's published works.

Commenting on it later, Solzhenitsyn would write: "If I could have set in train just the things suggested there . . . it would have meant a change not only for me but in the whole literary situation, and in time not merely the literary situation. . . . Although my heart yearned for something more, something decisive, still, those who change the course of history are the gradualists, in whose hands the fabric of events does not tear. If there were any possibility of changing the situation in our country smoothly, we ought to reconcile ourselves to it and do just that."[78] Solzhenitsyn was waiting for a suitable moment to start the process of publishing *The Gulag Archipelago* in the West. He knew that the book would never appear in the USSR, and that when it did come out in the West, it would be far too late for any kind of compromise with the authorities. At that moment, however—like an experienced politician—he was prepared to temporarily put aside the plan of openly going to war and ascertain whether for the time being he might be able to wring significant concessions from the authorities by taking the path of compromise.

It quickly became apparent that this road was closed. The Kremlin was not willing to play the game proposed in the letter to Suslov. Solzhenitsyn cherished the opportunity of addressing the world at the Nobel ceremony. On the other hand, however, he was afraid that if he traveled to accept the award, the authorities might block his return to Russia. He discussed with Swedish diplomats a possibility of having the ceremony in the Swedish embassy in Moscow. But the Swedes wanted to avoid politically charged public statements by the writer, pointing out that they "had to maintain good relations with the local authorities."[79] The Swedish officials even suggested a private ceremony in Solzhenitsyn's Moscow flat, but the writer considered this an insult to the Nobel Prize. Instead, he wrote a letter that was to be read out at the ceremonial Nobel dinner in Stockholm and had it smuggled out of the USSR. The letter ended with the following words: "I cannot close my eyes to the remarkable fact that the day of the Nobel Prize presentation coincides with Human Rights Day. . . . Everybody present in the Stockholm City Hall must see a symbolic meaning in this. So let none at this festive table forget that political prisoners are on hunger strike this very day in defense of rights that have been curtailed or trampled underfoot."[80]

At the Nobel Prize ceremony, the secretary to the Royal Academy Karl Ragnar Gierow cited praise in honor of Solzhenitsyn. Among other sources, he quoted the earlier positive remarks on *Ivan Denisovich* in *Pravda*. He then read out the letter from the absent laureate. He left out the last sentence on the hunger strike.

The Avalanche

On September 1, 1973, Solzhenitsyn's friend Efim Etkind called him from Leningrad at his Moscow apartment. He gave him the disturbing news that the KGB had found a typescript of *The Gulag Archipelago*. In early August, the KGB had arrested Elizaveta Voronyanskaya, a brave sixty-seven-year-old woman who had long worked with Solzhenitsyn typing out parts of *Archipelago*. Voronyanskaya knew that one of the typewritten copies was hidden near Leningrad in the town of Luga at the dacha of Leonid Samutin—a former Gulag inmate whose memoirs Solzhenitsyn had used in writing *Gulag Archipelago*. Voronyanskaya was interrogated for five days and nights. She finally revealed the secret. She was released but remained under the eye of the KGB. Two weeks later she was dead. It is almost certain that she had taken her own life.

For several years, Solzhenitsyn had been delaying the final decision to publish *The Gulag Archipelago*, although the Russian version, smuggled to the West, was ready for publication, and translations into the major Western languages besides English were well advanced. There were various reasons for the delay on the part of the Nobel laureate. Yet when he learned that the KGB now had a copy of the work, he immediately felt that he had crossed his Rubicon. "I had glimpsed the finger of God," he later recalled. "Sleepest thou, idle servant? The time has long since come and gone. Reveal it to the world!"[81] So he acted immediately. He secretly sent his agent in Zürich, Fritz Heeb, instructions to publish. On September 5, he officially announced to Western correspondents in Moscow that his new book entitled *The Gulag Archipelago* would shortly be published in the West. Finally, on December 29, 1973, Solzhenitsyn received the news by telephone that the first volume of the work had appeared that day in Paris.

Once the KGB had a copy of *Archipelago*, Solzhenitsyn's games with the Kremlin, based on his hopes of expanding the boundaries of free speech in the USSR, were over. There was nothing left for the writer but to raise his visor and show his real, previously concealed face. Only now could the world see the real Solzhenitsyn—the relentless exposer of communist evil, determined to fulfill his life's mission: to testify to the world about the inhuman truth of the Gulag in the name of its victims. *The Gulag Archipelago* was a work of camp literature designed on a hitherto unprecedented scale. It was composed of Solzhenitsyn's own reminiscences, complemented by the accounts of 227 other survivors. This huge trove of human experiences had been enriched by various sources available to the author. The result was an extensive "summa" of the Gulag, representing its history as well as a great variety of personal fates of its numerous victims.

Solzhenitsyn's work was based on two principal narrative planes intersecting with each other. The first one was a vast historical plane, showing the origins of the Soviet camp system, its aims, its internal organization, as well as its evolution. Readers of *The Gulag Archipelago* were presented with a historical sketch of the system of forced labor in the USSR—its successive stages, marked by administrative regulations, resolutions, decrees, and decisions, on the basis of which hundreds of thousands and even millions of people were sent to the camps. This narrative often shaded into a broad study of the geography, sociology, anthropology, and ethics of this vast "archipelago" of enslavement and exploitation. In Solzhenitsyn's work, the history of the Gulag was inseparable from the history of the Soviet system itself—it constituted the very core of the communist utopia in power.

This grand scheme of history interconnects in the book with the realm of human experience. The reader is constantly overwhelmed with the wealth of personal stories and individual accounts presented here. These accounts are composed following the order of the successive stages of a single victim's typical fate: arrest, investigation, interrogation, torture, prison, sentence, transport, life in the camps, hunger, murderous work, violence, brainwashing, penal servitude, exile, death, and so on. Like most Gulag memoirs by escapees and émigrés—and unlike the accounts written during the thaw in hopes for publication in the USSR—*The Gulag Archipelago* directly asked the question of the sources of the historic evil of the Gulag and did not shy away from direct answers. The book's subtitle, *An Experiment in Literary Investigation*, did not just mean a formal experiment in writing on the borderline of literature and history. The result of this "investigation" was a quite specific act of indictment, aimed not at some euphemistic "cult of personality" or "period of errors and distortions" but straight at the heart of communism, at its ideology and practices, starting from the shots fired in October 1917 from the cruiser *Aurora*.

Solzhenitsyn presented the hell of the Gulag as the quintessence of the Soviet historical experiment. The camps, the terror, the persecutions, and crimes against humanity were depicted as parts of the essence of communism without which it could not exist. Violence and contempt for human life—when life is viewed from the ideological perspective—represent, in Solzhenitsyn's view, the very core of communism. In *The Gulag Archipelago*, Solzhenitsyn not only aimed at exposing Soviet communism as evil by its nature but also emphasized the dependence of this system on lies. He reexamined the propaganda image of the Gulag and reminded his readers about the *perekovka* and its forgotten classics, such as Gorky's *Solovki*, Pogodin's *Aristocrats*, or the *White Sea Canal*. Finally, he presented a scathing image of Western sympathizers of the USSR, who for decades dismissed or legitimized the Gulag to the world.

It was at once realized, both in the West as well as in the Kremlin, that Solzhenitsyn's work was not only the most outstanding record so far of human experience in the camps but that it was a devastating critique of all Soviet communism. A commentator in a German newspaper foretold: "The time may come when we date the beginning of the collapse of the Soviet system from the appearance of *Gulag*."[82] Another German newspaper—this time a communist one—admitted that Solzhenitsyn's work had put "a burning question mark over fifty years of Soviet power, over the whole Soviet experiment from 1918 on."[83] Radio Liberty and Radio Free Europe soon began to broadcast *The Gulag Archipelago* in installments for listeners in the USSR and countries of Eastern Europe.

The Soviet TASS agency attacked Solzhenitsyn's book immediately after its appearance in Paris. In the agency's opinion, the writer's aim was "to poison the atmosphere of détente, to sow mistrust between peoples, to blacken the Soviet Union, its people, its policies." *The Gulag Archipelago* was called "a malicious slander against our socialist state," as well as "the foundation and pivot of the anti-Soviet campaign that is being spread throughout the pages of foreign newspapers." Soviet propagandists explained to the world that Solzhenitsyn's book found favor in the West only with the right-wing bourgeois press, which also praises the "fascist junta in Chile . . . the bloody reaction in Greece and the crimes of South African racists."[84]

Right after the New Year, following the appearance of *The Gulag Archipelago* in Paris, a major vilification campaign began in the Soviet media. Given the possibility of immediate arrest or other forms of persecution by the authorities, Solzhenitsyn was in constant touch with Western correspondents in Moscow, informing them of his situation. In an interview with the weekly *Time*, he parried the Soviet authorities' attack, explaining to the Western public that he was not in any way opposed to international détente, just as long as it took place "between nations and not their oppressors." He also said: "Everyone must stop cooperating with the lie. . . . In our country, the lie has become not just a moral category, but a pillar of the state. In recoiling from the lie, we are performing a moral, not a political act."[85] The Soviet media reacted according to their tradition; they outstripped each other in hurling epithets at the writer. "Traitor," "Vlasovite," "Judas," "fascist," "handmaiden of American imperialism," and "whore" were some of the most popular.

Western media responded immediately, leaving no doubt as to their positive attitude toward Solzhenitsyn. On January 22, there was a demonstration by American intellectuals in front of the National Press Club building in Washington in support of the author of *The Gulag Archipelago*. The very next day the Russian language service of the BBC and Deutsche Welle followed Radio Liberty and began broadcasting *Archipelago*. Less than a week later, the German translation of Solzhenitsyn's work appeared, followed two weeks later by the Swedish one. The first copies smuggled into the Soviet Union began their secret life in Moscow, passing silently from one impatient hand to another. The London *Times* published an interview with Andrei Sakharov in which the Russian physicist described *The Gulag Archipelago* as "a stone that will finally shatter the wall dividing mankind. It is a wall of mistrust and lack of understanding created by lies, wickedness, cowardice, and stupidity. . . . This stone has been cast by a sure and powerful hand."[86]

Meanwhile, the men in the Kremlin debated how to handle this mess. As early as January 7, at a two-hour meeting of the Politburo, Brezhnev raised the subject of *The Gulag Archipelago*. Although seemingly none of those present, including Brezhnev himself, had yet read Solzhenitsyn's work, the general secretary had a ready-made opinion on it, calling it a "contemptuous anti-Soviet lampoon."[87] Everyone agreed that the author needed to be punished. The only question was how. The main factor restraining the Soviet leadership's imagination on the subject was the realization that the West would not let the matter drop. Aleksei Kosygin and Nikolai Podgorny proposed a trial, followed by a sentence, and then sending Solzhenitsyn to a camp. Kosygin suggested Verkhoyansk, the coldest place on earth, where in 1892 a temperature of −68° Celsius had been recorded—the lowest single-day temperature outside Antarctica. The Soviet dignitary expected that both the climate and location of Verkhoyansk would discourage Western correspondents from taking too close an interest in the fate of the author of *Archipelago*. Yuri Andropov, however, insisted that Solzhenitsyn be forcibly removed from the USSR. Brezhnev decided to postpone for a time a final decision on punishment.

A month passed. Andropov began to urge Brezhnev not to delay any longer since positive views on *The Gulag Archipelago* were multiplying among intellectual elites in the West. This could only embolden Solzhenitsyn and other dissidents even more. Referring to the still-unresolved decision on camp or deportation, Andropov remarked: "Either way there will be losses. But unfortunately there is no other way out, since Solzhenitsyn's impunity is causing us more damage within the country than would be caused internationally if he were deported or arrested."[88] Of course, deporting Solzhenitsyn abroad would not silence him for good—a camp in Verkhoyansk would definitely do that. But at the same time, expelling him from the USSR would not expose the Soviet leadership to the same level of Western criticism as sending the author of *The Gulag Archipelago* back to the Gulag. Finally, the decision was made in favor of the expulsion. A summit meeting between Brezhnev and Nixon was planned for the spring. The Kremlin's high hopes were resting on the policy of détente championed by Nixon and Kissinger. Solzhenitsyn could not have known that the interest the West had for years shown in him probably now saved his life.

Solzhenitsyn was twice summoned to the prosecutor's office, and twice he did not show up. He was expecting to be arrested. Western correspondents were in constant contact with him, awaiting further developments. On February 12, eight KGB agents burst into Solzhenitsyn's Moscow flat with orders to arrest him. The KGB men took him to the Lefortovo Prison. The deputy prosecutor general of the USSR, Mikhail Malyarov, read out the charges from Article 64, covering treason, which carried a sentence ranging from ten years to the death penalty. Solzhenitsyn refused to sign the confirmation of having his charges presented to him and stated that he would not cooperate with the authorities in an investigation and trial.

The next morning, after spending a night in the cells in Lefortovo, he was issued a new suit, shirt, tie, coat, and fur hat—just like in Stalin's day prisoners were sometimes dressed for a show trial or for a meeting with their family. Solzhenitsyn initially expected a meeting with the highest Soviet authorities. "Where was I going? I had no doubt about it. To see the government, that very Politburo of theirs, of which Mayakovsky had once dreamed," he later recalled his own thoughts. "At long last we would have our first–and last–discussion.... The conversation would be a serious one, perhaps the most important of my life."[89] He was wrong. Prosecutor Malyarov read out a decree from the Presidium of the Supreme Soviet of the USSR, depriving him of Soviet citizenship and calling for his immediate expulsion from the USSR "for the systematic execution of actions incompatible with Soviet citizenship and harmful to the USSR."[90]

An Aeroflot aircraft was waiting at Sheremetyevo Airport. After a two-and-a-half-hour flight, they landed in Frankfurt-am-Main. The KGB men led him out to the steps. Suddenly he was left on his own, without an escort. A representative of the West Germany Foreign Ministry was waiting for him on the tarmac. Escorted by German police officers, the author of *The Gulag Archipelago* was taken to the house of his German friend, the Nobel laureate Heinrich Böll in Langenbroich in the suburbs of Bonn. While the motorcade was still en route from the airport, news of Solzhenitsyn's deportation had reached the media, and the Russian Nobel laureate was welcomed in Langenbroich not only by Böll but by a crowd of journalists, cameramen, TV crews, and paparazzi that swelled by the minute. Solzhenitsyn's sudden expulsion to Germany was a media event, and the world waited impatiently for more news—above all, for words from the writer himself.

The fact that for years Solzhenitsyn and Böll had shared a real friendship can be seen as a fine example of human brotherhood transcending political differences. In terms of political convictions, they differed on more or less everything. Heinrich Böll was an unshakeable leftist and one of the most implacable critics of the bourgeois West. He belonged to the group of Western writers most strongly criticized by the very same people who passionately supported Solzhenitsyn. And yet, political views had not prevented Böll from visiting Solzhenitsyn in Moscow back in 1972. Back then, Solzhenitsyn had already trusted Böll to such an extent that he asked him to countersign his will and to smuggle it outside the USSR.

In all honesty, Böll's understanding of Solzhenitsyn's works did not differ much from those Western commentators who managed to find in them illustrations of the main creed of the thaw—that Stalin's "errors" had been exposed and overcome, and the Soviet system was back on its right track leading to a bright future. In his review of *The Gulag Archipelago*, Böll wrote: "We should not for a moment forget that it ends in 1956. . . . While no sensible person can wish for an overthrow in the Soviet Union, we all see a change as desirable. . . . Since the author shows no trace of self-righteousness, this book should be no cause for self-righteousness on the part of any of its readers. We should not forget either this or the fact that it ends in 1956."[91]

Four years before Solzhenitsyn's expulsion, Böll had written in a review of *The First Circle*: "It was written for the liberation of Socialism. We have not the slightest cause to gloat over *The First Circle* as depicting Stalinist outrages, absurdities, and entanglements. We have more reason to wonder whether a Western author could be as brilliantly successful in revealing the world of the unsuspecting and the world of the silent sufferers within our own tangled complexities."[92] It must be noted that in Solzhenitsyn's eyes, making this kind of moral equivalence between the Western world and Communism was unacceptable, and he fought against it his whole life. However, both Solzhenitsyn and Böll remained respectful and loyal to one another despite all the differences in their views.

In his writing career, Solzhenitsyn had previously wanted to gain public attention in the West since that allowed him to fulfill his life's mission: to tell the world the truth about Soviet communism and the Gulag. Now, when the writer found himself in the world's spotlight, he was taken aback by the trivial forms that this attention took. The hordes of reporters, paparazzi, and cameramen trailing behind him—shouting out to him, noisily milling around day and night in front of his hideout, relentlessly disturbing the peace at all hours—overwhelmed and shocked him. Disconcerted by this endless media scrum, he finally shouted out: "You're worse than the KGB! Go away. I want to be alone!"[93]

Looking around for a suitable place to live in the West, Solzhenitsyn promptly visited Zurich, then took the train to Copenhagen, followed by a crossing on the ferry to Oslo. The trip took on the character of a triumphal procession; crowds of reporters greeted Solzhenitsyn at each stage, while the papers, radio, and television were full of reports on all possible details of his life and current situation. Solzhenitsyn had an allergic reaction to this Western sensationalism surrounding his person. He retained a sense of complete solemnity about the matters for which he was fighting and had no intention of abandoning this sense in the name of media popularity. When he was shown Aleksander Ford's film based on *The First Circle*, he criticized it for being superficial and kitschy.

He preferred Caspar Wrede's film version of *One Day in the Life of Ivan Deniso-vich*, which he watched later in Finland. It could be noticed that, starting with his initial encounter with the Western media circus just after his expulsion from the USSR, Solzhenitsyn was becoming increasingly anxious as to whether the Western world was, in fact, capable of understanding the terrible experiences of communism at a level deeper than media sensationalism and melodrama, and—even more generally—whether contemporary Western culture was in any state to think seriously about man and the world. The taste of Western freedom turned out for the author of *The Gulag Archipelago* at the very least strange, and his initial reaction was strongly ambivalent.

Meanwhile, the Western political world was reacting to the writer's expulsion from the USSR. The governments of West Germany, Great Britain, France, and Norway offered Solzhenitsyn political asylum. Canadian Prime Minister Pierre Trudeau suggested that he settle in Canada. Even the communist parties of Italy, Sweden, and Yugoslavia expressed solidarity with the exiled writer. In this context, the US administration's silence was significant. President Nixon was one of the few Western leaders not to express any support for Solzhenit-syn, and the United States refrained from offering asylum. Clearly, the White House, engaged in the policy of détente with the USSR, was anxious that mak-ing principled public steps regarding Solzhenitsyn, a relentless critic of Soviet communism, might discourage the Soviet leadership from disarmament talks and other policies leading to a political rapprochement. Nixon was preparing for the spring summit with Brezhnev, and the American government seemed to prefer avoiding any possible complications. As to Brezhnev and his Politburo, they had been concerned about the American reactions enough to forego Sol-zhenitsyn's imprisonment in Verkhoyansk but not enough to drop the idea of having him arrested and spectacularly expelled from the country.

Brezhnev's American partners hastened to reassure the Soviet general sec-retary that he had not much to worry about. Three days after Solzhenitsyn's expulsion from Russia, the principal architect of American foreign policy, Henry Kissinger, made it clear that "our human, moral and critical concern for Mr. Sol-zhenitsyn and people of similar convictions should [not] affect the day-to-day conduct of our foreign policy."[94] The previous day, the British *Guardian* had gone even further along the path of political caution, actually praising the Kremlin for forcibly deporting Solzhenitsyn. "The Soviet government has be-haved humanely," wrote the paper.[95] Of course, given that the government could have responded to *The Gulag Archipelago* by killing, torturing, or sending Solzhenitsyn to forced labor in the frozen north, it is hard to disagree with the British newspaper: anything else seems humane in comparison.

The White House's attitude to Solzhenitsyn did not change after Nixon, discredited by Watergate, departed the Oval Office. Kissinger's policies and attitudes to the USSR were continued under President Ford. When, after an American edition of *Archipelago* appeared, Solzhenitsyn visited the United States in June 1975 at the invitation of the AFL-CIO, President Ford did not invite him to the White House, despite the clear expectations of a significant segment of American public opinion. The White House justified its decision by saying the president avoided "meetings without substance." Solzhenitsyn's biographer D.M. Thomas later remarked: "Ford's intellect probably could not find anything useful to talk about with the author of *The Gulag Archipelago*."[96] Simon Winchester, the *Guardian*'s man in Washington, praised Ford, who, in his view, showed "integrity and realism" by refusing to meet with this "shaggy author" and "hairy polemicist" who had become the "darling of the redneck population" after speaking for an hour to thousands of "sagging beer bellies."[97] Winchester was referring to American workers and trade union members. The US Congress did not share President Ford's approach. In October 1975, the US Senate unanimously passed a resolution to confer honorary US citizenship on Solzhenitsyn. The only other person to have received it before was Winston Churchill. The resolution passed to the House Committee of the Judiciary, where the State Department under Kissinger strongly recommended against it. It was dropped.

The Kremlin authorities had no intention of leaving the issue of Western reactions to *The Gulag Archipelago* without a suitable response. The aggressive clamor filling the Soviet press from the moment the KGB found the manuscript did not seem to persuade Western public opinion. The Soviet authorities were eager, however, to discredit Solzhenitsyn in the West and were aware that for this they needed methods subtler than simply showering him with epithets. And so Soviet propaganda used people close to the writer and thus potentially credible in the eyes of the West. The authorities immediately sought out Solzhenitsyn's former friend from his younger days, Nikolai Vitkevich, the very same person with whom he had carelessly corresponded in 1945, leading to both of them being sentenced to the camps. Vitkevich was a professor and chairman of the chemistry department in a large scientific institute in Bryansk. For anyone even vaguely acquainted with Soviet reality there was no doubt that Vitkevich's position and career were on the line when he agreed to criticize Solzhenitsyn in an interview for the *Christian Science Monitor*.

At the same time, the KGB took a closer interest in Solzhenitsyn's former wife, Natalya Reshetovskaya. With the aid of persuasion and pressure, she was induced to vent freely her personal feelings about a man who had recently left her for another woman (Solzhenitsyn divorced Reshetovskaya in March 1973 and then married Natalya Svetlova in April.) In order to make it easier for her, the authorities, working through the Novosti press agency, invited Robert Lacontre, the correspondent of *Le Figaro*, to Reshetovskaya's apartment in Ryazan'. During the interview, she explained to the astonished Frenchman that her husband's work, which she had herself helped to type, had no historical value. It was based not on facts but on camp "folklore": that is, rumors and gossip by former inmates, full of exaggeration with more than a fair share of embroidery. Soon, Reshetovskaya's memoirs appeared, in which Solzhenitsyn comes across as a man full of character defects. The book was speedily brought out in English in 1975.[98] Other critical opinions on Solzhenitsyn were gathered from some of his friends and acquaintances who had been pressured in one way or another. These collected essays (including accounts from people like Malyarov, the prosecutor) were published in English in a volume entitled *The Last Circle*.[99]

While the KGB was busy finding and preparing these materials, Nikolai Yakovlev created a model representation of the Soviet propaganda on Solzhenitsyn for Western consumption. As early as February 13, 1974—that is, the day of the author's deportation—the Soviet publication *Golos Rodiny*, whose task was to influence Russian émigré circles, published an article by Yakovlev on Solzhenitsyn that was reprinted in *Literaturnaya Gazeta* a week later. The Nobel laureate was portrayed as a fanatical ideologue sheltering under the disguise of a writer. Moreover, it turned out that he had his own reasons for harboring hatred for the Soviet authorities. Yakovlev recalled that Solzhenitsyn came from landowning bourgeois stock destroyed by the Bolshevik revolution and Soviet power. Accordingly, circumstance dictated that he must have grown up in an atmosphere hostile toward Bolshevism. It was hardly surprising, therefore, that throughout his life he had been an implacable, although initially covert, enemy of the working class and of its homeland. There was a reason, after all, that he'd been put in a camp. *The Gulag Archipelago* was a book filled with distortions. It breathed hatred toward the system of social justice that had taken away the privileges of people like him. The author of *Archipelago* had shown by his attitudes that he was an ally and tool of the world bourgeoisie, which would not hesitate to unleash nuclear war in the hope of destroying the USSR. Thus, Solzhenitsyn and his books were a threat to world peace and détente.

One might say, perversely or not, that Solzhenitsyn had in some ways made it easier for those who were inclined to see him as an enemy of détente between East and West. After his expulsion, he frequently criticized the détente as a Soviet simulacrum and, at the same time, a cover for Western policies and attitudes of appeasement toward the USSR. He also made his mark as a critic of the West, reproaching the free world for succumbing to a sense of false security and losing moral courage. Criticism of the West from a procommunist and pro-Soviet standpoint was a traditional prerogative of Western intellectuals. This resolutely nonleftist criticism of the West from Solzhenitsyn, however, aroused visible annoyance in broad swathes of the Western intellectual and media world. At the same time, the traditionalist views expounded by Solzhenitsyn in many of his statements garnered him considerable respect from some conservative opinion makers, for whom he became something of a distant patron.

While Solzhenitsyn the publicist was arousing controversy, Solzhenitsyn the Gulag witness had permanently entered the West's intellectual and moral consciousness. *The Gulag Archipelago* was molding this consciousness and changing history as had few literary works in history. Those who had expected back in 1974 that *The Gulag Archipelago* might spell the beginning of the end of Soviet communism had been right. From the perspective of time, this can be seen even more clearly. Solzhenitsyn's work represented a moral blow to Soviet ideology from which it never recovered. Soviet communism never managed to find an effective response to Solzhenitsyn. In the West, the word "Gulag" became inextricably linked with communism and the Soviet Union. In March 1974, George Kennan wrote a review of *The Gulag Archipelago* in the *New York Review of Books*, in which he called Solzhenitsyn's book "the greatest and most powerful single indictment of a political regime ever to be levelled in modern times." He went on: "This merciless indictment is too devastating to be ignored. The Soviet leaders cannot, just by ignoring it themselves or attempting to smother it with falsehood, consign it to oblivion or cause it to remain without consequences. It will stick there, with increasing discomfort, until it has done its work."[100]

And indeed it did. It seems that two factors came together to achieve this result. One was the character of Solzhenitsyn's work itself: its scope, the scale and depth of the human experience it revealed, as well as the passion with which the author presented his revelations. But at the same time, the unusual role played by *The Gulag Archipelago* in the world depended on the particular context in which Solzhenitsyn was received in the West. After all, much had been known of the Gulag before Solzhenitsyn. He was by no means the first author who exposed the Gulag before the eyes of Western audiences. And yet Western public opinion had more often than not dismissed this topic and managed to find reasons for rationalizing, denying, and even glamorizing the camps along with other Soviet crimes. The process whereby many Western opinion makers abandoned pro-Soviet attitudes and accepted Solzhenitsyn's testimony was gradual and internally complex. As Michael Scammell points out, what made a great impression in the West was the fact that *The Gulag Archipelago* had been written with "the unique authority of someone who had lived through and survived the system (and even been a part of it for a while), who had seen it from inside—not by one of the dozens of Westerners, or even emigres or refugees, who had chronicled these monstrosities from a greater distance."[101]

But that was not all. At the time when *The Gulag Archipelago* came out, Solzhenitsyn was not someone who had just come to light as a witness to the terrible truth about the Soviets. He was a writer with a world-class reputation. He had been noticed in the West thanks to his tale about Ivan Denisovich. Accounts of the Gulag like *Ivan Denisovich*, which avoided direct criticism of the Soviet system, allowed many Western readers the moral comfort of sympathizing with victims of the Gulag without an accompanying need to revise their own sympathetic attitude toward Soviet communism. Becoming more and more attached to Solzhenitsyn, they found themselves supporting him and other Soviet dissidents. Thus, many Western sympathizers of Solzhenitsyn gradually lost hope in the Soviet system. As their disappointment with Soviet communism grew, they remained unaware for some time that Solzhenitsyn was not interested in reforming the Soviet system but in morally exposing it. By the time *The Gulag Archipelago* revealed Solzhenitsyn's true position on the matter, they often no longer had any reason not to accept it.

The Gulag Archipelago made a particularly strong impression in France—the country where public opinion, and especially the intellectual elites, had resisted the truth the longest. There, Solzhenitsyn's book led to a major breakthrough in thinking about the world. Gustaw Herling-Grudziński, whose *A World Apart* had been waiting in France since 1951 to be published—it came out there only in 1985, that is, eleven years after *the Gulag Archipelago*—described the significance of Solzhenitsyn's book in this country: "Solzhenitsyn played a huge part; *The Gulag Archipelago* changed Europe. . . . It was a revolution. I categorically assert that anyone writing a book about France of that time and who devotes a chapter to French intellectuals will have to write about Solzhenitsyn's book, for its appearance in Paris was a real revolution."[102] Under the influence of Solzhenitsyn's book, a series of prominent French intellectuals publicly announced their breakup with communism. In April 1975, Solzhenitsyn appeared on Bernard Pivot's TV show "Apostrophes." The same year a former Marxist named André Glucksmann condemned communism in a book under the revealing title *La Cuisinière et le mangeur d'hommes: Essai sur les rapports entre l'Etat, le marxisme et les camps de concentration* (The stove and the man eater: an essay on relations between the state, Marxism and concentration camps). In his book, Glucksmann argued, similarly to Solzhenitsyn, that the criminal practices of Soviet totalitarianism stemmed not only from Stalin's policies, and not even from Lenin's ideas, but from the very DNA of communist ideology: namely, the thought of Karl Marx. Michel Foucault, who in the early 1950s had started his philosophical career as a member of the French Communist Party, now responded to a question about his attitude toward Marxism: "Don't talk to me about Marx! I don't want to hear about this man anymore. . . . I've had enough of Marx!"[103] Bernard-Henri Lévy commented that *The Gulag Archipelago,* "barely published, sufficed to overturn our ideological landscape and reverse reference points."[104] Georges Suffert, editor of *Le Point,* admitted that *The Gulag Archipelago* "forever eclipsed the beacon of communism."[105] In 1976, the French Communist Party—perhaps the Kremlin's most faithful daughter in the West—officially condemned not just the Gulag of Stalin's day but even the camps and *psikhushki* of Brezhnev's. Hilton Kramer commented on the breakthrough that *The Gulag Archipelago* made in France: "It will forever remain one of the ironic lessons of history that the moral force that finally shattered the influence of Sartre and the French Left on their home ground came not from any effective dissent in the intellectual capitals of the West but from a heroic survivor of the very system whose evils they had long denied."[106]

Let the following incident serve as an example of the real earthquake experienced by the French cultural elites as a result of Solzhenitsyn. On the evening of June 21, 1977, while President Giscard d'Estaing was welcoming Brezhnev at a state banquet in the Elysée Palace, a rival event was taking place in the small Théâtre Récamier in Paris, at which French intellectuals were meeting with dissidents expelled from the USSR, including Vladimir Bukovsky, Natalya Gorbanevskaya, and Andrei Sinyavsky. Among the organizers of this event were André Glucksman, Eugène Ionesco, Gilles Deleuze, Michel Foucault, as well as—yes—Jean-Paul Sartre and Simone de Beauvoir.

The Gulag Archipelago not only changed the image of Soviet communism in the eyes of the West. To a certain extent it also influenced the West's thinking about itself, at least for the time being. Describing the nightmare of the Gulag, Solzhenitsyn reflected on its roots that lay within the Western world of ideas. Thus, the book became part of fundamental Western ideological debates. Weighing the question of whether the totalitarian evil of the Gulag stemmed directly from the very ideology of communism, or whether it was rather a product of its peculiar Russian implementation—that is, stained with the prerevolutionary Russian tradition of autocracy and disregard for the individual—Solzhenitsyn provided an unambiguous answer. For him, the source of the evil was communism itself, and Russia was its victim. The main critical thrust in *The Gulag Archipelago* was aimed at the phenomenon of ideology, understood as part of the Western heritage. Thus, Solzhenitsyn's exposé of Soviet communism in *The Gulag Archipelago* challenged Western audiences to historical and ideological self-reflection.

Solzhenitsyn emphasized the dependence of the totalitarian nightmare on ideological traditions that described the human reality of good and evil in the language of social abstractions—the same language with which followers of these traditions in the twentieth century formulated their radical programs to solve humanity's eternal ills. In *The Gulag Archipelago* he wrote:

> To do evil a human being must first of all believe that what he is doing is good, or else, that it's a well-considered act in conformity with natural law. Fortunately, it is in the nature of the human being to seek a *justification* for his actions. . . . Macbeth's self-justifications were feeble and his conscience devoured him. . . . The imagination and the spiritual strength of Shakespeare's evildoers stopped short at a dozen corpses. Because they had no ideology. . . . Ideology–that is what gives the evildoer the necessary steadfastness and determination. That is the social theory which helps to make his acts seem good instead of bad in his own and others' eyes, so that he won't hear reproaches and curses but will receive praise and honors. That was how the agents of the Inquisition fortified their wills: by invoking Christianity; the conquerors of foreign lands, by extolling the grandeur of their Motherland; the colonizers, by civilization; the Nazis, by race; and the Jacobins (early and late), by equality, brotherhood, and the happiness of future generations. Thanks to *ideology*, the twentieth century was fated to experience evildoing on a scale calculated in the millions. This cannot be denied, nor passed over, not suppressed.[107]

The hell of the Gulag and communism's other crimes was rooted in ideological thinking, according to Solzhenitsyn. This sort of thinking tends to externalize evil and project it onto the world of abstract social entities—class, race, nation—instead of seeking the sources of evil in man himself. Solzhenitsyn wrote: "If only it were all so simple! If only there were evil people somewhere insidiously committing evil deeds, and it were necessary only to separate them from the rest of us and destroy them. But the line dividing good and evil cuts through the heart of every human being. And who is willing to destroy a piece of his own heart?"[108]

Henceforth Solzhenitsyn would be perceived in the West as a relentless critic of a Western tradition of drawing radical political and moral conclusions from social theories. *The Gulag Archipelago*'s principal intellectual contribution to Western moral self-reflection was perhaps grasped in the most accurate way by Raymond Aron: "Solzhenitsyn's message can be summarized, it seems to me, in two fundamental sentences. There is something worse than poverty and repression and that something is the Lie; the lesson this century teaches us is to recognize the deadly snare of ideology, the illusion that men and social organizations can be transformed at a stroke."[109]

Emphasizing the Western roots of an ideology whose natural fruit was, in Solzhenitsyn's view, the Gulag, the Russian writer ensured that this subject was no longer exotic in the West. Whether agreeing with Solzhenitsyn or not, it was impossible to ignore him. Thanks to the great number of accounts by Gulag inmates already in circulation, people in the West had had long before Solzhenitsyn an opportunity to support and morally identify with victims of Soviet enslavement. How and when they took advantage of this opportunity was another matter. Now on an unprecedented scale they also could ponder the idea that the Gulag was the work of people whose thought processes had not necessarily been all that removed from standards and concepts common at the time in the West. The Western reader of *The Gulag Archipelago* was faced with the challenge to abandon the comfortable position of an external observer of a terrible, yet somewhat exotic event, and instead view communism as a universal tragedy. In the world depicted by Solzhenitsyn, the roots of the totalitarian evil lie deeply within all of us, irrespective of our geographical location. Just as with the roots of goodness that demands that we stand in defense of victims, condemn murders, and expose falsehood.

Coda

When the body of Anatoly Marchenko, who had died in prison, was buried in the municipal cemetery in Chistopol in December 1986, no one knew that he was probably the last victim of the Gulag. Within a few days, news of Marchenko's death traveled around the world's media. The West reacted with indignation and disbelief. After all, for over a year now the new leader in the Kremlin had been Mikhail Gorbachev—a man openly dissociating himself from his predecessors' oppressive policies and announcing before the world an unprecedented experiment: building communism without relying on violence and lies. Much was expected of Gorbachev in the West. Communism's critics were expecting what they viewed as the inevitable death of the Bolshevik project. A diminishing number of Soviet sympathizers and communist believers could again hope briefly for communism "with a human face." The world in general was breathing more easily in the conviction that Gorbachev was actively working to avert an apocalyptic confrontation between the world superpowers. In short, Gorbachev's promises spelled hope.

From the moment *The Gulag Archipelago* first appeared, the debate in the West over Soviet crimes had become for all intents and purposes settled. To be sure, there was still no lack of voices contesting the facts about the Gulag and other Soviet crimes, but they had become increasingly marginalized. These pro-Soviet sentiments were additionally weakened by Soviet intervention in Afghanistan in 1979, and the crackdown by the communist military regime in Poland against the Solidarity workers' movement in 1981 effectively ended the détente between the East and the West. Andropov's tightening of the screws in the USSR in the early 1980s had further diminished the significance of pro-Soviet voices in Western public debate. The real motives for making concessions toward the USSR remained only business interests and fear of the unthinkable: mutual annihilation. Gorbachev was very timely with his *perestroika* and *glasnost*.

Against the backdrop of the new Soviet leader's sweet-sounding promises, the news of Marchenko's death in December 1986 came as a shock. Gorbachev's credibility was imperiled. In this situation, he made the only decision capable of saving his humanitarian image: he ordered the release of all political prisoners still held in the camps. As far as we can tell, his order was obeyed. So perhaps we can say that by the start of 1987 the Gulag had ceased to exist.

Of course, all hopes of building communism "with a human face" turned out to be vain. Less than three years after the USSR's release of political prisoners, the people of Soviet-bloc countries of Eastern Europe concluded that they were no longer threatened with Soviet armed intervention. This spelled the end of communism in Eastern Europe. It took only two more years for the Soviet communist state to collapse.

These historic changes in Russia and Eastern Europe were accompanied by a recovery of collective memory. The formerly banned truth about communist crimes became more accessible with each passing day, publicized through the memoirs of survivors who were eager to finally tell their stories without fear of repercussions. Many once-secret archives were opened, although many documents were destroyed or stolen by the retreating communists. Overall, however, the voices of communism's victims finally entered and reshaped public discourses, and countless secrets were revealed. Soon historians could start writing histories of communism, no longer limited by the necessity of relying on speculation and conjectures.

Following immediately on the heels of these revelations, however, came the question that reverberated through the public debates in the postcommunist East and democratic West alike: Should these traumatic memories be cultivated and explored, or should they instead be forgotten and kept far from public attention? "Let's choose the future!" "Enough dwelling on the past traumas. Let's leave history for historians": these and similar slogans appeared at the center of many public debates, as if the famous maxim by Santayana—that those who forget history are doomed to repeat it—had lost its validity as soon as communist crimes were exposed. The advocates of oblivion emphasized the point that remembering past atrocities and wrongdoings only deepens divisions in societies instead of healing them—something which repressing these memories supposedly is capable of doing.

While this central divide between the guardians of memory and advocates of oblivion characterized public debates on communist crimes both in the West and the postcommunist East, it played different roles in different discourses. In the West, these crimes were seen as a historical topic for historians to explore and argue over. Although the long-lasting legacy of dismissals and denials of Soviet wrongdoing still lingered on in some academic and intellectual contexts, the topic itself was fundamentally viewed from the outside perspective of a researcher examining the evidence more or less dispassionately. In postcommunist countries, however, these discourses have been anything but dispassionate. There, cultural memories of communist atrocities immediately turned into crucial building blocks in the process of constructing new contemporary collective identities. The traumas of communism—suffered by many and long suppressed in public discourse—provided crucial themes for new community-building narratives.

It soon became apparent, however, that the ways in which memories of communist crimes impacted new discourses of identity in Eastern Europe and Russia differed profoundly. In Eastern European countries, communism was treated above all as an evil imposed by an external Soviet force. The overthrow of communism was celebrated in each of these countries primarily as the throwing off of a foreign yoke. As a result, the new historical narratives of these societies, which shaped a new sense of collective identity, began developing above all in opposition to that external oppressive force of Soviet communism. Even though communist criminals in Eastern Europe had in fact been recruited mostly from local communities, these figures tended to be publicly remembered as people merely carrying out the will of their Soviet overlords. This emphasis of public memory offered a somewhat convenient opportunity of forming a new sense of community largely around the stories of communism's victims. As for their communist oppressors, they were for the most part symbolically excluded from this community as traitors and foreign agents.

In the case of Russia, however, the narrative was quite different. Following the collapse of the Soviet Union, the desire to learn the truth about Bolshevik crimes appeared strong, but after less than a decade it was supplanted by a powerful and active desire to forget. Clearly, an essential difference between Russia and other countries of the former Soviet bloc was that communism had not been brought into Russia by foreign invaders. Thus the sources of totalitarian evil could not be conveniently placed outside the boundaries of Russians' new postcommunist identity. Russia was a country of both victims and victimizers. Furthermore, the Soviet Union's tragic history was rife with examples of perpetrators becoming victims, while victims sometimes themselves became perpetrators. In Lenin's and Stalin's empire, suffering from crimes and committing crimes (or assisting in them in myriad ways) often became so intimately intertwined that it often seemed almost impossible to disentangle them, especially years later. Around a decade after the end of the USSR, it became clear that most of Russian society preferred to forget the confusing dark side of their Soviet legacy.

There is nothing unusual in such an attitude. Some Western countries could easily draw on their own experiences to understand this aspect of contemporary Russian society. Those who are touched by the tragedy of civil wars, fratricidal conflicts, and criminal regimes often seek out oblivion in their attempts to live in the shadow of the past. Such an experience was not alien to Spain, Greece, and Northern Ireland, to mention just a few European examples. Yet once again Russia has confounded outside observers. What could be viewed as a familiar pattern shared by many societies has turned out to be yet another Russian enigma. Since Vladimir Putin took power in Russia in 2000, the apparent majority of Russian society has not only seemed oblivious toward Soviet crimes of the (not so distant) past but has expressed nostalgic admiration toward the greatest mass murderer and oppressor of Russians in history: Stalin. One explanation frequently trotted out is that Stalin's achievements at building the Soviet superpower had given many Russians the feeling of *dignity* and *pride* that they so sorely missed after this superpower's collapse. In light of such explanations, a question cannot remain unasked: Was this particular feeling really worth the lives of millions of innocent men, women and children? And does it justify forgetting them now?

Undoubtedly, attempts to grasp this phenomenon must be the task of many books yet to come. For people in the West today, these emotions and attitudes seem puzzling, even perplexing. On the other hand, however, this seemingly incomprehensible phenomenon is taking place in Russia—that is, in a country that the West has long been accustomed to see as a place that cannot be described using ordinary Western concepts and values. As we have seen in this book, a common reaction on the part of many people in the West toward such a feeling of cognitive helplessness has often been a reflexive questioning of their own cognitive criteria. Thus far, however, nobody in the West seems inclined to share the Russian nostalgia for Stalin. Does this mean that the long-lasting Western mystique of Russia is giving way to a new, more rational view?

Not so fast. Perhaps the Western mystique of Russia might have withered away, at least in its recognizable twentieth-century forms, but rationality may not be the most useful word for describing the contemporary condition of the communicative universe in Russia and the West alike. One must not forget that we have already entered a new global media world, one in which many of the once-familiar patterns of knowledge and reasoning are rapidly losing their power and consistency. This newly emerging communicative universe has recently been named the "post-truth" world by its critics. But, as a matter of fact, the "post-truth" world is not a new phenomenon at all. Some of its vital roots are firmly planted in the history of Soviet communism. The story told in this book of Soviet crimes under Western eyes provides ample illustration of the "post-truth" world being established well before this phrase was ever coined.

On the surface, nothing seems more dissimilar than the monolithic domain of Soviet ideology and propaganda, on the one hand, and the multilateral and chaotic universe of the contemporary global media stream on the other. What they do have in common, however, is their potentially corroding impact on the notion of truth as a value in and of itself and on our commitment to its pursuit. In Soviet communism, the prerogative to distinguish truth from falsehood was entirely appropriated by the totalitarian authorities. The rest of society was punished for unauthorized attempts to speak the truth or to try to independently establish it. During the most oppressive period of Soviet history, Stalinism, the official Soviet "truth" had, in fact, a dual nature, reflecting two different primary audiences to which it was addressed. The Western audience, which had little or no opportunity to verify Soviet propaganda by comparing it to Soviet reality, was fed fabrications and ideological arguments that it was expected to believe and espouse. To this end a rich arsenal of lies and deception was used.

The Soviet people, however, could not be affected by these lies in the way many Westerners were, since the Soviet people knew Soviet reality from their own everyday experience. And yet they were required under fear of severe punishments to disbelieve their own senses and reason whenever these faculties seemed at odds with a current ideological message. And so, starving Soviet peasants were expected to disbelieve the testimony of their own stomachs and sing enthusiastically about the abundance of their lives under collectivization. Exhausted slaves of the White Sea Canal were supposed to work themselves to death while cheerfully expressing gratitude to their Bolshevik masters for allowing them to build communism. During the purges, Soviet citizens were expected to erase their memories daily and replace them with new versions in order to properly identify who was a Soviet hero and who was an enemy of the people. In short, Soviet people under Stalin had lived in a "post-truth" world long before the phrase was coined in the West.

In this way, the Stalinist communicative universe became reminiscent of a surrealist play, one in which the commitment to truth, or even a pretension thereof, was no longer binding. The Soviet public—held at gunpoint—was trained to replace, without signs of resistance, the notion of truth with the surrealist poetics enforced by the authorities. This paradigm worked, however, only as long as the gun was aimed at the Soviet public. As soon as the direct fear of severe punishment was relaxed, the ostensible commitment to ideology evaporated too. The only place where Soviet ideology was still sometimes taken seriously was the West.

Putin's Russia dropped the deadweight of communist ideology but inherited and revived Stalin's surrealist poetics of public discourse in a new, twenty-first-century context. In Putin's "post-truth" universe, people are exposed via government propaganda to a relentless overdose of internally inconsistent and mutually contradictory messages and images. But this inner inconsistency and self-contradiction are not treated as disqualifying or even compromising. Peter Pomerantsev, who spent several years working in the inner circles of Putin's media at the Ostankino TV station, describes the version of reality produced there as a universe in which "nothing is true and everything is possible." "The whole line between fact and fiction . . . has become irrelevant," he comments. "The lies are told so often that after a while you find yourself nodding because it's hard to get your head around the idea that they are lying quite so much and quite so brazenly—and at some level you feel that if Ostankino can lie so much and get away with it, doesn't that mean they have real power to define what is true and what isn't? Wouldn't you do better just to nod anyway?"[1] Pomerantsev echoes—almost certainly unknowingly—the words of Barbara Skarga, the Polish prisoner of the Gulag in 1944–1956, quoted above. "You know," she wrote, "a small lie is always exposed, but a big one has a strange persuasive power. It is easy to believe it because it is hard to imagine the authorities would be capable of such colossal mystification."[2]

Skarga tried to demystify the persuasive power of the big Soviet lie over so many Western observers. In her view, it was based on the West's difficulty in imagining that a political regime can lie so freely with no fear of being exposed and publicly embarrassed. For Stalin's subjects, however, the big Soviet lie—as brazen and shameless as it was—constituted, most importantly, a sign of the regime's power to arbitrarily determine and dictate the truth. It was a demonstration of the regime's ultimate invulnerability to exposure and embarrassment. And this is how, in Pomerantsev's view, the government propaganda works in Russia today. This is the world of Baron Münchausen, who overwhelms his audience with a dazzling barrage of perhaps not-quite-believable but nevertheless captivating and emotionally charged stories, reports, images, and commentary. In this universe, everything seems possible because the limiting burden of truth is lifted from the shoulders of both the speaker and his audience—as long as the audience understands, of course, who does the talking and who listens and nods. Here even the cult of the Holy Mother Russia manages to coexist harmoniously with the cult of Stalin, the atheist usurper who killed far more Russian Orthodox people and desecrated more Russian churches than all the medieval Mongolian rulers combined.

The domestic version of Putin's "post-truth" universe revolves around the nostalgic myth of the Soviet empire whose inhabitants supposedly enjoyed the respect (meaning fear) of the rest of the world. The collapse of the Soviet Union was the greatest misfortune of the twentieth century because it deprived the Russian people of this respect. This loss must be reversed by all means necessary. This myth of the stolen glory and its central motif of Russia rising from its knees seem to have won Putin significant support among the Russian public. But Putin's "post-truth" universe is not limited to Russian domestic public discourse. On the contrary, it melds itself into the fabric of the global media universe. "The Kremlin switches messages at will to its advantage," Pomerantsev comments, "climbing inside everything: European right-wing nationalists are seduced with anti-EU message; the Far Left is co-opted with tales of fighting US hegemony; US religious conservatives are convinced by the Kremlin's fight against homosexuality. And the result is an array of videos and voices, working away at global audiences from different angles, producing a cumulative echo chamber."[3]

Today, Putin—perhaps inspired by his own propaganda—is launching an all-out invasion of Ukraine. His army is destroying Ukrainian cities, killing civilians, and committing atrocities practically in full view of the twenty-first-century media world. The global exposure does not seem to discourage the Russian propaganda, however, which presents this war of aggression through a surrealist lens: while the Ukrainians are officially denied the right to exist as a nation, the Russian authorities describe the invasion as the liberation of Ukraine from the Nazis. According to various sources, Putin's support among his countrymen seems to be high as the assault continues. However, the opposite is true in the West. At this moment, Western public opinion seems unusually united in its unwillingness to accept Putin's lies regarding the war. How long will this recent Western commitment to truth last? How can we cultivate it today and build on it in the future?

For once, we might start by learning from the past.

NOTES

Introduction: Escape from Truth

1. Alexander J. Taylor, ed., *M. T. Ciceronis Orationes* (Philadelphia: Towar and Hogan, 1826), 299.

2. Friedrich Nietzsche, *Unzeitgemässe Betrachtungen* (Munich: Goldmann, 1999).

3. Wislawa Szymborska, *View with a Grain of Sand: Selected Poems*, trans. Stanislaw Baranczak and Clare Cavanagh (San Diego: Houghton Mifflin Harcourt, 1995), 179–180.

4. Terrence Des Pres, *The Survivor: An Anatomy of Life in the Death Camps* (Oxford: Oxford University Press, 1976), 35.

5. Nadezhda Mandelshtam, *Hope against Hope*, trans. Max Hayward (New York: Scribner, 1970), 48.

6. Bruno Bettelheim, *Surviving* (New York: Knopf, 1979), 97.

7. Antoni Ekart, *Vanished without Trace: The Story of Seven Years in Soviet Russia*, trans. E. Sykes and E. D. Virpsha (London: Max Parrish, 1954), 12.

8. Primo Levi, *Survival in Auschwitz: The Nazi Assault on Humanity*, trans. Stuart Woolf (New York: Simon and Schuster, 1996), 11.

9. See Andrzej Żbikowski, *Karski* (Warsaw: Świat Książki, 2011); E. Thomas Wood and Stanislaw Jankowski, *Karski: One Man Tried to Stop the Holocaust* (New York: Wiley and Sons, 1994); David Wyman, *The Abandonment of the Jews: America and the Holocaust, 1941–1945* (New York: The New Press, 2007); David Wyman and Charles Rosenzveig, eds., *The World Reacts to the Holocaust* (Baltimore: Johns Hopkins University Press, 1996).

10. Iulii Margolin, *Puteshestvie w stranu ze-ka* (New York: Izdatel'stvo imeni Chekhova, 1952), 413.

11. A notable exception was the discovery of the hard evidence of Stalin's crimes (mass graves and piles of unburied bodies) by the Germans during their invasion of the Soviet and Soviet-occupied lands begun in 1941. During World War II, the Nazis publicized and tried to exploit evidence of Soviet mass killings in Lwów (Lviv), Vynnytsia, Katyn, and other locations. The Western powers refused to acknowledge and examine this evidence. See Anna Cienciala, Natalia Lebedeva, and Wojciech Materski, eds., *Katyn: A Crime Without Punishment* (New Haven: Yale University Press, 2007); Jerzy Węgierski, *Lwów pod okupacją sowiecką* (Warsaw: Editions Spotkania, 1991).

12. Maurice Hindus, *The Great Offensive* (New York: Smith and Haas, 1933), 305, 306.

13. Robert Conquest, *The Great Terror: A Reassessment* (Oxford: Oxford University Press, 1990), 470.

14. Martin Malia, *Russia Under Western Eyes: From the Bronze Horseman to Lenin Mausoleum* (Cambridge, MA: Harvard University Press, 1999), 307. Writing about the numbers of Stalin's victims, Malia refers to Robert Conquest, *The Great Terror: A Reassessment* (Oxford: Oxford University Press, 1990), epilogue; Alec Nove, "The Scale of the Purges," in Nove, ed., *The Stalin Phenomenon* (New York: St. Martin's Press, 1993), 29–33; Nove, "Victims of Stalinism: How Many?" in J. Arch Getty and Roberta Manning, eds. *Stalinist Terror: New Perspectives* (New York: Cambridge University Press, 1993); Stéphane Courtois et al., *Le livre noir du communisme: Crimes, terreur, répression* (Paris: Éditions Robert Laffont, 1997). On more recent discussion of the numbers, see Timothy Snyder, *Bloodlands: Europe Between Hitler and Stalin* (New York: Basic Books, 2010).

15. François Furet, *The Passing of an Illusion: The Idea of Communism in the Twentieth Century* (Chicago: University of Chicago Press, 1999), 148.

16. Barbara Skarga, *Po wyzwoleniu . . . (1944–1956)* (Warsaw: Aletheia, 2000), 199.

17. Sylvia Margulies, *The Pilgrimage to Russia: The Soviet Union and the Treatment of Foreigners, 1924–1937* (Madison: University of Wisconsin Press, 1968), 155.

18. See Eugene Lyons, "To Tell or Not to Tell," *Harper's*, Vol. CLXXI (June 1935), reprinted in Peter Filene, ed., *American Views of Soviet Russia 1917–1965* (Belmont: Dorsey Press, 1968), 104; Antoni Słonimski, *Moja podróż do Rosji* (Warszawa: Rój, 1932), 196–197.

19. See Fedor M. Dostoevskii, "Zapiski iz podpol'ia," in F. M. Dostoevskii, *Sobranie sochinenii* (Leningrad: Akademiia Nauk SSSR, 1989), 4:460.

20. Martin Amis, *Koba the Dread: Laughter and the Twenty Million* (New York: Vintage, 2002), 273. The problem of self-deception has been at the center of philosophical as well as psychological debates. A chief proponent of the idea of the ultimate intentionality (rationality) of self-deception, Donald Davidson,

maintains that a person *A* deceives him or herself if: (1) *A* concludes that the totality of the data available to that person supports the conviction *not p*. (2) *A* maintains that *not p*. (3) the conviction that *not p* makes *A* uncomfortable. (4) For this reason, *A* develops motivation to search for arguments supporting *p*. (5) *A* intentionally acts in order to strengthen the desired conviction *p*. (6) As a result of 5, *A* becomes convinced that *p*. (7) In order to construct and maintain the conviction *p*, *A* must violate the necessity of referring, in developing a new conviction, to the totality of the data available to him. (8) *A* is guilty of a self-induced weak substantiation of his own conviction. See D. Davidson, "Deception and Division," in *The Multiple Self*, ed. J. Elster (Cambridge: Cambridge University Press, 1988), 78–92. For more contributions to the debate, see A. O. Rorty, B. P. McLaughlin, eds. *Perspectives on Self-Deception* (Berkeley: University of California Press, 1988); A. Barnes, *Seeing Through Self-Deception* (Cambridge: Cambridge University Press, 1997); H. Fingarette, *Seeing Through Self-Deception* (Berkeley: University of California Press, 2000); A. R. Mele, *Self-Deception Unmasked* (Princeton, NJ: Princeton University Press, 2001); Robert Piłat, *Oszukiwanie samego siebie: Mózg a podmiot przekonań* (Warsaw: IFiS PAN, 2009). For psychological perspectives closely related to the debate, see D. Goleman, *Vital Lies, Simple Truths: The Psychology of Self-Deception* (New York: Simon and Schuster, 1985); William Hirstein, *Brain Fiction: Self-Deception and the Riddle of Confabulation* (Cambridge, MA: MIT Press, 2005). On willful self-deception by some communist victims of the Gulag, see Nanci Adler, *Keeping Faith with the Party: Communist Believers Return from the Gulag* (Bloomington: Indiana University Press, 2012).

21. See David A. Sprintzen and Adrian Van Den Hoven, eds., *Sartre and Camus: A Historic Confrontation* (Amherst, NY: Humanity Books, 2004).

22. Hannah Arendt, *The Origins of Totalitarianism* (New York: Harcourt Brace, 1951), 334.

23. See Dariusz Tolczyk, *See No Evil: Literary Cover-Ups and Discoveries of the Soviet Camp Experience* (New Haven: Yale University Press, 1999).

24. Tim Tzouliadis, *The Forsaken: An American Tragedy in Stalin's Russia* (New York: Penguin, 2008), 172. See also Robert Conquest, *The Great Terror: A Reassessment* (London: Hutchinson, 1990), 249.

25. See Owen Lattimore, "New Road to Asia," *National Geographic* (December 1944); Henry A. Wallace, *Soviet Asia Mission* (New York: Reynal & Hitchcock, 1946).

26. Amis, *Koba the Dread*, 272.

27. Richard Pipes, *Russia under the Bolshevik Regime* (New York: Vintage, 1995), 209.

28. *L'Express*, November 9, 1956.

1. Dreaming of Russia

1. Martin Malia, *Russia under Western Eyes: From the Bronze Horseman to the Lenin Mausoleum* (Cambridge, MA: Harvard University Press, 1999), 46.

2. Voltaire, *Histoire de l'Empire de Russie sous Pierre le Grand* (Geneva: Cramer, 1759), 1:1–2.

3. Voltaire, *Histoire de l'Empire de Russie sous Pierre le Grand* (Geneva: Cramer, 1763), 2:276.

4. Fedor Tiutchev, *Polnoe sobranie stikhotvorenii* (Leningrad: Sovetskii pisatel', 1987), 229.

5. Adam Mickiewicz, *Poems by Adam Mickiewicz*, trans. by various hands and edited by George Rapall Noyes (New York: Polish Institute of Arts and Sciences in America, 1943), 338. Mickiewicz was arrested by the Russian authorities in Wilno (Vilnius) and exiled to central Russia for his political involvement as a student. He spent more than four years in Russia (1824–1829).

6. Ibid., 350.

7. *Pushkin Threefold*, trans. Walter Arndt (Ann Arbor: Ardis, 1972), 142.

8. Friedrich Nietzsche, *Nachlass* in *Werke in Drei Bänden* (Munich: C. Hanser Verlag, 1966), 3: 690.

9. Friedrich Nietzsche, *Sämtliche Werke in Zwölf Bänden* (Stuttgart: Kroner, 1964), 11:365.

10. Quoted in Malia, *Russia under Western Eyes*, 214.

11. Ibid., 185.

12. Jan Kucharzewski, *Od białego do czerwonego caratu* (London: Veritas, 1989), 30.

13. Ibid., 31.

14. Ibid.

15. Aleksandr Gertsen, *Sobranie sochinenii v tridtsati tomakh* (Moscow: Izdatel'stvo Akademii Nauk SSSR, 1954), 2:311–312, 340.

16. Joseph Conrad, *Under Western Eyes* (Cologne: Könemann, 2000), 342, 343.

2. Ex Oriente Lux

1. More accurately the *GULag*. The name is an abbreviation of *Glavnoe Upravlenie Lagerei* (The main camp administration).

2. Richard Pipes, *The Russian Revolution* (New York: Knopf, 1990), 838.

3. Michał Heller, *Świat obozów koncentracyjnych a literatura sowiecka* (Paris: Kultura, 1974), 49.

4. *Cheka* is the acronym for *Chrezvychainaia komissiia po bor'be s kontrrevoliutsiei i sabotazhom* [The extraordinary commission for combatting counter-revolution and sabotage].

5. "Resolution on Red Terror" as cited in Pipes, *The Russian Revolution*, 833.

6. Andrzej Kamiński, *Koszmar niewolnictwa. Obozy koncentracyjne od 1896 do dziś. Analiza* (Warsaw: Przedświt, 1990), 34–35.

7. Quotation from Martin Amis, *Koba the Dread: Laughter and Twenty Million* (New York: Vintage, 2002), 50–53. The names of places and people were inaccurately transcribed into English in the cable.

8. Heller, *Świat obozów koncentracyjnych a literatura sowiecka*, 48.

9. *Istoricheskii arkhiv*, no. 1 (1958): 10. Cited in Pipes, *The Russian Revolution*, 834.

10. *Dekrety sovetskoi vlasti* (Moscow, 1958), V:69–70. See also Pipes, *The Russian Revolution*.

11. Donald Rayfield, *Stalin and His Hangmen: The Tyrant and Those Who Killed For Him* (New York: Random, 2004), 78.

12. Anne Applebaum, *Gulag: A History* (New York: Doubleday, 2003), 12.

13. See David Dallin and Boris Nicolaevsky, *Forced Labor in Soviet Russia* (New Haven: Yale University Press, 1947).

14. Anton Chekhov, *The Island: A Journey to Sakhalin* (New York: Washington Square Press, 1967), xix–xx.

15. See Aleksandr Yakovlev, *Krestosev* (Moscow: Vagrius, 2000).

16. NEP or New Economic Policy.

17. Nikita Okhotin and Arsenii Roginskii, eds., *Sistema ispravitel'no-trudovykh lagerei v SSSR, 1923–1960: Spravochnik* (Moscow: Memorial, 1998), 317.

18. A. S. Malsagoff, *An Island Hell: A Soviet Prison in the Far North* (London: A.M. Philpot, 1926).

19. Yakovlev, *Krestosev*, 188.

20. Rayfield, *Stalin and His Hangmen*, 78. See V. I. Lenin, *Polnoe sobranie sochinenii* (Moscow: Izdatel'stvo politicheskoi literatury, 1975), vol. 51.

21. See Michael Jakobson, *Origins of the Gulag: The Soviet Prison System, 1917–1934* (Lexington: University Press of Kentucky, 2015), 18–26.

22. Andrey Sinyavsky, *The Soviet Civilization* (New York: Arcade, 1991), 120.

23. Nikolai Bukharin, *Teoriia istoricheskogo materializma* (Moscow: Gosizdat, 1921).

24. Evgenii Preobrazhenskii, *O morali i klassovykh normakh* (Moscow: Gosizdat, 1923).

25. Sinyavsky, *The Soviet Civilization*, 124.

26. Quotation from Amis, *Koba the Dread*, 253.

27. Vasilii Kniazev, *Krasnoe evangelie* (Petrograd: Izdatel'stvo Petrogradskogo Soveta rabochikh i krasnoarmeiskikh deputatov, 1918), 15, 19, 34.

28. Vladimir Mayakovsky, *Selected Poems*, trans. by James H. McGavran (Evanston: Northwestern University Press, 2013), 205–207. (V. Maiakovskii, *Izbrannye proizvedeniia v dvukh tomakh* [Moscow: Gosizdat, 1953], 2:71.)

29. Vladimir Mayakovsky, *Mayakovsky—Plays*, trans. by Guy Daniels (Evanston: Northwestern University Press, 1995), 88–89. (V. Maiakovskii, *Teatr i kino* [Moscow: Gosizdat, 1954], 1:181.)

30. As quoted in Rayfield, *Stalin and His Hangmen*, 80.

31. Applebaum, *Gulag*, 9.

32. Demian Bednyi, *Sobranie sochinenii v vos'mi tomakh* (Moskva: Khudozhestvennaia literatura, 1964), 3:185.

33. Quoted in Tadeusz Klimowicz, *Przewodnik po współczesnej literaturze rosyjskiej i jej okolicach, 1917–1996* (Wrocław: Towarzystwo Przyjaciół Polonistyki Wrocławskiej, 1996), 303. The aesthetics of this description by Pilnyak recall vividly those used later in Nazi depictions of SS-men—also presented as an élite group of strong and handsome supermen.

34. Vladimir Maiakovskii, "Khorosho," in *Izbrannoe* (Minsk: Mastatskaia Litaratura, 1983), 339.

35. See Klimowicz, *Przewodnik*, 54–55.

36. Aleksandr Tarasov-Rodionov, *Opal'nye povesti* (New York: Izdatel'stvo im. Chekhova, 1955), 375.

37. Fedor Stepun, *Byvshee i nesbyvsheesia* (London: Overseas Publications Interchange, 1990), 2:221.

38. Klimowicz, *Przewodnik*, 303.

39. Rayfield, *Stalin and His Hangmen*, 82.

40. Valerii Shambarov, *Gosudarstvo i revoliutsii* (Moscow: Algoritm, 2001), 17.

41. Rayfield, *Stalin and His Hangmen*, 80.

42. Klimowicz, *Przewodnik*, 303.

43. Martin Malia, *Russia under Western Eyes: From the Bronze Horseman to the Lenin Mausoleum* (Cambridge, MA: Harvard University Press, 1999), 246.

44. Jacques Sadoul, *Vive la République des Soviets!* (Moscow: 1918); *Notes sur la révolution bolchevique, Octobre 1917-Janvier 1919* (Paris: Éditions de la Sirene, 1919).

45. Malia, *Russia Under Western Eyes*, 340. See also John M. Thompson, *Russia, Bolshevism, and the Versailles Peace* (Princeton: Princeton University Press, 1966), 176, and Richard Pipes, *Russia under the Bolshevik Regime* (New York: Vintage, 1995), 67.

46. Lincoln Steffens, *Letters* (New York: Harcourt, Brace & Co. 1938), 2:759.

47. Pierre Pascal, *Mon journal de Russie 1916–1918* (Paris: Éditions de l'Age d'Homme, 1975), 1: 247.

48. Pierre Pascal, *En Russie rouge* (Paris: Éditions de la librairie de l'Humanité, 1921), 6. Pascal later changed his views on Soviet communism.

49. William C. Bullitt, *The Bullitt Mission to Russia: Testimony before the Committee on Foreign Relations, U.S. Senate* (New York: B.W. Huebsch, 1919), 58, 50.

50. Bullitt, *The Bullitt Mission to Russia*, 115.

51. Louise Bryant, *Mirrors of Moscow* (New York: Macmillan, 1937), 48–49.

52. Bryant, *Mirrors of Moscow* (New York: Selzer, 1923), 54.

53. Louis Aragon, "Le Front rouge," quoted in Stéphane Courtois et al., *The Black Book of Communism* (Cambridge, MA: Harvard University Press, 1999), 727.

54. Courtois et al., *The Black Book of Communism*, 292.

55. Rayfield, *Stalin and His Hangmen*, 230.

56. Bertolt Brecht, *Die Massnahme* [The measures taken]; English quotation from Timothy Garton Ash, "Comrade Brecht," in Timothy Garton Ash, *The Uses of Adversity: Essays on the Fate of Central Europe* (New York: Random House, 1990), 32. Brecht's play was published in the USSR in 1934. Bertolt Brecht, *Epicheskie dramy*, trans S. Tretiakov (Moscow-Leningrad, 1934), 175.

57. Malia, *Russia Under Western Eyes*, 349.

58. Ibid., 350.

59. Ted Morgan, *Reds: McCarthyism in Twentieth-Century America* (New York: Random House, 2003), 75.

60. Xenia Joukoff Eudin and Harold H. Fisher, *Soviet Russia and the West, 1920–1927: A Documentary Survey* (Stanford, CA: Stanford University Press, 1957), 69. See also George F. Kennan, *Russia and the West Under Lenin and Stalin* (Boston: Little Brown, 1960), 206.

61. Pipes, *Russia under the Bolshevik Regime*, 215.

62. Simon Liberman, *Building Lenin's Russia* (Chicago: University of Chicago Press, 1945), 133.

63. Pipes, *Russia under the Bolshevik Regime*, 215 (Stinnes); Józef Mackiewicz, *The Triumph of Provocation* (New Haven, CT: Yale University Press, 2009), 85 (Annenkov).

64. Pipes, *Russia under the Bolshevik Regime*, 219.

65. *Times*, February 11, 1920.

66. Pipes, *Russia under the Bolshevik Regime*, 207.

67. *New York Times*, May 10, 1921.

68. Gerald Freund, *Unholy Alliance* (New York: Harcourt, Brace & Co, 1957), 129.

69. Malcolm Muggeridge, *Chronicles of Wasted Time: The Green Stick* (New York: William Morrow, 1973), 223.

70. *Survey* No. 41 (April 1962), 16; Pipes, *Russia under the Bolshevik Regime*, 233–234.

71. Malcolm Muggeridge, *Russian Journal*, 19 November 1932, Archives of the Hoover Institution, 72.

72. *Times*, July 25, 1927.

73. *Izvestiia TsK KPSS* (1990), no. 4, 192–193.

74. Andrei Kalpashnikov, *Prisoner of Trotsky* (New York: Doubleday, 1920).

75. Elgin E. Groseclose, "The Prisons of Despair: An Experience in the Russian Cheka," *Atlantic Monthly*, December 1923.

76. S. Malsagoff, *An Island Hell: A Soviet Prison in the Far North* (London: Philpot, 1926); J.D. Bessonov, *Mes 26 prisons et mon évasion de Solovki* (Paris: Payot, 1928); English translation: *My Twenty-Six Prisons and My Escape from Solovetski* (London: J. Cape, 1928)].

77. Pipes, *The Russian Revolution*, 839–840.

78. Pipes, *Russia under the Bolshevik Regime*, 225.

79. *Times*, June 22, 1922.

80. Applebaum, *Gulag*, 15.

81. *Le Metallurgiste*, May 1923.

82. Alexander Berkman, ed., *Letters from Russian Prisons* (New York: A. & C. Boni, 1925), 92.

83. Ibid., 101.

84. *Times*, August 5, 1924.

85. Ibid.

86. *Times*, January 31, 1925.

87. Berkman, *Letters from Russian Prisons*.

88. Ibid., 5.

89. Ibid.

90. Ibid., 7.

91. Ibid., 10.

92. Ibid., 16.

93. Ibid., 8.

94. Ibid., 11.

95. Ibid., 9.

96. Ibid., 14.

97. Ibid., 12.

98. Ibid., 13.

99. Ibid., 11–12.

100. Ibid., 7.

101. Ibid., 14.

102. Ibid., 6.

103. Ibid., 11.

104. See Applebaum, *Gulag*, 24.

105. Galina M. Ivanova, *Labor Camp Socialism: The Gulag in the Soviet Totalitarian System* (New York: Routledge, 2015), 20.

3. In the Soviet Theater of Life

1. Eugene Lyons, *The Red Decade* (New Rochelle: Arlington House, 1970 [1941]), 111.

2. Robert Tucker, *Stalin in Power: The Revolution from Above* (New York: Norton, 1990), 64.

3. S. A. Krasilnikov, "Rozhdenie Gulaga: diskusii v verkhnikh eshelonakh vlasti," *Istoricheskii Arkhiv* no. 4 (1997), 145. Quoted in English in Anne Applebaum, *Gulag: A History* (New York: Anchor Books, 2004), 74.

4. See I. Stalin, *Materialy ob ispol'zovanii truda ugolovno-zakliuchennykh*, Tsentral'nyi Gosudarstvennyi Arkhiv Rossiiskoi Federatsii, f. 393, op. 1, ed. khr. 285, 1.31.

5. Internal Soviet sources estimated the number of famine deaths at 5.5 million. Recent estimates by historians consider this figure as either correct or somewhat low. See Dana G. Dalrymple, "The Soviet Famine of 1932–1934," *Soviet Studies* 15, no. 3 (1964), 259; Timothy Snyder, *Bloodlands: Europe between Hitler and Stalin* (New York: Basic Books, 2010), 53; Norman M. Naimark, *Stalin's Genocides: Human Rights and Crimes against Humanity* (Princeton, NJ: Princeton University Press, 2010); Omelian Rudnytski, Natalia Levchuk, Oleh Wolowyna, Pavlo Shevchuk, and Alla Kovbasiuk, "Demography of a Man-made Human Catastrophe: The Case of Massive Famine in Ukraine 1932–1933," *Canadian Studies in Population* 42, no. 1–2 (2015).

6. Krasilnikov, "Rozhdenie Gulaga," 145–146.

7. "Debate on Report—The Immediate Tasks of the Communists in the Trade Union Movement, 12th Session, 6th ECCI Plenum, March 2, 1926," *Imprecorr*, March 25, 1926, 351. See also Sophie Coeure, *La grande lueur a l'Est. Les francais et l'Union sovietique 1917–1939* (Paris: Seuil, 1999).

8. Konstantin Umansky's career spanned over many years and various posts. In the 1920s, he served as a TASS (*Telegrafnaia Agentsiia Sovetskogo Soiuza*) (Telegraphic agency of the Soviet Union) correspondent in Rome, Paris, and Geneva. In the early 1930s, he headed the Press and Information Department in the People's Commissariat of Foreign Affairs. An important part of his job was to censor foreign correspondents' reports from the Soviet Union. In 1936, he became the VOKS (*Vsesoiuznoe obshchestvo kul'turnoi sviazi s zagranitsei*) (All-union society for cultural relations with foreign countries) representative in the United States and, in 1939, Soviet ambassador in Washington, DC. In 1943, he became Soviet ambassador to Mexico and died in a plane crash in 1945.

9. A. I. Rykov, "Zamechaniia k proektu rezoliutsii. Sovershenno konspirativno," RGASPI f. 495, op. 99, d. 12 ll. 15–16, quoted in Michael David-Fox, "The 'Heroic Life' of a Friend of Stalinism: Romain Rolland and Soviet Culture," *Slavonica* 11, no. 1 (April 2005), 17.

10. *New York Times*, August 15, 1930.

11. David Dallin and Boris Nicolaevsky, *Forced Labor in Soviet Russia* (New Haven, CT: Yale University Press, 1947), 220.

12. *New York Times*, July 6, 1930.

13. Dallin and Nicolaevsky, *Forced Labor in Soviet Russia*, 224–225.

14. *New York Times*, December 18, 1930.

15. *New York Times*, March 7, 1931.

16. *New York Times*, January 20, 1931.

17. Sir Alan Pim and Edward Bateson, *Report on Russian Timber Camps* (London: E. Benn, 1931).

18. See A. Gorcheva, *Pressa Gulaga (1918–1955)* (Moscow: Izdatel'stvo Moskovskogo universiteta, 1996).

19. Nick Baron, "Conflict and Complicity: The Expansion of the Karelian Gulag, 1923–1933," *Cahiers du Monde Russe* 42/2–4 (April–December 2001), 643; Applebaum, *Gulag*, 65, 582. Regarding the national mortality rates in the Gulag during the construction of the White Sea Canal, the archives of the Department of Prisoner Registration list 13,197 deaths in 1932 (4.81 percent mortality rate) and 67,297 deaths in 1933 (15.3 percent mortality rate). These records do not reflect deaths in prisons and in transport and do not include special exiles.

20. Iwan Solonewitsch, *Die Verlorenen. Eine Chronik namenlosen Leidens. Russland im Zwangsarbeitslager 1933* (Berlin: Essener Verlagsanstalt, 1937); Iwan Soloniewicz, *Rosja w obozie koncentracyjnym* (Lwow: Sekretariat Porozumiewawczy Polskich Organizacyj Spolecznych, 1937); Ivan Solonevich, *Russia in Chains* (London: Williams and Norgate, 1938); Ivan Solonevich, *The Soviet Paradise Lost* (New York: Paisley Press, 1938); Ivan Solonevich, *Les barbelés rouges. Trois Russes s'évadent des bagnes soviétiques* (Paris: Les Éditions de France, 1938); I. Solonewitsch, *Et folk i laenker* (Copenhagen: H. Hagerup, 1939).

21. Solonevich, *The Soviet Paradise Lost*, 155–156.

22. Barbara Skarga, *Po wyzwoleniu . . . (1944–1956)* (Warsaw: Aletheia, 2000), 84, 86.

23. Jules Margoline, *La condition inhumaine: Cinq ans dans les camps de concentration sovietiques* (Paris: Calman Levy, 1949), 42–43. English quote from Stéphan Courtois et al., *The Black Book of Comunism: Crimes, Terror, Repressions* (Cambridge, MA: Harvard University Press, 1999), 318.

24. Maksim Gor'kii, *Nesvoevremennye mysli* in *Novaia zhizn'* 1917–1918 (Maxim Gorky, *Untimely Thoughts: Essays on Revolution, Culture, and the Bolsheviks, 1917–1918* [New Haven, CT: Yale University Press, 1995].

25. Among those who recalled this episode was the eminent philologist Dmitry Likhachev, then a prisoner of the Solovki camp. He talked about it in an interview included in Marina Goldovskaia's documentary film *Vlast' solovetskaia* (Mosfilm, 1995).

26. *Literaturnaia Gazeta*, August 3, 1994, 6.

27. Maksim Gor'kii, "Solovki," in Gor'kii, *Sobranie sochinenii v 30 tomakh* (Moscow: 1952), 17:231.

28. Ibid.

29. Ibid. For more detailed discussion of Gorky's "Solovki," see Dariusz Tolczyk, *See No Evil: Literary Cover-Ups and Discoveries of the Soviet Camp Experience* (New Haven, CT: Yale University Press, 1999).

30. Shklovsky could not take part in the group journey of the 120 writers, but he managed to travel to the Canal separately in order to join the team working on *Belomor.*

31. Quoted from Frank Westerman, *Inżynierowie dusz* (Warsaw: Iskry, 2007), 54.

32. The alphabetical list of the authors includes: B. Agapov, S. Alymov, L. Averbakh, A. Berzin, S. Budantsev, S. Dikovsky, N. Dmitrev, A. Erlich, K. Finn, E. Gabrilovich, N. Garnich, G. Gauzner, S. Gekht, K. Gorbunov, M. Gorky, V. Inber, Vsev. Ivanov, B. Jasienski, V. Kataev, Z. Khatsrevin, G. Korabelnikov, M. Kozakov, B. Lapin, A. Lebedenko, D. S. Mirsky, L. Nikulin, B. Pertsov, Y. Rykachev, V. Shklovsky, L. Slavin, A. Tikhonov, A. Tolstoy, N. Yurgich, K. Zelinsky, and M. Zoshchenko.

33. For more detailed discussion of *Belomor,* see Cyntia Ruder, *Making History for Stalin: The Story of the Belomor Canal* (Gainesville: University Press of Florida, 1998), and Tolczyk, *See No Evil.*

34. L. Auerbach et al., *Belomor: An Account of the Construction of the New Canal Between the White Sea and the Baltic Sea,* ed. Maxim Gorky, L. Auerbach, and S. G. Firin, trans. Amabel Williams-Ellis (New York: H. Smith and R. Haas, 1935), v, vii.

35. *New York Times,* November 26, 1935.

36. Nikolai Pogodin, *Sobranie sochinenii* (Moscow: Iskusstvo, 1972), 1:410. The English quotation is from Ben Blake, ed., *Four Soviet Plays* (New York: Benjamin Bloom, 1972), 301–302.

37. Pogodin, *Sobranie sochinenii,* 1: 411–412. Blake, *Four Soviet Plays,* 303–304.

38. The English translation of *The Aristocrats* by Anthony Wixley and Robert S. Carr was published in 1937. Nikolai Pogodin, *The Aristocrats* (London: Lawrence and Wishart, 1937).

39. *New York Times,* February 20, 1937.

40. S. A. Malsagoff, *An Island Hell: A Soviet Prison in the Far North* (London: Philipot, 1926).

41. Anne Applebaum, "Dead Souls," *Weekly Standard* (December 13, 1999). Raymond Duguet, *Un bagne en Russie rouge* (Paris: Jules Talandier, 1928).

42. Y. D. Bessonov, *Mes 26 prisons et mon évasion de Solovki* (Paris: Payot, 1928), published in English as *My Twenty-Six Prisons and My Escape from Solovetski* (London: J. Cape, 1929); Boris Cederholm, *Au pays du NEP et de la Tcheka. Dans les prisons de l'U.R.S.S.* (Paris: J. Talandier, 1928), published in English as *In the Clutches of the Cheka* (Boston: Houghton Mifflin, 1929).

43. William A. Fairburn, *Forced Labor in Soviet Russia* (New York: Nation Press, 1931); The Duchess of Atholl, M.P., *The Conscription of a People* (London: Philipp Allan, 1931); Pim and Bateson, *Reports on Russian Timber Camps.*

44. *Out of the Deep: Letters from Soviet Timber Camps* (London: Geoffrey Bles, 1933); Essad-Bey (Leo Nussimbaum), *OGPU—The Plot Against the World* (New York: Viking, 1933).

45. Tatiana Tchernavina, *Escape from the Soviets* (New York: Dutton, 1934).

46. Vladimir Tchernavin, *I Speak for the Silent* (Boston: Hale Cushman & Flint, 1935).

47. Olga Dmitrievna [pseud.], *Red Gaols* (London: Burns Oates & Washbourne, 1935); Dmitrievna, *18 Jahre Sowjetherrschaft* (Vienna, 1936). George Kitchin, *Prisoner of the OGPU* (New York: Longmans, 1935).

48. Julia de Beausobre, *The Woman Who Would Not Die* (London: Chatto & Windus, 1938).

49. Ante Ciliga, *Au pays du grand mensonge* (Paris: Gallimard, 1938); first English edition: *The Russian Enigma* (London: Labour Book, 1940). See also Panait Istrati, *Vers l'autre flamme après seize mois dans l'URSS* (Paris: Rieder, 1929).

50. Pro-Soviet books were printed in the West in mass quantities at the time. For instance, the Left Book Club Series, published by Victor Gollancz, had fifty thousand regular subscribers.

51. John P. Diggins, *The American Left in the Twentieth Century* (New York: Harcourt Brace Jovanovich, 1973), 110. See also Paul Hollander, *Political Pilgrims: Western Intellectuals in Search of the Good Society* (New Brunswick: Transaction, 1998), 78.

52. Scott Nearing, *The Making of a Radical* (New York: Harper & Row, 1972), 202.

53. See Ernst Glaeser and F. G. Weiskopf, eds., *The Country Without Unemployment* (New York: International, 1931), a Soviet-propaganda photo album with captions in English, German, and French.

54. Edmund Wilson, "An Appeal to Progressives," *New Republic*, January 14, 1931.

55. Hugh Dalton, *The Fateful Years* (London: Frederic Muller, 1957), quoted in Kingsley Martin, *Editor: A Volume of Autobiography* (London: Hutchinson, 1968), 60.

56. Granville Hicks, *Where We Came Out* (New York: Viking, 1954), 25.

57. John Dos Passos, *The Theme Is Freedom* (New York: Dodd Mead, 1956), 67–68.

58. Eric J. Hobsbawm, *Revolutionaries* (New York: New Press, 1973), 27.

59. Antoni Slonimski, *Moja podróż do Rosji* (Warszawa: Rój, 1932), 196–197.

60. Peter Filene, ed., *American Views of Soviet Russia: 1917–1965* (Chapel Hill: University of North Carolina Press, 1968), 99.

61. Ibid., 101, 102, 103.

62. Ibid., 104.

63. Ibid.

64. Ibid., 107, 108.

65. *New York Times*, October 25, 1931.

66. John Lewis Gaddis, *Russia, the Soviet Union, and the United States* (New York: McGraw-Hill, 1990), 114.

67. *Moscow News*, January 12, 1932. See also Tim Tzouliadis, *The Forsaken: An American Tragedy in Stalin's Russia* (New York: Penguin, 2008), 13.

68. Filene, *American Views of Soviet Russia*, 106.

69. Stephen Spender, *Forward from Liberalism* (London: Victor Gollancz, 1937), 202.

70. Paul Johnson, *Intellectuals* (New York: Harper & Row, 1988), 156.

71. Malcolm Muggeridge, *The Sun Never Sets* (New York: Random House, 1940), 291. See also Alfred Kazin, *Starting Out in the Thirties* (Boston: Atlantic, 1965), 85; Hollander, *Political Pilgrims*, 81.

72. André Gide, *Littérature engagée* (Paris: Gallimard, 1950), 24.

73. George Orwell, *Homage to Catalonia* (London: Sacker and Warburg, 1938).

74. Martin, *Editor*, 215.

4. Wonderland

1. Richard Pipes, *Russia under the Bolshevik Regime* (New York: Vintage, 1995), 209.

2. Ibid., 210.

3. Ibid.

4. In 1931–1932 the International Union of Revolutionary Writers published the journal *Literatura mirovoi revoliutsii* [Literature of the world revolution] in Russian, German, French, and English. National branches of the Union were established in many countries.

5. Liam O'Flaherty, *I Went to Russia* (New York: Harcourt Brace, 1931), 222.

6. O. D. Kameneva, "Tov. Moskvinu. TsKVKP(b). Sov. sekretno. 5 ianvaria 1928," GARFf.5283, op. 1a, d. 118, l. 1–3, quoted in Michael David-Fox, *Showcasing the Great Experiment: Cultural Diplomacy and Western Visitors to the Soviet Union, 1921–1941* (Oxford: Oxford University Press, 2012), 34.

7. David-Fox, *Showcasing the Great Experiment*, 59.

8. O'Flaherty, *I Went to Russia*, 259–260.

9. David-Fox, *Showcasing the Great Experiment*, 105.

10. Ibid., 106.

11. *Low's Russian Sketchbook: Drawings by Low, Texts by Kingsley Martin* (London: Victor Gollancz, 1932), 9.

12. Malcolm Muggeridge, *Chronicles of Wasted Time* (London: Collins, 1972), 211, 212–213. See also Paul Hollander, *Political Pilgrims: Western Intellectuals in Search of the Good Society* (New Brunswick, NJ: Transaction Publishers, 1998), 105.

13. Julian Huxley, *A Scientist Among the Soviets* (London: Harper, 1932), 4–5.

14. John Strachey, *The Coming Struggle for Power* (New York: Covici, 1935), 360.

15. Lion Feuchtwanger, *Moscow 1937: My Visit Described for My Friends* (New York: Viking, 1937), 3, 149–150.

16. Malcolm Muggeridge, *Sun Never Sets* (New York: Random House, 1940), 79. See also Hollander, *Political Pilgrims*, 102.

17. George A. Burrell, *An American Engineer Looks at Russia* (Boston: Stratford, 1932), 21.

18. Ludmila Stern, *Western Intellectuals and the Soviet Union, 1920–1940: From Red Square to the Left Bank* (New York: Routledge, 2007), 23.

19. Jean-Richard and Marguerite Bloch, *Journal du voyage en URSS*, September 17, 1934; quoted in Stern, *Western Intellectuals and the Soviet Union, 1920–1940*, 23.

20. O'Flaherty, *I Went to Russia*, 215.

21. For example, John Dewey, who extolled the Soviets for their progressive educational system (until he changed his mind around 1937), visited the Soviet Union in the summer of 1928. He noted with amazement that practically everybody he met seemed to know who he was—not just Soviet intellectuals but also ordinary people, such as schoolteachers, office clerks, and factory workers. See "John Dewey in Russia," *The Survey* 61 (December 15, 1928), 349.

22. H. G. Wells, *An Experiment in Autobiography: Discoveries and Conclusions of a Very Ordinary Brain* (New York: Little, Brown, 1984), 215.

23. Eugene Lyons, *Assignment in Utopia* (New York: Harcourt Brace, 1937), 328.

24. Lyons, *Assignment in Utopia*, 218.

25. Richard Crossman, ed., *The God that Failed: Six Studies in Communism* (London: Hamilton, 1950), 65. See also Sylvia Margulies, *The Pilgrimage to Russia: The Soviet Union and the Treatment of Foreigners, 1924–1937* (Madison: University of Wisconsin Press, 1968), 88–89. Paying Western writers large sums in Soviet currency seemed to have yet another effect, in addition to bribing them and manipulating their sense of vanity. It created one more string tying them to the Soviets. These writers could spend those small fortunes only in the Soviet Union. Thus, they felt motivated to return, often repeatedly, in order to use previously unspent money.

26. Hollander, *Political Pilgrims*, 105.

27. Margulies, *The Pilgrimage to Russia*, 126.

28. Ella Winter, *Red Virtue: Human Relations in the New Russia* (New York: Harcourt Brace, 1933), 206.

29. Maurice Hindus, *The Great Offensive* (New York: Smith and Haas, 1933), 305, 306.

30. *New York Times*, February 3, 1931.

31. Sherwood Eddy, *The Challenge of Russia* (New York: Farrar and Rinehart, 1931), 104, 107. See also Hollander, *Political Pilgrims*, 145.

32. Anna Louise Strong, *This Soviet World* (New York: Holt, 1936), 256.

33. Tim Tzouliadis, *The Forsaken: An American Tragedy in Stalin's Russia* (New York: Penguin, 2008), 13.

34. *New York Times*, October 11, 1936.

35. Pat Sloan, *Soviet Democracy* (London: Left Book Club, 1937), 111.

36. Pat Sloan, *Russia Without Illusions*, preface by Beatrice Webb (London: F. Muller, 1938), 246.

37. Harold Laski, *Law and Justice in Soviet Russia* (London: L. and V. Woolf at the Hogarth Press, 1935), 21.

38. Ibid., 28.

39. G. B. Shaw, *The Rationalization of Russia* (Bloomington: Indiana University Press, 1964 [1931]), 92. See also Hollander, *Political Pilgrims*, 146–147.

40. Shaw, *The Rationalization of Russia*, 91.

41. D. N. Pritt, "The Russian Legal System," in *Twelve Studies in Soviet Russia*, ed. Margaret Cole (London: V. Gollancz, 1933), 162, 163, 164.

42. Strong, *This Soviet World*, 262.

43. See Timothy Snyder, *Bloodlands: Europe between Hitler and Stalin* (New York: Basic Books, 2010), 27–28.

44. Ibid., 34.

45. Viktor Danilov, Roberta Manning, and Lynne Viola, eds., *Tragediia sovetskoi derevni: dokumenty i materialy* (Moscow: ROSSPEN, 1999–2002), 3:649.

46. Snyder, *Bloodlands*, 50.

47. Ibid., 38–39.

48. Arthur Koestler, *The Yogi and the Commissar* (New York: Macmillan, 1946), 137.

49. Gareth Jones, *Experiences in Russia 1931: A Diary* (Pittsburgh: Alton Press, 1932).

50. *Manchester Guardian*, March 30, 1933.

51. *New York Times*, September 14, 1933.

52. *New York Times*, November 8, 1933. Gareth Jones was abducted during his trip to Inner Mongolia and killed under unclear circumstances on August 12, 1935.

53. In the opinion of Tim Tzouliadis, "it was Walter Duranty, more than any other individual, who persuaded Franklin Roosevelt of the wisdom of granting

diplomatic recognition to the Soviet government. Even before [Roosevelt's] inauguration, he spent long hours briefing the president-elect on 'the Soviet experiment.'" Tzouliadis, *The Forsaken*, 55.

54. *New York Times*, May 3, 1932.

55. S. J. Taylor, *Stalin's Apologist: Walter Duranty, New York Times' Man in Moscow* (New York: Oxford University Press, 1990), 221.

56. Lyons, *Assignment in Utopia*, 576.

57. Fred Kupferman, *Au pays des Soviets. Le voyage français en Union soviétique, 1917–1939* (Paris: Gallimard Juillard, 1979), 88; English quote from François Furet, *The Passing of an Illusion: The Idea of Communism in the Twentieth Century* (Chicago: University of Chicago Press, 1999), 147.

58. Lyons, *Assignment in Utopia*, 67.

59. Malcolm Muggeridge, "Russian Journal" (Hoover Institution Archive), September 28, 1932, 15; quoted in Robert Service, *Comrades! A History of World Communism* (Cambridge, MA: Harvard University Press, 2007), 206.

60. "Letters to the Editor: Social Conditions in Russia (Recent Visitors' Tribute)," *Manchester Guardian*, March 2, 1933.

61. Norman and Jeanne Mackenzie, eds., *The Diary of Beatrice Webb* (Cambridge, MA: Belknap Press, 1982), 4:414.

62. *The Diary of Beatrice Webb*, 4:301.

63. Sidney and Beatrice Webb, *Soviet Communism: A New Civilisation* (London: Left Book Club, 1937), 268.

64. Webb, *Soviet Communism*, 563.

65. Robert Conquest, *The Harvest of Sorrow: Soviet Collectivization and the Terror-Famine* (London: Hutchinson, 1986), 317.

66. Webb, *Soviet Communism*, 591, 594.

67. Ibid., 591.

68. "Otchet o poseshchenii S. Vebba," reprinted in A. V. Golubev et al., *Rossiia i Zapad: Formirovanie vneshnepoliticheskikh stereotipov v soznanii rossiiskogo obshchestva pervoi poloviny XX veka* (Moscow: Institut Istorii RAN, 1998), 227–228.

69. *The Diary of Beatrice Webb*, 4:495.

70. *New York Times*, April 14, 1935.

71. Jerzy Gliksman, *Tell the West* (New York: Gresham, 1948), 172.

72. Ibid., 172–173.

73. Ibid., 173.

74. Ibid., 173.

75. Ibid., 176.

76. Ibid., 178.

77. Ibid.

78. Ibid., 245–246.

79. Ibid., 351–352.

80. Victor Serge, *Soviet 1929* [vol. 2 of Panait Istrati, *Vers l'autre flamme*] (Paris: Rieder, 1929).

81. Furet, *The Passing of an Illusion*, 214–215.

82. Gaetano Salvemini, "Pour la liberté de l'esprit," *Les Humbles* (July 7, 1935), 5–9; English Quotation from Furet, *The Passing of an Illusion*, 286.

83. Salvemini, ibid. English quotation from Vitaly Shentalinsky, *Arrested Voices: Resurrecting the Disappeared Writers of the Soviet Regime* (New York: Free Press, 1996), 39.

84. Michael David-Fox, "The 'Heroic Life' of a Friend of Stalinism: Romain Rolland and Soviet Culture," *Slavonica*, 11 no. (April 1, 2005), 10. David-Fox presents a detailed discussion of Rolland's 1935 visit to the USSR and his conversation with Stalin based on a close analysis of recently available archival sources.

85. Furet, *The Passing of an Illusion*, 275.

86. See David-Fox, "The 'Heroic Life' of a Friend of Stalinism: Romain Rolland and Soviet Culture," 20, 26 note 25.

87. "Moskovskii dnevnik Romena Rollana," *Voprosy literatury* no. 3 (1989), 36.

88. The official transcript of Rolland's conversation with Stalin, authorized by both, appeared in the appendix to Romain Rolland, *Voyage à Moscou: Juin-juillet 1935* (Paris: Albin Michel, 1992), 237–247.

89. "Moskovskii dnevnik Romena Rollana." See also Tadeusz Klimowicz, *Obywatele Arkadii. Losy pisarzy rosyjskich po roku 1917* (Wroclaw: Wydawnictwo Uniwersytetu Wroclawskiego, 1993), 55.

90. "Moskovskii dnevnik Romena Rollana." See also Klimowicz, *Obywatele Arkadii*, 55.

91. "Beseda t. Stalina s Romen Rollanom. 28. VI. 1935," RGASPl f. 558, op. 11, ed. khr. 775, l. 2; quoted in David-Fox, *Showcasing the Great Experiment*, 239.

92. Stern, *Western Intellectuals and the Soviet Union, 1920–1940*, 27.

93. David-Fox, *Showcasing the Great Experiment*, 241.

94. Klimowicz, *Obywatele Arkadii*, 129.

95. "Pis'mo Romen Rollana tovarishchu Stalinu. 20.VII.1935," RGALI f. 631, op. 11, d. 283, l. 13; quoted in David-Fox, "The 'Heroic Life' of a Friend of Stalinism," 19.

96. On January 29, 1936, glamorous celebrations of Rolland's seventieth birthday took place in Moscow. The writer did not attend, but his portrait was displayed next to the portraits of Stalin, Molotov, and Kaganovich in the grand hall of the Moscow Conservatory. The gala included musical enactments of excerpts from Rolland's works, poetry readings, scholarly accolades, the showing of a documentary film immortalizing his visit to the USSR, and celebratory speeches by his Soviet readers—distinguished writers as well as industrial workers. A recorded greeting by Rolland was played and applauded. The Soviet radio broadcasted this celebration, and the *Literaturnaia gazeta* devoted an entire

issue to it. A new biography of Rolland appeared in Soviet bookstores, and local branches of the Union of Soviet Writers organized similar ceremonies celebrating Rolland's birthday in a number of Soviet cities.

97. André Gide, *Afterthoughts on the USSR* (New York: Dial Press, 1938), 58.

98. Ibid., 59.

99. An English translation soon appeared. See Gide, *Return from the USSR* (New York: Knopf, 1937).

100. Gide, *Retour de l'U.R.S.S.* (Paris: Gallimard, 1936), 67.

101. *Commune* no. 43 (March 1937), 804.

102. *L'Humanité*, January 18, 1937.

103. Gide, *Retouches à mon Retour de l'U.R.S.S.* (Paris: Gallimard, 1937), 66.

104. John V. Fleming, *The Anti-Communist Manifestos: Four Books That Shaped the Cold War* (New York: Norton, 2009), 37.

105. See Gustaw Herling, *A World Apart* (New York: Penguin, 1996), 14.

5. Stalin Presents

1. Stéphane Courtois et al., *The Black Book of Communism: Crimes, Terror, Repression* (Cambridge, MA: Harvard University Press, 1999), 190.

2. See Norman Naimark, *Stalin's Genocides* (Princeton, NJ: Princeton University Press, 2011).

3. Tomasz Kizny, *La Grande Terreur en URSS 1937–1938* (Paris: Noir sur Blanc, 2013), introductory essay.

4. Anne Applebaum, *Gulag: A History* (New York: Anchor Books, 2004), 579.

5. See "Statisticheskie svedeniia o rasstrelannykh i zakhoronennykh na spetsobekte 'Butovskii poligon' v 1937–1938 gg.," in *Butovskii poligon 1937–1938. Kniga pamiati zhertv politicheskikh repressii*, vyp. 7 (Moscow, 2003), 311; vyp. 8 (2004), 396–397. See also Timothy Snyder, *Bloodlands: Europe between Hitler and Stalin* (New York: Basic Books, 2010), 86; Richard J. Evans, *The Third Reich in Power* (New York: Penguin, 2005), 69–70; Barry McLoughlin, "Mass Operations of the NKVD, 1937–8," in *Stalin's Terror: High Politics and Mass Repression in the Soviet Union*, ed. by Barry McLoughlin and Kevin McDermott (Houndsmill, UK: Palgrave, 2003), 130–131.

6. See Snyder, *Bloodlands*, 58–118.

7. Snyder, *Bloodlands*, 103–104. Snyder conservatively estimates the number of ethnic Poles among the victims of these killings as about eighty-five thousand. Even at this estimate, Poles, who composed less than 0.4 percent of the Soviet population, accounted for one-eighth of the mortal victims of the Great Terror in 1937–1938. This means that, according to Snyder's count, "Soviet Poles were about forty times more likely to die during the Great Terror than Soviet citizens generally" (104).

8. Ibid., 111.

9. Oleg Khlevniuk, *The History of the Gulag: From Collectivization to the Great Terror* (New Haven, CT: Yale University Press, 2004), 147. See also: Snyder, *Bloodlands*, 107.

10. Eugenia Ginzburg, *Journey into the Whirlwind* (New York: Harcourt Brace Jovanovich, 1967), 74.

11. On the mental strategies of Communist victims in the Gulag see Nanci Adler, *Keeping Faith with the Party: Communist Believers Return from the Gulag* (Bloomington: Indiana University Press, 2012).

12. See P. P. Poletaev, "Malen'kaia respublika," in *Bolshevo: Literaturnyi istoriko-kraevedcheskii al'manakh* (Bolshevo: Pisatel', 1994), 80.

13. See G. S. Smith, *D. S. Mirsky: A Russian-English Life, 1890–1939* (Oxford: Oxford University Press, 2000), 316.

14. Ibid., 318.

15. Ernest Hemingway, *For Whom the Bell Tolls* (New York: Scribner's Sons, 1940), 424.

16. Ibid., 231.

17. Ibid., 245. According to secret Soviet sources, Hemingway was successfully recruited by an NKVD intelligence agent, Jacob Golos, in 1940. Soviet intelligence referred to him under the code name "Argo." See John Earl Haynes, Harvey Klehr, and Alexander Vassiliev, *Spies: The Rise and Fall of the KGB in America* (New Haven, CT: Yale University Press, 2009); Nicholas Reynolds, *Writer, Sailor, Soldier, Spy: Ernest Hemingway's Secret Adventures, 1935–1961* (New York: HarperCollins, 2017), 81.

18. Upton Sinclair and Eugene Lyons, *Terror in Russia? Two Views* (New York: Rand School Press, 1938), 40.

19. Walter Krivitsky, *In Stalin's Secret Service: An Exposé of Russia's Secret Policies by the Former Chief of the Soviet Intelligence in Western Europe* (New York: Harper Bros., 1939 and reprints). See also Boris Nicolaevsky, *Power and the Soviet Elite* (New York: Farrar, 1965), 64.

20. It appeared in the United Kingdom as *I Was Stalin's Agent* (London: H. Hamilton, 1939).

21. See Garry Kern, *A Death in Washington: Walter G. Krivitsky and the Stalin Terror* (New York: Enigma Books, 2003).

22. Robert Conquest, *The Great Terror: A Reassessment* (Oxford: Oxford University Press, 2008), 464.

23. RGASPI, f. 17, op. 171, d. 448, l. 184. For detailed information about the deaths of Radek and Sokolnikov, see Nikita Pietrow, *Psy Stalina* (Warsaw: Demart, 2012), 43–52.

24. *Izvestiia*, March 12, 1938.

25. Jerome Davis, *Behind Soviet Power: Stalin and the Russians* (New York: Readers' Press, 1946), 31.

26. Upton Sinclair and Eugene Lyons, *Terror in Russia? Two Views* (New York: R. R. Smith, 1938), 60.

27. Lion Feuchtwanger, *Moscow 1937: My Visit Described for My Friends* (New York: Viking, 1937), 122–123.

28. Karavkina, December 14, 1936. GARF, VOKS, f. 5283, op. 8, d.290, l. 9, quoted in Ludmila Stern, *Western Intellectuals and the Soviet Union, 1920–1940: From Red Square to the Left Bank* (New York: Routledge, 2007), 166.

29. Ivo Banac, ed., *The Diary of Georgi Dimitrov 1933–1949* (New Haven: Yale University Press, 2003), 44, 51. See also David-Fox, *Showcasing the Great Experiment*, 275.

30. Karavkina, December 19, 1936. GARF, VOKS, f. 5283, op. 1, d. 334, l. 7, quoted in Stern, *Western Intellectuals and the Soviet Union, 1920–1940*, 168.

31. See Feuchtwanger, *Moscow 1937*, chapter 1.

32. Stern, *Western Intellectuals and the Soviet Union, 1920–1940*, 173.

33. John V. Fleming, *The Anti-Communist Manifestos: Four Books That Shaped the Cold War* (New York: Norton, 2009), 40.

34. Ibid., 39.

35. Brecht quoted by Sidney Hook in "Bert Brecht, Sidney Hook, and Stalin (Letter)," *Encounter* (March 1978), 93.

36. *The New Leader*, October 10, 1964.

37. Ronald Hayman, *Brecht: A Biography* (New York: Oxford University Press, 1983), 203.

38. *The New Leader*, December 30, 1968.

39. *L'Humanité*, January 6, 1937.

40. Rolland to Bloch, March 3, 1938; quoted in Stern, *Western Intellectuals and the Soviet Union, 1920–1940*, 33–34.

41. Courtois et al., *The Black Book of Communism*, 784, note 30.

42. Ibid., 346.

43. Susanne Leonhard, *Gestohlenes Leben. Schicksal einer politischen Emigrantin in der Sowjetunion* (Stuttgart: Steingrüben Verlag, 1959), 714.

44. Annie Kriegel and Stéphane Courtois, *Eugen Fried. Le grand secret du PCF* (Paris: Seuil, 1997), 293.

45. Barry McLoughlin and Kevin McDermott, *Stalin's Terror: High Politics and Mass Repression in the Soviet Union* (New York: Palgrave Macmillan, 2003), 65.

46. *Die Zukunft*, March 10, 1939.

47. Münzenberg's friends and his life companion, Babette Gross, were convinced that he was killed by Soviet agents. See Babette Gross, *Willie Münzenberg— eine politische Biographie* (Stuttgart: Deutsche Verlags-Anstalt, 1967).

48. N. Fedorov, "Dvigatel' 'Perekovki'. Nachal'nik Dmitlaga S. G. Firin," in *Butovskii poligon 1937–1938 gg. vyp.* 8 (Moscow, 2004), 54.

49. *Moscow Daily News*, May 11, 1937.

50. Jean Lacouture, *André Malraux* (New York: Pantheon, 1975), 230.

51. Robert Service, *Comrades! A History of World Communism* (Cambridge, MA: Harvard University Press, 2007), 206.

52. William C. Bullitt to Secretary of State, April 20, 1936. 861.01/2120, RG59, National Archives II, College Park, MD; quoted in Tzouliadis, *The Forsaken*, 73.

53. Leonard Leshuk, *US Intelligence Perceptions of Soviet Power, 1921–1946* (London: Frank Cass, 2003), 87. See also *Department of Commerce, Foreign Commerce and Navigation of the United States* (Washington, DC: US Government Printing Office, 1939).

54. Tzouliadis, *The Forsaken*, 120.

55. Joseph E. Davies, *Mission to Moscow* (New York: Pocket Books, 1943), 26.

56. Keith D. Eagles, *Ambassador Joseph E. Davies and American-Soviet Relations, 1937–1941* (New York: Garland, 1985), 82.

57. George Kennan, *Memoirs (1925–1950)* (New York: Bantam, 1969), 86.

58. George W. Baer, ed., *The Question of Trust: The Origins of U.S.-Soviet Diplomatic Relations. The Memoirs of Loy W. Henderson* (Palo Alto: Hoover Institution Press, 1986), 455.

59. To William Phillips, 12 February 1937, box 3, Davies Papers, Manuscript Division, Library of Congress; quoted in Norman E. Saul, *Friends or Foes? The United States and Soviet Russia, 1921–1941* (Lawrence: University Press of Kansas, 2005), 341.

60. To Sumner Welles, 10 July 1937, folder Davies, box 40, Welles Papers, Franklin Roosevelt Presidential Library; quoted in Saul, *Friends or Foes?*, 343.

61. Davies to Marvin McIntyre (personal and confidential), 6 October 1937, folder October, box 6, Davies Papers, Manuscript Division, Library of Congress; quoted in Saul, *Friends or Foes*, 345.

62. Marjorie Merriweather Post interview with Nettie Major, August 31, 1964. PM4(50) Hillwood Museum Archives, Washington, DC; quoted in Tzouliadis, *The Forsaken*, 120.

63. Davies, *Mission to Moscow* (New York: Pocket Books 1943), 217.

64. Alexander Dolgun (with Patrick Watson), *Alexander Dolgun's Story: An American in the Gulag* (London, 1975), 30.

65. Conquest, *The Great Terror*, 464.

66. *Neue Freie Presse*, January 30, 1937.

67. Terry A. Cooney, *The Rise of the New York Intellectuals: Partisan Review and Its Circle* (Madison: University of Wisconsin Press, 1986), 99–100.

68. John Dewey, *Not Guilty: Report of the Commission of Inquiry into the Charges Made Against Leon Trotsky* (New York: Harper, 1938).

69. Trotsky's address was delivered to the New York Hippodrome Meeting over the phone. See David North, *In Defense of Leon Trotsky* (Southfield, MI: Mehring Books, 2010), viii.

70. "An Open Letter to American Liberals," *Soviet Russia Today* VI (March, 1937), 14–15.

71. English quote in Courtois et al., *Black Book of Communism*, 296.

72. Ibid., 185.

73. Ibid.

74. Ibid.

75. Naturally, not everyone subscribed to this view. Among those who did not was the Pope Pius XI, who condemned Nazism and communism alike in his encyclicals *Mit brennender Sorge* and *Divini Redemptoris*, published on March 10 and 19, 1937.

76. *Nationalsozialistische Briefe*, October 1925, and *Völkischer Beobachter*, 14 November 14, 1925; also published in Joseph Goebbels, *Die zweite Revolution. Briefe an Zeitgenossen* (Zwickau: Streiter Verlag, 1926), 41. See also Walter Laqueur, *Russia and Germany: A Century of Conflict* (New Brunswick, NJ: Transaction, 1990), 163.

77. Otto Ernst Schüddekopf, *Linke Leute von Rechts* (Stuttgart: Kohlhammer, 1960), 194. See also Laqueur, *Russia and Germany*, 162.

78. See Michael Kellogg, *The Russian Roots of Nazism: White Russians and the Making of National Socialism, 1917–1945* (New York: Cambridge University Press, 2006).

79. Alfred Rosenberg, *Pest in Russland! Der Bolschewismus, seine Häupter, Handlanger und Opfer* (Munich: Deutscher Volksverlag, 1922).

80. Another early influence along the same lines came from the writer Dietrich Eckart. After Eckart's death in 1923, a dialog between him and Hitler was published, presenting their shared view of communism as a Jewish conspiracy. See Dietrich Eckart, *Der Bolschewismus von Moses bis Lenin: Zwiegespräch zwischen Adolf Hitler und mir* (Munich: Franz Eher Nachf, 1925).

81. Walter Laqueur and other historians have speculated whether or not Hitler "deliberately exaggerated the danger of Bolshevism . . . in order to shock the German middle classes and induce them to support Nazism." Laqueur, *Russia and Germany*, 171.

82. Ibid.

83. Martin Malia, *Russia Under Western Eyes: From the Bronze Horseman to the Lenin Mausoleum* (Cambridge, MA: Harvard University Press, 1999), 327.

84. Andrzej Kamiński, *Koszmar niewolnictwa. Obozy koncentracyjne od 1896 do dziś* (Warsaw: Przedswit, 1990), 81.

85. The catalogue for the exhibit *Kommunismus ohne Maske* (Munich: Eher, 1935), 7.

86. Hermann Fehst, *Bolschevismus und Judentum* [Bolshevism and Jewry] (Berlin: 1934); Theodor Adamheit, *Rote Armee, rote Weltrevolution, roter Imperialismus* [The Red Army, red world revolution, red imperialism] (Berln: Nibelungen-Verlag, 1935); Niels Närk, *Das bringt die Rote Armee* (Berlin: Nibelungen, 1936); Adolf Ehrt, *Der Weltbolschewismus: Ein internationales Gemeinschaftswerk über die bolschewistische Wühlarbeit und die Umsturzversuche der Comintern in allen Ländern* (Berlin: Nibelungen, 1936); Rudolf Kommoss, *Juden hinter Stalin* [Jews behind Stalin] (Berlin: Nibelungen-Verlag, 1938); Hermann Greife, *Sowjetforschung* (Berlin: Nibelungen, 1936), *Zwangsarbeit in der Sowjetunion* (Berlin: Nibelungen, 1936), *Die Klassenkampfpolitik der Sowjetregierung* (Berlin: Nibelungen, 1937), *Ist eine Entwicklung der Sowjetunion zum nationalen Staat möglich?* (Berlin: Junker & Dünhaupt, 1939).

87. Goebbels talked to his staff about it. See David Welch, *The Third Reich: Politics and Propaganda* (London: Routledge, 2002), 183–185; Jan C. Behrends, "Back from the USSR: The Anti-Comintern's Publications on Soviet Russia in Nazi Germany (1935–41)," *Kritika: Explorations in Russian and Eurasian History* 10 no. 3 (Summer 2009), 539.

88. Alfred Laubenheimer, ed., *Und Du siehst die Sowjets richtig: Berichte von deutschen und ausländischen Spezialisten aus der UdSSR* (Berlin: Nibelungen, 1935).

89. Maria de Smeth, *Unfreiwillige Reise nach Moskau* (Berlin: Nibelungen, 1939).

90. *Werkmeister im Paradies: 4 Jahre im Traktorenwerk Charkow* (Berlin: Nibelungen, 1937).

91. Peter Nikolajew, *Bauern unter Hammer und Sichel: Bauer, Partisan, Verbannter, Flüchtling* (Berlin: Nibelungen, 1936); Maria Kraft, *In der Gewalt der Bolschewisten: Leidensjahre einer deutschen Frau in der Sowjet-Union* (Berlin: Nibelungen, 1938).

92. Wladimir Unischewski, *Wettlauf mit der GP* (Berlin: Nibelungen, 1939); Vladimir Unishevsky, *Red Pilot: Memoirs of a Soviet Airman* (London: Right Book Club, 1940); Georg Kravetz, *Fünf Jahre Sowjetflieger* (Berlin: Nibelungen, 1939).

93. Karl Albrecht, *Der verratene Sozialismus: Zehn Jahre als hoher Staatsbeamter in der Sowjetunion* (Berlin: Nibelungen, 1938). The book had ten editions before the summer of 1939; its publication was stopped during the Nazi-Soviet alliance of 1939–1941. After the German invasion of the USSR, it was republished again and translated into Russian as *Sud'by liudskie v podvalakh* (1942). Two million copies were in print by 1944.

94. Ibid., 644.

95. Agricola [Alexander Baumeister], *Das endlose Gefängnis: Erinnerungen des Finnländers Georg Kitchin aus den Kerkeren der Sowjetunion* (Berlin: Nibelungen, 1936).

96. *Grosse antibolschewistische Ausstellung* (Berlin: Verlag für Kultur—u. Wirtschefswerbung Daenell & Co., 1937).

97. Ibid.

98. Laqueur, *Russia and Germany*, 188.

99. Ibid., 196.

100. Otto Autenrieth, *Bismarck II. Der Roman der deutschen Zukunft* (Munich: Verlag Heimatland, 1921), 184. See also Kaminski, *Koszmar niewolnictwa*, 81–82.

101. Bert Branden [Herbert Blank], *Achtung, Hier Deutschland! Der Roman zu Zeit* (Berlin: Kampf Verlag, 1930), 114.

6. A Black-and-White Western

1. François Furet, *The Passing of an Illusion: The Idea of Communism in the Twentieth Century* (Chicago: University of Chicago Press, 1999), 321.

2. Natalia Lebedeva and Mikhail Narinskii, eds., *Komintern i vtoraia mirovaia voina* (Moscow: Pamiatniki istoricheskoi mysli, 1994), 1:277–278.

3. Ibid., 40.

4. Jerzy Łojek, *Agresja 17 września 1939* (Warsaw: Wojskowy Instytut Wydawniczy, 1990), 195. In response to French communists' pro-Soviet and pro-German position in September 1939, the French government delegalized the French Communist Party. See Stephane Courtois and Marc Lazar, *Histoire du Parti communiste francais* (Paris: Presses Universitaires de France, 1995), 173.

5. Paul Johnson, *Intellectuals* (New York: Harper & Row, 1988), 285.

6. William O'Neil, *A Better World: The Great Schism: Stalinism and American Intellectuals* (New York: Touchstone, 1982), 26.

7. Melvyn Leffler, *The Specter of Communism: The United States and the Origins of the Cold War, 1917–1953* (New York: Hill and Wang, 1994).

8. Zbigniew Siemaszko, "The Mass Deportations of the Polish Population to the USSR, 1940–1941," in *The Soviet Takeover of the Polish Eastern Provinces, 1939–1941*, ed. Keith Sword (New York: Palgrave, 1991), 234, n. 9.

9. Marian Czuchnowski, *Tyfus, teraz słowiki* (London: Modern Writing, 1951), 28.

10. Ibid.

11. Jerzy Gliksman, *Tell the West* (New York: Gresham, 1948), 219, 220, 221.

12. Beata Obertyńska, *W domu niewoli* (Warsaw: Czytelnik, 1991 [Rome: 1946]), 13.

13. Stéphane Courtois et al., *The Black Book of Communism* (Cambridge, MA: Harvard University Press, 1999), 372.

14. Furet, *The Passing of an Illusion*, 330.

15. Louis Fischer, *The Road to Yalta: Soviet Foreign Relations, 1941–1945* (New York: Harper & Row, 1972), 57.

16. John Colville, *The Fringes of Power: 10 Downing Street Diaries, 1939–55* (New York: Norton, 1985), 404.

17. *The Presidential Diaries of Henry Morgenthau, Jr., 1939–1945*, p. 1093, FDR Library, Hyde Park, New York. Quoted in Warren F. Kimball, *The Juggler: Franklin Roosevelt as Wartime Statesman* (Princeton, NJ: Princeton University Press, 1991), 7. See too Tim Tzouliadis, *The Forsaken: An American Tragedy in Stalin's Russia* (New York: Penguin, 2008), 228.

18. *New Statesman*, July 5, 1941.

19. G.D.H. Cole, *Europe, Russia, and the Future* (London: Macmillan, 1942), 8, 9.

20. Quotation taken from Isabelle Tombs, "Erlich and Alter, 'The Sacco and Vanzetti of the USSR': An Episode in the Wartime History of International Socialism," *Journal of Contemporary History* 23 (1988), 538.

21. Richard C. Lukas, *The Strange Allies: The United States and Poland 1941–45* (Knoxville: University of Tennessee Press, 1978), 91.

22. Clayton Koppes and Gregory D. Black, *Hollywood Goes to War: How Politics and Propaganda Shaped World War II Movies* (New York: Free Press, 1987), 219.

23. Tzouliadis, *The Forsaken*, 196–197.

24. Joseph Davies, *Mission to Moscow* (New York: Simon and Schuster, 1941), 357.

25. John Maynard, *The Russian Peasant and Other Studies* (London: Victor Gollancz, 1947), 196.

26. Koppes and Black, *Hollywood Goes to War*, 191.

27. Ibid., 207.

28. See David Culbert, *Mission to Moscow* (Madison: University of Wisconsin Press, 1980), 33.

29. Ibid., 31.

30. William Henry Chamberlin, *American Mercury*, March 1944, 271.

31. Elizabeth Barker, *Churchill and Eden at War* (New York: St. Martin's Press, 1978), 227.

32. George F. Kennan and John Lukacs, *George F. Kennan and the Origins of the Containment, 1944–1946* (Columbia: University of Missouri Press, 1997), 34–35.

33. George F. Kennan, "Comment," *Survey*, Winter–Spring 1975, 31.

34. Nikolai Tolstoy, *Stalin's Secret War* (New York: Holt, Rinehart & Winston, 1981), 289.

35. Lynne Olson and Stanley Cloud, *A Question of Honor: The Kościuszko Squadron: Forgotten Heroes of World War II* (New York: Alfred Knopf, 2003), 163.

36. Jan Zumbach, a Polish fighter pilot from 303 Squadron, appeared on a billboard advertising British War Bonds.

37. Tadeusz Piotrowski, *The Polish Deportees of World War II: Recollections of Removal to the Soviet Union and Dispersal Throughout the World* (Jefferson, NC: McFarland, 2004), 9.

38. Romuald Wernik, *Białe noce i czarne dnie* (London: Polska Fundacja Kulturalna, 1987), 7.

39. Keith Sword, *Deportation and Exile: Poles in the Soviet Union 1939–1948* (New York: St. Martin's Press, 1984), 48.

40. Piotrowski, *The Polish Deportees of World War II*, 9.

41. Ibid.

42. The eminent British military historian, Sir John Keegan, characterized Anders's army as "one of the most courageous combat formations of this war." See John Keegan, *Six Armies in Normandy: From D-Day to the Liberation of Paris* (New York: Viking, 1982), 262.

43. Quotations from Tzouliadis, *The Forsaken*, 200, 202.

44. Klaus Hergt, *Exiled to Siberia: A Polish Child's World War II Journey* (Cheboygan, MI: Crescent Lake, 2000), 182–183. The account's final details suggest that the boy's mother had been a victim of cannibalism.

45. The German author of the 2000 interview with the boy, Hank Birecki, writes that after such an American reception, Hank never spoke about his childhood. He only decided to talk about it fifty years later.

46. Quotation from Włodzimierz Bolecki, *"Inny świat" Gustawa Herlinga-Grudzińskiego* (Warsaw: WSiP, 1997), 23.

47. Tadeusz Wittlin, *Diabeł w raju* (Warsaw: Polonia, 1990), 74.

48. George Orwell, *The Complete Works of George Orwell*, vol. 17 (London: Secker & Warburg, 1998), 254.

49. Ibid., 258.

50. *Daily Worker*, March 20, 1943.

51. *Nova Svoboda*, April 7, 1943. See also Tombs, "Erlich and Alter, 'The Sacco and Vanzetti of the USSR,'" 544.

52. Anna Cienciala, Natalia Lebedeva, and Wojciech Materski, eds., *Katyń: A Crime Without Punishment* (New Haven, CT: Yale University Press, 2007), 118, 120.

53. Ibid., 306–307.

54. *Pravda*, April 19, 1943.

55. *Correspondence between the Chairman of the Council of Ministers of the USSR and the President of the USA and the Prime Minister of Great Britain During the Great Patriotic War of 1941–1945* (Moscow: Gosizdat 1957), 1:120–121.

56. Ibid., 2:61–62.

57. Martin Gilbert, *Winston S. Churchill*, vol. 7, *Road to Victory, 1941–45* (London: Heineman, 1986), 385.

58. *Documents on Polish-Soviet Relations, 1939–1945* (London: Heinemann, 1961), 2:700.

59. Allen Paul, *Katyn: The Untold Story of Stalin's Polish Massacre* (New York: Macmillan, 1991), 304.

60. Ibid.

61. US Department of State, *Foreign Relations of the United States*, Washington, DC 1995, vol. 3 (1943), 396.

62. Lloyd C. Gardner, *Spheres of Influence: The Great Powers Partition Europe, from Munich to Yalta* (Chicago: Ivan R. Dee, 1993), 209.

63. US Department of State, *Foreign Relations of the United States*, vol. 3 (1943), 395.

64. Paul, *Katyń*, 304–305.

65. Ibid., 302–303.

66. "The Soviet-Polish Break," *Life*, May 10, 1943, 30.

67. "Poles vs. Reds," *Newsweek*, May 10, 1943, 29. The theme of Polish cavalry attacking German tanks was a fabrication of Nazi propaganda circulated during the German invasion of Poland in September 1939.

68. Olson and Cloud, *A Question of Honor*, 268.

69. Roman Umiastowski, *Poland, Russia and Great Britain, 1941–1945* (London: Holis and Carter, 1946), 126.

70. Janusz K. Zawodny, *Death in the Forest* (Notre Dame: Notre Dame University Press, 1962), 158.

71. Alexander Werth, *Russia at War, 1941–1945* (New York: Dutton, 1964), 663.

72. Władimir Abarinow, *Oprawcy z Katynia* (Kraków: Znak, 2007), 185.

73. Werth, *Russia at War, 1941–1945*, 661–662. Nicholas was the Metropolitan of Kiev and not Moscow.

74. Paul, *Katyn*, 259.

75. Paul, *Katyn*, 258–259.

76. Ibid.

77. See Abarinow, *Oprawcy z Katynia*, 223–224. See also John Earl Haynes and Harvey Klehr, *Venona: Decoding Soviet Espionage in America* (New Haven: Yale University Press, 1999), 155–156.

78. Zawodny, *Death in the Forest*, 65. See also G. M. Gilbert, *Nuremberg Diary* (New York: Farrar Straus, 1947), 136.

79. Herbert Romerstein, "Tuszowanie Katynia," *Polska the Times*, March 8–9, 2008, 22.

80. Daria Nałęcz, Władimir Kozłow et al., eds., *Katyń. Dokumenty zbrodni*, vols. 1–4 (Warsaw: Naczelna Dyrekcja Archiwów Państwowych, 1995–2006).

81. Tzouliadis, *The Forsaken*, 171.

82. Ibid., 172.

83. Ibid., 207.

84. Elinor Lipper, *Eleven Years in Soviet Prison Camps* (Chicago: Regnery, 1951), 115.

85. Olga Adamova-Sliozberg, *Put'* (Moscow: Vozvrashchenie, 1993), 66.

86. Henry A. Wallace, *Soviet Asia Mission* (New York: Reynal & Hitchcock, 1946), 33.

87. Lipper, *Eleven Years in Soviet Prison Camps*, 115.

88. Wallace, *Soviet Asia Mission*, 34.

89. Anne Applebaum, *Gulag: A History* (New York: Doubleday, 2003), 168.

90. Tzouliadis, *The Forsaken*, 208.

91. Lipper, *Eleven Years in Soviet Prison Camps*, 93, 95.

92. Simeon Vilensky, ed., *Osventsim bez pechei* (Moscow: Vozvrashchenie, 1996), 10–16. See also Glinka's remarks in *Kolyma*, documentary film by Mikhail Mikheyev, 1992.

93. Janusz Bardach (with Kathleen Gleason), *Man Is Wolf to Man: Surviving Stalin's Gulag* (London: Scribner, 1998), 191.

94. Wallace, *Soviet Asia Mission*, 34.

95. Ibid., 34.

96. Lipper, *Eleven Years in Soviet Prison Camps*, 112.

97. Wallace, *Soviet Asia Mission*, 35.

98. Thomas Sgovio, *Dear America! Why I Turned Against Communism* (Kenmore, NY: Partners' Press, 1979), 160–161.

99. Wallace, *Soviet Asia Mission*, 35–36.

100. Bardach, *Man Is Wolf to Man*, 235.

101. Applebaum, *Gulag*, 443.

102. Varlam Shalamov, *Kolyma Tales*, trans. by John Glad (New York: Penguin, 1994), 278.

103. Ibid., 280–283.

104. Wallace, *Soviet Asia Mission*, 35.

105. Lipper, *Eleven Years in Soviet Prison Camps*, 112.

106. Wallace, *Soviet Asia Mission*, 36.

107. Lipper, *Eleven Years in Soviet Prison Camps*, 267.

108. Sgovio, *Dear America!*, 251.

109. Lipper, *Eleven Years in Soviet Prison Camps*, 269.

110. Wallace, *Soviet Asia Mission*, 212.

111. Applebaum, *Gulag*, 442.

112. Ted Morgan, *Reds: McCarthyism in Twentieth-Century America* (New York: Random House, 2003), 398–399. Karakhan himself was arrested by the NKVD during Stalin's purges and executed on September 20, 1937.

113. Ibid.

114. *Pacific Affairs*, September 1938.

115. Haynes and Klehr, *Venona*, 43, 146–150.

116. *National Geographic*, December 1944. See also Morgan, *Reds*, 399.

117. Lipper, *Eleven Years in Soviet Prison Camps*, 116.

118. Ibid.

7. The Curtain Falls, the Show Goes On

1. Stéphane Courtois et al., *The Black Book of Communism: Crimes, Terror, Repression* (Cambridge, MA: Harvard University Press), 216–217.

2. Ibid., 222.

3. Ibid.

4. Anne Applebaum, *Gulag: A History* (New York: Doubleday, 2003), 582–583.

5. Ibid., 579, 581–582. See also J. Otto Pohl, *The Stalinist Penal System* (Jefferson, NC: McFarland, 1997), 15; V. N. Zemskov, "Arkhipelag Gulag glazami pisatelia i statistika," *Argumenty i fakty* no. 45, 1989.

6. Courtois et al., *The Black Book of Communism*, 230.

7. Ibid., 229–231, 320–322.

8. Sven Steenberg, *Vlasov* (New York: Knopf, 1970), 221.

9. Nicholas Bethell, *The Last Secret: The Delivery to Stalin of Over Two Million Russians by Britain and the United States* (New York: Basic Books, 1974), 110.

10. Ibid., 90.

11. Ibid., 92.

12. Ibid., 95.

13. Ibid., 125.

14. Ibid., 127.

15. Ibid., 128.

16. Ibid., 132.

17. Ibid., 136, 145.

18. Ibid., 141.

19. Ibid., 140.

20. Ibid., 147.

21. Ibid., 150.

22. Dennis Hills, *Tyrants and Mountains: A Reckless Life* (London: Murray, 1992), 103–108, 137–140.

23. Bethell, *The Last Secret*, 179.

24. Steenberg, *Vlasov*, 224.

25. Courtois et al., *The Black Book of Communism*, 323.

26. Ibid., 321.

27. Quotation from Steenberg, *Vlasov*, 222.

28. *Winston Churchill: His Complete Speeches, 1897–1963* (London: Chelsea, 1974), 7:293.

29. Martin Malia, *Russia Under Western Eyes: From the Bronze Horseman to the Lenin Mausoleum* (Cambridge, MA: Harvard University Press, 1999), 359.

30. David Dallin and Boris Nicolaevsky, *Forced Labor in Soviet Russia* (New Haven, CT: Yale University Press, 1947). Russian Mensheviks in the West were very active in alerting Western public opinion to Bolshevik atrocities. Besides publishing the journal *Sotsialisticheskii Vestnik*, they collaborated with *The New Leader*. See Andre Liebich, *From the Other Shore* (Cambridge, MA: Harvard University Press, 1997).

31. *Chicago Tribune*, August 31, 1947.

32. *Chicago Tribune*, February 23, 1947. See also Zoe Zajdlerowa, *The Dark Side of the Moon* (London: Faber, 1946).

33. Jozef Czapski, *Souvenirs de Starobielsk* (Paris: Collection Temoignages, 1945); Ada Halpern, *Liberation—Russian Style* (London: MaxLove, 1945); also published as *Conducted Tour* (London: Sheed & Ward, 1945); Polish edition: *Spokojne życie* (Rome: Oddział Kultury i Prasy 2 Korpusu, 1946). See also Kazimierz Zamorski, *Dwa tajne biura 2 Korpusu* (London: Oficyna Poetów i Malarzy, 1990).

34. Sylwester Mora and Piotr Zwierniak, *La Justice soviétique* (Rome: Magi-Spinetti, 1945) and *Giustizia Sovietica* (Rome: Magi-Spinetti, 1945). N. N. Nikitin, *Why I Could Not Live in Soviet Russia* (Boston: Scollary, 1945).

35. Jerzy Gliksman, *Tell the West* (New York: Gresham, 1948). Antoni Ekart, *Echappé de Russie* (Paris: Hachette, 1949) [English edition: *Vanished Without a Trace* (London: Max Parrish, 1954)]. Jules Margolin, *La condition inhumaine* (Paris: Calmann-Levi, 1949).

36. Vladimir Petrov, *Soviet Gold: My Life as a Slave Laborer in the Siberian Mines* (New York: Farrar Straus, 1949).

37. Margarete Buber-Neumann, *Under Two Dictators* (London: Victor Gollancz, 1949), *Als Gefangene bei Stalin und Hitler* (Munich: Verlag der Zwolf, 1949), *Déportée en Sibérie* (Paris: Seuil, 1949).

38. Alex Weissberg, *The Accused* (New York: Simon and Schuster, 1951). Elinor Lipper, *Eleven Years in Soviet Prison Camps* (Chicago: Regnery, 1951); it had earlier appeared in a German edition, *Elf Jahre in sowjetischen Gefangnissen und Lagern* (Zurich: Oprecht, 1950). Gustaw Herling-Grudzinski, *A World Apart* (London: Heinemann, 1951).

39. Anatol Krakowiecki, *Kolyma. Les bagnes de l'or* (Paris: Les iles d'or, 1952).

40. *Slave Labor in Russia.* Report of the International Labor Relations Committee of the 66th Convention of the American Federation of Labor, San Francisco 1947, 31.

41. See *Report of the Ad Hoc Committee on Forced Labour* (Geneva: ILO, 1953).

42. Quoted in William H. Chamberlin, "Slave Laborers in Siberia: A Red 'Uncle Tom's Cabin,'" *Chicago Tribune*, November 20, 1949.

43. Iulia Beausobre, *The Woman Who Could Not Die* (London: V. Gollancz, 1948 [1938]), 7.

44. Ted Morgan, *Reds: McCarthyism in Twentieth-Century America* (New York: Random House, 2003), 400.

45. Graham White and John Maze, *Henry A. Wallace: His Search for a New World Order* (Chapel Hill: University of North Carolina Press, 1995), 296. See too Tim Tzouliadis, *The Forsaken: An American Tragedy in Stalin's Russia* (New York: Penguin, 2008), 329.

46. Owen Lattimore, *Ordeal by Slander* (Boston: Little Brown, 1950).

47. See Lattimore, *Ordeal by Slander* (editorial note to a 1971 reprint).

48. Paul Hollander, *Political Pilgrims: Western Intellectuals in Search of the Good Society* (New Brunswick: Transaction, 1998), 158.

49. Malia, *Russia Under Western Eyes*, 318.

50. See Elizabeth Kimball MacLean, *Joseph E. Davies: Envoy to the Soviets* (Westport, CT: Praeger, 1992), 125; Tzouliadis, *The Forsaken*, 275–276.

51. Ludmilla Thorne, "Introduction to the Transaction Edition," in Victor Kravchenko, *I Chose Justice* (New Brunswick, NJ: Transaction, 1989), xi.

52. John V. Fleming, *The Anti-Communist Manifestos: Four Books That Shaped the Cold War* (New York: Norton, 2009), 192–199; Gary Kern, *The Kravchenko Case: One Man's War Against Stalin* (New York: Enigma Books, 2007), 42–50.

53. Kravchenko, *I Chose Justice*, 12.

54. Ibid., 26.

55. Ibid., 36.

56. Ibid., 382.

57. Ibid., 379.

58. Ibid., 12.

59. Ibid., 55.

60. Hewlett Johnson, *The Socialist Sixth of the World* (London: Victor Gollancz, 1939), 367.

61. Nina Berberova, *Poslednye i pervye. Delo Kravchenko* (Moscow: Izdatel'stvo im. Sabashnikovykh, 2000), 243.

62. Kravchenko, *I Chose Justice*, 48.

63. Ibid., 300, 301.

64. Ibid., 273, 274, 275.

65. John V. Fleming, *The Anti-Communist Manifestos: Four Books That Shaped the Cold War* (New York: Norton, 2009), 244.

66. Ibid.

67. *The God That Failed*, ed. by Richard Crossman (New York: Harpers, 1949), 255.

68. *Times*, January 26, 1966. See also Robert Conquest, *The Great Terror: A Reassessment* (Oxford: Oxford University Press, 1990), 473.

69. Conquest, *The Great Terror*, 474.

70. Ibid., 475. See also Tzouliadis, *The Forsaken*, 277.

71. Buber-Neumann, *Under Two Dictators*, xii.

72. Conquest, *The Great Terror*, 473.

73. Ernest Hemingway, *For Whom the Bell Tolls* (New York: Scribner's Sons, 1940), 230. See also Leona Toker, *Return from the Archipelago: Narratives of Gulag Survivors* (Bloomington: Indiana University Press, 2000), 43.

74. Valentin Gonzalez, Julian Gorkin, *El Campesino: Life and Death in Soviet Russia* (New York: Putnam, 1952). See also the camp memoirs of another witness in the Rousset trial: Susanne Leonhard, *Gestohlenes Leben: Schicksal einer politischen Emigrantin in der Sowjetunion* (Frankfurt: Europäische Verlagsanstalt, 1956).

75. See Malia, *Russia under Western Eyes*, 367; Conquest, *The Great Terror*, 472. See also Annie Cohen-Solal, *Sartre: A Life* (New York: Pantheon, 1987).

76. Conquest, *The Great Terror*, 472.

77. *Les Temps modernes* (1950), issues 51, 57.

78. Jean-Paul Sartre, *Situations IV* (Paris: Gallimard, 1964), 104.

79. Courtois, et al., *The Black Book of Communism*, 750.

80. *Libération*, July 15–20, 1954. See also Paul Johnson, *Intellectuals* (New York: Harper Row, 1988), 243–244.

81. Jean-Paul Sartre, *Situations X* (Paris: Gallimard, 1976), 220. See also Johnson, ibid.

82. Gustaw Herling, *A World Apart* (New York: Penguin, 1996), 131.

83. Lev Shestov, *Umozrenie i otkrovenie. Religioznaia filosofiia Vladimira Solov'eva i drugie stat'i* (Paris: YMCA Press, 1964), 321.

84. Fyodor Dostoevsky, *The House of the Dead*, trans. David McDuff (New York: Penguin, 1985), 110.

85. Herling, *A World Apart*, ix (Bertrand Russell's preface to the first edition).

86. Gustaw Herling-Grudziński and Włodzimierz Bolecki, *Rozmowy w Dragonei* (Warsaw: Szpak, 1997), 103.

87. Ibid.

88. Ibid., 100.

89. Włodzimierz Bolecki, „*Inny świat*"*Gustawa Herlinga-Grudzińskiego* (Warsaw: WSiP, 1997), 31.

90. Ibid., 101.

8. The Passing of an Illusion?

1. See *Times*, March 7 and 11, 1953.

2. Quoted in Martin Esslin, *Bertolt Brecht: A Choice of Evils* (London: Eyre and Spottiswoode, 1959), 162.

3. Ol'ga Adamova-Sliozberg, *Put'* (Moscow: Vozvrashchenie, 1993), 80.

4. Barbara Skarga, *Po wyzwoleniu . . . (1944–1956)* (Warsaw: Aletheia, 2000), 227.

5. Walter J. Ciszek, *With God in Russia* (New York: Image Books, 1966), 221.

6. Ibid., 240.

7. Liubov Bershadskaia, *Rastoptannye zhizni. Rasskaz byvshei politzakliuchennoi* (Paris: Piat' kontinentov, 1975), 95.

8. Galina Ivanova, *Labor Camp Socialism* (Armonk, NY: Routledge, 2000), 124. See also Anne Applebaum, *Gulag: A History* (New York: Doubleday, 2003), 479.

9. Quoted in Paul Johnson, *Intellectuals* (New York: Harper & Row, 1988), 191.

10. *L'Express* November 9, 1956. Quoted in Francois Furet, *The Passing of an Illusion: The Idea of Communism in the Twentieth Century* (Chicago: University of Chicago Press, 1999), 556–557, n.24.

11. Richard Pipes, *Russia Under the Bolshevik Regime* (New York: Vintage, 1995), 211.

12. Martin Malia, *Russia Under Western Eyes: From the Bronze Horseman to the Lenin Mausoleum* (Cambridge, MA: Harvard University Press, 1999), 377.

13. Ibid.

14. Joseph Scholmer, *Vorkuta* (New York: Widenfeld and Nicolson, 1954); *La grève de Vorkuta* (Paris: Amiot Dumont, 1954).

15. *US News and World Report*, March 21, 1958.

16. Jean Nicolas, *Onze ans au paradis* (Paris: Artheme Fayard, 1958).

17. John Noble, *I Was a Slave in Russia* (New York: Devin-Adair, 1960).

18. Walter J. Ciszek, *With God in Russia* (New York: America Press, 1964).

19. Victor Herman, *Coming Out of the Ice* (New York: Harcourt Brace, 1978).

20. Alexander Dolgun with Patrick Watson, *Alexander Dolgun's Story: An American in the Gulag* (New York: Knopf, 1975).

21. Aino Kuusinen, *Der Gott stürzt seine Engel* (Minich: Fritz Molden, 1972); *Before and After Stalin: A Personal Account of Soviet Russia from 1926 to the 1960s*

(London: M. Joseph, 1974); *The Rings of Destiny* (New York: William Morrow, 1974).

22. Menachem Begin, *White Nights: The Story of a Prisoner in Russia* (London: Macdonald, 1957 [republished New York: Harper & Row, 1977]); first Hebrew edition: *Be-lelot levanim* (Jerusalem: Karni, 1953).

23. See Viktor Shklovskii, "Perekovka na kanale Volga-Moskva," in *Bolshevistskaia Pechat'*, no. 1, 1937.

24. Aleksandr Solzhenitsyn, *The Oak and the Calf: Sketches of Literary Life in the Soviet Union* (New York: Harper and Row, 1980), 42. See also Alexis Klimoff, ed., *Critical Companion to Solzhenitsyn's* One Day in the Life of Ivan Denisovich (Evanston, IL: Northwestern University Press, 1997), 99; Vladimir Lakshin, Novyi Mir *vo vremena Khrushcheva. Dnevnik i poputnoe* (Moscow: Knizhnaia palata, 1991).

25. *Literaturnaia Gazeta*, January 10, 1963.

26. *Literaturnaia Gazeta*, June 4, 1964.

27. *Izvestiia*, January 15, 1964.

28. Eugenia Ginzburg, *Journey into the Whirlwind* (New York: Harcourt Brace Jovanovich, 1967), 3.

29. Ibid., 417–418. The introduction appeared in English translation as the epilogue.

30. Olga Cooke and Rimma Volynska, "An Interview with Vasilii Aksenov," in *Canadian American Slavic Studies* no. 1 (2005), 25. At the time of the publication of Solzhenitsyn's *One Day in the Life of Ivan Denisovich* and shortly afterward, several works of Gulag literature written by survivors appeared in the USSR. They followed the Khrushchevian party line and presented the camp experiences of communist believers whose faith was never undermined despite their ordeals in the Gulag. These works included Georgii Shelest, "Kolymskie zapisi," *Znamia* 9 (1964); Iurii Piliar, "Liudi ostaiutsia liud'mi," *Iunost'*, 6, 7, 8 (1963), 3, 4, 5 (1964); Andrei Aldan-Semenov, "Barel'ef na skale," *Moskva* 7 (1964); Boris D'iakov, "Povest' o perezhitom," *Oktiabr'*, 7 (1964); Aleksandr Gorbatov, *Gody i voiny* (Moscow: Voenizdat, 1965). However, these works were not translated and published abroad, with the exception of Gorbatov's memoir. See Alexander Gorbatov, *Years off my Life* (London: Constable, 1964).

31. Eugenia Ginzburg, *Within the Whirlwind* (New York: Harcourt Brace Jovanovich, 1981), 419.

32. The Russian original came out in Milan in 1979.

33. Ginzburg, *Within the Whirlwind*, 423.

34. Ibid., 153.

35. *Washington Post*, February 15, 1974.

36. Anne Applebaum, *Gulag: A History* (New York: Doubleday, 2003), 530.

37. *The Third Wave: Russian Literature in Emigration*, ed. by Olga Matich and Michael Heim (Ann Arbor: Ardis, 1984), 125.

38. Joseph Brodsky, *Less Than One* (New York: Farrar, Straus and Giroux, 1987), 26–27.

39. Tadeusz Klimowicz, *Obywatele Arkadii. Losy pisarzy rosyjskich po roku 1917* (Wrocław: Wydawnictwo Uniwersytetu Wrocławskiego, 1993), 98.

40. Klimowicz, *Obywatele Arkadii*, 99.

41. Michael Browne, ed., *Ferment in the Ukraine* (Woodhaven, NY: Macmillan, 1971), 3. See also Applebaum, *Gulag*, 533.

42. Applebaum, Ibid.

43. Quotation from Tadeusz Klimowicz, *Przewodnik po współczesnej literaturze rosyjskiej i jej okolicach (1917–1996)* (Wrocław: Towarzystwo Przyjaciół Polonistyki Wrocławskiej, 1996), 399.

44. *Sąd idzie! Stenogram z procesu A. Siniawskiego i J. Daniela (A. Terca i M. Arżaka). Moskwa, luty 1966* (Paris: Kultura, 1966), 104.

45. Ibid., 117–118.

46. Quotation from Klimowicz, *Obywatele Arkadii*, 103.

47. Ibid., 99.

48. *Times*, January 31, 1966.

49. Pavel Litvinov, ed., *The Trial of the Four: A Collection of Materials on the Case of Galanskov, Ginzburg, Dobrovolsky and Lashkova, 1967–68* (New York: Viking, 1972), 227.

50. Anatoly Marchenko, *My Testimony* (New York: Dutton, 1969), 1, 3.

51. *On the Death of Prisoner of Conscience Anatoly Marchenko* (Amnesty International Press Release). Quoted in Applebaum, *Gulag*, 559.

52. Andrei Amalrik, *Involuntary Journey to Siberia* (New York: Harcourt Brace Jovanovich, 1970).

53. Pyotr Yakir, *A Childhood in Prison* (New York: Macmillan, 1972).

54. Quotation from Klimowicz, *Przewodnik*, 256.

55. Quotation from Klimowicz, *Przewodnik*, 683.

56. Vladimir Bukovsky, *To Build a Castle: My Life as a Dissenter* (New York: Viking, 1978), 357.

57. Petr Grigorenko, *Mysli sumasshedshego* (Amsterdam: Fond im. Gertsena, 1973); *The Grigorenko Papers* (Boulder, CO: Westview, 1976).

58. Zhores Medvedev and Roy Medvedev, *A Question of Madness* (London: Macmillan, 1971); Gennady Shimanov, *Notes from the Red House* (Montreal: Russian Orthodox Church Outside of Russia in Canada, 1971).

59. Quotation from Jakub Kumoch, "Władimir Bukowski—bicz na samodzierżawców," in *Rzeczpospolita*, February 24, 2007.

60. Ibid.

61. *Izvestiia*, October 24, 1971.

62. *The Observer*, September 9, 1973.

63. Andrei Grigorenko, "In Time of Trouble: The Life of P. G. Grigorenko's Family During His Persecution," in *The Grigorenko Papers*. See also Paul Hollander, *Political Pilgrims: Western Intellectuals in Search of the Good Society* (New Brunswick, NJ: Transaction, 1998), 383.

64. Sidney Bloch and Peter Reddaway, *Russia's Political Hospitals: The Abuse of Psychiatry in the Soviet Union* (London: Victor Gollancz, 1977), 121.

65. *New York Times*, October 16, 1973.

66. *Stern*, October 31, 1973, 26.

67. Bloch and Reddaway, *Russia's Political Hospitals*, 122.

68. Ibid.

69. *Stern*, October 31, 1973. For more see Bloch and Reddaway, *Russia's Political Hospitals*, 123–124.

70. Ibid.

71. See *Daily Express*, November 9, 1973; *Paris Match*, November 10, 1973.

72. *Guardian*, September 29, 1973; *Soviet News*, October 9, 1973. See also Bloch, Reddaway, *Russia's Political Hospitals*, 309.

73. *Guardian*, November 17, 1973.

74. Applebaum, *Gulag*, 551.

75. Leopold Labedz, *Solzhenitsyn: A Documentary Record* (Bloomington: Indiana University Press, 1973), 224.

76. Quotation from Michael Scammell, *Solzhenitsyn: A Biography* (New York: Norton, 1984), 683.

77. Labedz, *Solzhenitsyn*, 242.

78. Aleksandr Solzhenitsyn, *The Oak and the Calf* (London: Collins, 1979), 303.

79. Scammell, *Solzhenitsyn*, 715.

80. Solzhenitsyn, *The Oak and the Calf*, 497.

81. Solzhenitsyn, *The Oak and the Calf*, 349.

82. Solzhenitsyn, *The Oak and the Calf*, 389.

83. Ibid.

84. *Times*, January 3 and 4, 1974.

85. Solzhenitsyn, *The Oak and the Calf*, 532–534.

86. *Times*, January 25, 1974.

87. D.M. Thomas, *Alexander Solzhenitsyn: A Century in His Life* (New York: St. Martin's Press, 1998), 420.

88. Thomas, *Alexander Solzhenitsyn*, 423.

89. Scammell, *Solzhenitsyn*, 840.

90. Ibid.

91. Heinrich Böll, *Missing Persons and Other Essays* (London: McGraw-Hill, 1977), 169–170.

92. Thomas, *Alexander Solzhenitsyn*, 421.

93. Scammell, *Solzhenitsyn*, 851.

94. *Washington Post*, February 15, 1974.

95. *Guardian*, February 14, 1974.

96. Thomas, *Alexander Solzhenitsyn*, 433.

97. Ibid.

98. Natalya Reshetovskaya, *Sanya: My Life with Alexander Solzhenitsyn* (Indianapolis: Bobbs-Merrill, 1975).

99. *The Last Circle* (Moscow: Novosti Press Agency Publishing House, 1974).

100. *New York Review of Books*, March 21, 1974.

101. Scammell, *Solzhenitsyn*, 877.

102. Gustaw Herling-Grudziński and Włodzimierz Bolecki, *Rozmowy w Dragonei* (Warsaw: Szpak, 1997), 115.

103. Quotation from Didier Eribon, *Michel Foucault* (Cambridge, MA: Harvard University Press, 1991), 266.

104. Bernard-Henri Lévy, *La barbarie `a visage humain* (Paris: Grasset, 1977), 165.

105. Scammell, *Solzhenitsyn*, 877.

106. Hilton Kramer, "The Flowers on Sartre's Grave," *Commentary*, July 1993.

107. Aleksandr I. Solzhenitsyn, *The Gulag Archipelago*, vol. 1 (New York: Harper and Row, 1974), 173–174.

108. Ibid., 168.

109. Raymond Aron, "Alexander Solzhenitsyn and European Leftism," in *In Defense of Political Reason. Essays by Raymond Aron*, ed. by Daniel J. Mahoney (Lanham, MD: Rowman & Littlefield, 1994), 123.

Coda

1. Peter Pomerantsev, *Nothing Is True and Everything Is Possible: The Surreal Heart of the New Russia* (New York: Public Affairs, 2014), 230–231.

2. Barbara Skarga, *Po wyzwoleniu… (1944–1956)* (Warsaw: Aleteia, 2000), 199.

3. Pomerantsev, *Nothing Is True and Everything Is Possible*, 234.

BIBLIOGRAPHY

Abarinow, Władimir. *Oprawcy z Katynia*. Kraków: Znak, 2007.

Abuses of Psychiatry for Political Repression in the Soviet Union. Washington, DC: US Government Printing Office, 1972.

Acheson, Judy. *Young America Looks at Russia*. New York: Frederick Stokes, 1932.

Adamova-Sliozberg, Olga. *Put'*. Moscow: Vozvrashchenie, 1993.

Adler, Nanci. *The Gulag Survivor*. New Brunswick, NJ: Transaction, 2002.

———. *Keeping Faith with the Party: Communist Believers Return from the Gulag*. Bloomington: Indiana University Press, 2012.

Albrecht, Karl. *Der verratene Sozialismus: Zehn Jahre als hoher Staatsbeamter in der Sowjetunion*. Berlin: Nibelungen, 1938.

Amalrik, Andrei. *Involuntary Journey to Siberia*. Translated by Manya Harrari and Max Hayward. New York: Harcourt Brace Jovanovich, 1970.

———. *Will the USSR Survive until 1984?* Translated by Peter Reddaway. London: Pelican, 1970.

Amis, Martin. *Koba the Dread: Laughter and the Twenty Million*. New York: Vintage, 2002.

Applebaum, Anne. *Gulag: A History*. New York: Doubleday, 2003.

———. *Red Famine: Stalin's War on Ukraine*. New York: Doubleday, 2017.

Arendt, Hannah. *The Origins of Totalitarianism*. New York: Harcourt Brace, 1951.

Aron, Raymond. *The Opium of the Intellectuals*. Translated by Terence Kilmartin. New York: Doubleday, 1957.

Ash, Timothy Garton. *The Uses of Adversity: Essays on the Fate of Central Europe*. New York: Random House, 1990.

Ashmead-Bartlet, E. *The Riddle of Russia*. London: Cassell, 1929.

Baberowski, Jörg. *Der rote Terror. Die Geschichte des Stalinismus*. Munich: DVA, 2003.

———. *Verbannte Erde. Stalins Herrschaft der Gewalt*. Munich: C. H. Beck, 2012.

Bakirov, E., and Valerii Shantsev, eds. *Butovskii poligon 1937–1938. Kniga pamiati zhertv politicheskikh repressii*, vols. 1–8. Moscow: Panorama, 1998–2004.

Barbusse, Henri. *Staline. Un monde nouveau vu 'a travers un homme*. Paris, 1936; English edition: *Stalin: A New World Seen through the Man*. Translated by Vyvyan Holland. New York: Macmillan, 1936.

Bardach, Janusz (with Kathleen Gleason). *Man Is Wolf to Man: Surviving Stalin's Gulag*. London: Scribner, 1998.

Barker, Elizabeth. *Churchill and Eden at War*. New York: St. Martin's Press, 1978.

Barnes, Annette. *Seeing Through Self-Deception*. Cambridge: Cambridge University Press, 1997.

Bateson, Edward, and Alan Pim. *Report on Russian Timber Camps*. London: E. Benn, 1931.

Beal, Fred. *Proletarian Journey*. New York: Hillman-Curl, 1937.

Beausobre, Julia de. *The Woman Who Would Not Die*. London: Chatto & Windus, 1938.

Bednyi, Demian. *Sobranie sochinenii v vos'mi tomakh*. Moscow: Khudozhestvennaia literatura, 1964.

Begin, Menachem. *White Nights: The Story of a Prisoner in Russia*. Translated by Katie Kaplan. London: Macdonald, 1957.

Behrends, Jan C. "Back from the USSR: The Anti-Comintern's Publications on Soviet Russia in Nazi Germany (1935–41)." *Kritika: Explorations in Russian and Eurasian History* 10, no. 3 (Summer 2009): 527–56.

Berberova, Nina. *Poslednie i pervye. Delo Kravchenko*. Moscow: Izdatel'stvo im. Sabashnikovykh, 2000.

Berger, Joseph. *Nothing But the Truth*. New York: John Day, 1971.

Berkman, Alexander, ed. *Letters from Russian Prisons*. New York: A. & C. Boni, 1925.

Bershadskaia, Liubov. *Rastoptannye zhizni. Rasskaz byvshei politzakliuchennoi*. Paris: Piat' kontinentov, 1975.

Bessonov, Yuri. *My Twenty-Six Prisons and My Escape from Solovetski*. London: J. Cape, 1928; French edition: *Mes 26 prisons et mon évasion de Solovki*. Paris: Payot, 1928.

Bethell, Nicholas. *The Last Secret: The Delivery to Stalin of Over Two Million Russians by Britain and the United States*. New York: Basic Books, 1974.

Bettelheim, Bruno. *Surviving*. New York: Knopf, 1979.

Bevan, Aneurin, John Strachey, George Strauss, and Virginia Woolf. *What We Saw in Russia*. London: Hogarth Press, 1931.

Bloch, Sidney, and Peter Reddaway. *Russia's Political Hospitals: The Abuse of Psychiatry in the Soviet Union*. London: Victor Gollancz, 1977.

Blok, Aleksandr. *Dvenadtsat'*. St. Petersburg: Alkonost, 1918.

Bolecki, Włodzimierz. *"Inny świat" Gustawa Herlinga-Grudzińskiego.* Warsaw: WSiP, 1997.

Böll, Heinrich. *Missing Persons and Other Essays.* Translated by Leila Vennewitz. London: McGraw-Hill, 1977.

Bollinger, Martin. *Stalin's Slave Ships: Kolyma, the Gulag Fleet and the Role of the West.* Westport, CT: Praeger, 2003.

Bolshevo: Literaturnyi istoriko-kraevedcheskii al'manakh. Bolshevo: Pisatel', 1994.

Bouré, Julien. *Vu et entendu en URSS.* Paris: Les Éditions des Presses Modernes, 1938.

Brodsky, Joseph. *Less Than One.* New York: Farrar, Straus and Giroux, 1987.

Bryant, Louise. *Mirrors of Moscow.* New York: Selzer, 1923.

Buber-Neumann, Margarete. *Under Two Dictators.* Translated by Edward Fitzgerald. London: Victor Gollancz, 1949; German edition: *Als Gefangene bei Stalin und Hitler.* Munich: Verlag der Zwolf, 1949; French edition: *Déportée en Sibérie.* Paris: Seuil, 1949.

Buca, Edward. *Vorkuta.* Translated by Michael Lisinski and Kennedy Wells. London: Constable, 1976.

Bukharin, Nikolai. *Teoriia istoricheskogo materializma.* Moscow: Gosizdat, 1921.

Bukharin, Nikolai, and Evgenii Preobrazhenskii, *Azbuka kommunizma.* St. Petersburg: Gosizdat, 1920; First German and English editions: 1921 and 1922.

Bukovsky, Vladimir. *To Build a Castle: My Life as a Dissenter.* Translated by Michael Scammell. New York: Viking, 1978.

——— [Boukovsky, Vladimir], ed. *Une nouvelle maladie mentale en URSS: l'opposition.* Paris: Seuil, 1971.

Bukovsky, Vladimir, and Semyon Gluzman. *A Manual of Psychiatry for Political Dissidents.* London: Amnesty International, 1975.

Bullitt, William C. *The Bullitt Mission to Russia: Testimony before the Committee on Foreign Relations, U.S. Senate.* New York: B.W. Huebsch, 1919.

Burrell, George A. *An American Engineer Looks at Russia.* Boston: Stratford, 1932.

Buxhoeveden, Baroness Sophie. *Left Behind: Fourteen Months in Siberia during the Revolution, December 1917–February 1919.* London: Longmans Green, 1929.

Buxton, D. F. *The Challenge of Bolshevism: A New Social Ideal.* London: Allen and Unwin, 1928.

Callcott, Mary Stevenson. *Russian Justice.* New York: Macmillan, 1935.

Caute, David. *The Fellow-Travelers: Intellectual Friends of Communism.* New Haven, CT: Yale University Press, 1988.

Cederholm, Boris. *In the Clutches of the Cheka.* Translated by F. H. Lyons. Boston: Houghton Mifflin, 1929; *Au pays du NEP et de la Tcheka. Dans les prisons de l'U.R.S.S.* Paris: J. Talandier, 1928.

Chalidze, Valery. *To Defend These Rights: Human Rights and the Soviet Union.* Translated by Guy Daniels. New York: Random House, 1975.

Chamberlin, William Henry. *Russia's Iron Age.* Boston: Little Brown, 1934.

Chatterjee, Choi, and Beth Holmgren, eds. *Americans Experience Russia: Encountering the Enigma, 1917 to the Present.* Abingdon, VT: Routledge, 2012.

Chekhov, Anton. *The Island: A Journey to Sakhalin.* Translated by Brian Reeve. New York: Washington Square Press, 1967.

Chukovskaya, Lydia. *Sofia Petrovna.* First published in English as *The Deserted House.* Translated by Aline Werth. New York: Dutton, 1967.

Cienciala, Anna, Natalia Lebedeva, and Wojciech Materski, eds. *Katyn: A Crime without Punishment.* New Haven, CT: Yale University Press, 2007.

Ciliga, Ante. *The Russian Enigma.* Translated by Tony Kahn. London: Labour Book, 1940; *Au pays du grand mensonge.* Paris: Gallimard, 1938.

Ciszek, Walter J. *With God in Russia.* New York: America Press, 1964.

Citrine, Walter. *I Search for Truth in Russia.* London: Routledge, 1936.

Clément, Olivier. *The Spirit of Solzhenitsyn.* Translated by Sarah Fawcet and Paul Burns. London: Search Press, 1976.

Coeuré, Sophie. *La grande lueur à l'Est. Les Français et l'Union Sovietique 1917–1939.* Paris: Seuil, 1999.

Cohen-Solal, Annie. *Sartre: A Life.* New York: Pantheon, 1987.

Cole, G. D. H. *Europe, Russia, and the Future.* London: Macmillan, 1942.

Cole, Margaret, ed. *Twelve Studies in Soviet Russia.* London: V. Gollancz, 1933.

Colville, John. *The Fringes of Power: 10 Downing Street Diaries 1939–55.* New York: Norton, 1985.

Conolly, Violet. *Soviet Tempo: A Journal of Travel in Russia.* London: Sheed and Ward, 1937.

Conquest, Robert. *The Great Terror: A Reassessment.* Oxford: Oxford University Press, 1990.

———. *The Harvest of Sorrow: Soviet Collectivization and the Terror-Famine.* London: Hutchinson, 1986.

———. *Kolyma: The Arctic Death Camps.* New York: Viking, 1978.

———. *The Soviet Deportation of Nationalities.* London: Macmillan, 1960.

Conrad, Joseph. *Under Western Eyes.* Cologne: Könemann, 2000.

Cooney, Terry A. *The Rise of the New York Intellectuals: Partisan Review and Its Circle.* Madison: University of Wisconsin Press, 1986.

Correspondence between the Chairman of the Council of Ministers of the USSR and the President of the USA and the Prime Minister of Great Britain during the Great Patriotic War of 1941–1945. Moscow: Gosizdat 1957.

Corvin-Romanski, Andrew. *Prisoners of the Night.* Translated by Walter M. Besterman and Blair Taylor. Boston: Bobbs-Merrill, 1948.

Counts, George. *A Ford Crosses Soviet Russia.* Boston: Stratford, 1930.

Courtois, Stéphane, Nicolas Werth, Jean-Louis Panné, Andrzej Paczkowski, Karel Bartosek, and Jean-Louis Margolin. *The Black Book of Communism: Crimes, Terror, Repression.* Translated by Jonathan Murphy and Mark Kramer. Cambridge, MA: Harvard University Press, 1999.

Crossman, Richard, ed. *The God That Failed: Six Studies in Communism.* London: Hamilton, 1950.

Culbert, David. *Mission to Moscow.* Madison: University of Wisconsin Press, 1980.

Custine, Astolphe Marquis de. *La Russie en 1939.* Paris: Libraire d'Amyot, 1846.

———. *Letters from Russia.* Translated by Robin Buss. New York: Penguin, 2014.

Czapski, Joseph. *The Inhuman Land.* Translated by Gerald Hopkins. London: Chatto and Windus, 1951; French: *Terre inhumaine.* Paris: self, 1949.

———. *Souvenirs de Starobielsk.* Paris: Collection Temoignages, 1945.

Czuchnowski, Marian. *Tyfus, teraz słowiki.* London: Modern Writing, 1951.

Dallin, David, and Boris Nicolaevsky. *Forced Labor in Soviet Russia.* New Haven, CT: Yale University Press, 1947.

Dalton, Hugh. *The Fateful Years.* London: Frederic Muller, 1957.

Daniel, Yuli. *Prison Poems.* Translated by David Burg and Arthur Boyars. London: O'Hara, 1971.

Danilov, Viktor, Roberta Manning, and Lynne Viola, eds. *Tragediia sovetskoi derevni: dokumenty i materialy.* Moscow: ROSSPEN, 1999–2002.

David-Fox, Michael. "The 'Heroic Life' of a Friend of Stalinism: Romain Rolland and Soviet Culture." *Slavonica* 11, no. 1 (April 2005): 3–29.

———. *Showcasing the Great Experiment: Cultural Diplomacy and Western Visitors to the Soviet Union, 1921–1941.* Oxford: Oxford University Press, 2012.

Davies, Joseph E. *Mission to Moscow.* New York: Simon and Schuster, 1941.

Davis, Jerome. *Behind Soviet Power: Stalin and the Russians.* New York: Readers' Press, 1946.

———. *The New Russia.* New York: John Day, 1933.

Dekrety sovetskoi vlasti. Sbornik materialov. Moscow: Akademiia Nauk SSSR/ Rossiiskoi Federatsii, vols. 1–18, 1957–2009.

Des Pres, Terrence. *The Survivor: An Anatomy of Life in the Death Camps.* Oxford: Oxford University Press, 1976.

Dewey, John. *Impressions of Soviet Russia and the Revolutionary World: Mexico-China-Turkey.* New York: New Republic, 1929.

———. *Not Guilty: Report of the Commission of Inquiry into the Charges Made against Leon Trotsky.* New York: Harper, 1938.

Diggins, John P. *The American Left in the Twentieth Century.* New York: Harcourt Brace Jovanovich, 1973.

Djilas, Milovan. *Conversations with Stalin.* Translated by Michael Petrovich. New York: Harcourt Brace, 1962.

Dmitrievna, Olga. *Red Gaols.* London: Burns Oates & Washbourne, 1935; *18 Jahre Sowjetherrschaft.* Vienna, 1936.

Dolgun, Alexander (with Patrick Watson). *Alexander Dolgun's Story: An American in the Gulag.* New York: Knopf, 1975.

Dombrovsky, Yury. *The Keeper of Antiquities.* Translated by Michael Glenny. London: Longmans, 1969.

Dos Passos, John. *The Theme Is Freedom.* New York: Dodd Mead, 1956.

Dostoevskii, Fedor [Dostoevsky, Fyodor]. "Zapiski iz metrvogo doma," "Zapiski iz podpol'ia." In *Sobranie sochinenii,* vols. 3–4. Leningrad: Akademiia Nauk SSSR, 1989.

Dreiser, Theodore. *Dreiser Looks at Russia.* New York: Horace Liveright, 1928.

Duchess of Athol, M.P. *The Conscription of a People.* London: Philipp Allan, 1931.

Duguet, Raymond. *Un bagne en Russie rouge.* Paris: Jules Talandier, 1928.

Dunlop, John, Richard Haugh, and Alexis Klimoff, eds. *Alexander Solzhenitsyn: Critical Essays and Documentary Materials.* New York: Macmillan, 1975.

Duranty, Walter. *Duranty Reports Russia.* New York: Viking, 1934.

———. *The Kremlin and the People.* New York: Reynal and Hitchcock, 1941.

———. *USSR.* New York: J. B. Lippincott, 1944.

Eagles, Keith D. *Ambassador Joseph E. Davies and American-Soviet Relations, 1937–1941.* New York: Garland, 1985.

Eckart, Dietrich. *Der Bolschewismus von Moses bis Lenin: Zwiegespräch zwischen Adolf Hitler und mir.* Munich: Franz Eher Nachf, 1925.

Eddy, Sherwood. *The Challenge of Russia.* New York: Farrar and Rinehart, 1931.

Ekart, Antoni. *Vanished without Trace: The Story of Seven Years in Soviet Russia.* Translated by E. Sykes and E. D. Virpsha. London: Max Parrish, 1954; French edition: *Echappé de Russie.* Paris: Hachette, 1949.

Elster, Jon, ed. *The Multiple Self.* Cambridge: Cambridge University Press, 1988.

Epstein, Edward Jay. *Dossier: The Secret History of Armand Hammer.* New York: Carroll & Graf, 1999.

Erenburg, Il'ia. *Zhizn' i gibel' Nikolaia Kurbova.* Berlin: Gelikon, 1923.

Essad-Bey (Leo Nussimbaum). *OGPU—The Plot against the World.* Translated by Huntley Patterson. New York: Viking, 1933.

Esslin, Martin. *Bertolt Brecht: A Choice of Evils.* London: Eyre and Spottiswoode, 1959.

Evstafeev, Alexander. *Why I Escaped from Soviet Russia.* Seattle: Privately printed, 1937.

Fairburn, William A. *Forced Labor in Soviet Russia.* New York: Nation, 1931.

Fehling, Helmut. *One Great Prison: The Story Behind Russia's Unreleased POWs.* Boston: Beacon, 1951.

Feiler, Arthur. *The Experiment of Bolshevism.* Translated by H. J. Stenning. London: Allen & Unwin, 1930.

Feuchtwanger, Lion. *Moscow 1937: My Visit Described for My Friends.* Translated by Irene Josephy. New York: Viking, 1937.

Filene, Peter. *Americans and the Soviet Experiment, 1917–1933.* Cambridge, MA: Harvard University Press, 1967.

———, ed. *American Views of Soviet Russia 1917–1965.* Belmont: Dorsey, 1968.

Fischer, Louis. *The Road to Yalta: Soviet Foreign Relations, 1941–1945.* New York: Harper & Row, 1972.

———. *Soviet Journey.* New York: H. Smith and R. Haas, 1935.

Fittkau, Gerhard. *My Thirty-Third Year.* New York: Farrar Straus, 1958.

Fleming, John V. *The Anti-Communist Manifestos: Four Books That Shaped the Cold War.* New York: Norton, 2009.

Frank, Waldo. *Dawn in Russia.* New York: Scribner's Sons, 1932.

Freund, Gerald. *Unholy Alliance.* New York: Harcourt, Brace & Co, 1957.

Furet, François. *The Passing of an Illusion: The Idea of Communism in the Twentieth Century.* Translated by Deborah Furet. Chicago: University of Chicago Press, 1999.

Gaddis, John Lewis. *Russia, the Soviet Union, and the United States.* New York: McGraw-Hill, 1990.

Gardner, Lloyd C. *Spheres of Influence: The Great Powers Partition Europe, from Munich to Yalta.* Chicago: Ivan R. Dee, 1993.

General Sikorski Historical Institute, ed. *Documents on Polish-Soviet Relations, 1939–1945.* London: Heinemann, 1967.

Getty, J. Arch, and Roberta Manning, eds. *Stalinist Terror: New Perspectives.* New York: Cambridge University Press, 1993.

Gide, André. *Afterthoughts on the USSR.* New York: Dial Press, 1938; *Retouches à mon Retour de l'URSS.* Paris: Gallimard, 1937.

———. *Littérature engagée.* Paris: Gallimard, 1950.

———. *Return from the USSR.* New York: Knopf, 1937; *Retour de l'URSS.* Paris: Gallimard, 1936.

Gilbert, G. M. *Nuremberg Diary.* New York: Farrar Straus, 1947.

Gilbert, Martin. *Winston S. Churchill,* vol. 7, *Road to Victory, 1941–45.* London: Heineman, 1986.

Gilboa, Joshua. *Confess! Confess!: Eight Years in Soviet Prisons.* Translated by Dov Ben Aba. Boston: Little, Brown, 1968.

Ginzburg, Eugenia. *Journey into the Whirlwind.* Translated by Paul Stevenson and Max Hayward. New York: Harcourt Brace Jovanovich, 1967.

———. *Within the Whirlwind.* Translated by Ian Boland. New York: Harcourt Brace Jovanovich, 1981.

Glaeser, Ernst, and F. G. Weiskopf, eds. *The Country without Unemployment*. New York: International, 1931.

Gliksman, Jerzy. *Tell the West*. New York: Gresham, 1948.

Glucksmann, André. *La cuisiniere et le mangeur d'hommes. Essai sur l'Etat, le marxisme et les camps de concentration*. Paris: Seuil, 1975.

Goldman, Emma. *My Disillusionment in Russia*. New York: Doubleday, 1923.

Gollancz, Victor, ed. *The Betrayal of the Left: An Examination and Refutation of Communist Policy from October 1939 to January 1941*. London: V. Gollancz, 1941.

Golubev, A. V. *Rossiia i Zapad: Formirovanie vneshnepoliticheskikh stereotipov v soznanii rossiiskogo obshchestva pervoi poloviny XX veka*. Moscow: Institut Istorii RAN, 1998.

Gonzalez, Valentin, and Julian Gorkin. *El Campesino: Life and Death in Soviet Russia*. Translated by Ilsa Barea. New York: Putnam, 1952.

Gorbatov, Alexander. *Years Off My Life: Memoirs of General of the Soviet Army*. Translated by Gordon Clough and Anthony Cash. London: Constable, 1964.

Gorcheva, A. *Pressa Gulaga (1918–1955)*. Moscow: Izdat. Moskovskogo universiteta, 1996.

Gorky, Maxim. *Untimely Thoughts: Essays on Revolution, Culture, and the Bolsheviks, 1917–1918*. Translated by Herman Ermolaev. New Haven, CT: Yale University Press, 1995.

Gorky [Gor'kii], Maksim. "Solovki." In *Sobranie sochinenii v 30 tomakh*, vol. 17. Moscow: Gos. izdat. khud. literatury, 1952.

Gorky [Gor'kii], Maksim, Leopol'd Averbakh, Semen Firin, eds., *Belomorsko-Baltiiskii Kanal imeni Stalina: Istoriia stroitel'stva*. Moscow: GIZ, 1934. English version: *Belomor: An Account of the Construction of the New Canal between the White Sea and the Baltic Sea*. Edited by Amabel Williams-Ellis. New York: H. Smith and R. Haas, 1935.

Grémion, Pierre. *Intelligence de l'anicommunisme: Le Congrés pour la liberté de la culture à Paris, 1950–1975*. Paris: Fayard, 1995.

Grigorenko, Petro. *Memoirs*. Translated by Thomas Whitney. New York: Norton, 1982.

———. *Mysli sumasshedshego*. Amsterdam: Fond im. Gertsena, 1973; English selection: *The Grigorenko Papers*. Boulder, CO: Westview, 1976.

Gross, Babette. *Willie Münzenberg—eine politische Biographie*. Stuttgart: Deutsche Verlags-Anstalt, 1967.

Grossman, Vasily. *Forever Flowing*. Translated by Thomas Whitney. New York: Harper & Row, 1972.

———. *Life and Fate*. Translated by Robert Chandler. New York: Harper & Row, 1985.

Haldane, Charlotte. *Truth Will Out*. New York: Vanguard, 1950.

Halpern, Ada. *Liberation—Russian Style*. London: Maxlove, 1945, also published as *Conducted Tour*. London: Sheed & Ward, 1945.

Hammer, Armand. *Hammer by Armand Hammer with Neil Lyndon*. New York: G. P. Putnam's Sons, 1987.

Harper, Paul V. *The Russia I Believe In: Memoirs of Samuel N. Harper, 1902–1941*. Chicago: University of Chicago Press, 1945.

Hayman, Ronald. *Brecht: A Biography*. New York: Oxford University Press, 1983.

Haynes, John Earl, and Harvey Klehr. *In Denial: Historians, Communism and Espionage*. New York: Encounter Books, 2005.

———. *Venona: Decoding Soviet Espionage in America*. New Haven, CT: Yale University Press, 1999.

Haynes, John Earl, Harvey Klehr, and Kyril M. Anderson. *The Soviet World of American Communism*. New Haven, CT: Yale University Press, 1998.

Hecker, Julius F. *The Communist Answer to the World's Needs*. London: Chapman and Hall, 1935.

———. *Religion and Communism: A Study of Religion and Atheism in Soviet Russia*. London: Chapman and Hall, 1933.

———. *Religion under the Soviets*. New York: Vanguard, 1927.

Heller [Geller], Mikhail. *Kontsentratsionnyi mir i sovetskaia literatura*. London: Overseas Publications Interchange, 1974.

Hemingway, Ernest. *For Whom the Bell Tolls*. New York: Scribner's Sons, 1940.

Henderson, Loy. *The Question of Trust: The Origins of U.S.-Soviet Diplomatic Relations. The Memoirs of Loy W. Henderson*. Palo Alto: Hoover Institution Press, 1986.

Hergt, Klaus. *Exiled to Siberia: A Polish Child's World War II Journey*. Cheboygan, MI: Crescent Lake, 2000.

Herling [Herling-Grudziński], Gustaw. *A World Apart*. Translated by Andrzej Ciołkosz. London: Heinemann, 1951.

Herling [Herling-Grudziński], Gustaw, and Włodzimierz Bolecki. *Rozmowy w Dragonei*. Warsaw: Szpak, 1997.

Herman, Victor. *Coming Out of the Ice*. New York: Harcourt Brace, 1978.

[Herzen, Aleksandr] Gertsen, Aleksandr. *Sobranie sochinenii v tridtsati tomakh*. Moscow: Izdatel'stvo Akademii Nauk SSSR, 1954.

Hicks, Granville. *Where We Came Out*. New York: Viking, 1954.

Hills, Denis. *Tyrants and Mountains: A Reckless Life*. London: Murray, 1992.

Hindus, Maurice. *The Great Offensive*. New York: Smith and Haas, 1933.

Hobsbawm, Eric J. *Revolutionaries*. New York: New Press, 1973.

Hodgkin, H. T. *Seeing Ourselves through Russia: A Book for Private and Group Study*. New York: R. Long and R. Smith, 1932.

Hollander, Paul. *The End of Commitment: Intellectuals, Revolutionaries and Political Morality*. Chicago: Ivan R. Dee, 2006.

———, ed. *From the Gulag to the Killing Fields: Personal Accounts of Political Violence and Repression in Communist States.* Wilmington, DE: ISI Books, 2006.

———. *Political Pilgrims: Western Intellectuals in Search of the Good Society.* New Brunswick, NJ: Transaction, 1998.

Holmgren, Beth. *Women's Works in Stalin's Times: On Lidiia Chukovskaia and Nedezhda Mandelstam.* Bloomington: Indiana University Press, 1993.

Hook, Sidney, Vladimir Bukovsky, and Paul Hollander. *Soviet Hypocrisy and Western Gullibility.* Washington, DC: Ethics and Public Policy Center, 1987.

Howe, Irving, and Louis Coser. *The American Communist Party: A Critical History, 1919–1957.* Boston: Beacon, 1957.

Huxley, Julian. *A Scientist among the Soviets.* London: Harper, 1932.

Istrati, Panait. *Russia Unveiled.* Translated by R. J. S. Curtis. London: Allen & Unwin, 1931.

———. *Vers l'autre flamme après seize mois dans l'URSS.* Paris: Rieder, 1929.

Ivanova, Galina M. *Labor Camp Socialism: The Gulag in the Soviet Totalitarian System.* Translated by Carol Flath. New York: Routledge, 2015.

Jackowska, Anna Maria. *Sowiety na ławie oskarżonych. Polskie uczestnictwo w propagandowej zimnej wojnie we Francji w latach 1947–1952.* Warsaw: Instytut Pamięci Narodowej, 2018.

Jakobson, Michael. *Origins of the Gulag: The Soviet Prison System, 1917–1934.* Lexington: University Press of Kentucky, 2015.

Johnson, Hewlett. *The Socialist Sixth of the World.* London: Victor Gollancz, 1939.

———. *Soviet Russia since the War.* London: Boni and Gaer, 1947.

Johnson, Paul. *Intellectuals: From Marx and Tolstoy to Sartre and Chomsky.* New York: Harper & Row, 1988.

Jones, Gareth. *Experiences in Russia 1931: A Diary.* Pittsburgh: Alton, 1932.

Joukoff-Eudin, Xenia, and Harold H. Fisher. *Soviet Russia and the West, 1920–1927: A Documentary Survey.* Stanford, CA: Stanford University Press, 1957.

Judt, Tony. *Past Imperfect: French Intellectuals, 1944–1956.* Berkeley: University of California Press, 1992.

———, with Timothy Snyder. *Thinking the Twentieth Century.* New York: Penguin, 2013.

Kalpashnikov, Andrei. *Prisoner of Trotsky.* New York: Doubleday, 1920.

Kamiński, Andrzej. *Koszmar niewolnictwa. Obozy koncentracyjne od 1896 do dziś. Analiza.* Warsaw: Przedświt, 1990.

Kazin, Alfred. *Starting Out in the Thirties.* Boston: Atlantic, 1965.

Keeton, George W. *The Problem of the Moscow Trial.* London: A. & C. Black, 1933.

Kellogg, Michael. *The Russian Roots of Nazism: White Russians and the Making of National Socialism, 1917–1945.* New York: Cambridge University Press, 2006.

Kenez, Peter. *The Birth of the Propaganda State: Soviet Methods of Mass Mobilization, 1917–1929.* Cambridge: Cambridge University Press, 1985.

Kengor, Paul. *Dupes: How America's Adversaries Have Manipulated Progressives for a Century.* Wilmington, DE: ISI Books, 2010.

Kennan, George F. *Memoirs (1925–1950).* New York: Bantam, 1969.

———. *Russia and the West under Lenin and Stalin.* Boston: Little Brown, 1961.

Kennan, George F., and John Lukacs. *George F. Kennan and the Origins of the Containment, 1944–1946.* Columbia: University of Missouri Press, 1997.

Kern, Garry. *A Death in Washington: Walter G. Krivitsky and the Stalin Terror.* New York: Enigma, 2003.

———. *The Kravchenko Case: One Man's War on Stalin.* New York: Enigma, 2007.

Khlevniuk, Oleg. *The History of the Gulag: From Collectivization to the Great Terror.* Translated by Vadim Staklo. New Haven, CT: Yale University Press, 2004.

———. *Stalin: New Biography of a Dictator.* Translated by Nora Seligman Favorov. New Haven, CT: Yale University Press, 2015.

Kimball, Warren F. *The Juggler: Franklin Roosevelt as Wartime Statesman.* Princeton, NJ: Princeton University Press, 1991.

Kin, Viktor. *Izbrannoe.* Moscow: Sovetskii pisatel', 1965.

Kitchin, George. *Prisoner of the OGPU.* New York: Longmans, 1935.

Kizny, Tomasz. *La Grande Terreur en URSS 1937–1938.* Paris: Noir sur Blanc, 2013.

Klimoff, Alexis, ed. *Critical Companion to Solzhenitsyn's* One Day in the Life of Ivan Denisovich. Evanston, IL: Northwestern University Press, 1997.

Klimowicz, Tadeusz. *Obywatele Arkadii. Losy pisarzy rosyjskich po roku 1917.* Wrocław: Wydawnictwo Uniwersytetu Wrocławskiego, 1993.

———. *Przewodnik po współczesnej literaturze rosyjskiej i jej okolicach, 1917–1996.* Wrocław: Towarzystwo Przyjaciół Polonistyki Wrocławskiej, 1996.

Kmiecik, Jerzy. *A Boy in the Gulag.* London: Quartet, 1983.

Kniazev, Vasilii. *Krasnoe evangelie.* Petrograd: Izdatel'stvo Petrogradskogo Soveta rabochikh i krasnoarmeiskikh deputatov, 1918.

Koerber, Lenka. *Soviet Russia Fights Crime.* London: Routledge, 1934.

Koestler, Arthur. *Darkness at Noon.* Translated by Daphne Hardy. London: Macmillan, 1940.

———. *The Invisible Writing.* New York: Macmillan, 1954.

———. *The Yogi and the Commissar, and Other Essays.* New York: Macmillan, 1946.

Kolakowski, Leszek. *Main Currents of Marxism.* Translated by P. S. Falla. Oxford: Oxford University Press, 1978.

Kopelev, Lev. *Ease My Sorrows.* Translated by Antonina Bois. New York: Random House, 1983.

———. *No Jail for Thought.* Translated by Anthony Austin. London: Secker and Warburg, 1977.

Koppes, Clayton, and Gregory D. Black. *Hollywood Goes to War: How Politics and Propaganda Shaped World War II Movies.* New York: Free Press, 1987.

Kotkin, Stephen. *Magnetic Mountain: Stalinism as a Civilization.* Berkeley: University of California Press, 1997.

———. *Stalin: Paradoxes of Power, 1878–1928.* New York: Penguin, 2014.

———. *Stalin: Waiting for Hitler, 1929–1941.* New York: Penguin, 2017.

Krakowiecki, Anatol. *Kolyma. Les bagnes de l'or.* Paris: Les iles d'or, 1952.

Kravchenko, Victor. *I Chose Freedom.* New York: Scribner's Sons, 1946.

———. *I Chose Justice.* New York: Scribner's Sons, 1950.

Kriegel, Annie, and Stéphane Courtois. *Eugen Fried. Le grand secret du PCF.* Paris: Seuil, 1997.

Krivitsky, Walter. *In Stalin's Secret Service: An Exposé of Russia's Secret Policies by the Former Chief of the Soviet Intelligence in Western Europe.* Translated by Boris Shub. New York: Harper Bros. 1939.

Kucharzewski, Jan. *Od białego do czerwonego caratu.* London: Veritas, 1989.

Kupferman, Fred. *Au pays des Soviets. Le voyage français en Union soviétique, 1917–1939.* Paris: Gallimard Juillard, 1979.

Kuran, Timur. *Private Truths, Public Lies: The Social Consequences of Preference Falsification.* Cambridge, MA: Harvard University Press, 1997.

Kuromiya, Hiroaki. *Voices of the Dead: Stalin's Great Terror in the 1930s.* New Haven, CT: Yale University Press, 2007.

Kuusinen, Aino. *Before and after Stalin: A Personal Account of Soviet Russia from 1926 to the 1960s.* Translated by Paul Stevenson. London: M. Joseph, 1974; American edition: *The Rings of Destiny.* New York: William Morrow, 1974; German edition: *Der Gott stürzt seine Engel.* Vienna: Fritz Molden, 1972.

Kuznetsov, Eduard. *Prison Diaries.* Translated by Howard Spie. New York: Stein and Day, 1973.

Labedz, Leopold. *Solzhenitsyn: A Documentary Record.* Bloomington: Indiana University Press, 1973.

Lacouture, Jean. *André Malraux.* New York: Pantheon, 1975.

Lakshin, Vladimir. *Novyi Mir vo vremena Khrushcheva. Dnevnik i poputnoe.* Moscow: Knizhnaia palata, 1991.

Lamont, Corliss, and Margaret Lamont. *Russia Day by Day.* New York: Covivi, 1933.

Lane, Arthur Bliss. *I Saw Freedom Betrayed.* New York: Regency, 1949.

———. *I Saw Poland Betrayed.* Indianapolis: Bobbs Merrill, 1948.

Laqueur, Walter. *Russia and Germany: A Century of Conflict.* New Brunswick, NJ: Transaction, 1990.

Laski, Harold. *Law and Justice in Soviet Russia*. London: L. and V. Woolf at the Hogarth Press, 1935.

The Last Circle. Moscow: Novosti Press Agency Publishing House, 1974.

Lattimore, Owen. "New Road to Asia." *National Geographic* 86, no. 6 (December 1944): 641–76.

———. *Ordeal by Slander*. Boston: Little Brown, 1950.

Laubenheimer, Alfred, ed. *Und Du siehst die Sowjets richtig: Berichte von deutschen und ausländischen Spezialisten aus der UdSSR*. Berlin: Nibelungen, 1935.

Lebedeva, Natal'ia, and Mikhail Narinskii, eds. *Komintern i vtoraia mirovaia voina*. Moscow: Pamiatniki istoricheskoi mysli, 1994.

Leipman, Flora. *The Long Journey Home*. London: Corgi, 1987.

Lenin, Vladimir I. *Polnoye sobranie sochinenii*. Moscow: Izdatel'stvo politicheskoi literatury, vols. 1–55, 1958–1966.

Leonhard, Susanne. *Gestohlenes Leben. Schicksal einer politischen Emigrantin in der Sowjetunion*. Stuttgart: Steingrüben Verlag, 1959.

Levi, Primo. *Survival in Auschwitz: The Nazi Assault on Humanity*. Translated by Stuart Woolf. New York: Simon and Schuster, 1996.

Lévy, Bernard-Henri. *La barbarie à visage humain*. Paris: Grasset, 1977.

Liberman, Simon. *Building Lenin's Russia*. Chicago: University of Chicago Press, 1945.

Liebich, André. *From the Other Shore: Russian Social Democracy after 1921*. Cambridge, MA: Harvard University Press, 1997.

Lipper, Elinor. *Eleven Years in Soviet Prison Camps*. Translated by Richard and Clara Winston. Chicago: Regnery, 1951; German edition: *Elf Jahre in sowjetischen Gefangnissen und Lagern*. Zurich: Oprecht, 1950.

Littlepage, John D., and Demaree Bess. *In Search of Soviet Gold*. New York: Harcourt Brace, 1938.

Litvinov, Pavel, ed. *The Trial of the Four: A Collection of Materials on the Case of Galanskov, Ginzburg, Dobrovolsky and Lashkova, 1967–68*. New York: Viking, 1972.

Loder, John de Vere. *Bolshevism in Perspective*. London: Allen & Unwin, 1931.

Łojek, Jerzy. *Agresja 17 września 1939*. Warsaw: Wojskowy Instytut Wydawniczy, 1990.

Lottman, Herbert. *The Left Bank: Writers, Artists, and Politics from the Popular Front to the Cold War*. Chicago: University of Chicago Press, 1982.

Lovenstein, Meno. *American Opinion of Soviet Russia*. Washington, DC: American Council of Public Affairs, 1941.

Low's Russian Sketchbook. Drawings by Low and text by Kingsley Martin. London: Victor Gollancz, 1932.

Lukas, Richard C. *The Strange Allies: The United States and Poland, 1941–45*. Knoxville: University of Tennessee Press, 1978.

Lyons, Eugene. *Assignment in Utopia*. New York: Harcourt Brace, 1937.

———. *The Red Decade*. New Rochelle: Arlington House, 1970.

Mackiewicz, Józef. *The Triumph of Provocation*. Translated by Jerzy Hauptman, S. D. Lukac and Martin Dewhirst. New Haven, CT: Yale University Press, 2009.

Malia, Martin. *Russia under Western Eyes: From the Bronze Horseman to Lenin Mausoleum*. Cambridge, MA: Harvard University Press, 1999.

Malsagoff, Sozerko. *An Island Hell: A Soviet Prison in the Far North*. Translated by F. H. Lyon. London: A. M. Philpot, 1926.

Mandelshtam, Nadezhda. *Hope against Hope*. Translated by Max Hayward. New York: Scribner, 1970.

Marchenko, Anatoly. *From Tarusa to Siberia*. Translated by Joshua Rubenstein. Royal Oak, Michigan: Strathcona, 1980.

———. *My Testimony*. Translated by Michael Scammell. New York: Dutton, 1969.

———. *To Live Like Everyone*. Translated by Paul Goldberg. New York: Henry Holt, 1989.

Margolin, Iulii. *Puteshestvie w stranu ze-ka*. New York: Izdatel'stvo imeni Chekhova, 1952; French edition: Jules Margoline. *La condition inhumaine: Cinq ans dans les camps de concentration sovietiques*. Translated by Nina Berberova and Mina Journot. Paris: Calmann-Lévy, 1949.

Margulies, Sylvia. *The Pilgrimage to Russia: The Soviet Union and the Treatment of Foreigners, 1924–1937*. Madison: University of Wisconsin Press, 1968.

Martin, Kingsley. *Editor: A Volume of Autobiography*. London: Hutchinson, 1968.

Matich, Olga, and Michael Heim, eds. *The Third Wave: Russian Literature in Emigration*. Ann Arbor: Ardis, 1984.

Maiakovskii, Vladimir. *Izbrannye proizvedeniia v dvukh tomakh*. Moscow: Gosizdat 1953.

———. *Teatr i kino*. Moscow: Gosizdat, 1954.

Mayakovsky, Vladimir. *Mayakovsky—Plays*. Translated by Guy Daniels. Evanston, IL: Northwestern University Press, 1995.

———. *Selected Poems*. Translated by James H. McGavran. Evanston: Northwestern University Press, 2013.

Maynard, John. *The Russian Peasant and Other Studies*. London: Victor Gollancz, 1947.

McLoughlin, Barry, and Kevin McDermott, eds. *Stalin's Terror: High Politics and Mass Repression in the Soviet Union*. Houndsmill, UK: Palgrave, 2003.

Medvedev, Zhores. *Ten Years after Ivan Denisovich*. Translated by Hilary Sternberg. London: Macmillan, 1973.

Medvedev, Zhores, and Roy Medvedev. *A Question of Madness*. Translated by Ellen de Kadt. London: Macmillan, 1971.

Mele, Alfred. *Self-Deception Unmasked*. Princeton: Princeton U Press, 2001.

Mickiewicz, Adam. *Poems by Adam Mickiewicz.* Translated by various translators and edited by George Rapall Noyes. New York: The Polish Institute of Arts and Sciences in America, 1943.

Miles, F. S. *Changing Russia.* London: Marshall, Morgen and Scott, 1936.

Moën, Lars. *Are You Going to Russia?* London: Chapman & Hall, 1934.

Mora, Sylwester, and Piotr Zwierniak [Kazimierz Zamorski and Stanisław Starzewski]. *La Justice soviétique.* Rome: Magi-Spinetti, 1945 and *Giustizia Sovietica.* Rome: Magi-Spinetti, 1945.

Morgan, Claude. *Les Don Quichotte et les autres.* Paris: Roblot, 1979.

Morgan, Ted. *Reds: McCarthyism in Twentieth-Century America.* New York: Random House, 2003.

Muggeridge, Malcolm. *Chronicles of Wasted Time: The Green Stick.* New York: William Morrow, 1973.

———. *The Sun Never Sets.* New York: Random House, 1940.

———. *Winter in Moscow.* Boston: Little Brown, 1934.

Naimark, Norman M. *Stalin's Genocides: Human Rights and Crimes against Humanity.* Princeton, NJ: Princeton University Press, 2010.

Nałęcz, Daria, Władimir Kozłow, Wojciech Materski, Bolesław Woszczyński, Rudolf Pichoja, and Aleksander Gieysztor, eds. *Katyń. Dokumenty zbrodni,* vols. 1–4. Warsaw: Naczelna Dyrekcja Archiwów Państwowych, 1995–2006.

Nearing, Scott. *The Making of a Radical.* New York: Harper & Row, 1972.

Nicolaevsky, Boris. *Power and the Soviet Elite.* New York: Farrar, 1965.

Nicolas, Jean. *Onze ans au paradis.* Paris: Artheme Fayard, 1958.

Nietzsche, Friedrich. *Nachlass* in *Werke in Drei Bänden.* Munich: C. Hanser Verlag, 1966.

———. *Sämtliche Werke in Zwölf Bänden.* Stuttgart: Kroner, 1964.

———. *Unzeitgemässe Betrachtungen.* München: Goldmann, 1999.

Nikitin, N. N. *Why I Could Not Live in Soviet Russia.* Boston: Scollary, 1945.

Noble, John. *I Found God in Soviet Russia.* New York: St. Martin's Press, 1959.

———. *I Was a Slave in Russia.* New York: Devin-Adair, 1956.

Nove, Alec, ed. *The Stalin Phenomenon.* New York: St. Martin's Press, 1993.

Obertyńska, Beata. *W domu niewoli.* Warsaw: Czytelnik, 1991.

O'Flaherty, Liam. *I Went to Russia.* New York: Harcourt Brace, 1931.

Okhotin, Nikita, and Arsenii Roginskii, eds. *Sistema ispravitel'no-trudovykh lagerei v SSSR, 1923–1960: Spravochnik.* Moscow: Memorial, 1998.

Olson, Lynne, and Stanley Cloud. *A Question of Honor: The Kościuszko Squadron: Forgotten Heroes of World War II.* New York: Alfred Knopf, 2003.

O'Neil, William. *A Better World: The Great Schism: Stalinism and American Intellectuals.* New York: Touchstone, 1982.

Orwell, George. *Animal Farm.* London: Secker and Warburg, 1945.

———. *Homage to Catalonia.* London: Sacker and Warburg, 1938.

———. *Nineteen Eighty-Four*. London: Sacker and Warburg, 1949.

Out of the Deep: Letters from Soviet Timber Camps. London: G. Bles, 1933.

Panin, Dmitry. *The Notebooks of Sologdin*. Translated by John Moore. New York: Harcourt Brace, 1976.

Pares, Bernard. *Moscow Admits a Critic*. London: T. Nelson, 1936.

Pascal, Pierre. *En Russie rouge*. Paris: Éditions de la librairie de l'Humanité, 1921.

———. *Mon journal de Russie 1916–1918*. Paris: Éditions de l'Age d'Homme, 1975.

Paul, Allen. *Katyn: Stalin's Massacre and the Triumph of Truth*. DeKalb: Northern Illinois University Press, 2010.

———. *Katyn: The Untold Story of Stalin's Polish Massacre*. New York: Macmillan, 1991.

Petrov, Vladimir. *Soviet Gold: My Life as a Slave Laborer in the Siberian Mines*. Translated by David Chavchavadze. New York: Farrar Straus, 1949; *It Happens in Russia*. London: Eyre & Spottiswoode, 1951.

Pietrow, Nikita. *Psy Stalina*. Warsaw: Demart, 2012.

Piotrowski, Tadeusz. *The Polish Deportees of World War II: Recollections of Removal to the Soviet Union and Dispersal throughout the World*. Jefferson, NC: McFarland, 2004.

Pipes, Richard. *The Russian Revolution*. New York: Knopf, 1990.

———. *Russia under the Bolshevik Regime*. New York: Vintage, 1995.

———. *The Unknown Lenin: From the Secret Archive*. New Haven, CT: Yale University Press, 1998.

Pogodin, Nikolai. "Aristokraty." In *Sobranie sochinenii*, vol. 1. Moscow: Iskusstvo, 1972; English version: Nikolai Pogodin, *The Aristocrats*. Translated by Anthony Wixley and Robert S. Carr. London: Lawrence and Wishart, 1937.

Preobrazhenskii, Evgenii. *O morali i klassovykh normakh*. Moscow: Gosizdat, 1923.

Prisoners of Conscience in the USSR: Their Treatment and Conditions. Nottingham: Amnesty International, Gamble Press, 1975.

Prychodko, Nicholas. *One of the Fifteen Million*. Boston: Little Brown, 1952.

Pushkin, Aleksandr. *Pushkin Threefold*. Edited and translated by Walter Arndt. Ann Arbor: Ardis, 1972.

Rawicz, Slavomir. *The Long Walk*. London: Constable, 1956.

Rayfield, Donald. *Stalin and His Hangmen: The Tyrant and Those Who Killed for Him*. New York: Random House, 2004.

Reddaway, Peter, ed. *Uncensored Russia: The Human Rights Movement in the Soviet Union: The Annotated Text of the Unofficial Moscow Journal "A Chronicle of Current Events," nos. 1-11*. London: Andre Deutsch, 1972.

Reed, John. *Red Russia: The Triumph of the Bolsheviki*. London: Workers' Socialist Federation, 1919.

————. *Ten Days that Shook the World*. New York: Boni and Liveright, 1919.

Reshetovskaya, Natalya. *Sanya: My Life with Alexander Solzhenitsyn*. Translated by Elena Ivanhoff. Indianapolis: Bobbs-Merrill, 1975.

Rigoulot, Pierre. *Les paupiéres lourdes. Les Français face au goulag: aveuglements et indignations*. Paris: Editions universitaires, 1991.

Rigoulot, Pierre, and I. Yannakakis. *Un pavé dans l'histoire. Le débat français sur "Le livre noir du communisme."* Paris: Laffont, 1998.

Robeson, Paul. *Paul Robeson Speaks*. Edited by Philip S. Foner. London: Quartet, 1978.

Robinson, Robert. *Black on Red: My 44 Years Inside the Soviet Union*. Washington, DC: Acropolis, 1988.

Roeder, Bernhardt. *Katorga: An Aspect of Modern Slavery*. Translated by Lionel Kochan. London: Heinemann, 1958.

Rolland, Romain. "Moskovskii dnevnik Romena Rollana." *Voprosy literatury*, no. 3 (1989).

————. *Voyage à Moscou: Juin-juillet 1935*. Paris: Albin Michel, 1992.

Rorty, Amelie Oksenberg, and Brian P. McLaughlin, eds. *Perspectives on Self-Deception*. Berkeley: University of California Press, 1988.

Rosenberg, Alfred. *Pest in Russland! Der Bolschewismus, seine Häupter, Handlanger und Opfer*. Munich: Deutscher Volksverlag, 1922.

Rosenberg, Suzanne. *A Soviet Odyssey*. Oxford: Oxford University Press, 1988.

Rossi, Jacques. *Spravochnik po GULagu. Istoricheskii slovar' penitentsiarnykh institutsii i terminov*. Moskva: Prosvet, 1991.

Ruder, Cyntia. *Making History for Stalin: The Story of the Belomor Canal*. Gainesville: University Press of Florida, 1998.

Rukeyser, Walter Arnold. *Working for the Soviets*. New York: Covici-Friede, 1932.

Sąd idzie! Stenogram z procesu A. Siniawskiego i J. Daniela (A. Terca i M. Arżaka). Moskwa, luty 1966. Paris: Kultura, 1966.

Sadoul, Jacques. *Notes sur la révolution bolchevique, Octobre 1917–Janvier 1919*. Paris: Éditions de la Sirene, 1919.

————. *Vive la République des Soviets!* Moscow: Editions du Comité de la IIIe Internationale, 1918.

Sakharov, Andrei. *Memoirs*. Translated by Richard Lourie. New York: Knopf, 1990.

Sartre, Jean-Paul. *Situations IV*. Paris: Gallimard, 1964.

————. *Situations X*. Paris: Gallimard, 1976.

Scammell, Michael. *Koestler: The Literary and Political Odyssey of a Twentieth-Century Skeptic*. New York: Random House, 2009.

————. *Solzhenitsyn: A Biography*. New York: Norton, 1984.

Scheffer, Paul. *Seven Years in Soviet Russia*. Translated by Arthur Livingston. London: Putnam, 1931.

Schlögel, Karl. *Moscow 1937.* Translated by Rodney Livingstone. New York: Polity, 2014.

Scholmer, Joseph. *Vorkuta.* Translated by Robert Knee. New York: Weidenfeld and Nicolson, 1954; French edition: *La grève de Vorkuta.* Paris: Amiot Dumont, 1954.

Seibert, Theodor. *Red Russia.* Translated by Eden and Cedar Paul. London: Allen & Unwin, 1932.

Serge, Victor. *Soviet 1929.* Vol. 2 of Panait Istrati, *Vers l'autre flamme.* Paris: Rieder, 1929.

Service, Robert. *Comrades! A History of World Communism.* Cambridge, MA: Harvard University Press, 2007.

———. *Lenin: A Biography.* Cambridge, MA: Belknap Press, 2002.

———. *Spies and Commissars: The Early Years of the Russian Revolution.* New York: Public Affairs, 2013.

Sgovio, Thomas. *Dear America! Why I Turned against Communism.* Kenmore, NY: Partners' Press, 1979.

Shalamov, Varlam. *Kolyma Tales.* Translated by John Glad. New York: Penguin, 1994.

Shambarov, Valerii. *Gosudarstvo i revoliutsii.* Moscow: Algoritm, 2001.

Sharansky, Natan. *Fear No Evil.* Translated by Stephani Hoffman. New York: Random House, 1988.

Shaw, G. B. *The Rationalization of Russia.* Bloomington: Indiana University Press, [1931] 1964.

Shentalinsky, Vitaly. *Arrested Voices: Resurrecting the Disappeared Writers of the Soviet Regime.* New York: Free Press, 1996.

Shestov, Lev. *Umozrenie i otkrovenie. Religioznaia filosofiia Vladimira Solov'eva i drugie stat'i.* Paris: YMCA Press, 1964.

Shimanov, Gennady. *Notes from the Red House.* Montreal: Russian Orthodox Church Outside of Russia in Canada, 1971.

Sinclair, Upton, and Eugene Lyons. *Terror in Russia? Two Views.* New York: R. R. Smith, 1938.

Sinyavsky, Andrey [Tertz, Abram]. *The Soviet Civilization.* Translated by Joanna Turnbull. New York: Arcade, 1991.

———. *A Voice from the Chorus.* Translated by Kyril Fitzlyon and Max Hayward. London: Collins and Harvill, 1976.

Skarga, Barbara. *Po wyzwoleniu . . . (1944–1956).* Warsaw: Aletheia, 2000.

Slave Labor in Russia. Report of the International Labor Relations Committee of the 66th Convention of the American Federation of Labor, San Francisco 1947.

Sloan, Pat. *Russia without Illusions.* Preface by Beatrice Webb. London: F. Muller, 1938.

———. *Soviet Democracy.* London: Left Book Club, 1937.

Słonimski, Antoni. *Moja podróż do Rosji*. Warsaw: Rój, 1932.

Smeth, Maria de. *Unfreiwillige Reise nach Moskau*. Berlin: Nibelungen, 1939.

Smith, C. A. *Escape from Paradise*. London: Hollis and Carter, 1954.

Smith, G. S. *D. S. Mirsky: A Russian-English Life, 1890–1939*. Oxford: Oxford University Press, 2000.

Snyder, Timothy. *Bloodlands: Europe between Hitler and Stalin*. New York: Basic Books, 2010.

Solonevich, Ivan. *Russia in Chains*. Translated by Warren Harrow. London: Williams and Norgate, 1938; American edition: *The Soviet Paradise Lost*. New York: Paisley Press, 1938.

Solonevich, Tamara. *Zapiski sovetskoi perevodchitsy*. Sofia: Golos Rossii, 1937.

Solzhenitsyn, Aleksandr. *Cancer Ward*. Translated by Nicholas Bethell and David Burg. London: Bodley Head, 1968–69.

———. *The First Circle*. Translated by Michael Guybon. London: Collins and Harvill, 1969.

———. *The Gulag Archipelago*, vols. 1–2. Translated by Thomas Whitney. New York: Harper and Row, 1974–1975; vol. 3 translated by H. T. Willetts. New York: Harper and Row, 1978.

———. *Invisible Allies*. Translated by Alexis Klimoff and Michael Nicholson. Washington, DC: Counterpoint, 1995.

———. *Letter to the Soviet Leaders*. Translated by Hilary Sternberg. London: Fontana, 1975.

———. *The Oak and the Calf: Sketches of Literary Life in the Soviet Union*. Translated by H. T. Willetts. New York: Harper and Row, 1980.

———. *One Day in the Life of Ivan Denisovich*. Translated by Max Hayward and Ronald Hingley. New York: Praeger, 1963.

Spender, Stephen. *Forward from Liberalism*. London: Victor Gollancz, 1937.

Sprintzen, David A., and Adrian Van Den Hoven, eds. *Sartre and Camus: A Historic Confrontation*. Amherst, NY: Humanity, 2004.

Stajner, Karlo. *Seven Thousand Days in Siberia*. Translated by Joel Agee. New York: Farrar, Straus & Giroux, 1988.

Stalin, Iosif V. *Materialy ob ispol'zovanii truda ugolovno-zakliuchennykh*, Tsentralnyi Gosudarstvennyi Arkhiv Rossiiskoi Federatsii, f. 393, op. 1, ed. khr. 285, 1.31.

Steenberg, Sven. *Vlasov*. New York: Knopf, 1970.

Steffens, Lincoln. *Letters*. New York: Harcourt, Brace & Co. 1938.

Stekol, Harry. *Humanity Made to Order*. New York: Furman, 1937.

Stepun, Fedor. *Byvshee i nesbyvsheesia*. London: Overseas Publications Interchange, 1990.

Stern, Ludmila. *Western Intellectuals and the Soviet Union, 1920–1940: From Red Square to the Left Bank*. New York: Routledge, 2007.

Strachey, John. *The Coming Struggle for Power*. New York: Covici, 1935.

Strong, Anna Louise. *This Soviet World*. New York: Holt, 1936.

Sword, Keith, ed. *The Soviet Takeover of the Polish Eastern Provinces, 1939–1941*. New York: Palgrave, 1991.

Sworzeń, Marian. *Czarna ikona Biełomor. Kanał Białomorski: Dzieje, ludzie, słowa*. Warszawa: Sic, 2017.

Szymborska, Wislawa. *View with a Grain of Sand: Selected Poems*. Translated by Stanislaw Baranczak and Clare Cavanagh. San Diego: Houghton Mifflin Harcourt, 1995.

Tarasov-Rodionov, Aleksandr. *Opal'nye povesti*. New York: Izdatel'stvo im. Chekhova, 1955.

Tarsis, Valery. *The Bluebottle*. Translated by Thomas Jones and David Alger. London: Collins and Harvill, 1962.

———. *Ward 7*. Translated by Katya Brown. New York: Dutton, 1965.

Taylor, Alexander J., ed. *M. T. Ciceronis Orationes*. Philadelphia: Towar and Hogan, 1826.

Taylor, S. J. *Stalin's Apologist: Walter Duranty, New York Times' Man in Moscow*. New York: Oxford University Press, 1990.

Tchernavin, Vladimir. *I Speak for the Silent*. Translated by Nicholas Oushakov. Boston: Hale Cushman & Flint, 1935.

Tchernavina, Tatiana. *Escape from the Soviets*. Translated by N. Alexander. New York: Dutton, 1934.

Thomas, D. M. *Alexander Solzhenitsyn: A Century in His Life*. New York: St. Martin's Press, 1998.

Thompson, Dorothy. *The New Russia*. New York: H. Holt, 1928.

Thompson, John M. *Russia, Bolshevism, and the Versailles Peace*. Princeton, NJ: Princeton University Press, 1966.

Tiutchev, Fedor. *Polnoe sobranie stikhotvorenii*. Leningrad: Sovetskii pisatel', 1987.

Todorov, Tzvetan. *Facing the Extreme: Moral Life in the Concentration Camps*. Translated by Arthur Denner and Abigail Pollak. New York: Holt, 1996.

Toker, Leona. *Return from the Archipelago: Narratives of Gulag Survivors*. Bloomington: Indiana University Press, 2000.

Tolczyk, Dariusz. *See No Evil: Literary Cover-Ups and Discoveries of the Soviet Camp Experience*. New Haven, CT: Yale University Press, 1999.

Tolstoy, Nikolai. *Stalin's Secret War*. New York: Holt, Rinehart & Winston, 1981.

Tombs, Isabelle. "Erlich and Alter, 'The Sacco and Vanzetti of the USSR': An Episode in the Wartime History of International Socialism." *Journal of Contemporary History* 23 (1988): 531–49.

Tucker, Robert. *Stalin in Power: The Revolution from Above*. New York: Norton, 1990.

Tzouliadis, Tim. *The Forsaken: An American Tragedy in Stalin's Russia*. New York: Penguin, 2008.

Umiastowski, Roman. *Poland, Russia and Great Britain, 1941–1945.* Translated by Joanna Aldridge. London: Holis and Carter, 1946.

Valtin, Jan. *Out of the Night* New York: Alliance Book Corp., 1941.

Vilensky, Simeon, ed. *Osventsim bez pechei.* Moscow: Vozvrashchenie, 1996.

———, ed. *Till My Tale is Told: Women's Memoirs of the Gulag.* Translated by John Crowfoot, Marjorie Farquharson, Catriona Kelly, Sally Laird, and Cathy Porter. Bloomington: Indiana University Press, 1999.

Vinogradov, B. *Desiat' let kapitalisticheskogo okruzheniia SSSR.* Moscow: Gosizdat, 1926.

Viola, Lynne. *Stalinist Perpetrators on Trial: Scenes from the Great Terror in Soviet Ukraine.* Oxford: Oxford University Press, 2017.

Vladimov, Georgi. *Faithful Ruslan.* Translated by Michael Glenny. New York: Simon and Schuster, 1979.

Vogeler, Robert, with Leigh White. *I Was Stalin's Prisoner.* New York: Harcourt Brace, 1952.

Voltaire. *Histoire de l'Empire de Russie sous Pierre le Grand.* Genève: Cramer, 1759–1763.

Voznesenskaya, Julia, ed. *Letters of Love: Women Political Prisoners in Exile and the Camps.* Translated by Roger and Angela Keyes. London: Quartet, 1989.

Vuivovich, V. *Mezhdunarodnoe rabochee dvizhenie i Kommunisticheskii Internatsional.* Moscow: Gosizdat, 1926.

Vutkovskii, V. *Inostrannye kontsessii v narodnom khoziaistve SSSR.* Moscow: Gosizdat, 1928.

Wallace, Henry A. *Soviet Asia Mission.* New York: Reynal & Hitchcock, 1946.

Ward, Harry F. *The Soviet Spirit.* New York: International, 1944.

Wat, Alexander. *My Century: The Odyssey of a Polish Intellectual.* Translated by Richard Lourie. New York: Norton, 1990.

Waters, John E. *Red Justice.* Madison, Wisconsin: Privately printed, 1933.

Waydenfeld, Stefan. *The Ice Road: An Epic Journey from Stalinist Labor Camps to Freedom.* London: Mainstream, 1999.

Webb, Beatrice. *The Diary of Beatrice Webb.* Cambridge, MA: Belknap Press, 1982.

Webb, Sidney, and Beatrice Webb. *Soviet Communism: A New Civilisation.* London: Left Book Club, 1937.

Węgierski, Jerzy. *Lwów pod okupacją sowiecką.* Warsaw: Editions Spotkania, 1991.

Weissberg, Alex. *The Accused.* Translated by Edward Fitzgerald. New York: Simon and Schuster, 1951.

Welch, David. *The Third Reich: Politics and Propaganda.* London: Routledge, 2002.

Wells, H. G. *An Experiment in Autobiography: Discoveries and Conclusions of a Very Ordinary Brain.* New York: Little, Brown 1984.

Werth, Alexander. *Russia at War, 1941–1945*. New York: Dutton, 1964.

Westerman, Frank. *Inżynierowie dusz*. Warsaw: Iskry, 2007.

White, Graham, and John Maze. *Henry A. Wallace: His Search for a New World Order*. Chapel Hill: University of North Carolina Press, 1995.

Wicksteed, Alexander. *Life under the Soviets*. London: John Lane, 1928.

Wigmans, Johan. *Ten Years in Russia and Siberia*. Translated by Arnout de Waal. London: Darton, Longman and Todd, 1964.

Wilkins, Mira, and Frank E. Hill. *American Business Abroad: Ford on Six Continents*. Detroit: Wayne State University Press, 1964.

Williams, Albert Rhys. *The Soviets*. New York: Harcourt Brace, 1937.

Winter, Ella. *I Saw the Russian People*. Boston: Little, Brown, 1945.

———. *Red Virtue: Human Relations in the New Russia*. New York: Harcourt Brace, 1933.

Wittlin, Tadeusz. *Diabeł w raju*. Warsaw: Polonia, 1990.

Wolin, Simon, and Robert M. Slusser, eds. *The Soviet Secret Police*. New York: Praeger, 1958.

Wood, E. Thomas, and Stanislaw Jankowski. *Karski: One Man Tried to Stop the Holocaust*. New York: Wiley and Sons, 1994.

Wood, Neal. *Communism and British Intellectuals*. London: Victor Gollancz, 1959.

Wyman, David. *The Abandonment of the Jews: America and the Holocaust, 1941–1945*. New York: The New Press, 2007.

Wyman, David, and Charles Rosenzveig, eds. *The World Reacts to the Holocaust*. Baltimore: Johns Hopkins University Press, 1996.

Yakir, Pyotr. *A Childhood in Prison*. Translated by Richard Lourie. New York: Macmillan, 1972.

[Yakovlev] Iakovlev, Aleksandr. *Krestosev*. Moscow: Vagrius, 2000.

Yvon, M. *L'URSS telle qu'elle est*. Paris: Gallimard, 1938.

Zaitsev, Cyrille. *Herriot en Russie*. Paris: Nouvelle Éditions-Latins, 1933.

[Zajdlerowa, Zoe]. *The Dark Side of the Moon*. London: Faber, 1946.

Zamorski, Kazimierz. *Dwa tajne biura 2 Korpusu*. London: Oficyna Poetów i Malarzy, 1990.

Zawodny, Janusz K. *Death in the Forest*. Notre Dame: Notre Dame University Press, 1962.

Żbikowski, Andrzej. *Karski*. Warsaw: Świat Książki, 2011.

Zeman, Zbynek, ed. *A Chronicle of Current Events, nos. 16–58, 60–64*. London: Amnesty International, 1984.

Zhivov, M., ed. *Glazami inostrantsev. Inostrannye pisateli o Sovetskom Soiuze*. Moscow, 1932.

INDEX

Dariusz Tolczyk is Professor of Slavic Languages and Literatures at the University of Virginia. His books include *See No Evil: Literary Cover-Ups and Discoveries of the Soviet Camp Experience* and *Gułag w oczach Zachodu* [The Gulag under Western eyes].

For Indiana University Press

Jennika Baines, Acquisitions Editor

Emma Getz, Editorial Assistant

Brian Carroll, Rights Manager

Sophia Hebert, Assistant Acquisitions Editor

Brenna Hosman, Production Coordinator

Katie Huggins, Production Manager

Darja Malcolm-Clarke, Project Manager/Editor

Bethany Mowry, Acquisitions Editor

Dan Pyle, Online Publishing Manager

Rachel Rosolina, Marketing and Publicity Manager

Pamela Rude, Senior Artist and Book Designer